WORKSHOPS IN COMPUTING

Series edited by C. J. van Rijsbergen

Kei Davis and John Hughes (Eds.)

Functional Programming

Proceedings of the 1989 Glasgow Workshop

21–23 August 1989, Fraserburgh, Scotland

Published in collaboration with the
British Computer Society

BCS

Springer-Verlag
London Berlin Heidelberg New York
Paris Tokyo Hong Kong

Kei Davis, MSc
Department of Computing Science
University of Glasgow
Glasgow, G12 8QQ, Scotland

John Hughes, BA, DipCompSci, DPhil
Department of Computing Science
University of Glasgow
Glasgow, G12 8QQ, Scotland

ISBN–13:978–3–540–19609–9

British Library Cataloguing in Publication Data
Functional programming: proceedings of the 1989 Glasgow workshop, 21–23 August 1989. – (Workshops in computing)
1. Computer systems. Functional programming
I. Davis, Kei *1961–* II. Hughes, John *1958–* III. British Computer Society
IV. Series
005.1
ISBN–13:978–3–540–19609–9

Library of Congress Cataloging-in-Publication Data
Functional programming: proceedings of the 1989 Glasgow workshop. 21–23 August 1989 / Kei Davis & John Hughes (eds.)
p. cm. – (Workshops in computing)
"Published in collaboration with the British Computer Society."
Includes index.
ISBN–13:978–3–540–19609–9 e-ISBN–13:978–1–4471–3166–3
DOI: 10.1007/978–1–4471–3166–3
1. Functional programming (Computer science) – Congresses.
I. Davis, Kei, 1961– . II. Hughes, John, 1958– . III. British Computer Society. IV. Series.
QA76.62.F86 1990
005.1'1–dc20 90–9946
CIP

2128/3916–543210 Printed on acid-free paper

Preface

The second Glasgow workshop on functional programming was held in Fraserburgh, Scotland, in August 1989, continuing a planned annual tradition established the year before. The workshop was attended by the members of the functional programming groups at Glasgow and Stirling Universities, together with a smaller number of invited participants from other Universities and from industry. The twenty six papers in this volume cover almost all of the talks given. Our interests in compile-time analysis, program transformation, partial evaluation, types, parallelism and language design are all well represented.

The workshop was organised by Guy Argo, Kei Davis, Kevin Hammond and John Launchbury, all of the University of Glasgow. I am grateful to them all for their efforts.

It is also a pleasure to thank our industrial sponsors: British Telecom Research Labs, Ipswich; ICL, West Gorton; and the Hewlett Packard Laboratory, Bristol. Their financial support made the workshop possible.

Glasgow, Scotland
March 1990

John Hughes

Contents

A New Method for Strictness Analysis on Non-Flat Domains *

Simon B Jones[†] Daniel Le Metayer[‡]

Keywords Functional programming, optimization, strictness analysis, abstract interpretation

1 Introduction

A great deal of effort is currently being directed towards the development of optimization techniques for functional languages. In particular, for lazy languages strictness analysis is capable of yielding performance improvements by indicating where function arguments may safely be evaluated before (or concurrently with) function application without altering the meaning of a program; the optimization that results is the avoidance of the run time construction and detection of closures (or better utilization of a multiprocessor machine). An indication of the possible gains to be made can be seen in experiments reported in [1], where improvements in execution speed ranging from about three to twenty times were observed.

There are two sides of strictness analysis to be investigated: methods for performing the strictness analysis, and exploitation of the results of the analysis. In this paper we shall address the former, in particular in the case of lazily evaluated data structures; Wadler discusses this problem in [2]. Our approach to this problem is novel in that it is based on an abstract domain of very general *necessity patterns* which allow us to

- model in great detail the requirements that a function has for the components of the data structures which form its arguments,
- generate finite abstract domains in a systematic way (to enable the computation of fixpoints at compile time), and in a way that can be easily customized for the application.

We refer to the analysis using necessity patterns as *necessity analysis.* This is essentially a form of *backwards analysis* [3] but carried out in a different framework.

---

†Dept of Computing Science, University of Stirling, Scotland. Email: sbj@uk.ac.stir.cs

‡IRISA, Campus Universitaire de Beaulieu, Rennes, France. Email: lemetayer@irisa.fr

2 Language Syntax and Semantics

We consider a straightforward first-order purely functional language with lists.

The abstract syntax of the language is as follows:

```
c, p : Con                                                (constants)
x : Id                                                    (variable identifiers)
f : Fv                                                    (function variables)
e : Exp                                                   (expressions)
Exp ::= c | x | p(e1,...,en) | f(e1,...,en)
pr : Prog                                                 (programs)
Prog ::= { f1(x11,...)=e1
                ...
           fn(xn1,...)=en }
```

Con contains primitive functions (p) such as **cons**, **head**, **tail**, **eq**, **null**, **cond**, +, ..., and constants such as the integers, booleans and special values such as nil, the empty list. The concrete syntax of the language is similar except that infix notation may be used for operators such as eq and +, and conditional expressions will be written more traditionally using if_then_else_.

We do not give a formal standard semantics for the language here. We assume a straightforward non-strict semantics in which arguments to primitive and user-defined functions are not necessarily evaluated at call time. Primitive functions such as + and eq force full evaluation of both their arguments, cond forces its first argument, and head, tail and null partially force their arguments (just enough to determine their result, that is until the argument is found to be the result of a cons or nil).

3 Formalizing Necessity Analysis

3.1 An Abstract Domain of Necessity Patterns

The necessity interpretation is defined on a domain of patterns P: 0 represents a part of a structure which may not be needed for the evaluation being analysed, and 1 represents a part of a structure which will certainly be needed; a pair corresponds to a needed structure which may contain unneeded substructures: (1,0) represents a structure whose root cell and head are needed but whose tail may not be needed. Note that patterns (1,1) and 1 represent the same information (a structure all of whose substructures are needed); on the other hand (0,0) and 0 have different meanings: (0,0) specifies a cell that is needed whereas none of its substructures is needed, and 0 specifies a completely unneeded structure.

The domain P is defined more formally as the least solution of the following equation:

```
P = {0,1} + (P x P)
```

If p1 and p2 are elements of P then (p1,p2) denotes the corresponding element of P x P.

The elements of P are ordered as follows:

```
0 < (x,y) < 1
(x1,y1) <= (x2,y2)  iff  x1 <= x2 and y1 <= y2
```

We use the operations cons, head and tail to compose and decompose elements of P:

```
cons(1,1) = 1
cons(x,y) = (x,y)                          (x<>1 or y<>1)
head(0) = 0           head(1) = 1
head((x,y)) = x
tail(0) = 0           tail(1) = 1
tail((x,y)) = y
```

The least element of the domain is 0, and the greatest element is 1. It is easy to show that the domain is a complete lattice.

The operators least upper bound (lub) and greatest lower bound (glb) are useful for combining patterns:

```
"lub"           1 lub x = 1       x lub 1 = 1
                0 lub x = x       x lub 0 = x
                (a,b) lub (c,d) = cons(a lub c, b lub d)

"glb"           1 glb x = x      x and 1 = x
                0 glb x = 0      x and 0 = 0
                (a,b) glb (c,d) = cons(a and c, b and d)
```

It is convenient to use tuples of patterns [p1,...,pn] to define the necessity interpretation. Pattern matching notation is used to access the components of a tuple p:

```
let [r1,...,rn] = p
in ... ri ....
```

When combining tuples of patterns, operators lub and glb are applied pairwise to the component patterns:

```
[p1,...,pn] lub [q1,...,qn] = [p1 lub q1, ..., pn lub qn]
[p1,...,pn] glb [q1,...,qn] = [p1 glb q1, ..., pn glb qn]
```

3.2 The Abstract Intepretation N

Now we introduce the abstract interpretation N, called the *necessity interpretation*. This associates with each function f an abstract function Nf which maps a pattern specifying those parts of the result of f which are required to a tuple of patterns specifying those parts of the arguments that are necessary for this computation.

Let us take a simple example. The function:

```
f(x,y) = cons(head(x),tail(y))
```

gives an abstract function:

```
Nf(r) =  [cons(head(r),0), cons(0,tail(r))]
```

which, when applied to 1, that is "the whole result is needed", gives:

```
Nf(1) = [cons(head(1),0), cons(0,tail(1))]
      = [(1,0), (0,1)]
```

which may be interpreted as "only the tail of the first argument and the head of the second argument may not be needed".

Definition: Necessity interpretation N

In the following r denotes a necessity pattern (element of P). Exp is the domain of expressions and Id the domain of variable identifiers.

Each function f(x1,...,xn)=e has an associated abstract function

```
Nf(r)=[N[e][x1]r, ..., N[e][xn]r]
```

The interpretation N[e][xi]r, defined by the rules below, calculates a necessity pattern specifying which parts of the value bound to the variable xi are needed in order to compute those parts of the value of e specified by r.

```
N : Exp -> Id -> P -> P
N[e][x] 0 = 0                                                     (1)
N[x][x] r = r                                                     (2)
N[y][x] r = 0           (x <> y)                                  (3)
N[c][x] r = 0           (c constant)                              (4)
N[cons(e1,e2)][x] r = N[e1][x] head(r) lub N[e2][x] tail(r)       (5)
N[if null(x) then e2 else e3][x] r = cons(0,0) lub N[e3][x] r     (6)
N[if e1 then e2 else e3][x] r =                                   (7)
                    N[e1][x] 1 lub (N[e2][x] r glb N[e3][x] r)
N[p(e1,...,en)][x] r =                         (p is primitive)   (8)
                    let [r1,...,rn] = Np(r)
                    in N[e1][x] r1 lub ... lub N[en][x] rn
```

```
N[f(e1,...,en)][x] r =                                              (9)
                let [r1,...,rn] = Nf(r)
                in N[e1][x] r1 lub ... lub N[en][x] rn
Nhead(r) = [cons(r,0)]                                             (10)
Ntail(r) = [cons(0,r)]                                             (11)
Nnull(r) = [cons(0,0)]                                             (12)
Neq(r)   = [1,1]                                                   (13)
N+(r)    = [1,1]                                                   (14)
```

Note: Rules (2)-(14) apply only if r<>0.

We may informally justify these rules as follows:

Rule (1) expresses the fact that if no part of the value of e is needed then no part of the value of x is needed. (This rule is included as an optimization: it is used in preference to rules (2)–(14) if r=0; these rules would otherwise have to explicitly yield 0 if r=0.)

Rule (2): If we need r of the value of the expression x then we need r of the value of the variable x.

Rule (3): If x and y are different variables then no part of x is needed to evaluate the expression y.

Rule (4): No part of x is needed to evaluate the constant c.

Rule (5): The part of a variable x required to evaluate the part r of an expression cons(e1,e2) is the sum of the parts required to evaluate the part head(r) of e1 and the part tail(r) of e2. For example if only the head of the result is required (r = (1,0)) then only those parts of x needed for the expression e1 have to be considered (since N[e2][x] tail(r) = 0).

Rule (6): In order to test whether x is null, we must access its root cell (but no more), giving necessity pattern (0,0). If it *is* null then e2 cannot access any more of x than the null test. If it is not null then, in addition, e3 may access further into the structure of x. This is a special case of the conditional expression, rule (7), which has been further optimized by reference to the standard semantics of our functional language; this prevents the abstract interpretation losing too much information in this common case (which rule (7) would do).

Rule (7): A conditional expression must access enough of x to compute the full boolean value of e1. In addition, those parts of x that would be accessed by evaluating the part r of *both* e2 and e3 are certainly needed by the whole expression. Note that any part of x needed by e2 but not e3, or vice versa, is not certainly needed by the whole expression; hence the use of glb.

Rule (8) and rule (9): How much of x is needed to compute the part r of the result of a function application (either primitive p, or user defined f) where x may appear in the argument expressions? The abstracted form of the function (Np or Nf) is applied to r to yield a tuple r' specifying which parts of each of its arguments are needed; the part of x needed is then the sum of the parts needed for evaluation of the needed parts of each of the arguments.

Rules (10) to (14) are the abstract forms of typical primitive functions. These are straightforward. For example: if we need r of the head of the value of e, then we need cons(r,0) of the value of e (since we have no need of its tail); if we need r of the result of +, then we need all of both of its arguments. The special cases when r = 0 are dealt with by rule (1).

3.3 An Example

Let us illustrate the necessity interpretation by analysing the example of the reverse function defined as follows:

```
reverse(l) = if null(l) then nil
             else append(reverse(tail(l)),cons(head(l),nil))
append(l1,l2) = if null(l1) then l2
                else cons(head(l1),append(tail(l1),l2))
```

N yields the following derivations:

```
Nreverse(0) = [0]
Nreverse(r) = let [r'1,r'2] = Nappend(r)
                  [r'']     = Nreverse(r'1)
               in [cons(head(r'2), r'')]
Nappend(0) = [0,0]
Nappend(r) = let [r'1,r'2] = Nappend(tail(r))
             in [cons(head(r),r'1), r glb r'2]
```

Thus for example we may calculate:

```
Nreverse(1) = [1]
```

We should interpret this as telling us, correctly (and in this case rather obviously), that if we need the entire result of reverse then we need the whole of its argument to be calculated.

Perhaps more interestingly, if we define:

```
f(l) = head(append(l,l))
```

then we obtain:

```
Nf(0) = [0]
Nf(r) = [ N[head(append(l,l))][l] r ]
      = [ let [r'1,r'2] = Nappend(cons(r,0)) in r'1 lub r'2 ]
```

Now

```
Nappend((r,0)) = let [r'1,r'2] = Nappend(0)
                 in [ cons(r,r'1), (r,0) glb r'2 ]
               = [(r,0), 0]
```

So

```
Nf(0) = [0]
Nf(r) = [(r,0) lub 0]
      = [(r,0)]
```

which we interpret as telling us that, in general, if we need the part `r` of the result of applying `f` then we need the part `(r,0)` of the argument of `f`.

In particular:

```
Nf(1) =  [(1,0)]
```

which we interpret as telling us that we only need the head of the argument in order to calculate the whole result of `f`.

4 Finite Domains and Compile-Time Analysis of Strictness

4.1 Finite Domains and Fixed Points

The functions `Nf` defined by the interpretation `N` are, in general, recursive if the original function `f(x1,...)=e` is recursive. These functions are defined on the infinite domain of patterns `P` which is a complete lattice; a fixed point solution can therefore be defined in the usual way by successive iterations of the abstract function `Nf(r) = [N[e][x1]r,...]`. We start with the *greatest* function over `P` (here `Nf0(r)=[1,...]`), since we wish to *maximize* the necessity information about each argument, consistent with the function definition; thus we are dealing with *greatest fixed points.*

However, in order to exploit the results of strictness analysis we must compute this fixed point at compile-time, which can only be achieved if the domain is finite. For this reason we now define a family of finite domains `Pn`, which are contained in `P`:

```
P0 = {0,1}
Pn+1 = Pn + (Pn x Pn)
```

For example:

```
P1 = {0, 1, (0,0), (0,1), (1,0), (1,1)}
```

It is easy to show that these domains are also complete lattices. For each `Pi` an abstraction mapping `Mi` may be defined from elements of `P` to the elements of `Pi` that approximate them:

```
Mi  : P -> Pi
Mi p = the greatest element of Pi which is weaker than p
                (this element exists since p is an element of P)
```

For example:

```
M0 (0,1) = 0
M1 (0,(0,0)) = (0,0)
M1 (0,(0,(0,0))) = (0,0)
M1 (1,(0,0)) = (1,0)
```

`Mi p` is weaker than `p` to ensure correctness (safety): our approximation must *not overestimate* the necessity of a component of a data structure, otherwise in the intended implementation we may be led to forcing early evaluation of an undefined expression which in fact is not needed; in this case the implemented language would be more strict than intended.

`Mi p` is the greatest of the weaker elements so that the element is as accurate as possible: if we *understimate* the necessity for a component of a data structure then the intended implementation may expensively delay evaluation of a component which is known to be needed.

All primitive functions `pf` defined on `P` (e.g. `cons`, `head`, ...) are also defined on each `Pi` as `pfi(p1,..,pn) = Mi(pf(p1,...,pn))`. For example, in the domain `P0 cons(0,0) = 0`, and in the domain `P1 cons((0,1),1) = (0,1)`.

A different member of the family of finite domains may be appropriate for each particular program which is analysed. The larger members will be able to provide a more detailed analysis of any given program, but will require more work in the computation of fixed points. We suspect that `P1` may be adequate for many purposes, but more experiments need to be carried out to verify this.

4.2 Examples

Let us consider the greatest fixed points of `Nappend` and `Nreverse`, from above, in the finite domain `P1`.

In several iterations we easily find:

```
Nappend(0)      = [0,0]                    (1)
Nappend((0,0)) = [(0,0),0]                 (2)
Nappend((0,1)) = [(0,1),(0,1)]             (3)
Nappend((1,0)) = [(1,0),0]                 (4)
Nappend((1,1)) = [1,(1,1)]                 (5)
Nappend(1)      = [1,1]                    (6)

Nreverse(0)      = [0]                     (7)
Nreverse((0,0)) = [(0,0)]                  (8)
Nreverse((0,1)) = [(0,0)]                  (9)
Nreverse((1,0)) = [(0,0)]                  (10)
```

```
Nreverse((1,1)) = [1]                                                  (11)
Nreverse(1)     = [1]                                                  (12)
```

These results correctly reflect our intuition, although some are quite subtle. (6) and (12) tell us, not surprisingly, that if we need the whole of the results of **reverse** and **append** then we need the whole of their arguments. Perhaps the most intriguing is (3): if we need the root cell and tail of the result of append then we certainly need the root cell and tail of both arguments, but nothing else; in particular, we do not *necessarily* need the head of the second argument, which seems surprising until we realise that the first argument may be null, in which case the head of the second argument may not be needed. The analysis is thus seen to be quite powerful.

Although our aim here is not to discuss methods of optimization based on this form of strictness analysis, we can at least suggest one possibility. Let us suppose that we are compiling the function **f(x1,...)=e**, and that we have found the fixed point of **Nf** in domain Pn. For each argument **xi** of **f** we may calculate that part of **xi** which is needed for *all* uses of **f** as follows: we take the least upper bound of the necessity patterns [r1, ..., rn] from Nf(r) for all r in Pn except 0 (if we are actually applying **f** then it is because we certainly need *some* of its result). The resulting pattern specifies those parts of the actual argument corresponding to **xi** which can safely be evaluated before applying **f**. If the pattern is 1 then f is hyperstrict in that argument, although in general we would expect something weaker such as (1,0), specifying that the first item in the list is needed.

To illustrate this possibility for optimization we may consider two alternative versions of a function which filters a list to keep all the items with value 1 and to reject all others. The first version **keepones** is a standard recursion, and the second **keepones'** employs an accumulating parameter:

```
keepones(l) = if null(l) then nil else
              if head(l)=1 then cons(1,keepones(tail(l)))
                           else keepones(tail(l))

keepones'(l,l') = if null(l) then l' else
                  if head(l)=1 then keepones(tail(l),cons(1,l'))
                               else keepones(tail(l),l')
```

N yields the following abstract functions:

```
Nkeepones(0) = [0]
Nkeepones(r) = [ let [r']=Nkeepones(tail(r)) in cons(1,r')
                 glb let [r']=Nkeepones(r) in cons(1,r')    ]

Nkeepones'(0) = [0,0]
Nkeepones'(r) =
    [ let [r'1,r'2]=Nkeepones'(r) in cons(1,r'1),
      let [r'1,r'2]=Nkeepones'(r) in r glb tail(r'2) and r'2 ]
```

The greatest fixed points of these functions in `P1` are:

```
Nkeepones(0)       = [0]
Nkeepones((0,0)) = [(1,0)]
Nkeepones((0,1)) = [1]
Nkeepones((1,0)) = [(1,0)]
Nkeepones((1,1)) = [1]
Nkeepones(1)       = [1]

Nkeepones'(0)       = [0,0]
Nkeepones'((0,0)) = [1,0]
Nkeepones'((0,1)) = [1,(0,1)]
Nkeepones'((1,0)) = [1,0]
Nkeepones'((1,1)) = [1,1]
Nkeepones'(1)       = [1,1]
```

From this we can see that **keepones'** is strict in its first argument no matter what pattern of use we intend making of its result; **keepones** is not strict in this way. Thus we would compile a call of **keepones'** to have a delayed second argument, but an evaluated first argument.

5 Discussion

In our domain `P` of necessity patterns we can make a finer distinction between cases than [4] which cannot describe accurately the necessity of a function like **head** which does not treat all elements of a list in the same way). In our approach the finite abstract domains required in optimization can be derived systematically from `P`.

A partial lattice of strictness patterns has been proposed independently by Hall and Wise [5] where a particular symbol, **$**, is used to indicate strictness at the root of a list and bottom to represent non-strictness. So the pattern `(0,1)` in our setting would correspond to **$(bottom, $ x)** for any **x**. `0` in our domain corresponds to bottom in Hall's and Wise's domain but they do not have the counterpart of `1` (the greatest value in their domain is the least fixed point of `f x = $(x x)`. Furthermore they do not proceed by abstract interpretation as we do, but transform source functions directly into functions with strictness annotations.

[6] presents a powerful and general method based on projections. The paper includes a proof of the propagation rules for *contexts*, which should be applicable to the necessity analysis rules described in this paper.

There is a sense in which [5], [4] and this paper are alternative formulations of the same approach. The pattern/context propagation rules are essentially the same. The differences are in the choice of patterns; in [5] *regular* patterns are used, [4] uses a more restricted set, and this paper we use a smaller set still.

Further work has to be done to fully assess the relative power of these proposals.

Acknowledgement

We would like to thank John Hughes for his comments on this paper.

References

1. Fairbairn J. Removing redundant laziness from supercombinators. Proc of the Workshop on Implementation of Functional Languages, Aspenaes, Sweden, 1985, pp 181-189.

2. Abramsky S, Hankin C. Abstract interpretation of declarative languages. Ellis Horwood, 1987.

3. Hughes J. Backwards analysis of functional programs. University of Glasgow, Dept of Computing Science, research report CSC/87/R3, March 1987.

4. Wadler PL. Strictness on non-flat domains (by abstract interpretation over finite domains). In: [2], pp 266-275.

5. Hall CV, Wise D. Compiling strictness into streams. Proc of the Conference on the Principles of Programming Languages, 1987, pp 132-143.

6. Wadler PL, Hughes RJM. Projections for strictness analysis. Proc of 3rd Int Conf on Functional Programming and Computer Architecture, Portland, Oregon, September 1987, pp 385-407.

Backwards Strictness Analysis: Proved and Improved

Kei Davis
Philip Wadler

Dept. of Computing Science
University of Glasgow
Glasgow G12 8QQ
United Kingdom

Abstract

Given a syntax tree representing an expression, and some information regarding that expression, a *backwards analysis* will involve propagating the information (with appropriate transformation) towards the leaves of the tree, to yield information about the subexpressions. Here, the information at the root will describe the required definedness of the value of the expression, with the results of the analysis describing the definedness of the values lower in the tree sufficient or necessary to meet the condition at the root. In *Projections for Strictness Analysis* [1], such an analysis is described in which the information at each node is encoded by a special kind of function called a *projection*, with the results of the analysis revealing strictness information about the expression. This paper describes a more general and powerful technique, and provides proofs that both techniques meet a corresponding generalisation of the safety condition described in [1].

1 Introduction

The theory developed in [1] is prerequisite to the development in this paper. To make our presentation reasonably self-contained, this introduction includes a brief summary of much of the content of [1].

A *projection* is an idempotent function on domains that removes information from its argument, but does not change its type. Formally, a projection α is a continuous function which for every u in its domain,

$$\alpha\ u \sqsubseteq u$$
$$\alpha\ (\alpha\ u) = \alpha\ u$$

Projections form a complete lattice under the ordering $\sqsubseteq$, with the identity function ID as the greatest element and BOT, defined by $BOT\ u = \bot$ for all u, as the least. (The greatest lower bound $\alpha \sqcap \beta$ of two projections α and β is defined to be the the greatest *projection* less than both α and β; the greatest such function will not necessarily be a projection.) In this paper, α and β (sometimes subscripted) will always denote projections.

Consider the following projections on pairs, defined for all values u and v.

$$\begin{aligned} F\ (u,v) &= (u,\bot) \\ S\ (u,v) &= (\bot,v) \end{aligned}$$

Then

$$\begin{aligned} (F \sqcup S)\ (u,v) = (u,v) \\ (F \sqcap S)\ (u,v) = (\bot,\bot) \end{aligned}$$

so $F \sqcup S = ID$.

A projection may be interpreted as specifying a degree of required definedness of its argument by regarding that part of its argument which is mapped to $\bot$ as not needed, and that part left unchanged as needed. Suppose that f is a function from pairs to pairs, and that we are only concerned with the first component of the result of some application of f. Then that instance of f may be safely replaced by $F \circ f$. Here the composition with F serves to make explicit the requirement (or lack thereof) on the result of f; f is said to be evaluated in *context* F (the terms context and projection will be used interchangably.)

The context in which a function is evaluated may allow its argument to be less defined than in the general case. For example, suppose that

$$f\ (u,v) = (v,u).$$

Then for f in context F it is safe to apply S to its argument, that is,

$$F \circ f = F \circ f \circ S.$$

If for projections α and β we have $\alpha \circ f = \alpha \circ f \circ \beta$, we write $f : \alpha \Rightarrow \beta$. It is easy to show that

$$f : \alpha \Rightarrow \beta \textit{ iff } \alpha \circ f \sqsubseteq f \circ \beta.$$

Here β may be thought of as a conservative estimate of what information may be discarded from the argument of f without affecting the result, assuming some amount of information to be discarded from the result. Note that β is is not uniquely determined by f and α, since, for example, for any f and α, $f : \alpha \Rightarrow ID$.

So far we have shown how projections might be used to specify how much of an argument to a function is sufficient in a particular context, but not how much of the argument is necessary, that is, in what part of its argument a function is strict. We wish additionally to encode in a projection the information that a value must have some minimum degree of definedness, that is, that some part of the value must be more defined than $\bot$.

To specify necessity with projections we extend our domains by the addition of a new element that we will call $\lightning$. We will interpret $\alpha\ u = \lightning$ to mean that α *requires* a value more defined than u. All functions will be strict in $\lightning$, that is, that $f\ \lightning = \lightning$ for all f. Simple strictness is defined with the projection STR, where STR maps $\bot$ to $\lightning$, but acts as the identity on all other values.

Since STR is a projection we must have $STR\ \bot \sqsubseteq \bot$; since $\lightning \neq \bot$, it must be that $\lightning \sqsubset \bot$. Thus $\lightning$ is a new bottom element to be added to every domain

D; this new domain is just D lifted, written $D_{\lightning}$. Every function $f : D_1 \rightarrow D_2$ is extended to a function in $D_{1\lightning} \rightarrow D_{2\lightning}$ by making f strict in $\lightning$.

We can use STR to define strictness:

$$f : STR \Rightarrow STR \textit{ iff } f \textit{ is strict.}$$

Another useful projection is ABS, defined by

$$\begin{aligned} ABS\,\lightning &= \lightning \\ ABS\; u &= \bot,\; u \neq \lightning \end{aligned}$$

If f makes no use of its argument, then $f : STR \Rightarrow ABS$. Also, for all f, $f : ABS \Rightarrow ABS$.

The least projection $FAIL$ is defined by

$$FAIL\, u = \lightning, \text{ all } u$$

Since every function is strict in $\lightning$, we have that for all f, $f : FAIL \Rightarrow FAIL$.

For projection α, $STR \sqcap \alpha$ will be called the *strict part* of α; if α is equal to its strict part then α will be called *strict*. The nonstrict form of α is $\alpha \sqcup ABS$. We need only consider strictness analysis in a strict context, since for all f and α,

$$\textit{if } f : (\alpha \sqcap STR) \Rightarrow \beta \textit{ then } f : (\alpha \sqcup ABS) \Rightarrow (\beta \sqcup ABS)$$

The discussion so far generalises to functions of several arguments, but the notation $f : \alpha \Rightarrow \beta$ is no longer adequate since we will want to consider separate projections to be applied to each of the arguments of f.

We define an operator & to be the same as $\sqcup$ except strict in $\lightning$. That is

$$\begin{aligned} u \,\&\, v &= u \sqcup v,\; u \neq \lightning \textit{ and } v \neq \lightning \\ &= \lightning \qquad\;\; ,\; u = \lightning \textit{ or } v = \lightning \end{aligned}$$

Each of the operators $\sqcup$ and & distributes over the another.

Other useful projections are those that require constructor values. For any sum-of-products type with constructors $c_1, \ldots, c_m$, any strict projection on that type can be expressed as the least upper bound of projections $P_1, \ldots, P_m$, where

$$P_i\; (c_j\; v_1\; \ldots\; v_{a_j}) = \lightning,\; i \neq j$$

However, we will restrict our treatment to projections of the form $C_i\; \alpha_1\; \ldots\; \alpha_{m_i}$ where

$$\begin{aligned} C_i\; \alpha_1\; \ldots\; \alpha_{a_i}\; (c_j\; v_1\; \ldots\; v_{a_j}) &= c_j\; (\alpha_1\; v_1)\; \ldots\; (\alpha_{a_j}\; c_{a_j}),\; i = j \\ &= \lightning \qquad\qquad\qquad\qquad\quad ,\; i \neq j \end{aligned}$$

and the lub's of sets of these projections. For each type, this restricted set of projections forms a complete lattice, and any element can be expressed as $FAIL$ or

$$\bigsqcup_{i=1}^{m} C_i\; \alpha_{i,1}\; \ldots\; \alpha_{i,a_i}.$$

For all such projection functions C,

$$(C\; \alpha_1\; \ldots\; \alpha_a) \sqcup (C\; \beta_1\; \ldots\; \beta_a) \sqsubseteq C\; (\alpha_1 \sqcup \beta_1)\; \ldots\; (\alpha_a \sqcup \beta_a)$$

$$(C\; \alpha_1\; \ldots\; \alpha_a) \,\&\, (C\; \beta_1\; \ldots\; \beta_a) = C\; (\alpha_1 \,\&\, \beta_1)\; \ldots\; (\alpha_a \,\&\, \beta_a)$$

and if any of the α_i is *FAIL* then $C\ \alpha_1\ \ldots\ \alpha_a$ is *FAIL*. Also,

$$(C_i\ \alpha_1\ \ldots\ \alpha_{a_i})\ \&\ (C_j\ \beta_1\ \ldots\ \beta_{a_j}) = FAIL,\ i \neq j$$

$$(C_i\ \alpha_1\ \ldots\ \alpha_{a_i}) \sqcap (C_j\ \beta_1\ \ldots\ \beta_{a_j}) = FAIL,\ i \neq j$$

As an aside, this restriction excludes exactly those projections that encode an interdependence between values comprising a product type. An example is the projection on pairs of integers defined by

$$\begin{aligned} P\ (1,2) &= (1,2) \\ P\ (2,1) &= (2,1) \\ P\ (x,y) &= \lightning,\ \textit{otherwise} \end{aligned}$$

Finally, we will call unary functions from projections to projections *projection transformers*.

2 Expressions and Programs

The analysis will be for a first-order functional language. The abstract syntax for this language is as follows.

Abstract Syntax

$x \in Var$	Variables
$c \in Constr$	Constructors
$f \in Fv$	Function variables
$p \in Pfv$	Strict primitive function variables
$e \in Exp$	Expressions
$d \in Dfns$	Sets of function definitions

$$\begin{aligned} e ::= \ & x \\ & \mid c\ e_1\ \ldots\ e_n \\ & \mid f\ e_1\ \ldots\ e_n \\ & \mid p\ e_1\ \ldots\ e_n \\ & \mid \textbf{case}\ e_0\ \textbf{of} \\ & \qquad c_1\ x_{1,1}\ \ldots\ x_{1,a_1} \Rightarrow e_1 \\ & \qquad \vdots \\ & \qquad c_m\ x_{m,1}\ \ldots\ x_{m,a_m} \Rightarrow e_m \end{aligned}$$

$$d ::= \{f_i\ x_1\ \ldots\ x_{n_i} = e_i \mid 1 \leq i \leq n\}$$

Nullary primitive functions and nullary constructors will provide constants in the language.

The following semantics is given for this language.

Semantic Domains

$Val = Bool + \sum_{i=1}^{n}(c_i\ Val^{a_i})$	$\{c_i \mid 1 \leq i \leq n\}$ a set of constructors, c_i has arity a_i
$LVal = Val_{\lightning}$	domain for strictness analysis
$Fun = \bigcup_{i=0}^{\infty} (LVal^i \rightarrow LVal)$	first order functions
$Fenv = Fv \rightarrow Fun$	function variable environment
$Venv = Var \rightarrow LVal$	bound variable environment

Semantic Functions

$$
\begin{array}{lllllll}
\mathcal{E} & :: \mathit{Exp} & \rightarrow & \mathit{Venv} & \rightarrow & \mathit{Fenv} & \rightarrow \mathit{LVal} \\
\mathcal{E}_{dfns} & :: \mathit{Dfns} & \rightarrow & \mathit{Fenv} & & & \\
\mathcal{C} & :: \mathit{Constr} & \rightarrow & \mathit{Fun} & & & \\
\mathcal{P} & :: \mathit{Pfv} & \rightarrow & \mathit{Fun} & & &
\end{array}
$$

In the following and in the rest of the paper, the $\overline{z}$ will be used as shorthand for $z_1, \ldots, z_k$, and $[\overline{x}/\overline{y}]$ for $[x_i/y_i \mid 1 \le i \le k]$, where k is implicit from the context. Extension of variable environments is denoted by juxtaposition, for example $\rho[x/y]$ or $\rho_1\rho_2$.

For reasons to be made clear later, we require that if $\daleth$ is in the range of ρ, then $\mathcal{E}[\![e]\!]\ \rho\ \sigma\ =\ \daleth$. Assuming that $\daleth$ is not in the range of ρ, $\mathcal{E}$ is defined as follows.

$$\mathcal{E}[\![x]\!]\ \rho\ \sigma\ =\ \rho[\![x]\!]$$

$$\mathcal{E}[\![c\ e_1\ \ldots\ e_n]\!]\ \rho\ \sigma\ =\ \mathcal{C}[\![c]\!]\ (\mathcal{E}[\![e_1]\!]\ \rho\ \sigma)\ \ldots\ (\mathcal{E}[\![e_n]\!]\ \rho\ \sigma)$$

$$\mathcal{E}[\![p\ e_1\ \ldots\ e_n]\!]\ \rho\ \sigma\ =\ \mathcal{P}[\![p]\!]\ (\mathcal{E}[\![e_1]\!]\ \rho\ \sigma)\ \ldots\ (\mathcal{E}[\![e_n]\!]\ \rho\ \sigma)$$

$$\mathcal{E}[\![f\ e_1\ \ldots\ e_n]\!]\ \rho\ \sigma\ =\ \sigma[\![f]\!]\ (\mathcal{E}[\![e_1]\!]\ \rho\ \sigma)\ \ldots\ (\mathcal{E}[\![e_n]\!]\ \rho\ \sigma)$$

$$
\begin{array}{l}
\mathcal{E}[\![\textbf{case}\ e_0\ \textbf{of} \\
\quad c_1\ x_{1,1}\ \ldots\ x_{1,a_1}\ \Rightarrow\ e_1 \\
\quad\ \vdots \\
\quad c_m\ x_{m,1}\ \ldots\ x_{m,a_m}\ \Rightarrow\ e_m]\!]\ \rho\ \sigma \\
\ = \mathcal{E}[\![e_i]\!]\ \rho[(sel_{i,1}\ v)/x_{i,1},\ \ldots\ ,(sel_{i,a_i}\ v)/x_{i,a_i}]\ \sigma,\ \mathit{if}\ isc_i\ v\ (1 \le i \le n) \\
\ = \bot \qquad\qquad\qquad\qquad\qquad\qquad\qquad\qquad\qquad ,\ \mathit{otherwise} \\
\qquad \mathit{where}\ v\ =\ \mathcal{E}[\![e_0]\!]\ \rho\ \sigma
\end{array}
$$

$$
\begin{array}{l}
\mathcal{E}_{dfns}[\![\{f_i\ x_1\ \ldots\ x_{n_i}\ =\ e_i \mid 1 \le i \le n\}]\!] \\
\ =\ \mathit{fix}\ (\lambda\sigma.[(\lambda y_1 \ldots y_{n_i}.\mathcal{E}[\![e_i]\!]\ [\overline{y}/\overline{x}]\ \sigma)/f_i \mid 1 \le i \le n])
\end{array}
$$

The function $sel_{i,j}$ for each i and j is the projection from the product type formed by the constructor c_i onto its jth component, and isc_i, for each i, is the discriminator that for an argument of a sum type for which one of the summands is the product type formed by the constructor c_i, yields *true* if its argument projected onto that product type is not $\bot$, and yields *false* otherwise.

Since every function (including the conditional) is strict in $\daleth$, the least fixed point of any recursive function is the constant function returning $\daleth$. To avoid this we require that *fix* in the definition of $\mathcal{E}_{dfns}$ yield the least fixed point (a function environment) such that each function in its range yields $\bot$ rather than $\daleth$ whenever its arguments are all not equal to $\daleth$.

3 The Semantic Function $\mathcal{B}$

Let e be an expression, σ be a function environment, τ be a projection transformer, and x be a variable. Then τ ***is safe for** x **with respect to** e **at** σ* if for all projections α and variable environments ρ,

$$\alpha\ (\mathcal{E}[\![e]\!]\ \rho\ \sigma)\ \sqsubseteq\ \mathcal{E}[\![e]\!]\ (\rho[\tau\ \alpha\ (\rho[\![x]\!])/x])\ \sigma$$

Roughly, this states that τ is safe for x with respect to e at σ if, in the evaluation of e, using $\tau\ \alpha\ (\rho[\![x]\!])$ in place of $\rho[\![x]\!]$ gives at least as defined a result as applying α to the value of e. If e were the body of the definition of the function f, and x the name of its only argument, then this condition would be exactly the same as

$$\forall \alpha . f : \alpha\ \Rightarrow\ \tau\ \alpha$$

We consider some examples.

$\lambda\alpha.ID$ is safe for x with respect to every expression e.

$\lambda\alpha.FAIL$ is safe for x with respect to no expression e.

$\lambda\alpha.ABS$ is safe for x with respect to every expression e in which x is not free.

$\lambda\alpha.\alpha$ is safe for x with respect to x.

The first example states that it is always safe to leave the value of a variable unchanged. For the second example it is helpful to refer to the definition of safety above. The variable environment on the right-hand side of the inequality will always map x to $\lightning$, so the value of the right-hand side will always be $\lightning$. However, we can always choose α and ρ such that the left-hand side is at least $\bot$. The third example states that it is always safe to map variables not present in the expression to $\bot$. The fourth is easily interpreted.

Our goal is to give another semantics $\mathcal{B}$ for expressions that yields such a τ. Whereas $\mathcal{E}$ maps an expression e to a value (an element of *LVal*), we expect $\mathcal{B}$ to map the same expression e to a projection transformer that, with respect to a given variable, is safe for e. We will carry further the idea of replacing occurrences of *LVal* in the type of $\mathcal{E}$ by the type of projection transformers to give the type of $\mathcal{B}$. The variable environment for $\mathcal{B}$ will map variables to projection transformers, and the function environment for $\mathcal{B}$ will map variables to functions from projection transformers to projection transformers. Just as the function environment σ for $\mathcal{E}$ is defined in terms of $\mathcal{E}$ applied to a set of function definitions, the function environment ψ for $\mathcal{B}$ will be analogously defined in terms of $\mathcal{B}$ applied to the same set of function definitions. This is summarised in the following.

Semantic Domains

$Proj\ \subseteq\ LVal\ \rightarrow\ LVal$	projections
$Ptran\ =\ Proj\ \rightarrow\ Proj$	projection transformers
$Ptfun\ =\ \bigcup_{i=0}^{\infty}\ (Ptran^{i}\ \rightarrow\ Ptran)$	first order functions on projection transformers
$Bfenv\ =\ Fv\ \rightarrow\ Ptfun$	function variable environment
$Bvenv\ =\ Var\ \rightarrow\ Ptran$	bound variable environment

Semantic Functions

$$\begin{array}{lll} \mathcal{B} & :: Exp \rightarrow Bvenv \rightarrow Bfenv \rightarrow Ptran \\ \mathcal{B}_{dfns} & :: Prog \rightarrow Bfenv \\ \mathcal{C}_{\mathcal{B}} & :: Constr \rightarrow Ptfun \\ \mathcal{P}_{\mathcal{B}} & :: Pfv \rightarrow Ptfun \end{array}$$

Before giving the definition of $\mathcal{B}$, we make precise the condition that $\mathcal{B}$ should satisfy. Let x be a variable and e be an expression with free variables $\overline{z}$. In the term $\mathcal{E}[\![e]\!]\ \rho\ \sigma$, the variable environment ρ maps variables to values. In the corresponding term $\mathcal{B}[\![e]\!]\ \phi\ \psi$, the variable environment ϕ maps each variable z_i to a projection transformer that is safe for x with respect to z_i. (As was shown in the examples above, if $x = z_i$, then $\lambda\alpha.\alpha$ is safe, otherwise $\lambda\alpha.ABS$ is safe.) For such a θ, we would intend that $\mathcal{B}[\![e]\!]\ \phi\ \psi$ be safe for x with respect to e. This is in fact a special case of what we require of $\mathcal{B}$—we generalise by requiring ϕ to map each variable z_i to a projection transformer τ_i that is safe for x with respect to a given expression e_i (instead of just z_i), and requiring that $\mathcal{B}[\![e]\!]\ \phi\ \psi$ be safe for x with respect to $e[\overline{e}/\overline{z}]$ (instead of $e[\overline{z}/\overline{z}]$, that is, e.)

More precisely, for all projections α, expressions e with free variables $\overline{z}$, variables x, expressions $\overline{e}$ and projection transformers $\overline{\tau}$ such that τ_i is safe for x with respect to e_i at σ for each i, we require that $\mathcal{B}[\![e]\!]\ [\overline{\tau}/\overline{z}]\ \psi$ be safe for x with respect to $e[\overline{e}/\overline{z}]$ at σ, where for some set of function definitions d, $\psi = \mathcal{B}_{dfns}[\![d]\!]$ and $\sigma = \mathcal{E}_{dfns}[\![d]\!]$. This is the *safety condition* for $\mathcal{B}$.

Given such a $\mathcal{B}$, then for the definition

$$f\ x_1\ \ldots\ x_n = e$$

define $f^{\mathcal{B}}$ by

$$f^{\mathcal{B}} = \lambda\tau_1\ \ldots\ \tau_n.\ \mathcal{B}[\![e]\!]\ [\tau_1/x_1,\ldots,\tau_n/x_n]\ \psi$$

then

$$f^{\mathcal{B}}\ (\lambda\alpha.ABS)\ \ldots\ (\lambda\alpha.ABS)\ (\lambda\alpha.\alpha)\ (\lambda\alpha.ABS)\ \ldots\ (\lambda\alpha.ABS)$$

is safe for x_j, where $(\lambda\alpha.\alpha)$ above is in the jth position: we reason as follows. Let the x_i be the subexpressions e_i of e as above. For $x_i \neq x_j$, $(\lambda\alpha.ABS)$ is safe for x_j with respect to x_i, and $(\lambda\alpha.\alpha)$ is safe for x_j with respect to x_j.

Rules for $\mathcal{B}$

We introduce another operator $\triangleright$ to simplify the definition of $\mathcal{B}$. As shown in the introduction, it is safe to set

$$\mathcal{B}[\![e]\!]\ \phi\ \psi\ (\alpha \sqcup ABS) = ABS \sqcup (\mathcal{B}[\![e]\!]\ \phi\ \psi\ (\alpha \sqcap STR))$$

$$\mathcal{B}[\![e]\!]\ \phi\ \psi\ FAIL = FAIL$$

$$\mathcal{B}[\![e]\!]\ \phi\ \psi\ ABS = ABS$$

Let α be strict and not *FAIL*, and define $\triangleright$ by

$$\begin{array}{rl} FAIL & \triangleright\ \beta = FAIL \\ ABS & \triangleright\ \beta = ABS \\ (ABS \sqcup \alpha) & \triangleright\ \beta = ABS \sqcup \beta \\ \alpha & \triangleright\ \beta = \beta \end{array}$$

Now the three previous statements may be summarised by the statement that it is always safe to set

$$\mathcal{B}[\![e]\!]\ \phi\ \psi\ \alpha\ =\ \alpha\ \rhd\ \mathcal{B}[\![e]\!]\ \phi\ \psi\ (\alpha \sqcap STR)$$

In the definition of $\mathcal{B}$ this rule will be implicit, and arguments like α here will be assumed to be strict and not *FAIL*. The same assumption will be made of all projection transformers, so that, for example, $\lambda\alpha.ABS$ really means $\lambda\alpha.\alpha\ \rhd\ ABS$.

We will assume that ψ is the result of applying $\mathcal{B}_{dfns}$ to some set of function definitions. We will require that for all τ in the range of ϕ, $\tau\ \alpha\ =\ \alpha\ \rhd \tau\ (\alpha \sqcap STR)$ for all projections α, and that $\tau\ \alpha\ \&\ \tau\ \beta\ =\ \tau\ (\alpha\ \&\ \beta)$ for all projections α and β. A projection transformer with these properties will be called *well behaved.* Later we will show that $\mathcal{B}$ is well behaved if the elements of the range of its argument ϕ are; in practice this assumption poses no restriction since these elements will be such well behaved projection transformers as $\lambda\alpha.ABS$ or $\lambda\alpha.\alpha$, or the results of applying $\mathcal{B}$ to these.

For the sake of brevity, ϕ_{ABS} will denote the environment that maps all variables to $\lambda\alpha.ABS$, and for all variables x, ϕ_x will denote the environment that maps x to $\lambda\alpha.\alpha$ and all other variables to $\lambda\alpha.ABS$.

$$\mathcal{B}[\![x]\!]\ \phi\ \psi\ =\ \phi[\![x]\!]$$

$$\mathcal{B}[\![c\ e_1\ \ldots\ e_n]\!]\ \phi\ \psi\ =\ \mathcal{C}_{\mathcal{B}}[\![c]\!]\ (\mathcal{B}[\![e_1]\!]\ \phi\ \psi)\ \ldots\ (\mathcal{B}[\![e_n]\!]\ \phi\ \psi)$$

$$\mathcal{B}[\![p\ e_1\ \ldots\ e_n]\!]\ \phi\ \psi\ =\ \mathcal{P}_{\mathcal{B}}[\![p]\!]\ (\mathcal{B}[\![e_1]\!]\ \phi\ \psi)\ \ldots\ (\mathcal{B}[\![e_n]\!]\ \phi\ \psi)$$

$$\mathcal{B}[\![f\ e_1\ \ldots\ e_n]\!]\ \phi\ \psi\ =\ \psi[\![f]\!]\ (\mathcal{B}[\![e_1]\!]\ \phi\ \psi)\ \ldots\ (\mathcal{B}[\![e_n]\!]\ \phi\ \psi)$$

$$\begin{aligned}
&\mathcal{B}[\![\textbf{case}\ e_0\ \textbf{of} \\
&\qquad c_1\ x_{1,1}\ \ldots\ x_{1,a_1}\ \Rightarrow\ e_1 \\
&\qquad \vdots \\
&\qquad c_m\ x_{m,1}\ \ldots\ x_{m,a_m}\ \Rightarrow\ e_m]\!]\ \phi\ \psi \\
&\quad =\ \lambda\alpha.\textstyle\bigsqcup_{i=1}^{m}\ (\quad \mathcal{B}[\![e_i]\!]\ \phi[(\lambda\alpha.ABS)/x_{i,j}\ |\ 1 \le j \le a_i]\ \psi\ \alpha \\
&\qquad\qquad\qquad \&\ \mathcal{B}[\![e_0]\!]\ \phi\ \psi(C_i\ (\mathcal{B}[\![e_i]\!]\ \phi_{x_{i,1}}\ \psi\ \alpha)\ \ldots\ (\mathcal{B}[\![e_i]\!]\ \phi_{x_{i,a_i}}\ \psi\ \alpha)))
\end{aligned}$$

$$\begin{aligned}
&\mathcal{B}_{dfns}[\![\{f_i\ x_{i,1}\ \ldots\ x_{i,n_i}\ =\ e_i\ |\ 1 \le i \le n\}]\!] \\
&\quad =\ \mathit{fix}\ (\lambda\psi.[(\lambda y_1 \ldots y_{n_i}.\mathcal{B}[\![e_i]\!]\ [\overline{y}/\overline{x}]\ \psi)/f_i\ |\ 1 \le i \le n])
\end{aligned}$$

For strict primitive functions p of arity n, define

$$\mathcal{P}_{\mathcal{B}}[\![p]\!]\ \tau_1\ \ldots\ \tau_n\ =\ \lambda\alpha.\&_{i=1}^{n}\ \mathcal{B}[\![e_i]\!]\ \phi\ \psi\ STR$$

For $n = 0$, this reduces to $\lambda\alpha.abs$.

For a constructor c_i of arity a_i belonging to a sum type of constructors $\{c_i\ |\ 1 \le i \le m\}$, define

$$\mathcal{C}_{\mathcal{B}}[\![c]\!]\ \tau_1\ \ldots\ \tau_n\ (\textstyle\bigsqcup_{j=1}^{m}\ C_j\ \alpha_{j,1}\ \ldots\ \alpha_{j,a_j})\ =\ \&_{j=1}^{a_i}\ \mathcal{B}[\![e_j]\!]\ \phi\ \psi\ \alpha_{i,j}$$

Here any of the $C_j\ \alpha_{j,1}\ \ldots\ \alpha_{j,a_j}$, for $1 \le j \le m$, may be taken to be *FAIL*. If $C_i\ \alpha_{i,1}\ \ldots\ \alpha_{i,a_i}$ is taken to be *FAIL*, then the result is *FAIL*.

4 Examples

We illustrate the application of the method with a simple example. Let

$$\begin{aligned} head\ xs \ = \ & \textbf{case}\ xs\ \textbf{of} \\ & y : ys \Rightarrow y \end{aligned}$$

We will assume that $\rhd$ is implicit in every lambda abstraction. Then

$$\begin{aligned} head^{\mathcal{B}}\ \tau &= \mathcal{B}[\![\textsf{case}\ xs\ \textsf{of}\ y : ys\ \Rightarrow\ y]\!]\ [\tau/xs]\ []\ \alpha \\ &= \lambda\alpha.\quad \mathcal{B}[\![xs]\!]\ [\tau/xs]\ []\ (CONS\ (\mathcal{B}[\![y]\!]\ \phi_y\ []\ \alpha)\ (\mathcal{B}[\![y]\!]\ \phi_{ys}\ []\ \alpha) \\ &\qquad \&\ \mathcal{B}[\![y]\!]\ [\tau/xs,\ (\lambda\alpha.ABS)/y,\ (\lambda\alpha.ABS)/ys]\ []\ \alpha \\ &= \lambda\alpha.\tau\ (CONS\ (\alpha\ \rhd\ \alpha)\ (\alpha\ \rhd\ ABS)) \\ &= \lambda\alpha.\tau\ (CONS\ \alpha\ ABS) \end{aligned}$$

To determine a projection transformer safe for xs with respect to $head\ xs$, apply apply $head^{\mathcal{B}}$ to $(\lambda\alpha.\alpha)$. Simplifying and removing the lambda-abstraction gives the following.

$$\begin{aligned} head^{\mathcal{B}}\ (\lambda\alpha.\alpha)\ \alpha &= \alpha\ \rhd\ \alpha\ \rhd\ CONS\ \alpha\ ABS \\ &\ \alpha\ \rhd\ CONS\ \alpha\ ABS \end{aligned}$$

Thus, for example, for $head\ xs$ in context STR, it is safe to evaluate xs in context $head^{\mathcal{B}}\ (\lambda\alpha.\alpha)\ STR\ =\ CONS\ STR\ ABS$, that is, to require that xs have the value $cons\ x\ y$ where $x \neq \bot$.

Defining $tail$ in an analogous way, we have $tail^{\mathcal{B}}\ \tau\ =\ \lambda\alpha.\tau\ (CONS\ ABS\ \alpha)$. Then the strictness of the expression $head\ (tail\ xs)$ with respect to xs is given by

$$\begin{aligned} &\mathcal{B}[\![head\ (tail\ xs)]\!]\ [(\lambda\alpha.\alpha)/xs]\ [head^{\mathcal{B}}/head,\ tail^{\mathcal{B}}/tail] \\ &\quad = head^{\mathcal{B}}\ (tail^{\mathcal{B}}\ (\lambda\alpha.\alpha)) \\ &\quad = \lambda\alpha.(CONS\ ABS\ (CONS\ \alpha\ ABS)) \end{aligned}$$

Next we consider the analysis of a recursive function. Let

$$\begin{aligned} last\ xs\ =\ & \textbf{case}\ xs\ \textbf{of} \\ & y : ys \Rightarrow \textbf{case}\ ys\ \textbf{of} \\ &\qquad\qquad\quad []\qquad \Rightarrow y \\ &\qquad\qquad\quad z : zs \Rightarrow last\ ys \end{aligned}$$

Then

$$\begin{aligned} last^{\mathcal{B}}\ \tau\ =\ & \tau\ (CONS\ (\alpha\ \sqcup\ last^{\mathcal{B}}\ (\lambda\alpha.ABS)) \\ & \qquad (NIL\ \sqcup\ (last^{\mathcal{B}}\ (\lambda\alpha.\alpha)\ \alpha\ \&\ CONS\ ABS\ ABS)))) \end{aligned}$$

Here the definition of $last^{\mathcal{B}}$ is recursive. Assuming that the domains of projections in which we are working are finite, then the domains of projection transformers and functions from projection transformers to projection transformers are also finite, so such equations may be solved by the usual fixedpoint iteration. The construction of such domains is discussed in [1]. In this case we have, for example,

$$\begin{aligned} last^{\mathcal{B}}\ (\lambda\alpha.\alpha)\ STR &= CONS\ (STR \sqcup ABS)\ (NIL \sqcup (last^{\mathcal{B}}\ (\lambda\alpha.\alpha)\ STR)) \\ &= \quad CONS\ ID\ NIL \\ &\quad \sqcup\ CONS\ ID\ (CONS\ ID\ NIL) \\ &\quad \sqcup\ CONS\ ID\ (CONS\ ID\ (CONS\ ID\ NIL)) \\ &\quad \sqcup \ldots \end{aligned}$$

5 Safety of $\mathcal{B}$

The argument ψ of $\mathcal{B}$ maps syntactic objects (function variables) to semantic values: the values given by applying $\mathcal{B}$ to the bodies of the (syntactic) definitions of the functions associated with the function variables. We can imagine, however, eliminating function variables from any given expression e to which $\mathcal{B}$ is applied by repeated substitution of function variables in e by the bodies of the corresponding functions. In general this process will generate infinite 'expressions'. This idea can be made sensible by defining a domain Ex of expressions,

$$\begin{aligned} Ex \;=\; & \;\; Var \\ & + Pfv\ Ex\ \ldots\ Ex \\ & + Constr\ Ex\ \ldots\ Ex \\ & + \textbf{case}\ Ex\ \textbf{of} \\ & \qquad Constr\ Var\ \ldots\ Var\ \Rightarrow\ Ex \\ & \qquad \vdots \\ & \qquad Constr\ Var\ \ldots\ Var\ \Rightarrow\ Ex \end{aligned}$$

and redefining $\mathcal{B}$ in the obvious way,

$$\mathcal{B}'\ ::\ Ex \rightarrow Bvenv \rightarrow Proj \rightarrow Proj$$

An obvious question is whether $\mathcal{B}[\![e]\!]\ \phi\ \psi$ has the same value as $\mathcal{B}'[\![e']\!]\ \phi$, where e' is the result of eliminating function variables from e by (possibly infinitely) substituting the function definitions from which ψ is derived. The question is explored by Stoy in [2] under the name of *syntactic recursion*. We state without further justification that the values are the same, as are those produced by $\mathcal{E}$ and the analogously redefined $\mathcal{E}'$. This fact will simplify proofs about certain properties of $\mathcal{B}$ by allowing the proofs to be cast in terms of $\mathcal{B}'$ and $\mathcal{E}'$.

5.1 A Property of &

The following is a useful property of &.

Proposition. For all e, ϕ, ψ, α, and β, let $\tau = \mathcal{B}[\![e]\!]\ \phi\ \psi$, then

$$(\tau\ \alpha)\ \&\ (\tau\ \beta) \;=\; \tau\ (\alpha\ \&\ \beta)$$

Proof. This proof uses the following scheme. Let P be the predicate on expressions

$$\begin{aligned} P(e) &= \forall\phi,\psi,\alpha,\beta.(\tau\ \alpha)\ \&\ (\tau\ \beta) \;=\; \tau\ (\alpha\ \&\ \beta) \\ & \quad \textit{where}\ \tau \;=\; \mathcal{B}[\![e]\!]\ \phi\ \psi \end{aligned}$$

The predicate P is recast in terms of $\mathcal{B}'$. The new predicate P' is shown to hold for $\bot_{Ex}$, and that for all elements e of Ex different from $\bot_{Ex}$, $P'(e)$ is implied by P' holding for all (immediate) subexpressions of e, so that, therefore, P' holds for all elements of Ex. From this we conclude that P holds for all elements of Exp and function environments ψ.

case $\bot_{Ex}$:

$$(\mathcal{B}'[\![\bot_{Ex}]\!]\ \phi\ \alpha)\ \&\ (\mathcal{B}'[\![\bot_{Ex}]\!]\ \phi\ \beta)$$

$$= \bot_{Proj}\ \&\ \bot_{Proj}$$

$$= \bot_{Proj}$$

$$= \mathcal{B}'[\![\bot_{Ex}]\!]\ \phi\ (\alpha\ \&\ \beta)$$

case x :

$$\mathcal{B}'[\![x]\!]\ \phi\ \alpha\ \&\ \mathcal{B}'[\![x]\!]\ \phi\ \beta$$

$$= \phi[\![x]\!]\ \alpha\ \&\ \phi[\![x]\!]\ \beta$$

$$= \phi[\![x]\!]\ (\alpha\ \&\ \beta)$$

$$= \mathcal{B}'[\![x]\!]\ \phi\ (\alpha\ \&\ \beta)$$

case p :

$$\mathcal{B}'[\![p]\!]\ \phi\ \alpha\ \&\ \mathcal{B}'[\![p]\!]\ \phi\ \beta$$

$$= (\lambda\alpha.ABS)\ \alpha\ \&\ (\lambda\alpha.ABS)\ \beta$$

$$= ABS$$

$$= (\lambda\alpha.ABS)\ (\alpha\ \&\ \beta)$$

$$= \mathcal{B}'[\![p]\!]\ \phi\ (\alpha\ \&\ \beta)$$

case $p\ e_1\ \ldots\ e_n$:

$$(\mathcal{B}'[\![p\ e_1\ \ldots\ e_n]\!]\ \phi\ \alpha)\ \&\ (\mathcal{B}'[\![p\ e_1\ \ldots\ e_n]\!]\ \phi\ \beta)$$

$$= (\&_{i=1}^{n}\ \mathcal{B}'[\![e_i]\!]\ \phi\ STR)\ \&\ (\&_{i=1}^{n}\ \mathcal{B}'[\![e_i]\!]\ \phi\ STR)$$

$$= (\&_{i=1}^{n}\ \mathcal{B}'[\![e_i]\!]\ \phi\ STR)$$

$$= \mathcal{B}'[\![p\ e_1\ \ldots\ e_n]\!]\ \phi\ (\alpha\ \&\ \beta)$$

case $c_i\ e_1\ \ldots\ e_{a_i}$:

$$\begin{aligned}&\mathcal{B}[\![c_i\ e_1\ \ldots\ e_{a_i}]\!]\ \phi\ \psi\ (\beta_1 \sqcup \bigsqcup_{j=1}^{m} C_j\ \alpha_{j,1}\ \ldots\ \alpha_{j,n_j})\\ \&\ &\mathcal{B}[\![c_i\ e_1\ \ldots\ e_{a_i}]\!]\ \phi\ \psi\ (\beta_2 \sqcup \bigsqcup_{j=1}^{m} C_j\ \beta_{j,1}\ \ldots\ \beta_{j,n_j})\end{aligned}$$

$$= (\&_{j=1}^{a_i}\ \mathcal{B}[\![e_j]\!]\ \phi\ \psi\ \alpha_{i,j})\ \&\ (\&_{j=1}^{n_i}\ \mathcal{B}[\![e_j]\!]\ \phi\ \psi\ \beta_{i,j})$$

$$= \&_{j=1}^{a_i}\ (\mathcal{B}[\![e_j]\!]\ \phi\ \psi\ \alpha_{i,j})\ \&\ \mathcal{B}[\![e_j]\!]\ \phi\ \psi\ \beta_{i,j})$$

{ by the induction hypothesis }

$$= \&_{j=1}^{a_i}\ (\mathcal{B}[\![e_j]\!]\ \phi\ \psi\ (\alpha_{i,j}\ \&\ \beta_{i,j}))$$

$$= \mathcal{B}[\![c_i\ e_1\ \ldots\ e_{a_i}]\!]\ \phi\ \psi\ (\beta_1 \sqcup \beta_2 \sqcup \bigsqcup_{j=1}^{m} C_j\ (\alpha_{j,1}\ \&\ \beta_{j,1})\ \ldots\ (\alpha_{j,n_j}\ \&\ \beta_{j,a_j}))$$

case case ... :

$$\begin{aligned}&\mathcal{B}'[\![\text{case}\ \ldots]\!]\ \phi\ \alpha\\ \&\ &\mathcal{B}'[\![\text{case}\ \ldots]\!]\ \phi\ \beta\end{aligned}$$

$$\begin{aligned}= \quad & \bigsqcup_{i=1}^{m} (\ \ \mathcal{B}'[\![e_i]\!]\ \phi[(\lambda\alpha.ABS)/x_{i,j} \mid 1 \le j \le a_i]\ \alpha \qquad (1)\\ & \qquad \&\ \mathcal{B}'[\![e_0]\!]\ \phi(C_i\ (\mathcal{B}'[\![e_i]\!]\ \phi_{v_{i,1}}\ \alpha)\ \ldots\ (\mathcal{B}'[\![e_i]\!]\ \phi_{v_{i,a_i}}\ \alpha)))\\ \&\ & \bigsqcup_{i=1}^{m} (\ \ \mathcal{B}'[\![e_i]\!]\ \phi[(\lambda\alpha.ABS)/x_{i,j} \mid 1 \le j \le a_i]\ \beta\\ & \qquad \&\ \mathcal{B}'[\![e_0]\!]\ \phi(C_i\ (\mathcal{B}'[\![e_i]\!]\ \phi_{v_{i,1}}\ \beta)\ \ldots\ (\mathcal{B}'[\![e_i]\!]\ \phi_{v_{i,a_i}}\ \beta)))\end{aligned}$$

Let

$$\tau_i = \mathcal{B}'[\![e_i]\!]\ \phi[(\lambda\alpha.ABS)/x_{i,j} \mid 1 \le j \le a_i]$$

and

$$\tau_{0,i} = \lambda\alpha.\mathcal{B}'[\![e_0]\!]\ \phi\ (C_i\ (\mathcal{B}'[\![e_i]\!]\ \phi_{v_{i,1}}\ \alpha)\ \ldots\ (\mathcal{B}'[\![e_i]\!]\ \phi_{v_{i,a_i}}\ \alpha)),\ 1 \le i \le m.$$

Then

$$(1) = (\bigsqcup_{i=1}^{m}(\tau_i\ \alpha\ \&\ \tau_{0,i}\ \alpha))\ \&\ (\bigsqcup_{i=1}^{m}(\tau_i\ \beta\ \&\ \tau_{0,i}\ \beta))$$

$$= \bigsqcup_{i=1}^{m} \bigsqcup_{j=1}^{m}(\tau_i\ \alpha\ \&\ \tau_{0,i}\ \alpha\ \&\ \tau_j\ \beta\ \&\ \tau_{0,j}\ \beta) \qquad (2)$$

Using the induction hypothesis we have that $\tau_i\ \alpha\ \&\ \tau_i\ \beta = \tau_i\ (\alpha\ \&\ \beta)$ and $\tau_{0,i}\ \alpha\ \&\ \tau_{0,j}\ \beta = FAIL,\ i \neq j$. So

$$(2) = \bigsqcup_{i=1}^{m}(\tau_i\ (\alpha\ \&\ \beta)\ \&\ \tau_{0,i}\ (\alpha\ \&\ \beta))$$

5.2 The Substitution Rule

Proposition.

$$\mathcal{B}[\![e_0[\overline{e}/\overline{z}]]\!]\ \phi\ \psi\ \alpha$$

$$\begin{aligned}\sqsubseteq \quad & \mathcal{B}[\![e_0]\!]\ \phi[(\lambda\alpha.ABS)/\overline{z}]\ \psi\ \alpha\\ \&\ & \&_{i=1}^{k}\ \mathcal{B}[\![e_0]\!]\ \phi_{ABS}[\mathcal{B}[\![e_i]\!]\ \phi\ \psi/z_i]\ \psi\ \alpha\end{aligned}$$

$$\begin{aligned}= \quad & \mathcal{B}[\![e_0]\!]\ \phi[(\lambda\alpha.ABS)/\overline{z}]\ \psi\ \alpha\\ \&\ & \&_{i=1}^{k}\ \mathcal{B}[\![e_i]\!]\ \phi\ \psi\ (\mathcal{B}[\![e_0]\!]\ \phi_{z_i}\ \psi\ \alpha)\end{aligned}$$

Proof. The assertion can be established by repeated application of the simpler rule following.

$$\mathcal{B}[\![e_0[e/z]]\!]\ \phi\ \psi\ \alpha$$

$$\begin{aligned}\sqsubseteq\quad & \mathcal{B}[\![e_0]\!]\ \phi[(\lambda\alpha.ABS)/z]\ \psi\ \alpha \\ & \&\ \mathcal{B}[\![e_0]\!]\ \phi_{ABS}[\mathcal{B}[\![e]\!]\ \phi\ \psi/z]\ \psi\ \alpha\end{aligned}$$

$$\begin{aligned}=\quad & \mathcal{B}[\![e_0]\!]\ \phi[(\lambda\alpha.ABS)/z]\ \psi\ \alpha \\ & \&\ \mathcal{B}[\![e]\!]\ \phi\ \psi\ (\mathcal{B}[\![e_0]\!]\ \phi_z\ \psi\ \alpha)\end{aligned}$$

The proof is by induction on e_0.

case $\perp_{Ex}$:

$$\mathcal{B}'[\![\perp_{Ex}[e/z]]\!]\ \phi\ \alpha$$

$$= \mathcal{B}'[\![\perp_{Ex}]\!]\ \phi\ \alpha$$

$$= \perp_{Proj}$$

$$\begin{aligned}=\quad & \mathcal{B}'[\![\perp_{Ex}]\!]\ \phi[(\lambda\alpha.ABS)/z]\ \alpha \\ & \&\ \mathcal{B}'[\![\perp_{Ex}]\!]\ \phi_{ABS}[\mathcal{B}[\![e]\!]\ \phi\ \psi/z]\ \alpha\end{aligned}$$

$$\begin{aligned}=\quad & \mathcal{B}'[\![\perp_{Ex}]\!]\ \phi[(\lambda\alpha.ABS)/z]\ \alpha \\ & \&\ \mathcal{B}'[\![e]\!]\ \phi\ (\mathcal{B}[\![\perp_{Ex}]\!]\ \phi_z\ \psi\ \alpha)\end{aligned}$$

case x, $x \neq z$:

$$\mathcal{B}'[\![x[e/z]]\!]\ \phi\ \alpha$$

$$= \mathcal{B}'[\![x]\!]\ \phi\ \alpha$$

$$= \phi[\![x]\!]\ \alpha$$

$$= \phi[\![x]\!]\ \alpha\ \&\ ABS \qquad (1)$$

$$= \mathcal{B}'[\![x]\!]\ \phi[(\lambda\alpha.ABS)/z]\ \alpha\ \&\ \mathcal{B}'[\![x]\!]\ \phi_{ABS}[\mathcal{B}'[\![e]\!]\ \phi/z]\ \alpha$$

and

$$(1) = \mathcal{B}'[\![x]\!]\ \phi[(\lambda\alpha.ABS)/z]\ \alpha\ \&\ \mathcal{B}'[\![e]\!]\ \phi\ (\mathcal{B}'[\![x]\!]\ \phi_z\ \alpha)$$

case z:

$$\mathcal{B}'[\![z[e/z]]\!]\ \phi\ \alpha$$

$$= \mathcal{B}'[\![e]\!]\ \phi\ \alpha$$

$$= ABS\ \&\ \mathcal{B}'[\![e]\!]\ \phi\ \alpha \qquad (1)$$

$$= \mathcal{B}'[\![z]\!]\ \phi[(\lambda\alpha.ABS)/z]\ \alpha\ \&\ \mathcal{B}'[\![z]\!]\ \phi_{ABS}[\mathcal{B}'[\![e]\!]\ \phi/z]\ \alpha$$

and

$$(1) = \mathcal{B}'[\![z]\!]\ \phi[(\lambda\alpha.ABS)/z]\ \alpha\ \&\ \mathcal{B}'[\![e]\!]\ \phi\ (\mathcal{B}'[\![z]\!]\ \phi_z\ \alpha)$$

case p: (straightforward)

case $p\ e_1\ \ldots\ e_n$: (straightforward)

case $c\ e_1\ \ldots\ e_n$: (straightforward)

case **case** ...:

$$\mathcal{B}'[\![(\textbf{case}\ \ldots)[e/z]]\!]\ \phi\ \alpha$$

$$\begin{aligned} = \mathcal{B}'[\![\textbf{case}\ e_0[e/z]\ \textbf{of}\ & c_1\ x_{1,1}\ \ldots\ x_{1,a_1} \Rightarrow e_1[e/z] \\ & \vdots \\ & c_m\ x_{m,1}\ \ldots\ x_{m,a_m} \Rightarrow e_m[e/z]]\!]\ \phi\ \alpha \end{aligned}$$

$$\begin{aligned} = \textstyle\bigsqcup_{i=1}^{m} (\ & \mathcal{B}'[\![e_i[e/z]]\!]\ \phi[(\lambda\alpha.ABS)/x_{i,j} \mid 1 \le j \le a_i]\ \alpha \\ & \&\ \mathcal{B}'[\![e_0[e/z]]\!]\ \phi\ (C_i\ (\mathcal{B}'[\![e_i[e/z]]\!]\ \phi_{x_{i,1}}\ \alpha)\ \ldots\ (\mathcal{B}'[\![e_i[e/z]]\!]\ \phi_{x_{i,a_i}}\ \alpha))) \end{aligned}$$

$$\begin{aligned} = \textstyle\bigsqcup_{i=1}^{m} (\ & \mathcal{B}'[\![e_i[e/z]]\!]\ \phi[(\lambda\alpha.ABS)/x_{i,j} \mid 1 \le j \le a_i]\ \alpha \\ & \&\ \mathcal{B}'[\![e_0[e/z]]\!]\ \phi\ (C_i\ (\mathcal{B}'[\![e_i]\!]\ \phi_{x_{i,1}}\ \alpha)\ \ldots\ (\mathcal{B}'[\![e_i]\!]\ \phi_{x_{i,a_i}}\ \alpha))) \qquad (1) \end{aligned}$$

We have assumed that the $x_{i,j}$, $1 \le i \le m$, $1 \le j \le a_i$, are not free in e, to avoid unintended variable capture. Since $\mathcal{B}'[\![e]\!]\ \phi_y = (\lambda\alpha.ABS)$ for every expression e and variable y if y is not free in e, each subterm $\mathcal{B}'[\![e_i[e/z]]\!]\ \phi_{x_{i,j}}$ above is equal to $\mathcal{B}'[\![e_i]\!]\ \phi_{x_{i,j}}$; this justifies the last equality. Writing β_i for $C_i\ (\mathcal{B}'[\![e_i]\!]\ \phi_{x_{i,1}}\ \alpha)\ \ldots\ (\mathcal{B}'[\![e_i]\!]\ \phi_{x_{i,a_i}}\ \alpha)$, we have by the induction hypothesis

$$\begin{aligned} (1) \sqsubseteq \textstyle\bigsqcup_{i=1}^{m} (\ & \mathcal{B}'[\![e_i]\!]\ \phi[(\lambda\alpha.ABS)/x_{i,j} \mid 1 \le j \le a_i][(\lambda\alpha.ABS)/z]\ \alpha \\ & \&\ \mathcal{B}'[\![e_i]\!]\ \phi_{ABS}[\mathcal{B}'[\![e]\!]\ \phi/z]\ \alpha \\ & \&\ \mathcal{B}'[\![e_0]\!]\ \phi[(\lambda\alpha.ABS)/z]\ \beta_i \\ & \&\ \mathcal{B}'[\![e_0]\!]\ \phi_{ABS}[\mathcal{B}'[\![e]\!]\ \phi/z]\ \beta_i) \end{aligned}$$

Writing

$$\begin{aligned} & \tau_i \text{ for } \mathcal{B}'[\![e_i]\!]\ \phi[(\lambda\alpha.ABS)/x_{i,j} \mid 1 \le j \le a_i][(\lambda\alpha.ABS)/z],\ 1 \le i \le m \\ & \tau_0 \text{ for } \mathcal{B}'[\![e_0]\!]\ \phi[(\lambda\alpha.ABS)/z] \\ & \theta_i \text{ for } \mathcal{B}'[\![e_i]\!]\ \phi_{ABS}[\mathcal{B}'[\![e]\!]\ \phi/z], \qquad 1 \le i \le m \\ & \theta_0 \text{ for } \mathcal{B}'[\![e_0]\!]\ \phi_{ABS}[\mathcal{B}'[\![e]\!]\ \phi/z] \end{aligned}$$

the last expression is

$$\bigsqcup_{i=1}^{m} (\tau_i\ \alpha\ \&\ \theta_i\ \alpha\ \&\ \tau_0\ \beta_i\ \&\ \theta_0\ \beta_i)$$

$$\sqsubseteq \bigsqcup_{i=1}^{m}\bigsqcup_{j=1}^{n} (\tau_i\ \alpha\ \&\ \theta_i\ \alpha\ \&\ \tau_0\ \beta_j\ \&\ \theta_0\ \beta_j)$$

$$= (\bigsqcup_{i=1}^{m} (\tau_i\ \alpha\ \&\ \tau_0\ \beta_i))\ \&\ (\bigsqcup_{i=1}^{n} (\theta_i\ \alpha\ \&\ \theta_0\ \beta_i))$$

$$\begin{aligned} = \quad & (\textstyle\bigsqcup_{i=1}^{m} (\ \mathcal{B}'[\![e_i]\!]\ \phi[(\lambda\alpha.ABS)/x_{i,j} \mid 1 \le j \le a_i][(\lambda\alpha.ABS)/z]\ \alpha \qquad (1)\\ & \qquad \&\ \mathcal{B}'[\![e_0]\!]\ \phi[(\lambda\alpha.ABS)/z]\ \beta_i))\\ & \&\ (\textstyle\bigsqcup_{i=1}^{m} (\ \mathcal{B}'[\![e_i]\!]\ \phi_{ABS}[\mathcal{B}'[\![e]\!]\ \phi/z]\ \alpha\\ & \qquad \&\ \mathcal{B}'[\![e_0]\!]\ \phi_{ABS}[\mathcal{B}'[\![e]\!]\ \phi/z]\ \beta_i))\end{aligned}$$

$$= (\mathcal{B}'[\![\textbf{case}\ \ldots]\!]\ \phi[(\lambda\alpha.ABS)/z]\ \alpha)\ \&\ (\mathcal{B}'[\![\textbf{case}\ \ldots]\!]\ \phi_{ABS}[\mathcal{B}'[\![e]\!]\ \phi/z]\ \alpha)$$

$$= \mathcal{B}'[\![(\textbf{case}\ \ldots)[e/z]]\!]\ \phi\ \alpha$$

Also,

$$\begin{aligned} & \{\text{ by the induction hypothesis }\}\\ (1) = \quad & (\textstyle\bigsqcup_{i=1}^{m} \quad (\mathcal{B}'[\![e_i]\!]\ \phi[(\lambda\alpha.ABS)/x_{i,j} \mid 1 \le j \le a_i][(\lambda\alpha.ABS)/z]\ \alpha)\\ & \qquad \&\ (\mathcal{B}'[\![e_0]\!]\ \phi[(\lambda\alpha.ABS)/z]\ \beta_i))\\ & \&\ (\textstyle\bigsqcup_{i=1}^{m} \quad (\mathcal{B}'[\![e_0]\!]\ \phi\ (\mathcal{B}'[\![e_i]\!]\ \phi_z\ \alpha)\\ & \qquad \&\ (\mathcal{B}'[\![e_0]\!]\ \phi\ (\mathcal{B}'[\![e_i]\!]\ \phi\ \beta_i))\end{aligned}$$

$$\begin{aligned} = \quad & (\textstyle\bigsqcup_{i=1}^{m} (\mathcal{B}'[\![e_i]\!]\ \phi_{ABS}\phi[(\lambda\alpha.ABS)/z]\ \alpha)\ \&\ (\mathcal{B}'[\![e_0]\!]\ \phi[(\lambda\alpha.ABS)/z]\ \beta_i))\\ & \&\ (\textstyle\bigsqcup_{i=1}^{m} (\mathcal{B}'[\![e_0]\!]\ \phi\ ((\mathcal{B}'[\![e_i]\!]\ \phi_z\ \alpha) \qquad \&\ (\mathcal{B}'[\![e_i]\!]\ \phi\ \beta_i))))\end{aligned}$$

$$= (\mathcal{B}'[\![\textbf{case}\ \ldots]\!]\ \phi[(\lambda\alpha.ABS)/z]\ \alpha)\ \&\ (\mathcal{B}'[\![e]\!]\ \phi\ (\mathcal{B}'[\![\textbf{case}\ \ldots]\!]\ \phi_z\ \alpha))$$

5.3 Proof of Safety

Proposition. $\mathcal{B}$ satisfies its safety condition, that is, for all projections α, expressions e with free variables $\overline{z}$, variables x, expressions $\overline{e}$ and projection transformers $\overline{\tau}$ such that τ_i is safe for x with respect to e_i for each i, $1 \le i \le k$, and $\tau = \mathcal{B}[\![e]\!]\ [\overline{\tau}/\overline{z}]\ \psi$, we have

$$\alpha\ (\mathcal{E}[\![e[\overline{e}/\overline{z}]]\!]\ \rho\ \sigma) \sqsubseteq \mathcal{E}[\![e[\overline{e}/\overline{z}]]\!]\ (\rho[\tau\ \alpha\ (\rho[\![x]\!])/x])\ \sigma$$

Proof. Again, the proof is in terms of $\mathcal{B}'$ and $\mathcal{E}'$, by syntactic recursion on the expression e. The symbols *LHS* and *RHS* will be used to stand for instances of the left-hand and right-hand sides, respectively, of the above inequality.

case $\bot_{Ex}$:

$$LHS = \alpha\ (\mathcal{E}'[\![\bot_{Ex}[\overline{e}/\overline{z}]]\!]\ \rho)$$

$$= \alpha\ \bot$$

$$= \text{ʿ}$$

$$\sqsubseteq RHS$$

case z_i, $1 \leq i \leq k$:

$$\alpha\ (\mathcal{E}'[\![z_i[\overline{e}/\overline{z}]]\!]\ \rho)$$

$$= \alpha\ (\mathcal{E}'[\![e_i]\!]\ \rho)$$

{ by the assumption that τ_i is safe for x with respect to e_i }

$$\sqsubseteq \mathcal{E}'[\![e_i]\!]\ (\rho[\tau_i\ \alpha\ (\rho[\![x]\!])/x])$$

$\{\ \tau = \tau_i = \mathcal{B}'[\![z_i]\!]\ [\overline{\tau}/\overline{z}]\ \}$

$$= \mathcal{E}'[\![e_i]\!]\ (\rho[\tau\ \alpha\ (\rho[\![x]\!])/x])$$

case p:

$$\alpha\ (\mathcal{E}'[\![p[\overline{e}/\overline{z}]]\!]\ \rho)$$

$$= \alpha\ (\mathcal{E}'[\![p]\!]\ \rho)$$

$$\sqsubseteq \mathcal{E}'[\![p]\!]\ \rho[(\lambda\alpha.ABS)\ \alpha\ (\rho[\![x]\!])/x]$$

$$= \mathcal{E}'[\![p]\!]\ \rho[\tau\ \alpha\ (\rho[\![x]\!])/x]$$

case $p\ w_1\ \ldots\ w_n$:

$$LHS = \alpha\ (\mathcal{E}'[\![(p\ w_1\ \ldots\ w_m)[\overline{e}/\overline{z}]]\!]\ \rho)$$

$$= \alpha\ (\mathcal{E}'[\![p\ (w_1[\overline{e}/\overline{z}])\ \ldots\ (w_m[\overline{e}/\overline{z}])]\!]\ \rho)$$

$$= \alpha\ (\mathcal{E}'[\![p\ y_1\ \ldots\ y_m]\!]\ [\mathcal{E}'[\![w_i[\overline{e}/\overline{z}]]\!]\ \rho/y_i \mid 1 \leq i \leq m])$$

{ since p is strict }

$$\sqsubseteq \mathcal{E}'[\![p\ y_1\ \ldots\ y_m]\!]\ [STR\ (\mathcal{E}'[\![w_i[\overline{e}/\overline{z}]]\!]\ \rho)/y_i \mid 1 \leq i \leq m](1)$$

Let $\theta_i = \mathcal{B}'[\![w_i[\overline{\tau}/\overline{z}]]\!]$, $1 \leq i \leq m$. By the induction hypothesis, each θ_i is safe for x with respect to $w_i[\overline{e}/\overline{z}]$, so

$$(1) \sqsubseteq \mathcal{E}'[\![p\ y_1\ \ldots\ y_m]\!]\ \mathcal{E}'[\![w_i[\overline{e}/\overline{z}]]\!]\ [\theta_i\ STR\ (\rho[\![x]\!])/x]/y_i \mid 1 \leq i \leq m] \qquad (2)$$

If $\theta_i\ STR\ (\rho[\![x]\!]) = \text{ኁ}$ for any i, then by the definition of $\mathcal{E}'$ we have that this last term is equal to ኁ. Suppose then that $\theta_i\ STR\ (\rho[\![x]\!]) = \text{ኁ}$ for no i. Then for any j,

$$\tau\ \alpha\ (\rho[\![x]\!])$$

$$= \mathcal{B}'[\![p\ w_1\ \ldots\ w_m]\!]\ [\overline{\tau}/\overline{z}]\ \alpha\ (\rho[\![x]\!])$$

$$= \&_{i=1}^{m}\ (\theta_i\ STR)\ (\rho[\![x]\!])$$

$$= \bigsqcup_{i=1}^{m}\ (\theta_i\ STR)\ (\rho[\![x]\!])$$

$$\sqsupseteq \theta_j\ STR\ (\rho[\![x]\!])$$

So, by monotonicity,

$$(2) \sqsubseteq \mathcal{E}'[\![p\ y_1\ \dots\ y_m]\!]\ \mathcal{E}'[\![w_i[\overline{e}/\overline{z}]]\!]\ [\tau\ \alpha\ (\rho[\![x]\!])/x]/y_i \mid 1 \leq i \leq m]$$

$$= RHS$$

case $c\ w_1\ \dots\ w_a$:

$$LHS = \alpha\ (\mathcal{E}'[\![(c\ w_1\ \dots\ w_n)[\overline{e}/\overline{z}]]\!]\ \rho)$$

$$= \alpha\ (\mathcal{C}[\![c]\!]\ (\mathcal{E}'[\![w_1[\overline{e}/\overline{z}]]\!]\ \rho)\ \dots\ (\mathcal{E}'[\![w_n[\overline{e}/\overline{z}]]\!]\ \rho)) \qquad (1)$$

If (1) $\neq$ ↿, then α can be expressed as

$$\alpha \ = \ \beta(\bigsqcup_{i=1}^{m} C_i\ \alpha_{i,1}\ \dots\ \alpha_{i,a_i})$$

and C_i matches c for some i. Let this C_i be denoted by C, a_i by a, and $\alpha_{i,j}$ by α_j for $1 \leq j \leq a_i$. Then

$$(1) \ = \ \mathcal{C}[\![c]\!]\ (\alpha_1\ (\mathcal{E}'[\![w_1[\overline{e}/\overline{z}]]\!]\ \rho))\ \dots\ (\alpha_a\ (\mathcal{E}'[\![w_a[\overline{e}/\overline{z}]]\!]\ \rho)) \qquad (2)$$

Let $\theta_i \ = \ \mathcal{B}'[\![w_i]\!]\ [\overline{\tau}/\overline{z}]$, $1 \leq i \leq a$. By the induction hypothesis, θ_i is safe for x with respect to $w_i[\overline{e}/\overline{z}]$ for each i, so

$$(2) \ \sqsubseteq \ \mathcal{C}[\![c]\!]\ (\mathcal{E}'[\![w_1[\overline{e}/\overline{z}]]\!]\ \rho[\theta_1\ \alpha_1\ (\rho[\![x]\!])/x])\ \dots\ (\mathcal{E}'[\![w_a[\overline{e}/\overline{z}]]\!]\ \rho[\theta_1\ \alpha_a\ (\rho[\![x]\!])/x]) \qquad (3)$$

If $\theta_i\ \alpha_i\ (\rho[\![x]\!]) \ = $ ↿ for some i, then (3) $=$ ↿ $\sqsubseteq$ RHS. Otherwise, for any j,

$$\theta_j\ \alpha_j\ (\rho[\![x]\!])$$

$$\sqsubseteq \bigsqcup_{i=1}^{n} \theta_i\ \alpha_i\ (\rho[\![x]\!])$$

$$= \&_{i=1}^{n}\ \theta_i\ \alpha_i\ (\rho[\![x]\!])$$

So, for $\beta \ = \ \&_{i=1}^{a}\ (\theta_i\ \alpha_i)$,

$$(3) \ \sqsubseteq \ \mathcal{C}[\![c]\!]\ (\mathcal{E}'[\![w_1[\overline{e}/\overline{z}]]\!]\ \rho[\beta\ (\rho[\![x]\!])/x])\ \dots\ (\mathcal{E}'[\![w_n[\overline{e}/\overline{z}]]\!]\ \rho[\beta\ (\rho[\![x]\!])/x])$$

And by monotonicity we have

$$\beta \ \sqsubseteq \ \mathcal{B}'[\![c\ e_1\ \dots\ e_n]\!]\ [\overline{\tau}/\overline{z}]\ \alpha$$

The case rule

We can derive the *case* rule without reference to the induction hypothesis.

Consider the left-hand side of the inequality we wish to show, and the definition of $\mathcal{E}'$. We may assume that either $e_0[\overline{e}/\overline{z}]$ has been reduced to head-normal form, or that is has no such form. If it has no such normal form, or if that form does not match one of patterns, then the left-hand side of the inequality is ↿, and the inequality is satisfied for any value of the right-hand side. Assuming that $e_0[\overline{e}/\overline{z}]$ is in head-normal form, we have for some i,

$$\begin{aligned} \tau = \mathcal{B}[\![\text{case } c_i\ e_{i,1}\ \dots\ e_{i,a_i}\ \text{of} \qquad & \qquad (1) \\ c_1\ x_{1,1}\ \dots\ x_{1,a_1}\ \Rightarrow\ e_1 & \\ \vdots \qquad & \\ c_m\ x_{m,1}\ \dots\ x_{m,a_m}\ \Rightarrow\ e_m]\!]\ \phi\ \alpha & \end{aligned}$$

Now τ is certainly safe if

$$\tau \sqsupseteq \mathcal{B}'[\![e_i[e_{i,1}/x_{i,1} \ \dots \ e_{i,a_i}/x_{i,a_i}]]\!] \ \phi \ \alpha \qquad (2)$$

By definition,

$$\begin{aligned}(1) = \bigsqcup_{j=1}^{m} (\quad & \mathcal{B}'[\![e_j]\!] \ \phi[(\lambda\alpha.ABS)/x_{i,j} \mid 1 \le j \le a_i] \ \alpha \\ & \& \ \mathcal{B}'[\![c_j \ e_{j,1} \ \dots \ e_{j,a_j}]\!] \ \phi \ (C_i \ (\mathcal{B}'[\![e_j]\!] \ \phi_{x_{j,1}} \ \alpha) \ \dots \ (\mathcal{B}'[\![e_j]\!] \ \phi_{x_{j,a_i}} \ \alpha))\end{aligned}$$

$$= (\mathcal{B}'[\![e_i]\!] \ \phi[(\lambda\alpha.ABS)/x_{i,j} \mid 1 \le j \le a_i] \ \alpha) \ \& \ (\&_{j=1}^{a_i} \ \mathcal{B}'[\![e_j]\!] \ \phi_{x_{i,j}} \ \alpha)$$

{ by the substitution rule }
$= (2)$

6 $\mathcal{A}$

The analysis described in [1] may be recast in terms with the same functionality as $\mathcal{B}$. We will call the analysis in this form $\mathcal{A}$.

The analysis in [1] gives separate rules for *if* and *case*, such that the rule for *if* gives a weaker analysis than for the semantically equivalent *case* expression. We choose therefore to ignore the *if* rule altogether.

The rules for $\mathcal{A}$ are exactly the same as for $\mathcal{B}$ except that we require that the variable environment ϕ for $\mathcal{A}$ map no more than a single variable to a value different from $\lambda\alpha.ABS$. The rules for $\mathcal{A}$ may be derived from the rules for $\mathcal{B}$ by replacing occurrences of $\mathcal{B}$ on the left-hand sides of the rules by $\mathcal{A}$, those on the right-hand sides by $\mathcal{A}'$, and adding the rule

$$\mathcal{A}'[\![e]\!] \ [\overline{\tau}/\overline{z}] \ \psi \ = \ \&_{i=1}^{n} \ \mathcal{A}[\![e]\!] \ \phi_{ABS}[\tau_i/z_i] \ \psi$$

We wish to show that $\mathcal{A}$ gives a weaker analysis than $\mathcal{B}$, in the sense that

$$\mathcal{B}[\![e]\!] \ \phi \ \psi \ \alpha \ \sqsubseteq \ \mathcal{A}[\![e]\!] \ \phi \ \psi \ \alpha$$

for all appropriate values of e, ϕ, ψ, and α, from which the safety of $\mathcal{A}$ is immediate. In fact we show a more general result. By monotonicity of & we have

$$(\mathcal{B}[\![e]\!] \ \phi_1 \ \psi) \ \& \ (\mathcal{B}[\![e]\!] \ \phi_2 \ \psi) \ \sqsubseteq \ \mathcal{B}[\![e]\!] \ (\phi_1 \ \& \ \phi_2) \ \psi$$

where ϕ_1 & ϕ_2 is defined for ϕ_1 and ϕ_2 having the same domain, and for every element z of this domain,

$$(\phi_1 \ \& \ \phi_2)[\![z]\!] \ = \ \phi_1[\![z]\!] \ \& \ \phi_2[\![z]\!]$$

The weakness of $\mathcal{A}$ relative to $\mathcal{B}$ results from its considering function arguments separately. This may be demonstrated by encapsulating a *case* expression in a function definition. Suppose that we have the function definition

$$\begin{aligned} f \ x \ y \ z \ = \ & \text{case } x \text{ of} \\ & \quad true \Rightarrow y \\ & \quad false \Rightarrow z \end{aligned}$$

and analyse strictness with respect to y in the call $f \ x \ y \ y$. We have

$$f^{\mathcal{A}} \ (\lambda\alpha.ABS) \ (\lambda\alpha.\alpha) \ (\lambda\alpha.\alpha) \ STR \ = \ ID$$

$$f^{\mathcal{B}} \ (\lambda\alpha.ABS) \ (\lambda\alpha.\alpha) \ (\lambda\alpha.\alpha) \ STR \ = \ STR$$

that is, $\mathcal{B}$ shows the call to be strict in y, but $\mathcal{A}$ does not.

7 Conclusion

The weakness of $\mathcal{A}$ relative to $\mathcal{B}$ results from the consideration of function arguments individually, rather than jointly as in $\mathcal{B}$. This is exemplified by the *if* example.

Just as for forwards strictness analysis, we may construct a lattice of approximations between $\mathcal{A}$ and $\mathcal{B}$ (see [3].) In the forwards analysis, the real strength of the computationally difficult analysis (the one corresponding to $\mathcal{B}$) only becomes apparent for higher-order analyses—we anticipate the same for backwards analysis. Extension of the backwards analysis to the higher-order case seems to be the next logical step in the development.

More information and background on backwards analysis may be found in [4, 5, 6, 7, 8, 9].

References

[1] Wadler, P., and Hughes, R.J.M., 1987. *Projections for Strictness Analysis.* Report 35, Programming Methodology Group, Department of Computer Sciences, Chalmers University of Technology and University of Göteborg, Göteborg, Sweden.

[2] Stoy, Joseph E: *Denotational Semantics: The Scott-Strachey Approach to Programming Language Theory.* The MIT Press, Cambridge, Massachusetts, 1977.

[3] Davis, K. "Trading accuracy for efficiency in forwards strictness analysis." Unpublished manuscript, 1989.

[4] Hughes, R.J.M. "Strictness detection in non-flat domains." In *Proceedings of the Workshop on Programs a Data Objects* (Copenhagen). H. Ganzinger and N. Jones, eds. LNCS 217. Springer-Verlag, Berlin, 1985

[5] Hughes, R.J.M. *Backwards Analysis of Functional Programs.* Departmental Research Report CSC/87/R3, Department of Computing Science, University of Glasgow, 1987.

[6] Hughes, R.J.M. "Analysing strictness by abstract interpretation of continuations." Chapter 4 of Abramsky, S. and Hankin, C. (eds.). *Abstract Interpretation of Declarative Languages.* Ellis-Horwood, 1987.

[7] Hughes, R.J.M. "Compile-time analysis of functional programs." In *Proc. Year of Programming Summer School on Declarative Programming,* (Austin, Texas), 1987, David Turner (ed.), Addison-Wesley 1989.

[8] Hughes, R.J.M. "Projections for polymorphic strictness analysis." 1989.

[9] Hughes, R.J.M. and Ferguson, A. "An iterative powerdomain construction." In *Draft Proceedings of the 1989 Glasgow Workshop on Functional Programming* (Fraserburgh, Scotland). 1989.

Abstract Interpretation of Polymorphic Functions

Gebreselassie Baraki and John Hughes
Department of Computing Science
University of Glasgow
Glasgow G12 8QQ

Abstract

Abstract interpretation is one of the popular techniques used in doing program analysis. In this paper, we define an abstract interpretation of polymorphic functions which may be used to perform strictness analysis. The abstract functions of polymorphic functions are again polymorphic. Finally it is proved that the abstract interpretation is safe.

1. Introduction

Experience has shown that efficient implementations of lazy functional languages must rely on powerful semantic analysis. In particular, strictness analysis has proved to be very important. A function f is said to be strict if $f \perp = \perp$; the arguments of strict functions can be passed by value instead of by need, enabling more efficient code to be generated.

The analysis technique we are interested in is *abstract interpretation* [1]. Intuitively, we run the program to be analysed on *abstract* or *partial* information about its inputs, giving partial information about its results. The mapping of abstract inputs to abstract outputs can give all sorts of information about the computational behaviour of the program. Abstract values range over finite *abstract domains*, which means that infinite loops in the abstract computation are detectable.

Mycroft was the first to use abstract interpretation to perform strictness analysis of functional programs [2]. The analysis applied only to first-order functions over flat domains. Burn, Hankin and Abramsky extended this to strictness analysis of higher-order functions over flat domains [3]. Wadler showed how lazy lists (a non-flat domain) can be incorporated [4], and Abramsky proved that the result of the analysis of any monomorphic instance of a polymorphic function can be used at all instances [5] (but not the abstract function).

If different instances of a polymorphic function are used in many places in a program, analysis may have to be performed as many times to compute an abstract function for each instance. This potential inefficiency was pointed out by Burn, and later by Hughes [6]. Hughes also developed a method by which the abstract function of any instance can be computed from that of the simplest. However, the method works only for first-order functions.

In this note an abstract interpretation of a polymorphic language is proposed. The language is the second-order λ-calculus with constants. Unlike the untyped λ-calculus, it has two variable binding operators : one for types and the other for values. Polymorphic functions are represented as functions of types. We describe our abstraction in two steps. First we define an abstraction of the type system. This maps each type into the type of its abstract values. This mapping is then used to define the abstraction of expressions. Finally a textual abstraction is defined and shown to be *safe*.

Bruce and Meyer define second-order functional domains [7]. They show that such domains model the second-order λ-calculus. $\wp\omega$, the structure which was used to model the untyped λ-calculus by Scott [8], can be turned into a second-order functional domain. From now on, we assume that this is the model used in defining the semantics of the second-order λ-calculus.

2. The language

As we said above, we work with second-order λ-calculus. The main novel feature of this language is the use of a type binding operator. Consequently application of expressions to types is defined. Before providing the syntax of the language we introduce the type system.

Types

We restrict ourselves to one base type **int**, the type of integers, and assume that there are infinitely many type variables.

Definition The *second-order types* are inductively defined by :

(i) a base type or a type variable is a type.

(ii) if α and β are types then $\alpha \to \beta$ is a type.

(iii) if t is a type variable and α is a type then $\forall t.\alpha$ is a type.

An occurrence of a type variable t in a type α is said to be *bound* if it is inside a sub-type of the form $\forall t.\beta$, otherwise it is *free* . For any types α and σ and a type variable t, $\alpha[\sigma/t]$ is used to denote the result of substituting σ for every free occurrence of t in α. Substitution is defined by the following rules:

$t[\sigma/t]$	$= \sigma$
$s[\sigma/t]$	= s, if s is a variable different from t or a base type
$(\alpha \to \beta)[\sigma/t]$	$= (\alpha[\sigma/t]) \to (\beta[\sigma/t])$
$(\forall t.\alpha)[\sigma/t]$	$= \forall t.\alpha$
$(\forall s.\alpha)[\sigma/t]$	$= \forall s.(\alpha[\sigma/t])$, if $s \neq t$, and s not free in σ or t not free in α
$(\forall s.\alpha)[\sigma/t]$	$= \forall z.(\alpha[z/s])([\sigma/t])$, if $s \neq t$ and s free in σ and t free in α

Two types are said to be equivalent if one can be obtained from the other by renaming bound variables.

Terms

Since **int** is the only base type the only constants of the language are the natural numbers. We assume that there are infinitely many variables.

Definition The *second-order λ-terms* are inductively defined by :

(i) every constant and variable is a term.

(ii) if M and N are terms, so is (MN).

(iii) if x is a variable, α a type and M a term then $(\lambda x \in \alpha.M)$ is a term.

(iv) if M is a term and α is a type then $M[\alpha]$ is a term .

(v) If t is a type variable and M a term then $\Lambda t.M$ is a term.

$M[\alpha]$ stands for the application of the term M to the type α and Λ is the type binding operator.

An occurrence of a term variable x in a term M is said to be *bound* if it is inside a sub-term of the form $\lambda x \in \alpha.N$, otherwise it is *free*. An occurrence of a type variable t in a term M is *bound* if it is inside a sub-term of the form $\Lambda t.N$, otherwise it is *free*.

For any terms M and N and a variable x, M[N/x] denotes the result of substituting N for every free occurrence of x in M. Substitution is given by the following rules:

y[L/y]	=	L
x[L/y]	=	x, if x is a constant or a variable different from y
(MN)[L/y]	=	(M[L/y])(N[L/y])
$(\lambda x \in \alpha.M)[L/x]$	=	$\lambda x \in \alpha.M$
$(\lambda x \in \alpha.M)[L/y]$	=	$\lambda x \in \alpha.(M[L/y])$, if x is not free in L or y not free in M
$(\lambda x \in \alpha.M)[L/y]$	=	$(\lambda u \in \alpha.M[u/x])([L/y]$, if x is free in L and y free in M
$(M[\alpha])[L/y]$	=	$(M[L/y])[\alpha]$
$(\Lambda t.M)[L/y]$	=	$\Lambda t.(M[L/y])$

It also makes sense to define substitution of a type σ for every occurrence of a type variable t in a term M. The result of this substitution is denoted by $M[\sigma/t]$. Since the words '*bound*' and '*free*' are used in three different ways, it is important to note that we have three different forms of substitution. Which form we are using at a particular point is usually obvious from context.

β-reduction

In the untyped λ-calculus, β-reduction is the main vehicle for performing computations. In the second-order λ-calculus we have two forms of abstraction: one with respect to (term) variables and another with respect to type variables. Hence it is possible to define two forms of β-reduction :

$$(\lambda x \in \alpha.M)N \quad = \quad M[N/x]$$
$$(\Lambda t.M)[\alpha] \quad = \quad M[\alpha/t]$$

α-conversion and η-contraction can also be defined with respect to the two abstractions in a straight forward way.

remark

(i) The second-order λ-calculus is strongly normalisable. However, programming languages based on it usually allow recursive definitions. With recursion, some non-terminating computations become definable in the language. Even without recursion, it makes sense to talk about strictness of functions because of its operational significance. To say that a function is strict means that it needs to evaluate its argument.

To study strictness analysis we introduce $\perp$ to the language as a new constant and give it the type $\forall t.t$. It is now necessary to extend the definition of reduction, as follows :

$$\begin{aligned}
\bot[\forall t.\sigma][\alpha] &= \bot[\sigma[\alpha/t]] \\
\lambda x \in \alpha.\ \bot[\beta] &= \bot[\alpha\text{->}\beta] \\
\Lambda t.\ \bot[\sigma] &= \bot[\forall t.\sigma] \\
\bot_{\alpha\text{->}\beta}(x) &= \bot_{\beta} \\
\bot[\alpha\text{->}\beta]\ x &= \bot[\beta] \\
\bot &= \bot[\forall t.t]
\end{aligned}$$

(ii) Some of the properties and functions which we will define are recursive on the structure of types. Thus whenever we use the reduction rule $(\Lambda t.M)[\alpha] = M[\alpha/t]$, α will not be allowed to be a polymorphic type. Otherwise well known problems of circularity, which are difficult to get read of, will arise. Obviously this assumption results in a language which is weaker than the full second-order λ-calculus.

An ordering on terms

We now introduce an ordering, $\leq$, on values of terms. $\leq$ is defined by cases on types. Let a and b be values of terms of the same type.

(i) **int**

$a \leq b$ if and only if $a = b$ or $a = \bot$

(ii) $\alpha \text{->} \beta$

$a \leq b$ if and only if $a(x) \leq b(x)$ for all x

(iii) $\forall t.\alpha$

$a \leq b$ if and only if $a[\beta] \leq b[\beta]$ for all types β

It is easy to show that $\leq$ is a partial order.

A language for abstract functions

We need a language to express abstract functions. This will also be a version of the second-order λ-calculus, in which the only base type is **2**. The terms of type **2** are 0 and 1. We define an ordering on terms in the usual way, starting from $0 \leq 1$. The terms of each type in this language form a lattice and thus we will call these types lattice types. To distinguish the two languages explicitly we write the type binding operator as $\mathbf{\Lambda}$ and quantification over types as $\mathbf{\forall}$.

3. Abstraction

In the analysis described in [3] an abstraction of the semantic domain, which is a mapping into a domain whose summands are finite lattices, is defined. The abstract interpretation which we define here is given as a mapping of expressions of the original language into expressions of the language with lattice types. But types appear in expressions in this case. Thus we first provide a mapping, *Abs*, from types into lattice types. This map will be used in defining the abstraction of values.

Mapping types into lattice types

We define the function *Abs* from the original type system into the new type system by structural induction.

$$Abs\ \mathbf{int} = \mathbf{2}$$
$$Abs\ t = t$$
$$Abs\ \alpha \text{->} \beta = Abs\ \alpha \text{->} Abs\ \beta$$
$$Abs\ \forall t.\alpha = \forall t.(Abs\ \alpha)$$

Note that we map type variables into themselves. Strictly speaking, we should introduce a new class of lattice type variables. But then it would be necessary to do some kind of substitution every time we map polymorphic types. For simplicity we use the same class of variable names and the context in which they appear should make it clear as to how they are used.

An important property which will be used in the future is the following :

Lemma 3.1 For any types τ, σ and a type variable t :

$$(Abs\ \sigma)[(Abs\ \tau)/t] = Abs\ (\sigma[\tau/t])$$

Proof

We proceed by structural induction on types.

(i) $\sigma = \mathbf{int}$

the result holds trivially.

(ii) $\sigma = \alpha \text{->} \beta$

$$\begin{aligned}(Abs\ \alpha \text{->} \beta)[(Abs\ \tau)/t] &= (Abs\ \alpha \text{->} Abs\ \beta)[(Abs\ \tau)/t] \\ &= (Abs\ \alpha)\ [(Abs\ \tau)/t] \text{->} (Abs\ \beta)\ [(Abs\ \tau)/t] \\ &= (Abs\ (\alpha[\tau/t])) \text{->} (Abs\ (\beta[\tau/t])) \\ &= Abs\ (\alpha[\tau/t] \text{->} \beta[\tau/t]) \\ &= Abs\ ((\alpha \text{->} \beta)[\tau/t])\end{aligned}$$

(iii) $\sigma = \forall s.\beta$

$$\begin{aligned}(Abs\ (\forall s.\beta))\ [(Abs\ \tau)/t] &= (\forall s.(Abs\ \beta))[(Abs\ \tau)/t] \\ &= \forall s.((Abs\ \beta)\ [(Abs\ \tau)/t] \\ &= \forall s.(Abs\ \beta[\tau/t])\end{aligned}$$

But

$$\begin{aligned}Abs\ ((\forall s.\beta)[\tau/t]) &= Abs\ (\forall s.\beta[\tau/t]) \\ &= \forall s.(Abs\ \beta[\tau/t])\end{aligned}$$

Abstraction of expressions

Having defined the mapping from types into lattice types, we now define the abstraction. Given any type, the abstraction maps objects of the type to objects of the corresponding lattice type. That is for any type α we define $abs_\alpha : \alpha \to Abs\ \alpha$. Before defining this mapping we introduce some notation and definitions.

As in [3], for any set of values A of type α we define the downward closure, A^*, of A and $\mathbb{P}A$ as follows :

$A^* = \{ x \in \alpha \,/\, x \le a \text{ ,for some } a \in A\}$, and

$\mathbb{P}A$ = the set of all non-empty subsets of A which are downward closed.

For any function $f : X \to Y$, $\mathbb{P}f : \mathbb{P}X \to \mathbb{P}Y$ is defined by $(\mathbb{P}f)(U) = \{f(a) \,/\, a \in U\}^*$.

We also use a mapping $conc_\alpha : Abs\ \alpha \to \mathbb{P}\alpha$. $conc_\alpha$ takes an abstract value and gives the set of all values of type α whose abstract values are below the abstract value we started with. More precisely : $conc_\alpha\ a = \{ x \in \alpha \,/\, abs_\alpha\, x \le a \}$.

We define the abstraction by type recursion.

$$abs_{int}\ \bot = 0$$
$$abs_{int}\ x = 1,\ x \ne \bot$$

$$abs_{\alpha \to \beta} = \lambda f. \bigsqcup \circ \mathbb{P}(abs_\beta \circ f) \circ conc_\alpha$$

$$abs_{\forall t.\alpha}\ x = \Lambda u. \bigsqcup_{\{\sigma / Abs\ \sigma = u\}} abs_{\alpha[\sigma/t]}\ x[\sigma]$$

The fact that we have only one base type in the original language implies that there is one to one correspondence between types and lattice types. Thus the expression $\{\sigma / Abs\ \sigma = u\}$, which appears in the last equation, is a singleton and hence we do not need to take least upper bounds. However it is better to keep it as it is, because the proofs in this paper would remain the same even if we extend the language by introducing more base types.

Some properties of the abstraction

Proposition 3.2

$$(abs_{\alpha \to \beta}\, f)(abs_\alpha\, a) \ge abs_\beta\,(f(a))$$

Proof

$$\begin{aligned}(abs_{\alpha \to \beta}\, f)(abs_\alpha\, a) &= (\textstyle\bigsqcup \circ \mathbb{P}(abs_\beta \circ f) \circ conc_\alpha)(abs_\alpha(a)) \\ &= \textstyle\bigsqcup \{ abs_\beta\,(f(u)) \,/\, abs_\alpha(u) \le abs_\alpha(a) \}^* \\ &\ge abs_\beta\,(f(a))\end{aligned}$$

Proposition 3.3

For any type α : $(abs_{\forall t.\beta}\ x)[Abs\ \ \alpha] \geq abs_{\beta[\alpha/t]}\ x[\alpha]$

Proof

$$(abs_{\forall t.\beta}\ x)[Abs\ \ \alpha] = (\Lambda u. \bigsqcup_{\{\sigma/\ Abs\ \ \sigma = u\}} abs_{\beta[\sigma/t]}\ x[\sigma])\ [Abs\ \ \alpha]$$
$$= \bigsqcup_{\{\sigma/\ Abs\ \ \sigma = Abs\ \ \alpha\}} abs_{\beta[\sigma/t]}\ x[\sigma]$$
$$\geq abs_{\beta[\alpha/t]}\ x[\alpha]$$

4. Abstract interpretation

Our motivation for this work has been the desire to have polymorphic abstract functions. Although results of the analysis of a monomorphic instance of a polymorphic function may be applied to all instances, abstract functions may carry more information (see [6]).
In what follows an abstract interpretation of polymorphic functions will be defined.

The textual abstraction, *tabs*

Again the definition of *tabs* is given by structural induction :

tabs (c)	=	*abs* (c), if c is a constant
tabs (x)	=	x
tabs ($\lambda x \in \alpha$. e)	=	$\lambda x \in$ (*Abs* α). (*tabs* e)
tabs (MN)	=	(*tabs* M) (*tabs* N)
tabs (M[α])	=	(*tabs* M) [*Abs* α]
tabs (Λt.e)	=	Λu. (*tabs* e)[u/t]

5. Safety

The textual abstraction is defined on program texts whereas the map *abs* may be regarded as being defined on semantic objects. It makes sense to introduce the notion of *safety* for the abstract interpretation. *tabs* is safe if it is at least as defined as *abs*. That is for any expression e : *abs* e $\leq$ *tabs* e. We will state and prove a theorem which is a sufficient condition for safety.

Theorem

For any type variables $\{t_i\}$, term variables $\{x_j\}$, types $\{\tau_i\}$, terms (or values) $\{v_j\}$ and expression e the following holds :

$$abs\ (e[\tau_i/t_i][v_j/x_j]) \ \leq\ (tabs\ e)[(Abs\ \tau_i)/t_i][(abs\ v_j)/x_j]$$

Proof

In the proof we will omit the type subscript of *abs*.
We proceed by structural induction on terms

(i) the case where e is a variable or a constant is trivial.

(ii) $(\mathit{tabs}\ (e_1 e_2))[(\mathit{Abs}\ \tau_i)/t_i][(\mathit{abs}\ v_j)/x_j]$

$= \{$ definition of *tabs* $\}$

$((\mathit{tabs}\ e_1)(\mathit{tabs}\ e_2))\ [(\mathit{Abs}\ \tau_i)/t_i][(\mathit{abs}\ v_j)/x_j]$

$= \{$ property of substitution $\}$

$((\mathit{tabs}\ e_1)\ [(\mathit{Abs}\ \tau_i)/t_i][(\mathit{abs}\ v_j)/x_j])((\mathit{tabs}\ e_2)\ [(\mathit{Abs}\ \tau_i)/t_i][(\mathit{abs}\ v_j)/x_j])$

$\geq \{$ induction assumption $\}$

$(\mathit{abs}\ (e_1[\tau_i/t_i][v_j/x_j]))\ (\mathit{abs}\ (e_2[\tau_i/t_i][v_j/x_j]))$

$\geq \{$ proposition 3.2 $\}$

$\mathit{abs}\ ((e_1[\tau_i/t_i][v_j/x_j])\ (e_2[\tau_i/t_i][v_j/x_j]))$

$= \{$ property of substitution $\}$

$\mathit{abs}\ ((e_1 e_2)[\tau_i/t_i][v_j/x_j])$

(iii) Assume that $\lambda x \in \alpha.\ e$ is of type $\alpha \text{->} \beta$

$(\mathit{abs}\ ((\lambda x \in \alpha.\ e)[\tau_i/t_i][v_j/x_j]))(a)$

$= \{$ definition of *abs* $\}$

$\bigsqcup \{\mathit{abs}_{\beta[\tau i/ti]}\ ((\lambda x \in \alpha[\tau_i/t_i].\ (e\ [\tau_i/t_i][v_j/x_j]))(v))\ /\mathit{abs}_{\alpha[\tau i/ti]}(v) \leq a\}^*$

$= \{\ \beta$-reduction $\}$

$\bigsqcup \{\mathit{abs}_{\beta[\tau i/ti]}\ (e\ [\tau_i/t_i][v_j/x_j, v/x])\ /\ \mathit{abs}_{\alpha[\tau i/ti]}(v) \leq a\}^*$

By induction assumption we have :

For all v with $\mathit{abs}_{\alpha[\tau i/ti]}(v) \leq a$

$\mathit{abs}_{\beta[\tau i/ti]}\ (e\ [\tau_i/t_i][v_j/x_j, v/x])$

$\leq (\mathit{tabs}\ e)[(\mathit{Abs}\ \tau_i)/t_i][(\mathit{abs}\ v_j)/x_j, (\mathit{abs}\ v)/x]$

$\leq (\mathit{tabs}\ e)[(\mathit{Abs}\ \tau_i)/t_i][(\mathit{abs}\ v_j)/x_j, a/x]$

Therefore

$(\mathit{abs}\ ((\lambda x \in \alpha.\ e)[\tau_i/t_i][v_j/x_j]))(a) \leq (\mathit{tabs}\ e)[(\mathit{Abs}\ \tau_i)/t_i][(\mathit{abs}\ v_j)/x_j, a/x]$

But

$((\mathit{tabs}\ (\lambda x \in \alpha.\ e)\ )[(\mathit{Abs}\ \tau_i)/t_i][(\mathit{abs}\ v_j)/x_j])(a)$

$= (\lambda x \in \mathit{Abs}\ \alpha.\ ((\mathit{tabs}\ e)\ [(\mathit{Abs}\ \tau_i)/t_i][(\mathit{abs}\ v_j)/x_j]))(a)$

$= (\mathit{tabs}\ e)\ [(\mathit{Abs}\ \tau_i)/t_i][(\mathit{abs}\ v_j)/x_j, a/x]$

Hence we have the desired inequality.

(iv) $\mathit{abs}\ ((\Lambda t.e)[\tau_i/t_i][v_j/x_j])$

$= \mathit{abs}\ (\Lambda t.(e[\tau_i/t_i][v_j/x_j]))$

$= \Lambda u. \bigsqcup_{\{\alpha / \mathit{Abs}\ \alpha = u\}} \mathit{abs}_{\beta[\alpha/t]}\ e[\tau_i/t_i, \alpha/t][v_j/x_j]$

By induction assumption, for each type α with *Abs* $\alpha = u$:

$$\mathit{abs}_{\beta[\alpha/t]}\ e[\tau_i/t_i, \alpha/t][v_j/x_j] \leq (\mathit{tabs}\ e)[(\mathit{Abs}\ \tau_i)/t_i, (\mathit{Abs}\ \alpha)/t][(\mathit{abs}\ v_j)/x_j]$$

For each u the expression on the right-hand side is fixed and hence the least upper bound of the left-hand side over α with *Abs* $\alpha = u$ will be bounded by it.
On the other hand :

$(\mathit{tabs}\ (\Lambda t.e))[(\mathit{Abs}\ \tau_i)/t_i][(\mathit{abs}\ v_j)/x_j]$

$= (\Lambda u.\ (\mathit{tabs}\ e)[u/t])[(\mathit{Abs}\ \tau_i)/t_i][(\mathit{abs}\ v_j)/x_j]$

$= \Lambda u.\ ((\mathit{tabs}\ e)[u/t, (\mathit{Abs}\ \tau_i)/t_i][(\mathit{abs}\ v_j)/x_j])$

Therefore

$\mathit{abs}\ ((\Lambda t.e)[t_i/t_i][v_j/x_j]) \leq (\mathit{tabs}\ (\Lambda t.e))[(\mathit{Abs}\ \tau_i)/t_i][(\mathit{abs}\ v_j)/x_j]$

(v) $\mathit{abs}\ ((M[\alpha])[\tau_i/t_i][v_j/x_j])$

$= \{$ property of substitution $\}$

$\mathit{abs}\ ((M\ [\tau_i/t_i][v_j/x_j])[\alpha[\tau_i/t_i]])$

$\leq \{$ proposition 3.3 $\}$

$(\mathit{abs}\ (M\ [\tau_i/t_i][v_j/x_j]))[\mathit{Abs}\ (\alpha[\tau_i/t_i])]$

$\leq \{$ induction assumption $\}$

$((\mathit{tabs}\ \ M)[(\mathit{Abs}\ \tau_i)/t_i][(\mathit{abs}\ v_j)/x_j])[\mathit{Abs}\ (\alpha[\tau_i/t_i])]$

$= \{$ lemma 3.1 $\}$

$((\mathit{tabs}\ \ M)[(\mathit{Abs}\ \tau_i)/t_i][(\mathit{abs}\ v_j)/x_j])[(\mathit{Abs}\ \alpha)[(\mathit{Abs}\ \tau_i)/t_i]]$

$= \{$ property of substitution $\}$

$((\mathit{tabs}\ \ M)[\mathit{Abs}\ \alpha])[(\mathit{Abs}\ \tau_i)/t_i][(\mathit{abs}\ v_j)/x_j]$

$= \{$ definition of *tabs* $\}$

$(\mathit{tabs}\ M[\alpha])[(\mathit{Abs}\ \tau_i)/t_i][(\mathit{abs}\ v_j)/x_j]$

6. Conclusions and future work

We have described an abstract interpretation of a polymorphic language where the abstract functions of polymorphic functions are polymorphic. However, a useful analysis of a practical programming language must deal with recursion, which we have not treated. At the moment we are studying ways of introducing recursion.

References

[1] Cousot P, R. Cousot : static determination of dynamic properties of

programs. In : Proceedings of the 2nd International Symposium on Programming. 1976

[2] Mycroft A : the theory and practice of transforming call-by-need into call-by-value. In : Proceedings of the 4th International Symposium on Programming. Springer, Berlin Heidelberg New York, 1980 (Lecture notes in computer science no. 83)

[3] Burn G. L, Hankin C. L, S. Abramsky. Strictness analysis for higher order functions. Science of Computer Programming 1986;7:249-278

[4] Wadler P : strictness analysis on non-flat domains. In : Abramsky S. and C. Hankin (eds) Abstract Interpretation of Declarative Languages. Ellis-Horwood, 1987

[5] Abramsky S : strictness analysis and polymorphic invariance. In : Proceedings of the DIKU Workshop on programs as data objects. Springer, Berlin Heidelberg New York,1986 (Lecture notes in computer science no. 217)

[6] Hughes J : abstract interpretation of first-order polymorphic functions. In : Proceedings of the Glasgow Workshop on Functional Programming. 1988

[7] Bruce K. B, A. R Meyer : the semantics of second order polymorphic lambda calculus. In : Proceedings of the International Symposium on the Semantics of Data Types. Springer, Berlin Heidelberg New York, 1984 (Lecture notes in computer science no. 173)

[8] Scott D. Data types as lattices. SIAM Journal of Computing 1976;5: 522-587

An Iterative Powerdomain Construction

A. B. Ferguson and R. J. M. Hughes

Abstract

A finite domain for the abstract interpretation of lazy lists is known, but is not easily generalisable to other lazy data structures. A construction for finite abstract domains is presented which is quite general, based on the notion of a 'set of elements'. The abstraction for elements is given, and a new powerdomain is developed. Finally, a means of iterative calculation of the sub-domain which contains all the 'useful' points is arrived at.

1 Introduction

Only recently have strictness analysis techniques been developed to deal with non-flat domains: that is to say that early methods (such as Mycroft's [1]) deal only with data types which are either completely undefined, or are completely defined, and structures which are more complex must necessarily be treated in the same way to be analysed in such a framework. Clearly this loses potential strictness information, since this means that for lists, say, all that could be discovered is whether a function is strict or not, i.e. whether it is safe to evaluate its argument into head normal form.

It would clearly be desirable to obtain further strictness information for such data types, firstly to improve the general accuracy of the analysis (so that we do not immediately lose information about an object simply by virtue of it having been encapsulated in a list), and also to allow list or other such arguments to be pre-evaluated to a greater extent, to further reduce the cost of building closures. In particular, we would like to be able to identify the following kinds of strictness in lists, i.e. whether for a given list argument it is safe to evaluate:

- To head-normal form. Ordinary strictness.
- To head-normal form, and also to evaluate the first element (either completely, or to some specified degree).
- The spine of the list. Tail strictness.
- The spine, and each of the elements (to whatever degree). Hyper-strictness.

Other kinds of strictness are possible also: we might for instance take the view that head strictness means that if a particular *Cons* cell is created, then its head must necessarily be evaluated too. This can be done in the projections approach to strictness analysis [2]. We will not consider this or any other possible schema in the present paper. Here we will use the framework for abstract interpretation developed by Burn, Hankin and Abramsky [3].

In order to perform abstract interpretation on lazy lists, and other non-flat data structures, an abstract domain must be constructed, which (for conventional techniques at any rate) must be finite. Thus the obvious idea of representing an abstract list (say) by a list of abstract values is infeasible, as this would necessarily be infinite. One solution is to ignore order completely, which would enable simple strictness, tail strictness, and head-tail strictness (hyper-strictness) to be captured. Such a framework would necessarily fail to treat head-strictness, since this is an order-dependent property (as well as more out-of-the-ordinary forms of strictness, such as being strict in alternate elements). (Although Burn, it might be noted, has a scheme for combining a method of this kind with one for head-strictness [4].)

One such treatment is that of Wadler [5], which uses the domain $(\mathbf{2}_\perp)_\perp$ for abstract lists of flat elements, with the following interpretation of the points (bottommost first, writing $\hat{f}$ for the abstract version of the function f being analysed):

$\perp$, corresponding to the list domain bottom, with $\hat{f}\perp = \perp$ meaning simple strictness;

∞, corresponding to infinite and partial lists, i.e. those ending in bottom, with $\hat{f}\,\infty = \perp$ meaning tail strictness;

$0\in$, corresponding to finite lists (terminated by *Nil*) with one or more elements being bottom, with $\hat{f}\,0\in\ = \perp$ meaning hyper-strictness;

$1\in$, corresponding to total lists, so that $\hat{f}\,1\in\ = \perp$ means the function implements abort.

For lists of some general type t, the domain used is $(\hat{t}_\perp)_\perp$, where $\hat{t}$ is the abstract domain for the element type. The bottommost two points have the same interpretation as before, and each of the others is of the form $e\in$, meaning that the greatest lower bound of the abstract values of the elements of the list is e. For some other types, such as trees, a similar approach may be used.

This works well for flat lists, but does not generalise to arbitrary data-structures, and only in an ad hoc fashion to lists of non-flat structures. The basic difficulty is that the four point domain is chosen essentially for its correspondence to the desired strictness information for lists, and as a result is an arbitrary choice of domain with regard to some other type, as it does not take account of the type's structure. The four point domain may be rationalised as follows: regard a value of the recursive type as a collection of elements, held together with some other structure. We then interpret the bottom point as being the usual bottom, i.e. no defined elements, no defined structure. The point ∞ we interpret as being a partly defined structure. The remaining points are those where the structure is total, the particular point corresponding to the least defined element.

This approach can be extended only to data structures which fit the same general pattern, such as list- and tree-like types. For other types, particularly more complex ones, we have no guarantee that it is at all useful to regard a value of the type in this fashion.

A further problem is the lack of accuracy of the analysis obtained on lists of compound objects. Consider some function which maps some operator whose abstraction is lub down a list of pairs. If we analyse this function's behaviour over the lists with elements having abstractions $(0,0)$ in one case, and in the other, two elements with abstractions $(0,1)$ and $(1,0)$, we will find we are unable to distinguish between them, as both are represented by the same point, $(0,0)\in$. Wadler's technique cannot discover any strictness which would depend on discovering the function to be undefined on the former, but not on the latter. We might hope that a technique which used a more exact representation for compound objects would allow more strictness to be discovered in such cases.

2 Overview

It would clearly be desirable to have an abstraction which would work for any type described by the usual type-formation operators. Our basic idea is to abstract the structure as a set of elements. This would in principle allow the construction of finite domains, by the aforementioned expedient of forgetting the ordering inherent in the concrete values. However, the notions of both 'set' and 'element' need to be refined.

Our approach differs from that of Wadler in two key ways: firstly we represent a value by sets of (something related to) the base domain, rather than single values of the base domain, to which are added further points. This avoids the need to take greatest lower bounds while abstracting a list, which necessarily worsens the approximation. Instead we can retain (essentially) all the information about the components of our data type, though discarding ordering information.

Further, we generalise away from the idea of elements, and simply consider the smallest useful subcomponent of a data structure, corresponding essentially to a single level of recursion. This allows us to avoid difficulties with types which are not parameterised, or are on more than one type variable, or otherwise have a non-straightforward structure which would complicate the notion of an 'element' *per se*.

Consider the simplest useful example, lists of some flat type, *Int*, say. In Wadler's scheme, we have two points for partial list structures, and two points corresponding to the abstract domain for the base type, representing the least defined points in lists with complete 'tails'. In our approach, we seek to treat each of these symmetrically, by capturing list structure in whether our sets contain something corresponding to *Nil*, and definedness of elements as part of *Cons*'s. Every value of this type must consist of a number of instances of the 'body' of the recursive type, nested inside one another as recursive tails. If we discard the tails, but retain each of the bodies, then we can form sets of these as our first step in calculating abstract values. We will call these bodies ***chunks***.

In our example, the possible chunks are $\perp$, *Nil*, and objects of the form $Cons\, h\, \cdot$. Clearly we must consider all possibilities for the element h in this last case, but the tail we have thrown away entirely. Since the type *Int* has as its abstraction the two point domain, this leaves us two possibilities for the abstraction of *Cons* chunks, which we will write as $0:$ and $1:$. The abstractions of $\perp$ and *Nil* we will write as respectively $\perp$ and $[\,]$. Each recursive level of a list must consist of one of these, so in principle all we need do is to form a set of all the chunks in a value, and abstract each individually.

We can form sets of these chunks to represnt the same concrete values as each of the points of Wadler's abstract domain.

$$
\begin{aligned}
\perp &:: \{\perp\} \\
\infty &:: \{\perp, 1{:}\} \\
0\!\in &:: \{[\,], 0{:}, 1{:}\}
\end{aligned}
$$

$$1\in \;::\; \{[\,],1{:}\}$$

One complication is that it is necessary to use a chunk domain which is lub-closed, in order to have any reasonable expectation that our final abstract domain will have properly defined lubs. Thus we will have to add extra points to our chunk domain, as the four chunks above do not form a lattice. More seriously, we cannot of course use 'sets' at all, but must use a powerdomain construction of some kind. We will consider the usual finite powerdomains, the Hoare, Smyth and Plotkin constructions.

The three standard powerdomains offer the widest possible range of 'granularity' of construction: the Hoare and Smyth domains are the 'coarsest-grained' possible (that is, they distinguish the fewest points), while the Plotkin powerdomain is the 'finest-grained' (distinguishes the most points possible). It turns out that we shall need a powerdomain of intermediate granularity for our purposes, which we later construct.

In the Hoare powerdomain, each point is a downward-closed set. Thus a given set is represented by adding in all the elements approximating its members. The Smyth powerdomain, analogously, consists of upward-closed sets. This means that we can use the Hoare powerdomain to represent upper bounds, ('best-case' scenarios), and the Smyth for lower bounds ('worst-case'). Unfortunately, neither of these is sufficiently exact for our purposes, since we require both kinds of bound. In order to distinguish between $\perp$ and ∞ we need an upper bound ("could some of the structure be defined?"), but we need lower bounds to distinguish between the other two points ("might some of the elements be undefined?"). Thus in the Hoare powerdomain $0\in$ and $1\in$ would become the single point "Some elements of the list may be defined", while in the Smyth powerdomain, $\perp$ and ∞ would be merged into "Some of the list structure may be undefined". Thus we need a powerdomain which captures interval information in some way.

The Plotkin powerdomain contains points which are convex sets. The representative of a given set is obtained by adding all points which lie between any two drawn from it. This enables us to distinguish each of the four desired sets. Unfortunately, minimal upper bounds are non-unique in this powerdomain, a least upper bound operation being essential for abstract interpretation. Also, this domain contains too many points, both in the sense of being very large and potentially costly to analyse, and that it differentiates between sets of chunks which are, for the purposes of abstract interpretation, essentially the same.

3 Language

Consider the following set of domain-forming operators:

$$\begin{aligned} t \;::=\;& \mathbf{1} \\ \mid\;& \mathit{Int} \\ \mid\;& t_1 \oplus t_2 \\ \mid\;& t_1 \times t_2 \\ \mid\;& t_\perp \\ \mid\;& \mu v.t(v) \end{aligned}$$

where **1** is the one-point domain, Int the integers plus bottom, $\oplus$ is coalesced sum, $\times$ is (unlifted) product, and $t_\bot$ lifting. Recursive domains are formed by the μ operator.

We will use our type formation operators as functors, so that we may write for example $f \times g$, where f and g are functions, to mean the function over pairs which applies f to the left component, and g to the right.

We will use a language with the following zeroth order terms:

$$
\begin{array}{rcl}
e & ::= & \cdot \\
& | & zero \mid succ \mid iszero \mid pred \\
& | & inl\ e \mid inr\ e \mid isl\ e \mid outl\ e \mid outr\ e \\
& | & (e_1, e_2) \mid fst\ e \mid snd\ e \\
& | & abort \mid lift\ e \mid drop\ e \\
& | & wrap\ e \mid unwrap\ e
\end{array}
$$

The terms in our language are (monomorphically) typed as follows (we will not consider how we will actually obtain type information in practice, and will omit type subscripts):

$$
\begin{array}{rcl}
& \vdash & \cdot : \mathbf{1} \\
\\
& \vdash & zero : Int \\
e : Int & \vdash & succ\ e : Int \\
n : Int, e_1 : t, e_2 : t & \vdash & iszero\ n\ e_1\ e_2 : t \\
e : Int & \vdash & pred\ e : Int \\
\\
e : t_1 & \vdash & inl_{t_2}\ e : t_1 \oplus t_2 \\
e : t_2 & \vdash & inr_{t_1}\ e : t_1 \oplus t_2 \\
e : t_1 \oplus t_2 & \vdash & isl\ e : Int \\
e : t_1 \oplus t_2 & \vdash & outl\ e : t_1 \\
e : t_1 \oplus t_2 & \vdash & outr\ e : t_2 \\
\\
e_1 : t_1, e_2 : t_2 & \vdash & (e_1, e_2) : t_1 \times t_2 \\
e : t_1 \times t_2 & \vdash & fst\ e : t_1 \\
e : t_1 \times t_2 & \vdash & snd\ e : t_2 \\
\\
& \vdash & abort_t : t_\bot \\
e : t & \vdash & lift\ e : t_\bot \\
e : t_\bot & \vdash & drop\ e : t \\
\\
e : t(\mu v.t(v)) & \vdash & wrap\ e : \mu v.t(v)) \\
e : \mu v.t(v)) & \vdash & unwrap\ e : t(\mu v.t(v))
\end{array}
$$

We now take our language to be that of first order recursion equations over these terms.

We will use the type abstractions below:

$$\begin{aligned}
\widehat{\mathbf{1}} &= \mathbf{1} \\
\widehat{Int} &= \mathbf{1}_\perp \\
(\widehat{A \oplus B}) &= \widehat{A} \times \widehat{B} \\
(\widehat{A \times B}) &= \widehat{A} \times \widehat{B} \\
\widehat{A_\perp} &= (\widehat{A})_\perp
\end{aligned}$$

We define the abstraction maps as follows:

$$\begin{aligned}
abs_T &: T \to \widehat{T} \\
abs_{\mathbf{1}} &= id \\
abs_{Int} &= \Delta \\
abs_{s \oplus t} &= < abs_s \circ outl, abs_t \circ outr > \\
abs_{s \times t} &= abs_s \times abs_t \\
abs_{t_\perp} &= (abs_t)_\perp
\end{aligned}$$

That is, we abstract the singleton domain by itself, products by products of abstract domains, and lifted domains by lifted abstract domains. Primitive flat domains such as *Int* (others such as *Bool* will generally be included also) will be abstracted as the two-point domain $\mathbf{2} \mathrel{\hat{=}} \mathbf{1}_\perp$, the points of which we shall write as 0 for the bottom point, and 1 for the top. The abstraction map used is the definedness function Δ ($\Delta n \mathrel{\hat{=}} if\ n = \perp\ then\ 0\ else\ 1$). The interpretation is that 0 represents the domain bottom, and 1 all others (and by downward-closure, the whole of the concrete domain).

Product is used to abstract sum because the domain must be closed under least upper bound, so points must be added to make this domain a lattice. Thus a pair $(p, \perp)$ represents the value $inl\ p$, while a point (p_1, p_2) represents $inl\ p_1 \sqcup inr\ p_2$.

It is unfortunate to note that the desired abstraction for primitive domains differs from what would be obtained by first constructing the domain from the sum and lift operators, and then abstracting as above, as it turns out that the corresponding abstract domains would include extra points corresponding to each of the total values of the concrete domain.

Define concretisation in terms of the above:

$$\begin{aligned}
Conc &: \widehat{T} \to \mathcal{P}(T) \\
Conc\ x &= \{l : abs\ l \sqsubseteq x\}
\end{aligned}$$

We may now define abstraction over sets of values as follows:

$$\begin{aligned}
Abs &: \mathcal{P}(T) \to \widehat{T} \\
Abs &= \bigsqcup \circ \mathcal{P} abs
\end{aligned}$$

4 Chunks

The intuition behind the construction is that abstract values be sets of abstract elements. However, this is not sufficient to usefully describe a concrete value, since there is 'other stuff' in there as well. Even the simplest case, lists, contain not just the element type, but also a terminating value, which may be either *Nil* or $\bot$. Since this is precisely the information required for detecting tail strictness, it is necessary to include these objects in the abstract value. The solution is to consider the data structure to be a collections of 'chunks', each of which has a number of successors determined by the type (its subcomponents). Since we wish to ignore the ordering of the chunks, we may simply remove these 'successor links' from the original type to obtain the type for the chunks.

Thus for a type $\mu v.F(v)$, if we unfold the recursion one level, we obtain objects of type $F(\mu v.F(v))$. We may now remove the tails from the type by replacing that part of the type with the 'dot' type. This gives us concrete chunks of type $F(\mathbf{1})$, which we can then abstract by the usual means. Since we wish 'sets' of these objects, the abstract values are then of type $\mathcal{P}\widehat{F(\mathbf{1})}$, for some suitably chosen powerdomain constructor $\mathcal{P}$.

In particular, for lists, we have

$$List\, t = \mu l.\mathbf{1}_\bot \oplus (t \times l)_\bot$$

Chunks are therefore of type $\mathbf{1}_\bot \oplus (t \times \mathbf{1})_\bot$, which is isomorphic to $\mathbf{1}_\bot \oplus t_\bot$. Choosing some flat type for t, an abstract chunk is of type $\mathbf{1}_\bot \times \mathbf{2}_\bot$.

We interpret these chunks as follows:

$\bot \,\hat{=}\, abs \bot = (\bot, \bot)$ – the chunk corresponding to an undefined list

$[\,] \,\hat{=}\, abs\ Nil = abs(inl(lift\cdot)) = (lift\cdot, \bot)$ – the chunk corresponding to the empty list

$0{:}\ \hat{=}\, abs(Cons\ \bot\ \cdot) = abs(inr(lift 0)) = (\bot, lift 0)$ – a *Cons* chunk, containing an undefined element

$1{:}\ \hat{=}\, abs(Cons\ (lift\, v)\ \cdot) = abs(inr(lift 1)) = (\bot, lift 1)$ – a *Cons* chunk containing a defined element

$[\,] \sqcup 0{:} = (lift\cdot, \bot) \sqcup (\bot, lift 0) = (lift\cdot, lift 0)$ – the upper bound of empty list and undefined element

$[\,] \sqcup 1{:} = (lift\cdot, \bot) \sqcup (\bot, lift 1) = (lift\cdot, lift 1)$ – the upper bound of empty list and defined element

It is now necessary, given a concrete value of some type to calculate the set of chunks corresponding to it. Firstly, given such a value, we need to obtain the 'topmost' chunk. We may define a function *top* to do this as follows, using the functor F to map the constant $\mathbf{1}$ function over the given value:

$$\begin{aligned} top_F &: F(t) \rightarrow F(1) \\ top_F &= F(t \mapsto \mathbf{1}) \end{aligned}$$

We must also be able to recover the set of recursive tails that *top* throws away, in order that we may extract the chunks from these as well. The function *tails* essentially throws away an amount of its arguments given by its index (which is a parameterised type), and yields a set of residuals:

$$\begin{aligned}
tails_F &: F(t) \to \mathcal{P}(t) \\
tails_{t\mapsto t}\; val &= \{val\} \\
tails_{t\mapsto \mathbf{1}}\; val &= \{\} \\
tails_{t\mapsto F(t)\oplus G(t)}\; \bot &= \{\} \\
tails_{t\mapsto F(t)\oplus G(t)}\; (inl\; val) &= tails_F\; val \\
tails_{t\mapsto F(t)\oplus G(t)}\; (inr\; val) &= tails_G\; val \\
tails_{t\mapsto F(t)\times G(t)}\; (v_1, v_2) &= tails_F\; v_1 \cup tails_G\; v_2 \\
tails_{t\mapsto \mu v.F(v)(t)}\; (wrap\; val) &= tails_{t\mapsto F(\mu v.F(v)(t))}\; val
\end{aligned}$$

We can now define abstraction over recursive types as follows:

$$abs_{\mu t.F(t)} = flatten_F \circ F\, abs_{\mu t.F(t)} \circ unwrap$$

$$\begin{aligned}
flatten_F &: F(\mathcal{P}(\widehat{F(\mathbf{1})})) \to \mathcal{P}(\widehat{F(\mathbf{1})}) \\
flatten_F\; val &= \{abs(top_F\; val)\} \cup tails_F\; val
\end{aligned}$$

This first abstracts each of the recursive tails, mapping the abstraction across the tails 'in place', and then 'flattens out' the resultant object, by forming a set of its tails, and adding in the abstraction of the topmost chunk. These definitions necessitate the choice of some powerdomain: for the moment the Plotkin powerdomain will suffice, since all we require is that $\{\cdot\}$ and $\bigcup$ exist, and are continuous. Later, however, we will be using a different powerdomain. Note that as the Plotkin powerdomain does not contain the point $\{\}$, the function tails does not return a point in the powerdomain, but simply a set of chunks. The abstraction function itself however, must necessarily return an element of some domain, so we need to perform the appropriate closure operations to obtain one of Plotkin's points.

For lists ($List\; t = \mu l.\mathbf{1}_\bot \oplus (t \times l)_\bot$), we have the following:

$$top_{t\mapsto \mathbf{1}_\bot \oplus (t\times l)_\bot}\; e = head\; e$$

and

$$tails_{t\mapsto \mathbf{1}_\bot \oplus (t\times l)_\bot}\; e = \{tail\; e\}$$

from which we obtain

$$flatten_{t\mapsto \mathbf{1}_\bot \oplus (t\times l)_\bot}\; e = \{abs_t(head\; e), tail\; e\}$$

and

$$abs_{List\; t} = \{abs_t(head\; e)\} \cup abs_{List\; t}(tail\; e)$$

much as we would expect.

5 A new powerdomain

Since our objective is to construct a *domain*, we must construct our sets of chunks by a suitably chosen powerdomain. We shall examine each of the three standard powerdomains in turn.

In the Hoare powerdomain, each point is a downward-closed set. The points are ordered by the relation

$$S \sqsubseteq_H T \triangleq \forall s \in S. \exists t \in T. s \sqsubseteq t$$

Thus a given set is represented by adding in all the elements approximating its members. So we would have to represent $1\in$ by $\{\perp, [\,], 0:, 1:\}$, which would make it indistinguishable from $0\in$. This is clearly not suitable for our purposes.

The Smyth powerdomain, analogously, consists of upward-closed sets. The ordering is:

$$S \sqsubseteq_S T \triangleq \forall t \in T. \exists s \in S. s \sqsubseteq t$$

This would make our chunk sets for $\perp$ and ∞ indistinguishable, as both would include all possible chunks $(\{\perp, [\,], 0:, [\,] \sqcup 0:, 1:, [\,] \sqcup 1:\})$.

The Plotkin powerdomain, containing points which are convex sets, has representatives of the four desired sets which remain distinct. The ordering here is:

$$S \sqsubseteq_{EM} T \triangleq S \sqsubseteq_H T \& S \sqsubseteq_S T$$

However, a least upper bound operation is needed, and the Plotkin lacks this. For example, consider the type $t ::= A\ t \mid B\ t \mid C\ t$, written as $\mu t.t_\perp \oplus t_\perp \oplus t_\perp$ using our domain forming operators. This has abstraction $\mathcal{P}(\mathbf{2} \times \mathbf{2} \times \mathbf{2})$. Write $a = abs(A\cdot), b = abs(B\cdot), c = abs(C\cdot)$. Now consider the sets $\{a, b\}$ and $\{a, c\}$ The sets $\{a, b \sqcup c\}$ and $\{a, a \sqcup b, a \sqcup c\}$ are both upper bounds, and are incomparable – in fact both are minimal upper bounds.

Also, a smaller domain is desirable. In particular, sets of chunks which are essentially the same for our purposes, such as $\{[\,], 0:\}$ and $\{[\,], 0:, [\,] \sqcup 0:\}$, would hopefully be equated.

Both of these problems may be addressed by considering a subdomain of the Plotkin powerdomain in which each of the points is closed under $\sqcup$ (as well under convexity). We may justify this on an intuitive basis by observing that we do not really care about the distinction between sets of chunks differing only by points which are the lubs of others points in the sets. For example, if we know that the chunks [] and $0:$ are present, then we might as well assume that $[] \sqcup 0:$ will be too. Since these sets have a pointed aspect 'sloping up to' a single greatest value, call them *cones*. There are clearly fewer of these than in the whole Plotkin powerdomain, and they merge points which differ only in whether the corresponding sets contain least upper bounds of some of the other elements. Furthermore, they still distinguish between each of the desired points of the list domain, and least upper bound exists for the Cone powerdomain.

The Cone powerdomain is of intermediate granularity and size between the Plotkin and Smyth powerdomains, and in particular it can be seen that Cone is a subdomain of Plotkin, and Smyth a subdomain of Cone.

We will now give our construction of the Cone powerdomain. We will follow Plotkin in our choice of base domains, with an additional restriction. Our construction will work for any SFP object (see [6]) in which lubs exist, and will give a similar result. We will consider only finite domains, and in our application they always will be.

We will say a point of the Plotkin powerdomain is a *cone* if the set S of elements is closed under least upper bound. That is,

$$coneS \hat{=} x \in S \wedge y \in S \Rightarrow x \sqcup y \in S$$

Now consider the function *conify*, which performs lub-closure:

$$conifyS \hat{=} \{\bigsqcup S' | \{\} \subset S' \subseteq S\}$$

Lemma 1 *applying conify to any point yields a cone.*

Proof: let $C = conifyS$. Then $x, y \in C \Rightarrow x = \bigsqcup X, y = \bigsqcup Y$ for some $\{\} \subset X, Y \subseteq S$. Therefore $x \sqcup y = \bigsqcup X \sqcup \bigsqcup Y = \bigsqcup(X \cup Y)$, and so $x \sqcup y \in C$, since $\{\} \subset X \cup Y \subseteq S$. Therefore $coneC$.

We now observe that cones are the fixed points of *conify*, that is, that the conification of any cone is itself.

Lemma 2 $coneC \Rightarrow conifyC = C$.

Proof: Consider a cone C. If $x \in C$, then clearly $x \in conifyC$, and hence $C \subseteq conifyC$.

Now consider $x \in conifyC$. Then $x = \bigsqcup X$ for some $\{\} \subset X \subseteq C$, i.e., $x = x_1 \sqcup x_2 \sqcup \ldots \sqcup x_n$, and by repeated use of the cone property, $x \in C$. So $conifyC \subseteq C$, and therefore $C = conifyC$.

Lemma 3 *conify is monotonic.*

Proof: Suppose $S \sqsubseteq T$. Now consider $x \in conifyS$. Then $x = \bigsqcup X$ for some $\{\} \subset X \subseteq S$. But since $S \sqsubseteq_H T$, $X \sqsubseteq_H T$ and $x = \bigsqcup X \sqsubseteq \bigsqcup T = \bigsqcup(conifyT) \in conifyT$. So $conifyS \sqsubseteq_H conifyT$.

Similarly, if $x \in conifyT$, then $x = \bigsqcup X$ for some $\{\} \subset X \subseteq T$. Since $S \sqsubseteq_S T$, there exists $\{\} \subset Y \subseteq S$ such that $Y \sqsubseteq_S X$. Then $y = \bigsqcup Y \in conifyS \sqsubseteq x$. Thus $conifyS \sqsubseteq conifyT$, and hence *conify* is monotonic.

Theorem 1 *conify is a closure.*

Observe that *conify* is continuous (as it is a monotonic function over finite domains and greater than the identity (since $x \in S \Rightarrow x \in conifyS$, and $x \in conifyS \Rightarrow x = \bigsqcup X, X \subseteq S \Rightarrow x' \in X \sqsubseteq x$), *conify* is a *closure*, and hence its image is a subdomain of the Plotkin powerdomain.

It remains to show that the Cone powerdomain has lubs. Consider the pointwise lub of two cones S and T

$$P = \{x \sqcup y | x \in S \wedge y \in T\}$$

Lemma 4 P *is a cone.*

Proof: $p, q \in P \Rightarrow p = x \sqcup y, q = z \sqcup w$, where $x, z \in S, y, w \in T$. So $p \sqcup q = (x \sqcup y) \sqcup (z \sqcup w) = (x \sqcup z) \sqcup (y \sqcup w)$. But $coneS \Rightarrow s = (x \sqcup z) \in S$, $coneT \Rightarrow t = (y \sqcup w) \in T$. Therefore $p \sqcup q = s \sqcup t \in P$, and $coneP$.

Lemma 5 *P is an upper bound for S and T.*

Proof: Given $s \in S$, take $s \sqsubseteq s \sqcup t$ for any $t \in T$. So $S \sqsubseteq_H P$. If $p \in P$, then $p = s \sqcup t$ for some $s \in S, t \in T$. So take $s \sqsubseteq p$, and thus $S \sqsubseteq_S T$. So $S \sqsubseteq P$, and similarly for T.

Theorem 2 $P = S \sqcup T$

Proof: Suppose U is an upper bound for S and T, i.e. a cone such that $S \sqsubseteq U$ and $T \sqsubseteq U$. Show that $P \sqsubseteq U$, i.e. P is *least* upper bound.

Consider some $p \in P$. Then $p = s \sqcup t$ for some $s \in S, t \in T$. Since $S \sqsubseteq_H U, \exists s' \in U.s \sqsubseteq s'$, and similarly $T \sqsubseteq_H U \Rightarrow \exists t' \in U.t \sqsubseteq t'$. So $p \sqsubseteq s' \sqcup t'$. But since U is a cone, $s' \sqcup t' \in U$, and hence $P \sqsubseteq_H U$.

Now consider $u \in U$. Since $S \sqsubseteq_S U, \exists s \in S.s \sqsubseteq u$, and similarly $\exists t \in T.t \sqsubseteq u$. Since $s \sqcup t \in P$, $P \sqsubseteq_S U$. Thus $P \sqsubseteq U$ as required.

Note that as lubs exist, greatest lower bounds exist also as a consequence. Thus the Cone powerdomain construction, unlike the Plotkin, will give a lattice wherever the base domain is a lattice.

It is of course necessary that we have $\{\cdot\}$ and $\biguplus$. These can be defined simply by calculating them in the Plotkin powerdomain, and then translating into the Cone.

An interesting question is whether recursive domain equations involving the Cone powerdomain can be solved, as can those involving the Plotkin. This is not immediately clear, since Plotkin's universal domain does not have lubs, and hence is not an object which fits in the Cone framework. It may be possible to solve domain equations in the Plotkin powerdomain, and then convert these domains to corresponding Cone ones, or it may be necessary to use a different universal domain. At any rate it is tempting to suspect solutions do exist, though the question is not relevant here, and we do not attempt any claim on the matter.

6 The structure of the powerdomain

Despite the inclusion of only lub-closed sets, the Cone powerdomain for lists is still rather large, containing 22 points. Closer examination reveals this to be because our construction includes points which cannot possibly occur in practice. For example, a number of sets do not contain either $\perp$ or *Nil*, whereas any concrete list must have such a chunk. Similarly, some contain both, and since lists are linear structures, may contain only one such terminating chunk. If all such points are removed, we are left with a domain of nine points, corresponding to the following sets:

$\perp = \{\perp\}$
: The bottom element of the list domain, corresponding to that point of Wadler's domain.

NIL = {[ ]}
: The empty list.

INF0 = $\{\perp, 0{:}\}$
: Infinite lists containing only undefined elements

$\text{FIN}^{+}0 = \{[\,], 0{:}, [\,] \sqcup 0{:}\}$
: Non-empty finite lists containing only undefined elements.

INF1 = $\{\bot,\ 0{:},\ 1{:}\}$
Infinite lists of defined values. Corresponds to Wadler's point ∞.

FIN0 = $\{[\,],\ [\,]\sqcup 0{:}\}$
Finite lists containing only undefined elements.

FIN$^+$(0 − 1) = $\{[\,],\ 0{:},\ [\,]\sqcup 0{:},\ 1{:},\ [\,]\sqcup 1{:}\}$
Non-empty finite lists containing some undefined values. Corresponds to the point $0\in$ in Wadler's domain.

FIN$^+$1 = $\{[\,],\ 1{:},\ [\,]\sqcup 0{:},\ [\,]\sqcup 1{:}\}$
Non-empty finite lists containing only defined values.

FIN1 = $\{[\,],\ [\,]\sqcup 0{:},\ [\,]\sqcup 1{:}\}$
Finite lists of defined values. Corresponds to $1\in$.

Thus five 'new' points are introduced, all of which are potentially useful in that they are possible abstract values for actual lists, although their utility in detecting strictness is not uniformly obvious. This larger domain will clearly be more expensive to analyse, although it should be noted the height of the domain, which is the relevant metric for estimating the complexity of the associated analysis, is only two greater than previously. Thus the other three extra points are essentially free.

To see how the new points could be useful, consider first INF0, and the list indexing function (!). We have that INF0 $\hat{!}1 = 0$, enabling us to deduce that $[a\ldots]!i$ is strict in a, not possible in Wadler's domain (since $\infty\hat{!}1 = 1$). Similarly FIN0 $\hat{!}1 = 0$, which gives us that $(map(a+)xs)!$ is strict in a also. In Wadler's domain, we discover that $0\in\hat{!}1 = 1$, and so no strictness is discovered.

7 Refining the powerdomain

As we have observed, the Cone powerdomain contains many points which are superfluous for our abstract interpretation. We will now construct a domain which contains only the points that we are interested in, that is, those which are the abstractions of some sets of concrete values.

Thus we wish to calculate the range of Abs. Writing $f(\!|X|\!)$ for $\{fx | x \in X\}$:

$$\begin{aligned}
rng(Abs_{\mu t.F(t)}) &= rng(\bigsqcup \circ \mathcal{P}abs_{\mu t.F(t)})\\
&= \bigsqcup \circ \mathcal{P}abs_{\mu t.F(t)}(\!|\mathcal{P}\mu t.F(t)|\!)\\
&= \bigsqcup(\!|\mathcal{P}abs_{\mu t.F(t)}(\!|\mathcal{P}\mu t.F(t)|\!)|\!)\\
&= \bigsqcup(\!|\mathcal{P}(abs_{\mu t.F(t)}(\!|\mu t.F(t)|\!))|\!)\\
&= \bigsqcup(\!|\mathcal{P}(rng(abs_{\mu t.F(t)}))|\!)
\end{aligned}$$

Note that this is simply the range of abs, closed under lub.

We now calculate the image of abs

$$\begin{aligned}
rng(abs_{\mu t.F(t)}) &= abs_{\mu t.F(t)}(\!|\mu t.F(t)|\!)\\
&= flatten_F \circ F abs_{\mu t.F(t)} \circ unwrap(\!|\mu t.F(t)|\!)\\
&= flatten_F(\!|F abs_{\mu t.F(t)}(\!|unwrap(\!|\mu t.F(t)|\!)|\!)|\!)
\end{aligned}$$

$$
\begin{aligned}
&= flatten_F (\!| F abs_{\mu t.F(t)} (\!| F(\mu t.F(t)) |\!) |\!) \\
&= flatten_F (\!| F(abs_{\mu t.F(t)} (\!| \mu t.F(t) |\!)) |\!) \\
&= \mu D. flatten_F (\!| F D |\!)
\end{aligned}
$$

In order to see how to calculate the points of a particular Cone powerdomain which will be needed for analysing values of a particular type, it is necessary to consider not just the abstract chunk type, but also the original type itself. For example, lists and binary trees have identical chunks (since the degree of branching of a chunk is immaterial), but the tree powerdomain will contain sets that the list one does not, because concrete trees may be 'terminated' by both Leaves and bottoms, in different places, and thus their abstract versions may be sets containing both chunks.

We will calculate the required sub-domain by starting with an initial approximation of $\{\{\bot\}\}$, the sub-domain containing only the bottommost point of the powerdomain. We will calculate successive approximations as follows: given a type expression $\mu v.F(v)$, and an approximation to the powerdomain of chunks, S, by applying F to S, resulting in a set of objects isomorphic to the concrete domain, but in which the tails are represented by a set of abstract chunks. We then flatten each of the points by taking the topmost (concrete) chunk of this object, applying the abstraction function, and adding the result to the set of chunks obtained by taking the union of each tail of the point.

Since our initial approximation of $\{\{\bot\}\}$ is minimal, the function being iterated is monotonic increasing under $\subseteq$. That is, each approximation is a superset of its predecessor, and as these are bounded above by the full Cone powerdomain, the sequence of approximations must converge.

Applying this to the list type yields the nine-point sub-domain described earlier. With binary trees, an eleven point domain is obtained, equal to that for lists with the addition of the points

$$\{\bot, [], 0:, [] \sqcup 0:\} \text{ and } \{\bot, [], 0:, [] \sqcup 0:, 0:, [] \sqcup 1:\}$$

Namely those points which contain at least one branch, and both a Leaf chunk and a bottom chunk. The construction still excludes those points containing neither possible terminating chunk, and the set with both, but no branch, amounting to eleven points in total.

Thus we can calculate $rng(Abs)$ as described above. However, can we guarantee that it is a domain? To see that we can, consider the function $Abs \circ Conc$. This is monotonic and continuous, as both Abs and $Conc$ are. From their definitions:

$$
\begin{aligned}
(Abs \circ Conc)x &= \bigsqcup(\mathcal{P}abs\{l | absl \sqsubseteq x\}) \\
&= \bigsqcup\{absl | absl \sqsubseteq x\} \\
&= \bigsqcup\{x' | x' \sqsubseteq x; x \in rng(abs)\} \\
&\sqsubseteq \bigsqcup\{x' | x' \sqsubseteq x\} \\
&= x
\end{aligned}
$$

Thus $Abs \circ Conc \sqsubseteq id$. Now consider $Conc \circ Abs$, which is also monotonic and continuous, and a downwards closed set X:

$$x \in X \;\Rightarrow\; absx \in \{absx' | x' \in X\}$$

$$
\begin{aligned}
&\Rightarrow \ absx \sqsubseteq \bigsqcup\{absx' | x' \in X\} \\
&\Rightarrow \ x \in \{l | l \sqsubseteq absx \in \bigsqcup\{absx' | x' \in X\}\} \\
&\Rightarrow \ x \in \{l | absl \sqsubseteq (\bigsqcup \circ \mathcal{P}abs)X\}\} \\
&\Rightarrow \ x \in (Conc \circ Abs)X \\
&\Rightarrow \ X \subseteq (Conc \circ Abs)X \\
&\Rightarrow \ X \sqsubseteq (Conc \circ Abs)X
\end{aligned}
$$

So $id \sqsubseteq Conc \circ Abs$.

From $Conc \sqsubseteq Conc$ and $Abs \circ Conc \sqsubseteq id$ we now have

$$Conc \circ Abs \circ Conc \sqsubseteq Conc$$

and by monotonicity of Abs,

$$Abs \circ Conc \circ Abs \circ Conc \sqsubseteq Abs \circ Conc$$

From $id \sqsubseteq Conc \circ Abs$, $Conc \sqsubseteq Conc \circ Abs \circ Conc$, and hence

$$Abs \circ Conc \sqsubseteq Abs \circ Conc \circ Abs \circ Conc$$

From the above two, we have

$$Abs \circ Conc = Abs \circ Conc \circ Abs \circ Conc$$

and thus $Abs \circ Conc$ is idempotent. It is thus a retraction over $\mathcal{P}(F(\mathbf{1}))$, and so its image is a subdomain. It is in fact a projection, not a closure, so we need to use the fact that it is a function over finite domains.

Similarly, from $Abs \sqsubseteq Abs$ and $Abs \circ Conc \sqsubseteq id$ we obtain that

$$Abs \circ Conc \circ Abs \sqsubseteq Abs$$

and from $id \sqsubseteq Conc \circ Abs$,

$$Abs \sqsubseteq Abs \circ Conc \circ Abs$$

So $Abs = Abs \circ Conc \circ Abs$.

Now consider the range of Abs once more:

$$
\begin{aligned}
rng(Abs) &= rng(Abs \circ Conc \circ Abs) \\
&\subseteq rng(Abs \circ Conc) \\
&\subseteq rng(Abs)
\end{aligned}
$$

Thus $rng(Abs) = rng(Abs \circ Conc)$. Since $Abs \circ Conc$ is a projection, then $rng(Abs)$ is a domain, as required.

8 Conclusions

A general construction for an abstract domain for the forwards analysis of any lazy algebraic type has been presented, generalising previous work. The accuracy of our analysis will be at least somewhat better than existing techniques, although how much of a gain is achievable in practice is not yet established. Certainly our technique is significantly more generally applicable. The computational cost involved is also an open question, but is certain to be at least somewhat higher than that of its forerunner.

A powerdomain has been constructed which lies between two well known others in granularity. This may be useful in other applications where least upper bound is needed together with a high degree of distinction between sets of elements.

Intuitively, there should be a non-iterative characterisation of the sub-domain construction, based on the degree of branching of each chunk. It is left to future work to show that it is possible to do this in a fashion equivalent to the treatment here.

References

[1] A. Mycroft, The Theory and Practice of Transforming Call-by-Need into Call by Value, *Proc. International Symposium on Programming*, Springer LNCS 83, 1980.

[2] Philip Wadler and John Hughes, Projections for Strictness Analysis *Functional Programming Languages and Computer Architectures*, LNCS 274, Springer-Verlag, 1987. G. Kahn ed,

[3] G. L. Burn, C. L. Hankin, S. Abramsky, The Theory of Strictness Analysis for Higher-order Functions, *Workshop on Programs as Data Objects*, Copenhagen, Springer LNCS 217, 1985.

[4] Geoffrey Burn, A New Domain For Head-Strictness, *correspondence.*

[5] Phil Wadler, Strictness analysis on non-flat domains (by Abstract interpretation over finite domains), *Abstract Interpretation of Declarative Languages*, Ellis Horwood, 1987

[6] G. D. Plotkin, A Powerdomain Construction, *SIAM Journal of Computing* Vol. 5, No. 3, September 1976.

Complexity Analysis for a Lazy Higher-Order Language

David Sands*

Department of Computing, Imperial College
180 Queens Gate, London SW7 2BZ
email: ds@uk.ac.ic.doc

Abstract

This paper is concerned with the time-analysis of functional programs. Techniques which enable us to reason formally about a program's execution costs have had relatively little attention in the study of functional programming. We concentrate here on the construction of equations which compute the time-complexity of expressions in a lazy higher-order language.

The problem with higher-order functions is that complexity is dependent on the cost of applying functional parameters. Structures called *cost-closures* are introduced to allow us to model both functional parameters *and* the cost of their application.

The problem with laziness is that complexity is dependent on *context*. Projections are used to characterise the context in which an expression is evaluated, and cost-equations are parameterised by this context-description to give a compositional time-analysis. Using this form of context information we introduce two types of time-equation: *sufficient-time* equations and *necessary-time* equations, which together provide bounds on the exact time-complexity.

1 Introduction

This paper is concerned with the time-analysis of functional programs. Techniques which enable us to reason formally about a program's execution costs have had relatively little attention in the study of functional programming. There has been some interest in the mechanisation of program cost analysis, perhaps the main examples being [1, 2, 3]. These works describe systems which analyse cost by first constructing (recursive) equations which describe the time-complexity of a functional program in a strict first-order language. A closed form expression for cost is obtained in some cases by mechanised manipulation (transformation) of these equations. The average-case solution of such equations is considered in [4, 5]. We concentrate here on the *first* part of this process—the construction of equations which compute the time-complexity of a given program. For programs written a first-order strict (*i.e.* call-by-value) language this is very straightforward. In the first part of this paper we show how to deal with a strict higher-order language (a fuller development can be

*This work was partially supported by ESPRIT Basic Research Action P3124

found in [6]). In the remainder of the paper we adapt these ideas to a lazy language. This extension is based on Wadler's use of *context-analysis* in the construction of time equations for a lazy first-order language [7].

The aim is to develop a calculus that enables us to reason about time-complexity. Given a program (which we will consider to be any expression, plus a set of mutually recursive function definitions), the problem is to find a means of constructing equations which describe the cost (in terms of the number of certain elementary operations) of evaluating any expression. In this paper we choose to express cost in terms of the number of non-primitive function applications. One advantage of deriving cost-equations which are themselves expressed in a functional language is that they are amenable to a rich class of program transformation and analysis techniques *c.f.* [2, 3]—this paper retains the functional flavour of these approaches.

The paper is organised as follows. In section 2 we consider the analysis of first and higher-order strict languages. Section 3 introduces a description of *context* that will be used in the analysis of lazy languages. Section 4 presents *sufficient-time* analysis, an upper-bound analysis for a lazy first-order language, which uses contexts that describe information that is *sufficient* to compute a value. Section 5 presents *necessary-time* analysis, a corresponding lower-bound analysis. Section 6 extends these ideas to a higher-order language.

2 Strict Time Analysis

In this section we consider the analysis of strict languages. A full presentation is given in [6].

2.1 A First Order Language

Firstly we define a simple first-order functional language. We consider a set of mutually recursive function definitions of the form

$$f_i(x_1, \ldots, x_{n_i}) = e_i$$

and an expression to be evaluated in the context of these definitions. Expressions have the following syntax:

$$e \ ::= \ f(e_1, \ldots, e_j) \mid \mathit{ident} \mid \mathit{const} \mid \texttt{if } e_1 \texttt{ then } e_2 \texttt{ else } e_3$$

Where f is one of the user-defined functions f_i, or a strict primitive function or constructor p.

For each equation of the form $f_i(x_1, \ldots, x_{n_i}) = e_i$ it is straightforward to construct an equation taking the same arguments as the original function, which computes the cost (in terms of the number of non-primitive function calls) of applying f_i to a tuple of values. The *cost equation* (or *cost-function*) is defined as:

$$cf_i(x_1, \ldots, x_{n_i}) = 1 + \mathcal{T}[\![e_i]\!]$$

where $\mathcal{T}$ is a syntax-directed abstraction given in figure 1. These rules clearly reflect the call-by-value evaluation order. For example, in the rule for application, we sum

$$\begin{array}{rcl} \mathcal{T}[\![const]\!] & = & \mathcal{T}[\![ident]\!] \;=\; 0 \\ \mathcal{T}[\![\texttt{if } e_1 \texttt{ then } e_2 \texttt{ else } e_3]\!] & = & \mathcal{T}[\![e_1]\!] + \texttt{if } e_1 \texttt{ then } \mathcal{T}[\![e_2]\!] \texttt{ else } \mathcal{T}[\![e_3]\!] \\ \mathcal{T}[\![p(e_1 \ldots e_n)]\!] & = & \mathcal{T}[\![e_1]\!] + \cdots + \mathcal{T}[\![e_n]\!] \\ \mathcal{T}[\![f_i(e_1 \ldots e_n)]\!] & = & cf_i(e_1 \ldots e_n) + \mathcal{T}[\![e_1]\!] + \cdots + \mathcal{T}[\![e_n]\!] \end{array}$$

Figure 1: First-Order Strict Cost Definition

the cost of evaluating the arguments, in addition to the function application. (*N.B.* We will use infix notation to ease presentation throughout this paper)

Syntax directed derivations of this form, for similar first order languages can be found in [1, 2, 3]. These works focus on some automatic techniques by which the recursive cost-equations can be manipulated to achieve non-recursive equations.

Example

As a simple example of the above scheme, consider the list-append function defined as:

```
append(x,y) = if null(x) then y else cons(hd(x), append(tl(x),y))
```

From this definition, applying $\mathcal{T}$ we obtain the cost-function which computes the number of non-primitive function applications:

```
cappend(x,y) = 1 + if null(x) then 0 else cappend(tl(x),y)
             = 1 + length(x)
```

The aim of the systems described in the papers cited above is to derive just such a closed-form expression, by means of program transformation. This paper focuses on the process of obtaining the initial cost-functions, for languages using higher-order functions and laziness—a necessary precursor to the derivation of closed-form equations describing, for example, average-case complexity.

2.2 A Higher-Order Curried Language

In this section we outline a means of deriving cost programs for a higher-order language. The time-equations are derived via two mappings. The first modifies the original equations so that functional values are augmented with information needed to describe the cost of their application. The second constructs the time-equations using these modified equations.

Firstly we define our language. We have function definitions of the form

$$f_i\, e_1 \ldots e_{n_i} = exp_i$$

along with curried primitive functions p_i (of arity m_i). The syntax of expressions is given in figure 2.

For each definition $f_i\, x_1 \ldots x_{n_i} = exp_i$ we wish to construct a cost function

$$cf_i\, x_1 \ldots x_{n_i} = exp_i'$$

exp	::=	*exp e*	(application)
	|	*e*	
e	::=	f_i	(function)
	|	*p*	(primitive function)
	|	*x*	(identifier)
	|	*c*	(constant)
	|	(*exp*)	(parenthesis)
	|	**if** e_1 **then** e_2 **else** e_3	(conditional)

Figure 2: Expression Syntax

which computes the cost of applying f_i to n_i values.

Suppose we wish to construct a cost-function for an apply function defined as: `apply f x = f x`. The cost function associated with `apply` should have the form:

$$\texttt{Capply(f,x)} = 1 + \textit{the cost of applying } \texttt{f} \textit{ to } \texttt{x}.$$

But how do we *syntactically* refer to the cost function associated with `f`?

Cost–Closures

In order to reason about the cost of application of functions, as well as the functions themselves, we introduce structures called *cost-closures*. A cost-closure is a triple (f, cf, a) of a function f, its associated cost-function cf and some arity information a. Together with cost-closures we define two (left associative) infix functions `@` and `c@` which define the application of cost-closures and the cost of application. Functions `@` and `c@` satisfy:

$$(f, cf, a) \mathbin{\texttt{@}} e = \begin{cases} f\ e & \text{if } a = 1 \\ (f\ e, cf\ e, a-1) & \text{otherwise} \end{cases}$$

$$(f, cf, n) \mathbin{\texttt{c@}} e = \begin{cases} cf\ e & \text{if } n = 1 \\ 0 & \text{otherwise} \end{cases}$$

The arity component of the cost-closure, and its use in the definition of `c@` is explained by the fact that for reasons of efficiency and simplicity, there is no evaluation of the body of a function until the function is supplied with at least the number of arguments in it's definition (this avoids the potentially expensive resolution of name clashes, and is thus a feature of most functional language implementations).

Cost-closures are used in the following way. We define two syntax-directed translation functions $\mathcal{V}$ and $\mathcal{T}$. The purpose of $\mathcal{V}$ (figure 4) is to modify the original program so that all functional objects are translated into cost-closures, and to perform application via `@`. $\mathcal{T}$ (figure 5) defines the cost-functions, using `c@`. The cost of evaluating any expression *exp* with respect to definitions $f_i\, x_1 \ldots x_{n_i} = exp_i$, $i = 1, \ldots, k$ is then defined by the program given in figure 3. $\mathcal{V}$ is defined on the structure of expressions *exp* and *e*. $\mathcal{T}$ is consequently defined over the syntax of expressions generated by $\mathcal{V}$.

$$
\begin{aligned}
f'_1\, x_1 \ldots x n_1 &= \mathcal{V}[\![e_1]\!] \\
&\vdots \\
f'_k\, x_1 \ldots x n_k &= \mathcal{V}[\![e_k]\!] \\
cf'_1\, x_1 \ldots x n_1 &= 1 + \mathcal{T} \circ \mathcal{V}[\![e_1]\!] \\
&\vdots \\
cf'_k\, x_1 \ldots x n_k &= 1 + \mathcal{T} \circ \mathcal{V}[\![e_k]\!]
\end{aligned}
$$

$$\mathcal{T} \circ \mathcal{V}[\![e]\!]$$

Figure 3: Higher-Order Cost-Program Scheme

Some Optimisations

The code derived by the above translation schemes is rather more cumbersome than is necessary. This is because we introduce more @'s and c@'s than are necessary. Some straightforward optimisations simplify the cost program considerably, and can be defined according to the syntactic structure of expressions [6].

Example

The following simple example illustrates the derivation (and the optimisation):

```
map f x = if (null x) then nil
          else (cons (f (hd x)) (map f (tl x)))
```

The cost-function derived from this is:

```
cmap f x = 1 + ((null,cnull,1) c@ x) +
           if ((null,cnull,1) @ x) then nil
           else (((cons,ccons,2) c@ (f @ ((hd,chd,1) @ x)))
           + ((cons,ccons,2)@(f @ ((hd,chd,1)@ x)) c@
             ((map',cmap,2)@ f @ ((tl,ctl,1)@ x)))
           + f c@ ((hd,chd,1)@ x) + ((hd,chd,1)c@ x)
           + ((map',cmap,2)@ f c@ ((tl,ctl,1)@ x))
           + ((map',cmap,2)c@ f) + ((tl,ctl,1)c@ x) )
```

Using simple optimisation schemes, we get the equivalent cost-function definition:

```
cmap f x = 1 + if (null x) then 0
               else (f c@ (hd x)) + (cmap f (tl x))
```

$$\begin{aligned}
\mathcal{V}[\![exp\ e]\!] &= \mathcal{V}[\![exp]\!]\ \texttt{@}\ \mathcal{V}[\![e]\!] \\
\mathcal{V}[\![\texttt{if}\ e_1\ \texttt{then}\ e_2\ \texttt{else}\ e_3]\!] &= \texttt{if}\ \mathcal{V}[\![e_1]\!]\ \texttt{then}\ \mathcal{V}[\![e_2]\!]\ \texttt{else}\ \mathcal{V}[\![e_3]\!] \\
\mathcal{V}[\![(exp)]\!] &= (\mathcal{V}[\![exp]\!]) \\
\mathcal{V}[\![f_i]\!] &= (f_i'\ ,\ cf_i\ ,\ n_i\ ) \\
\mathcal{V}[\![p_i]\!] &= (p_i\ ,\ cp_i\ ,\ m_i\ ) \\
\mathcal{V}[\![c]\!] &= c \\
\mathcal{V}[\![x]\!] &= x
\end{aligned}$$

Figure 4: Function Modification Map, $\mathcal{V}$

$$\begin{aligned}
\mathcal{T}[\![exp'\ \texttt{@}\ e']\!] &= \mathcal{T}[\![exp']\!]\ +\ \mathcal{T}[\![e']\!]\ +\ (exp'\ \texttt{c@}\ e') \\
\mathcal{T}[\![\texttt{if}\ e_1'\ \texttt{then}\ e_2'\ \texttt{else}\ e_3']\!] &= \mathcal{T}[\![e_1']\!]\ +\ \texttt{if}\ e_1'\ \texttt{then}\ \mathcal{T}[\![e_2']\!]\ \texttt{else}\ \mathcal{T}[\![e_3']\!] \\
\mathcal{T}[\![(exp')]\!] &= (\mathcal{T}[\![exp']\!]) \\
\mathcal{T}[\![(p_i\ ,\ cp_i\ ,\ m_i\ )]\!] &= \mathcal{T}[\![(f_i\ ,\ cf_i\ ,\ n_i\ )]\!]\ =\ 0 \\
\mathcal{T}[\![c]\!] &= \mathcal{T}[\![x]\!]\ =\ 0
\end{aligned}$$

Figure 5: Cost-Expression Construction Map, $\mathcal{T}$

2.3 Correctness

The derived program computes the number of times a certain "step" is performed in the evaluation of the program. In this section we formalise our intuitive model of "evaluation steps" via an *operational semantics.* We prove that the number of steps our derived program computes is correct with respect to the actual operational behaviour of the original program.

Semantics

The (dynamic) operational semantics for our language is defined by an inference system (a set of rules and axioms) in the style of *Natural Semantics* [8].

Step-counting

In order to reason about complexity we define a dynamic semantics so that the evaluation of an expression gives a pair of the value, and the number of reductions of non-primitive functions, (which corresponds to the use of a particular rule in the semantics). In this "step-counting semantics", given in figure 6 the rules define judgements of the form

$$\rho \vdash_\phi exp \xrightarrow{s} \langle v, t \rangle$$

which is read as

> Given environment ρ and function environment ϕ, evaluating exp yeilds value v, with t reductions of non-primitive function applications.

$$\textbf{SApp.1} \quad \frac{\rho \vdash_\phi exp \rightarrow \langle (f, n', \rho'), n_1 \rangle \quad \rho \vdash_\phi e \rightarrow \langle v', n_2 \rangle}{\rho \vdash_\phi exp\ e \rightarrow \langle (f, n' - 1, \rho' + +v'), n_1 + n_2 \rangle} \text{ if } n' > 1$$

$$\textbf{SApp.2} \quad \frac{\begin{array}{c}\rho \vdash_\phi exp \rightarrow \langle (f_i, 1, \rho'), n_1 \rangle \\ \rho \vdash_\phi e \rightarrow \langle v', n_2 \rangle \quad \rho' {+\!\!+} v' \vdash_\phi \phi(f_i) \rightarrow \langle v, n_3 \rangle\end{array}}{\rho \vdash_\phi exp\ e \rightarrow \langle v, n_1 + n_2 + n_3 + 1 \rangle}$$

$$\textbf{SApp.3} \quad \frac{\rho \vdash_\phi exp \rightarrow \langle (p_i, 1, \rho'), n_1 \rangle \quad \rho \vdash_\phi e \rightarrow \langle v', n_2 \rangle}{\rho \vdash_\phi exp\ e \rightarrow \langle v, n_1 + n_2 \rangle \quad \text{if Apply}(p_i, (\rho' {+\!\!+} v')) = v}$$

$$\textbf{SCond.1} \quad \frac{\rho \vdash_\phi e_1 \rightarrow \langle \texttt{true}, n_1 \rangle \quad \rho \vdash_\phi e_2 \rightarrow \langle v, n_2 \rangle}{\rho \vdash_\phi \texttt{if } e_1 \texttt{ then } e_2 \texttt{ else } e_3 \rightarrow \langle v, n_1 + n_2 \rangle}$$

$$\textbf{SCond.2} \quad \frac{\rho \vdash_\phi e_1 \rightarrow \langle \texttt{false}, n_1 \rangle \quad \rho \vdash_\phi e_3 \rightarrow \langle v, n_2 \rangle}{\rho \vdash_\phi \texttt{if } e_1 \texttt{ then } e_2 \texttt{ else } e_3 \rightarrow \langle v, n_1 + n_2 \rangle}$$

$$\textbf{SBrac} \quad \frac{\rho \vdash_\phi exp \rightarrow \langle v, n \rangle}{\rho \vdash_\phi (exp) \rightarrow \langle v, n \rangle}$$

$$\textbf{SUserf} \quad \rho \vdash_\phi f_i \rightarrow \langle (f_i, n_i, \langle\rangle), 0 \rangle$$

$$\textbf{SPrimf} \quad \rho \vdash_\phi p_i \rightarrow \langle (p_i, m_i, \langle\rangle), 0 \rangle$$
(where $m_i = arity(p_i)$)

$$\textbf{SIdent} \quad \rho \vdash_\phi x_j \rightarrow \langle \rho_j, 0 \rangle$$

$$\textbf{SConst} \quad \rho \vdash_\phi c \rightarrow \langle c, 0 \rangle$$

Figure 6: Step-Counting Semantics

This generalises a standard semantics (not given here) whose judgements are of the form:

$$\rho \vdash_\phi exp \rightarrow v$$

Here we sketch some of the details in order to state the correctness theorem.

Environments

The environment to the left of the turnstile is used to map identifiers onto values. This environment is represented by a list, $\langle v_1, \ldots, v_n \rangle$ where the i_{th} element, v_i, is the value bound to identifier x_i. ρ is a list of values, where ρ_i denotes the i_{th} element, and $\rho {+\!\!+} v$ extends ρ with value v.

We will assume that we have constructed a function-environment which maps the function-names to the right-hand-side of their definition. Informally we parameterise the turnstile in the sentences by this environment—it would be straightforward to include the construction of this environment in the semantic rules.

In the following we will use ϕ' to denote the function-environment of the cost-program (see figure 3) corresponding to some function environment ϕ.

Closures

Closures represent values of function-type. A closure is a triple of the form (f, n, ρ) consisting of a function name, f, an (incomplete) environment, ρ, and an arity n (> 0) representing the number of values required to make the environment complete.

To relate values in the cost-program to values in the original program, (this includes environments, which are by definition lists of values) we define a convenient mapping:

DEFINITION 2.1

$$v^{cc} = \begin{cases} \langle v_1^{cc}, \cdots, v_k^{cc} \rangle & \textit{if } v = \langle v_1, \cdots, v_k \rangle \\ \langle (f', n, \rho^{cc}), (cf, n, \rho^{cc}), n \rangle & \textit{if } v = (f, n, \rho) \\ v & \textit{otherwise} \end{cases}$$

Thus function values (closures) are related to a three element list (a cost-closure) in the cost program. (We are taking the semantics of a cost closure to be that of a three element list in order to show that we do not need an extended language to implement them)

The following lemma establishes that $\mathcal{V}[\![\cdot]\!]$ preserves the meaning of programs (modulo ^{cc}):

LEMMA 2.2 *For all expressions exp, if there exists a value v such that*

$$\rho \vdash_\phi exp \rightarrow v$$

then

$$\rho^{cc} \vdash_{\phi'} \mathcal{V}[\![exp]\!] \rightarrow v^{cc}$$

The main correctness theorem is as follows:

THEOREM 2.3 *For all expressions exp, and value environments ρ, if there exists a value v such that*

$$\rho \vdash_\phi exp \xrightarrow{s} \langle v, t \rangle$$

for some t, then

$$\rho^{cc} \vdash_{\phi'} \mathcal{T} \circ \mathcal{V}[\![exp]\!] \rightarrow t$$

Note that this is not a total correctness ($\Longleftrightarrow$)—it says nothing about nontermination or run-time errors in the evaluation of the original program. It is easy to see that nontermination will be inherited by the cost program, whereas run-time errors (*e.g.* `hd(nil)`) may not, and so the cost-program may be more defined than the original.

The proofs of the lemma and the main theorem follow by induction on the structure of the proofs (derivations) in the operational semantics. These are given in full in [6].

3 Lazy Time Analysis: Describing Context

A major obstacle in the time-analysis of lazy languages is the problem of *context sensitivity:* the cost of evaluating an expression depends on the context in which it is used. In order to give a *compositional* treatment of the analysis of lazy-evaluation we must take into account some description of context.

3.1 Modelling Contexts with Projections

The formulation of a context which will be used in our time analysis is that provided by Wadler and Hughes [9] in the analysis of *strictness.* Wadler shows how this formulation of context can be useful for time analysis in [7]. Here we provide an introduction to the use of *projections* to model contexts. For a fuller development the reader is referred to [9]; a more formal development, together with enhanced analysis techniques is given in [10].

The basic problem is, given a function, how much information do we require from the argument in order to determine a certain amount of information about the result. Projections, in the domain theoretic sense, can provide a concise description of both the amount of information which is *sufficient* and the amount which is *necessary.*

DEFINITION **3.1** *A projection, α, is a continuous function from a domain $\mathcal{D}$ onto itself, such that $\alpha \sqsubseteq \mathrm{ID}_{\mathcal{D}}$ and $\alpha \circ \alpha = \alpha$, where $\mathrm{ID}_{\mathcal{D}}$ is the identity function on $\mathcal{D}$*

In other words, given an object u, a projection removes information from that object ($\alpha u \sqsubseteq u$), but once this information has been removed further application has no effect ($\alpha(\alpha u) = \alpha u$). A projection is used to represent a context, where the information removed represents information not needed by that context.

In the following the terms *projection* and *context* will be synonymous, and will be ranged over by α and β.

DEFINITION **3.2 Safe Projections:** *Given a (first order) function, f, of n arguments, if*

$$\alpha(f(u_1,\ldots,u_n)) = \alpha(f(u_1,\ldots,(\beta u_i),\ldots u_n))$$

for all objects $u_1,\ldots,u_n$, then we say that in context α, β is a safe context for the i'th argument of f. *This is abbreviated by $f^i : \alpha \Rightarrow \beta$.*

Lifted Projections

We will require that projections describe two types of information: what information is *sufficient*, and what information is *necessary.* In order to describe the latter, Wadler and Hughes introduce a new domain element, $\lightning$, called "abort". The interpretation of $\alpha u = \lightning$ is that context α requires a value more defined than u. To make this work, we must have $\lightning \sqsubset \bot$ and all functions are naturally-extended to be strict in $\lightning$, *i.e.*, $f(u_1,\ldots,\lightning,\ldots,u_n) = \lightning$. These technical devices are explained more formally in [11] in terms of *lifting.*

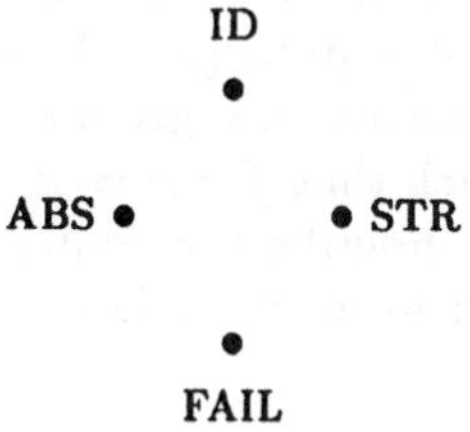

$$\text{ID}\,u = u$$

$$\text{STR}\,u = \begin{cases} \lightning & \text{if } u = \bot \text{ or } u = \lightning \\ u & \text{otherwise} \end{cases}$$

$$\text{ABS}\,u = \begin{cases} \lightning & \text{if } u = \lightning \\ \bot & \text{otherwise} \end{cases}$$

$$\text{FAIL}\,u = \lightning$$

Figure 7: The Projection Lattice

The Projection Lattice

A projection $\alpha : \mathcal{D}_{\lightning} \to \mathcal{D}_{\lightning}$, is called *a projection over $\mathcal{D}$*. Projections over any domain form a lattice, with ordering $\sqsubseteq$, containing at least the points given in figure 7.

DEFINITION 3.3 *A* strict projection *is any projection α such that* $\alpha(\bot) = \lightning$

The largest of such projections is STR, giving us an alternative definition of strict projections: a projection α is strict if and only if $\alpha \sqsubseteq$ STR. Of the non-strict projections, the smallest is the projection ABS. This context is important since if it is safe to evaluate an expression in the context ABS, then the value of the expression will not be needed. FAIL is the unsatisfiable context.

There may be infinitely many projections, which are all either strict (FAIL $\sqsubseteq \alpha \sqsubseteq$ STR) or non-strict (ABS $\sqsubseteq \alpha \sqsubseteq$ ID). The four projections above will be used "polymorphically" to represent the corresponding projection over the appropriate domain.

Given two projections $\alpha \sqsubset \beta$, α represents a more precise description of a context than β. The context ID is therefore the least informative. Furthermore, if it is safe to evaluate some expression in a context α, then it is always safe to evaluate in a context $\beta, \alpha \sqsubseteq \beta$.

Contexts for Lists

The following projections are useful for building contexts over the non-flat domain of lists $\mathcal{D}^*$ of elements from some domain $\mathcal{D}$:

$$\text{NIL}\,u = \begin{cases} nil & \text{if } u = nil \\ \lightning & \text{otherwise} \end{cases}$$

$$\text{CONS}\,\alpha\,\beta\,u = \begin{cases} cons(\alpha\,x)(\beta\,xs) & \text{if } u = cons\ x\ xs \\ \lightning & \text{otherwise} \end{cases}$$

NIL is the context which requires an empty-list, and CONS $\alpha\,\beta$ is the context which requires a non-empty list whose head is needed in context α and whose tail is needed in context β. For example, the context (CONS STR ABS) requires a non-empty list whose first element is needed, and the rest is not.

Context Analysis

Analysing context is a *backwards analysis:* given a context α for a function f, what can we say about the contexts of the arguments? We need to propagate the information about the result of a function *backwards* to it's arguments. *i.e.*, given a function f of arity n, and a context α we need to find each β_i such that $f^i : \alpha \Rightarrow \beta_i$.

Ideally we need to find the smallest β_i, since these describe the contexts most precisely. In order to give a computable approximation we may settle for *some* β_i satisfying the above property.

Projection Transformers

A function of α yielding such a β_i is called a *projection transformer.* We will adopt the following notation: The projection-transformer written $f^{\#i}$ is a function satisfying $f^i : \alpha \Rightarrow f^{\#i}\alpha$. *N.B.* Strictly speaking we should distinguish between the syntactic objects—the program defining f, and the semantic objects—the projections, and the denotations given by some semantic function. Following the style of [9] we will mix these entities for notational convenience.

Rules for defining recursive equations for the projection transformers are given in [9]—an important result here is that a solution to these equations can be determined *automatically* if we work with finite lattices of projections, although it is not difficult to modify the equations to give more accurate projection equations (which are harder to solve).

4 Sufficient-Time Analysis

In this section we show how context information can be used to aid the time analysis of a lazy first-order language; Sufficient-time analysis (with some minor differences) corresponds to the time analysis presented in [7]. The information obtained by the backwards analysis is used to derive equations which compute an upper bound to the precise cost of a given program. This upper-bound is obtained by using information which tells us what values are *sufficient* to compute an expression. We call the resulting analysis a *sufficient-time* analysis.

4.1 Context-Parameterised Cost Functions

As in the first-order time analysis of section 2, we will define a *cost-function*, cf_i, for each function f_i defined in the original program. As before the cost functions will take as parameters the original arguments to the functions, but in addition they will be parameterised by a *context*, representing the context in which the functions are evaluated.

How can cost-functions make use of context ?

We know that any expression in the context ABS will be ignored, so the cost in this context is zero. In any other context the cost of a function application will be (approximated above by) $1+$ the cost of evaluating the body of the function, in that context.

$$\begin{array}{rcl}
\mathcal{T}_s[\![c]\!]\alpha & = & \mathcal{T}_s[\![x]\!]\alpha \;=\; 0 \\
\mathcal{T}_s[\![\texttt{if } e_1 \texttt{ then } e_2 \texttt{ else } e_3]\!]\alpha & = & \alpha \hookrightarrow_s \mathcal{T}_s[\![e_1]\!]\mathrm{ID} + \texttt{if } e_1 \texttt{ then } \mathcal{T}_s[\![e_2]\!]\alpha \texttt{ else } \mathcal{T}_s[\![e_3]\!]\alpha \\
\mathcal{T}_s[\![p(e_1 \ldots e_n)]\!]\alpha & = & \mathcal{T}_s[\![e_1]\!](p^{\#1}\alpha) + \cdots + \mathcal{T}_s[\![e_n]\!](p^{\#n}\alpha) \\
\mathcal{T}_s[\![f_i(e_1 \ldots e_n)]\!]\alpha & = & \mathcal{T}_s[\![e_1]\!](f_i{}^{\#1}\alpha) + \cdots + \mathcal{T}_s[\![e_n]\!](f_i{}^{\#n}\alpha) \\
 & & + cf_i(e_1 \ldots e_n, \alpha)
\end{array}$$

Figure 8: Definition of $\mathcal{T}_s$

We define the cost functions associated with each function $f_i(x_1 \ldots x_{n_i}) = e_i$ to be

$$cf_i(x_1, \ldots, x_{n_i}, \alpha) = \alpha \hookrightarrow_s 1 + \mathcal{T}_s[\![e_i]\!]\alpha$$

where we introduce the notation $\alpha \hookrightarrow_s e$ to abbreviate cost e "guarded" by context α:

$$\alpha \hookrightarrow_s e = \begin{cases} 0 & \text{if } \alpha = \mathrm{ABS} \\ e & \text{otherwise} \end{cases}$$

The syntactic map $\mathcal{T}_s$ defined in figure 8 is very similar to that defined in figure 1, but is defined with respect to a particular context. $\mathcal{T}_s[\![e]\!]\ \alpha$ defines the cost of evaluating expression e in context α. It makes use of the context transformers $f_i{}^{\#1} \ldots f_i{}^{\#n_i}$ defined for each function f_i, which satisfy the required safety criterion. In particular it will be appropriate to set $f^{\#m}(\mathrm{ABS}) = \mathrm{ABS}$, since if the result of a function is not needed, then neither are its arguments.

The rule for function application tells us that the cost of evaluating a function application is the associated cost-function applied to the arguments (and the context) plus the sum of evaluating the arguments in the contexts prescribed by the context-transformers.

The conditional expression, like any other, has zero cost in the context ABS (guaranteed by the use of $\hookrightarrow_s$). Otherwise we sum the cost of evaluating the condition (which may or may not be evaluated, hence the safe-context for boolean values ID, *c.f.* [7]) plus either the cost of the alternate or the consequent, depending on the *value* of the condition.

The cost of evaluating any expression in the context ABS is zero, so we have:

PROPOSITION 4.1 *For every expression e,* $\mathcal{T}_s[\![e]\!]\mathrm{ABS} = 0$

PROOF Straightforward structural induction in e □

A Small Example

Consider the expression: `hd(cons(not(true),`*exp*`))`, where

```
not(x) = if x then false else true
```

and *exp* represents some arbitrary expression. The cost-function for not is

$$\begin{array}{rcl}
\texttt{cnot}(\texttt{x},\alpha) & = & \alpha \hookrightarrow_s \texttt{1 + (}\ \alpha \hookrightarrow_s \texttt{0 + if x then 0 else 0)} \\
 & = & \alpha \hookrightarrow_s \texttt{1}
\end{array}$$

We assume a boolean-valued program is evaluated in the context STR, and so the cost program is defined by: $\mathcal{T}_s$[[hd(cons(not(true), *exp*))]] STR, which is, by definition

$$\texttt{cnot(true, cons}^{\#1}\texttt{(hd}^{\#1}\texttt{(STR)))} + 0 + \mathcal{T}_s[\![exp]\!]\ \texttt{cons}^{\#2}\texttt{(hd}^{\#1}\texttt{(STR))}$$

The context transformers for the primitive functions satisfy

$$\texttt{hd}^{\#1}(\alpha) = \text{CONS } \alpha \text{ ABS} \qquad \texttt{cons}^{\#1}(\text{CONS } \alpha\ \beta) = \alpha \qquad \texttt{cons}^{\#2}(\text{CONS } \alpha\ \beta) = \beta$$

and so the cost is cnot(true , STR) + $\mathcal{T}_s[\![exp]\!]$ ABS $= 1$, for any expression *exp*.

4.2 Approximation and Safety

What are the precise properties of the cost programs? Here we consider the approximation and correctness properties of the "lazy" cost-program.

Approximation

The expression $\mathcal{T}_s[\![e]\!]\alpha$ gives an upper-bound estimate to the cost of lazy evaluation of e in context α. The cost expressions formed by $\mathcal{T}_s$ are refinements of the call-by-value cost-expressions (section 2) in which subexpressions whose values are not needed do not contribute to the cost equation. Since the safety condition for projections does not specify that we require the smallest possible projection, the context ABS may be approximated by any larger projection. This approximation is reflected in the cost-program as an over-estimation of cost. (In the extreme case the context transformers are such that the context ABS is *never* derived in the cost-program, and so the value of the cost program is the same as that given by the strict derivation of figure 1.) Note also that in computing the cost of a function application $f(e)$ in context α the cost due to e will only be counted *once*. The context of e, $f^{\#1}(\alpha)$ will be the net context of the possible contexts in which e is shared, and so the process properly models call-by-*need*.

Safety

Whenever the cost-program terminates yielding a value, that value is indeed an upper bound to the time cost of evaluating the program lazily. A problem with this analysis method is that there are cases when the cost-program does not yield a value when it should do so. Firstly the cost-program may not terminate even when the program does—non-terminating cost expressions can be thought of as "computing" the worst possible upper-bound to the cost. However the approximation in the cost-program can lead to arbitrary run-time errors (*i.e.* not just nontermination). In the next section we introduce *necessary-time* equations which allow us to place a lower-bound on the precise complexity and which have better termination properties.

5 Necessary-Time Analysis

So far we have outlined the use of contexts to derive equations which can give an upper-bound to the time-complexity of an expression in a particular context. As mentioned previously, this idea is based on [7]. The cost-functions which compute this sufficient-complexity are only partially correct in the sense that if they compute a value, then that value is indeed an upper-bound to the time-cost of a program. There is potentially much more information about context using the projections described: *strict* contexts allow us to describe the amount of information which is *necessary* to compute a value. In this section we show how the use of this information can give us equations which describe a lower bound to the precise time-cost (the *necessary-time*) and which overcome the termination deficiencies of sufficient-time analysis. The key to sufficient-time analysis is the use of the context ABS to deduce that an expression will not be evaluated. The key to *necessary-time* is the operational interpretation of the *strict* projections.

5.1 Necessary-Cost Functions

In order to construct functions which compute the necessary-cost of evaluating a function in a particular context, we make the following operational connection between expressions which can be safely evaluated in a strict context, and their operational behaviour.

- If it is safe to evaluate an expression of the form $f(e_1, \ldots, e_n)$ in a strict context, then operationally, we know that this outermost application must be reduced.

Conversely, if an expression is evaluated in a non-strict context then that expression *may or may not* be reduced (only the context ABS allows us to conclude that it *definitely* will not).

Motivated by this observation, we now define the necessary-cost. The cost of evaluating an expression e in a context α is given by $\mathcal{T}_n[\![e]\!]\alpha$ where $\mathcal{T}_n$ is once again a mapping defined over the syntax of expressions, and assuming some safe context transformers for the user-defined functions.

For each function definition of the form

$$f_i(x_1 \ldots x_{n_i}) = e_i$$

we will define an associated necessary-cost-function

$$cf_i(x_1, \ldots, x_{n_i}, \alpha) = \alpha \hookrightarrow_n 1 + \mathcal{T}_n[\![e_i]\!]\alpha$$

where we use the notation $\alpha \hookrightarrow_n e$ to abbreviate necessary-cost e modulo context α:

$$\alpha \hookrightarrow_n e = \begin{cases} e & \text{if } \alpha \sqsubseteq \text{STR} \\ 0 & \text{otherwise} \end{cases}$$

The definition of $\mathcal{T}_n$ is given in figure 9. The rules are very similar to the definitions for $\mathcal{T}_s$ but we use $\hookrightarrow_n$ in place of $\hookrightarrow_s$. The only other difference is in the translation for the conditional expression.

PROPOSITION 5.1 *For all contexts α, if $\alpha \sqsubseteq$ STR then*

$$\alpha(\texttt{if } u_1 \texttt{ then } u_2 \texttt{ else } u_3) = \alpha(\texttt{if } \text{STR}(u_1) \texttt{ then } u_2 \texttt{ else } u_3)$$

PROOF Straightforward by cases according, $u_1 \sqsupset \bot$ and $u_1 \sqsubseteq \bot$ □

This tells us that in any strict context it is safe to evaluate the condition in the context STR, and thus gives us the appropriate context for determining the cost due to the condition in the conditional expression.

$$
\begin{aligned}
\mathcal{T}_n[\![const]\!]\alpha &= \mathcal{T}_n[\![ident]\!]\alpha \;=\; 0 \\
\mathcal{T}_n[\![\texttt{if } e_1 \texttt{ then } e_2 \texttt{ else } e_3]\!]\alpha &= \alpha \hookrightarrow_n \mathcal{T}_n[\![e_1]\!]\mathrm{STR} \\
&\quad + \texttt{if } e_1 \texttt{ then } \mathcal{T}_n[\![e_2]\!]\alpha \texttt{ else } \mathcal{T}_n[\![e_3]\!]\alpha \\
\mathcal{T}_n[\![p(e_1 \ldots e_n)]\!]\alpha &= \mathcal{T}_n[\![e_1]\!](p^{\#1}\alpha) + \cdots + \mathcal{T}_n[\![e_n]\!](p^{\#n}\alpha) \\
\mathcal{T}_n[\![f_i(e_1 \ldots e_n)]\!]\alpha &= \mathcal{T}_n[\![e_1]\!](f_i^{\#1}\alpha) + \cdots + \mathcal{T}_n[\![e_n]\!](f_i^{\#n}\alpha) \\
&\quad + cf_i(e_1 \ldots e_n, \alpha)
\end{aligned}
$$

Figure 9: Definition of $\mathcal{T}_n$

5.2 Example

As a example of necessary-time analysis we use insertion-sort (as in [7]). The definitions are given in figure 10. The necessary-time equations constructed according to

```
insert(x,xs)  =  if null(xs) then cons(x,nil)
                 else if x < hd(xs) then cons(x,xs)
                      else cons(hd(xs),insert(x,tl(xs)))
sort(xs)      =  if null(xs) then nil
                 else insert(hd(xs),sort(tl(xs)))
min(xs)       =  hd(sort(xs))
```

Figure 10: Insertion Sort

$\mathcal{T}_n$ are given in figure 11: In this example we wish to consider the cost of evaluating

```
cinsert(x,xs,α)  =  α ↪n 1 + if null(xs) then 0
                             else if x < hd(xs) then 0
                                  else cinsert(x,tl(xs),cons#2(α))
csort(xs,α)      =  α ↪n 1 + if null(xs) then 0
                             else cinsert(hd(xs),sort(tl(xs)),α) +
                             csort(tl(xs),insert#2(α))
cmin(xs,α)       =  α ↪n 1 + csort(xs,hd#1(α))
```

Figure 11: Necessary-Cost Functions

min in a strict context. We are not particularly concerned here with the techniques for deriving the safe projection transformers. We note however that the projection transformers needed in this example are members of the finite domains for lists (and integers) described in [9] for the purpose of strictness analysis, and as such can be determined mechanically by fixpoint iteration. The equations we require are:

$$\mathrm{hd}^{\#1}(\mathrm{STR}) = \mathrm{CONS\ STR\ ABS}$$

$$\begin{aligned} \texttt{cons}^{\#2}(\text{CONS STR ABS}) &= \text{ABS} \\ \texttt{insert}^{\#2}(\text{CONS STR ABS}) &= \text{CONS STR ABS} \end{aligned}$$

Now we examine the cost of `min`:

```
cmin(xs,STR) = STR ↪n 1 + csort(xs,hd#1(STR))
             = 1 + csort(xs,CONS STR ABS)
```

```
csort(xs,CONS STR ABS)
  = 1 + if null(xs) then 0
        else cinsert(hd(xs),sort(tl(xs)),CONS STR ABS) +
             csort(tl(xs),insert#2(CONS STR ABS))
  = 1 + if null(xs) then 0
        else cinsert(hd(xs),sort(tl(xs)),CONS STR ABS) +
             csort(tl(xs),CONS STR ABS)
cinsert(y,ys,CONS STR ABS)
  = 1 + if null(ys) then 0
        else if y < hd(ys) then 0
             else cinsert(y,tl(ys),cons#2(CONS STR ABS))
  = 1 + if null(ys) then 0
        else if y < hd(ys) then 0
             else cinsert(y,tl(ys),ABS)
  = 1
```

and so

```
csort(xs,CONS STR ABS) = 1 + if null(xs) then 0
                             else 1 + csort(tl(xs),CONS STR ABS)
```

This simple recurrence has the exact solution `1 + 2*length(xs)` and so

```
cmin(xs,STR) = 2 + 2*length(xs)
```

In this example the sufficient-time equations derive the same result, since the contexts (CONS STR ABS) and STR are very precise (*i.e.* they are the smallest safe projections). Therefore we can conclude that this is the *exact* time complexity.

5.3 Approximation and Safety

The expression $\mathcal{T}_n[\![e]\!]\alpha$ gives a lower-bound estimate to the cost of the lazy evaluation of e in context α. For a non-strict context α the lower bound must be zero since an expression in such a context *may or may not* need to be evaluated. Proposition 5.2 below establishes this property.

PROPOSITION 5.2 *For every expression e*, $\text{ABS} \sqsubseteq \alpha \sqsubseteq \text{ID} \Rightarrow \mathcal{T}_n[\![e]\!]\alpha = 0$

PROOF Structural induction in *e*. □

Safety

The necessary-cost programs enjoy better termination properties than the sufficient-cost programs, being at least as well defined as the original program. We state this property in the following way:

THEOREM 5.3 *Given mutually recursive functions $f_1, \ldots f_m$, defined by equations:*

$$f_i(x_1, \ldots, x_{n_i}) = e_i, \; i = 1 \ldots m$$

then for all objects $u_1, \ldots u_{n_i}$, and contexts α

$$\alpha(f_i(u_1, \ldots, u_{n_i})) \sqsupset \bot \Rightarrow cf_i(u_1, \ldots, u_{n_i}, \alpha) \sqsupset \bot$$

where cf_i is defined by the equation $cf_i(x_1, \ldots, x_{n_i}, \alpha) = \alpha \hookrightarrow_n \mathcal{T}_n[\![e_i]\!]\alpha$

PROOF Omitted—a fixed point induction over the functions and cost-functions simultaneously. □

6 Higher-Order Lazy Time-Analysis

In this section we develop an extension to the techniques for lazy time analysis to incorporate higher-order functions. This is achieved by adaptation of the higher-order analysis given in section 2, illustrated with a conservative extension to the context information available for first-order functions.

6.1 Context Information

The extension of lazy-time analysis to higher-order functions also needs context information. Here we immediately run into some problems. The techniques which we have assumed so far, concerning the form and derivation of context transformers, cannot be directly extended to higher-order functions. Consider, for example, an instance of the apply function, `apply f x`, in some context α. The problem here is that there is no useful context information that can be propagated to `x` (by any context function $\mathtt{apply}^{\#2}$) which is *independent* of the function f.

Wray's thesis [12] shows how to handle a "second order" language (for strictness analysis) by additional parameterization of the context transformers to include the context transformers for functional arguments. An approach to fully higher-order backwards analysis is outlined in [13]. This is based on a mixture of abstract interpretation (forwards analysis) and first-order backwards analysis. For the purposes of this section it will not be necessary to introduce these devices. Instead we will demonstrate our methods with a sufficient-time analysis using a very simple extension of the context information to higher-order functions. It is expected that the information provided by a full development of context analysis for higher-order functions could be accommodated in the time analysis we present here.

The language we use here is defined by the same grammar as that of the higher-order language in section 2.

6.2 The Projection Transformers

The method we shall describe for constructing the time equations will require the use of the same style of projection transformers that are used for the first-order analysis—for each function definition f_i we will require projection transformers ${f_i}^{\#k}$ such that ${f_i}^k\alpha \Rightarrow ({f_i}^{\#k}\alpha)$.

Since we are working with a higher-order language, we may expect expressions of the form

$$f_i\, e_1 \ldots e_{n_i} e_{n_i+1} \ldots e_m$$

Here the contexts propagated to expressions $e_1 \ldots e_{n_i}$ are determined by the projection transformers of f_i. For a conservative estimate we know it is safe to propagate the context ID to the expressions $e_{n_i+1} \ldots e_m$. In fact, the analysis we present will be able to use more precise information in this instance.

Objects of function type will also require projections to describe the context in which they are needed. A projection of a function gives a function which has less defined results on some of its arguments. For the purpose of time analysis it is sufficient to use the four-point context domain to describe the amount of evaluation of a functional argument (*i.e.* all or nothing). In an expression of the form *exp e* in a context α, we can safely set the context for *exp* to be a mapping of α into the four-point domain for functions. For convenience we define a functional $\diamond$ to perform this task:

$$\diamond\alpha = \begin{cases} \text{FAIL} & \text{if } \alpha = \text{FAIL} \\ \text{ABS} & \text{if } \alpha = \text{ABS} \\ \text{STR} & \text{if FAIL} \sqsubset \alpha \sqsubseteq \text{STR} \\ \text{ID} & \text{if ABS} \sqsubset \alpha \sqsubseteq \text{ID} \end{cases}$$

6.3 Accumulating Cost-Functions

As in the strict higher-order language we will define for each function in the language a cost function, constructed via two syntactic maps. The first, $\mathcal{V}_L$, plays the same rôle as that of $\mathcal{V}$ in the higher-order strict language — it constructs cost-closures and makes their application explicit via an apply function $@_L$. The second, $\mathcal{T}_L$, is used to define the cost-expressions. In the following we use the term *cost-expression* to refer to objects of type *context* $\rightarrow$ *cost*. The definitions of $\mathcal{V}_L$ and $\mathcal{T}_L$ are given in figures 12 and 13. These definitions will be explained in the following sections.

User-defined functions

For each function defined $f_i\, x_1 \ldots x_{n_i} = e_i$ we define a sufficient-cost function to be

$$cf_i\, \langle x_1, c_1\rangle \ldots \langle x_{n_i}, c_{n_i}\rangle\, \alpha = \alpha \hookrightarrow_s 1 + \mathcal{T}_L \circ \mathcal{V}_L[\![e_i]\!]\, \alpha + c_1({f_i}^{\#1}\alpha) + \ldots + c_{n_i}({f_i}^{\#n_i}\alpha)$$

In addition to the context-transformers, the cost functions require modified versions of functions themselves: $f_i'\, x_1 \ldots x_{n_i} = \mathcal{V}_L[\![e_i]\!]$

Application and it's Cost

The cost-functions defined above now have additional parameterisation in the form of cost-expressions paired with each argument. We will explain this choice by considering the cost associated with function application *exp e*.

In the higher-order strict language, application is first translated to $exp' \mathbin{@} e'$ (were exp' is defined according to $\mathcal{V}$) and the cost of evaluation is

$$\mathcal{T}[\![exp']\!] + \mathcal{T}[\![e']\!] + exp' \mathbin{c@} e'$$

Suppose we begin by re-using $\mathcal{V}$, and we attempt to define (with respect to some context β) a lazy version of $\mathcal{T}$, $\mathcal{T}_L$.

In the rule for $\mathcal{T}_L[\![exp' \mathbin{@} e']\!]\ \beta$ we must propagate the context β to the appropriate cost-expressions. We can map β into a four-point domain (overloading $\Diamond$) to get a safe context for the function exp'. We do not know the appropriate context for e', but we can always safely use the context ID and set

$$\mathcal{T}_L[\![exp' \mathbin{@} e']\!]\beta = \mathcal{T}_L[\![exp']\!]\Diamond\beta + \mathcal{T}_L[\![e']\!]\mathrm{ID} + (exp' \mathbin{c@} e')\,\beta$$

Two major problems make this rule unsatisfactory.

1. No useful context information is propagated to e'. The information we have available is the projection transformers, but this is not used since we do not in general know which projection transformer is appropriate.

2. If we have a partial application, for example if exp' is (cons,ccons,2) then e may not be evaluated at all.

We solve both of these problems by passing both the argument, *and* the cost-expression to the cost function. It is then the cost function's task to apply the appropriate context (which is determined by the projection transformers of the function) to these cost expressions—see the cost-function scheme above. We introduce new versions of @ and c@ to accommodate these requirements.

Cost-closures and the apply function

For these reasons we need to define a new version of $\mathcal{V}$ and a different version of the function @. The "lazy" version of $\mathcal{V}$, $\mathcal{V}_L$ is defined in figure 12. Because, in the rule for application, the cost-closure $\mathcal{V}_L[\![exp]\!]$ is applied to the cost-expression $\mathcal{T}_L[\![e]\!]$, we need a new version of the @ function which satisfies:

$$(f, cf, a) \mathbin{@_L} \langle e, ce\rangle = \begin{cases} f\ e & \text{if } a = 1 \\ (f\ e, cf\ \langle e, ce\rangle, a-1) & \text{otherwise} \end{cases}$$

Note that cost-closures retain the same *function–costfunction–arity* structure.

Defining the cost-expressions

Figure 13 also defines cost-expressions via a mapping $\mathcal{T}_L$. A significant difference here is that we do not make the definition with respect to a particular context. This is because we wish to pass cost-expressions (functions *context* $\rightarrow$ *cost*) to the cost-functions without applying them to a particular context.

To define $\mathcal{T}_L$ we define a couple of useful functions:

- Addition of cost expressions: we use a specialised addition operator, $\Diamond\!\!+$, which (for the left operand) maps the context into the four-point projection domain of the left operand: $(ce_1 \Diamond\!\!+ ce_2)\,\alpha = (ce_1(\Diamond\alpha)) + (ce_2\,\alpha)$. By allowing $\Diamond$ to be polymorphic, $\Diamond\!\!+$ is associative.

- The null cost-expression: the function $\overline{0}$ gives zero-cost in any context, so $\overline{0}\ \alpha = 0$ for any α.

Consider the rule for application:

$$\mathcal{T}_L[\![exp'\ @_L\ \langle e', ce'\rangle]\!] = \mathcal{T}_L[\![exp']\!] \diamond\!\!+ (exp'\ c@_L\ \langle e', ce'\rangle)$$

If we apply this expression to a context β, we get

$$\mathcal{T}_L[\![exp']\!] \diamond \beta + (exp'\ c@_L\ \langle e', ce'\rangle)\ \beta$$

To ensure $c@_L$ gives us a cost expression, only a small change is needed in the definition of $c@$

$$(f, cf, n)\ c@_L\ \langle e, ce\rangle = \begin{cases} cf\ \langle e, ce\rangle & \text{if } n = 1 \\ \overline{0} & \text{otherwise} \end{cases}$$

$$\begin{array}{rcl}
\mathcal{V}_L[\![exp\ e]\!] & = & \mathcal{V}_L[\![exp]\!]\ @_L\ \langle \mathcal{V}_L[\![e]\!], \mathcal{T}_L \circ \mathcal{V}_L[\![e]\!]\rangle \\
\mathcal{V}_L[\![\texttt{if}\ e_1\ \texttt{then}\ e_2\ \texttt{else}\ e_3]\!] & = & \texttt{if}\ \mathcal{V}_L[\![e_1]\!]\ \texttt{then}\ \mathcal{V}_L[\![e_2]\!]\ \texttt{else}\ \mathcal{V}_L[\![e_3]\!] \\
\mathcal{V}_L[\![(exp)]\!] & = & (\mathcal{V}_L[\![exp]\!]) \\
\mathcal{V}_L[\![f_i]\!] & = & (f_i'\ ,\ cf_i\ ,\ n_i\ ) \\
\mathcal{V}_L[\![p_i]\!] & = & (p_i\ ,\ cp_i\ ,\ m_i\ ) \\
\mathcal{V}_L[\![c]\!] & = & c \\
\mathcal{V}_L[\![x]\!] & = & x
\end{array}$$

Figure 12: The function modification map

$$\begin{array}{rcl}
\mathcal{T}_L[\![exp'\ @_L\ \langle e', ce'\rangle]\!] & = & \mathcal{T}_L[\![exp']\!] \diamond\!\!+ (exp'\ c@_L\ \langle e', ce'\rangle) \\
\mathcal{T}_L[\![\texttt{if}\ e_1'\ \texttt{then}\ e_2'\ \texttt{else}\ e_3']\!] & = & \mathcal{T}_L[\![e_1']\!] \diamond\!\!+ \texttt{if}\ e_1'\ \texttt{then}\ \mathcal{T}_L[\![e_2']\!]\texttt{else}\ \mathcal{T}_L[\![e_3']\!] \\
\mathcal{T}_L[\![(exp')]\!] & = & (\mathcal{T}_L[\![exp']\!]) \\
\mathcal{T}_L[\![(p_i\ ,\ cp_i\ ,\ m_i\ )]\!] & = & \mathcal{T}_L[\![(f_i\ ,\ cf_i\ ,\ n_i\ )]\!] = \overline{0} \\
\mathcal{T}_L[\![c]\!] & = & \mathcal{T}_L[\![x]\!] = \overline{0}
\end{array}$$

Figure 13: The cost-function construction map

Primitive functions

The cost-function associated with a primitive function p_i of arity m_i is

$$cp_i\ \langle x_1, c_1\rangle \ldots \langle x_{m_i}, c_{m_i}\rangle\ \alpha = c_1(p_i{}^{\#1}\alpha) + \ldots + c_{m_i}(p_i{}^{\#m_i}\alpha)$$

Applying the above schemes in the construction of time-equations requires that we remove (partially evaluate) unnecessary instances of $@_L$, and $c@_L$, as we outlined in section 2.2. In addition we need to specialise functions to remove unnecessary parameters—this is because of the additional parameterisation involved in both modified functions, and cost-functions. The (somewhat lengthy) examples have been omitted, but it is worth noting that the process could benefit from some simple mechanical support.

7 Conclusions

We have presented a method of analysing the time complexity of a lazy higher-order functional language. The techniques for a strict higher-order language are more fully developed in [6]. We have extended of these ideas to give a treatment of lazy higher-order languages, based upon [7]: projections are used to characterise the context in which an expression is evaluated, and cost-equations are parameterised on this context-description. We have introduced two types of time-equation: *sufficient-time* equations (corresponding to the equations in [7]), and *necessary-time* equations, which together provide bounds on the exact time-complexity.

7.1 Related Work

Higher-Order Functions

Analysing the time-complexity of higher-order functions is considered by Shultis [14]. He begins with a non-standard denotational semantics which models both value and cost. A slightly less cumbersome logic is then defined for reasoning about cost by the direct manipulation of expression syntax. The logic is "tested" against the model by using an implementation of the semantics—no formal connection is provided between the logic and the model (in fact correctness could not be established without first restricting the language to typable expressions, although this is not mentioned in the paper).

A means of analysing higher-order functions, rather more in the "functional" style of the approach taken here, can be found in [15]. Le Métayer's solution involves defining a family of cost-functions for each function in the original script, for which the ith cost-function computes the cost of applying the function to its ith argument (in this respect it is closer to Shultis' approach). The syntax-directed rules for obtaining the cost functions require that cost function definitions are constructed dynamically. In addition, unlike the techniques presented here the analysis cannot handle lists of functions, or non-polymorphically typable functions.

In [16] Talcott is concerned with providing tools for reasoning about intensional properties of programs (like cost). To this end, *computation structures*, *derived properties* and *derived programs* are introduced. These simply correspond to a *proof* or derivation in an operational semantics, *properties of the proof* (computed by the step-counting semantics), and *cost-programs* respectively. This framework enables derived programs computing cost to be constructed mechanically, but only for a first-order subset of the lisp-like language used. We reason about the intensional properties of programs in a more straightforward way, without the need for any extra machinery other than the relatively familiar "symbol pushing" involved in operational semantics (see [17]).

Lazy Evaluation

A (non-compositional) means of analysing a call-by-name language is considered in [15]. Le Métayer's solution involves transforming a call-by-name program into a strongly equivalent one with call-by-value semantics. The call-by-value program can be analysed using "strict" techniques (such as those presented in section 2). The translation, however, makes the program significantly more complex, and it not clear that the translation preserves the number of steps that are being counted in the analysis.

Bjerner's time analysis for programs in the language of Martin-Löf type-theory [18] has relevance to the analysis of first-order lazy functional languages, and provided inspiration for Wadler's work. His operational model of contexts, *evaluation degrees* could form an alternative basis for the work presented here. More recently, Bjerner and Holmström [19] have adapted the ideas in [18] to give a calculus for the time analysis of a first-order functional language. The equations used to describe context are *precise*, thus specifying an *exact* time-analysis. The problem here is that the equations cannot be solved mechanically. The main correctness theorem developed (independently) in [19] (apart from the correctness of the context equations) corresponds very closely to theorem 5.3—if we view their model of context (called "demands") as projections, we get a class of projections for which necessary and sufficient times will always be equal. Equations for this class of "exact" projections can be derived with a straightforward modification of the projection equations in [9].

7.2 Further Work

Higher-Order Context Information

The use of first-order context analysis in the analysis of a higher-order language means that, even though cost-expressions are passed as arguments so they are applied to the appropriate context, there are many cases where the contexts derived for higher-order functions are not sufficiently precise. Consider the following function definition: For satisfiable contexts α, the `apply` function (`apply f x = f x`) has the following projection transformers: $\texttt{apply}^{\#1}\alpha = \Diamond\alpha$, and $\texttt{apply}^{\#2}\alpha = \mathrm{ID}$.

Without knowing about the context of the function `apply`, the context for x is approximated by the least informative context ID.

The sufficient-time equation constructed with these projection transformers is

$$\texttt{capply <f,fc> <x,xc>}\ \alpha \ = \ \alpha \hookrightarrow_s 1 + \texttt{fc}(\Diamond\alpha) + \texttt{xc}\ \mathrm{ID} + (\texttt{f c@}_L\texttt{<x,}\bar{0}\texttt{>})\ \alpha$$

The lack of accurate projection transformers means that the cost-expression `xc` is applied to the imprecise context ID—it is not difficult to construct examples where this gives an unsatisfactory time analysis. Context-analyses for higher-order languages are not well-developed. As mentioned before, Wray's strictness analysis handles "second order" functions—projection equations can be extended to handle such functions, and the resulting context descriptions can be used by cost-functions presented here. Fully higher-order analyses still present problems for the construction of both approximate and precise context equations.

An alternative solution to this problem further utilises the technique of "passing" cost-expressions. The expression bound to `x` in the function `apply` above is evaluated in the context of the function bound to `f`, so we can pass the cost expression on to the cost function associated with `f` as follows:

$$\texttt{capply <f,fc> <x,xc>}\ \alpha \ = \ \alpha \hookrightarrow_s \ \texttt{1 + fc(}\Diamond\alpha\texttt{) + (f c}@_L\texttt{<x,xc>)}\ \alpha$$

To generalise this technique we must check that any parameter whose cost-expression we wish to propagate is not shared (*i.e.* it is not required in more than one context). For a sufficient-time analysis we could propagate to all contexts, while in a necessary-time analysis we could choose to propagate the cost expression to a single context. In addition we need to determine when the propagation is necessary, since unnecessary propagation (*i.e.* when the context information is sufficiently precise) decreases the compositionality of cost-functions with no additional benefit.

Acknowledgements

Thanks to Jesper Andersen, Chris Hankin, Sebastian Hunt and Daniel Le Métayer for their useful suggestions relating to earlier drafts of this paper.

References

[1] B. Wegbreit. Mechanical program analysis. *C.ACM*, 18:528–539, September 1975.

[2] D. LeMétayer. Mechanical analysis of program complexity. In *ACM SIGPLAN 85 Symposium*, July 1985.

[3] M. Rosendahl. Automatic complexity analysis. In *Functional Programming Languages and computer architecture, conference proceedings.* ACM press, 1989.

[4] T. Hickey and J. Cohen. Automating program analysis. *J. ACM*, 35:185–220, January 1988.

[5] P. Flajolet. Mathematical methods in the analysis of algorithms and data structures. Repport 400, INRIA, Le Chesnay, France, May 1985.

[6] D. Sands. Complexity analysis for a higher order language. Technical Report DOC 88/14, Imperial College, October 1988.

[7] P. Wadler. Strictness analysis aids time analysis. In *15th ACM Symposium on Principals of Programming Languages*, January 1988.

[8] G. Kahn. Natural semantics. In *Proceedings of Symposium on Theoretical Aspects of Computer Science*, pages 22–39. Springer Verlag, 1987. LNCS 247.

[9] P. Wadler and R. J. M. Hughes. Projections for strictness analysis. In *1987 Conference on Functional Programming and Computer Architecture*, Portland, Oregon, September 1987.

[10] K. Davis and P. Wadler. Backwards strictness analysis: Proved and improved. In *Proceedings of Glasgow Workshop on Functional Programming*, August 1989.

[11] G.L. Burn. A relationship between abstract interpretation and projection analysis (extended abstract). In *17th ACM Symposium on Principals of Programming Languages*, January 1990.

[12] S. C. Wray. Programming techniques for functional languages. Technical Report 92, University of Cambridge Computer Laboratory, June 1986.

[13] R. J. M. Hughes. Backwards analysis of functional programs. DoC Research Report CSC/87/R3, University of Glasgow, March 1987.

[14] J. Shultis. On the complexity of higher-order programs. Technical Report CU-CS-288, University of Colorado, Febuary 1985.

[15] D. LeMétayer. Analysis of functional programs by program transformation. In *Second France–Japan Artificial Intelligence and Computer Science Symposium.* North–Holland, 1988.

[16] C. Talcott. Derived properties and derived programs. Technical report, Stanford, 1985.

[17] G. D. Plotkin. A structured approach to operational semantics. Technical Report DAIMI FN–19, Computer Science Department, Aahus University, Denmark, September 1981.

[18] B. Bjerner. *Time Complexity of Programs in Type Theory.* PhD thesis, Chalmers University of Technology, 1989.

[19] B. Bjerner and S. Holmström. A compositional approach to time analysis of first order lazy functional programs. In *Functional Programming Languages and computer architecture, conference proceedings.* ACM press, 1989.

Deriving the fast Fourier algorithm by calculation

Geraint Jones
Programming Research Group
11 Keble Road
Oxford OX1 3QD

Abstract

This paper reports an explanation of an intricate algorithm in the terms of a potentially mechanisable rigorous-development method. It uses notations and techniques of Sheeran [1] and Bird and Meertens [2, 3]. We have claimed that these techniques are applicable to digital signal processing circuits, and have previously applied them to regular array circuits [4, 5, 6].

This paper shows that they can deal with an apparently very different and more complex algorithm: the fast Fourier transform. Similar papers to this one [7, 8, 9] perform most of the same calculations, but experiment with different ways of expressing the algorithms and their development.

Twenty-five years ago Cooley and Tukey rediscovered an optimising technique usually attributed to Gauss, who used it in hand calculation. They applied the technique to the discrete Fourier transform, reducing an apparently $O(n^2)$ problem to the almost instantly ubiquitous $O(n \log n)$ 'fast Fourier transform' [10]. The fast Fourier transform is not of course a different transform, but a fast implementation of the discrete transform.

Its greatest virtue lies in that it can be executed in $O(\log n)$ time on $O(n)$ processors in a uniform way – it lends itself to a low-latency high-throughput pipelined hardware implementation. Indeed, a footnote to the Cooley–Tukey paper records that a hardware implementation was underway as the paper was published, specifically that a component for evaluating a four-point transform had been 'designed by R. E. Miller and S. Winograd of the IBM Watson Research Centre'.

The unfortunate disadvantage of the fast algorithm is that although the fundamental idea is simple, the detail of its efficient implementation is very hard to understand. That efficiency depends on intricate permutations which rearrange data to maximise the sharing of work done in calculating intermediate results. Presentations of the algorithm abound in mysterious artefacts like the reversal of bits in subscripts [11], and the translation of parts of subscripts from time space to frequency space [12]. More recent descriptions of implementations seem to gloss over the problem, either referring the reader back to older presentations [13], or apparently assuming that the algorithm – because it is well known – must be well understood [14].

This paper reports some success in describing the derivation of the the Cooley–Tukey fast Fourier algorithm from the specification of the discrete Fourier transform.

A functional programming notation was used to express the discrete transform, and the fast algorithm has been calculated from it by equational reasoning. The calculation has been carried out in some detail as part of the feasibility study for a mechanical circuit-designer's assistant. The style of the calculation is such that we believe that the process of deriving a reasonable layout of an implementing circuit from our final program would also be mechanisable.

The discrete Fourier transform

The discrete Fourier transform is defined in terms of the arithmetic on an integral domain. You can think of arithmetic on complex numbers, for a definite example, although there are applications where finite fields or vector spaces over integral domains are appropriate. The derivation depends only on the algebraic properties of the arithmetic, not on the underlying arithmetic itself, so everything said here about the algorithm will be true for finite fields and vector spaces as well.

The discrete Fourier transform of a vector x of length n is a vector y of the same length for which

$$y_j = \sum_{k:0\leqslant k<n} \omega^{j\times k} \times x_k$$

where ω is a principal n-th root of unity. (In the example of complex numbers, you can think of $\omega = e^{2\pi i/n}$.) The result, y, is sometimes called the 'frequency spectrum' of the sample x.

Even if the powers of ω are pre-calculated, it would appear that $O(n^2)$ multiplications are required to evaluate the whole of y for any x. The fast algorithm avoids many of these by making use of the fact that $\omega^n = 1$. The discovery made by Cooley and Tukey was that if n is composite, the calculation can be divided into what amounts to a number of smaller Fourier transforms. Suppose $n = p \times q$, then by a change of variables

$$\begin{aligned}
y_{pa+b} &= \sum_{c:0\leqslant c<p}\ \sum_{d:0\leqslant d<q} \omega^{(pa+b)(qc+d)} x_{qc+d} \\
&= \sum_{c:0\leqslant c<p}\ \sum_{d:0\leqslant d<q} (\omega^{pq})^{ac}(\omega^{p})^{ad}(\omega^{q})^{bc}\omega^{bd} x_{qc+d} \\
&= \sum_{d:0\leqslant d<q} (\omega^{p})^{ad}\omega^{bd} \sum_{c:0\leqslant c<p} (\omega^{q})^{bc} x_{qc+d}
\end{aligned}$$

Since ω^q is a p-th root of unity, and ω^p is a q-th root of unity, it is not surprising that the above calculation leads to an implementation in which p-sized and q-sized transforms appear. It is harder, however, to see what that implementation might be.

A notation for describing circuits

To simplify calculation with algorithms, we write and work with expressions which represent not data values, but functions. This requires a variety of operators for combining functions – algorithms, or circuits, depending on whether you think we are designing programs or hardware – rather than the more usual operators which act on data.

The basic operation on circuits is composition, $f \cdot g$ defined by $(f \cdot g)x = f(gx)$, which you can think of as connecting the output of g to the input of f. We have previously [7] tried explaining this development in terms of 'reverse composition', $f \,;\, g = g \cdot f$, which is easier to read left-to-right as an operational description, but which fits less well with our other notational conventions.

All our data are organised in finite lists – or vectors – and many of the operators in this paper describe the way that a function operating on a signal is manipulated to make a function which operates on a list of signals. In this way we avoid having to manipulate subscript expressions or individual components of the vectors. For example, $f * x$ read 'f map x', is defined by $(f * x)_i = f x_i$ and represents the replication of the circuit f so that each instance can be connected to one of each of the signal sources in the list x. We write $f*$, or sometimes $(f*)$ for the replicated circuits – the function that takes the list x as input and returns the list $f * x$. Similarly, $f**$ means $(f*)*$ which is a circuit that expects a list of lists of signals – a column of rows, say – and applies $f*$ to each row, which is to say that it applies f to each element of each row. Very occasionally we will be driven to write $(*)$ for the function which when applied to f returns $f*$, that is $(*)f = f*$.

One of the more useful properties of map is that it distributes over composition: $(f \cdot g)* = f* \cdot g*$ irrespective of the particular functions f and g. Moreover, if f and g commute, that is if $f \cdot g = g \cdot f$, then $f* \cdot g* = (f \cdot g)* = (g \cdot f)* = g* \cdot f*$ so $f*$ and $g*$ commute, and so do $f**$ and $g**$, and so on. All our calculations are of essentially this form, and rely on a rich collection of laws none of them significantly more complex than these.

The concatenation of lists, $x +\!\!+\, y$ is the list consisting of the elements of x followed by those of y. (All our lists are of finite length.) A function like $f*$ is called a homomorphism of lists because $f * (x +\!\!+\, y) = (f * x) +\!\!+\, (f * y)$. Homomorphisms are clearly ideal candidates for parallel implementation.

Reduction is a generalisation of the way that the $\sum$ operator applies addition to a list of values. We write $\oplus / x$, read 'the $\oplus$ reduce of x', for the value of $x_0 \oplus x_1 \oplus x_2 \oplus \ldots$ but only when $\oplus$ is associative so that it does not matter in what order the $\oplus$ operations are applied. (We follow a convention of Bird and Meertens that the symbols $\oplus$, $\otimes$ and so on are not specific operators but are usually operator variables, just as f, g and so on are function variables, and x, y and so on are data variables.) Flatten, $+\!\!+/$, is the operation which joins a list of lists to make a single list, and the generalisation of the homomorphism property of map is that $f* \cdot +\!\!+/ = +\!\!+/ \cdot f**$. In the case of the usual arithmetic operations $+$ and $\times$, for which $n \times (x + y) = (n \times x) + (n \times y)$, it is similarly the case that $n\times \cdot +/ = +/ \cdot n \times *$. This is called the distribution of $\times$ over $+$, so we will also say that $*$ distributes over $+\!\!+$.

For any operation $\oplus$, its reduction can be divided over $+\!\!+$ because $\oplus / (x +\!\!+\, y) = (\oplus / x) \oplus (\oplus / y)$, and more generally $\oplus/ \cdot +\!\!+/ = \oplus/ \cdot \oplus / *$. That means that you can reduce a list of lists either by concatenating the rows and reducing the whole, or by reducing each of the rows and then reducing the list of results. The equality $\oplus/ \cdot +\!\!+/ = \oplus/ \cdot \oplus / *$ therefore captures the essence of the associativity of the $\oplus$ operation.

If x and y are lists of the same length $x \Upsilon_{\oplus} y$, read as 'x zip-with-$\oplus$ y', is the point-by-point operation defined by $(x \Upsilon_{\oplus} y)_i = x_i \oplus y_i$. This is another replication operation like map, which produces an operation that has a naturally parallel implementation. An example is Υ_{+} which is the usual point-by-point addition of vectors.

Some notation specific to this algorithm

In the course of the calculation of the fast Fourier algorithm, we identified a number of useful operations which may not be familiar to the users of the Bird–Meertens calculus. Much of the work of the development is encapsulated in the algebra of these operations.

The transposition of lists of lists is here written И, defined by $(\text{И}x)_{ij} = x_{ji}$. (You can calculate many of its properties from Bird's and Meertens' observation that $\text{И} = \Upsilon_{+\!\!+}/ \cdot 1\copyright **$ where $1 \copyright x$ is the list of length one whose only element is x.) Throughout the theory underlying this paper, lists of lists have to be 'rectangular' with every sublist having the same length. In that case it follows from the definitions that for any binary $\oplus$, $\Upsilon_{\oplus}/ = \oplus / * \cdot \text{И}$. That is, if given a column of rows, you can $\Upsilon_{\oplus}$ the rows together column by column by transposing the rows and columns, and then $\oplus$-ing along each of the rows. Consider now

$$
\begin{aligned}
\Upsilon_{+}/ \cdot n\times ** \;&= \{\text{ transposition rule for } \Upsilon_{+}/ \,\} \\
&\quad +/* \cdot \text{И} \cdot n\times ** \\
&= \{\text{ map acts pointwise, so } \text{И} \cdot f ** = f ** \cdot \text{И} \,\} \\
&\quad +/* \cdot n\times ** \cdot \text{И} \\
&= \{\text{ map distributes over composition } \} \\
&\quad (+/ \cdot n \times *)* \cdot \text{И} \\
&= \{\text{ multiplication distributes over addition } \} \\
&\quad (n\times \cdot +/)* \cdot \text{И} \\
&= \{\text{ map distributes over composition } \} \\
&\quad n \times * \cdot +/* \cdot \text{И} \\
&= \{\text{ transposition rule for } \Upsilon_{+}/ \,\} \\
&\quad n \times * \cdot \Upsilon_{+}/
\end{aligned}
$$

so showing that $n \times *$, which is the multiplication of vectors by the scalar n, distributes over Υ_{+}, which is the point-by-point addition of vectors. The calculation shows that this is a consequence of the distribution property of scalar addition and multiplication.

Transposition is useful in capturing other properties of operations. For example, if as well as being associative $\oplus$ is a commutative operation – that is if $x \oplus y = y \oplus x$ – you can choose to $\oplus$-reduce an array of values either by rows and then columns, or by columns and then rows, that is $\oplus/ \cdot \Upsilon_{\oplus}/ = \oplus/ \cdot \oplus / * \cdot \text{И} = \oplus/ \cdot \oplus / *$. This equality captures the essence of the commutativity of $\oplus$. (Bird describes operators for which $\oplus/ \cdot \Upsilon_{\otimes}/ = \otimes/ \cdot \oplus / *$ by saying that $\oplus$ *abides* with $\otimes$, so commutative operators are ones which abide with themselves.)

Some of the properties of the $*$ operation are shared by operators that have previously usually been used to explain the skewing of data in time [15, 16]. The triangle operation is defined by $(f \vartriangle x)_i = f^i x_i$ where f^i represents i repeated applications of f, and the block operation $(f \square x)_i = f^{\#x} x_i$ where $\#x$ is the length of x. We will call $*$, $\vartriangle$, and $\square$ *pointwise* operations.

If $\oplus$ and $\otimes$ are any two pointwise operators, and if f and g are two functions that commute – that is, if $f \cdot g = g \cdot f$ – then so do $f\oplus$ and $g\otimes$ – that is, $f\oplus \cdot g\otimes = g\otimes \cdot f\oplus$ – and by repeated application of this same theorem, so do any pair of terms like $f \vartriangle * \vartriangle *$ and $f \square \vartriangle \vartriangle *$. Again, if f and g commute and $\oplus$ is pointwise, then $(f \cdot g)\oplus = f\oplus \cdot g\oplus$ and so on, which is reminiscent of the distribution of $*$ over composition. If $\oplus$ and $\otimes$ are pointwise operations, $f \oplus \otimes \cdot И = И \cdot f \otimes \oplus$, which is a general form of an earlier observation that $f ** \cdot И = И \cdot f **$.

Of course, not all the properties of $*$ are shared by pointwise operations, and it is possible to relax some of the preconditions of these results if it is known that one of the pointwise operators is map. Given functions which do not quite commute, say $f \cdot g = g \cdot h$, then for any pointwise $\oplus$ operation $f\oplus \cdot g* = g* \cdot h\oplus$ even if $f \neq h$.

To construct constant lists $n \circledcirc x$, read 'n copies of x', is a list of length n, each element of which is x. Although it is an apparently unusual operation, it has properties which are familiar-looking when cast in algebraic terms, for $(m+n) \circledcirc x = (m \circledcirc x) +\!\!\!+ (n \circledcirc x)$ and $n \circledcirc (x \oplus y) = (n \circledcirc x) \Upsilon_{\oplus} (n \circledcirc y)$. For any f it is clearly the case that $n\circledcirc \cdot f = f* \cdot n\circledcirc$ because if you want n copies of the output of a circuit, you can just as easily fan out the output of one instance of the circuit or fan out the input to a number of copies of the circuit. Although you might expect only to use this equation to optimise by replacing the right-hand side by the left, it can also be used left to right so as to increase the amount of parallelism, perhaps in the hope that the $f*$ term can be combined with some later processing to achieve a global simplification.

Because transposition is effectively an interleaving operation, it interacts quite regularly with the copying operator. Copying a list and interleaving the copies is the same as making individual copies of the elements of the list, $И \cdot n\circledcirc = n \circledcirc *$, and replicating the rows of a transposed list of lists is related to replicating the entire list by $n \circledcirc * \cdot И = И \cdot n\circledcirc \cdot И = И \cdot И* \cdot n\circledcirc$. Other interactions between these operations can be calculated from these and from earlier equations.

Calculating with functions of specific types

The width (or period) of a Fourier transform is of course a part of the calculation. It transpires that in reasoning about the algorithm, say $\mathcal{F}$, it is necessary to be able to refer this width, which is of course the length of the argument, x. However, the argument does not normally appear in the calculations, which deal with $\mathcal{F}$ rather than with $\mathcal{F}x$ which is the value of the output. There are two apparent alternative techniques for dealing with this. One possibility which suggests itself is to handle the width information as a part of the type of the expression, and perform a parallel calculation of the type alongside the manipulation of the algorithm-valued expression.

The other possibility – explored in reference [7] – is to code the type, where necessary, by introducing functions which are the identities on just that type. This technique makes the type-calculation uniform with the algorithm-calculation, and is probably the right approach to use in implementing mechanical tools to support the calculation. On the other hand, it makes the formulae appear rather strange, and leads to some unnatural manipulations.

Most exponents of this sort of calculation tend to be rather vague about details of type, for example writing the name of a polymorphic function in a calculation even when the calculation is valid only for particular instances. Their calculations are usually supported by an informal natural-language commentary about the restrictions. In this paper, the presentation is a compromise between these approaches: we write type-restrictions in the function-expressions, but will not be quite as careful with the type restrictions as with the values. To do this is simply to cast a cloak of notational formality over the informality of a running commentary.

If f is a function which takes arguments of type α and if β is a subtype of α, the function $f \upharpoonleft \beta$ is that which agrees with f but is applicable only to values in β, and to all values in β. Similarly, if f returns values of α' and if β' is a subtype of α', the function $\beta' \upharpoonright f$ is the largest which agrees with f but returns values in β'. (Small letters from early in the Greek alphabet are type variables in this paper.)

Occasionally $f \cdot g$ is written even when the domain of f is strictly smaller than the range of values returned by g, intending by that to indicate a restriction of g. The cost of this otherwise harmless convention is that even if g is a bijection, it is not necessarily the case that $f = (f \cdot g) \cdot g^{-1}$. On the other hand, it is always the case that $(f \upharpoonleft \alpha) \cdot g = (f \upharpoonleft \alpha) \cdot (\alpha \upharpoonright g) = f \cdot (\alpha \upharpoonright g)$. Moreover, restriction associates with composition, $(f \cdot g) \upharpoonleft \alpha = f \cdot (g \upharpoonleft \alpha)$ and $\alpha \upharpoonright (f \cdot g) = (\alpha \upharpoonright f) \cdot g$, so all the brackets can be left out, and if you prefer you can read the restrictions as compositions with identity functions.

The types that need to be named in this calculation are all the types of zeroth order objects: values of the integral domain over which the arithmetic is defined, lists of these, and lists of lists and so on. The type of lists (of any length), each component of which is of type α, would usually be written α^*, making a pun between the list-type constructor and the operation of mapping over lists. The subtype of that type containing just lists of length n each component of which is of type α, would similarly be written α^n. So, for example, $\alpha^{*,p}$ is the type of p-lists of lists of α values; $\alpha^{q,*}$ is the type of lists of q-lists of α values; and $\alpha^{q,p}$ is the type of p-lists of q-lists of α values. This last type is the greatest common subtype of the preceding two, and in general the greatest common subtype – intersection – of two types satisfies $\alpha^{x,y} \cap \beta^{p,q} = (\alpha \cap \beta)^{(x \sqcup p),(y \sqcup q)}$ where $*$ is now also punned with the bottom of the flat lattice of natural numbers. This gives a way of factoring type restrictions, for example $f \upharpoonleft (\alpha \cap \beta) = f \upharpoonleft \alpha \upharpoonleft \beta$.

The calculations in this paper use a number of rules about the interaction between specific operations and type restriction, for example that $\text{И} \upharpoonleft \alpha^{x,y} = \alpha^{y,x} \upharpoonright \text{И}$, that $n© \upharpoonleft \alpha = \alpha^n \upharpoonright n©$, and that $f\Box \upharpoonleft \alpha^n = f^n{*} \upharpoonleft \alpha^n$, for any proper natural number n. Moreover, if f is homogeneous on α, that is if $f \upharpoonleft \alpha = \alpha \upharpoonright f$, and if $\oplus$ is pointwise, then $f\oplus$ is homogeneous on α^* and on each α^n.

For the most part, in this paper the only part of a type which is relevant is whether it is a list type, or the number of components in that list. Accordingly we shall usually omit the base type, writing $f \upharpoonleft *, p$ for the restriction of f to p-lists of lists; $f \upharpoonleft q, *$ for the restriction of f to lists of q-lists; and so on.

Since $\#(x \mathbin{+\!\!+} y) = (\# x) + (\# y)$, it follows that $\# \cdot \mathbin{+\!\!+}/ = +/ \cdot \# *$ and so that $\mathbin{+\!\!+}/ \upharpoonright n, m = n \times m \rceil \mathbin{+\!\!+}/ \upharpoonright n, m$. Notice that you cannot in general compare these last two functions with $n \times m \rceil \mathbin{+\!\!+}/$ since they are applicable only to lists of length m with sublists of length n, whereas $n \times m \rceil \mathbin{+\!\!+}/$ can flatten any rectangular list of lists with a total length of $n \times m$, and there will be other factorisations of this product unless n and m are equal primes.

Casting the algorithm in the notation

The first task in a calculation dealing with an algorithm is to cast the specification in the notation that will be used to handle the development. There are two things which we do in this stage.

One part appears to be largely a process of eliminating subscripts, since the usual convention is to specify separately each co-ordinate of an output vector. The conventional understanding of a specification of the form $y_i = \ldots$ is that the subscript is universally quantified, so that this one equation formally represents a number of different equations, one for each value of i. To make clear that an algorithm operates uniformly at all co-ordinates of its output we write a single equation which defines the whole list of output values. This means that we need (temporarily) a notation for lists, which we write $\langle i : 0 \leqslant i < n : x_i \rangle$ for the list of length n, the ith element of which is x_i.

The other part of the translation is to manipulate the specification - which is usually an expression describing the output of a calculation for a given input - into the form of an application to that input of an expression representing the algorithm. The manipulation of the algorithm can then proceed without reference to the particular input.

The discrete Fourier transform was specified by

$$y_j = \sum_{k:0 \leqslant k < n} \omega^{j \times k} \times x_k$$

by which was meant that the output y should be defined for each j in the range $0 \leqslant j < n$, so meaning that

$$\begin{aligned}
y &= \langle j : 0 \leqslant j < n : \textstyle\sum \langle k : 0 \leqslant k < n : \omega^{j \times k} \times x_k \rangle\rangle \\
&= \{ \text{meaning of summation, meaning of arithmetic exponentiation} \} \\
&\quad \langle j : 0 \leqslant j < n : + / \langle k : 0 \leqslant k < n : (\omega^j)^k \times x_k \rangle\rangle \\
&= \{ \text{meaning of } * \text{ and associativity of } \times \} \\
&\quad +/ * \langle j : 0 \leqslant j < n : \langle k : 0 \leqslant k < n : ((\omega \times)^j)^k x_k \rangle\rangle \\
&= \{ \text{meaning of } \triangle \} \\
&\quad +/ * \langle j : 0 \leqslant j < n : (\omega \times)^j \triangle\, x \rangle \\
&= \{ \text{distribution of } \triangle \text{ over commuting composition, meaning of } \copyright \} \\
&\quad +/ * \langle j : 0 \leqslant j < n : ((\omega \times) \triangle)^j (n \copyright x)_j \rangle \\
&= \{ \text{meaning of the } \triangle \text{ operator} \} \\
&\quad +/ * (((\omega \times) \triangle) \triangle (n \copyright x))
\end{aligned}$$

$= \{$ meaning of composition $\}$

$((+/*) \cdot (((\omega\times)\triangle)\triangle) \cdot (n©))x$

$= \{$ conventions about parentheses $\}$

$(+/* \cdot \omega\times \triangle \triangle \cdot n©)x$

Since ω depends on n, because $\omega^n = 1$, we will write $\omega\times$ using a new operator ς for which $n \varsigma z = \omega \times z$. This operation has the property, which will be useful later, that $((p \times q)\varsigma)^q = (p\varsigma)$.

The term $+/* \cdot n\varsigma \triangle \triangle \cdot n©$ represents the discrete Fourier transform algorithm, but is only applicable to lists of length n, so we will calculate from the definition

$$\mathcal{F} \restriction n \quad = \quad +/* \cdot n\varsigma \triangle \triangle \cdot n© \restriction n$$

Dividing large problems into smaller ones

Suppose f is an algorithm or circuit for calculating some list-valued function of a list of values. If it is possible to express f in the form $+\!\!+/ \cdot g$, then g is an algorithm for constructing the same result in parts, and may be implementable by a number of independent parts. For example, $(m \times n)© = +\!\!+/ \cdot m© \cdot n© = +\!\!+/ \cdot n © * \cdot m©$ describes a divide-and-conquer strategy for fanning out a signal $m \times n$ times by first making m copies, and then independently fanning each of those out n times.

Similarly, $f \cdot +\!\!+/$ is an algorithm which constructs the same result as f from a partition of the same input into a rectangular list of lists. If it is possible to 'simplify' $f \cdot +\!\!+/$ into a form which has a parallel implementation, that gives a strategy for dividing the calculation of f. A particularly useful result in the present case is that $f\triangle \cdot +\!\!+/ = +\!\!+/ \cdot f \square \triangle \cdot f \triangle *$ which means that $f\triangle$ can be implemented by a number of (smaller) independent instances of $f\triangle$ and a triangular array of $f\square$ components. (Notice that this equality depends the decision to allow lists of lists only where every sublist has the same length.)

In the course of factorising the discrete Fourier transform, this rule is applied twice to an instance of an expression of the form $f \triangle \triangle$.

$f \triangle \triangle \cdot +\!\!+/ \cdot +\!\!+/ **$

$= \{$ factorising $\triangle \}$

$+\!\!+/ \cdot f\triangle \square \triangle \cdot f\triangle \triangle * \cdot +\!\!+/ **$

$= \{$ factorising $\triangle$ and properties of $*$ and pointwise operators $\}$

$+\!\!+/ \cdot f\triangle \square \triangle \cdot +\!\!+/ ** \cdot (f \square \triangle \cdot f \triangle *) \triangle *$

$= \{$ again $\}$

$+\!\!+/ \cdot +\!\!+/ ** \cdot (f \square \triangle \cdot f \triangle *) \square \triangle \cdot (f \square \triangle \cdot f \triangle *) \triangle *$

$= \{$ commuting pointwise terms $\}$

$+\!\!+/ \cdot +\!\!+/ ** \cdot f \square \triangle \square \triangle \cdot f \triangle * \square \triangle \cdot f \square \triangle \triangle * \cdot f \triangle * \triangle *$

This factorisation corresponds to the two changes of variables in the earlier calculation with summations. Notice that all four of the terms in f commute, because all of the operators in them are pointwise.

Since the f in question is $n\varsigma$, this is the point to observe that some powers of f are going to be cancellable, specifically that

$$\begin{aligned} n\varsigma \,\square \triangle \square \triangle \upharpoonright q,*,p,* &= n\varsigma^{n} * \triangle * \triangle \upharpoonright q,*,p,* \\ &= 1\varsigma * \triangle * \triangle \upharpoonright q,*,p,* \\ &= 1\varsigma * * * * \upharpoonright q,*,p,* \end{aligned}$$

where 1ς is the identity on the type underlying the arithmetic.

Dividing the discrete Fourier transform

Suppose that $n = p \times q$. The factorisation of the n-point transform proceeds, as suggested above, by simplifying a specific instance of $\mathcal{F} \upharpoonright n \cdot +\!\!+/$. The particular instance is chosen – with hindsight, of course – so that a term can be cancelled later.

$$\begin{aligned}
& \mathcal{F} \upharpoonright n \cdot +\!\!+/ \upharpoonright q,p \\
&\quad = \{\text{ definition }\} \\
&\qquad +/* \cdot n\varsigma \triangle \triangle \cdot n\copyright \upharpoonright p \times q \cdot +\!\!+/ \upharpoonright q,p \\
&\quad = \{\text{ absorbing restriction, factorising } \copyright \} \\
&\qquad +/* \cdot n\varsigma \triangle \triangle \cdot +\!\!+/ \cdot q\copyright \cdot p\copyright \cdot +\!\!+/ \upharpoonright q,p \\
&\quad = \{\text{ properties of } \copyright \text{ and } * \} \\
&\qquad +/* \cdot n\varsigma \triangle \triangle \cdot +\!\!+/ \cdot +\!\!+/** \cdot q\copyright \cdot p\copyright \upharpoonright q,p \\
&\quad = \{\text{ earlier calculation }\} \\
&\qquad +/* \cdot +\!\!+/ \cdot +\!\!+/** \cdot K \cdot q\copyright \cdot p\copyright \upharpoonright q,p \\
&\qquad \text{where } K = n\varsigma \,\square \triangle \square \triangle \cdot n\varsigma \triangle * \square \triangle \cdot n\varsigma \,\square \triangle \triangle * \cdot n\varsigma \triangle * \triangle * \\
&\quad = \{\ f* \text{ is a homomorphism }\} \\
&\qquad +\!\!+/ \cdot +/** \cdot +\!\!+/** \cdot K \cdot q\copyright \cdot p\copyright \upharpoonright q,p \\
&\quad = \{\ * \text{ distributes over composition, } + \text{ is associative }\} \\
&\qquad +\!\!+/ \cdot (+/ \cdot +/*)** \cdot K \cdot q\copyright \cdot p\copyright \upharpoonright q,p
\end{aligned}$$

But then, because $q\copyright \cdot p\copyright \upharpoonright q,p = q,p,p,q \upharpoonleft q\copyright \cdot p\copyright$ the instance of K is applied only to values of type q,p,p,q.

$$\begin{aligned}
K \upharpoonright q,p,p,q \;&= \{\text{ homogeneity of } n\varsigma \text{ and pointwise operations }\} \\
&\qquad (p \times q)\varsigma \,\square \triangle \square \triangle \upharpoonright q,p,p,q \cdot (p \times q)\varsigma \triangle * \square \triangle \upharpoonright q,p,p,q \,\cdot \\
&\qquad (p \times q)\varsigma \,\square \triangle \triangle * \upharpoonright q,p,p,q \cdot (p \times q)\varsigma \triangle * \triangle * \upharpoonright q,p,p,q \\
&= \{\text{ properties of } \square \text{ and pointwise operators }\} \\
&\qquad (p \times q)\varsigma^{p \times q} * \triangle * \triangle \upharpoonright q,p,p,q \cdot (p \times q)\varsigma^{p} \triangle * * \triangle \upharpoonright q,p,p,q \,\cdot \\
&\qquad (p \times q)\varsigma^{q} * \triangle \triangle * \upharpoonright q,p,p,q \cdot (p \times q)\varsigma \triangle * \triangle * \upharpoonright q,p,p,q \\
&= \{\text{ properties of } \varsigma \} \\
&\qquad 1\varsigma * \triangle * \triangle \upharpoonright q,p,p,q \cdot q\varsigma \triangle * * \triangle \upharpoonright q,p,p,q \,\cdot \\
&\qquad p\varsigma * \triangle \triangle * \upharpoonright q,p,p,q \cdot n\varsigma \triangle * \triangle * \upharpoonright q,p,p,q \\
&= \{\ 1\varsigma \text{ is cancellable, and commuting terms }\} \\
&\qquad *,*,p,q \upharpoonleft q\varsigma \triangle * * \triangle \cdot n\varsigma \triangle * \triangle * \cdot p\varsigma * \triangle \triangle * \upharpoonright q,p,*,*
\end{aligned}$$

Substituting back into the main calculation

$$\begin{aligned}
\mathcal{F} \upharpoonright n \cdot +\!\!+/ \upharpoonright q,p &= +\!\!+/ \cdot (+/ \cdot + / *) ** \upharpoonright *,*,p,q \cdot \\
&\quad q\varsigma \triangle ** \triangle \cdot n\varsigma \triangle * \triangle * \cdot p\varsigma * \triangle \triangle * \cdot \\
&\quad q,p,*,* \upharpoonleft q\copyright \cdot p\copyright \upharpoonright q,p \\
&= +\!\!+/ \upharpoonright p,q \cdot (+/ \cdot + / *) ** \cdot \\
&\quad q\varsigma \triangle ** \triangle \cdot n\varsigma \triangle * \triangle * \cdot p\varsigma * \triangle \triangle * \cdot \\
&\quad q\copyright \cdot p\copyright \upharpoonright q,p
\end{aligned}$$

The strategy from this point is to use the equality $k\copyright \cdot f = f* \cdot k\copyright$, and the distributivity of ς over addition, that is $+/ \cdot k\varsigma* = k\varsigma \cdot +/$ to simplify by eliminating some of the $*$ operators from the expression. To do this the order of some of the operators must be changed by composing both sides with a transposition.

$$\begin{aligned}
\mathcal{F} \upharpoonright n \cdot +\!\!+/ \upharpoonright q,p \cdot \text{И} &= +\!\!+/ \upharpoonright p,q \cdot (+/ \cdot + / *) ** \cdot \\
&\quad q\varsigma \triangle ** \triangle \cdot n\varsigma \triangle * \triangle * \cdot p\varsigma * \triangle \triangle * \cdot \\
&\quad q\copyright \cdot p\copyright \cdot \text{И} \upharpoonright p,q \\
&= \{ \text{transposing pointwise operations} \} \\
&\quad +\!\!+/ \upharpoonright p,q \cdot (+/ \cdot + / *) ** \cdot \text{И} ** \cdot \\
&\quad q\varsigma * \triangle * \triangle \cdot n\varsigma * \triangle \triangle * \cdot p\varsigma \triangle * \triangle * \cdot \\
&\quad q\copyright \cdot p\copyright \upharpoonright p,q \\
&= \{ \text{commutativity of } + \} \\
&\quad +\!\!+/ \upharpoonright p,q \cdot (+/ \cdot + / *) ** \cdot \\
&\quad q\varsigma * \triangle * \triangle \cdot n\varsigma * \triangle \triangle * \cdot p\varsigma \triangle * \triangle * \cdot \\
&\quad q\copyright \cdot p\copyright \upharpoonright p,q \\
&= \{ \text{distributivity of } \varsigma \text{ over } + \} \\
&\quad +\!\!+/ \upharpoonright p,q \cdot +/ ** \cdot q\varsigma\triangle * \triangle \cdot n\varsigma\triangle \triangle * \cdot \\
&\quad +/*** \cdot p\varsigma \triangle * \triangle * \cdot q\copyright \cdot p\copyright \upharpoonright p,q \\
&= \{ \text{carrying } q\copyright \text{ across } * \} \\
&\quad +\!\!+/ \upharpoonright p,q \cdot \\
&\quad +/ ** \cdot q\varsigma\triangle * \triangle \cdot q\copyright \cdot n\varsigma \triangle \triangle \cdot \\
&\quad +/ ** \cdot p\varsigma\triangle * \triangle \cdot p\copyright \upharpoonright p,q \\
&= \{ \text{factorising and distributing restriction} \} \\
&\quad +\!\!+/ \upharpoonright p,q \cdot \\
&\quad +/ ** \cdot q\varsigma\triangle * \triangle \cdot q\copyright \upharpoonright q,* \cdot \\
&\quad n\varsigma \triangle \triangle \cdot \\
&\quad +/ ** \cdot p\varsigma\triangle * \triangle \cdot p\copyright \upharpoonright p,*
\end{aligned}$$

There are two occurrences of similar expressions in the right-hand side, differing only in the parameter p or q. Each of these can be shown in the same way to satisfy

$$\begin{aligned}
+/ ** \cdot k\varsigma\triangle * \triangle \cdot k\copyright \upharpoonright k,* &= \{ k\copyright \upharpoonright *,* = \text{И} \cdot k \copyright * \} \\
&\quad +/ ** \cdot k\varsigma\triangle * \triangle \cdot \text{И} \cdot k \copyright * \upharpoonright k,*
\end{aligned}$$

$$
\begin{aligned}
&= \{\text{ transposition of pointwise operations }\}\\
&\quad \mathcal{N} \cdot +/ ** \cdot k\varsigma \triangle \triangle * \cdot k \circledcirc * \upharpoonright k, *\\
&= \{ * \text{ distributes over composition }\}\\
&\quad \mathcal{N} \cdot (+/* \cdot k\varsigma \triangle \triangle \cdot k \circledcirc \upharpoonright k) *\\
&= \{\text{ definition }\}\\
&\quad \mathcal{N} \cdot (\mathcal{F} \upharpoonright k)*
\end{aligned}
$$

so showing that

$$\mathcal{F} \upharpoonright n \cdot +\!\!+/ \upharpoonright q,p \cdot \mathcal{N} \;=\; +\!\!+/ \upharpoonright p,q \cdot \mathcal{N} \cdot (\mathcal{F} \upharpoonright q)* \cdot n\varsigma \triangle \triangle \cdot \mathcal{N} \cdot (\mathcal{F} \upharpoonright p)*$$

Now $\mathcal{N}$ is its own inverse, and so can be carried over to the other side of the equation. Moreover, $+\!\!+/ \upharpoonright q,p$ is a bijection onto the set of $q \times p$-lists – which is anyway the domain of $\mathcal{F} \upharpoonright (p \times q)$ – and so can be inverted.

$$
\begin{aligned}
\mathcal{F} \upharpoonright n \;&=\; +\!\!+/ \upharpoonright p,q \cdot \mathcal{N} \cdot (\mathcal{F} \upharpoonright q)* \cdot n\varsigma \triangle \triangle \cdot \mathcal{N} \cdot (\mathcal{F} \upharpoonright p)* \cdot \mathcal{N} \cdot (+\!\!+/ \upharpoonright q,p)^{-1}\\
&=\; +\!\!+/ \upharpoonright p,q \cdot \mathcal{N} \cdot (\mathcal{F} \upharpoonright q)* \cdot n\varsigma \triangle \triangle \cdot \mathcal{N} \cdot (\mathcal{F} \upharpoonright p)* \cdot \mathcal{N} \cdot q,p \upharpoonright (+\!\!+/)^{-1}
\end{aligned}
$$

Allowing for a slight abuse of notation, the bizarre looking function $q,p \upharpoonright (+\!\!+/)^{-1}$ is that which takes a list of length n and divides it into p chunks each of length q. The remaining asymmetry in the expression is annoying, but merely superficial for of course $n\varsigma \triangle \triangle \cdot \mathcal{N} = \mathcal{N} \cdot n\varsigma \triangle \triangle$.

The decomposition of $\mathcal{F} \upharpoonright n$ can be read – taking terms from right to left – as a divide-and-conquer algorithm for implementing transforms of composite width: divide the input into p chunks of length q; interleave them; apply an array (of q) independent p-point transforms; interleave the results; modify by scaling the $\langle i,j\rangle$-th signal by $(n\varsigma)^{i \times j}$; apply an array (of p) independent q-point transforms; interleave the results; and finally concatenate the q resulting lists, each of which is of length p, into a single n-list. This is the algorithm known as the 'fast Fourier transform'.

It is the contention of this paper that this equation shows much more clearly than the manipulation of summations that a discrete Fourier transform can be implemented by a divide-and-conquer algorithm using a number of smaller transforms of the same kind.

Twiddling

Leaving aside the rearrangement of the data, on unwinding the recursive calls it transpires that all the substantial work performed by the fast Fourier transform algorithm is in the application of $n\varsigma \triangle \triangle \upharpoonright p,q$.

Suppose that $\oplus$ and $\otimes$ are operators that *cross-associate*, in the sense that $(x \oplus y) \otimes z \;=\; x \oplus (y \otimes z)$, and that $\otimes$ has a left unit $\iota_\otimes$, then it can easily be shown by induction on k that $(x\oplus)^k \;=\; ((x\oplus)^k \iota_\otimes)\otimes$. Since each component of $\iota_{\Upsilon_\otimes}$ is necessarily $\iota_\otimes$, it follows immediately that $x \oplus \triangle = (x\oplus \triangle\, \iota_{\Upsilon_\otimes})\Upsilon_\otimes$.

Again, since the associativity of $\Upsilon_\otimes$ follows from that of $\otimes$, and since any associative operator cross-associates with itself,

$$
\begin{aligned}
x\oplus \triangle \triangle \;&= \{\text{ applying the lemma to } \oplus \text{ and the inner } \triangle \}\\
&\quad (x\oplus \triangle\, \iota_{\Upsilon_\otimes})\; \Upsilon_\otimes \triangle
\end{aligned}
$$

$= \{$ applying the lemma to $\Upsilon_\otimes$ and the outer $\triangle\}$
$((x\oplus \triangle\, \iota_{\Upsilon_\otimes})\, \Upsilon_\otimes\, \triangle \iota_{\Upsilon_{\Upsilon_\otimes}})\, \Upsilon_{\Upsilon_\otimes}$
$= \{$ inverting the lemma, for $\oplus$ and the inner $\triangle\}$
$(x \oplus \triangle\, \triangle\, \iota_{\Upsilon_{\Upsilon_\otimes}})\Upsilon_{\Upsilon_\otimes}$

This decomposition gives an algorithm for calculating $x\oplus \triangle\, \triangle$ by an $O(p\times q) = O(n)$ linear-time application of $\Upsilon_{\Upsilon_\otimes}$ to the signal and a term which depends only on the size of the circuit.

In the case of the Fourier transform, this term is an array of elements of the underlying integral domain – frequently referred to mysteriously as the 'twiddle factors' – which can therefore be pre-calculated. The $\otimes$ operation corresponding to ς is the multiplication on the integral domain, and its left unit is the unit of the domain, so

$$n\varsigma \triangle \triangle \restriction p,q \quad = \quad (n \varsigma \triangle \triangle \mathbf{1})\Upsilon_{\Upsilon_\times}$$

where $\mathbf{1}$ is the appropriately-sized (two-dimensional) array of ones. The $n \varsigma \triangle \triangle \mathbf{1}$ term is the array of twiddle factors, and they can be applied by about $p \times q$ multipliers arranged according to $\Upsilon_{\Upsilon_\times}$. To be precise, only $(p-1)\times(q-1)$ multipliers can be needed since $p + q - 1$ of the twiddle factors are guaranteed to be one.

Outline of an implementation

The usual recursive 'butterfly' implementation of the fast Fourier transform applies only to transforms on vectors of length 2^n for some n. This is because it is very easy to do two-point transforms: because minus one is the principal square root of unity, the two-point transform $\Phi = \mathcal{F} \restriction 2$ takes $\langle x_0, x_1\rangle$ into $\langle x_0 + x_1, x_0 - x_1\rangle$ and requires no multiplications.

For higher powers of two, it uses the factorisation

$$\mathcal{F} \restriction 2n \quad = \quad +\!\!+/ \restriction 2,n \cdot И \cdot (\mathcal{F} \restriction n)* \cdot (2n \varsigma \triangle \triangle \mathbf{1})\Upsilon_{\Upsilon_\times} \cdot И \cdot \Phi* \cdot И \cdot n,2 \,\rceil\, (+\!\!+/)^{-1}$$

The function $n,2 \,\rceil\, (+\!\!+/)^{-1}$ divides its input into halves of length n, and $+\!\!+/ \restriction 2,n$ joins a list of n pairs. The only explicit multiplications in this factorisation are in the $\Upsilon_{\Upsilon_\times}$ operator, and can be implemented by an array of $2n$ multiplications only $n - 1$ of which are non-trivial. The factorisation is used recursively on the $\mathcal{F} \restriction n$ term until only two-point transforms remain.

The usual way of implementing this algorithm – that is, the usual way of laying out the circuit – is to divide $\mathcal{F}$ into two parts: let $\mathcal{F} = \mathcal{S} \cdot \mathcal{F}'$ where

$$\mathcal{F}' \restriction 2n \quad = \quad +\!\!+/ \restriction n,2 \cdot (\mathcal{F}' \restriction n)* \cdot (2n \varsigma \triangle \triangle \mathbf{1})\Upsilon_{\Upsilon_\times} \cdot И \cdot \Phi* \cdot И \cdot n,2 \,\rceil\, (+\!\!+/)^{-1}$$

(A transposition has been omitted from the left-hand end of the expression, which explains the type of the final catenation.) Sheeran [17, 18] gives a solution, usually known as a 'butterfly' circuit, to the recursion

$$\mathcal{B} \restriction 2n \quad = \quad +\!\!+/ \restriction n,2 \cdot (\mathcal{B} \restriction n)* \cdot И \cdot \Phi* \cdot И \cdot n,2 \,\rceil\, (+\!\!+/)^{-1}$$

which is almost the same as that for $\mathcal{F}'$. The solution need only be adjusted – perhaps using Luk's heterogeneous constructors [19] – to accommodate the twiddle factors. Alternately, the twiddle factors might be calculated in a pre-pass using another co-located butterfly of the same shape as $\mathcal{B}$.

Similarly, the solution to

$$\mathcal{S} \upharpoonright 2n \quad = \quad +\!\!\!+/ \upharpoonright 2, n \cdot \mathcal{U} \cdot (\mathcal{S} \upharpoonright n) * \cdot n, 2 \urcorner +\!\!\!+/$$

is a permutation. It is that very thorough shuffle which appears inscrutably in implementations of the fast transform, and which reverses the bits of the index of the position of a value in a vector.

It should also be clear from this paper that the butterfly implementation can be extended to input of any width n, given only implementations of $\mathcal{F} \upharpoonright p$ for each prime p which divides n. This generalization is also suggested by Cooley and Tukey.

Estimation of costs

The reason that the 'fast' algorithm is so called is that it requires a significant number fewer of the basic arithmetic operations. As shown, you can implement $n\varsigma \triangle \triangle \upharpoonright p, q$ for a given n by $(p-1) \times (q-1)$ circuits which multiply by constants, and $+/* \upharpoonright p, q$ by $(p-1) \times q$ adders. Accordingly, the algorithm suggested by

$$\mathcal{F} \upharpoonright n \quad = \quad +/* \cdot n\varsigma \triangle \triangle \cdot n© \upharpoonright n$$

seems to require $(n-1)^2$ multipliers and $n \times (n-1)$ adders.

Suppose the fast algorithm requires at most M_k multipliers and A_k adders to implement $\mathcal{F}_k$, for $k < n$, then if n is composite, then for any factorisation into p and q

$$\mathcal{F} \upharpoonright n \quad = \quad +\!\!\!+/ \upharpoonright p, q \cdot \mathcal{U} \cdot (\mathcal{F} \upharpoonright q) * \cdot n\varsigma \triangle \triangle \cdot \mathcal{U} \cdot (\mathcal{F} \upharpoonright p) * \cdot \mathcal{U} \cdot q, p \urcorner (+\!\!\!+/)^{-1}$$

gives an algorithm which shows that

$$\begin{aligned} M_n &\leqslant p \times M_q + (p-1) \times (q-1) + q \times M_p \\ A_n &\leqslant p \times A_q + q \times A_p \end{aligned}$$

Each of these gives a bound of $O(n \log n)$ on the number of active components.

In the specific case of the power-of-two sized transform, the number of multiplications (discounting mere sign-changes) can be shown to be $(n \log n)/(2 \log 2) - n + 1$, and the number of additions (or subtractions) is $n \log n$.

Transforms over vectors

Having set up the mechanism, it is worth showing that we can also explain within this formalism the sense in which the fast transform is related to transforms on vectors. Let $\mathcal{G}$ be the discrete Fourier transform, abstracted on the arithmetic operations:

$$\mathcal{G}(\oplus, \otimes) \upharpoonright n \quad = \quad \oplus/* \cdot n\otimes \triangle \triangle \cdot n© \upharpoonright n$$

A term in the factorisation of a discrete Fourier transform has the form

$$
\begin{aligned}
\text{И} \cdot (\mathcal{G}(\oplus, \otimes) \upharpoonleft n)* \cdot \text{И} &= \{ \text{definition} \} \\
& \quad \text{И} \cdot (\oplus/* \cdot n\otimes \triangle \triangle \cdot n\copyright \upharpoonleft n)* \cdot \text{И} \\
&= \{ \text{distribution of } * \text{ over composition} \} \\
& \quad \text{И} \cdot \oplus/ ** \cdot n\otimes \triangle \triangle* \cdot n \copyright * \upharpoonleft n, * \cdot \text{И} \\
&= \{ \text{transposition exchanges pointwise operators} \} \\
& \quad \oplus/ ** \cdot n\otimes \triangle *\triangle \cdot \text{И} \cdot n \copyright * \upharpoonleft n, * \cdot \text{И} \\
&= \{ \text{properties of transpose and } \copyright \} \\
& \quad \oplus/ ** \cdot n \otimes \triangle * \triangle \cdot n\copyright \upharpoonleft n, * \cdot \text{И} \\
&= \{ \text{properties of transpose and } \copyright \} \\
& \quad \oplus/ ** \cdot n \otimes \triangle * \triangle \cdot \text{И}* \cdot n\copyright \upharpoonleft *, n \\
&= \{ \text{transposition exchanges pointwise operators} \} \\
& \quad \oplus/ ** \cdot \text{И}* \cdot n \otimes * \triangle \triangle \cdot n\copyright \upharpoonleft n \\
&= \{ \text{transposition rule for } \Upsilon_{\oplus}/ \} \\
& \quad \Upsilon_{\oplus}/* \cdot (n \otimes *) \triangle \triangle \cdot n\copyright \upharpoonleft n \\
&= \{ \text{definition} \} \\
& \quad \mathcal{G}(\Upsilon_{\oplus}, (*) \cdot (\otimes)) \upharpoonleft n
\end{aligned}
$$

but if $n\otimes$ is a scaling of a value of some type, then $((*) \cdot (\otimes))n = (*)((\otimes)n) = (n\otimes)*$ is the corresponding scaling of vectors of that type; and if $\oplus$ is addition of values of some type, then $\Upsilon_{\oplus}$ is addition of vectors of that type.

This has related a number of scalar transforms on interleaved samples to a transform on vectors of samples. You can therefore, if you so wish, see the term $\text{И} \cdot (\mathcal{F} \upharpoonleft n)* \cdot \text{И}$ in the factorisation of the transform as an n-point vector-valued transform operating on a list of n vectors.

Summary

A notation has been presented for describing circuits, and a framework for reasoning about them. This framework was previously known to be able to deal with simple, regular circuits of the sort that have little wiring in their layout. Having suggested that these techniques were suitable for designing digital signal-processing circuits, it was necessary to show that they could deal with existing signal processing components.

The specification of the discrete Fourier transform was translated into the notation; and a summary was given of a calculation from that specification of the fast Fourier transform algorithm. The details of the calculation appear in another paper [20], where it is conducted at a level that could be explained to a very simple mechanical proof checker. Reference [7] contains essentially the same summary of the calculation as is in the present paper, but in a different notation. The presentation given here seems to be a little more natural, at least to users of the Bird-Meertens formalism.

Because all of the reasoning is based on the algebra of the operators, and not on the specific operators or type of data, the calculation is independent of the choice of that type. Although the calculation might have seemed to be about a circuit that would transform a constant input vector, earlier work [21] has shown that the algebra is unchanged by a systematic re-interpretation of all the operators as ones that operate, for example, on time-sequences. (This re-interpretation is known elsewhere as as 'lifting' [22].) It follows that our development of the fast algorithm applies equally well to a circuit that would operate on a time-sequence of sample vectors.

Although the detailed calculation – like any calculation carried out in great detail – is difficult to follow, we contend that

$$\begin{aligned}&\mathcal{F} \upharpoonright (p \times q)\\ &= \;\; +\!\!+/ \upharpoonright p,q \cdot \mathcal{N} \cdot (\mathcal{F} \upharpoonright q)* \cdot ((p \times q) \varsigma \triangle \triangle 1) \Upsilon_{\Upsilon_\times} \cdot \mathcal{N} \cdot (\mathcal{F} \upharpoonright p)* \cdot \mathcal{N} \cdot q, p \upharpoonleft (+\!\!+/)^{-1}\end{aligned}$$

shows much more clearly than any expression describing the output (rather than the circuit) that a discrete Fourier transform can be implemented by a divide-and-conquer strategy which yields a number of smaller transforms of the same kind.

The derivation of this equation proved also to be necessary in writing a program to implement the fast Fourier transform: without the equation it would be hard to understand the program; without the derivation it would be hard to believe the equation. The relevant fragment of the program is

```
fft (+/) ($igma) = f
                         where f   xs = f' xs,  if prime (#xs)
                                      = f'' xs, otherwise
                               f'     = dft (+/) ($igma)
                               f'' xs = ((++/) . (|/|) . (f *) .
                                          (((n $igma) /\) /\) .
                                         (|/|) . (f *) . (|/|) . (\++)) xs
                                        where n      = #xs
                                              (\++) = into (factor n)
```

A complete Orwell [23] program demonstrating the execution of this function appears as an appendix to this paper.

Performing the detailed derivation of fast Fourier transform from the specification has shown that it is reasonable to expect to be able to perform this derivation using the sort of machine assistance available for supporting array designs in the same style. It might also be possible to extend this to mechanical layout of high-wire circuits like the butterfly implementation of the fast Fourier transform, including allocation of the correct twiddle factor to the correct multiplier. Although this necessarily detailed study of the fast Fourier algorithm has revealed structure which was not previously so clear, the principal outcome of the work is to support our claim that our functional circuit-design style can indeed deal with another kind of digital signal processing circuit.

I am grateful to Mary Sheeran, for having spared me the necessity of the other half of this work; Lambert Meertens, for some unfortunate notational advice which I have nevertheless taken to my heart; and to the squiggolists at the Programming Research Group, for tolerating this calculation in its unruly adolescence.

References

[1] Sheeran M. *Design and verification of regular synchronous circuits*, IEE Proceedings, vol. 133, Pt. E, No. 5, September 1986, pp 295–304

[2] Bird RS. *An introduction to the theory of lists*, In: Broy M (ed) *Logic of programming and calculi of discrete design*, Springer, 1987, pp 3–42

[3] Bird RS. *Lectures on constructive functional programming*, Oxford University Computing Laboratory Programming Research Group technical monograph PRG–69, September 1988

[4] Luk W, Jones G. *The derivation of regular synchronous circuits*, In: Bromley K, Kung S-Y, Schwarzlander E. *Proceedings of the international conference on systolic arrays*, IEEE Computer Society Press, 1988, pp 305–314

[5] Luk W, Jones G. *From specification to parametrised architectures*, In: Milne GJ (ed) *The fusion of hardware design and verification*, North-Holland, 1988, pp 267–288

[6] Sheeran M, Jones G. *Relations + higher-order functions = hardware descriptions*, Proc. CompEuro 89, Hamburg, May 1987 pp 303–306

[7] Jones G. *Calculating the fast Fourier transform as a divide and conquer algorithm*, (unpublished)

[8] Jones G. *Factorising Fourier for fastness*, (privately circulated draft of present paper)

[9] Jones G. *Constructing the fast Fourier transform by calculating with the algorithm*, working paper for the STOP summer school on *Constructive Algorithmics*, Ameland, September 1989

[10] Cooley JW, Tukey JW. *An algorithm for the machine computation of complex Fourier series*, Mathematics of Computation, **19**, 1965, pp 297–301

[11] Aho AV, Hopcroft JE, Ullman JD. *The design and analysis of computer algorithms*, Addison–Wesley, 1974

[12] Smith SG. *Fourier transform machines*, In: Denyer P, Renshaw D. *VLSI signal processing; a bit-serial approach*, Addison–Wesley, 1985, pp 147–199

[13] Ullman JD. *Computational aspects of VLSI*, Computer Science Press, 1984

[14] Chandy KM, Misra J. *Parallel program design – a foundation*, Addison–Wesley, 1988

[15] Jones G, Luk W. *Exploring designs by circuit transformation*, In: Moore W, McCabe A, Urquhart R (eds) Proceedings of the first international workshop on *Systolic Arrays*, Adam Hilger, 1987, pp 91–98

[16] Sheeran M. *Retiming and slowdown in Ruby*, In: Milne GJ (ed) *The fusion of hardware design and verification*, North-Holland, 1988, pp 289–308

[17] Sheeran M. *Describing hardware algorithms in Ruby*, In: David et al (eds) Proceedings IFIP WG10.1 workshop on *Concepts and Characteristics of Declarative Systems*, Budapest, 1988

[18] Sheeran M, Jones G. *Butterfly algorithms*, (in hand)

[19] Luk W. *Parametrised design for regular processor arrays*, D.Phil. thesis, Oxford University, 1988

[20] Jones G. *Fast Fourier transform by program transformation of the discrete Fourier transform*, (submitted for publication)

[21] Jones G, Sheeran M. *Timeless truths about sequential circuits*, In: Tewksbury SK, Dickinson BW, Schwartz SC (eds) *Concurrent computations: algorithms, architectures and technology*, Plenum Press, 1988, pp 245–259

[22] Backhouse RC. *Making formality work for us*, Technical Report CS 8907, Department of Mathematics and Computing Science, University of Groningen, 1989

[23] Wadler PL, Miller Q. *An introduction to Orwell 5.00*, Oxford University Programming Research Group, 1988

An Orwell script for fast Fourier transform

```
This script contains implementations of the discrete Fourier transform,
        dft -- an quadratic implementation close to the specification
        fft -- an O(n.logn) recursive implementation
        vft -- a sketch of an optimisation of the same
as described in the accompanying paper.  There are also code to exercise
them and examples of its use.
                                                          gj 3.ix.1989
Operator declarations
---------------------

The odd graphics which are used as operators have to be introduced at the
top of the script.

Although * is used thoughout this script for 'map', it has to be bound
in local definitions because its use has been pre-empted by predefined
numeric multiplication.  Otherwise it would have been defined here by

  %right   90  *
  (*) :: (a -> b) -> [a] -> [b]
  (*) = map

The triangle operator satisfies (f /\ x)!i = (f^i) (x!i), but is defined
recursively

> %right   90  /\
> (/\) :: (a -> a) -> [a] -> [a]
> f /\    []  = []
> f /\ (x:xs) = x : (f /\ (f * xs))
>                where (*) = map

Transposition satisfies (|/| xss)!i!j = xss!j!i
```

```
> %prefix |/|
> (|/|) :: [[a]] -> [[a]]
> |/| xss = [ [x]   | x      <-     hd xss                  ], if #xss = 1
>         = [  x:xs | (x,xs) <- zip (hd xss, |/| (tl xss)) ], if #xss > 1
```

The operator +/ will be used to stand for a various addition-reductions, and although no value is given here, it needs to be declared to be a prefix operator

```
> %prefix +/
```

List catenation and its inverse

Catenation of lists, written ++/ in the paper, is implemented by the primitive concat = foldr (++) [] for speed

```
> %prefix ++/
> (++/) :: [[a]] -> [a]
> (++/) = concat
```

It is inverted by two functions, 'by' and 'into': (by n xs) is used only if #xs is divisible by n, and returns a list of lists of length n which when concatenated return xs

```
> by :: num -> [a] -> [[a]]
> by n xs = [],                                  if xs = []
>         = take n xs : by n (drop n xs), if #xs >= n
```

and (into n xs) is used only if #xs is divisible by n, and returns a list of length n of lists which when concatenated return xs

```
> into :: num -> [a] -> [[a]]
> into n xs = by (#xs $div n) xs
```

Instances of by and into will be represented by the \++ operator (which is written as the inverse of ++/ in the paper) here introduced by

```
> %prefix \++
```

Fourier transform

The Fourier transform of xs is obtained by summing xs_i.w^(i.j); the transform is implemented by (dft (+/) ($igma)) where (n $igma) is a function that represents multiplication by the n-th root of unity, and ((+/) xs) represents the sum of the elements of xs.

```
> dft :: ([a] -> a) -> (num -> a -> a) -> ([a] -> [a])
> dft (+/) ($igma) xs = (((+/) *) . (((n $igma) /\) /\) . (n $copy)) xs
>                       where n   = #xs
>                             (*) = map
```

and the fast transform is obtained by a divide-and-conquer strategy applied to composite width vectors, falling back on the use of dft in the other cases

```
> fft :: ([a] -> a) -> (num -> a -> a) -> ([a] -> [a])
> fft (+/) ($igma) = f
>                    where f   xs = f' xs, if prime (#xs)
>                                 = f'' xs, otherwise
>                          f'     = dft (+/) ($igma)
>                          f'' xs = ((++/) . (|/|) . (f *) .
>                                     (((n $igma) /\) /\) .
>                                    (|/|) . (f *) . (|/|) . (\++)) xs
>                                   where n      = #xs
>                                         (\++) = into (factor n)
>                                         (*)    = map
```

Here, the factor of n chosen for division of xs is (factor n) which is the largest factor of n less than its square root, that is

```
> factor n = (last . divides n . belowroot n) [1..n]
>            where divides n   = filter ((= 0) . (n $mod))
>                  belowroot n = takewhile ((<= n) . sq)
>                                where sq x = x * x
```

and n is prime iff this factor is one.

```
> prime n = factor n = 1
```

(I know it could be made more efficient, but I was writing for clarity!)

You might try to replace the term ((|/|) . (f *) . (|/|)), according to the paper, by (fft (((+/) *) . (|/|)) ((*) . ($igma))), and indeed

```
  vft :: ([a] -> a) -> (num -> a -> a) -> ([a] -> [a])
  vft (+/) ($igma) = f
                     where f   xs = f' xs,  if prime (#xs)
                                  = f'' xs, otherwise
                           f'     = dft (+/) ($igma)
                           f'' xs = ((++/) . (|/|) . (f *) .
                                       (((n $igma) /\) /\) .
                                             f''' . (\++)) xs
                                    where n      = #xs
                                          (\++) = into (factor n)
                                          (*)    = map
                           f'''   = vft vsum vsigma
                                    where vsum   = ((+/) *) . (|/|)
                                                   where (*) = map
                                          vsigma = (*) . ($igma)
                                                   where (*) = map
```

would work were it not for the fact that the recursive call leads to an ill-founded type recursion: the arguments of the recursive call of vft oblige it to have a type

```
        ([[a]] -> [a]) -> (num -> [a] -> [a]) -> ([[a]] -> [[a]])
```

You can make a definition which uses this algorithm for one factorisation and then falls back on the earlier algorithm:

```
> vft :: ([a] -> a) -> (num -> a -> a) -> ([a] -> [a])
> vft (+/) ($igma) = f
>                 where f   xs = f' xs,  if prime (#xs)
>                              = f'' xs, otherwise
>                       f'     = dft (+/) ($igma)
>                       f'' xs = ((++/) . (|/|) . (f *) .
>                                    (((n $igma) /\) /\) .
>                                         f''' . (\++)) xs
>                            where n        = #xs
>                                  (\++) = into (factor n)
>                                  (*)    = map
>                       f'''   = fft vsum vsigma
>                            where vsum   = ((+/) *) . (|/|)
>                                           where (*) = map
>                                  vsigma = (*) . ($igma)
>                                           where (*) = map
```

The large number of bindings of (*) are again an artefact of the type checking, since the uses have different types.

A symbolic example

The arithmetic in the example is going to be over formal polynomials in a given root of unity, that root being the smallest one to be used in a given program. The polynomial -- necessarily of finite degree -- is represented by a list of its coefficients, in decreasing order of power of the root.

```
> poly a == [a]
```

Multiplication of such a polynomial by the given root of unity moves the coefficient of the highest power of the root to the end of the list -- as the coefficient of unity in the result -- and shifts the other coefficients left by one place.

```
> shift :: [a] -> [a]
> shift (x:xs) = xs ++ [x]
```

If p divides #xs, then (p $sigma xs) represents xs times the p-th principal root of unity: this is achieved by shifting the coefficients by one p-th of their length.

```
> ($igma) :: num -> poly a -> poly a
> (p $igma) = (++/) . shift . into p
```

The sum of two formal polynomial values is the pointwise sum of the coefficients; since each of these coefficients will be represented by a list of terms, they can just be concatenated to represent addition. The sum of a list of polynomials can either be implemented by a fold of a zipwith, or more conveniently for the present purposes by the equivalent

```
> (+/) :: [poly a] -> poly a
> (+/) = ((++/) *) . (|/|) where (*) = map
```

Demonstration code

To demonstrate the symbolic Fourier transform code, it will be exercised on polynomials, of degree less than n, over lists of integers; the presence of the number i in the j-th coefficient of a polynomial (indexed of course from the right-hand end) will be taken to represent a formal variable x_i times the j-th power of w -- a formal n-th root of unity.

```
> index == num
> coeff == [index]
```

A vector of length n, of formal polynomials of degree less than n, will be laid out by translating each of the polynomials into strings and laying them out one to a line.

```
> showvec :: [poly coeff] -> string
> showvec = layn . map showpoly
```

Each polynomial is represented by displaying the terms with non-zero (non-empty) coefficients, and punctuating with '+' signs.

```
> showpoly :: poly coeff -> string
> showpoly = stringfold " + " . map showterm . index
>            where index xs
>                    = [ (x,i) | (x,i) <- zip(reverse xs,[0..]); x ~= []]
```

Each term is represented by the coefficient times 'w' to a power.

```
> showterm :: (coeff, num) -> string
> showterm (x,i) = showcoeff x,                              if i = 0
>                = bracket showcoeff x ++ ".w^" ++ show i, if i > 0
>                  where bracket f x = f x,               if #x = 1
>                                    = "(" ++ f x ++ ")", if #x > 1
```

Each coefficient is represented as a list of variables punctuated with '+' signs. The call of 'sort' arranges that the variables appear in order of index -- it happens that no variable will appear twice in any coefficient, but in principle this function could collect the multiplicity of a variable and pass it to 'showvar'.

```
> showcoeff :: coeff -> string
> showcoeff = stringfold "+" . map showvar . sort
```

Each variable is represented by 'x' followed by its index.

```
> showvar :: index -> string
> showvar i = "x" ++ show i
```

The function 'stringfold' inserts the representation of an operator in the places in the representation of an expression corresponding to a reduction of that operator.

```
> stringfold :: string -> [string] -> string
> stringfold op = foldr1 (infix op)
>                 where infix op l r = l ++ op ++ r
```

The input to which an n-point transform will be applied is to represent a list of n polynomials, the i-th of which represents x_i (as the coefficient of unity in a formal polynomial of degree n-1).

```
> input :: num -> [poly num]
> input n = [ nulls ++ [[i]] | i <- [1..n] ] where nulls = copy (n-1) []
```

Execution of the example code

For example, the input for an eight-point transform is demonstrated by

```
? (showvec . input) 8

   1) x1
   2) x2
   3) x3
   4) x4
   5) x5
   6) x6
   7) x7
   8) x8
```

The specification applied to this input returns

```
? (showvec . dft (+/) ($igma) . input) 8

   1) x1+x2+x3+x4+x5+x6+x7+x8
   2) x1 + x2.w^1 + x3.w^2 + x4.w^3 + x5.w^4 + x6.w^5 + x7.w^6 + x8.w^7
   3) x1+x5 + (x2+x6).w^2 + (x3+x7).w^4 + (x4+x8).w^6
   4) x1 + x4.w^1 + x7.w^2 + x2.w^3 + x5.w^4 + x8.w^5 + x3.w^6 + x6.w^7
```

```
5) x1+x3+x5+x7 + (x2+x4+x6+x8).w^4
6) x1 + x6.w^1 + x3.w^2 + x8.w^3 + x5.w^4 + x2.w^5 + x7.w^6 + x4.w^7
7) x1+x5 + (x4+x8).w^2 + (x3+x7).w^4 + (x2+x6).w^6
8) x1 + x8.w^1 + x7.w^2 + x6.w^3 + x5.w^4 + x4.w^5 + x3.w^6 + x2.w^7
```

as do the similar expressions in fft and vft.

For what it is worth, on a Sun3 the costs are approximately:

```
(showvec.dft(+/)($igma).input) 8    66 CPU seconds, 166 000 reductions
(showvec.fft(+/)($igma).input) 8     4.8 seconds,     9 600 reductions
(showvec.vft(+/)($igma).input) 8     5.0 seconds,     9 400 reductions
```

NB: these costs will not scale as O(n^2) and O(n.log n) because direct implementation of ((w /\) /\) requires O(n^4) applications of 'w' each of which might cost O(n). In a practical implementation it would be necessary to do something more sensible.

Chemical Reaction as a Computational Model

Jean-Pierre Banâtre, Daniel Le Métayer

IRISA/INRIA
campus de Beaulieu
35042 Rennes, FRANCE
jbanatre/lemetayer@irisa.fr

Abstract: We present a new formalism called GAMMA which relies on the chemical reaction metaphor; the only data structure is the multiset and the computation can be seen as a succession of chemical reactions consuming elements of the multiset and producing new elements according to specific rules. We show the relevance of this formalism with respect to program development by proposing a systematic program derivation method.

1 Introduction

The cost of software development has become a major expense in the application of computers. Experience has shown that more than half of all programming effort and resources is spent in correcting errors in programs [7]. One solution to alleviate this problem is to resort to a method of program verification based on sound mathematical principles. However the proof of an already existing program turns out to be a far from easy task. It is now admitted that the development of correct programs requires the application of a systematic procedure. As stated in [9], a program and its proof should be developed hand-in-hand, with the proof usually leading the way. The last two decades have brought a better understanding of the fundamental concepts of systematic program development [6,9]. However these concepts have been formulated in an imperative language framework. We believe that this makes program derivation more difficult because it imposes the introduction of two different kinds of sequentiality in the same step:

- the sequentiality that is implied by the logic of the program and
- the sequentiality that is imposed by the computing model.

We claim that these two concerns should be separated; a program should first be derived in a high level language in which no superfluous constraint (that is to say sequentiality which is not relevant to the logic of the program) has to be introduced. This language can then be implemented on various kinds of machines: it is only at this stage that the extra sequentiality imposed by a particular computing model will be taken into account.

The question to answer now concerns the definition of this high level language;

there are essentially two different approaches:

- the imperative approach (languages with explicit control features) and
- the declarative approach (languages without any explicit control structure).

Our belief is that the imperative approach is not well suited to the systematic design of programs because it entails an operational reasoning which is difficult to master. Functional languages represent a first example of high level non imperative formalism; however functional languages encourage the use of recursion in data structures and in programs and this recursion turns out to be a disguised form of sequentiality. Consider for example the problem of designing a functional program to find the maximum element of a set. Typically the set will be represented as a list and the result will be evaluated by a recursive walk through this list. This sequential decomposition is not relevant to the specification of the problem (the elements of the set could be processed in any given order): it is again imposed by the idiosyncrasies of the language which provides recursion as the unique structuring tool.

It should be clear that the recursive nature of programs reflects the recursive nature of data structures; so we decided to start with the less constraining data structure facility: the multiset. There is no form of hierarchy in a multiset and there may be several occurrences of the same element. The control structure associated should reflect this absence of sequentiality and should entail some kind of chaotic model of execution. In order to give an intuitive description of the Γ operator we use the chemical reaction metaphor: a computation may be seen as a succession of applications of reactions which consume elements of the multiset and produce new ones according to particular rules. The computation ends when no more reaction can occur. When the condition holds for several disjoint subsets, the reactions can take place in any order or even simultaneously; so GAMMA programs often contain a great deal of implicit parallelism. This may be seen as an important advantage as far as implementation is concerned because it makes GAMMA an attractive candidate for execution on parallel processors. We shall not dwell on this here (the interested reader may refer to [1] for further information on the parallel implementation of GAMMA) but rather consider the benefit of implicit parallelism with respect to systematic program construction.

The GAMMA formalism is introduced more formally in section 2. In section 3 we describe the associated program development strategy and we apply it to the derivation of a sorting program. Section 4 contains a comparison with related work and investigates possible areas for further research.

2 The GAMMA Model

The GAMMA model can be described as a multiset transformer: the computation is a succession of applications of rules which consume elements out of the multiset while producing new elements into the multiset. The computation ends when no rule can be applied. The basic information structuring facility is the multiset which is the same as a set except that it may contain multiple occurrences of the same element [10]. The notation {...} will be used to represent multisets; there is no ambiguity since we never use simple sets in this paper. The basic operations on multisets are the following:

- *union*: the number of occurrences of an element in $M_1 \cup M_2$ is the sum of its numbers of occurrences in M_1 and M_2.
- *difference*: the number of occurrences of an element in $M_1 - M_2$ is the difference of its numbers of occurrences in M_1 and M_2.
- *non deterministic selection*: *oneof*(*M*) yields one arbitrarily selected element of *M*.

The Γ operator can be defined formally in the following way:

$$\Gamma((R_1,A_1),...,(R_m,A_m))\ (M) = oneof\,(\Gamma^s\ ((R_1,A_1),...,(R_m,A_m))\ (M)) \quad \textbf{where}$$
$$\Gamma^s((R_1,A_1),...,(R_m,A_m))\ (M) =$$
$$\{M' \mid (\exists\, x_1,...,x_n \in M,\ \exists\ i \in [1,m] \textbf{ such that } R_i\,(x_1,...,x_n) \textbf{ and}$$
$$M' \in \Gamma^s\,((R_1,A_1),...,(R_m,A_m))\,((M - \{x_1,...,x_n\}) \cup A_i\,(x_1,...,x_n))) \textbf{ or}$$
$$(M' = M \textbf{ and } \forall\, i \in [1,m],\ \forall\, x_1,...,x_n \in M,\ \neg R_i\,(x_1,...,x_n))\}$$

$\Gamma^s((R_1,A_1),...,(R_m,A_m))\ (M)$ represents the set of the possible (multiset) results of the program $\Gamma((R_1,A_1),...,(R_m,A_m))\ (M)$. Functions R_i (called "reaction conditions") are boolean functions specifying under which circumstances some elements of the multiset can react. Functions A_i ("actions") describe the effect of the reactions. The above definition indicates that if one or several reaction conditions hold for several subsets at the same time, the choice which is made among them is not deterministic. However appropriate restrictions on the definition of conditions R_i and actions A_i may ensure determinacy; this point is not developed here. If the reaction condition holds for several disjoint subsets the reactions can also take place simultaneously. This important property, which confers a high level of implicit parallelism to GAMMA programs, is due to the fact that actions have a local effect: they substitute in the multiset the consumed elements by the produced elements, independently of the rest of the multiset. In order to state this property more formally , we give an alternative definition for Γ in which parallelism is made explicit:

$$\Gamma^p\,((R_1,A_1),...,(R_m,A_m))\,(M) =$$
$$\{M' \mid (\ \exists\, M_1,...,M_n \textbf{ such that } M = M_1 \cup \ ....\ \cup M_n\ ,\ \exists\ i1,\ ...,\ in \in N,$$
$$\exists\ M'_1 \in \Gamma_{i1}\,((R_1,A_1),...,(R_m,A_m))\,(M_1)$$
$$...$$
$$\exists\ M'_n \in \Gamma_{in}\,((R_1,A_1),...,(R_m,A_m))\,(M_n)$$
$$M' \in \Gamma^p\,((R_1,A_1),...,(R_m,A_m))\,(M'_1 \cup \ ....\ \cup M'_n\,)) \textbf{ or}$$
$$(\,M' = M \ \textbf{ and } \forall\, i \in [1,m],\ \forall\, x_1,..,x_n \in M\ ,\ \neg R_i(x_1,..,x_n))\}$$

where

$$\Gamma_i\,((R_1,A_1),...,(R_m,A_m))\,(M) = \textbf{ if } i = 0 \textbf{ then } \{M\} \textbf{ else}$$
$$\{M' \mid (\exists\, x_1,..,x_n \in M\,, \exists\ j \in [1,m] \textbf{ such that } R_j\,(x_1,..,x_n) \textbf{ and}$$
$$M' \in \Gamma_{i\text{-}1}((R_1,A_1),...,(R_m,A_m))\,((M - \{x_1,..,x_n\}) \cup A_j\,(x_1,..,x_n))) \textbf{ or}$$
$$(M' = M \ \textbf{ and } \forall\, j \in [1,m],\ \forall\, x_1,..,x_n \in M\ ,\ \neg\, R_j\,(x_1,..,x_n))\}$$

It is easy to show that:

$$\Gamma^p((R_1,A_1),...,(R_m,A_m))\,(M) = \Gamma^s((R_1,A_1),...,(R_m,A_m))\,(M)$$

$\Gamma_i((R_1,A_1),...,(R_m,A_m))\,(M)$ is the set of multisets that can be obtained by at most i reactions and $\Gamma^p((R_1,A_1),...,(R_m,A_m))\,(M)$ is defined like $\Gamma^s((R_1,A_1),...,(R_m,A_m))\,(M)$ except that it makes explicit the fact that reactions can be performed independently on several disjoint subsets.

Let us now take two examples to illustrate the programming style entailed by the GAMMA model.

Example 1

The function computing the prime numbers less than or equal to n can be written in a concise and elegant way in GAMMA:

$$prime\_numbers(n) = \Gamma((R,A))\,(\{2,..,n\}) \quad \textbf{where}$$
$$R\,(x_1,x_2) = multiple\,(x_1,x_2)$$
$$A\,(x_1,x_2) = \{x_2\}$$

where *multiple* (x_1,x_2) is true if and only if x_1 is a multiple of x_2. The following figure describes the computation of *prime_numbers* (8). Two reacting elements are connected by a line. Of course this is one among the possible paths leading to the result.

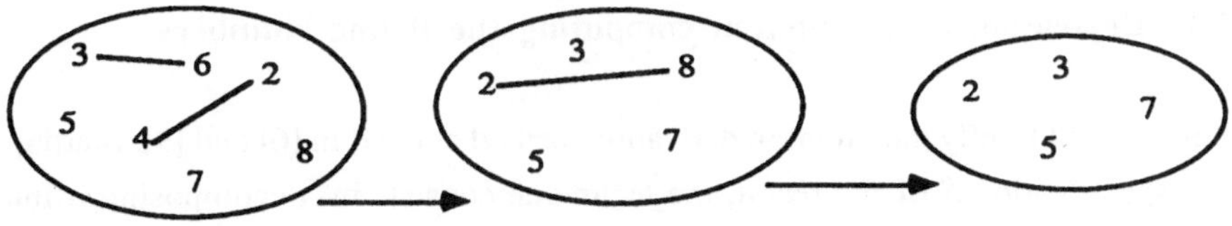

Example 2

Let us consider the problem of sorting a sequence of values. The sequence is represented as a multiset *M* of couples (*index, value*) where the index *x.i* of an element *x* gives the position of the value *x.v*. All indexes are distinct and in a range [1,..,*card*(*M*)]. The GAMMA program is the following:

$$sort\,(M) = \Gamma\,((R,A))\,(M) \quad \textbf{where}$$
$$R\,(x,y) = (x.i > y.i \ \textbf{and}\ x.v < y.v)$$
$$A\,(x,y) = \{(y.i,\ x.v)\,,\,(x.i,\ y.v)\}$$

The following figure describes a possible computation of

sort ({(4, 8), (2, 5), (3, 9), (1, 13), (5, 9)})

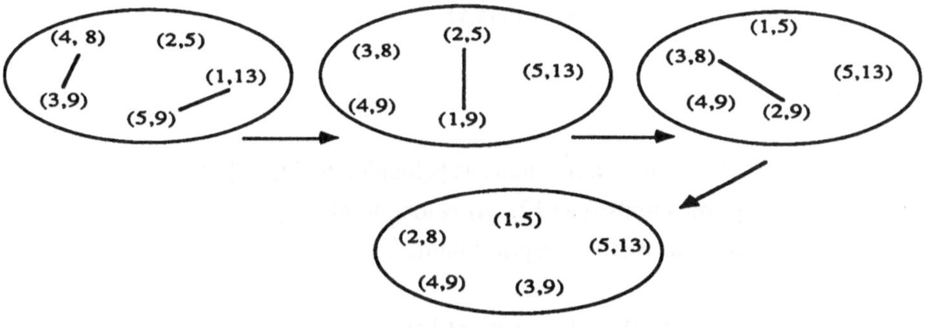

A stable state is reached as no couple of elements satisfies the reaction condition. Of course this is only one of the possible sequences of configurations leading to the result. This program can be seen as a generalized form of the exchange sort algorithm as any couple of ill-ordered elements can exchange their positions at any time.

3 Program Derivation

In order to introduce the derivation method, we first describe intuitively the development of the program computing the prime numbers given in the previous section. Then we present the method precisely and illustrate it with the derivation of a sorting program.

3.1 Derivation of a Function computing the Prime Numbers

Let us recall briefly the program derivation method defined in [6] and [9]. Starting from the specification S of the result, the technique consists in decomposing it into two formulae I and V such that I **and** $V \Leftrightarrow S$. I (for invariant), is a weakened form of S and remains true throughout the computation (in particular, I holds at the initial and final steps), whereas V (for variant) is the property to be established by the computation.
The second step is the derivation of an iterative command: $*[\neg V \rightarrow P]$ which means that while $\neg V$ is true, the sequence P of instructions is performed; it is requested that the evaluation of P does not invalidate the invariant. To prove the total correctness of the derived iteration, a termination function is associated with the sequence P, this function is lower bounded and must be decreased at each evaluation of P. Let us describe along these lines the derivation of a GAMMA program computing the prime numbers upto a given integer n.
The initial multiset is $\{2,..,n\}$, and the specification S of the result M may be :

(1) $\forall x \in M, \; x \in \{2,..,n\}$

(2) $\forall x \in \{2,..,n\}, \; (\forall y \in \{2,..,n\} \; \neg multiple(x,y)) \Rightarrow x \in M$

(3) $\forall x, y \in M, \; \neg multiple(x,y)$

That is to say :

> M must contain only elements belonging to $\{2,..,n\}$ (1),
> all prime numbers in $\{2,..,n\}$ belong to M (2),
> each element of M is a prime number (3).

We choose I = (1) **and** (2) as the invariant because it holds for the set $\{2,..,n\}$. The computation has to progress as long as the variant V = (3) does not hold; in other words, as long as the formula $\neg V = \exists x, y \in M, \; multiple(x,y)$ is true. This is expressed by a reaction condition $R(x,y) = multiple(x,y)$. The associated action has to preserve the invariant and to transform the multiset in "the right direction" (so as to reach in a finite number of steps a state satisfying the variant). According to the invariant, the action can neither add a value (1), nor remove the value y because it may be a prime number (2); so the only possible action is $A(x,y) = \{y\}$. This action maintains the invariant I; furthermore, an application of the action removes an element from M, so we can choose as a termination function the cardinal of M. The derived program is :

$$\begin{aligned} prime\_numbers(n) &= \Gamma((R,A))\ (\{2,..,n\}) \qquad \textbf{where} \\ R(x,y) &= multiple(x,y) \\ A(x,y) &= \{y\} \end{aligned}$$

Next section describes more precisely the derivation method suggested by this example.

3.2 The Derivation Method

Our derivation method is inspired by Dijkstra and Gries 's works [6,9]; however the non imperative nature of GAMMA makes it possible to stay at a descriptive level, avoiding the need to fix unnecessary details about the control of programs.

The derivation method is decomposed into four stages. The first one is the transformation of the specification and its split into an invariant and a variant. In the second step, the reaction condition is derived from the variant. The third step is the deduction of the action from the invariant and the variant. The last step is the derivation of a well-founded ordering from the action and the invariant.

(0) Specification

The specification is expressed in a first order logic language. The basic data structure is the multiset, so if specific data structures are needed they have to be encoded into a multiset.

(1) Transformation and split of the specification

The specification S is first transformed into a conjunction of formulae. The specification can then be split into two properties I (Invariant) and V (Variant) such that $S = I$ **and** V. The invariant is chosen as the part of S which can easily be established by an initialisation program. The only trivial initial multiset is a constant multiset; so the strategy consists in constructing the initial multiset from constant multisets occuring in the specification. If such multisets do not occur in the specification or if the initialisation does not lead to a successful derivation, then the initial multiset must be produced by an initial GAMMA program; so in general the derived program may be a composition of GAMMA programs, each one establishing a part of the specification while maintaining the previously established parts. The variant should be a formula of the form:

$$\forall x_1, ..., x_n \in M\ ,\quad P(x_1,...,x_n)$$

where n is a constant value and $P(x_1,...,x_n)$ does not contain any quantifier. The motivation for this restriction will appear in step (2). If the variant may be decomposed into a conjunction of formulae, some of them being satisfied by the intial multiset, a useful strategy consists in reinforcing the invariant (and weakening the variant) with the formulae which hold for the initial multiset. For instance, a relation:

$$P(x,y) = \forall x\,, y \in M\,,\ \ C(x,y) \Rightarrow g(x) = g(y)$$

can be transformed into:

$$P(x,y) = P_1(x,y) \textbf{ and } P_2(x,y)$$
$$P_1(x,y) = \forall x\,, y \in M\,,\ \ C(x,y) \Rightarrow g(x) \le g(y)$$
$$P_2(x,y) = \forall x\,, y \in M\,,\ \ C(x,y) \Rightarrow g(x) \ge g(y)$$

If the variant is P, and P_1 holds for the initial state then P_1 can be added to the invariant and the variant becomes P_2.

(2) Reaction condition

If the variant is of the form

$$\forall x_1\,, \ldots, x_n \in M\,,\ \ P(x_1,\ldots,x_n)$$

where $P(x_1,\ldots,x_n)$ does not involve any quantifier, then its negation is:

$$\exists\, x_1\,, \ldots, x_n \in M\,,\ \ \neg P(x_1,\ldots,x_n)$$

and $\neg P(x_1,\ldots,x_n)$ is a local condition depending only on the values of $x_1,\ldots,x_n$, so a reaction condition R can be derived in a straightforward way:

$$R(x_1,\ldots,x_n) = \neg P(x_1,\ldots,x_n)$$

So the restriction to formulae $P(x_1,\ldots,x_n)$ which do not involve any quantifier is the expression in the derivation process of the fact that GAMMA programs must be described only in terms of local computations. Last let us notice that when V is a conjunction of formulae, several reaction conditions will be derived.

(3) Action

The strategy used to derive the action consists in choosing a modification of the multiset that validates the variant locally (that is to say on the multiset of the produced elements), while maintaining the invariant. This seems to be a sensible strategy since the goal of the action is to modify the multiset in such a way that the variant eventually becomes true. However the variant is a global property on the multiset whereas the effect of the action is only local; so the best one can expect from the action is that it validates the variant locally. Furthermore it turns out that this restriction generally allows us to derive a unique possible action.

(4) Well-founded ordering

The fact that the action validates locally the variant does not necessarily imply that the variant will eventually be satisfied globally. In order to ensure termination we have to provide a well-founded ordering (an ordering such that there is no infinite descending sequences of elements) and to show that the application of an action strictly decreases the multiset according to this ordering. When the action is such that the number of produced elements is strictly smaller than the number of consumed elements the well-founded ordering is clearly the usual integer ordering on the cardinal of the multiset. When it is not the case we use a result from [5] allowing the derivation of a well-founded ordering on multisets from a well-founded ordering on the elements of the multiset. Let > be an ordering on S and >> be the ordering on multisets $\mathcal{M}(S)$ defined in the following way:

$$\begin{aligned} & M >> M' \\ & \quad \Leftrightarrow \exists X \in \mathcal{M}(S), \exists Y \in \mathcal{M}(S) \text{ such that} \\ & \qquad (X \neq \{\} \text{ and } M \supseteq X \text{ and } M' = (M - X) \cup Y \\ & \qquad\qquad \text{and } \forall y \in Y, \exists x \in X \;\; x > y)) \end{aligned}$$

The ordering >> on $\mathcal{M}(S)$ is well-founded if and only if the ordering > on S is well-founded. This result is fortunate since GAMMA programs behave exactly in this way, by removing elements from the multiset and inserting new elements. So our strategy consists in trying to deduce well-founded orderings on the elements of the multiset such that each element produced by the action may be associated with a strictly greater element consumed by the action. We proceed in two steps; first we deduce all the relations corresponding to the possible associations between consumed elements and produced elements. The second step consists in proving that one of these relations may be extended into a well-founded ordering; this second step is sometimes non-trivial but the problem is made easier by the fact that, thanks to Dershowitz-Manna multiset ordering, we only have to reason locally (that is to say on the ordering on elements instead of the multiset ordering).

Let us point out that a particular configuration (I,V) may not lead to a program; so a derivation may fail, for instance in step (3) when no action fulfilling the requirements can be discovered. In this case, it may be necessary to make a new attempt from to step (1) and to choose another initial state, and/or consider another decomposition (I',V'). To illustrate the derivation method, we develop in the next section a sorting algorithm.

3.3 Derivation of a Sorting Algorithm

We first have to choose a representation of the data in terms of multisets and to express the specification of a well-ordered set of elements.

(0) Specification

A natural data structure to describe a sorted set of values is the sequence. This sequence must be encoded within a multiset; let us choose a multiset M of couples (*index, value*), where the index $x.i$ of an element x gives the position of the value $x.v$ in the sequence. Let M_0 be the initial multiset of values; a possible specification of the result M is :

(1) $\forall x, y \in M, \;\; x.i < y.i \Rightarrow x.v \leq y.v$

(2) $M.i = \{1, ..., card(M_0)\}$

(3) $M.v = M_0$

where $M.v$ is the multiset of the values of the elements of M and $M.i$ is the multiset of indexes of elements of M. This specification expresses the fact that all elements are sorted (1), indexes are unique and in the range $[1,..,card(M_0)]$ (2), and the multiset of values is unchanged (3).

The next step of derivation consists in splitting the specification into an invariant property and a variant property. There are many possibilities, let us investigate only one of them.

(1) Split of the specification

According to the strategy presented above, the initial multiset must be constructed in a trivial way from multiset constants occurring in the specification. The specification of the sorting algorithm involves two multiset constants M_0 and $\{1, ..., card(M_0)\}$. Properties (2) and (3) can easily be established by a GAMMA program; let us call *init* the program computing this cartesian product. We shall consider it as a basic multiset operator. If such an operator were not available in the language we would have to derive the corresponding GAMMA program. As the invariant must hold in the initial state, a natural decomposition of S is V = (1) and I = (2) and (3). The invariant means that each value is associated with a unique index in the range $[1..card(M_0)]$. As long as the variant does not hold, the virtual sequence of values is ill-ordered, so the reaction condition has to express the fact that V does not hold.

(2) Reaction condition

Let us recall the definition of the variant V:

$$\forall x, y \in M, \quad x.i < y.i \Rightarrow x.v \leq y.v$$

The variant is of the form:

$$\forall x_1, \ldots, x_n \in M, \quad P(x_1, \ldots, x_n)$$

So the reaction condition can be derived in a straightforward way from its negation:

$$\neg V = (\exists x, y \in M, \quad x.i < y.i \textbf{ and } x.v > y.v)$$
$$R(x,y) = x.i < y.i \textbf{ and } x.v > y.v$$

(3) Action

The action must transform the multiset while maintaining the invariant. Furthermore, according to our strategy the action must validate locally the variant, which means that the values produced by the action must be well-ordered. The invariant property expresses the fact that the action cannot remove or add any value or index, so the only possible action is to exchange the positions $x.i$ and $y.i$ of the elements selected by the reaction condition. Fortunately this unique possible choice also fulfills the requirement that the values produced must be well-ordered. This can be written :

$$A(x,y) = \{(x.i, y.v), (y.i, x.v)\}$$

The elements $(x.i, x.v)$ and $(y.i, y.v)$ of the multiset are replaced by the elements $(x.i, y.v)$ and $(y.i, x.v)$. So we have derived the following sorting program :

$$sort\,(M_0) = \Gamma((R,A))\ \ (init(M_0)) \qquad \textbf{where}$$
$$R(x,y) = (x.i < y.i \textbf{ and } x.v > y.v)$$
$$A(x,y) = \{(x.i,y.v), (y.i,x.v)\}$$

(4) Well-founded ordering

Our strategy consists in enumerating the possible relations that could be extended into a multiset ordering according to Dershowitz-Manna theorem in such a way that the action strictly decreases the multiset. This means that each element produced by the action must be smaller than one of the removed elements. Since the action consumes two elements $(x.i,x.v)$ and $(y.i,y.v)$ and produces two elements $(x.i,y.v)$ and $(y.i,x.v)$ we have four possible choices here; we have to find an ordering « such that:

(C_1)	$((x.i,y.v) \ll (x.i,x.v)$ **and** $(y.i,x.v) \ll (x.i,x.v))$	or
(C_2)	$((x.i,y.v) \ll (x.i,x.v)$ **and** $(y.i,x.v) \ll (y.i,y.v))$	or
(C_3)	$((x.i,y.v) \ll (y.i,y.v)$ **and** $(y.i,x.v) \ll (x.i,x.v))$	or
(C_4)	$((x.i,y.v) \ll (y.i,y.v)$ **and** $(y.i,x.v) \ll (y.i,y.v))$	

Let us examine property (C_1) first; since the reaction condition is $(x.i < y.i$ **and** $x.v > y.v)$, we first try to derive a relation R_1 such that:

$$(x.i < y.i \textbf{ and } x.v > y.v) \Rightarrow R_1((x.i,y.v), (x.i,x.v)) \textbf{ and}$$
$$(x.i < y.i \textbf{ and } x.v > y.v) \Rightarrow R_1((y.i,x.v), (x.i,x.v))$$

which can be reformulated in the following way:

$$(a.i = b.i \textbf{ and } b.v > a.v) \Rightarrow R_1(a, b) \textbf{ and}$$
$$(a.v = b.v \textbf{ and } a.i > b.i) \Rightarrow R_1(a, b)$$

A trivial solution is the function R_1 defined as follows:

$$R_1(a,b) \Leftrightarrow (a.i = b.i \textbf{ and } b.v > a.v) \text{ or } (a.i > b.i \textbf{ and } a.v = b.v)$$

In order to obtain an ordering, we take now the reflexive and transitive closure of R_1:

$$R'_1(a,b) \Leftrightarrow (a.i \geq b.i \textbf{ and } b.v \geq a.v)$$

It is clear that R'_1 is antisymmetric, so it is an ordering. This ordering is well-founded (the sets of values and indexes are finite), so the corresponding ordering on multisets is also well-founded. By construction this ordering is such that each element produced by the reaction condition can be associated with a strictly greater consumed element, so the action strictly decreases the multiset and we have provided a termination proof of the derived GAMMA program.

Relation (C_3) could have been chosen as well to derive a well-founded multiset ordering but relations (C_2) and (C_4) would not have been successfull because the reflexive and transitive closure of the derived relation is not antisymmetric.

We should notice that the specification of this problem could be split in different ways leading to different GAMMA programs. Another solution is to take (1) and (3) as invariant and (2) as variant; a straightforward initialisation of the multiset is $init'(M_0) = \{(x,1), x \in M_0\}$ which associates each value with index 1. We obtain the following program:

$$
\begin{aligned}
sort'(M_0) &= \Gamma((R,A))\ \ (init'(M_0)) \qquad\qquad \textbf{where}\\
R(x,y) &= (x.i = y.i \ \textbf{ and } \ x.v < y.v)\\
A(x,y) &= \{(x.i, x.v), (y.i{+}1, y.v)\}
\end{aligned}
$$

Indexes are successively incremented until they have reached the position corresponding to the associated value.

We believe that the freedom provided by the use of multisets allows us to derive in a natural way programs that would be much more difficult to discover using more constrained data structures. The use of lists for example implicitly entails the fact that property (2) (all indexes are unique and in the range $[1,..,card(M_0)]$) is a part of the invariant; this precludes (or at least makes far less natural) the derivation of programs like *sort'* which handles multisets with non unique indexes.

4 Conclusion

Several formalisms bearing some similarities to GAMMA have been proposed recently. Let us mention:

- The *associons* model [12]: an associon is a tuple of names defining a relation between entities represented by these names. The state of the computation can be changed by the creation of new associons representing new relations deduced from the already existing ones.
- UNITY [3]: a UNITY program is essentially a declaration of variables and a set of multiple-assignment statements. Program execution consists in selecting nondeterministically some assignment statement, executing it and going on forever.
- Linda [2,8]: Linda is a simple communication model in which processes communicate by adding and removing tuples in a tuple space.

The main originality of GAMMA in comparison with the associons model and UNITY is the locality property (reactions operate only on their arguments, independently of the rest of the multiset) which makes program derivation and parallel implementation [1] easier. However, these proposals seem to denote a current trend towards a very high level programming style which tends to separate program design and implementation concerns.

Several research areas are currently being investigated; they concern principally (1) the design of a GAMMA progamming environment and (2) the implementation of GAMMA.

(1) A system for GAMMA program development

The program derivation method presented in this paper is the basis of a GAMMA program development system currently under implementation. An interesting area of investigation concerns the design of a suitable programmer interface for semi-automatic program derivation. Such an interface would allow the representation of relevant pieces of information concerning the development process such as invariant and variant properties, a record of choices already investigated and of the choices still to be considered... It would also be desirable to put forward a method allowing the analysis of failures in the program development process. Last but not least, we are currently investigating the design of a unified framework for the formalization of the derivation process itself.

(2) implementation of GAMMA

The evaluation of GAMMA programs involves two different kinds of tasks:

- the search for elements of the multiset satisfying the reaction condition,
- the application of the action to these elements.

The first task is particularly difficult to implement efficiently as it necessitates forming all possible tuples of elements in order to check for the reaction condition.

Two prototype implementations have been carried out in sequential and parallel environments. The sequential implementation consists in adding the Γ operator to the ML language and generating ML programs from GAMMA programs. Although not very efficient, as no special optimizations were included, this implementation is a platform for GAMMA program development and experimentation.

A second implementation has been carried out on the Intel iPSC2 32-nodes multiprocessor machine. The action is clearly a local operation: it can be carried out independently of the rest of the multiset. So the main problem to tackle in designing a parallel implementation is the distribution of the search process. We have chosen to exclude the duplication of values as it entails tricky coherence problems and a loss of locality. So, the values are spread over the processors and they move through the network in order to allow the examination of all the tuples. We have defined a communication protocol and proved important properties such as the absence of deadlock and the detection of termination. A more complete description of this implementation can be found in [1]. It should be clear, however, that the key step in the design of a really efficient implementation of GAMMA is the analysis of programs in order to decrease the number of tuples to be examined in order to detect a reaction condition. This analysis is currently investigated. The main idea is to try to derive a topology of the multiset in order to isolate for each element a small number of "neighbours" which may potentially be associated with it in a reaction. This clustering technique may have dramatic effects on the execution times [4].

References

[1] Banâtre J.-P., Coutant A., Le Métayer D., A Parallel Machine for Multiset Transformation and its Programming Style, Future Generation Computer Systems, North-Holland, 1988, pp. 133-144.

[2] Carriero N., Gelernter D., Linda in Context, Comm. of the ACM 32, 4, April 1989, pp. 444-458.

[3] Chandy M., Misra J., Parallel Program Design: a Foundation, Addison-Wesley Publishing Company, 1988.

[4] Creveuil C., Moguerou G., Dérivation d'un algorithme de segmentation d'images: un exemple d'application du formalisme GAMMA, Technical Report INRIA, N°1049, June 1989.

[5] Dershowitz N., Manna Z., Proving termination with Multiset Orderings, Comm. of the ACM, 22, 8, August 1979, pp. 465-476.

[6] Dijkstra E. W., A Discipline of Programming, Prentice-Hall, Englewood Cliffs, N.J., 1976.

[7] Dromey R.G., How to Solve it by Computer?, Prentice Hall, 1982.

[8] Gelernter D., Generative Communication in Linda, ACM Transactions on Programming Languages and Systems, vol. 7, N° 1, January 1985, pp. 80-112.

[9] Gries D., The Science of Programming, Springer Verlag, New York, 1981.

[10] Knuth D., Seminumerical Algoritms. The Art of Computer Programming, Addison Wesley Publishing Company, 1969.

[11] Manna Z., Waldinger R., Synthesis: Dreams ⇒ Programs, IEEE trans. on Software Engineering, vol. SE-5, N° 4, July 1979, pp. 294-328.

[12] Rem M., Associons: A Program Notation with Tuples instead of Variables, ACM Transactions on Programming Languages and Systems, vol. 3, N° 3, July 1981, pp. 251-262.

Sketching a Constructive Definition of 'mix'

A.C. Reeves, C. Rattray
Department of Computing Science,
University of Stirling,
Stirling FK9 4LA

Abstract

Since the early seventies partial evaluation has been recognised as a powerful tool for constructing compilers. The ability to produce a partial evaluator for language L in language L *is* the ability to generate compilers and compiler generators. This paper uses the theory of sketches to produce a formal framework to describe the function specialisation phase of a partial evaluator for L in terms of the specification of L.

1 Introduction

Partial evaluation [1, 2] or mixed computation can be described informally as the process of 'doing as much evaluation as possible with, possibly, incomplete input'. If p is a program (function) whose input can be divided into two classes: S - static i.e. input which is fixed at a particular value, and D - dynamic i.e. input which is not fixed and may vary over all possible values of the correct type, the program p can be evaluated fully only if it is given both S and a particular value of D.

If only S is available the process of *partial evaluation* can be applied to p. The part of the computation of p which depends only on S is performed. The result of this process is a new specialised version of p whose input is the dynamic part of the input of p, D, and which, when it is applied to D, produces the same output as p applied to both S and D.

$$p\langle S, D\rangle = p_S\langle D\rangle$$

This specialised function p_S is known as a *residual program*. For example consider the function *power*

$$\begin{array}{lcll} \textit{power}\ x\ n & = & 1, & \textbf{if } n = 0 \\ & = & x * \textit{power}\ x\ (n-1), & \textbf{otherwise} \end{array}$$

This function raises x to the power of n. Suppose the value of n is fixed at 3 but the value of x is dynamic. Specialisation of *power* to its static input $n = 3$ produces the residual program

$$power'\ x \;=\; x * x * x * 1$$

because all computation except multiplication by x, which is dynamic, can be performed at partial evaluation time.

The ability to generate compilers, and compiler-compilers using a self-applicable partial evaluator, ie. a partial evaluator for the programming language S which is written in language S, has been extensively explored. A detailed background of this use of partial evaluation and its use in the wider field of program transformation and optimisation can be obtained from the following references: [3, 4, 5, 6, 7, 8].

The problem of specialising a program to some particular value of part of its input is not as simple as it might first appear. To specialise the *power* function to some fixed value of n the partial evaluator need only unfold recursive calls of *power* until the value of n falls to 0. Now consider the specialisation of *power* to some fixed value of x (say 5) rather than n. The ***obvious*** specialisation is

$$\begin{array}{lcll} power''\ n & = & 1, & \textbf{if } n = 0 \\ & = & 5 * power''(n-1), & \textbf{otherwise} \end{array}$$

but this specialisation cannot be produced by repeated unfolding of recursive calls because the value of n is dynamic and therefore never falls to 0. Specialisation by repeated unfolding will actually cause non-termination of the partial evaluator as it attempts to produce the infinite residual program shown below.

$$\begin{array}{lcll} power'''\ n & = & 1, & \textbf{if } n = 0 \\ & = & 5 * 1, & \textbf{if } n - 1 = 0 \\ & = & 5 * 5 * 1, & \textbf{if } n - 1 - 1 = 0 \\ & & \vdots & \\ & = & 5 * \cdots * 5 * 1, & \textbf{otherwise} \end{array}$$

The problem arises because the expression *power 5 n* where n is dynamic is itself dynamic and *must* not be unfolded at partial evaluation time. To overcome this problem a partial evaluation system must perform a process of binding time analysis on the program to be specialised to determine which sub-expressions in its body are static (reducible) and which are dynamic (irreducible). Broadly speaking there are two phases to partial evaluation:

1. a binding time analysis which determines which parts of the function are reducible and which are not. This paper does not address the problem of binding time analysis. For a formal treatment of binding time analysis see [9].

2. A function specialisation phase which takes the function to be specialised and the information produced by the binding time analysis phase and produces the specialised function. This phase is very closely related to a *self-interpreter*, i.e. an interpreter for the language S which is itself an S program. Function specialisation must behave exactly as a self-interpreter for the sub-expressions which have not been marked as irreducible by binding time analysis and must not reduce sub-expressions which are marked as irreducible. The exact nature

of the specialisation produced is highly dependent on the output from binding time analysis, but in general binding time analysis prevents the specialisation phase from producing an infinite residual program.

Research in partial evaluation has tended to concentrate on the development of efficient partial evaluators which produce good quality specialisations. The relationship between a language and its partial evaluator has not been examined in any great detail. This situation is illustrated by what is probably the most commonly used specification of a self-applicable partial evaluator given using the notation of Jones et al. If s is any S program and $S\ s\ d$ is the result of running s with input data d a self-applicable partial evaluator, **mix**, is an S program which satisfies the following:

$$Ss\langle d_1, d_2\rangle \equiv S(S\mathbf{mix}\langle s, d_1\rangle)d_2$$

where d_1 is the static part of the input to s and d_2 is the dynamic input. This definition simply states that $S\mathbf{mix}\langle s, d_1\rangle$ is the residual program generated using the S program s and its static input d_1. The specification, while correct, is not particularly helpful in the production of the partial evaluator **mix** because **mix** is not related to a known object in any obvious manner. The ideal specification of **mix** would allow it to be calculated from the definition of the language S. This paper is an attempt to use the theory of sketches to provide a non-language-specific framework in which calculation of the function specialisation phase of **mix** is possible.

The theory of sketches is outlined in section 2. Section 3 describes how sketches can be used to specify programming languages. In section 4, the function specialisation phase of a partial evaluator for a language specified using sketches is described using properties of the model which are non-language-specific. The final section, 5, discusses how the work should be developed and describes the pitfalls of the approach.

2 Sketches

The sequel assumes that the reader is familiar with the concepts of category, functor, natural transformation, and adjunction, no other knowledge of category theory is assumed. The interested reader is referred to [10, 11, 12].

2.1 Some Definitions

In essence a sketch is a (possibly finite) graph with some extra structure so that it can be used as a representation of a (potentially infinite) category. Sketches can also be used as a syntax for the specification of a data type and are defined by Wells and Barr [13] in the manner shown below.

Definition: Directed Graph.
A directed graph, G, is a pair of sets G_0 — nodes, and G_1 — edges together with two functions: $src : G_1 \rightarrow G_0$, which returns the source node of a given edge, and function $trg : G_1 \rightarrow G_0$ maps the edges to their target nodes. □

For example:

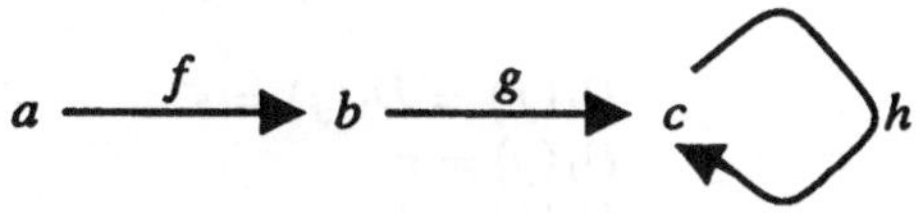

With G_0, G_1, *src*, and *trg* defined as:

$$G_0 = \{a, b, c\} \quad G_1 = \{f, g, h\}$$

$$\begin{array}{ll} src(f) = a & trg(f) = b \\ src(g) = b & trg(g) = c \\ src(h) = c & trg(h) = c \end{array}$$

The definition of a sketch requires the definition of a diagram. To define a diagram we must first define a graph homomorphism.

Definition: Graph Homomorphism.

Given graphs G and E, a graph homomorphism $H : G \rightarrow E$ is defined as a pair of functions $H_i : G_i \rightarrow E_i, i = 0, 1$ such that the following properties hold.

$$\forall\, e \in G_1 : H_0(src(e)) = src(H_1(e)) \text{ and } \forall\, e \in G_1 : H_0(trg(e)) = trg(H_1(e))$$

That is to say H preserves the connectivity of the graph G. □

A diagram can now be defined.

Definition: Diagram.

If d and G are graphs, a diagram of shape d in G is defined as a graph homomorphism $D : d \rightarrow G$. □

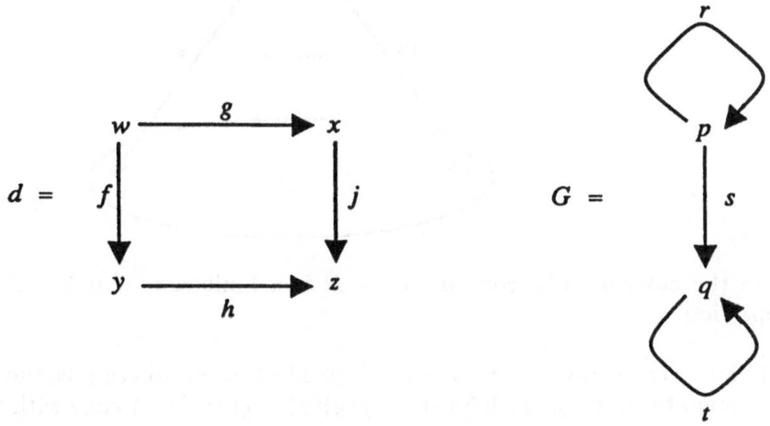

$$D : d \rightarrow G := (D_0, D_1)$$

where D_0 and D_1 are defined as

$$D_0(w) = D_0(x) = p$$
$$D_0(y) = D_0(z) = q$$

$$D_1(f) = D_1(j) = s$$
$$D_1(g) = r$$
$$D_1(h) = t$$

If all the edges, e, in the shape of a diagram are of the form $src(e) = trg(e)$, the diagram is said to be *discrete*.

A directed graph and a set of distinguished diagrams in that graph form two of the components of a sketch. The remaining two components are a set of cones and a set of cocones, defined below.

Definition: Cone.

A cone in a graph G consists of:

1. a diagram of shape d in G, $D : d \to G$. This diagram is called the *base* of the cone.
2. A node v of G, called the *vertex* of the cone.
3. A family of projection edges $p = \{p_i : v \to D(i)\}$ indexed by the nodes of d.

A cone with vertex v and base D is referred to as a cone from v to D or cone $p : v \to D$. □

Any cone $p : v \to D$ can be indicated by a diagram of the form

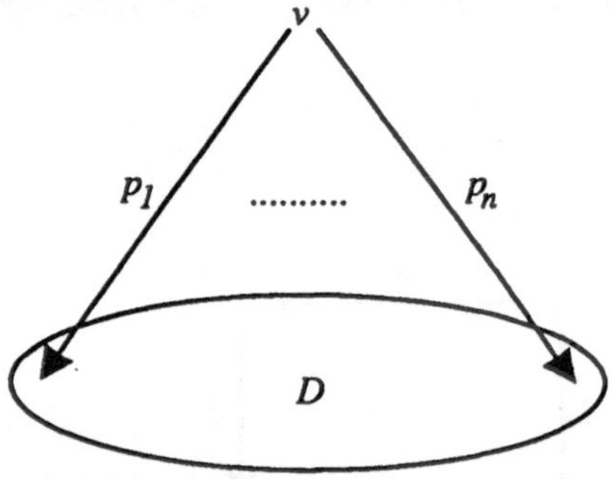

In the category C a cone $p : v \to D$ is a limit cone if it has two additional properties:

1. for every arrow $a : i \to j$ of d, $p_i; D(a) = p_j$ where ; is the composition operator of C and is defined as $(f; g)(x) = g(f(x))$. A cone with this property is called a *commutative cone*.
2. If $q : s \to D$ is a different commutative cone there is a unique arrow $u : s \to v$ such that $u; p_i = q_i$ for all nodes i of d. In the category of commutative cones over diagram D, the limit cone is the terminal object.

A limit cone over a discrete diagram, in any category, is called a *product cone* and its vertex is known as the *product* of the objects in its base. In **SET**, the category of sets, for example, the vertex of a limit cone over a discrete diagram is the cartesian product of the sets in its base.

The final component of a sketch is a set of cocones.

Definition: Cocone.
A cocone in a graph G consists of:

1. a diagram of shape d in G, $D : d \to G$. This diagram is called the *base*.
2. A node v of G, called the *vertex*.
3. A family of injections $in = \{in_i : D(i) \to v\}$ indexed by the nodes of d. □

In the category C a cocone is defined simply as a cone in the opposite category C^{op}. The colimit cocone over diagram D in the category C is defined as the initial object in the category of commutative cocones over diagram D. That is to say, if $j : D \to v$ is the colimit cocone over diagram $D : d \to G$ and $k : D \to s$ is another commutative cocone over D there is a unique arrow $u : v \to s$ such that $k_i = j_i; u$.

In any category the colimit cocone over a discrete diagram is the sum (coproduct) of the objects in its base. In *SET*, for example, the vertex of the colimit cocone is the disjoint union of the sets in its base.

These definitions of directed graph, diagram, cone, and cocone are combined to give the definition of a sketch.

Definition: Sketch.
A sketch is a 4 tuple (G, D, C, Co) consisting of a graph G, a set D of diagrams on G, a set C of cones on G, and a set Co of cocones on G. □

Definition: Sketch Morphism.
If $S_1 = (G_1, D_1, C_1, Co_1)$ and $S_2 = (G_2, D_2, C_2, Co_2)$ are sketches then a sketch morphism $F : S_1 \to S_2$ is a graph homomorphism which takes the diagrams in D_1 to diagrams in D_2, the cones in C_1 to cones in C_2, and cocones in Co_1 to cocones in Co_2. □

Given any category $\mathcal{C}$ there is a sketch underlying $\mathcal{C}$ defined as (G, D, C, Co) where G is the underlying graph of $\mathcal{C}$, D is the set of all commutative diagrams of $\mathcal{C}$, C is the set of all limit cones of $\mathcal{C}$, and Co is the set of all colimit cocones. This leads to the final definition in this section.

Definition: Model of a sketch.
A model of a sketch S is a sketch morphism $M : S \to |D|$ where $|D|$ is the sketch underlying some category D (typically *SET*). It follows that the diagrams of S will be taken to commutative diagrams of D, and the cones (cocones) of S will be taken to limit cones (colimit cocones) of D. □

Because a sketch is essentially a graph it does not have a composition operator so a sketch S with a finite number of edges can represent a category $M(S)$ with an infinite number of arrows produced by composing the images of the edges of S in M.

The models of a sketch form a category, the models of the sketch are the objects of the category and the arrows are natural transformations[1]. The category of models of sketch S in category C is denoted by $\mathbf{Mod}_{\mathbf{C}}(S)$; when $C = SET$ it is omitted.

There are two theorems which appear in [14] involving categories of models of a sketch which will be important in the description of a partial evaluator.

Theorem 1 *If $h : S \to T$ is a sketch morphism, then it determines a functor between the categories of models of* S *and* T, $h^*_{\mathbf{C}} : \mathbf{Mod}_{\mathbf{C}}(T) \to \mathbf{Mod}_{\mathbf{C}}(S)$ □

Proof: The functor $h^*_{\mathbf{C}} : \mathbf{Mod}_{\mathbf{C}}(T) \to \mathbf{Mod}_{\mathbf{C}}(S)$ is construced as:

$h^*_{\mathbf{C}}(M)$	$= h; M$	for all objects M of $\mathbf{Mod}_{\mathbf{C}}(T)$
$h^*_{\mathbf{C}}(f : M \to M')$	$= f : (h; M) \to (h; M')$	for all arrows $f : M \to M'$ □

The second theorem is proved by Barr and Wells in [15] for the class of finite product (FP) sketches modeled in *SET*, an FP sketch is a sketch without cocones and where all cones are over finite discrete diagrams.

Theorem 2 *If* S *and* T *are FP sketches and $h : S \to T$ is a sketch morphism, then h^* has a left adjoint* $h_{\#} : \mathbf{Mod}(S) \to \mathbf{Mod}(T)$. □

Proof: See [15], chapter 4.3, theorem 3. □

2.2 Sketches as a Syntax for Abstract Data Types

Currently, interest is growing in the use of sketches as a tool for the specification of abstract data types. Sketches appear to offer a tool which is far more powerful than any which is currently available. Two reasons for this are:

1. the equations (diagrams) of a sketch contain no variables and equational reasoning is therefore greatly simplified.

2. The existence of a set of cocones in a sketch allows the user to specify sorts as disjoint unions of other sorts, this can drastically reduce the complexity of a sketch. To quote from Wells and Barr [13].

   > "Having the ability to form disjoint unions makes it easy to define operations ... which are undefined on part of the datatype. We don't need to give it some artificial value such as 'error' — we just don't define it on the embarrassing part of the datatype, and in any model it is then not defined there and thus gives no trouble."

[1] Although a model of a sketch is not a functor, it is still possible to talk of arrows between models as natural transformations because the target of a model *is* a category.

Gray [14] shows how sketches of simple datatypes may be combined to form more complex datatypes such as: **SETofNAT**, and **SETofSETofNAT**.

A simple example, a sketch of the natural numbers with addition is included here to give a flavour of the use of sketches in the specification of abstract data types.

Example: Natural numbers with addition (*Nat*).

The definition of natural numbers requires two operations which construct elements of *nat*.

1. $0 : [] \rightarrow nat$ — which identifies a constant in the set of natural numbers.

2. $succ : nat \rightarrow nat$ — which, given a natural number, identifies its successor.

The constructor operations in the sketch are given as two arrows.

$$0 : \mathsf{T} \rightarrow nat$$
$$succ : nat \rightarrow nat$$

This implies the existence of two objects in the sketch graph, T — the object which is the vertex of the empty cone, and *nat* — the sort, natural numbers.

The arity of the addition operation is $+ : nat \times nat \rightarrow nat$. To describe this operation the cone N_2 is introduced.

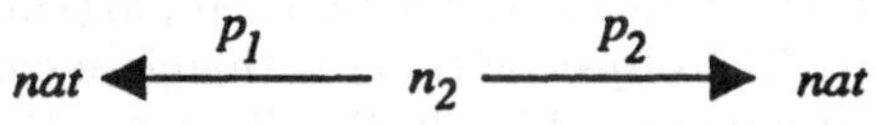

The the + operation is given as an arrow $+ : n_2 \rightarrow nat$. The graph of the sketch is therefore:

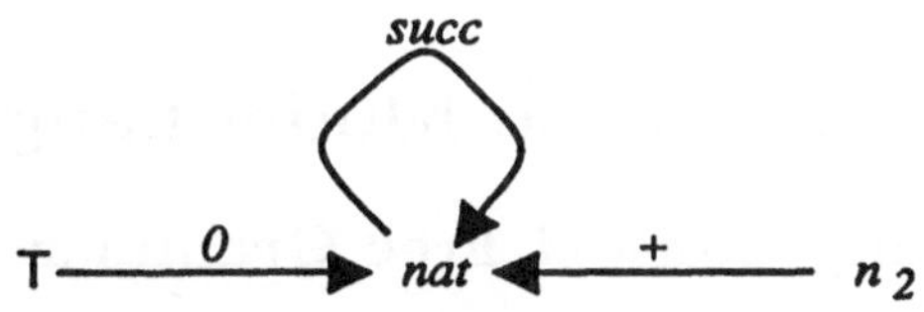

with appropriate identity arrows for each object. The set of cones is $\{\mathsf{T}, N_2\}$ and the set of cocones is empty for this sketch.

Two equations are needed to describe the + operation:

1. $\forall\, x \in nat : x + 0 = x$

2. $\forall\, x, y \in nat : x + succ(y) = succ(x + y)$

These equations become diagrams of the sketch, given below using a linear notation.

$$(id_{nat}, 0); + = id_{nat} \qquad D_1$$

At first sight the arrows $(0, id_{nat})$ and id_{nat} have different source objects, ie the source of id_{nat} is *nat* and the source of $(0, id_{nat})$ is the cone X:

$$nat \xleftarrow{p_1} X \xrightarrow{p_2} \top$$

It should be noted that the vertex of this cone is, in fact, isomorphic to *nat*. For this reason the cone X is not required in the set of cones for the sketch and diagram D_1 is well formed.

The second equation gives rise to the diagram:

$$(id_{nat}, succ); + = +; succ \qquad D_2$$

These are the only diagrams required for the sketch.

To give a semantics to the sketch we take its initial model, M, in **Mod**(Nat). This model takes the empty cone $\top$ to the limit cone over the empty diagram in *SET*. The vertex of this cone is, in fact, any singleton set. The set which is chosen by convention, is $\{\emptyset\}$. The cone N_2 is taken to the limit cone over the diagram

$$M(nat) \qquad\qquad M(nat)$$

and its vertex is therefore the cartesian product $M(nat) \times M(nat)$.

The arrow $M(0)$ is the constant function zero, $M(succ)$ is the successor function on natural numbers. The object $M(nat)$ is therefore constrained to be isomorphic to the set of natural numbers. Finally the diagrams D_1 and D_2 are taken to commutative diagrams which constrains $M(+)$ to be the function which adds pairs of natural numbers. $M(Nat)$ therefore has the semantics of natural numbers with addition and so *Nat* does indeed define the desired abstract data type.

3 Using Sketches to Model Language

3.1 Specifying Context Free Grammar

In [13] Wells and Barr describe a method of using sketches to specify context free grammars. The approach is based on the notion of a *context free* sketch, defined below. The approach used here is a combination of the approach of Wells and Barr and of Rus's work on an algebraic model of language [16, 17, 18].

In Rus's model the nonterminal symbols are the sorts of an algebra, and the terminal symbols are the operation symbols. For example a production rule

$$S \Rightarrow t_0 S_1 t_1 \ldots t_{n-1} S_n t_n$$

where t_i is a terminal symbol and S_i is a nonterminal symbol, is represented as an operation

$$t_0t_1 \ldots t_n : S_1, \ldots, S_n \rightarrow S$$

The operation symbol $t_0t_1 \ldots t_n$ is distributed over its operands $S_1, \ldots, S_n$ and produces a result S.

A similar model can be constructed using the context free sketches defined by Wells and Barr.

Definition: Context free sketch.
A sketch is context free if all of its nodes can be uniquely classified as either: a vertex node, a nonterminal node, or a terminal node.

1. A node is a vertex node if it is the vertex of one, and only one, cone, does not form part of the base of a cone, and is not the target of a constant.

2. A node which is not the vertex of any cone, and is not the target of a constant, is a nonterminal node.

3. A terminal node cannot be the vertex of a cone, and must be the target of exactly one constant arrow.

In addition to this partitioning of nodes, a context free sketch must not contain any diagrams or cocones. □

Every context free sketch must contain at least one nonterminal node, and if it contains any terminal nodes, it must contain the cone T.

The nonterminal nodes of the sketch specifying a context free grammar play the role of the nonterminals in the grammar. The production rules are represented by the arrows of the sketch. Each arrow is labeled to allow multiple production rules with the same start and end points. The terminal symbols of the grammar are not included in the sketch, so it specifies an abstract rather than a concrete syntax. This differs from the Wells and Barr sketches which can also specify concrete syntax.

If $p : LHS \Rightarrow RHS$ is a production rule, the arrow $p : RHS \rightarrow LHS$ represents it in the sketch. The arrows are therefore the production rules reversed. Vertex nodes are included to allow production rules with right hand sides which contain more than one symbol. For the sake of clarity we shall take certain liberties with the notation and omit the details of nonterminal nodes which are simply classes of terminal symbols, such as *integer* in most programming languages. These lexical details can be added by extending the sketch to include the regular expressions describing the nonterminals which represent a class of terminal symbols in the obvious manner. The extensions to the sketch can then be transformed into a family of constant arrows with the nonterminal node as their target. In such an extended sketch, the sentences of the language are all paths from the vertex of the cone T to the start symbol of the grammar.

In [13] Wells and Barr give a proof that the initial model of their, more general, sketch is indeed the language generated by a context free grammar.

Example: A simple expression syntax.
To illustrate the sketch of a context free grammar consider the simple expression syntax given below as a set of BNF production rules.

$$\langle Exp \rangle \Rightarrow \langle Exp \rangle + \langle Exp \rangle$$
$$\langle Exp \rangle \Rightarrow \langle Num \rangle$$

Since *Num* is a nonterminal consisting of a class of terminal symbols, details of its construction shall be omitted.

The sketch will contain two nonterminal nodes *Num* and *Exp*. Since one of the production rules has a right hand side containing two nonterminals there will also be a vertex node, given by the cone Exp_2.

In addition to the arrows given by the cone Exp_2 there are two arrows which correspond to production rules. These are: $is : Num \rightarrow Exp$, and '+' : $Exp_2 \rightarrow Exp$. The graph of the sketch is shown below.

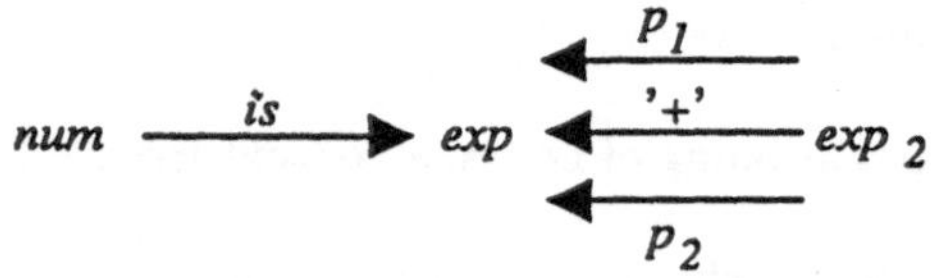

A model, *M*, of this sketch can be constructed by mapping the object *Num* to the set of strings identified by the family of nonterminals derived from the sketch extended to include the lexical information. The cone Exp_2 is taken to the limit cone over the following diagram.

$$M(exp) \qquad\qquad M(exp)$$

The vertex of the cone Exp_2 is therefore the cartesian product $M(exp) \times M(exp)$. $M(exp)$ is the set of abstract syntax trees of the language.

An abstract syntax tree is defined as a labeled, ordered, rooted tree such that:

1. if t is a string in V, the vocabulary of the language, then it is an abstract syntax tree.
2. If T is an abstract syntax tree with a leaf x labeled by a nonterminal N, and there is a production rule $p : N \Rightarrow s_1 \ldots s_n$. An abstract syntax tree T' is constructed from T by attaching nodes $s_1, \ldots, s_n$ in order as the children of x and relabeling node x with p, the name of the production rule.

The arrow $M(is)$ constructs abstract syntax trees given by rule 1 and the arrow M('+') constructs the trees given by rule 2, where '+' is used as the name of the production rule.

3.2 The Specification of a Language

The model of language described in this section is a categorical version of the algebraic model of language developed by Rus, and is based on the notions of a context free sketch with diagrams, defined below.

Definition: Context free sketch with diagrams.
A context free sketch with diagrams is any sketch, $S = (G, D, C, \emptyset)$, such that a context free sketch $S' = (G, \emptyset, C, \emptyset)$ is formed by deleting the diagrams D of S. □

Theorem 3 *If* $S' = (G, D, C, \emptyset)$ *is a context free sketch with diagrams and* $S = (G, \emptyset, C, \emptyset)$ *is a context free sketch, there is a sketch morphism* $\mathcal{E} : S \longrightarrow S'$ *which preserves the graph,* G, *and cones,* C. □

Proof: $\mathcal{E}(G, \emptyset, C, \emptyset) = (G, D, C, \emptyset)$ □

A language specification can be constructed using theorem 3, a context free sketch with diagrams and its corresponding context free sketch.

Definition: Language specification.
A language specification is a triple $L = (S, S', \mathcal{E} : S \longrightarrow S')$, where S' is a context free sketch with diagrams specifying the semantics of L. The sketch S is the context free sketch generated from S' by deleting the diagrams, S specifies the abstract syntax of L. The sketch morphism $\mathcal{E}$ is given by theorem 3. □

The language specified by a language definition $L = (S, S', \mathcal{E})$, is the language whose syntax *Syn* is given by the initial model, M_S, of S in *SET*. The semantics of L, *Sem*, is given by the initial model $M_{S'}$ in *SET*; the functor $\mathcal{E}^*$ induced by the sketch morphism $\mathcal{E}$ and theorem 1 associates a model of the syntax S with each model of the semantics and is called the *Learning Functor*. The evaluation function $\mathcal{E}_{\#} : \mathbf{Mod}(S) \longrightarrow \mathbf{Mod}(S')$ is its left adjoint and is given by theorem 2. It is a consequence of adjointness that left adjoints preserve initial objects so $\mathcal{E}_{\#}(Syn) = Sem$.

4 Sketching Partial Evaluators

By construction the learning functor $\mathcal{E}^*$ and evaluation functor $\mathcal{E}_{\#}$ form an adjunction $\mathcal{E}_{\#} \dashv \mathcal{E}^*$. This section shows how the properties of $\mathcal{E}^*$ and $\mathcal{E}_{\#}$ can be used to describe a partial evaluator for the language L.

Property 1 *If* $L = (S, S', \mathcal{E})$ *is a language specification,* Sem *is the initial model of* S' *in* $\mathbf{Mod_C}(S')$, *and* $\mathcal{E}^* : \mathbf{Mod_C}(S') \longrightarrow \mathbf{Mod_C}(S)$ *is the learning functor induced by theorem 1 then* $\mathcal{E}^*(\mathrm{Sem})(S) = \mathrm{Sem}(S')$. □

Proof: By definition $\mathcal{E}^*(M) = \mathcal{E}; M$ for all models M in $\mathbf{Mod}(S')$. So

$$\mathcal{E}^*(Sem)(S) = (\mathcal{E}; Sem)(S) = Sem(\mathcal{E}(S)) = Sem(S')$$

□

The object $\mathcal{E}^*(Sem)$ therefore uniquely encodes each function denotable in the semantics of L, (i.e. *Sem*). It should be remembered that $\mathcal{E}^*(Sem)$ is actually a model of the syntax of L *not* its semantics, and so describes L programs rather than their meanings. This model of the syntax can therefore be viewed as a *canonical* syntax for L since each function which is expressible (as a class of programs) in the full syntax *Syn* is uniquely expressible in $\mathcal{E}^*(Sem)$. The natural transformation η, the unit of the adjunction $\mathcal{E}_\# \dashv \mathcal{E}^*$, therefore identifies a mapping from the syntax of L to its canonical syntax. The basic purpose of the function specialisation phase of a partial evaluator is to compute this mapping, so η_{Syn} is the function specialisation phase of a partial evaluator for L.

5 Discussion

5.1 Summary

The theory of sketches can be used to construct a specification of the function specialisation phase of a partial evaluator for any given language regardless of the internal details of the language. The construction requires a model of language based on sketches where the semantics is specified by a context free sketch with diagrams S', the syntax is given by the corresponding context free sketch S. A sketch morphism $\mathcal{E}$ is also included to specify the evaluation of programs. The language specified by such a construction has the initial models of S and S' as its syntax and semantics respectively. Its evaluation function $\mathcal{E}_\#$ is given as the left adjoint of $\mathcal{E}^*$, the functor from $\mathbf{Mod}(S')$ to $\mathbf{Mod}(S)$ induced by $\mathcal{E}$.

Using this model of language, a function specialiser (the mapping from syntax to canonical syntax) is given as the arrow identified by the unit of the adjunction $\mathcal{E}_\# \dashv \mathcal{E}^*$ at the initial model of S. This method of specification of the function specialiser for a language allows a function specialiser to be specified precisely in terms of the language specification.

5.2 Problems: Not the Ideal 'mix'

There are a number of problems with the approach taken above, two of the major ones are described below.

5.2.1 Self-application

A large part of the power of partial evaluation as a compilation technique arises as a result of self-application. Compilation by partial evaluation is possible without the ability to apply a partial evaluator to itself, but it is not possible to use a partial evaluator to generate compilers or compiler generators without self-application.

Using the techniques described above the partial evaluator for a language L is specified as η_{Syn}, the arrow identified by the syntax of L (i.e. *Syn*), and by the unit of the adjunction formed by the evaluation and learning functors for L. This arrow is a morphism of models in the category $\mathbf{Mod}(S)$ where S is the sketch specifying the syntax of L, and does not itself exist as either a component of the syntax or the semantics of L. Since η_{Syn} is not part of L it cannot be an L program and is therefore not self-applicable.

There is possibly a way to solve this problem, because the arrow η_{Syn} is a morphism of models, ie. a natural transformation. Let $L = (S, S', \mathcal{E})$ be a language specification, *Syn* be its syntax and *Sem* its semantics. The objects $Syn(S)$ and $Sem(S')$ are not, in general, categories, but can be extended to categories by taking the intersections of all sub-categories of *SET* which contain them [19]. If $Sem(S')$ can be taken to a sub-category of $Syn(S)$ then the natural transformation η_{Syn} will identify arrows in $Syn(S)$ which are the components of a partial evaluator for the language L. The components of the natural transformation η_{Syn} would then belong to the syntax of L. This may be used as the starting point for a description of partial evaluation involving self-application, but more work needs to be done before this can be decided.

5.2.2 Binding Time Analysis

A large number of the specialisations produced by η_{Syn} will actually be infinite programs because of the lack of any binding time analysis phase. Binding time analysis is effectively an abstract interpretation of the programming language L and as such is likely to involve the internal details of its semantics. An interesting domain theoretic formalisation of binding time analysis in terms of dependent sums is given by Launchbury [9] and it may turn out to be a useful exercise to attempt to re-formulate this work in terms of sketches.

6 Acknowledgements

We would like to thank Alan Hamilton, Simon Jones, John Launchbury, and Peter Sestoft for several stimulating discussions of this work. Their suggestions and criticisms were most enlightening.

References

[1] Futamura Y.; ***Partial evaluation of computation process - An approach to a compiler-compiler***, Systems, Computers, Controls, Vol 2, No 5, 1971, pp 45–50.

[2] Ershov A.P.; ***On the partial computation principle***, Information processing letters, Vol 6, No 2, 1977, pp 38–41.

[3] Futamura Y.; ***Partial computation of programs***, Proc: RIMS Symposia on software science and engineering, Kyoto 1982, LNCS 147, pp 1–34, Springer-Verlag.

[4] Ershov A.P.; ***Mixed computation: Potential applications and problems for study***, Theoretical computer science, Vol 18, No 1, 1982, pp 41–67.

[5] Jones N.D., Sestoft P., Søndergaard H.; ***An experiment in partial evaluation: The generation of a compiler generator***, In: Rewriting techniques and applications, J.P. Jouannaud (Ed), 1985, LNCS 202, pp 124–140, Springer-Verlag.

[6] Jones N.D., Sestoft P., Søndergaard H.; *Mix: A self-applicable partial evaluator for experiments in compiler generation*, List and Symbolic Computation, Vol 2, No 1, 1989.

[7] Turchin V.F.; *Program transformation by supercompilation*, Programs as data objects, Proceedings of a workshop, Denmark, 1985, LNCS 217, pp 257–281, Springer-Verlag.

[8] Turchin V.F.; *The concept of a supercompiler*, ACM-TOPLAS, Vol 8, No 3, 1986, pp 292–325.

[9] Launchbury J.; *Domain Decomposition using Dependant Sums and its Application to Partial Evaluation*, This proceedings.

[10] Goldblatt R.; *Topoi, The categorical analysis of logic*, Revised edition, Studies in logic and the foundations of mathematics, Vol 98, Eds: J. Barwise, D. Kaplan, H.J. Keisler, P. Suppes, A.S. Troelstra, 1984, North-Holland.

[11] Mac Lane S.; *Categories for the working mathematician*, 1971, Springer-Verlag.

[12] Rydeheard D.E., Burstall R.M.; *Computational category theory*, Prentice Hall international series in computer science, Ed: C.A.R. Hoare, 1988.

[13] Wells C., Barr M.; *The formal description of data types using sketches*, Mathematical foundations of programming language semantics, Proc: 3rd workshop, Tulane University, New Orleans, Louisiana, 1987, LNCS 298, pp 386–413, Springer-Verlag.

[14] Gray J.W.; *Categorical aspects of data type constructors*, Theoretical computer science, Vol 50, No 2, 1987, pp 103–135.

[15] Barr M., Wells C.; *Toposes, Triples and Theories*, Springer-Verlag, 1985.

[16] Rus T.; *T.I.C.S. System: A compiler generator*, University of Iowa department of computer science technical report 83–08, 1983.

[17] Rus T.; *An alternative to C.F. grammar for language specification*, Proceedings of IEEE conference on computer languages, Oct 27–30, 1986, Miami beach, Florida.

[18] Rus T.; *An algebraic model of programming languages*, Computer languages, Vol 12, No3/4, 1987, pp 173–195.

[19] Higgins P.J.; *Categories and groupoids*, Van nostrand reinhold mathematical studies 32, Eds: P.R. Halmos, F.W. Gehring, 1971.

Transformation in a Non–Strict Language: An Approach to Instantiation

Colin Runciman, Mike Firth, Nigel Jagger
Department of Computer Science
University of York
York, Y01 5DD
United Kingdom

ABSTRACT

A problem arises when the usual rules of fold/unfold transformation are applied in a non–strict programming system. Case analysis by instantiation may alter strictness characteristics of the function being transformed, and hence alter the behaviour of programs. Although such behavioural changes can in general be quite subtle, they are all too apparent if the program is interactive, since I/O interleaving is closely tied to strictness properties. A two–phase solution to the problem is proposed. It comprises a suitable form of strictness analysis to determine whether a proposed instantiation is safe, and a procedure to re–formulate troublesome definitions so that, in effect, case analysis is shifted to a nearby safe context.

1. Introduction

We assume a purely functional programming language in the recursion equation style[1]. Data values are generated from constants and constructor functions. Functions other than constructors may be defined by cases in a series of clauses. In each clause the left hand side is an application of the function to particular argument *patterns*: constructions in which the atomic components may be variables as well as constants. The right hand side expresses the corresponding result in terms of the variables bound on the left.

The few programming symbols we shall use, and their meanings, are summarised below.

`->`	is by definition
`[]`	empty list
`h:t`	non–empty list with head `h`, and tail `t`
`[a,b,...,z]`	short for `a:b:...:z:[]`

The following symbols will also be used. They are not part of the programming language but are used to express properties of programs.

$\Rightarrow$	evaluates to (symbolically)
$\perp$	undefined value

A function is *strict* in some argument position if every application of the function with $\perp$ as the argument in that position yields only $\perp$ as the result.

An important characteristic of our programming system is that it admits *non-strict* functions. First of all, the constructors are non-strict. This means that input and output streams can be treated as *lazy lists*. Also computations involving lists of infinite length are possible. Explicitly defined functions may or may not be strict, but if defining clauses oblige an argument to be matched against a constructor pattern other than a simple variable, strictness is certain. This is simply explained in operational terms: the argument matching process implicit in the application of a function defined by cases cannot successfully evaluate a $\perp$ argument in order to determine its constructive form.

Example

Consider a simple interactive program that prompts its user to supply decimal numerals as successive inputs and produces corresponding roman numerals as outputs. It might be used as follows.

```
> 7
VII
> 9
IX
> etc
```

Ignoring the details of interpreting decimal numerals as numbers, the program can be viewed as a function with a list of numbers as argument, and a list of interleaved prompts numerals as result. Omitting also the details of the roman function that maps an individual number to an individual numeral, the following definitions suffice.

```
interoman ns -> interleave prompts (map roman ns)
interleave [] x -> []
interleave (h:t) x -> h : interleave x t
prompts -> "> " : prompts
map f [] -> []
map f (h:t) -> f h : map f t
```

Note that prompts is not a function, but an infinite list, in which every element has the same value – a string of characters used as a prompt.
□

In the context of this kind of programming system, we wish to carry out *fold/unfold transformations*. We assume that readers are familiar with the basic rules of fold/unfold, as first described by Burstall and Darlington[2]. The chief motive for such transformation is that, in principle, original definitions can be made using the simplest and clearest possible formulations free from the influence of efficiency concerns. These original definitions are then transformed into computationally cheaper forms using only rules that preserve the meaning of what is defined. Although the resulting final definitions may be quite intricate, confidence in their correctness can be based on the simple equivalent definitions from which they are derived. For the interoman example, one might hope to use *fold/unfold* to eliminate the three auxiliary definitions and save the costs associated with intermediate lists.

2. Problem

The problem is that application of unmodified fold/unfold in a non-strict language may yield a program that is not semantically equivalent to the original. In particular, results may differ when an argument is undefined or only partially defined. This is readily apparent when the program being transformed is interactive, because transformation upsets the interleaving of computer outputs with user inputs. To illustrate matters more closely, consider the `interoman` program once again.

Evaluation for Complete Inputs

If the *complete* list of inputs `[7, 9]` is known, it is straightforward to verify that the result of `interoman` is the expected list of outputs.

```
interoman [7, 9]
⇒ interleave prompts (map roman [7, 9])
⇒ interleave ("> ":prompts) (map roman [7, 9])
⇒ "> " : interleave (map roman [7, 9]) prompts
⇒ "> " : interleave (roman 7 : map roman [9]) prompts
⇒ "> " : "VII" : interleave prompts (map roman [9])
⇒ ... etc etc ...
with ["> ", "VII", "> ", "IX", "> "] as the final result.
```

But this list of outputs doesn't say anything about the *interactive* behaviour of the program, because it contains nothing to indicate the order of appearance of its items relative to the availability of items in the input. This information is actually buried in the derivation sequence, throughout which the unused input can be identified as the argument of `map roman` and the output so far can be seen at the left of the expression.

Evaluation for Partial Inputs

To obtain the precise status of the interaction at any point it suffices to determine for any given prefix of the input the corresponding prefix of the output. That is, we must be able to answer questions of the form "so far the user's input is such and such, what is the computer's output?". In a non-strict language, such input and output prefixes are proper values: they are *partial lists* whose structure beyond some point is ⊥. For example ⊥ itself can be viewed as a partial list describing the input available before the user has typed anything at all. If the single number 7 has been entered, the partial input list is `7:⊥`, and so on. For such partial inputs corresponding partial outputs can be derived.

```
interoman ⊥
⇒ interleave prompts ⊥
⇒ "> " : interleave ⊥ prompts
⇒ "> " : ⊥

interoman (7:⊥)
⇒ ... omitting intermediate details of derivation ...
⇒ "> " : "VII" : "> " : ⊥
```

Before the user has entered anything at all, the computer presents a prompt; after the user has entered a single number, the computer further presents the appropriate roman numeral and another prompt. This behaviour is as required.

Unqualified Fold/Unfold Case Analysis

Using the usual *instantiation* rule of *fold/unfold* a transformation of interoman may proceed by case analysis, as follows.

```
interoman []
⇒ interleave prompts []
⇒ ["> "]

interoman (n:ns)
⇒ interleave prompts (roman n : map roman ns)
⇒ "> " : roman n : interleave prompts (map roman ns)
```

Fold using the original defining clause for interoman.

```
interoman (n:ns) -> "> " : roman n : interoman ns
```

Putting the two cases together, one obtains a new definition of interoman, which we will refer to as interoman'.

```
interoman' [] -> ["> "]
interoman' (n:ns) -> "> " : roman n : interoman' ns
```

Superficially, the transformation appears to be successful. The three auxiliaries interleave, prompts and map have disappeared. For *complete* inputs the same complete outputs are produced as with the originally defined interoman.

However, the correct interactive behaviour has been lost. Consider again the two examples of *partial* inputs, this time using interoman'.

```
interoman' ⊥ ⇒ ⊥
interoman' (7:⊥) ⇒ "> " : "VII" : ⊥
```

There is no initial prompt. Prompts do appear, but precede successive outputs, not inputs.

What Went Wrong?

In a strict language, when transforming a function f defined over list arguments, it suffices to consider the cases f [] and f (h:t). These two cases cover all possible list values with the sole exception of ⊥, the completely undefined list. But omitting that case is correct, for then f ⊥ is undefined, that is f ⊥ ≡ ⊥, which is precisely the assumption of strictness.

In a non-strict language, f ⊥ must be properly considered as an additional case. Not only may f ⊥ itself have some defined value, but it also serves as a base case in the definition by recursion of the results of f for partial lists. However, instantiating a defining clause with left hand side f ⊥, although mathematically correct, is futile for the purposes of programmed definition. (The implicit comparison with ⊥ would, of course, be undecidable.)

Even in a non-strict language, however, many functions are strict in one or more arguments – a fact that is exploited to great effect in the compilation of programs for efficient execution[3]. And when *instantiation* is confined to variables in which the transformed function is *strict*, the implicit ⊥

result, arising from the omission of a ⊥-instantiated defining clause, is correct. Indeed, instantiation is correct *if and only if* the originally defined function was strict in the instantiated variable. But the function `interoman` is non–strict; hence the problem.

3. Solution

A practical solution requires two things. First, there is *enforcement*. We need some mechanism for determining whether strictness requirements are met. This mechanism can be used to provide a check, built into case analysis, that ensures only valid instantiation steps are carried out. The second requirement is *re–alignment*. When the strictness check fails, maybe the relevant definition can be re–structured into a form that does allow case analysis. The instantiation context cannot be identical to the original one, but it might be very close to it. We need a way to perform such re–structuring wherever possible.

3.1. Checking for Strictness

Widely accepted methods of testing for strictness use a static program analysis like *abstract interpretation*[4] or *backwards analysis*[5]. Such methods have been extensively used in compiler work but not, to our knowledge, in fold/unfold program transformation.

Although static analyses are only approximate, they give very useful results in practise. On the rare occasions when they do fail, it is always possible to try a more direct approach. Many of the situations which defeat the static approach may be easily handled by a combination of symbolic evaluation and full proof. Both the static and direct methods of detecting strictness may be fully automated. In the former case, some kind of fixpoint analysis is required eg. *frontier analysis*[6]. The direct method may be automated by combining a leftmost outermost strategy of lazy evaluation with a convergent term rewriting system.

If both these approaches to strictness fail to resolve the issue, then to be safe it must be assumed that the function is non–strict.

3.2. Dealing with Non–Strictness

When strictness cannot be demonstrated, simply forbidding an instantiation is not very helpful. What is needed is some way of re–arranging the definition being worked on so that instantiation *can* be performed, but in a strict context arranged to be as close to the original as possible. One solution is to re–formulate the relevant function definition in terms of strict auxiliary functions, and to transform some or all of these auxiliaries instead of transforming the main function. In order that as little as possible is lost by this shift of transformational effort from main function to auxiliaries, the auxiliaries should represent as much as possible of the computation.

Deriving Maximal Strict Auxiliaries

Given a clause in the definition of a function which includes some variable v on the left hand side, the following procedure may be used to reformulate the right hand side in terms of what we shall call *maximal strict auxiliaries* in v. The term *maximal* here needs a little amplification: the auxiliaries will correspond to largest units of computation that are *detectably* strict using our particular methods of strictness analysis.

Let e_0 be the expression forming the original RHS. The first step is to "peel away" any surface layer of computation that is clearly non–strict in v, performing all reductions that only require the information available in e_0 without any substitutions for variables.

(i) Unfold as far as possible in e_0 using the standard leftmost outermost strategy of lazy evaluation. Call the resulting expression e_1.

For some functions, an *infinite amount* of computation might be possible without any knowledge of any particular value for v (for example, if the function yields an infinite sequence of v's). In this case, performing all possible computation at transformation–time, as in step (i), is over–eager. One way to guard against this is to devise a coding of redexes onto some finite alphabet (eg. choose an alphabet of defined function names and code applications of f as "f"). Now modify the evaluation procedure to accept a ***reducible sub–alphabet*** as an additional parameter. For a "top–level" evaluation give the entire alphabet of redex codes as the value of this parameter, but to evaluate a contractum give an alphabet with the redex code removed. This simple device guarantees termination after a finite amount of reduction.

The next step is to identify the largest possible strict sub–expressions of e_1.

(ii) In a copy of e_1 substitute $\perp$ for each occurrence of v. Substitute $\perp$ for any application involving a $\perp$ argument and a function detected to be strict in the relevant argument position. Apply this substitution rule repeatedly until there is no function application left to which it could be applied. Call the resulting expression e_2.

Now for each $\perp$ symbol in e_2 that has been introduced as a result of the strict application rule, there will be a sub–expression strict in v at the corresponding position in e_1. These sub–expressions are candidates to be made into auxiliaries. Call the set of such sub–expressions S. If $S = \{e_1\}$, that is e_2 is itself $\perp$, then the main function is strict in v, so introducing strict auxiliaries is unnecessary. If, on the other hand, $S = \emptyset$ then no suitable strict auxiliaries can be determined. Assuming that neither of these conditions obtains, step (iii) involves making one or more auxiliary definitions.

(iii) For each expression e_S in S formulate a corresponding single–clause function definition. The LHS should be the application of a new function symbol with all variables free in e_S, but bound in the original defining clause, as arguments. The RHS should be e_S itself.

Now that the auxiliaries are defined, they should be used! In transformational terms, we must perform all possible *folds* using the new clauses.

(iv) Form e_3 from e_1 by replacing each subexpression in S by an application of the corresponding auxiliary defined in step (iii). Replace e_0, the original RHS of the main function definition, by e_3.

Example

Applying the above procedure to the interoman example, with ns as the variable v, the expressions and new definitions obtained are as follows.

(i)
```
interleave prompts (map roman ns)
⇒ interleave ("> " : prompts) (map roman ns)        (e0)
⇒ "> " : interleave (map roman ns) prompts          (e1)
```

(ii)
```
"> " : interleave (map roman ⊥) prompts
⇒ "> " : interleave ⊥ prompts
⇒ "> " : ⊥                                          (e2)
```

(iii) `aux ns -> interleave (map roman ns) prompts`

(iv) `interoman ns -> "> " : aux ns`

Whereas interoman is non-strict in ns, aux is strict. Appropriate transformation of aux proceeds in much the same way as the earlier (inappropriate) transformation of interoman.

```
aux []
⇒ interleave (map roman []) prompts
⇒ interleave [] prompts
⇒ []

aux (n:ns)
⇒ interleave (map roman (n:ns)) prompts
⇒ interleave (roman n : map roman ns) prompts
⇒ roman n : interleave prompts (map roman ns)
⇒ roman n : interleave ("> " : prompts) (map roman ns)
⇒ roman n : "> " : interleave (map roman ns) prompts
```

Fold using the original defining clause for the auxiliary aux.

```
aux (n:ns) -> roman n : "> " : aux ns
```

Fold using the reformulated defining clause for full interoman.

```
aux (n:ns) -> roman n : interoman ns
```

We arrive at the following completed program.

```
interoman ns -> "> " : aux ns
aux [] -> []
aux (n:ns) -> roman n : interoman ns
```

The result of transformation in this case is a "tight loop" between interoman, which is responsible for the production of prompts, and aux which generates the roman numerals.

□

4. Tupling of Strict Auxiliaries

The *tupling strategy*[7] is an important method for combining the computations of several different function applications that share a common argument. The idea is to introduce a new function that computes a tuple of results. At first, the definition of this function is expressed simply as a tuple of separate applications, but it may be transformed to share work between component computations, and ultimately to eliminate all uses of the original functions.

Example

```
average xs -> sum xs / len xs
sum [] -> 0
sum (x:xs) -> x + sum xs
len [] -> 0
len (x:xs) -> 1 + len xs
```

The tupling strategy suggests reformulating the definition of `average` as follows

```
average xs -> s / n
  where (s,n) -> sumlen xs
sumlen xs -> (sum xs, len xs)
```

from which a direct recursive definition of `sumlen` can be derived, avoiding the need for the auxiliaries `sum` and `len` to perform separate recursive computations over `xs`.

□

But transformation of `sumlen` must begin with case analysis by instantiation of `xs`: so is `sumlen` strict? The answer is "yes" if *both* `sum` *and* `len` are strict – which indeed they are. This assumes that tuples obey the equivalence

$$(\bot,\bot,...,\bot) \equiv \bot$$

which holds even in most non-strict languages.

So if the procedure of the previous section yields *several* maximal strict auxiliaries from a single non-strict function definition, the tupling strategy is one possible way to combine them. Also, to approximate the benefits of tupling several functions together where some of the functions are non-strict we can apply the tupling strategy to the maximal strict auxiliaries.

5. Concluding Remarks

We have solved a problem that arises when fold/unfold is applied in a non–strict language featuring pattern matching. Our solution has been implemented in our STARSHIP transformation support system[8]. For strictness analysis, we have combined Mycroft's first–order abstract interpretation[4] with Young and Hudak's method for finding fixpoints, known as pending analysis[9]. The latter is ideally suited to an interactive system since it gives rapid convergence. Indeed, Young and Hudak claim their method is >20 times faster than its nearest rival, the frontiers algorithm[6]. To make up for the inadequacies of the simple abstract interpretation, we include an additional phase of strictness detection which takes a more direct approach – combining symbolic lazy evaluation with a convergent term rewriting system. The cumulative power of the two complementary approaches seems to be sufficient to deal with most situations that arise in practise.

The method for isolating the maximal (detectably) strict auxiliaries has been implemented as an automated procedure available to the user. This has been tested on various examples. Clearly, the capabilities of the strictness detection algorithm are a vital factor in determining the effectiveness of our method. It could make the difference between a hardly worthwhile transformation scattered over several small auxiliaries and a very worthwhile one at a higher level. Indeed, for some examples, a weak strictness detection system may even prevent any transformation at all, even though non–trivial strict auxiliaries do exist. Our static strictness detection scheme could be extended (eg. to deal with higher–order functions and non–flat domains) but for the examples we have explored so far our present method seems to be quite effective.

Acknowledgements

Our work is funded by British Telecom PLC and the Science and Engineering Council of Great Britain.

References

1. D. A. Turner, "Recursion Equations as a Programming Language", in *Functional Programming and its Applications*, ed. J. Darlington, P. Henderson and D. A. Turner, Cambridge University Press (1982).
2. R. M. Burstall and J. Darlington, "A Transformation System for Developing Recursive Programs", *Journal of the ACM* **24**(1), pp. 44-67 (January 1977).
3. S. L. Peyton Jones, *The Implementation of Functional Languages*, Prentice–Hall (1987).
4. A. Mycroft, "Abstract Interpretation and Optimising Transformations for Applicative Languages", Ph. D. Thesis, CST-15-81, Unversity of Edinburgh, Department of Computer Science (December 1981).
5. R. J. M. Hughes and P. Wadler, "Projections for Strictness Analysis", pp. 385-407 in *Functional Programming Languages and Computer Architecture*, ed. G. Kahn, Springer Lecture Notes in Computer Science 274, Portland, Oregon (September 1987).
6. C. Martin and C. Hankin, "Finding Fixed Points in Finite Lattices", pp. 426-445 in *Functional Programming Languages and Computer Architecture*, ed. G. Kahn, Springer Lecture Notes in Computer Science 274, Portland, Oregon (September 1987).
7. A. Pettorossi, "Methodologies for Transformations and Memoing in Applicative Languages", PhD Thesis, Department of Computer Science, University of Edinburgh (October 1984).
8. M. A. Firth and C. Runciman, *Starship Version 0.2 Reference Manual*, Department of Computer Science, University of York (February 1990).
9. J. Young and P. Hudak, "Finding Fixpoints on Function Spaces", YALE/DCS/RR-505, Yale University Department of Computer Science (December 1986).

Referentially Transparent Database Languages

Phil Trinder
Oxford University *

Abstract

This paper explores the consequences of enforcing referential transparency in database languages. It is argued that preserving referential transparency is the fundamental difference between functional and procedural languages. The significant features of a database implemented, manipulated and queried using functional languages are briefly described. The consequences of preserving referential transparency in the implementation, manipulation and query languages are described.

1 Introduction

Some advantages often claimed for functional languages include data abstraction, pattern matching and higher-order functions. While these features are supported, they do not seem to be specific to functional languages. Data Abstraction originated in the procedural world [1], and is widely used there [2, 3, 4]. Pattern matching had its origins in procedural languages [5]. Many procedural languages also treat procedures as first class objects [6, 7].

Preserving referential transparency, however, does seem to be the fundamental difference between functional and procedural languages. The properties functional languages derive as a consequence of preserving referential transparency are well known. They include equational reasoning, which simplifies proof, transformation and derivation. Referential transparency eliminates side-effects, makes parallel evaluation simple and lazy evaluation possible. To preserve transparency, however, data structures must no longer be modified. Instead a new copy must be constructed, this is called *non-destructive update*.

Most of the properties derived from referential transparency are desirable for any programming language. In a database, however, large data structures are frequently modified and non-destructive update initially appears to be unreasonably expensive. By examining a database that is implemented, manipulated and queried in a functional language the costs and benefits of preserving referential transparency can be ascertained.

Data storage is important because almost all non-trivial programs manipulate permanent data. At present most declarative languages are guest languages

*Currently visiting at the Computing Science Department, Glasgow University, Glasgow G12 8QQ, Scotland. Email: trinder@uk.ac.glasgow.cs

on single-processor procedural machines, and able to preserve their data in the file system provided by the host machine. However, the interface to the file system that is provided by guest languages is primitive and often not referentially transparent. A guest functional language that adopted the proposals outlined in this paper would have rich, but declarative, data manipulation and query facilities.

Further, there are several machines, and more under development, that are designed to evaluate functional languages in parallel [8, 9, 10, 11]. To integrate with the declarative framework and thus be efficient on these machines, the manipulation and query languages must be implemented in a parallel functional language. From a database viewpoint, if parallel functional languages become a fast alternative to procedural languages, then it is desirable to implement databases in them. There is already some evidence that declarative multiprocessors, with their large memories, have potential for fast data manipulation [12].

The remainder of this paper is structured as follows. Section 2 gives a new, contracted, definition of referential transparency and describes its consequences for a programming language. Section 3 briefly describes the significant features of a functional database. Section 4 describes the impact of referential transparency on the implementation, manipulation and query languages of the database. Section 5 concludes.

2 Referential Transparency

2.1 Definition

The following definition is interesting only in that it is a contraction of an existing definition. Readers familiar with referential transparency and its consequences for programming languages may wish to omit both this subsection and the next.

Referential transparency is a fundamental property of mathematical notations. It was first described for propositions by Whitehead and Russell [13]. Quine defines when part of an English sentence is referentially transparent [14]. A three-clause definition suitable for a computing notation has been given by Stoy [15]. The following definition paraphrases only two of Stoy's clauses. The third clause is then deduced.

The only thing that matters about an expression is its **value**. ***Moreover, in the same context, the expression has the same value wherever it occurs.***

Referential transparency allows a simple definition of equality; two expressions are equal if they denote the same value. Because the value is the only important feature of an expression, any two equal expressions may be interchanged. For example, sin(1+5) can be replaced by sin(6). The significance of the qualification governing the context is as follows. An expression may have different values in contexts in which the values of its free variables differ. For example, if $x = 6$, then sin(1+5), sin(6) and sin(x) are all interchangeable, provided that sin(x) is not placed in some context where x has been defined to be some value other than 6.

An immediate consequence of our definition is that the value of a composite expression depends only on the *values* of its constituent expressions. Hence any sub-expression may be replaced by any other equal in value. This is the third clause of Stoy's definition. The ability to substitute one expression for another is termed *equational reasoning* and is central to mathematical thought. Substitution facilitates proof, and the transformation and derivation of programs [16].

2.2 Consequences

Let us examine the impact of enforcing referential transparency in a programming language. We start by considering some aspects of conventional, referentially opaque, languages in order to have a basis for comparison. In a referentially opaque language, programs compute by effect [17]. A program proceeds by repeatedly computing a value and assigning it to a location in the store. Because this behaviour is so close to a von Neumann architecture, such programs are efficient on conventional machines.

The first consequence of enforcing referential transparency is freedom from a detailed execution order. As the effect of a conventional language statement may depend on the current contents of the store, the order in which the statements are executed is crucial. This execution order must be specified by the programmer. In contrast, an expression in a transparent notation must always have the same value in the same context. In other words, the value of an expression is independent of the history of the computation. Hence the order in which the expressions within a program are evaluated is not significant. This determinism implies that a program is simpler because it need not contain detailed sequencing information. Further, both lazy and parallel evaluation become natural alternatives.

A second consequence is that referentially transparent programs may no longer have *side effects*. The side effects we mean are those actions a sub-¿program performs in addition to computing the desired value. Such actions include assignment to global variables and performing input or output. Side effects allow some actions such as input and output to be expressed neatly. However, unless the additional effects are well documented, they may not be anticipated by users of the subprogram. For this reason, the presence of unnecessary side effects is regarded as undesirable [17, 18, 19].

The third consequence of enforcing referential transparency is that assignment may no longer be used. This is because a variable is a simple expression. As such, our definition states that a variable must always have the same value in the same context. Assignment violates this requirement by changing the value associated with a variable. The loss of assignment is perhaps the most significant result of constraining a language to be referentially transparent. Assignment is a fundamental operation in a von Neumann machine. When disallowing its use in a machine we must expect to pay a heavy penalty.

We might, for example wish to decrement the balance in a bank account record. In a transparent language, a new name must be associated with the new value. We must construct a new account record containing the new balance, copy the unchanged information from the original record and give it a new name. This approach to modifying data is termed non-destructive update.

A destructive update or assignment could simply change the balance part of the existing record. The non-destructive update requires more space, as we have both the old and the new account records. The non-destructive update also requires more time, because we have to copy the unchanged information from the original account record into the new one.

The situation is even worse for database applications where we frequently wish to modify large data structures. Consider the task of updating a bank account record that is part of a structure containing thousands of similar records. A destructive update can simply alter the balance part of the specified record. A non-destructive update must create a new copy of the entire structure.

In summary, referential transparency facilitates reasoning about programs using proof, transformation and derivation. Transparent programs are free from a rigid evaluation order, making parallelism easier and lazy evaluation possible. Side effects are eliminated and a non-destructive update regime is enforced. Further discussions of referential transparency and its significance can be found in Bird and Wadler [16], Stoy [15] and Turner [20]. A full description of the suitability of functional languages for parallelism can be found in [21]. A description of the costs and benefits of lazy evaluation can be found in [17].

3 A Functional Database

The following description of a functional database is condensed from [22, 23, 24]. For simplicity the database is treated as a single class of data. The principles remain the same for a more realistic database. The papers cited above describe a more realistic database with, *inter alia*, facilities for multiple users and multiple classes of data.

3.1 Bulk Data Structures

A class is a homogeneous set of data items. In a persistent environment a class can be stored in a data structure. Because these structures are large they are termed bulk data structures. The structures used to represent the data are a crucial part of the database implementation.

3.1.1 Update cost

Operations that do not modify a data structure, for example looking up a value, can be implemented efficiently in a functional language. However, when a data structure is changed in a functional program a new version of the structure must be constructed. It appears to be prohibitively expensive to create a new version of a large data structure every time it is modified.

It is expensive to construct new versions of many data structures. For example, consider representing a class of data items as a list. Fortunately it is not necessary to create a new copy of every element in the list when creating a new version of it. While the new version of the list is logically completely separate from the old version, most implementations allow the old and new versions to *share* the unchanged part. This is best illustrated by an example. Consider the following representation of f, a list of names and values.

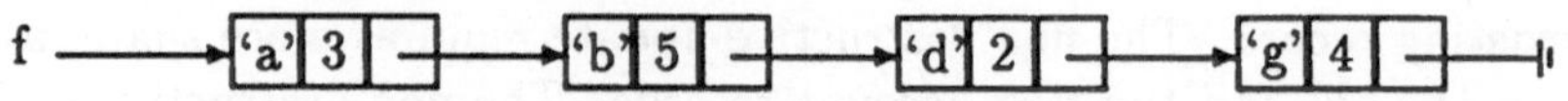

Constructing a new list with a value of 6 associated with 'b' gives

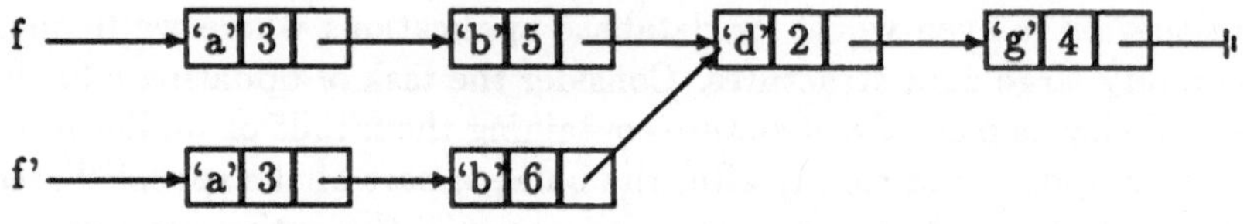

On average, when creating a new version of the list, half of the list will need to be reconstructed. If the list contains n records, this gives a time and space cost of $n/2$. Such high modification costs effectively prohibit the use of lists as a bulk data structure. Fortunately new versions of some data structures can be constructed cheaply.

3.1.2 Trees

A new version of a tree can be cheaply constructed. For simplicity a binary tree is described. In a more realistic database a B-tree [25, 26, 27] would be used. The distinction is not important for the techniques described here. A class can be viewed as a collection of records and there may be a key function that, given a record, will return its key value. If *Rt* and *Kt* are the record and key types then an abstract datatype, *Bdt*, for such a tree can be written

$$Bdt \;=\; record\, Rt \;\mid\; node\, Bdt\; Kt\; Bdt$$

Using this definition and ignoring some error reporting issues an operations that lookup and update a record can be written as follows.

$$\begin{aligned} lookup\;\; k'\;\; (record\, r) &= r,\; if\; key\, r \;=\; k' \\ &= error,\; otherwise \end{aligned}$$

$$\begin{aligned} lookup\;\; k'\;\; (node\, lt\; k\, rt) &= lookup\;\; k'\;\; lt,\; if\; k' \;\le\; k \\ &= lookup\;\; k'\;\; rt,\; otherwise \end{aligned}$$

$$\begin{aligned} update\;\; r'\;\; (record\, r) &= record\, r',\; if\; key\, r \;=\; key\, r' \\ &= error,\; otherwise \end{aligned}$$

$$\begin{aligned} update\;\; r'\;\; (node\, lt\; k\, rt) &= node\, (update\;\; r'\;\; lt)\; k\, rt,\; if\; key\, r' \;\le\; k \\ &= node\, lt\; k\; (update\;\; r'\;\; rt),\; otherwise \end{aligned}$$

3.1.3 Efficiency

Let us assume that the tree contains n records and is balanced. In this case its depth is $\log n$. The update function only requires to construct $\log n$ new nodes to create a new version of such a tree. This is because any unchanged nodes are shared between the old and the new versions and hence a new "spine" of the tree is all that need be constructed. This is best illustrated by the following diagrams. If the tree depicted in figure 1 is updated to associate a value of 3 with x, then the result is depicted in figure 2.

Figure 1: Original Tree

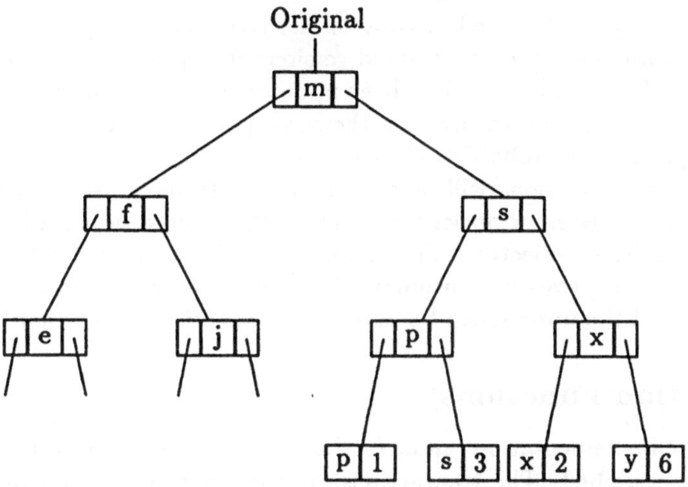

Figure 2: Original and New Trees

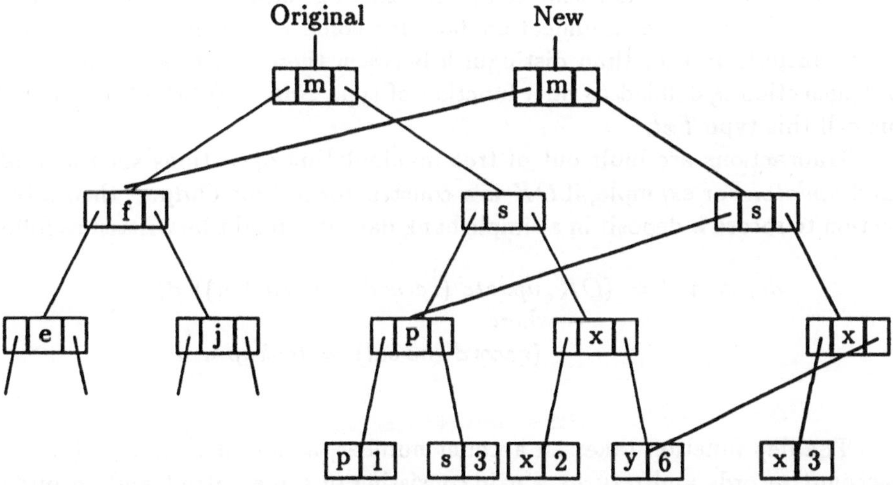

A time complexity of $\log n$ is the same as an imperative tree update. The non-destructive update has a larger constant factor, however, as the new nodes must be created and some unchanged information copied into them. Destructive update is, however, more space efficient than this naive approach as it requires no new nodes.

The functional update can be made more efficient. A *reference count* is used in garbage collection and records how many pointers there are to a data structure. This corresponds to how many logical copies of the data structure exist. A single reference count implies that there is only one copy and hence the original version need not be preserved if the data structure is updated. Some implementations [28] incorporate an optimisation whereby destructive update is used if there is only one reference to the data structure being modified. Clearly this optimisation can be used when the original version of a tree is not required and results in the functional update having the same time and space requirements as its procedural equivalent.

If non-destructive update is used, a copy of the tree can be kept cheaply because the nodes common to the new and old versions are shared. In the worst case, to keep a copy of a tree that has since been updated u times requires $u \log n$ nodes. In fact, as updates tend to occur in the same part of the database, or cluster, the average figure is probably well below this.

These cheap multiple versions will be shown to be extremely useful in the next Section. Once a version is no longer required the unused nodes will be reclaimed by the garbage collector. The significant points are that when a version is required it is preserved automatically and cheaply. Further, if a version is not required the update can be automatically performed efficiently.

3.2 Transaction Functions

Before the database implementation can be further described the transactions it processes must be described. The transactions are the manipulation language used to create and maintain the database. Transactions are either read-only queries or modifications that update the database. A query transaction can be expressed as a function from the database to a domain of answers. A modifying transaction is a function that takes the existing database and creates a new version. In case the modification fails for some reason it must also return some output. Rather than distinguish between these two types of transaction a transaction is defined to be a function of type $Bdt \rightarrow (Output \times Bdt)$. Let us call this type Txt.

Transactions are built out of tree manipulating operations such as *lookup* and *update*. For example, if OK is a constructor of type *Output*, then a transaction to record a deposit in a simple bank database might be written as follows.

$$\begin{aligned} dep\ a\ n\ d &= (OK, update\ (record\, ano\, (bal + n))\ d) \\ &\quad \text{where} \\ &\qquad (record\, ano\, bal) = lookup\ a\ d \end{aligned}$$

The dep function takes an account number, a sum of money and a tree of account records and returns a pair consisting of some output and an updated tree. The new tree is constructed by replacing the specified account record by an identical record, except that the balance has been incremented by the specified sum. Note that dep is of the correct type for a transaction function when it is partially applied to an account number and a sum of money, i.e. $dep\ a\ n$ has type $Bdt \rightarrow (Output \times Bdt)$.

A transaction to withdraw money from an account can be written in a similar manner. It is slightly more complex because a test must be made to ensure that there are sufficient funds to cover the withdrawal.

$$\begin{aligned} wdr\ a\ n\ d &= (OK, update\ (record\ ano\ (bal - n))\ d),\ if\ bal \geq n \\ &= (NoMoney,\ d),\ otherwise \\ &\qquad \text{where} \\ &\qquad\quad (record\ ano\ bal) = lookup\ a\ d \end{aligned}$$

3.3 Database Manager

3.3.1 Manager

The database manager is a stream processing function. It consumes a lazy list, or stream, of transaction functions and produces a stream of output. A simple version can be written as follows.

$$manager :: Dbt \rightarrow [Txt] \rightarrow [Output]$$

$$\begin{aligned} manager\ d\ (tx : txs) &= out : manager\ d'\ txs \\ &\qquad \text{where} \\ &\qquad\quad (out, d') = tx\ d \end{aligned}$$

The first transaction function in the input stream is applied to the database and a pair is returned as the result. The output component of the pair is placed in the output stream. The updated database, d', is given as the first argument to the recursive call to the manager. The manager function is partially applied to an initial database d_0 to obtain the stream processing function. Thus the expression $manager\ d_0$ is of type $[Txt] \rightarrow [Output]$. Because the manager function retains the modified database produced by each transaction function it has an evolving state.

3.3.2 Concurrency

A purely lazy, or demand-driven, evaluation of bulk-data operations does not lead to any concurrency. The operations are performed serially because there is only a single source of demand, or task. It is reasonable to assume that the result of all of the operations will be demanded. Thus a task can be sparked to evaluate a subsequent operation before the current operation has completed. This effect can be achieved using an eager constructor. An eager list constructor sparks tasks to evaluate both the head and the tail of the list concurrently. If the output-list constructor in the *manager* function is made eager, one task is sparked to evaluate the output of the current operation and another to evaluate the manager applied to subsequent transactions.

A pseudo-parallel database manager has been constructed. The implementation and the following results are described in [23]. The implementation demonstrates concurrency between individual operations such as *lookup* and *update*. The implementation also shows that the root of the tree forms a bottleneck. It does indicate, however, that because the root resides in primary memory, transactions can pass through the bottleneck at an acceptable rate. As a consequence of the bottleneck the rate of processing transactions is independent of the size of the database as long as all of the database resides in primary memory. Two problems that severely restrict concurrency were identified in [22]. Solutions to the problems were also proposed. The solutions use parallelism primitives, including a new primitive, *optif*. One of the problems is illustrated in the implementation. The new primitive *optif* has been implemented and is used to demonstrate a solution to the problem. Parallelism is obtained both within and between transactions written using *optif*.

Some form of exclusion is necessary to prevent concurrent transactions from interfering. Suppose one transaction updates part of the database and a second transaction depends on the new data. The second transaction cannot be allowed to read the new data until the first transaction has finished with it. A common imperative solution is for a transaction to lock all of the nodes it may change, so denying access to other transactions until the update is complete.

Exclusion occurs within the database manager as a result of *data dependency*. Recall that update is achieved by constructing a new version of the database. Until a node in the new version exists no other function can read its contents. Any process demanding, or depending on, a node that is being constructed is suspended until the node becomes available. Once the required data is available the demanding process is restarted. Both suspension and restart occur automatically within the parallel evaluator. Clearly the reading process can consume each node as it is produced by the update transaction. This gives rise to a 'pipelining' effect.

3.4 Query Processing

The tree representing a class of data can be flattened to produce a list of records. This list can then be processed using a list comprehension to answer queries. Recursive queries can be expressed by embedding the list comprehensions in recursive functions. Queries can be expressed as transactions by using the list comprehension as the body of a transaction function. For example if $members\, d$ returns the list of members records currently in the database d, then a transaction to retrieve all of the members with negative balances can be written as follows. Note that it is of type Txt.

$$negbal\ d\ =\ ([(name) \mid (name,\ address,\ balance) \leftarrow members\ d;\ balance\ < 0], d)$$

4 Impact of Referential Transparency

4.1 Implementation Language

Some of the consequences of enforcing referential transparency in the implementation language are straightforward. Lazy evaluation allows streams or lazy lists of transactions to be directed to the database manager. Another consequence not yet thoroughly explored concerns resilience, the task of recovering the database contents after a system failure. The multiple versions of the database generated by non-destructive update should make this simple. It is interesting to note that, whether or not a version of the database is preserved the functional *update* and *lookup* operations have the same efficiency as their procedural counterparts.

Two less obvious consequences concern concurrency and the choice of bulk data structures. Referential transparency guarantees that the concurrency in the implementation has simple semantics. The non-destructive update regime required by referential transparency allows an unusual degree of concurrency between transactions. Consider two transactions that appear adjacent in the managers input stream. The second transaction is said to *overtake* if, although it is applied to the database after the first, it may complete earlier in real time.

Section 3.3.2 described how data dependency prevented a transaction wishing to read a record from overtaking a transaction writing that record. A transaction that neither reads nor writes any record read or written by an earlier transaction does not depend on that transaction and can overtake. Let us consider the more interesting case of read- and write-transactions that read and write the same record. It is important to note that a write-transaction only writes entities, it does *not* read them beforehand. This sort of write-transaction is useful if the new value of the entity does not depend on the existing value.

Both a read-transaction and a write-transaction can overtake another read-transaction because there is no data dependency between them. Concurrency is provided by the eager output-list constructor in the database manager. The output from the initial read-transaction is placed in the output in parallel with the manager processing subsequent transactions. As the database is unchanged by the read-transaction it is immediately available for processing the following transaction. A following read can simply lookup the desired record. A write-transaction can construct a new version of the database without disrupting the previous read which is proceeding on its own version of the database. Although in real-time the read transaction may complete after the update transaction, logically it occurred first, i.e. on an earlier version of the database.

Most unusually, a write-transaction can overtake another write-transaction. The reason is that, even if they write the same record, there is no data-dependency between the writes at the leaf of the tree. Both transactions can construct new versions of the record independently. Overtaking at the leaves is significant because these are the parts of the tree most likely to be in secondary storage with a high access cost. The value written by the first transaction will not be visible to transactions after the second update. It will, however, be visible to any lookups between the first and second updates. Of course if the second write-transaction needs to read the value written by the first it must await the completion of the first transaction.

The implementation described in [23] is used to demonstrate the interaction of each combination of read- and write-transactions. In summary, let us compare the concurrency between read- and write-transactions permitted by data-dependency with that permitted by conventional locking schemes. The following table gives the concurrency permitted by each scheme

Concurrency Permitted	Locking	Data-Dependency
Read followed by Read	Y	Y
Read followed by Write	N	Y
Write followed by Read	N	N
Write followed by Write	N	Y

However a conventional write-lock permits both reading and writing of the entity locked. A read immediately followed by a write is a common sequence. This effect is achieved in the data manager by constructing a transaction-function that performs both a lookup and an update. For example *dep* has this form. This entails follwing the path in the tree to the entity twice. A more efficient solution is to introduce a new operation that follows the path to the entity only once, and the *replaces* the entity with a function of itself.

Data dependency permits greater concurrency than a locking scheme between lookups and replace operations. This is because a replace operation can inspect the original version of the entity and construct a new version of it without disturbing a lookup that is proceeding on the original version. An important use of this concurrency is to permit long read-only transactions to proceed without excluding updates. This is also illustrated in the implementation [23]. The concurrency between replace and lookup operations permitted by locking and data-dependency is summarised in the table below.

Concurrency Permitted	Locking	Data-Dependency
Read followed by Read	Y	Y
Read followed by Replace	N	Y
Replace followed by Read	N	N
Replace followed by Replace	N	N

The second major consequence of enforcing referential transparency is that a non-destructive update regime restricts the structures that can be used for bulk data storage to those that can be cheaply modified. In Section 3.1.1 lists were shown to be very expensive to modify. Conventional databases use hash files to provide fast, i.e. constant-time access to data. Unfortunately there seems to be no efficient means of modifying a hash file under a non-destructive regime. In contrast to the tree structures described above conventional databases often use graphical structures, i.e. structures with shared sub-structures. Nikhil has noted that non-destructive update of graph structures is expensive.

The example Nikhil uses to illustrate this point is that of several *course* objects that share the same *classroom* object. If the seating capacity of the classroom changes, a new version of each of the *course* objects that refer to it must be constructed. 'In general the transaction programmer must explicitly identify and rebuild every path from the root of the database to the "updated" object' [29].

The problem of modifying graphical structures is not as serious as it initially appears. Often there are only a few, well-defined paths from the root of the database to the updated object. Secondary indices are a common database structure with shared substructures, i.e. the records that both indices point to. In [23] a secondary index is shown to require a single additional access path to be maintained. As a result a secondary index can be maintained at a reasonable cost in time, space and programming effort. Further, not all operations are affected by the graph modification problem. Neither *lookup* nor *insert* are affected. It is demonstrated in [23] that deletion must either be performed non-destructively or a substantial complexity and access-time penalty is incurred.

The problem of modifying graphical structures can always be avoided by using a key to represent the graphical structure, rather than a pointer. For example, if a key identifying the *classroom* object was stored in each of the *course* objects a new version of the *course* objects would not be needed when a modified *classroom* object was created. Representing the graphical structure in this way costs access time because, instead of dereferencing a pointer, an index lookup must be performed. More significantly this type of representation introduces complexity for the programmer who must explicitly perform the lookup.

4.2 Transaction Language

Referential transparency makes guaranteeing the *totality* of transactions easy. A transaction is total if all of its actions are performed, or none of them are performed. The *wdr* transaction from Section 3.2 is an example of a total transaction. If there are sufficient funds *wdr* will *update* the account. If there are insufficient funds, it will abort, leaving the database unchanged. In the destructive update world considerable effort must be expended to guarantee totality. Typically a log of each transactions actions is maintained and if the transaction aborts the changes made so far must be reversed.

Under a non-destructive update regime the original database is preserved. Hence aborting the transaction is easy — the original database is simply re-instated. The transaction programmers task is simple because the original database is named, for example it is called *d* in *wdr*. As described in Section 3.1.3 the original version of the database can be retained cheaply.

Often a new transaction will be constructed out of existing transactions, this is called nesting. The changes made by a sub-transaction are only visible once its parent transaction has completed, i.e. committed. If the parent transaction fails then any changes made by its sub-transactions must be reversed. Achieving this behaviour is similar to guaranteeing totality and requires considerable work under a destructive regime. Because the original database can be named and cheaply preserved in the non-destructive database described above, reversing the parent and sub-transactions is easily accomplished. An example of a nested transaction can be found in [23].

Because the transactions are expressed in a referentially transparent notation they can be reasoned about easily. The queries described in Section 3.4 are transactions and the next subsection demonstrates how they can be transformed to encrease efficiency. It should also be possible to construct proofs about transactions. For example a transaction might be shown to preserve an invariant.

4.3 Query Language

A lazy evaluation strategy makes database queries faster [30]. Lazy evaluation provides two improvements over a naive strict evaluation strategy. Firstly, only as much of the query as is required is computed. Secondly, a naive, strict evaluator may traverse the list of records for each selection or projection encountered in a query. Buneman *et al* have shown that lazy evaluation causes a sequence of selections and projections to be performed in a single pass over the list. Lazy evaluation and parallel evaluation can coexist. A query can be lazily evaluated and, because it is a read-only transaction, the unchanged database is immediately available for processing subsequent eager transactions.

Because of the referential transparency of the list comprehension queries it is easy to transform them to improve efficiency. An equivalent transformation for each major improvement strategy identified in the database literature is given in [24, 23]. This means that existing algorithms that improve queries using several strategies can be applied to improve list comprehension queries. Space precludes a detailed description of the transformations. The correctness of the transformations can be proved.

5 Conclusion

Preserving referential transparency is seen as the property that distinguishes functional languages from procedural languages. By examining a database implemented, manipulated and queried in a functional language the consequences of preserving referential transparency in database languages have been explored.

Fast evaluation and the ease of transformation make preserving referential transparency in a query language desirable. The suitability of referentially transparent languages for implementing and manipulating databases is less clear. The transaction language is attractive because of its power and mathematical tractability. It is, however, dependent on the implementation language providing cheap multiple versions of the database.

As an implementation language, a parallel functional language has sufficient concurrency and clean semantics. Access to some important data structures can be implemented efficiently, classes of data and secondary indices are two examples. However, the non-destructive update regime limits the choice of data structures to those that can be modified efficiently. Some desirable data structures, such as closely-linked graphs cannot be modified efficiently and hence cannot be used in a functional database. The author believes that the data structures that can be modified efficiently are sufficient to support most database applications with acceptable efficiency. A more realistic implementation would provide a better understanding of the costs and benefits of enforcing referential transparency in the implementation and transaction languages.

References

[1] Birtwistle GM. Dahl OJ. Myhraug B. Nygaard K. Simula Begin. Auerbach, Philadelphia, 1973

[2] Albano A. Cardelli L. Orsini R. Galileo: A Strongly Typed Interactive Conceptual Language. ACM Transactions on Database Systems June 1985;10,2: 230-260

[3] American National Standards Institute Inc. The Programming Language Ada Reference Manual. Springer Verlag LNCS 155 1983

[4] Goldberg A. Robsen D. Smalltalk 80 The Language and its implementation. Addison Wesley, 1983

[5] Farber DJ. Griswold RE. Polonsky IP. SNOBOL, a String Manipulating Language. Journal of the ACM 1964;11,1: 21-30.

[6] Atkinson MP. et al. P.S. Algol Reference Manual 2nd Ed. University of Glasgow Computing Science PPR Report 12, 1985

[7] Harper R. Introduction to Standard ML. Edinburgh University Technical Report ECS-LFCS-86-14, November 1986

[8] Flagship Project — Alvey Proposal. Document Reference G0003 Issue 4, May 1985

[9] Burton FW. Sleep MR. Executing Functional Programs on a Virtual Tree of Processors. In: Proceedings of the ACM Conference on Functional Programming Languages and Computer Architecture, 1981

[10] Cox S. Glaser H. Reeve M. Compiling Functional Languages for the Transputer. In: Proceedings of the Glasgow Workshop on Functional Programming, Fraserburgh, Scotland, August 1989

[11] Peyton Jones SL. Using Futurebus in a Fifth Generation Computer. Microprocessors and Microsystems March 1986;10,2: 69-76.

[12] Robertson IB. Hope$^+$ on Flagship. In: Proceedings of the Glasgow Workshop on Functional Programming, Fraserburgh, Scotland, August 1989

[13] Whitehead AN. Russell B. Principia Mathematica, 2nd Ed. Vol I, Cambridge University Press, 1925, pp 665ff.

[14] Quine WV. Word and Object. MIT Press, 1960, pp 141ff.

[15] Stoy JE. Denotational Semantics. MIT Press, 1977

[16] Bird RS. Wadler PL. Introduction to Functional Programming. Prentice Hall, 1988

[17] Henderson P. Functional Programming Application and Implementation. Prentice Hall, 1980

[18] Ullman JD. Fundamental Concepts of Programming Systems. Addison Wesley, 1976

[19] Yeh RT. Current Trends in Programming Methodology Vol I. Prentice Hall, 1971, pp 40-42.

[20] Turner DA. Recursion Equations as a Programming Language. In: Functional Programming and its Application. Darlington J. Henderson P. Turner DA. (Eds) Cambridge University Press, 1982

[21] Peyton Jones SL. The Implementation of Functional Programming Languages. Prentice Hall, 1987

[22] Argo G. Fairbairn J. Hughes RJM. Launchbury EJ. Trinder PW. Implementing Functional Databases. In: Proceedings of the Workshop on Database Programming Languages, Roscoff, France September 1987

[23] Trinder PW. A Functional Database. D.Phil. thesis, Oxford University, 1989

[24] Trinder PW. Wadler PL. Improving List Comprehension Database Queries. In: Proceedings of TENCON'89, Bombay, India, November 1989

[25] Bayer R. McCreight E. Organisation and Maintenance of Large Ordered Indexes. Acta Informatica 1972;1,3: 173-189p

[26] Date CJ. An Introduction to Database Systems, 4th Ed. Addison Wesley, 1976

[27] Ullman JD. Principles of Database Systems. Pitman, 1980

[28] Stoy W. The Implementation of Functional Languages using Custom Hardware. Ph.D. thesis, Cambridge University, 1985

[29] Nikhil R. Semantics of Update in a FDBPL. In: Proceedings of the Workshop on Database Programming Languages, Roscoff, France, September 1987, 365-383.

[30] Buneman P. Nikhil R. Frankel R. An Implementation Technique for Database Query Languages. ACM Transactions on Database Systems June 1982;7,2: 164-187.

Imperative Effects from a Pure Functional Language

L. McLoughlin
Department of Computing,
Imperial College London,
London, UK
(lmjm@doc.ic.ac.uk)

E. S. Hayes[1]
Hewlett Packard Laboratories,
Bristol, UK
(esh@hplb.uucp)

August 16, 1989

Abstract

In most conventional programming languages a programmer has access to a large number of libraries of general and special purpose functions. In particular for performing various kinds of input and output operations. This paper shows a way in which these libraries can be accessed within the framework of a pure functional programming language.

Since the original motivation for the work was to be able to perform I/O in a pure way the arguments for our approach will be given from that point of view. Once this is done it is possible to use the same mechanism to call functions from most existing foreign programming languages.

An implementation of the functional programming language Hope, see [2] and [11], uses this technique, which has proven succesful in practice.

1 Introduction

When trying to explain functional programming languages to programmers versed in the lore of more conventional languages, such as C or Pascal, inter-language working, in particular I/O, is perhaps the most difficult area to describe.

The idea of referential transparency, that is a function called with a given set of arguments will always return the same result, is relatively simple and most programmers can still remember it from their school maths. Most of them agree for example, that the idea of a sine function returning a different result for the same arguments at different times is contrary to the spirit of mathematics. They can generally see how this property, that they once took for granted in maths, would be useful in reasoning about programs. This property is one of the primary motivations for using functional languages. It is therefore unfortunate to have to give up this property in order to perform I/O (as is often the case). At this point most programmers will suspect that something has gone wrong.

The general novice query about functional language I/O runs like this: if everything in the language can be done by calling a function why can't I call functions to do input and output? The problem with using such an approach can be demonstrated by thinking about a function to read a character from the keyboard. Each time the function is called it may return a different result. This means that the function is not referentially transparent and so any program which calls such a function is no longer pure. The reason is of course that there is an extra implicit argument to such a function (ie the state of the external system), this cannot be ignored by a functional program.

[1]This work was funded whilst at Westfield and Imperial Colleges of the University of London.

There have been several attempts to overcome these problems and still maintain the clean properties of functional languages. In this paper the existing approaches to solving these problem are described and then one solution, a variation of one used in Karlsson's Nebula operating system design[8], is discussed. This approach has been adopted for the Hope compiler developed at Imperial College.

2 History of the Work

The original adaptation of the Nebula continuation based method from streams to a single data structure was made in 1985-1986[2]. This style of using continuations was then implemented in a Hope compiler[3] in 1986-7. It was necessary to use continuations in this implementation as the target was a simulated parallel machine, so calling imperative routines was not possible.

These ideas were proposed and later adopted as the basis for the I/O mechanism for the Hope compiler[4] produced by the Alice Group at Imperial College.

Some of this material was originally presented at the seminar on *Functional Programming with Computer Graphics* at Middlesex Poly, London in November 1987.

An early draft was also circulated on the Functional Programming Mailing List[9] .

3 Related Work

In discussing related work we will limit ourselves solely to those systems that maintain referential transparency. Since this is the key feature that defines a functional language we felt that any mechanism which violates this property would prevent the language from being considered purely functional.

The existing pure systems that we have found break down into four categories:

history Functions in the program can update the history of I/O operations.

streams The program maps a lazy stream of input to a lazy stream of output

stream continuations The program maps a lazy stream of results to a lazy stream of requests

continuations The program maps a single input result to a new request

Each of the initial three categories is illustrated by way of its use in an existing functional language. The final category, which we are proposing is then discussed separately.

Hudak and Sundaresh[5] describes a system which maps from an input state to a stream of output states. However it seems to be only a syntactic variant on the *history* class of systems. In the same paper Hudak and Sundaresh give a full comparison of the various forms of pure I/O and show that they are equivalent in power.

3.1 History

In their paper Williams and Wimmers[13] describe a dialect of Backus's FP [1] that has four additional language primitives: `in`, `out`, `get` and `put` which act upon a device and a history. These primitives modify the history, which records all the I/O operations. The history is only accessible to these primitives. This restriction is necessary to prevent the programmer from keeping copies of the history, performing I/O operations on the different histories and thus setting the devices into an undefined state.

For example the `in` primitive is defined as:

[2] Sean Hayes, while a post graduate at Westfield and Imperial Colleges.

[3] Lee McLoughlin post graduate work and as part of a collaborative project with B.T.

```
in:(idevice,h) = (i,h')
```

In reads one object `i` from `idevice` which results in a change in the state of the history from `h` to `h'`.

Various FP operators are then redefined to take into account any I/O operation that may be performed by the functions it acts upon.

As an I/O proposal it is only deficient in one area. It fails to allow for asynchronous events, such as keyboard interrupts.

3.2 Streams

Streams are perhaps the most widely used of the pure I/O mechanisms in functional languages. Versions of it have been used by Hope[2] and Miranda [4] [12]. The latest language to be defined to use this mechanism is Haskell[6].

The idea behind the approach is that as a function is invoked, it is passed a structure (typically called a stream), which notionally contains all of the inputs the program will require. As in most cases these inputs are dependent on the outputs the program will produce, the inputs must be made available as they are demanded, which implies lazy evaluation of the input stream.

The program assumes the presence of another external function which is evaluated concurrently with the user function. This function has as one of its inputs the lazy stream being produced by the user function, and produces as part of its output the lazy stream forming the input to the user function. This external agent decodes the user requests and performs some appropriate action, and produces values (for example disk files) and gives them to the program.

The major drawback with the stream approach is that it relies on discipline in the user function:

- to ensure that it never attempts to access a part of the stream not yet available (otherwise the system will 'hang').
- to ensure that there are no references within the program to unwanted parts of the input stream, so that the external agent can be space efficient. (for example if the user were to copy a reference to the initial input stream, and keep it for the duration of the program, then the entire stream of replies would need to be maintained in store - which would be a problem if the communication was intended to be an infinite one).

3.3 Stream Continuations

The inspiration for our own model comes from that used in the Nebula system designed by Karlsson [8].

In Nebula a program is a function which maps a lazy list of system call results to a lazy list of system call requests. Although this may sound the wrong way (mapping results to the requests which generate them) a program needs to generate requests so that the surrounding system (normally the operating system) can perform them, hence the value of a program must be requests. Then in order for the program to use the results of the requests the surrounding system must pass them down to the program in some way. The only way in a functional system to do this is to pass the result down as a parameter to the program.

Each request needs to contain the name of the operation for the surrounding system to perform, any arguments required by that operation and the function to call with the result of the operation. The function that is given the result is the continuation, this is a construct used

[4] Miranda is a trademark of Research Software Ltd.

in denotational semantics to represent the rest of the program after a goto or a function call[3]. Here it is the rest of the program after the outside operation has been performed.

For example here is the definition of the library function read (taken from the Nebula paper):

```
[fileid -> integer -> (string -> replies -> calls) -> replies -> calls]
read file length cont sys =
        (READ, (file, length)), cont ([string](head sys)) (tail sys)
```

An object containing the request to perform and the arguments for that request is put at the head of a list of generated requests:

```
        (READ, (file, length)),
```

The result of this request is then taken off the head of the stream of incoming results and passed to the continuation function along with the remaining list of results, for future requests to use.

4 Continuations

The mechanism proposed is derived from the continuation system of Nebula. The primary difference is that instead of a continuously running program generating a list of system calls and being given a list of results, a program is written as a set of sub-programs, each returning a single request (with one or more embedded continuations). Each request will typically require the calling of a further program (one of the continuations).

More than one continuation may be specified in order to handle error cases, for example, or to post interrupt handlers. This is the method used in the hope compiler to allow programmer access to asynchronous events. Its drawback over the imperative approach is that only the state accessible at the time the continuation was posted can be used in the handler, this implies that if the current state is important, the handler must be continuously re-posted.

The advantage of the single return of an embedded continuation function over the stream models is that the approach is applicable in both language implementations with strict evaluation, and those that support lazy evaluation[5].

Consider the following view of the flow of control in an imperative program under a conventional operating system. In this view both the program and the operating system are run as co-routines sharing time on a single processor. This is not a complete picture of how an operating system runs a program. But it is sufficient for this explanation.

Before the program starts the operating system is running. To run the program the operating system is suspended and then the program is started. When the program wishes to perform an operating system call is passes a message to the operating system which encapsulates the call and its parameters and the program is suspended. Now the operating system starts to run again, services the request and sends a message back to program of the requests result. The program starts to run again with the result of the system call available to it.

With the continuation model a very similar set of steps is proposed, but with some key differences, see Figure one.

Before the functional program starts the operating system is running. To run the program the operating system is suspended and then the program is started, at expr1. When the program wishes to perform an operating system call is passes a message to the operating

[5]Whilst many researchers in the field would consider lazy evaluation mandatory for functional languages, the original definition of Hope for example, required strict evaluation.

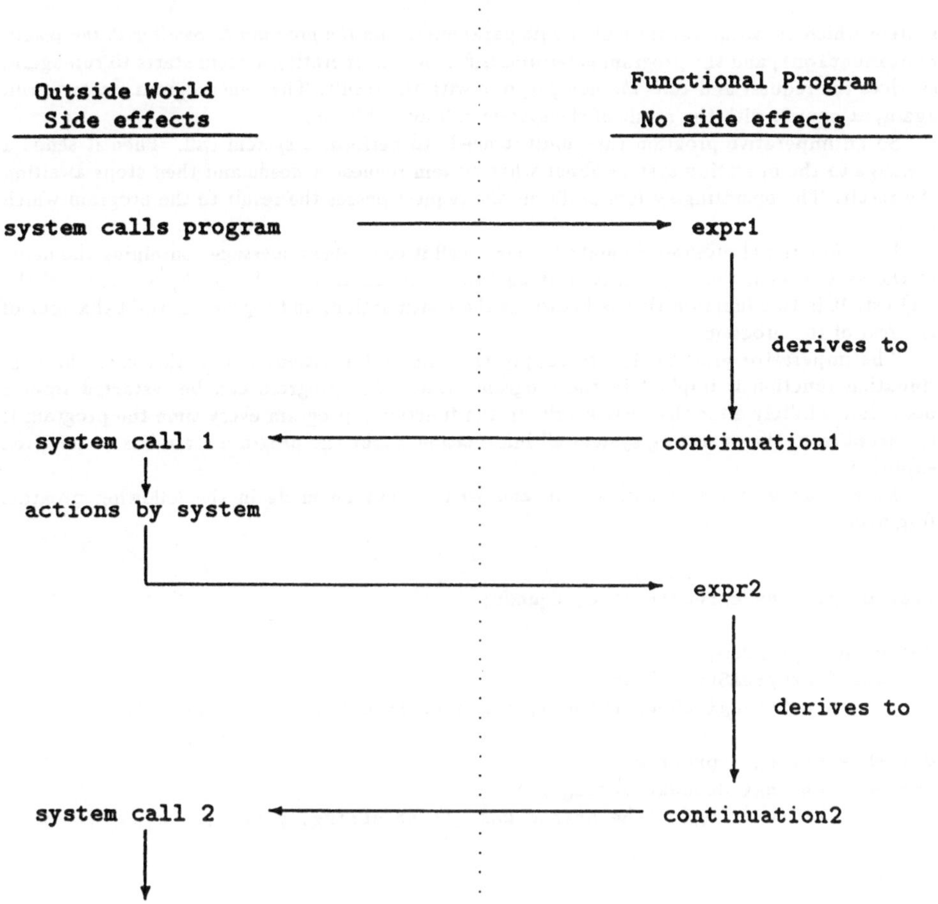

Figure 1: Functional I/O Model

system which encapsulates the call and its parameters *and the program to recall with the result*, `continuation1`, and the program is *terminated.* Now the operating system starts to run again, services the request and *calls the new program* with the result. The *new* program starts to run again, at `expr2`, with the result of the system call available to it.

So an imperative program runs until it needs to perform a system call. Then it sends a message to the operating system about what system request it needs and then stops awaiting the result. The operating system performs the request passes the result to the program which it restarts.

For a functional program to make a system call it generates a message containing the name of the system call, the arguments to it and the function to be called with the result of the request. It is this function that is known as the continuation, and represents the behaviour of the rest of the program.

The imperative program has to supply the same information, but in this case the continuation function is implicit in the program state. The program can be restarted from a point immediately after the system call. In the functional program every time the program is restarted from the operating system all information about the program state has to be given explicitly.

Here is an example of how a read and write might be made in the following program fragment.

```
...
type program == c_result -> c_request;

dec main : program;
--- main( ProgramStart ) <=
        ReadString( show_string ); ! A data item NOT a function call

dec show_string : program;
--- show_string( ReadOk( string ) ) <=
         WriteString( ''the string was: '' <> string, next );

...
```

The program is entered for the first time with a call of the function main. This function, and hence the program, generates a single item as its result. This is the data item:

```
ReadString
```

Part of this data item is the function to be called with the result of the read.

You can imagine this program being run by the operating system in the following way. It starts the program by performing the function call:

```
main( ProgramStart )
```

The program then generates a single data object and terminates:

```
ReadString( show_string )
```

The operating system performs the read string, successfully in this case, and starts to run the program again but this time by calling the function given as the continuation function with the result of the operation (suitably packaged for the type system). So it executes the function call:

```
show_string( ReadOk( string ) )
```

Eventually the program will terminate by returning an "exit" structure which, obviously, does not contain a continuation function.

A more interesting program is one that has to count the number of strings typed to it. In order to do this continuation function must not only use the result of the ReadString request it must also have access to a counter being used by the program.

In Hope the key to doing this is the use of **lambda**, unnamed, functions which can appear in expressions. In the example below, in **countstrings** the counter **lines** is in the environment of the continuation function for the ReadString request and so is available to this function.

```
type program == c_result -> c_request;

dec main : program;
--- main( ProgramStart ) <=
        countstrings ( 0 );

dec countstrings: num -> c_request;
--- countstrings( lines ) <=
        ReadString( lambda String( result ) =>
                        if result == ''stop''
                        then printcount( lines )
                        else countstrings( lines + 1 )
                    end );

dec printcount: num -> c_request;
--- printcount( lines ) <=
        PrintNum( lines, exit );
```

The continuation primitives used in the examples are not necessarily those we expect to be used in practice. On existing operating systems we would expect the continuations to reflect the libraries already available. On a novel architecture, or if the existing libraries are inappropriate, we will show that given a suitable set of continuation primitives, more complicated operations can be built from them, in exactly the same way as libraries are constructed in an imperative languages.

It has been argued[10] that the continuation model is not as expressive as a pure stream approach, in that it is possible to write an efficient general function which converts from a program written in a continuation style to one written in a stream style, but not vice versa.

This result is not surprising however, as the conversion from continuations to streams is an information losing transformation. The implicit model that the continuations support of a reply to given request being consumed before the next request is issued, and the fact that there is no possibility of holding on to previous transactions is easy to remove.

It is not so easy to build a function that introduces this information, as the possibility exists of the stream based function not being a "good citizen" and holding on to many copies of the stream or accessing the replies in a different order to that of the requests being sent.

5 Higher Order Functions and Continuations

It is possible to use the continuation model proposed here in two ways, both essential in a good programming model. First one can write higher order operators in order to construct more powerful operations from the basic ones. Second it is possible to write layers of library routines in terms of the basic provided mechanisms.

In the case of higher order operations, take for example an operator ';' which is similar to the use of semicolon in an imperative language.

```
FirstStatement ;
NextStatement
```

Here **FirstStatement** is run. This in some way will change the state of the program (perhaps by reading or writing to the user) once completed **NextStatement** is then run.

In a functional language **FirstStatement** and **NextStatement** are both functions. The standard way to combine two functions to form a new function which performs both actions is to use the compose operator (normally written as o).

Compose in Hope has the following definition:

```
typevar A, B, C;
dec compose : (B -> C) # (A -> B) -> (A -> C);
--- compose( f, g ) <=
                    lambda a => f( g( a ) ) end;
```

Let the operator ';' be this compose, so that in the construction **f ; g**, the function g becomes the continuation function for f.

Naively the **read** and **write** functions should then look like[6]:

```
type c_program == c_value -> c_request;

dec read : c_program -> c_request;
--- read rest <= READ( rest );

dec write : c_program -> c_value -> c_request;
--- write rest <= lambda arg => WRITE( arg, rest ) end;
```

But with this definition, although the composition **read ; write** is type correct[7], it is not possible to use this in larger constructions. For example the composition (**read ; write**) ; (**read ; write**) is not type correct.

The solution to this is to require all request constructing functions to take the same set of arguments. This leads to the following definitions, (note the extra, and unused, argument to **read**).

```
type c_program == c_value -> c_request;

dec read : c_program -> c_value -> c_request;
--- read rest <= lambda arg => READ( rest ) end;

dec write : c_program -> c_value -> c_request;
--- write rest <= lambda arg => WRITE( arg, rest ) end;
```

[6]The syntax of hope is deficient here, these examples would look better in a language which allowed currying in the patterns.

[7]subatitute A = B =(c_value → c_request), C = c_request

Now the composition (read ; write) : (read ; write) also has type

```
c_program -> c_value -> c_request;
```

the same as read and write. which allows arbitrary numbers of compositions.

Other Higher order operations are possible, for example the ';' operator could be used as the basis of a 'for loop' structurally similar to the countstrings example.

6 Simulating Variables

One use of continuations that has been suggested on the FP mailing list[7] is to use them to simulate variables.

The general idea is that a set of request functions is provided to map from strings (variable names) to values and to allow the updates of those values.

For example:

```
typedef variable == string;

! Get the value of the named variable
dec getv : variable # c_program -> c_request;
! Set the named variable to the given value
dec setv : variable # num # c_program -> c_request;
```

These functions can then be used to get and set named values. In a typed language such as Hope the type of these functions is problematic. If more than numbers have to be stored then an overloaded version of these functions for each additional type is required. Alternately some form of polymorphism could be incorporated to allow any type to be used, although this may cause some difficult implementation problems in storing such variables.

The advantage of these variables increases if I/O operations are defined in terms of them.

These could be provided simply with the following two functions, given that the problems mentioned above with function types and implementation could be solved.

```
! Get the value of the named variable from a file
dec readv : variable # file # c_program -> c_request;

! Write the value of the named variable to a file
dec writev : variable # file # c_program -> c_request;
```

For example the problem of passing a symbol table between the passes of a multi-pass compiler could be dealt with by having the symbol table as an imperative object manipulated by getv and savev. At the end of one pass the entire symbol table could be saved by:

```
... <= writev( ''symtab'', ''symtab.file'', exit );
```

Then at the start of the next pass the symbol table could be read in again with:

```
... <= readv( ''symtab'', ''symtab.file'', restofprog );
```

and further manipulated.

7 Libraries

It is also possible to build libraries of functions building on the primitives. For example, using the function **read** a function can be written which has the program behaviour of skipping through the input to match a given character, and then reading the next item.

```
dec readTo :  c_value -> (c_program -> c_value -> c_request);
--- readTo c <= (skip c) ; read
```

This seems like an attractive definition, provided skip can be defined. One possibility is:

```
dec skip :  c_value -> (c_program -> c_value -> c_request);
--- skip c <=
      lambda rest =>
        lambda arg =>
          (read(lambda val <=
                    if matches(val,c)
                    then rest val
                    else ((skip c) rest) val
               end))
          arg
        end
      end;
```

The only complication here is the passing of the unnamed function as the continuation of the read function, notice how this preserves the 'user' continuation **rest**.

8 Conclusions

This paper has described a simple method of incorporating foreign language calls into a functional language without compromising the pure semantics of the functional language. The external calls may have a non functional behaviour, but this is isolated from the functional part of the program.

The method essentially consists of viewing a program as a set of functions - each of which returns a data structure containing an embedded function (the continuation). This may be invoked by the external system with a reply to the request implied by the rest of the data structure.

The advantages of this method over other proposed schemes are

- It does not depend on lazy evaluation.
- It imposes a structure on the request/reply dialogue.
- It is possible to define higher order operations to combine request functions.
- It is possible to build library functions over the existing routines.

This method does not provide an answer to writing all software in a functional manner (it still does not deal with merging two streams fairly for example), nor does it imply that it is easier to reason about behaviours between function calls. We believe however, that the fact that the program is split up into a number of request generating *functions*, and that a certain discipline of protocol is enforced, may aid in designing, transforming, and reasoning about programs that have to access non-functional external systems.

Appendices

A Simple Implementation Using Strict let

This initial implementation is described as an example of how to implement continuations in a quick and simple way. It does not use good programming practice.

The first implementation of continuations in Hope was achieved by exploiting the fact that the initial implementation of Hope evaluated all let bound expressions, whether or not they were referenced in the body.

In:

```
let variable == expression
in expression
```

The variable initialising part of `let` statements were evaluated before the in part. By exploiting this the arguments to foreign functions could be evaluated before the function was called. This is necessary since conventional languages require values as arguments, and would be unable to evaluate expressions to values if passed lazily.

In addition to this an external language call routine was added `extcall`. This was built in to the Hope compiler in such a way that it was not available to users. This restricted access to foreign language functions to those that a continuation interface had been built for.

This implementation was completed in a couple of days just to test ideas. It was abandoned when the semantics of `let` statements were converted to be fully lazy.

Generally each available foreign language function had an interface implemented in a way similar to this for putchar:

```
--- os( putchar( val, rest ) ) <=
    let v == val          ! force evaluation of val into v
    in
        let result == extcall( PUTCHAR, v )
        in  os( rest( os_num( result ) ) );
```

The function first called by the operating system, finds suitable arguments and then calls the users main function. This then returns a continuation that is passed to os. A program is terminated by an `extcall` to a `exit` operating system call.

Although this relied on `let` forcing evaluation, this first implementation did prove most useful in testing out this variant of continuations and allowed test programs to be written.

It is important to realize that the details of the implementation were unknown to users they merely saw the type definitions for `syscall` and `sysresult`.

Here are the original definitions that were visible to programmers.

```
data sysresult ==
     os_ok ++
     os_args( num # list( list char ) ) ++        ! command line args
     os_num( num ) ++
     os_char( char ) ++
     os_real( real ) ++
     os_fail( num )
      ...

typedef program == sysresult -> syscall;
```

```
! System calls are actually performed by returning a system call tuple
! from the program.
! The vast majority of these routines have the following parameters:
! the arguments to the system/function call itself
! function to call with the result of the foreign call
! There are a few special exception (eg: exit, which terminates
! a program run).
data syscall ==
     ! unix system calls
     unix_exit( num ) ++
     ! test routines
     putchar( char # program ) ++
     getchar( program ) ++
     putnum( num # program ) ++
     getnum( program ) ++
     putreal( real # program ) ++
     getreal( program )
       ...
```

References

[1] J. W. Backus. *Can Programming be Liberated from the von Neumann Style* CACM 21(*8*), August 1978.

[2] R. M. Burstall, D. B. MacQueen and D. T. Sannella. *Hope: An Experimental Applicative Language.* Proc. Of 1980 LISP Conference. Stanford, Ca. Aug 1980

[3] Anthony J. Field and Peter G. Harrison. *Functional Programming.* Addison-Wesley. 1988

[4] Sean Hayes. *Hope+ Comments.* Imperial College Technical Memo IC/FPR/LANG/2.5.1/10 October 1986.

[5] Paul Hudak and Raman S. Sundaresh. *On the Expressiveness of Purely Functional I/O Systems* Research Report YALEDU/DCS/RR-665. December 1988.

[6] Paul Hudak and Phillip Wadler et al. *Report on the Functional Programming Language Haskell.* Technical Report YALEDU/DCS/RR-666. Yale University, January 1988.

[7] Evan Ireland and Andrew Dwelly. *Functional Programming mailing list* June 1988

[8] Kent Karlsson. *Nebula: A Functional Operating System* Chalmers University, Goteborg. 1981.

[9] Lee M. McLoughlin and Sean Hayes. *Interlanguage working from a pure Functional Language. Functional Programming mailing list* November 1988

[10] Simon Peyton Jones. *Functional Programming mailing list* April 1989

[11] Mark Tsang and Lee McLoughlin. *Hope Handbook.* Forward Intelligence Unit, British Telecom. Jan 1987.

[12] David Turner. *Miranda: a non-strict functional language with polymorphic types* In *Proc. Conference on Functional Programming Languages and Computer Architecture*, Nancy. *LNCS* **201**, Springer Verlag. 1985

[13] John H. Williams and Edward L. Wimmers. *Sacrificing Simplicity for Convenience: Where do you draw the line?* IBM Almaden Research Center. 1988.

Designing Data Structures

Alastair Reid

Abstract

The *design* (as opposed to the choice and use) of data structures has been the subject of relatively little study in the context of formal methods. In this paper, we introduce our ideas on how data structures are designed.

1 Introduction

The sciences do not try to explain, they hardly even try to interpret, they mainly make models. By a model is meant a mathematical construct which, with the addition of certain verbal interpretations, describes observed phenomena. The justification of such a mathematical construct is solely and precisely that it is expected to work.

— John von Neumann

Implementation of a specification using data refinement is (roughly speaking) based on repeatedly choosing part of the specification and replacing it with a refinement which does "at least as much" and is (presumably) more implementable or efficient. Choosing a refinement may often be viewed as mere selection of a previously developed refinement of a similar specification from some form of library; but occasionally a new refinement must be designed — thus extending the library. Unfortunately, very little has been written about how these new data structures may be designed — [1], [2] and [3] being the most notable exceptions.

This paper is an introduction to the way we think about the design of efficient data structures. We shall be concerned mostly with time efficiency although we recognise that space efficiency is also important. We begin by briefly describing our notation and semantics. We then examine in some detail an example implementation of a specification paying particular attention to the data structure and attempting to draw general conclusions from our analysis. Finally, we discuss some of the problems with our approach.

2 Definitions

Miranda is used for our example specification. We give a brief overview of Miranda notation below. Further details may be found in [4].

- $[A]$ is the set of all lists $[a_1, \ldots a_m]$ with elements drawn from A and $m \in \mathbb{N}$.
- $f :: A \rightarrow B$ states that f is a (Miranda) function with *source type* A and *target type* B.
- $(\text{++}) :: [A] \rightarrow ([A] \rightarrow [A])$; $[a_1, \ldots a_m] \text{++} [a_{m+1}, \ldots a_n] = [a_1, \ldots a_m, a_{m+1}, \ldots a_n]$.
- $\texttt{length} :: [A] \rightarrow \texttt{num}$; $\texttt{length}[a_1, \ldots a_m] = m$.

- **head** :: $[A] \rightarrow A$; $\mathbf{head}[a_1, \ldots a_m] = a_1$.
- **tail** :: $[A] \rightarrow [A]$; $\mathbf{tail}[a_1, a_2, \ldots a_m] = [a_2, \ldots a_m]$.
- **init** :: $[A] \rightarrow [A]$; $\mathbf{init}[a_1, \ldots a_{m-1}, a_m] = [a_1, \ldots a_{m-1}]$.

We may consider functions as sets of pairs in the usual set-theoretic way. For example, the functions which doubles every natural number is:

$$\text{double} = \{\langle 0,0\rangle, \langle 1,2\rangle, \langle 2,4\rangle, \langle 3,6\rangle, \ldots\}$$

For any function $f\colon A \rightarrow B$, $\mathit{dom}\, f = A$ and $\mathit{ran}\, f = B$.

We regard data structures as the representations of states. In order to apply our approach, we shall assume that the specifier has defined the following sets:

- A set X of *state names*.
- A set M of *modifiers*. Modifiers are names of total operations with arity $X \rightarrow X$. X is closed under application of the operations named in M.
- A set O of *observers*. Observers are names of total operations with domain X and range $\neq X$.

Informally, the basis for the specifier's choice of M and O is that modifiers are used to *change* the state and observers are used to *inspect* the state.

Our semantics (of specifications) is a special case of observational equivalence to the initial model of a specification.

Let R be a set of representations of the states named in X, *rep* a function mapping state names to representations, *imp* a function mapping operations (i.e. modifiers and observers) to their implementations. Then, we require that for all $m \in M$, $o \in O$ the diagrams in figures 1 and 2 commute.

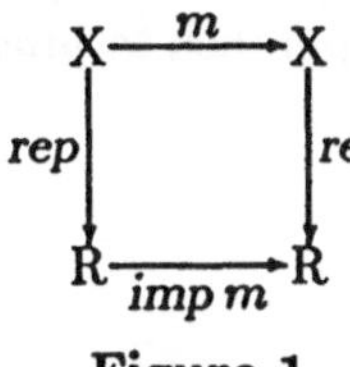

Figure 1

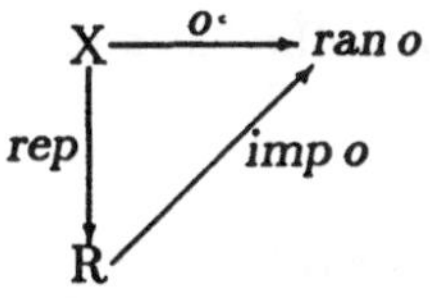

Figure 2

That is,

$$\mathit{Correct}(\langle \mathit{imp}, \mathit{rep}\rangle) \stackrel{\text{def}}{=} \forall x : X, m : M, o : O \bullet \; (\mathit{imp}\, m)(\mathit{rep}\, x) = \mathit{rep}(mx) \wedge (\mathit{imp}\, o)(\mathit{rep}\, x) = ox$$

One of the consequences of this definition is that representations must be adequate — that is only states which cannot be distinguished using the available operations (i.e. observers and modifiers) may have the same representation as each other. This is an important property because it allows us to test a representation independently of the implementations of the operations.

Formalising the notion of states being indistinguishable using only a set of observers O and any sequence of modifiers from $[M]$, we define the equivalence $\equiv (\mathrm{mod}\, O)$:

$$x \equiv y\, (\mathrm{mod}\, O) \stackrel{\text{def}}{=} \forall n : \mathbb{N}, m_1 \ldots m_n : M, o \colon O \bullet om_1 \ldots m_n x = om_1 \ldots m_n y$$

Given a representation function *rep*, we say that *rep is adequate* iff *Adequate*(*rep*).

$$Adequate(rep) \stackrel{\text{def}}{=} \forall x, y : X \bullet rep\, x = rep\, y \Rightarrow x \equiv y\, (\text{mod}\, O)$$

We mention the special case that, if *rep* is an injection, *rep* is adequate.

Finally, we intend that specifications will be implemented in a number of stages and therefore we assume that the representation of the target type of the observers will be performed separately (if at all).

3 Analysis Of A Data Structure

In order to gain a better understanding of data structures, we examine a typical implementation of a double ended queue — gradually reversing the design process which (we believe) created it.

We begin by giving an example specification and an implementation of it; relating some of the definitions given in the previous section to the specification. We then consider data structures, starting with structural aspects and then looking at the values stored in a data structure. Finally we summarise this section with an outline of our approach.

3.1 A Specification And Its Implementation

The queue specification is given in figure 3. For ease of comprehension we use Miranda for our specification. Our use of a programming language for the specification might prompt the reader to think of our *specification* as an *implementation*. We point out that the distinction between the two is rather fuzzy and that, since our approach is based on the *semantics* of the specification rather than on more *syntactic* aspects, any distinction which may exist between specifications and implementations is avoided. As a consequence we mention that it is perfectly legitimate to consider our method as a (somewhat indirect) approach to *program transformation*.

```
queue == [char]
taggedChar ::= Tagc char | Error
eq    ::  queue                        || empty queue
front ::  queue -> taggedChar          || front of queue
add   ::  num -> queue -> queue        || add to rear
rem   ::  queue -> queue               || remove from rear
deq   ::  queue -> queue               || dequeue from front
eq = []
front [] = Error
front q  = Tagc head q
rem [] = []
rem q  = init q
deq [] = []
deq q  = tail q
add a q = q ++ [a]
```

Figure 3

Note that we have used the composite type `taggedChar` to make `front` total. In our discussion, we shall occasionally refer to the length of a queue, this is simply the length of the list representing the queue in the specification.

In this example, the only sensible choice of state names is the set of all terms of type `queue` and, because of their arity and usage, `rem` and `deq` are modifiers and `front` is an observer. Intuitively, add is also a modifier; we use partial application to produce the functions (`add'a'`), (`add'b'`), ... which have the correct arity for modifiers.

The resulting sets are:

- $X = \{$`eq`, (`add'a'`)`eq`, (`add'b'`)`eq`, `deq`(`add'a'`)`eq`, (`add'c'`) `rem eq`, ...$\}$
- $M = \{$`rem`, `deq`, (`add'a'`), (`add'b'`), ...$\}$
- $O = \{$`front`$\}$

Our implementation (figure 4) is in a Pascalesque language and uses linked data structures. It is intended to be similar to implementations which would be derived by any competent programmer. Note that we have used the composite type `taggedChar` from the specification and that as we mentioned at the end of section 2, this type would have to be implemented (perhaps by a variant record) before the implementation could be used.

```
type    dq = record front, rear : ^cell end;
        cell =  record
                  item : num;
                  next, prev : ^cell
                end;
var     q:dq;

procedure EQ;
begin q.front := nil; q.rear := nil end;

function FRONT: taggedChar;
begin
  if q.front ≠ nil
    then FRONT :=  Tagc q.front^.item
    else FRONT :=  Error
end;

procedure ADD(x:char);
var t:^cell;
begin
  new(t); t^.item := x; t^.next:=nil; t^.prev := q.rear;
  if q.rear ≠ nil
    then q.rear^.next := t
    else q.front :=t;
  q.rear := t end
end;

procedure DEQ;
```

```
var t:^cell;
begin
  if q.front ≠ nil
    then begin
      t:=q.front; q.front := q.front^.next;
      if q.front ≠ nil
        then q.front^.prev := nil
        else q.rear:=nil;
      dispose(t)
  end
end;

procedure REM;
var t:^cell;
begin
  if q.rear ≠ nil
    then begin
      t:=q.rear; q.rear := q.rear^.prev;
      if q.rear ≠ nil
        then q.rear^.next:=nil
        else q.front:=nil;
      dispose(t)
  end
end;
```

Figure 4

We shall consider linked data structures as being made up of a number of *nodes* connected by unidirectional *links* and accessed from outside the structure by *entry points*. Figure 5 shows the representation used by the example implementation using the traditional style of data structure diagram [5, pp. 44–45].

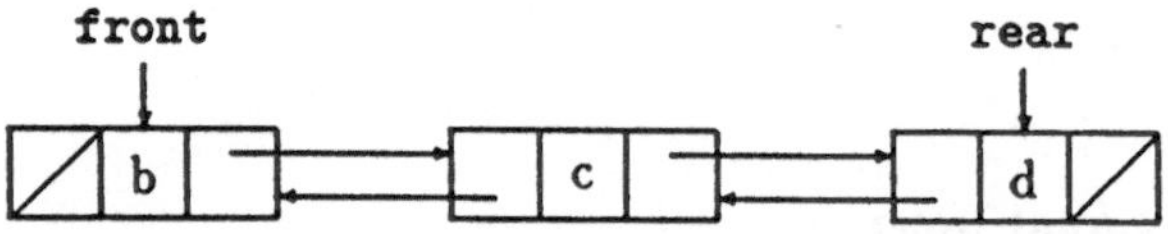

Figure 5

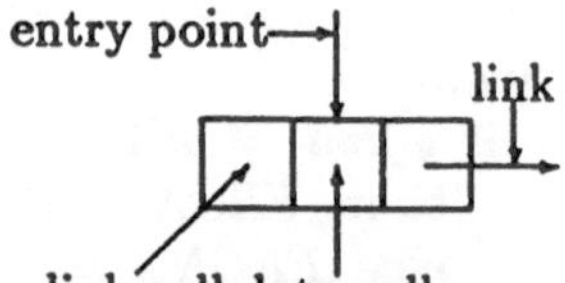

Key

Each node contains a number of labelled *link cells* (e.g. `prev` and `next`) and labelled *data cells* (e.g. `item`). We shall refer to the node pointed to by an entry point p as *the target of* p or as *the* p *node*. We shall refer to (the node containing) the link cell containing a link l as *the source (node/cell) of* l and the node pointed to by l as *the target node of* l. We allow the contents of a data cell to be structured using (variant) records, arrays, etc. and so, without loss of generality, we shall assume that each node contains a single data cell.

We define a *path* in a data structure to be a list of link labels. If there is a sequence of nodes $[n_0, \ldots n_m]$ joined by a sequence of links $[l_1, \ldots l_m]$ such that the source and target of each link l_i are n_{i-1} and n_i respectively, then we say there is *a path* $[p_1, \ldots p_m]$ *from* n_0 *to* n_m where p_i is the label of the link cell storing l_i.

For example, in figure 5, there are the following:

- a path [next, next] from the `front` node to the `rear` node;
- a path [prev, prev] from the `rear` node to the `front` node;
- a path [next, prev, next] from the `front` node to the central node;
- ⋮

In order to discuss efficiency, we require metrics. As a crude time metric, we shall count the number of primitive operations (traversal, removal, modification, etc. of entry points, links, values, etc.) and, as a space metric, the number of data cells, link cells and entry points in a representation.

3.2 Entry Points

Consider the use of entry points made by the implementations of observers and modifiers.

- Observers such as `FRONT` use entry points to determine which value to return. The position of observation points (i.e. entry points used by the observer) is therefore determined only by the choice of *representation of the current state*.
- Modifiers such as `ADD('e')` and `REM` use entry points to determine which change to make and then to make that change. Thus, the position of update points (i.e. entry points used to change the data structure) is determined by both *the representation of the current state* and *its relationship to the representations of the states derivable from it.*

Clearly the `rear` entry point is an update point; but the `front` entry point appears to be both an update point and an observation point. We believe that each entry point was introduced for a single specific purpose and that the `front` entry point is therefore the result of *fusing* two previously separate entry points — one an update point, the other an observation point.

We may generalise this idea of fusing two entry points with the same target to fusing two entry points with "nearby targets". We refine the term "nearby targets" with "approximation" which is defined as follows:

> Let b and c be entry points, p a path and R a class of representations of states. b p-approximates c in R iff in every representation $r \in R$, there is a path p from b to c.

For example, an entry point whose target is the penultimate node in a queue (i.e. the node adjacent to the `rear` node) is [prev]-approximated by the `rear` node (in all queues of length 2 or more). Such an entry point has indeed been "optimised out" — `REM` requires access to this node to allow the link to the old `rear` node to be removed.

We may generalise this notion still further by allowing the path defining the path from b to c to be a function of the representation. In this way, the `rear` entry point could be "optimised out" since it may be reached by following the `next` links from the `front` cell. Since the cost of this reduction in space is relatively high, this optimisation would probably not be justifiable purely in terms of the time-space tradeoff it represents. However, in examples like a priority queue [6, pp. 150–151] (or almost any other problem which is usually solved using some form of search) the cost of having an entry point at every cell where the implementation of a modifier may make a change is quite considerable e.g. every `ADD(x)` in a priority queue could require access to a different cell and so an individual entry point is required for every $x \in$ `char`. The only way to avoid this problem is to introduce loops using this generalisation of approximation (perhaps introducing additional structure to aid the location of the cell to be examined or modified). The problem of searching is a large one with many different solutions and so we shall not discuss it further here.

3.3 Links

We turn now to considering the use of links. With the exception of using links when one entry point approximates another, their sole purpose is to allow entry points to be moved when the implementation of a modifier is applied. This can be seen in the `prev` links whose only purpose (apart from the `[prev]`-approximation mentioned earlier) is to allow the `rear` update point to be moved when `REM` is applied.

From this it follows that after having:

1. chosen the parts of the representation of each state to be changed when the implementation of each modifier is applied; and
2. introduced entry points providing access to these points,

links are introduced between temporally adjacent targets of each entry point (where applying operations to the state corresponds to the flow of time). That is, if an entry point p points to a node b in the representation of some state x and p points to a node c in the representation of σx (for some $\sigma \in M$), then there should be a link from b to c in the representation of x (assuming c is in the representation of x).

Of course, since we have added new links to the representation, further changes will need to be made by the implementation of each modifier and so more entry points are introduced. If these cannot be fused with or approximated by the existing entry points, further links must be added requiring still more complex implementations of modifiers, more entry points, and so on ad infinitum. We thus see one of the other uses of fusion and approximation as being an *attempt* to avoid getting stuck in this loop.

Although it is not used in this example, there is a counterpart of entry point fusion for links. Clearly, if the links from two link cells b and c have the same target in all representations, they provide the same information and we may fuse the cells. Thus if there were links "running parallel to" the `next` links in the representation of the queue, we could fuse them with a substantial saving in space.

We may generalise this using *link approximation* in an analogous way to our generalisation of node fusion. We define link approximation as follows:

Let l be a link cell label, p a path and R a class of representations of states. p approximates l in R iff in every representation $r \in R$, for every l-link with source b and target c, there is a path p from b to c.

So far, we have discussed the "structural part" of the representation (i.e. links and entry points) and we have shown how the design of the structure is largely determined by:

- the *choice* of where to store the information required to make the observations; and
- the *choice* of where the modifiers access to change the representation.

We shall turn now to the "data part" of the representation where these choices are made.

3.4 Data Related Aspects Of Design

The task in designing the "data part" of an implementation is, essentially, deciding what features of the state to store in each representation so that the observers and the modifiers may be efficiently implemented. In this section, we look first at how we may represent the data part and then at the demands placed on the data part by correctness and efficiency requirements.

3.4.1 Adequate Data Parts

We would normally start the design with an adequate data part and add structure to it. As we add structure, some of the information in the data part is encoded in the structure and so we may simplify the data part. In this way, information is gradually moved from the data part into the structural part of the representation. When going the other way (i.e. removing the structure), information must be added to the data part so that we know what the contents of each node tells us about the state.

Since each representation is the result of applying a function (i.e. *rep*) to the state name, the contents of each node must also be a function of the state name. We shall label each node with a unique function *name* such that, in the representation of a state called x, the contents of the node labelled with a function name f, is the value denoted by $f(x)$. For example, in the representation of queues, we may label nodes as in figure 6

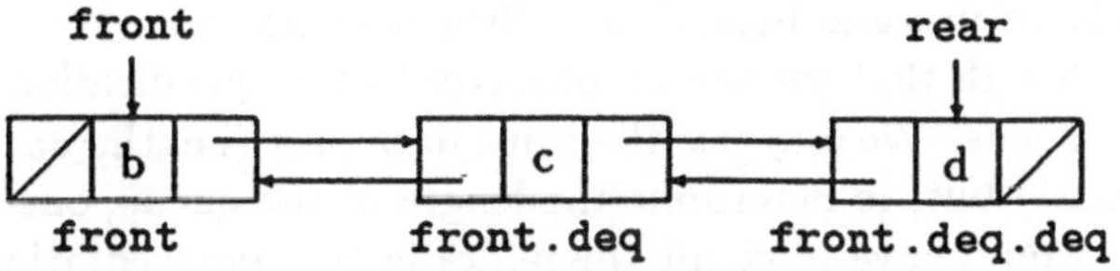

Figure 6

To put this more formally, let N be a set of node labels (i.e. function names), V the set of values that may be stored in a data cell and $F: N \rightarrow (X \rightarrow V)$ a naming function associating node labels with functions. We may describe the data part of the representation of a given state (wrt a given choice of F) using a function assiging values to node labels. We shall use the function $\textit{data-rep}_F\colon X \to (N \to V)$ for this purpose and note that $\textit{data-rep}_F\, x \subseteq \{\langle f, (F\, f)\, x\rangle \mid f \in N\}$.

In our queue example, we may name the functions using the function deqs:

$$\mathtt{deqs} = \{\langle 0, \mathtt{front}\rangle, \langle 1, \mathtt{front.deq}\rangle, \langle 2, \mathtt{front.deq.deq}\rangle, \ldots\}$$

This may be used to give the following description of the data part of the representation of queues:

$$\textit{data-rep}_{\mathtt{deqs}}\, x = \{\langle i, (\mathtt{deqs}\, i)\, x\rangle \mid 0 \leq i < \mathtt{length}\, x\}$$

We may readily see that this data part is adequate since, for any queue q:

$$q = [\mathtt{front}\, q, \mathtt{front.deq}\, q, \mathtt{front.deq.deq}\, q, \ldots]$$

i.e. the list used to represent the state in the specification may be reconstructed from the data part of the representation.

3.4.2 Efficient Data Parts

After adequacy, our next major concern is how efficiently the data structure may be used. There are two things contributing to the efficiency (or inefficiency) of the implementation of an operation: the number of nodes accessed and the difficulty of the manipulation of the values stored in them. Often the cost of manipulating the values is insignificant compared to the cost of gathering them and so we shall emphasise the cost of accessing nodes.

From this, we derive the following definition of efficiency:

> Let A and B be implementations of a specification and let S be a set of sequences of operations (i.e. modifiers and observers). *A is more efficient than B for S* if the number of nodes accessed when executing A's implementation of S is less than the number of nodes accessed when executing B's implementation of S.

If desired, this could be generalised by assigning a weight to every sequence and comparing the weighted sums of the number of nodes accessed to execute each sequence in A and B.

In order to achieve this efficiency goal, we would expect that a good data representation would require only a small number of nodes to be accessed in order to determine the result of any observation.

In our queue example, FRONT need only examine one node (at most) to determine which value to return and hence is an efficient operation.

Suppose though that we add an observer to the specification which returns the length of the queue. We may use the same data part (i.e. the data part given above is still adequate) but, to determine the length of the queue, one implementation of the observer would have to count the nodes in the representation and so would be rather inefficient. However, if we added another node (which stored the length of the queue) to the representation, we could implement the `length` operation more efficiently because the desired value (i.e. the length) can be calculated by examining a small number (1 here) of nodes.

If we ignore the choice of imperative implementation and do not consider implementations which *modify* the representation of the state, implementation of the modifiers is rather similar to implementation of the observers — requiring only the calculation of the value of each node in the new representation from those in the old representation. Since all new nodes and almost all old nodes have to be accessed by implementations of the modifiers, an efficient representation would usually have a small number of nodes. (We are also less justified in ignoring the cost of calculating each value.)

However, allowing the reuse of parts of the representation of a state in the representation of its successor states makes it possible to significantly increase the efficiency of implementations, if we can avoid accessing most of the nodes in the representation being modified. Since a node may only be modified if it is accessed, this means that in an efficient representation, most of the nodes in a state x must have the same contents (and links) as nodes in the representation of its successors σx (for $\sigma \in M$). For example, figure 7 shows the effect of the modifier DEQ on the data part of the representation in figure 6 and the way in which the nodes in the original representation are reused for the representation of the state after applying DEQ.

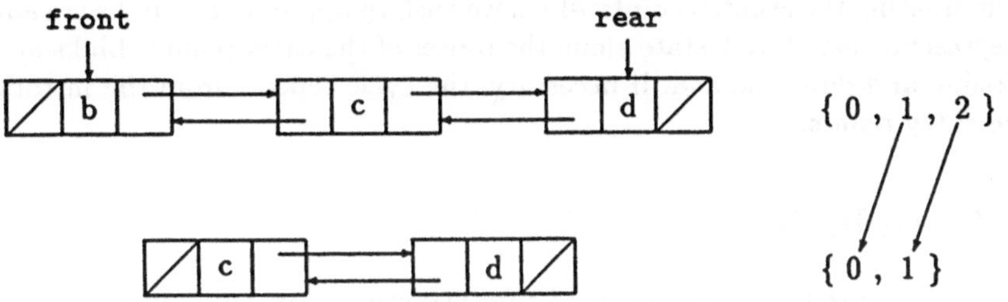

Figure 7

In this example, the choice of how to reuse nodes is obvious; in more complex examples, it is less so — often the data part must be redesigned to ensure that features of the state which change independently of each other are stored separately.

The above discussion deals with what appear to be the major issues in the design of the data part of an efficient representation:

- the data part should be adequate;
- it should be possible to calculate the result of an observation by examining a few nodes and so the representation should store features of the state closely related to what can be observed;
- it should be possible to modify a representation by accessing only a few nodes, and so the data parts of adjacent states (x and σx) should be very similar (i.e. there should be a one-to-one function $c_{x,\sigma}$: $dom(data\text{-}rep\, x) \rightarrow dom(data\text{-}rep\, \sigma x)$ which is defined for most of its domain and for which corresponding nodes have the same contents.
- there should be a description of how to calculate the successor of each representation which respects the correspondence between node labels (i.e. if $n \in dom(c_{x,\sigma})$, the node labelled n in the representation of x is reused as the node labelled $c_{x,\sigma}\, n$ in the representation of σx.)

We shall now consider the entire design process.

3.5 Summary

To summarise our analysis, when designing a data structure one should first choose the data part and then design a structure to manipulate and access it.

The data part of the representation should initially be adequate; it should store the information required by the implementation of the observers in a small number of nodes; and it should have similar representations for adjacent states.

Starting with an adequate data part, a description of how to calculate the result of applying an observation and of how to calculate the data part of a state from its predecessor, the structural part is gradually added. As structure is designed and added, the data part may be simplified by removing nodes or labels which are no longer required for adequacy.

Then, observation points are added to the representation of each state so that they provide access to the cells from which the result of observing that state is calculated. Similarily, update points are added, thus allowing the values of new cells to be calculated and various changes to be made. After fusing entry points and eliminating those entry points which we wish to approximate, links are added in the representation of each state along the routes of the entry points. Links are fused if possible and desirable and, if necessary, the cycle repeats from the introduction of the entry points.

4 Conclusions

We have presented our ideas on how data structures can be designed. At present we recognise the following limitations in our view of the design process:

1. Although we have an abstract machine (not reported here) which may be used to describe an implementation, further work is required to determine under which circumstances the "optimisations" described here actually do result in a more efficient implementation.

2. We have no clear idea of how a good data part may be designed. This is one of our major interests at the present moment.

3. Throughout our discussion, we have considered how to implement an observation of a particular state, how to change the representation of a particular state into one of its successors, etc. Generating an implementation, requires that we generalise the implementations of each observer and of each modifier into implementations which work for any state. Our approach currently does not consider such generalisation.

4. As yet we are unable to cope adequately with problems requiring some form of search/lookup for their solution. However, since our problem seems only to be the large (usually infinite) number of entry points introduced, it seems plausible that a few techniques for reducing the number of entry points (such as use of hash tables, search trees, etc.) would largely overcome this limitation.

5. We cannot handle specifications permitting a range of possible values for a given observation. (For example, a common observer for sets is a choice operation which returns one of the elements of the set it is applied to.) This

problem can be avoided by strengthening the specification until there is only a single value for every observation. However, this solution is not entirely satisfactory since the information required to make a good (i.e. efficiency inducing) choice of how to strengthen the implementation is not available until implementation has begun.

5 Acknowledgements

This work was strongly motivated by and based on work reported in [2] and [3]. It was financially supported by an SERC Research Studentship.

References

[1] Mary E. d'Imperio, Data Structures and their Representation in Storage, in Halpern, Shaw (editors), Annual Review in Automatic Programming, Volume 5, pp. 1–76, International Tracts in Computer Science and Technology and Their Applications, Pergamon Press Ltd., 1969.

[2] Muffy H. Thomas, Implementing Algebraically Specified Abstract Data Types in an Imperative Programming Language, in TAPSOFT '87, Pisa, Italy, Lecture Notes in Computer Science, Volume 250, Springer Verlag, 1987.

[3] Muffy H. Thomas, The Imperative Implementation of Algebraic Data Types, Research Report CSC/88/R4, Computing Science Department, University of Glasgow, 1987 (also, Ph.D. thesis, University of St. Andrews, 1987.)

[4] Richard J. Bird and Philip Wadler, An introduction to Functional Programming, Prentice-Hall, 1988.

[5] Aho, Hopcroft, Ullman, The Design and Analysis of Computer Algorithms, Addison Wesley, 1974.

[6] Donald Erwin Knuth, The Art Of Computer Programming, Volume 3, Sorting and Searching, Addison Wesley, 1973.

Describing Butterfly Networks in Ruby

Mary Sheeran
Computing Science Dept.
Glasgow University
Glasgow G12 8QQ, UK

Abstract

The Ruby design language is used to describe and reason about butterfly networks.

1 Introduction

A hardware algorithm is one that is suitable for implementation on silicon, either as a single chip or as a network of chips. Not all algorithms are suitable for direct implementation on silicon. A good hardware algorithm is characterised by a simple static 2-dimensional structure, and by efficient use of communication between components. A piece of data is usually read into the circuit once only, and it is passed around the circuit efficiently. Systolic and other regular array architectures bring this notion of hardware algorithm to its limit. They have simple regular 2-dimensional layouts, use only nearest neighbour connections, and make very efficient use of data by pumping it through the circuit . Previous work has shown that a functional language, μFP, and its relational successor, Ruby, are suitable for regular array design [1,2,3,4,5,6]. Many systolic algorithms have been developed using standard program transformation techniques. Luk's thesis [7] is an elegant exploration of the approach.

We extend that work by showing how Ruby is used to describe and reason about more complex (and interesting) networks of cells. We concentrate on what Ullman calls "organisations with high wire area" [8] and in particular on butterfly networks. Algorithms for these networks are usually presented in a rather informal and unsatisfactory way. Typically, the behaviour of a basic cell is presented either as a circuit diagram or as a piece of imperative code. A diagram is used to show how these cells are connected for a particular size of input. It is then asserted that this network of cells implements the required function. Usually, there is little or no justification of the assertion, and an explanation of how the network was *designed* is rare indeed. If we are to teach students to design good hardware algorithms, then we must find more precise ways of describing both the algorithms and how they are developed.

Ruby, with its set of transformation rules, is a good starting point because it captures information about both behaviour and structure. Behaviour and structure are intimately related in high wire area networks. A notation that has structural information added as an afterthought can fail to highlight this relationship. Most interesting networks have a recursive structure, and Ruby has an appropriate form of recursion. Although recursive hardware algorithms often have fairly simple iterative descriptions, we have found that recursive descriptions are easier to understand because they give more clues about how the algorithm was designed.

Butterfly networks are described informally in section 2. Section 3 introduces those aspects of Ruby that are used in this paper. (See [9] for a more general introduction to Ruby.) Section 4 shows how Ruby is used to describe and reason about butterfly networks. Section 5 takes Batcher's bitonic sorting algorithm as an example. Discussion and conclusions are given in section 6.

2 Butterfly Networks

The butterfly network has become familiar because of its association with the Fast Fourier Transform. We consider only the binary butterfly in which each cell (or processor or node) has four ports, two on each side. Cells at either end of the network are connected to two other cells, while internal cells have four connections. The network is arranged as k ranks, each with 2^{k-1} cells. It is the connections between the cells that make the network interesting, and also give rise to its name. The networks for $k = 2$ and $k = 3$ are shown in figure 1.

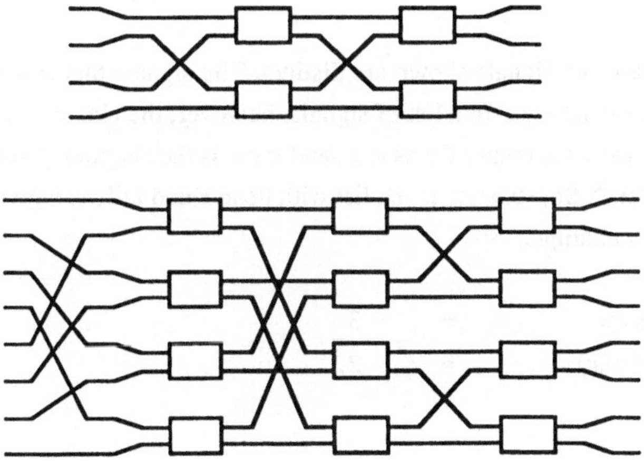

Figure 1 Butterfly networks

The butterfly network has two alternative recursive decompositions, as explained in section 4. The reader might like to find four different instances of a ($k = 2$) butterfly in the ($k = 3$) butterfly shown.

Butterfly cells can range from simple comparators to complex processors. Typical applications are sorting, Fast Fourier Transform [8,10] and the interconnection of processors and memories [11] or networks of processors. The butterfly is closely related to the Cube Connected Cycle and the hypercube, both of which have been used as the connection pattern in commercial supercomputers [12].

3 Ruby

3.1 Introduction

A Ruby circuit description is a binary relation between signals. For combinational circuits, we consider a signal to be a single data value. For sequential circuits, time must be taken into account, so signals correspond to streams of data values. Our design style has the nice property that circuit development is done in the same style for both combinational and sequential circuits. The algebraic laws about relations on data values are also true of relations on streams of data values. Thus, we use a transformational style whether we are designing sequential or combinational circuits. In this paper, we consider only combinational circuits (although the results apply equally well to sequential circuits).

A signal is atomic or is either a tuple or a list of signals. If *a*, *b* and *c* are signals, then the following are tuples of signals

(a) *(a,b)* *((a,b),c)* and *(a,b,c)*.

Note that the last two signals shown are distinct. The signals that make up a tuple need not all be of the same type. In a list of signals, however, the elements must all be of the same type. We write the empty list as < >, and *<x>* is the singleton list containing *x*. List append is written ^. So, *<x>^xs* is the list with head *x* and tail *xs*. # gives the length of a tuple or list. For example,

#<a,b,c>	=	3
#(<a,b>,c)	=	2.

3.2 Higher Order Functions for Circuit Construction

Circuit descriptions are built hierarchically, using higher order functions. Each higher order function has both a behavioural and a pictorial interpretation. By convention, circuits are drawn with their domain signal on the left and their range signal on the right. This matches the conventional use of

$$a \mathrm{R} b$$

for the assertion that the relation *R* relates the domain signal *a* to the range signal *b*.

Our first two higher order functions for constructing circuits are ordinary relational composition and relational inverse, defined in the usual way. ($\wedge$ is logical and.)

$$a \ (\mathrm{R} ; \mathrm{S}) \ c \quad =_{\mathrm{def}} \quad \exists b.\, a \mathrm{R} b \ \wedge \ b \mathrm{S} c$$
$$a \ (\mathrm{R}^{-1}) \ b \quad =_{\mathrm{def}} \quad b \mathrm{R} a$$

Composition is associative, so brackets can be omitted:

$$(\mathrm{R} ; \mathrm{S}) ; \mathrm{T} \quad = \quad \mathrm{R} ; (\mathrm{S} ; \mathrm{T}) \tag{1}$$

Note that $R ; R^{-1}$ is not, in general, the identity on the domain of R. Repeated composition is represented by the standard notation. For example, $R^3 = R ; R ; R$. The pictorial convention for relations causes *R ; S* to be drawn with *R* on the left, *S* on the right, and intermediate wires joined in the middle. For the same reason, relational inverse (the swapping of the domain and range) corresponds to flipping the circuit about a vertical axis. Flipping twice returns the circuit to its original position.

$$(\mathrm{R}^{-1})^{-1} \quad = \quad \mathrm{R} \tag{2}$$

The effect of flipping a composition is expressed by the equality

$$(\mathrm{R} ; \mathrm{S})^{-1} \quad = \quad \mathrm{S}^{-1} ; \mathrm{R}^{-1} \tag{3}$$

We reason about circuit behaviour by substituting equals for equals, using laws like this.

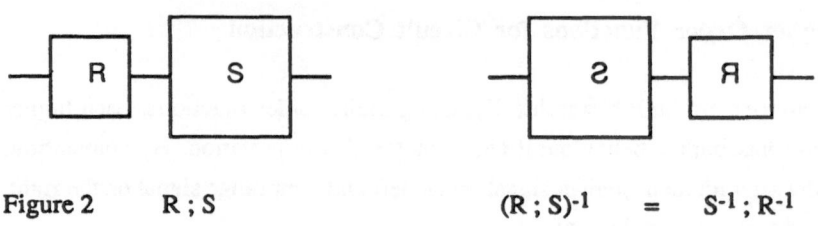

Figure 2 $R ; S$ $(R ; S)^{-1} = S^{-1} ; R^{-1}$

In the diagrams, the wires are abstract; they may carry compound signals. When the structure of a signal is known, this is indicated by the spacing between wires. So, for example, the elements of a list are equally spaced.

Our next higher order function, conjugate, is defined using composition and inverse.

$$R / S \quad =_{def} \quad R ; S ; R^{-1}$$

We prove two simple equalities about conjugate. The proofs of other algebraic laws are similar, except where indicated.

$$(R / S)^{-1} \quad = \quad R / (S^{-1}) \qquad (4)$$

Proof :

$(R / S)^{-1}$

= "def. /"

$(R ; S ; R^{-1})^{-1}$

= "by (1)"

$((R ; S) ; R^{-1})^{-1}$

= "by (3)"

$(R^{-1})^{-1} ; (R ; S)^{-1}$

= "by (2)"

$R ; (R ; S)^{-1}$

= "by (3)"

$R ; (S^{-1} ; R^{-1})$

= "by (1)"

$R ; S^{-1} ; R^{-1}$

= "def. /"

$R / (S^{-1})$ Q.E.D.

$$A / (R / S) \quad = \quad (A ; R) / S \qquad (5)$$

Proof:

$A / (R / S)$

$=$ "def. / twice"

$A ; (R ; S ; R^{-1}) ; A^{-1}$

$=$ "by (1)"

$(A ; R) ; S ; (R^{-1} ; A^{-1})$

$=$ "by (3)"

$(A ; R) ; S ; (A ; R)^{-1}$

$=$ "def. /"

$(A ; R) / S$ Q.E.D.

The identity on signals is written *id*. Some restricted identities are also useful. #n is the identity on lists of length n. For example, #1, the identity on singleton lists, is useful in recursive definitions (cf. section 3.4). We use restricted identites and conjugate together to restrict both the domain and range of a relation. For example, $\#2^k/R$ is the subrelation of *R* that relates a list of length 2^k to a list of length 2^k.

Circuits in which components operate independently on elements of a tuple of signals are described using the higher order function par. The parallel composition of two relations, *R* and *S*, is written [*R*, *S*]. The definition extends naturally to arbitrary tuples.

$$(a,b)\ [R, S]\ (c,d) \quad =_{def} \quad a\,R\,c \ \wedge\ b\,S\,d$$

Some properties of par are

$$[R, S] ; [T, V] \quad = \quad [R ; T,\ S ; V] \qquad (6)$$
$$[R, S]^{-1} \quad = \quad [R^{-1}, S^{-1}] \qquad (7)$$

Combining equations (6) and (7) gives

$$[B, C] / [R, S] \quad = \quad [B / R, C / S] \qquad (8)$$

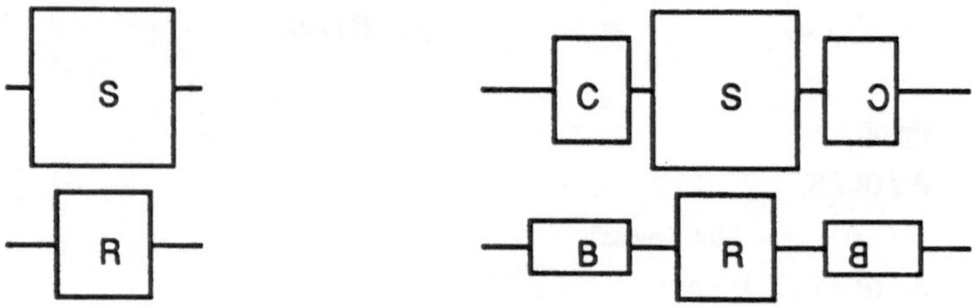

Figure 3 [R, S] [B, C] / [R, S] = [B / R, C / S]

Replication is introduced by the generic higher order function *map*. *Map R* replicates *R*, placing copies across a list of signals. It is generic in that it represents the class of circuits of this form. (Fig. 4 shows one representative of the class.) *Map R* is the smallest relation satisfying these constraints. We call a relation *homogeneous* if it relates only lists of equal length. The relation *map R* is always homogenous. (≡ is equality on predicates.)

$$\langle\rangle \;\; \text{map R} \;\; \langle\rangle$$
$$\langle a\rangle\hat{}\,as \;\; \text{map R} \;\; \langle b\rangle\hat{}\,bs \quad \equiv \quad a\,\text{R}\,b \;\wedge\; as\,(\text{map R})\,bs$$

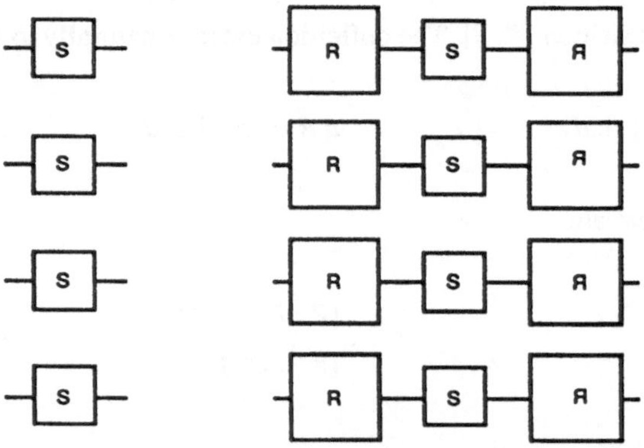

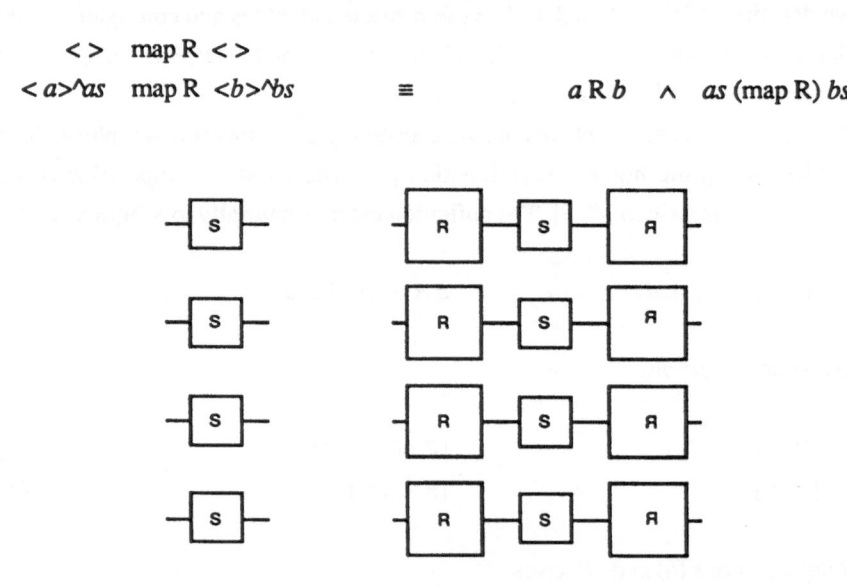

Figure 4 map S map R / map S = map (R / S)

The properties of map are similar to those of par.

$$(\text{map R})^{-1} \quad = \quad \text{map}\,(\text{R}^{-1}) \qquad (9)$$

$$(\text{map } R) \,/\, (\text{map } S) \quad = \quad \text{map } (R \,/\, S) \qquad (10)$$

Proof (by induction):

base case: $\langle\rangle\ (\text{map } R) / (\text{map } S)\ \langle\rangle$ "def. map, def. /, def. ;"

$\langle\rangle\ \text{map } (R / S)\ \langle\rangle$ "def. map"

step:

$\langle a\rangle \frown as\ \ (\text{map } R) / (\text{map } S)\ \ \langle b\rangle \frown bs$

$\equiv$ "def. /, def. ;, def. map"

$\exists c,cs,d,ds.\ \langle a\rangle \frown as\ (\text{map } R) \langle c\rangle \frown cs \ \wedge\ \langle c\rangle \frown cs\ (\text{map } S) \langle d\rangle \frown ds \ \wedge\ \langle d\rangle \frown ds\ (\text{map } R)^{-1} \langle b\rangle \frown bs$

$\equiv$ "def. map, by (9)"

$\exists c, d.\quad a\,R\,c \quad\wedge\quad c\,S\,d \quad\wedge\quad d\,R^{-1}\,b \quad\wedge$

$\exists cs, ds.\quad as\ (\text{map } R)\ cs \quad\wedge\quad cs\ (\text{map } S)\ ds \quad\wedge\quad ds\ (\text{map } R)^{-1}\ bs$

$\equiv$ "def. /, def. ;"

$a\,(R/S)\,b \quad\wedge\quad as\ (\text{map } R) / (\text{map } S)\ bs$

$\equiv$ "ind. hyp."

$a\,(R/S)\,b \quad\wedge\quad as\ \text{map } (R/S)\ bs$

$\equiv$ "def. map"

$\langle a\rangle \frown as\ \ \text{map } (R / S)\ \ \langle b\rangle \frown bs$ Q.E.D.

Ordinary relational union is useful, not as a circuit combining form, but as a way of building the relation for a single circuit. Thus, it does not have a pictorial interpretation. We use it in both recursive and iterative descriptions of circuits. ($\vee$ is logical or.)

$$a\,(R \dot{+} S)\,b \quad =_{\text{def}} \quad a\,R\,b \ \vee\ a\,S\,b$$

The higher order functions just defined (composition, inverse, conjugate, par, map and union) form the basis for this paper. A set of primitive circuits is assumed to be given. Depending on the application, these primitives might range from simple combinational gates to complex sequential components. For the sorter example, the only primitive needed is a comparator defined by

$$(a,b)\ \text{Cmp}\ (a,b) \quad , a \geq b$$
$$(a,b)\ \text{Cmp}\ (b,a) \quad , b \geq a$$

Here, we have assumed that *a* and *b* are just single numbers. If we wanted to deal with sequential circuits, *a* and *b* would have to be streams of numbers, and the comparator would have to operate pointwise on those streams. Even when we make this move to streams, the algebraic properties of the language are preserved. Thus, the techniques applied here to combinational circuits apply equally well to sequential ones. To preserve the algebraic properties of the language, the primitives must obey certain rules; they must exhibit a form of polymorphism. See [13] for further discussion of this point.

3.3 Quantifiers

It is useful to be able to compose a sequence of different but related circuits. For example, instead of R^4, we might want

R(0) ; R(1) ; R(2) ; R(3)

where each *R(i)* is possibly different. We do this by applying the quantifier ⨟ (corresponding to the binary combining form ;) to the indexed sequence of relations *‹R(0),R(1),R(2),R(3)›*. The shorthand for that sequence is *i<4.R(i)*. In general,

$$i{<}n.R(i) \quad =_{def} \quad \langle R(0),\ R(1),\ ..\ R(n-1)\rangle.$$

Here, *i* is a bound variable, while *n* is free and gives the number of elements in the sequence. Both *i* and *n* are natural numbers. We call a relation that does not depend on any parameters *closed*. We write

i.R(i)

for the unbounded sequence. The empty sequence is ‹ ›, and we append sequences using ^. Now, we can make quantifiers out of any of our binary combining forms in the same way as we make quantifiers from binary logical operators. Applying a quantifier to a sequence is the same as inserting the original combining form between elements of the sequence. If the sequence is empty, the result will be the identity of the combining form. We make quantifiers for relational composition and relational union. (Note that both composition and union are associative, so we could, if we wished, unwind the sequences from the other end.)

$$⨟\ \langle\ \rangle \quad =_{def} \quad id$$
$$⨟\ rs\ \hat{}\langle r\rangle \quad =_{def} \quad (⨟\ rs)\ ;\ r$$

example: $⨟\ i<4.R(i) = (⨟\ i<3.R(i))\ ;\ R(3)$
$= (⨟\ i<2.R(i))\ ;\ R(2)\ ;\ R(3)$
$= (⨟\ i<1.R(i))\ ;\ R(1)\ ;\ R(2)\ ;\ R(3)$
$= R(0)\ ;\ R(1)\ ;\ R(2)\ ;\ R(3)$

Strictly speaking, the fat composition should be labelled with a type. For example, if each *R(i)* is of type list of Integer to list of Integer (say) then fat compositon applied to the empty sequence is the identity on lists of Integers. Repeated composition is a special case of the heterogenous combinator. Here, *S* does not depend on *i*.

$$⨟\ i<n.S \quad = \quad S^n \qquad \text{(S closed)} \qquad (11)$$

Under certain conditions, we can cancel relations on internal arcs in a heterogeneous composition, converting it into a homogeneous one.

$$R^{-1}\ ;\ R^2 = R \quad \Rightarrow \quad ⨟\ i<k.(R^{i+1}/\ S) = (R\ ;\ S)^k\ ;\ R^{-k} \quad \text{(R,S closed)} \qquad (12)$$

The quantifier corresponding to relational union is Σ.

$$\Sigma \langle\ \rangle \quad =_{def} \quad \text{empty (the empty relation)}$$
$$\Sigma \langle r\rangle\text{^}rs \quad =_{def} \quad r + \Sigma\ rs$$

where + is relational union.

$$\Sigma k.R(k) \quad = \quad R(0) \ + \ \Sigma k.R(k+1) \qquad (13)$$

example: $\Sigma k.\#2^k = \#2^0 + \Sigma k.\#2^{k+1}$

$\Sigma k.\#2^k$ is the identity on lists whose length is a power of two, while $\Sigma k.\#2^{k+1}$ is the identity on lists whose length is 2^n for $n > 0$.

Because of the properties of relational union,

$$\Sigma i.S \quad = \quad S \qquad \text{(S closed)} \qquad (14)$$

Luk first introduced heterogeneous combinators in [7]. [2] discusses the algebraic properties and applications of these combinators.

3.4 Wiring Relations

The number of circuits that can be described using our small set of higher order functions is greatly increased by introducing some extra wiring relations. The relations *halve* and *pair* restructure a signal without affecting the component signals. *Halve* relates a list of even length to a pair containing the first and second halves of that list.

$$as \frown bs \ \text{halve}\ (cs, ds) \quad \equiv \quad \#as = \#bs \ \wedge \ as = cs \ \wedge \ bs = ds$$

example: $\langle 1,2,3,4,5,6,7,8\rangle$ halve $(\langle 1,2,3,4\rangle, \langle 5,6,7,8\rangle)$

We abbreviate a common use of *halve* and its repeated application.

$$R \mid S \quad =_{def} \quad \text{halve} / [R, S]$$
$$\text{two}^0\, R \quad =_{def} \quad R$$
$$\text{two}^{n+1}\, R \quad =_{def} \quad (\text{two}^n\, R) \mid (\text{two}^n\, R) \qquad (n \geq 0)$$

examples:

$$\text{two}\, R \quad = \quad R \mid R$$
$$\text{two}^3\, R \quad = \quad (\text{two}^2\, R) \mid (\text{two}^2\, R)$$
$$= \quad (\text{two}\, R \mid \text{two}\, R) \mid (\text{two}\, R \mid \text{two}\, R)$$
$$= \quad ((R \mid R) \mid (R \mid R)) \mid ((R \mid R) \mid (R \mid R))$$

$$\text{two}(\Sigma k.\#2^k) \quad = \quad (\Sigma k.\#2^k) \mid (\Sigma k.\#2^k)$$
$$= \quad \Sigma k.\#2^{k+1}$$

The relation *two R ; two S* is, in general, smaller than the relation *two(R ; S)*.

$$\text{two}\, R\, ;\, \text{two}\, S \quad \leq \quad \text{two}(R\, ;\, S) \qquad (15)$$

Consider

$$R \quad = \quad \{(\langle 1\rangle,\langle 1\rangle),(\langle 1\rangle,\langle 1,1\rangle)\}$$
$$S \quad = \quad \{(\langle 1\rangle,\langle 1\rangle),(\langle 1,1\rangle,\langle 2\rangle)\}$$
$$R\, ;\, S \quad = \quad \{(\langle 1\rangle,\langle 1\rangle),(\langle 1\rangle,\langle 2\rangle)\}$$
$$\text{two}\, R \quad = \quad \{(\langle 1,1\rangle,\langle 1,1\rangle),(\langle 1,1\rangle,\langle 1,1,1,1\rangle)\}$$
$$\text{two}\, S \quad = \quad \{(\langle 1,1\rangle,\langle 1,1\rangle),(\langle 1,1,1,1\rangle,\langle 2,2\rangle)\}$$
$$\text{two}\, R\, ;\, \text{two}\, S \quad = \quad \{(\langle 1,1\rangle,\langle 1,1\rangle),(\langle 1,1\rangle,\langle 2,2\rangle)\}$$
$$\text{two}(R\, ;\, S) \quad = \quad \{(\langle 1,1\rangle,\langle 1,1\rangle),(\langle 1,1\rangle,\langle 2,2\rangle),(\langle 1,1\rangle,\langle 1,2\rangle)\}$$

So,

$$\text{two } R \,;\, \text{two } S \quad < \quad \text{two}(R \,;\, S)$$

in this case. The strict equality does hold if at least one of *R* and *S* is homogeneous. In fact, many of the relations that we use are homogeneous, in which case we can exploit the fact that *two* distributes over composition.

$$⨾\, k<j.(\text{two } R(k)) \quad = \quad \text{two}(⨾\, k<j.R(k)) \quad (\forall k<j.R(k)\text{homogeneous}) \qquad (16)$$

Pair relates a list of length 2*n* to an *n*-list of pairs.

$$\langle\rangle \quad \text{pair} \quad \langle\rangle$$
$$\langle a1,a2\rangle\hat{}as \quad \text{pair} \quad \langle c\rangle\hat{}cs \quad \equiv \quad c = (a1,a2) \;\wedge\; as \text{ pair } cs$$

example: *<1,2,3,4,5,6,7,8>* pair *<(1,2),(3,4),(5,6),(7,8)>*

The *pair* conjugate of a *map* is a commonly used form. In *pmap R*, *R* must relate pairs to pairs.

$$\text{pmap } R \quad =_{\text{def}} \quad \text{pair} \,/\, (\text{map } R)$$

example: *<1,2,3,4,5,6,7,8>* pmap Cmp *<2,1,4,3,6,5,8,7>*

Note that *pmap Cmp* relates lists of integers of equal (even) length, while *map Cmp* relates equal length lists of pairs of integers.

The wiring relation *zip* is surprisingly useful. It is the special case of transposition that relates a pair of lists to a list of pairs. Unlike *halve* and *pair*, it corresponds to non-trivial wiring on the circuit. Again, it describes a class of circuits of varying sizes.

$$(\langle\rangle,\langle\rangle) \quad \text{zip} \quad \langle\rangle$$
$$(\langle a\rangle\hat{}as,\langle b\rangle\hat{}bs) \quad \text{zip} \quad \langle c\rangle\hat{}cs \quad \equiv \quad c = (a,b) \;\wedge\; (as,bs) \text{ zip } cs$$

example: *(<1,2,3,4>,<5,6,7,8>)* zip *<(1,5),(2,6),(3,7),(4,8)>*

$$\text{zip}^{-1} \,/\, [\text{map } R, \text{map } S] \quad = \quad \text{map } [R, S] \qquad (17)$$

The proof is by induction and is similar to the proof of equation (10). The diagram, of necessity, shows an instance of equation (17) corresponding to a particular size of domain and range. Note how the grouping of wires gives an indication of the structure of signals. The domain and range (of each circuit) is a 4-list of pairs. The domain and range of the subcircuit [*map R*, *map S*] is a pair of 4-lists; the two groups of 4 wires are separated to indicate this.

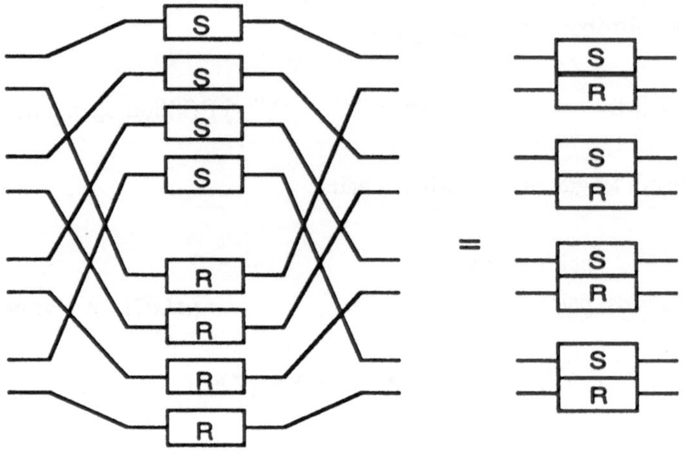

Figure 5 $\quad zip^{-1}$ / [map R, map S] $\quad = \quad$ map [R, S]

Consider a deck of cards. It can be riffled by dividing in half, interleaving to give 26 pairs, and then unpairing. Surprisingly, this operation (which is sometimes called the perfect shuffle) is often used in circuits. *Riffle*, a standard operation on lists, can be described using *halve*, *zip* and *pair*.

$$\text{riffle} \quad =_{def} \quad \text{halve ; zip ; pair}^{-1}$$

The relation riffle is homogeneous, and operates on even length lists.

$$\Sigma k.(\#2k \,/\, \text{riffle}) \quad = \quad \text{riffle} \qquad (18)$$

A common operation is the *riffle* conjugate of *pmap R*. Butterfly networks are built from this component.

$$\text{rpmap R} \quad =_{def} \quad \text{riffle} \,/\, (\text{pmap R})$$

Note that the *riffle* conjugate of a *map* has the same behaviour as the *map* itself, but operating on even length lists only.

$$\text{riffle} \,/\, (\text{map R}) \quad = \quad (\Sigma k.\#2k) \,/\, (\text{map R}) \qquad (19)$$

For lists of length 2^n, *riffle*^{n} is the identity.

$$\Sigma n.(\#2^n / \mathrm{riffle}^n) \quad = \quad \Sigma n.(\#2^n / \#2^n) \tag{20}$$

Informally, this equality is proved by noticing that for lists of length 2^n, riffling corresponds to a cyclic shift of the binary representation of the index of the list. So, for example, for 8-lists, element number 0 stays at position 0, but element number 3, say, moves to position 6, since shift(011) = 110. Clearly, *shift*^{n} is the identity on a binary number of length *n*. The inverse of *riffle* corresponds to a cyclic shift in the other direction, so

$$\Sigma n.(\#2^n / (\mathrm{riffle} \,;\, \mathrm{riffle}^{-1})) \quad = \quad \Sigma n.(\#2^n / \#2^n) \tag{21}$$

and

$$\Sigma n.(\#2^n / (\mathrm{riffle}^{-1} \,;\, \mathrm{riffle})) \quad = \quad \Sigma n.(\#2^n / \#2^n) \tag{22}$$

On lists whose length is a power of two, the relation *pmap R* relates by *R* those pairs of elements whose indices differ in the least significant bit, while *rpmap R* relates by *R* those pairs of elements whose indices differ in the most significant bit. By a similar argument, we can show that

$$i{<}n.(\#2^n / (\mathrm{riffle}^i / \mathrm{rpmap}\ R)) \quad = \quad i{<}n.(\#2^n / \mathrm{two}^i(\mathrm{rpmap}\ R)) \tag{23}$$

Here, we are asserting the equality of two sequences of relations. The following two equalites are consequences of equation (23).

$$i{<}n.(\#2^{n+1} / (\mathrm{riffle}^{i+1} / \mathrm{rpmap}\ R)) \quad = \quad i{<}n.(\#2^{n+1} / \mathrm{two}(\mathrm{riffle}^i / \mathrm{rpmap}\ R)) \tag{24}$$

$$i{<}n.(\#2^{n+1} / (\mathrm{riffle}^i / \mathrm{rpmap}\ R)) \quad = \quad i{<}n.(\#2^{n+1} / (\mathrm{riffle}^{-1} / \mathrm{two}(\mathrm{riffle}^i / \mathrm{rpmap}\ R))) \tag{25}$$

These informal appeals to the binary representation of indices are unattractive. We would like to avoid or at least minimise them. The key to this seems to be the choice of appropriate higher order functions. We hope to report on that work in a later paper.

The language introduced so far, with its higher order functions, primitives and wiring relations, is quite powerful. It can describe many standard circuits. However, its expressive power (and usefulness) is greatly increased by the addition of a simple form of recursion.

3.5 Recursion

A relation is defined inductively by a set of equations. The relation defined is the least one satisfying the equations. For example, a tree-shaped higher order function is defined as

$$\text{tree } F \;=_{def}\; \#1 \;+\; F\,;\,\text{two(tree } F)$$

Unwinding the recursion gives

$$\begin{aligned}\text{tree } F \;=\; \#1 \;&+\; F\,;\,\text{two } \#1\\ &+\; F\,;\,\text{two}(F\,;\,\text{two } \#1)\\ &+\; F\,;\,\text{two}(F\,;\,\text{two}(F\,;\,\text{two } \#1))\\ &+\; \ldots\end{aligned}$$

For homogeneous *F*, we can rewrite this description of the tree as

$$\begin{aligned}\text{tree } F \;=\; \#2^0 \;&+\; \#2^1 / F\\ &+\; \#2^2 / (F\,;\,\text{two } F)\\ &+\; \#2^3 / (F\,;\,\text{two } F\,;\,\text{two}^2 F)\\ &+\; \ldots\end{aligned}$$

giving an iterative view of the tree.

$$\text{tree } F \;=\; \Sigma k.(\#2^k / (\text{;}\, i{<}k.\text{two}^i F)) \qquad \text{(F homogeneous) (26)}$$

Because *two*^{i} *F* is homogeneous, we can also conjugate each rank.

$$\text{tree } F \;=\; \Sigma k.\,(\#2^k / (\text{;}\, i{<}k.(\#2^k / \text{two}^i F))) \qquad \text{(F homogeneous) (27)}$$

4 Butterfly Networks in Ruby

A butterfly network has more than one recursive decomposition; this is one of the reasons why butterfly networks are interesting. First, the definition of a binary butterfly network is given. Then, several alternative descriptions are derived, using the laws. It is assumed that *F* relates pairs to pairs. Note that *map F*, *pmap F* and *rpmap F* are all homogeneous.

4.1 The Butterfly Network as a Tree

A binary butterfly network is a tree of generic components.

$$»« F \quad =_{def} \quad \text{tree (rpmap F)}$$

Since *rpmap F* is homogeneous, we can also use iterative descriptions of *tree* ((26),(27)).

$$»« F \quad = \quad \Sigma k.(\#2^k/ (⨾\ i<k.two^i(\text{rpmap F}))) \qquad (28)$$

$$»« F \quad = \quad \Sigma k.(\#2^k/ (⨾\ i<k.(\#2^k/ two^i(\text{rpmap F})))) \qquad (29)$$

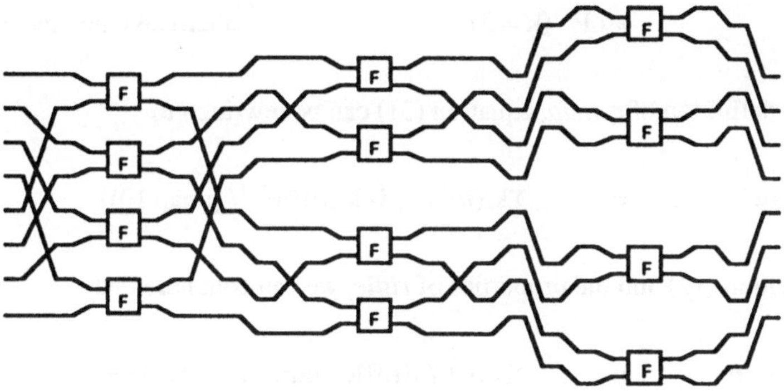

$\#8/ (two^0(\text{rpmap F}) \;;\; two^1(\text{rpmap F}) \;;\; two^2(\text{rpmap F}))$

Figure 6 »« F (k = 3) butterfly as tree

4.2 Other iterative views of the butterfly

Now, equation (23) is directly applicable to the sequence of relations to which ⨾ is applied in equation (29). This gives a different iterative description.

$$»« F \quad = \quad \Sigma k.(\#2^k/ (⨾\ i<k.(\#2^k/ (riffle^i/ \text{rpmap F})))) \qquad (30)$$

Again, because each rank is homogeneous, the conjugation of each rank can be removed.

$$»« F \quad = \quad \Sigma k.(\#2^k/ (⨾\ i<k.(riffle^i/ \text{rpmap F}))) \qquad (31)$$

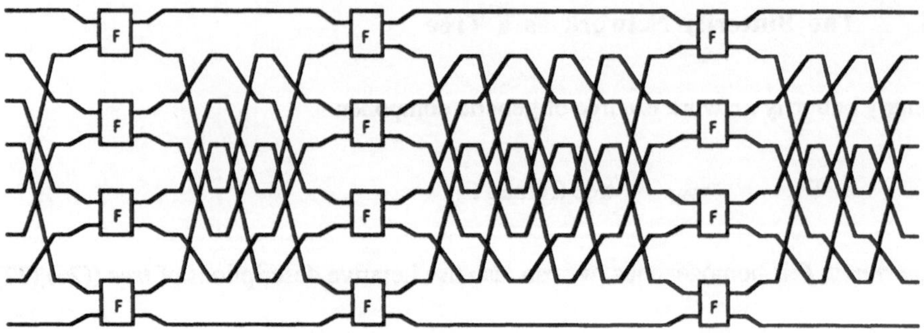

#8/ ($riffle^0$ / rpmap F ; $riffle^1$ / rpmap F ; $riffle^2$ / rpmap F) =
#8/ (riffle ; pmap F ; $riffle^{-1}$; $riffle^2$; pmap F ; $riffle^{-2}$; $riffle^3$; pmap F ; $riffle^{-3}$)

Figure 7 »« F (k = 3) alternative iterative view

Using the definition of *rpmap*, equation (31) can be rewritten to

$$»« F = \Sigma k.(\#2^k/ (⨾\ i<k.(riffle^{i+1}/\ pmap\ F))) \quad (32)$$

From equation (12) and the properties of *riffle*, we can conclude that

$$»« F = \Sigma k.(\#2^k/ ((riffle\ ;\ pmap\ F)^k\ ;\ riffle^{-k}))$$
$$= \Sigma k.(\#2^k/ (riffle\ ;\ pmap\ F)^k) \quad (33)$$

Thus, the buttefly and shuffle-exchange networks are equivalent.

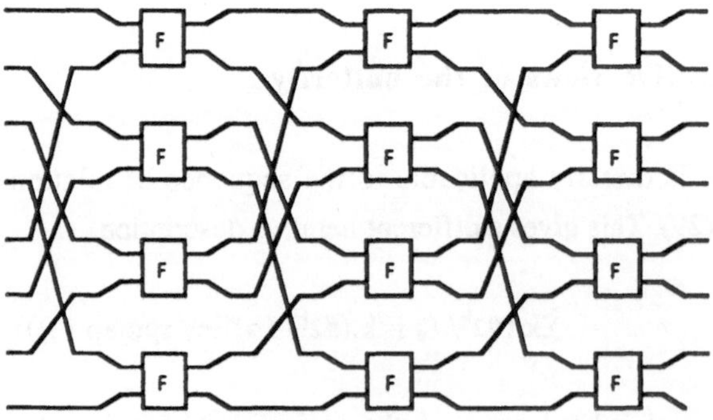

#8/ (riffle ; pmap F ; riffle ; pmap F ; riffle ; pmap F)

Figure 8 »« F (k = 3) butterfly as shuffle network

In some contexts, the shuffle network might be preferable, either because of its more regular layout or because it is more easily rolled up, so that a single piece of hardware can be thought of as serving as each rank in turn (cf. [11] for an interesting case study of the design of these types of network).

4.3 Recursive Views of the Butterfly

Unwinding the definition of tree gives us a recursive view of the butterfly.

$$\text{»« } F \quad = \quad \#1 \;+\; \text{rpmap } F \,;\, \text{two(»« } F) \qquad (34)$$

Fig. 9 illustrates this first recursive description for k = 3 (8 signals in domain and range). The outlined circuits are recursive calls of the butterfly.

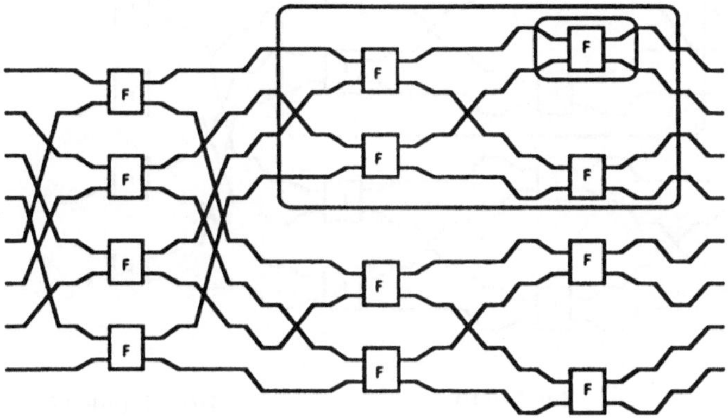

rpmap F ; two(»« F)

Figure 9 »« F (k = 3) recursive view

We can use the iterative descriptions to derive an alternative recursive decomposition.

»« F

= "by (31)"

$\Sigma k.(\#2^k/ (\fatsemi\ i<k.(\text{riffle}^i/ \text{ rpmap } F)))$

= "unwinding Σ"

$\Sigma k.(\#2^{k+1}/ (\fatsemi\ i<k+1.(\text{riffle}^i/ \text{ rpmap } F))) \quad + \quad \#2^0$

= "unwinding ⨾ from right"

$\Sigma k.(\#2^{k+1}/ ((\fatsemi\ i<k.(\text{riffle}^i/ \text{ rpmap } F)) \,;\, (\text{riffle}^{k+1}/ \text{ pmap } F))) \quad + \quad \#1$

= "homogeneity of riffle^i/ rpmap F, pmap F, (20)"

$$\Sigma k.(\#2^{k+1}/ (\fatsemi\ i<k.(\#2^{k+1}/ (\text{riffle}^{i}/ \text{rpmap } F))))\ ;\ \text{pmap } F \quad + \quad \#1$$

$=$ "by (25)"

$$\Sigma k.(\#2^{k+1}/ (\fatsemi\ i<k.(\#2^{k+1}/ (\text{riffle}^{-1}/ \text{two}(\text{riffle}^{i}/ \text{rpmap } F)))))\ ;\ \text{pmap } F\ +\ \#1$$

$=$ "homogeneity of riffle, properties of two"

$$\Sigma k.(\#2^{k+1}/ (\fatsemi\ i<k.(\text{riffle}^{-1}/ \text{two}(\text{riffle}^{i}/ \text{rpmap } F))))\ ;\ \text{pmap } F \quad + \quad \#1$$

$=$ "homogeneity of riffle, properties of two"

$$\text{riffle}^{-1}/ \text{two}(\Sigma k.(\#2^{k}/ (\fatsemi\ i<k.(\text{riffle}^{i}/ \text{rpmap } F))))\ ;\ \text{pmap } F \quad + \quad \#1$$

$=$ "by (31)"

$$\#1 \quad + \quad \text{riffle}^{-1}/ \text{two}(\text{»« } F)\ ;\ \text{pmap } F$$

$$\text{»« } F \quad = \quad \#1 \quad + \quad \text{riffle}^{-1}/ \text{two}(\text{»« } F)\ ;\ \text{pmap } F \qquad (35)$$

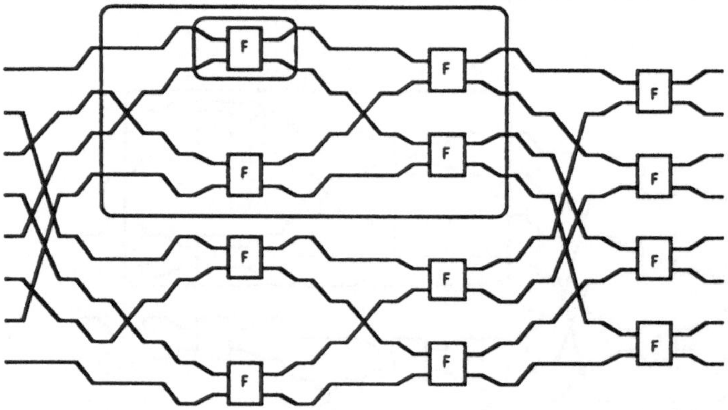

riffle^{-1}; two(»« F) ; riffle ; pmap F

Figure 10 »« F (k = 3) alternative recursive view

Having several alternative descriptions should make this mapping algorithms onto this network easier. In fact, the butterfly has several other recursive decompositions, though we will not discuss them here.

5 Example: a Sorting Network

Problem: design a sorter (into decreasing order) based on a simple comparator *Cmp*.

(a,b) Cmp *(a,b)* , $a \geq b$

(a,b) Cmp *(b,a)* , $b \geq a$

We should first check that we have not already unknowingly solved the problem. Is *»«Cmp* a sorter? For a given sequence (of length 2^n), *»«Cmp* can sort some, but in general not all, of its permutations. For example, it can sort the sequence <0,0,1,1>

<0,0,1,1> »« Cmp <1,1,0,0>

but it cannot sort the sequence <0,1,0,1>.

<0,1,0,1> »« Cmp <0,1,0,1>

One can prove by induction that *»«Cmp* sorts both increasing and decreasing sequences. It was Batcher who noticed that it can sort many other sequences [14]. The sequences that can be sorted by *»«Cmp* are called bitonic. To make a sorter, we need only work out how to permute an input sequence into *some* bitonic sequence, which can then be sorted by *»«Cmp*. Most of the bitonic sequences are of no interest to us. How do we choose a suitable form of bitonic sequence? The key is to use recursion. It would be best to use recursive calls of (smaller versions of) the entire sorter. The most obvious divide and conquer strategy doesn't work. A sequence consisting of two halves, each of which is sorted into decreasing order is *not* in general bitonic.

Batcher had a flash of inspiration that overcomes this stumbling block; a sequence whose halves are sorted into *opposite* orders (a *dec-inc* sequence) *is* bitonic [14]. This is the eureka step that gives rise to a classic algorithm. First, we define the identity on dec-inc sequences (of length 2^n, $n \geq 0$) in terms of *dec*, the identity on decreasing sequences. (*Rev* is the relation that reverses a sequence, so *inc* = *rev / dec* is the identity on increasing sequences.)

$$\text{dec-inc} \quad =_{def} \quad \#1 \quad + \quad (\text{dec} \mid \text{inc})$$

We must show that a dec-inc sequence is related by *»«Cmp* to its sorted permutation and to no other value. That is

dec-inc ; »« Cmp = dec-inc ; »« Cmp ; dec

The proof is by induction. We give its outline only.

Base case: the relations *dec-inc*, *»«Cmp* and *dec* all have #1 as their base cases, and

#1 ; #1 = #1 ; #1 ; #1

Step:
Notice that if we take a dec-inc sequence of length at least two, and unriffle it, we get two dec-inc sequences.

$$(\text{dec} \mid \text{inc}) ; \text{riffle}^{-1} \quad = \quad (\text{dec} \mid \text{inc}) ; \text{riffle}^{-1}; \text{two dec-inc} \tag{36}$$

By the inductive hypothesis, we can sort each of these sequences using »«*Cmp*.

$$(\text{dec} \mid \text{inc}) ; \text{riffle}^{-1}; \text{two}(\text{»« Cmp}) = (\text{dec} \mid \text{inc}) ; \text{riffle}^{-1}; \text{two}(\text{»« Cmp}) ; \text{two dec} \tag{37}$$

Moreover, we can permute the two appended decreasing sequences into a single sorted sequence simply by riffling and then exchanging adjacent elements if they are out of order.

$$\begin{aligned}&(\text{dec} \mid \text{inc}) ; \text{riffle}^{-1}; \text{two}(\text{»« Cmp}) ; \text{riffle} ; \text{pmap Cmp} \quad = \\ &(\text{dec} \mid \text{inc}) ; \text{riffle}^{-1}; \text{two}(\text{»« Cmp}) ; \text{riffle} ; \text{pmap Cmp} ; \text{dec}\end{aligned} \tag{38}$$

This assertion must be proved by using the properties of increasing and decreasing sequences. Examples of such proofs are given in [8]. The point to notice is that if the elements of a dec-inc sequence are coloured alternately red and blue, then the two smallest elements of the sequence must be coloured one red and one blue. They cannot be the same colour. Similarly, the next two largest elements must be one red and one blue, and so on. (Drawing he V-shaped graph of a dec-inc sequence should convince you of this.) So, the way to sort such a dec-inc sequence is to sort the red and blue parts (recursively), interleave the results, and exchange those red-blue pairs that are out of order. Equation (38) is a more precise way of saying this. Using equation (35), it can be rewritten to

$$(\text{dec} \mid \text{inc}) ; \text{»« Cmp} \quad = \quad (\text{dec} \mid \text{inc}) ; \text{»« Cmp} ; \text{dec} \tag{39}$$

From this and the base case, we can conclude that

$$\text{dec-inc} ; \text{»« Cmp} \quad = \quad \text{dec-inc} ; \text{»« Cmp} ; \text{dec} \tag{40}$$

To make a sorter, we need only work out how to permute an input sequence into a dec-inc one. So, we have reduced the problem to the design of *make-dec-inc* in

$$\text{sort} \quad =_{\text{def}} \quad \text{make-dec-inc} ; \text{»« Cmp}$$

The obvious way to make a dec-inc sequence is to make two recursive calls of the sorter. A sorter into increasing order is (literally) made by flipping a sorter into decreasing order about a horizontal axis. The definition of flip is left as an exercise.

$$\text{make-dec-inc} \quad =_{def} \quad \#1 \quad + \quad (\text{sort} \mid \text{flip(sort)})$$

The bitonic sorter has been much studied (cf. [15] for example). The point of this paper is not the algorithm itself but the way in which it has been presented using a notation that is both concise and easy to read. Algorithms like this are often explained using an imperative language with standard control structures. We find such explanations hard to understand. Our notation has the advantage that it is well suited to program transformation, which is a very powerful tool in circuit and algorithm design.

6 Discussion and Conclusions

Previous work on μFP and Ruby has concentrated on the design of regular array algorithms [1,3,4,5,6,7,9]. This paper extends the range of the calculus to "high wire area" networks. Algorithms for such networks have often been poorly described in the literature. Operational descriptions of the form "processor i in rank j does operation k at time t" fail to capture the essence of an algorithm. In particular, they lose sight of the beautiful recursive structure of many of these algorithms. (Note that the bitonic sorter uses recursion within the butterfly as well as direct recursive calls of sort.) Software designers use recursion as a matter of course. We think that hardware designers will come to use it more and more to develop, prove and present algorithms. It is very noticeable that that our recursive circuit descriptions look much nicer than our iterative ones. It is difficult to see how this could be avoided, as the iterative descriptions usually need bound variables, which clutter up the expressions. Certainly, more work needs to be done on the choice of notation.

In section 5, we simply presented a well known algorithm, pulling the eureka step out of a hat. We have not *derived* the algorithm from a specification. A derivation would be much more convincing, and we hope to produce one eventually. The most impressive work in this area is Geraint Jones' derivation of the fast Fourier transform by program transformation of the discrete Fourier transform [10].

Applications for which Ruby is suitable are characterised by a close relationship between structure and behaviour. However, with the advent of multiprocessors, algorithms with particular structures have become relevant to software designers. The distinction between hardware and software is becoming blurred. Although the basic cell used in the example is a combinational comparator, the techniques used would work equally well with more complicated sequential cells.

Related work can be found in [16,17]. Although Bird and Meertens design software algorithms (and use a notation that is even more concise than ours) the two approaches are similar in spirit. Work on the Bird-Meertens calculus provides a foundation for this kind of transformational approach.

Acknowledgements

This is a revised version of a paper that appeared as 'Describing Hardware Algorithms in Ruby' in Proc. IFIP TC10/WG10.1 Workshop on Concepts and Characteristics of Declarative Systems (David et al. eds.), North-Holland, 1989. Both the presentation and the notation have changed considerably; this paper supercedes the earlier one. Many thanks to Geraint Jones for help and support. Thanks to Wayne Luk, David Murphy and Simon Peyton Jones for their detailed comments.

This research is supported by SERC grant # GR/F 28939 (Relational Programming) and by SERC/IED grant # IED2/1/1759 (High Performance VLSI DSP Architectures). I gratefully acknowledge the support of a Royal Society of Edinburgh BP Research Fellowship.

References

1. Jones G, Luk W. Exploring designs by circuit transformation. In: Moore W, McCabe A, Urquhart R (eds.) *Systolic Arrays*. Adam Hilger, Bristol, 1986, pp. 91-98.

2. Luk W. Specifying and Developing Regular Heterogeneous Designs. In: Claesen LJM (ed) *Applied Formal Methods for Correct VLSI Design*. North-Holland, 1989.

3. Luk W, Jones G. The derivation of regular synchronous circuits. In: Bromley K, Kung SY, Schwartzlander (eds.) *Proc. Int. Conf. on Systolic Arrays*. IEEE Computer Society Press, 1988, pp. 305-314.

4. Luk W, Jones G. From specification to parametrised architectures. In: Milne GJ (ed.) *The fusion of hardware design and verification*. North-Holland, 1988, pp. 267-288.

5. Sheeran M. Designing Regular Array Architectures using Higher Order Functions. In: Jouannaud J-P (ed.) *Functional Programming Languages and Computer Architecture*, LNCS 201, Springer-Verlag, 1985, pp. 220-237.

6. Sheeran M. Retiming and Slowdown in Ruby. In: Milne GJ (ed.) *The fusion of hardware design and verification*. North-Holland, 1988, pp. 289-308.

7. Luk W. *Parametrised design for regular processor arrays*. D.Phil Thesis, Oxford University, Programming Research Group, Oxford, 1988.

8. Ullman JD. *Computational Aspects of VLSI*. Computer Science Press, 1984.

9. Sheeran M. Ruby - a language of relations and higher-order functions. In: Birtwistle G (ed.) *Proc. 3rd Banff workshop on hardware verification*. Springer-Verlag, to appear 1990.

10. Jones G. Deriving the fast Fourier algorithm by calculation. In: *Proc. Glasgow workshop on Functional Programming*, Springer-Verlag, 1990.

11. Weste N, Eshraghian K. *Principles of CMOS VLSI Design: A Systems Perspective*. Addison-Wesley, 1985.

12. Stone HS. *High-Performance Computer Architecture*. Addison-Wesley, 1987.

13. Jones G, Sheeran M. Timeless Truths about Sequential Circuits. In: Tewksbury SK, Dickinson BW, Schwartz SC (eds.) *Concurrent Computations: Algorithms, Architecture and Technology* . Plenum Press, New York, 1988, pp. 245-259.

14. Batcher KE. Sorting Networks and their Applications. In: *Proc. Spring Joint Computer Conference*, AFIPS, vol. 32, 1968.

15. Stone HS. Parallel Processing with the Perfect Shuffle. *IEEE Trans.Comp*. Vol. C-20, No. 2, 1971.

16. Bird RS. *Lectures on constructive functional programming*. Oxford University Computing Laboratory Programming Research Group technical monograph PRG-69, 1988.

17. Meertens LGLT. Constructing a Calculus of Programs. In: van de Snepscheut (ed.) Mathematics of Program Construction. LNCS 375, Springer-Verlag, 1989.

Implementation of a Non-Standard Interpretation System

Satnam Singh
The University of Glasgow

Abstract

Non-standard interpretation is used to describe and implement three interpretations of an example circuit to yield type checking and testability information. An implementation of a non-standard interpretation system which supports interpretations for testability analysis is described. Comparisons are made with an imperative implementation and it is shown that this technique allows prototype analysers to be constructed quickly.

1 Introduction

Abstract interpretation of functional programs has been exploited to obtain information from the syntactic structure which is then used to improve the execution speed of these programs. A generalisation of this technique, called *non-standard interpretation* is used here to analyse hardware descriptions. A non-standard interpretation system for a subset of the Ruby hardware description language has been implemented. This system supports various interpretations including simulation, type checking and testability analyses.

The primary role of a hardware description language is to describe a circuit's behaviour, so its syntax and semantics are in a convenient form for simulation. However, it is possible to place other interpretations on the source language text. Non-standard interpretation involves replacing the circuit primitives that describe the behaviour of the circuit (the *standard interpretation*) by other definitions. When the description is executed with suitably chosen alternative primitives and non-standard values, more information about the circuit may be obtained. For example, if each primitive were replaced by a delay and joins of wires were replaced by a primitive taking the longest delay, then running the circuit description would yield a function computing the longest delay at each output.

Ruby [1] is employed as an example of a relational hardware description language. Only a small subset of the language is used here to demonstrate non-standard interpretation. It is shown that relational languages can express more algorithms as simple non-standard interpretations than functional languages. The key feature which makes this possible is the bidirectional nature of the information flow in relational languages. We shall be concerned only with combinational circuits in this paper, so the sequential primitive D is omitted and feedback loops are not considered.

A non-standard interpretation system for analysing Ruby style descriptions has been implemented. At the core of the system are two interpreters for performing forward and backward (unidirectional) analyses of circuits. It is shown that it is possible to decompose some bidirectional (relational) analyses into several unidirectional (functional) analyses thus enabling a functional language to be used for the implementation. This is advantageous since executing an interpretation in some relational or logic style language like PROLOG is slower than using a functional language.

The forward and backward core interpreters are paramerterised on the behaviour of the nodes in the circuit. Different behaviours yield different (non-standard) interpretations for performing circuit analyses. The interpretation of the combining forms and wiring primitives are fixed for each core interpreter so they do not have to be respecified.

The technique also allows quick implementation of prototype analysers. The method does not require the circuit to be respecified in some other form. The possibility of inconsistency between different circuit descriptions is now avoided since only one description is employed for many analyses. This technique also allows analysis algorithms which are difficult to understand to be expressed more elegantly since they concentrate on what is happening at the nodes and nets and abstract away from how information is propagated through the wires.

2 Introduction to Ruby

2.1 A Ruby Subset

Ruby is a powerful hardware description language which allows regular synchronous circuits to be represented and manipulated easily. To demonstrate non-standard interpretation requires only a small subset of the language. A more detailed description of Ruby is available in [1].

Ruby models circuit primitives by relations between streams. Using streams, i.e. infinite sequence of values, allows sequential behaviour to be modelled elegantly [2]. Composite values may be constructed by tupling e.g. $(a, b, (c, d))$ is a tuple with three elements: a, b and the tuple (c, d) in that order. Signals are homogeneous streams of such data values: the nth value of s is denoted by $s(n)$. Construction of signals is denoted by angle $<>$ brackets and concatenation by $\hat{}$.

$$\begin{aligned} < a, b, < c, d >> (t) &= (a(t), b(t), (c(t), d(t))) \\ < a, b >\hat{}< c, d > &= < a, b, c, d > \\ <>\hat{}a &= a \\ < a, b >\hat{}<< c, d >> &= < a, b, < c, d >> \end{aligned}$$

In order to describe the types of signals, two type declarations are introduced. First, let *logic* be the type of the value carried by a single wire. Groups of wires are described by tupling and a *signal* is either a single wire or a tuple of wires:

$$signal := logic \mid < signal, \ldots, signal >$$

Ruby models circuits using predicates of the form $a\,R\,b$ where a is in the domain and b is in the range. The primitive gates have the following standard interpretations for behaviour:

$$\begin{array}{ll} x\ NOT\ y & \Leftrightarrow \forall t.\ y(t) = \overline{x(t)} \\ <a,b>\ AND\ c & \Leftrightarrow \forall t.\ c(t) = a(t) \wedge b(t) \\ <a,b>\ OR\ c & \Leftrightarrow \forall t.\ c(t) = a(t) \vee b(t) \end{array}$$

Primitive circuits are combined by using various combining forms. These are summarised below:

$$\begin{array}{lll} a\ F;G\ c & =_{def} \exists b.\ (a\ F\ b)\ \&\ (b\ G\ c) & \text{Serial Composition} \\ <a,b>\ [F,G]\ <c,d> & =_{def} (a\ F\ c)\ \&\ (b\ G\ d) & \text{Parallel Composition} \\ a\ fork\ <a,a> & =_{def} true & \text{Fork} \\ x\ id\ x & =_{def} true & \text{Identity relation} \end{array}$$

Serial composition binds more strongly than parallel composition. Ruby has many other combining forms and is suitable for describing hardware at a more abstract level than combinational gates.

The subset defined above is not currently implemented by a true relational (bidirectional) interpreter. Instead, two interpretations exist to model unidirectional information flow. One interpreter considers data flow from the inputs to the outputs (a *forward* interpretation) and the other models information flow from the outputs to the inputs (a *backward* interpreter). A forward interpretation of the standard subset Ruby semantics is identical to treating Ruby as if it were a functional hardware description language.

Sometimes considering Ruby to be a functional language (i.e. constraining the information to flow in the forward direction) is powerful enough and the forward interpretation may be used for this. For example, simulation, hazard detection and deductive fault simulation may be expressed by a forward interpretation. However, other analyses require more complex information flow e.g. SCOAP [5] testability measure. By combining forward and backward interpretations appropriately, more elaborate interpretations may be expressed. Expressing a bidirectional interpretation like SCOAP in terms of smaller unidirectional interpretations allows a more efficient implementation. The bidirectional interpretation requires a full relational backtracking system whereas the unidirectional interpretations may be implemented in a functional framework.

The interpretations presented in this paper, along with many others, have been implemented in Miranda [1] as part of a non-standard interpretation system which also include presentation functions and a parser for the subset given above.

2.2 An example circuit in Ruby

The circuit in Figure 1 is used to illustrate the interpretations presented later. Since it is often necessary to refer to particular instances of gates and internal wires (which are referred to by the gate that drives them) a method for uniquely identifying nodes is required. Rather than requiring Ruby expression to be annotated, the interpretation system automatically labels the nodes of circuits. A Ruby description of the demonstration circuit is given below.

$$[id, NOT; fork, id]; reorgl; [AND, OR]; AND$$
$$<a, <b,c>, d>\ reorgl\ << a,b>, <c,d>>$$

[1] Miranda is a trademark of Research Software Ltd.

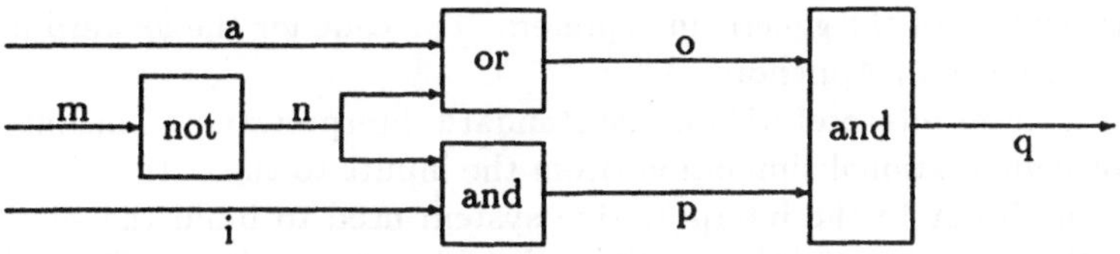

Figure 1: Demonstration circuit.

The result type of the expression to the left of *reorgl* is

$$< logic, < logic, logic >, logic >$$

and input type of the expression to the right of the *reorgl* is

$$<< logic, logic >, < logic, logic >>$$

The purpose of *reorgl* is to perform rewiring (restructuring a tuple) in order to facilitate serial composition.

2.3 Representing Signals

All the primitives in the implementation are defined over a data type, called `data` which describes Ruby style signals. It is defined as follows:

```
data * ::= ATOMIC * | TUPLE [data *] | Error [char]
```

The input to and output from a circuit or subcircuit is either some atomic entity e.g. a single logic value in simulation, represented by the `ATOMIC` constructor or a tuple of such values represented by the `TUPLE` constructor. An additional constructor `Error` is used by the interpretation system to help produce error messages.

This type is paramterised to allow circuits to take different types of input for various interpretations. For example, the standard interpretation associates logic values with wires, so the type of the forward and backward functions is `data logic -> data logic`. Here, `logic` is a type used to describe logic values. The type `logic` is defined as follows:

```
logic ::= L | H | U
```

A three-valued model is used: `L` for low, `H` for high and `U` for undefined values.

If *a*, *b*, *c* and *d* are values of the same type, then the Ruby signal $<< a, b >, c, d >$ is represented as:

```
TUPLE [TUPLE[ATOMIC a, ATOMIC b]], ATOMIC c, ATOMIC d]
```

2.4 The Combinational Interpretation

The interpretation system provides templates for performing forwards and backwards analyses. All the interpretations in this paper are implemented by using one or more instantiation of the generic interpreters. The code for the forward interpretation system is given in Appendix A.

The most natural interpretation is the standard interpretation. This interpretation performs combinational simulation (from the inputs to the outputs) of a Ruby expression. The input to the interpretation system used to build the simulator is given below. Some lines containing compiler directives are omitted. The definitions of the wiring functions are 'hardwired' because they tend not to vary from one interpretation to the other. Only the interpretations for the three logic gates have to be given. The type of the information carried by the wires is also given to the interpretation system (`logic` in this case). The labelling information for each gate is made available by the interpretation system through the first parameter of the defining function. The labels are represented by numbers and are used by interpretations that need to pass on information about internal nodes and wires.

```
> not_fn n x = log_not x
> and_fn n x y = log_and x y
> or_fn n x y = log_or x y

> log_and x y
>   = U, if (x=U) \/ (y=U)
>   = L, if (x=L) \/ (y=L)
>   = H, if (x=H) &  (y=H)

...
```

The definitions of `log_or` and `log_not` are similar.

The above interpretation is used to perform unidirectional combinational simulation. The following dialogue with the interpretation system demonstrates a simulation of the example circuit.

First, the input description is unparsed to display the circuit to be simulated. The circuit is called "cirl" and is extracted from a library called "frasenv".

```
Miranda write_ast (lookup frasenv "cir1")
[ID, NOT ; FORK, ID] ; reorg1  ; [AND, OR] ; AND
```

The combinational interperter is used to simulate the demonstration circuit for the input $< 1,1,0 >$. The result is not only the output of the circuit, but also the output of each node in the circuit. Each interpretation produces as output a result which has the same 'shape' as the circuit to be analysed. This is useful when information is required about internal nodes and wires.

```
Miranda write_logic (comb_sim frasenv "cir1" "<110>")
[1, 0 ; <0,0>, 0] ; <<1,0>,<0,0>> ; [0, 0] ; 0
```

Interpretations may be combined by the `cross` function. This is demonstrated by the following example which crosses the circuit description with the output value of each node to yield a circuit description annotated with output values.

```
Miranda wr_cross write_ast' (show_tuple show_logic) (cross cirl sim1)
[ID 1, NOT 0 ; FORK <0,0>, ID 0] ; reorg1  <<1,0>,<0,0>> ;
[AND 0, OR 0] ;  AND 0
Miranda
```

Simulation of a badly formed circuit fails. For example, the circuit $NOT; AND$ is accepted by the system but when it is interpreted a run time error is signaled. Badly formed or typed circuits may be detected by using an intepretation that checks that when two circuits are serially composed the result type of the first is compatible with the input type of the second.

3 Non-Standard Interpretation

3.1 Abstract Interpretation

Abstract interpretation allows additional information to be deduced from a program by executing an abstract version of the program. The archetypical example is the rule of signs ([3]).

Given the task "find the sign of 34 * (-5) * (-3993)" it is easy to find one method of working out the answer. Perform the arithmetic operations to find the result of the computation: the sign of the resulting number is the answer. By casual inspection, it is clear to a human that the required sign is positive because only the signs of the numbers are required to work out the final sign: the actual numbers are not important. It is possible to express the above calculation more abstractly by replacing positive numbers by a value that denotes positive numbers i.e. +ve and use -ve similarly for negative numbers. The operator * has to be replaced by × which performs the abstract operation:

$$\begin{aligned} +ve \times +ve &= +ve \\ -ve \times -ve &= +ve \\ -ve \times +ve &= -ve \\ +ve \times -ve &= -ve \end{aligned}$$

This abstract version is simpler and involves less work.

This technique is used in functional programming to obtain strictness information about programs i.e. to find out what expressions will definitely be evaluated. This information helps to optimise the run-time of lazy functional languages.

In abstract interpretation, an abstract version of the program is run on an abstract version of the input to produce an abstract version of the output. It should be possible to define an abstraction function from a concrete value to an abstract value. Non-standard interpretation is a more general technique which allows the standard primitives to be replaced by any other definition, whether more abstract or not. The new interpretation should be reasonable w.r.t. the standard interpretation. This new interpretation is run on non-standard input data which need not be related at all to the standard input data. The last two interpretations presented in this paper are non-standard interpretations.

3.2 Non-Standard Interpretation for Hardware Description Languages

The standard interpretation of a hardware description language describes the behaviour of the circuit. Consider the expression

$$AND; NOT$$

which describes the construction of a 2-input NAND gate. The standard semantics interprets AND by a relation that describes the logical behaviour of an AND gate, NOT by a relation that inverts its inputs and ; by the function that composes AND and NOT so that the output of the AND gate is used as the input to the NOT gate. The expression may be used to simulate a NAND gate by applying it to a stream of logic values. The stream of logic levels is the standard value.

By changing the interpretation, a different meaning may be found for the expression above. Consider the problem of computing the longest delay through a combinational network. This may be performed by interpreting the AND gate as a relation that chooses the larger of two input delays and then adds the delay due to the AND gate itself. This delay is the 'output' of the AND gate. Similarly, the interpretation of the NOT gate simply takes a delay as input and returns the delay plus the delay due to the NOT gate. This expression may be applied to tuples of delays which form the input to the AND gate. This tuple is a non-standard value.

This interpretation may be represented as follows assuming that the delays for NOT and AND gates are 5 and 10 respectively:

$$\begin{array}{ll} x\ NOT^{*}\ y & \Leftrightarrow y = x + 5 \\ <a, b>\ AND^{*}\ c & \Leftrightarrow c = max[a, b] + 10 \end{array}$$

The meaning of serial composition for the longest delay interpretation is the same as the meaning of serial composition in the standard interpretation. Assume that the *NAND* gate expression above is part of a larger circuit. Let the first input to the AND gate be a delay of 17 (i.e. it takes a maximum of 17 time units for a value to propagate from a primary input) and the delay at the second input be 9. Let us use the above interpretation to work out what the maximum delay at the output of the NOT gate will be:

$$\begin{array}{ll} <17, 9>\ AND^{*}\ c & \Leftrightarrow c = max[17, 9] + 10 = 27 \\ 27\ NOT^{*}\ y & \Leftrightarrow y = 27 + 5 = 32 \\ \text{therefore} <17, 9>\ AND^{*}; OR^{*}\ 32 & \end{array}$$

The interpretation used to compute the longest delay is simpler than the standard interpretation because it is possible to define an abstraction function from the standard interpretation to the delay interpretation. Some interpretations may use abstract versions of the standard primitives while others may be much more complicated than the standard interpretation. Indeed, a non-standard interpretation may use the standard interpretation itself.

4 A Simple Abstract Interpretation: Composition Checking

Composition (or type) checking is an example of an *abstract* interpretation because each primitive is 'recoded' to operate on an abstract version of the input to produce and abstract version of the output. The abstraction is from a value to its type.

An abstraction function from signal values to type values may be defined as follows:

$$
\begin{aligned}
abs[\![a]\!] &= logic \\
abs[\![< e_1, \ldots, e_n >]\!] &= < abs[\![e_1]\!], \ldots, abs[\![e_n]\!] >
\end{aligned}
$$

The above abstraction builds a tuple of the same shape as the standard tuple but each atomic element may only be *logic*. Informally, this is like rewriting the signal, but ignoring the actual atomic values and replacing them with a constant value that denotes a single 'wire'.

The other interpretations presented are not abstract interpretations. The abstraction function above *removes* information. The other interpretations add information or use non-standard values which are unrelated to the standard values.

Running the type checker with the example circuits gives the following output.

```
Miranda write_type (type_check frasenv "cir1")
[Logic, Logic ; <Logic,Logic>, Logic] ;
<<Logic,Logic>,<Logic,Logic>> ; [Logic, Logic] ; Logic
```

Each gate in the standard interpretation is replaced by a type expression giving the output type of the gate.

A bad composition causes the output to be an error value. By tracing backwards, it is possible to locate exactly where the bad composition is located. If the left *AND* gate in the demonstration circuit were replaced by a *NOT* gate the circuit becomes badly formed. This is because the input to the *NOT* gate is of type $< logic, logic >$ but *NOT* is only well defined for the input type *logic* i.e. it can only have a single wire along its input. From the same library "bad1" is such a circuit:

```
Miranda write_ast (lookup frasenv "bad1")
[ID, NOT ; FORK, ID] ; reorg1  ; [NOT, OR] ; AND
```

The following output is generated by the type checking interpreter when the circuit above is submitted:

```
Miranda  write_type (type_check frasenv "bad1")
Logic, Logic ; <Logic,Logic>, Logic] ;
<<Logic,Logic>,<Logic,Logic>> ; [
program error: NOT given shape <$,$> at node 6
```

The number 6 refers to the label assigned to the *NOT* gate by the forward interpreter.

5 Deductive Fault Simulation

5.1 Introduction to Deductive Fault Simulation

Testability of integrated circuits is concerned with identifying chips that are defective due to the manufacturing process. The effect of physical defects on a circuits behaviour is modelled by faults which express how the logical behaviour is affected e.g. by assuming that a wire remains stuck at a constant value. Tests are performed by applying test patterns: a sequence of inputs which determines whether a class of faults is present. Due to factors like deliberately built-in redundancy, not all faults may be detectable. The fraction of all possible faults revealed by a given set of test patterns is called the fault coverage. The effort required to test the circuit (the testability) is usually measured as the number of test patterns required to achieve a given fault coverage.

The single stuck-at fault model is used by the interpretations implemented. Circuits conforming to this model have only one stuck-at fault i.e. only one net may be stuck at 0 (s-a-0) or stuck at 1 (s-a-1). Generating enough test patterns to cover all stuck-at faults usually gives a very high fault coverage.

The task of generating a test pattern for a given fault is very expensive. Once a test pattern for a particular fault has been generated, it is usually the case that this test pattern will also reveal other faults. Employing the test pattern generation system to rediscover test patterns at great cost is not necessary. It is possible to perform some kind of analysis which examines a circuit for a given pattern in order to ascertain which faults it exposes.

A fault simulator takes as input a test pattern and produces as output a list of faults that can be detected by this pattern. Some fault simulators work by simulating defective versions of the circuit, whilst others simulate the working version and deduce from the correct behaviour which faults are detectable at the output. A deductive fault simulator [4], which simulates a working circuit, is implemented using non-standard interpretation.

Deductive fault simulation works by propagating lists which represent faults detected at predecessor gates. For each gate, the subset of faults that is passed has added to it the fault detectable at the output of the gate.

The output of each gate is the true logic value and a set of faults that the output line is sensitive to. The faults that are propagated through a 2-input *AND* gate for all 4 possible input values are characterised by set expressions. Each input to the *AND* gate is considered as carrying not only the true logic value, but also a set of faults that the input line is sensitive to. Let the logic inputs to the *AND* gate be x and y and let the fault sets be A and B respectively. Each pattern will be represented by writing xy/z where x and y are the input values and z is the output value.

- Pattern 00/0. Any fault that causes the output to be different from its true value is a detectable fault. In this case, the output has to be 1 for the effect of some previous fault to be detected. This requires both inputs to be 1 for the output to be 1 i.e. we want any fault that changes $(0 \rightarrow 1)$ both the first and second input. This means that we want the faults that are common to sets A and B i.e. $A \cap B$.

xy/z	Set Expression (for $< x,y > ANDz$)
00/0	$A \cap B \cup \{z_1\}$
01/0	$A \cap \overline{B} \cup \{z_1\}$
10/0	$\overline{A} \cap B \cup \{z_1\}$
11/1	$\overline{(\overline{A} \cap \overline{B})} \cup \{z_0\}$

Table 1: Set expressions for propagating faults through an AND gate.

xy/z	Set Expression (for $< x,y > ORz$)
00/0	$A \cup B \cup \{z_1\}$
01/0	$A \cup \overline{B} \cup \{z_0\}$
10/0	$\overline{A} \cup B \cup \{z_0\}$
11/1	$\overline{(\overline{A} \cup \overline{B})} \cup \{z_0\}$

Table 2: Set expressions for propagating faults through an OR gate.

- Pattern 01/0. We want to choose those faults that cause the output to change to 1 i.e. those faults that change the first input. It is wrong to simply choose all the faults in set A because some of these faults may also be in set B. Consider the effect of a fault in $A \cap B$: this causes the first input to be faulty $(0 \rightarrow 1)$ and the second input to be faulty $(1 \rightarrow 0)$. The result is that the output is still 0 (not different from its true value) so such faults are not detectable. We want those faults that are in A but not in B i.e. $A - (A \cap B)$. We may rewrite this as $A \cap \overline{B}$.

- Pattern 10/0. By a similar argument it can be seen that the faults propagated are represented by the set expression $B - (A \cap B)$ i.e. $\overline{A} \cap B$.

- Pattern 11/1. We now want to pass any faults that cause the output to become 0 i.e. faults that cause either of the inputs to be 0. The effect of any fault in A or B is to set one or more of the inputs to 0 so we can pass all the faults in A and B i.e. $A \cup B$. This may be rewritten as follows: $A \cup B = \overline{\overline{(A \cup B)}} = \overline{(\overline{A} \cap \overline{B})}$.

To each of the set expressions above we must remember to add the fault detectable at the output. The name of the output node is z, so the fault z stuck-at-0 is represented by z_0 and the fault z stuck-at1 is represented by z_1. The results obtained in the above analysis are summarised in Table 5.1. Intersection is understood to bind more strongly than union.

Notice the pattern:

- If $x = 1$ then A is complemented (lines 3 and 4).

- If $y = 1$ then B is complemented (lines 2 and 3).

- If $z = 1$ then the first part of the set expression is complemented (line 4).

The rules for an OR gate may be obtained by a similar analysis (Table 2).

These rules are similar to the rules for an AND gate except that intersection has been replaced by union and the output fault is different. An inverter will pass all faults at its input and add to the fault list the fault that may be detected at

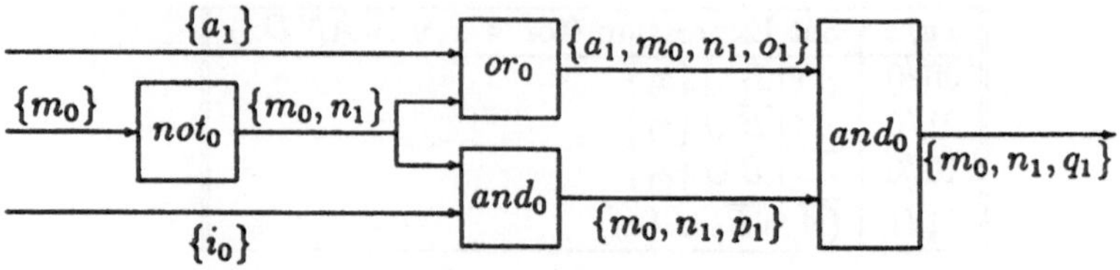

Figure 2: Deductive fault simulation example.

$(x, A)NOT(n)(y, C)$	$\Leftrightarrow C = x \cup \{n_{\overline{y}}\}\ \&\ y = \overline{x}$
$<(x, A),(y, B)> AND(n)(z, C)$	$\Leftrightarrow C = \neg_z(\neg_x A \cap \neg_y B) \cup \{n_{\overline{z}}\}\ \&\ z = x \wedge y$
$<(x, A),(y, B)> OR(n)(z, C)$	$\Leftrightarrow C = \neg_z(\neg_x A \cup \neg_y B) \cup \{n_{\overline{z}}\}\ \&\ z = x \vee y$

Table 3: Deductive Fault Simulation Primitives and Combining Forms in Ruby

its output. Any combinational circuit may be transformed into an AND-OR-NOT representation and then have deductive fault simulation performed on it by using the above method.

5.2 An Example of Deductive Fault Simulation

Figure 2 illustrates deductive fault simulation with the example circuit. The input pattern is $< 1, 1, 0 >$ and each gate in the figure is subscripted by the logic (standard) value of its output. The fault sets are shown propagating along the wires.

Consider the and gate with output node q (the large AND gate). The true output is 0 so we want to pass those faults that will set both the inputs to 1 i.e. we have to 'fault' both the inputs. These faults are obtained by taking the intersection of the two input fault sets (see the rules for an AND gate with pattern 00/0). Since this is the primary output of the circuit, the test pattern $< 1, 1, 0 >$ detects the faults given by the following set expression:

$$\{m_0, n_1, p_1\} \cap \{a_1, m_0, n_1, o_1\} \cup \{q_1\} = \{m_0, n_1, q_1\}$$

5.3 Implementing Deductive Fault Simulation

Assume that an abstract syntax tree representation for a combinational circuit given in Ruby exists. As mentioned earlier, each node has available to it a unique value for labeling. This value is made explicit by mentioning it as a parameter to each node e.g. $NOT(n)$ describes a NOT gate which has been assigned the label n. The interpretation system does this numbering automatically so each node is uniquely identified (and consequently each wire, which is identified by the node which drives it). Table 3 shows the interpretation used to implement deductive fault simulation.

Each gate is a predicate involving pairs containing a logic value and a fault set, a node label and the output which is also a pair of logic value. For example, the second line shows the rule for an AND gate which has two inputs. The first input is a pair containing a logic value x and an associated fault set A. The logic value at the output is z defined to be the logical conjunction of x and y and the fault set that is propagated is made up of applying the rules for deductive fault simulation. These conditionally negate set A if x is true and set B if y is true. The bracketed expression is also negated if the output z is true. Note: $\neg_x V$ means negate the set V w.r.t. $A \cup B$ if the boolean variable x is true. Finally, the fault detectable at the output is added to the propagation set. This is represented by the singleton set $\{n_{\bar{x}}\}$ which says that the node labeled by n is stuck at value $\bar{x}$ i.e. the opposite value from the working circuit.

In this interpretation the combining forms have the same interpretation as the combining forms in the standard interpretation. This interpretation 'includes' the standard interpretation. The non-standard values are tuples of sets (of faults) and logic values.

The above interpretation could be implemented in a relational framework using the above relations. However, since the relations are really unidirectional i.e. information only flows from the domain to the range, it is sufficient to implement each primitive by a function. The combining forms may also be implemented by unidirectional functions.

The Miranda code used to define and implement the deduction rules for the *AND* gate are given below. The conditional negation function cn actually works on logic values rather than booleans (assume that H is *true* and L is *false*).

```
> and_fn :: num -> (logic,[faulttype]) -> (logic,[faulttype])
>             -> (logic,[faulttype])
> and_fn n (x, fx) (y, fy)
>  = (outv, outfault n outv fo)
>    where
>    outv = log_and x y
>    fo = cn outv (intersection (cn x fx u) (cn y fy u)) u
>    u = union fx fy

> faulttype ::= SA0 num | SA1 num
> cn L fs u = fs
> cn H fs u = mkset (u--fs)
> union x y = mkset (x++y)
> outfault n L fs = (SA1 n) : fs
> outfault n H fs = (SA0 n) : fs
> intersection xs ys = [x | x <- xs ; member ys x]
```

The rules for an *OR* gate just require another 6 lines of code similar to the and_fn definition. Along with a 3 line definition for *NOT* this is all that is required by the interpretation system to perform deductive fault simulation. The rules for *id*, *fork* etc. are dealt with automatically since these are just 'wiring' functions that propagate information and change it's shape.

The definitions given above provide a clear and concise specification of deductive fault simulation. They may also be implemented naturally in a functional language. Non-standard interpretation has been used to make the deductive fault simulation method easier to understand and implement.

set0 (z) = min [**set0** (x), **set0** (y)] + 1	Rule 1
set1 (z) = **set1** (x) + **set1** (y) + 1	Rule 2
obsv (x) = **set1** (y) + **obsv** (z) + 1	Rule 3
obsv (y) = **set1** (x) + **obsv** (z) + 1	Rule 4

Table 4: SCOAP rules for $< x, y > ANDz$

set0 (z)	= **set0** (x) + **set0** (y) + 1
set1 (z)	= min [**set1** (x), **set1** (y)] + 1
obsv (x)	= **set0** (y) + **obsv** (z) + 1
obsv (y)	= **set0** (x) + **obsv** (z) + 1

(a)

set1 (y)	= **set0** (x) + 1
set0 (y)	= set1 (x) + 1
obsv (x)	= 1

(b)

Table 5: SCOAP rules for (a) $< x, y > OR\, z$ and (b) $x\, NOT\, y$

6 Testability Measure

6.1 The SCOAP Testability Measure

A means for estimating the "difficulty of testing" one realisation of a circuit compared to another is useful when deciding which is the better design. Analysing the subcircuits of a design to find which parts are inaccessible can help to redesign the circuit to improve access to internal nodes.

One simple measure of testability is the number of test patterns produced by running an automatic test pattern generation program (ATPG). However, test patterns are expensive to produce. An alternative is to use a testability measure program to estimate the testability of each node in the circuit. Testability measure programs use heuristics gleaned from running ATPG programs. This paper uses a testability measure called SCOAP [5].

The SCOAP testability measure assigns a 6-element vector to each node of the circuit. The six elements describe how easy it is to set a combinational or sequential node to 0 or 1 and how easy it is to propagate the value on some combinational or sequential node to an observable output. Since we are only concerned with the analysis of sequential circuits in this paper, we shall only be interested in obtaining 3 values for each node: [2]

set0 (n) : a measure of how easy it is to set node n to logic 0.
set1 (n) : a measure of how easy it is to set node n to logic 1.
obsv (n): a measure of how easy it is to observe the value at node n.

Large values for the above measures indicate poor controllability and observability. The rules in Table 4 are used to calculate the SCOAP values for the 2 input nodes and 1 output node of a 2 input AND gate.

[2]These values were called CC0 (**set0**), CC1 (**set1**) and CO (**obsv**) on the original literature.

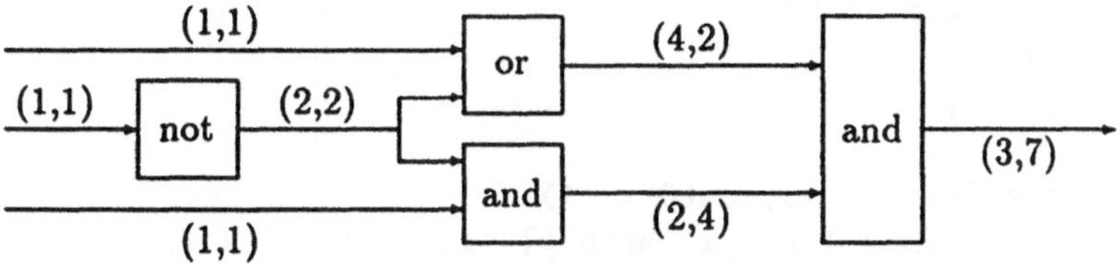

Figure 3: SCOAP controllability values for the example circuit.

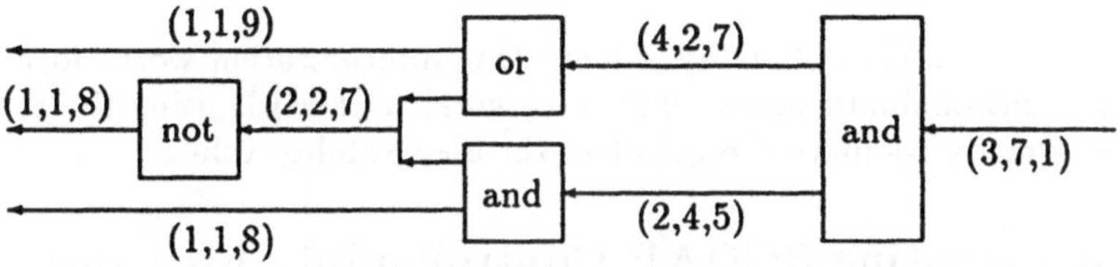

Figure 4: SCOAP observability and controllability values for the example circuit.

Rule 1 describes how easy it is to set the output z of an AND gate to 0 i.e. **set0**(z). This can be done by setting either of the inputs to 0. The SCOAP rules choose the input which is easier to set to 0 (i.e. has the lowest cost associated with it) and then adds 1 as a penalty for propagating the result past the AND gate. To set the output of an AND gate to 1 requires both the inputs to be set to 1. Thus, the formula for **set1**(z) adds the difficulty of setting both x and y to 1 and then adds a fixed penalty of 1 for the AND gate.

Rules 3 and 4 describe the observability costs for the input nodes x and y. To observe the value at node x, node y has to be set to 1 so that the output depends only on x. Thus a cost of **set1**(y) has to be incurred. Then we have to add the cost of transporting the value from the output of the AND gate z to an observable output. This can be recursively specified as **obsv**(z). Finally we add a penalty of 1 for propagating the value across the AND gate. Rule 4 is similar.

The rules for an OR gate are shown in Table 5(a). For primary inputs, **set0** and **set1** are defined to be 1 and for primary outputs **obsv** is 0. This reflects that fact that only one assignment has to be made to set a primary input to a particular value. Also, no assignments are required to observe an output. The controllability of the primary outputs and the observability of the primary inputs are values of little interest. Table 5(b) shows the rules for a NOT gate.

The actual costs returned by the SCOAP measure represent the number of combinational node assignments required to control/observe a given node plus some notion of depth. This is a heuristic that tries to estimate the difficulty of generating test patterns for the given node (i.e the *testability* of a node). SCOAP gives good values for small to medium circuits, but deviates from true values for larger circuits.

The rules in the tables above describe bidirectional information flow. A direct implementation requires a relational interpreter. It is possible to decompose SCOAP into two unidirectional interpretations. Notice that the controllability values may be implemented independently of the observability values. However, the observability

```
> cont_type == (num, num)
> set0 (x, y) = x
> set1 (x, y) = y

> not_fn n x = (set1 x +1, set0 x +1)
> and_fn n x y = (min [set0 x, set0 y] +1, (set1 x) + (set1 y) +1)
> or_fn n x y = ((set0 x) + (set0 y) +1, min [set1 x, set1 y] +1)
```

Figure 5: Source code for controllability interpretation.

values *depend* on the controllability values. One interpretation works forwards to compute the controllability values. The next works backwards using the controllability values already computed to calculate the observability values.

6.2 Implementing SCOAP Controllability Measure

An interpretation to compute only the controllability values can be easily constructed by directly transcribing the **set0** and **set1** rules into Miranda. The input code for the entire controllability interpretation, excluding `export` and `import` directives, is presented in Figure 5.

Running the controllability interpreter with the above circuit gives the following output:

```
Miranda write_set01 (sco_set frasenv "cir1" (TUPLE[inp,inp,inp]))
[set0=1 set1=1, set0=2 set1=2 ; <set0=2 set1=2,set0=2 set1=2>,
set0=1 set1=1] ; <<set0=1 set1=1,set0=2 set1=2>,
<set0=2 set1=2,set0=1 set1=1>> ; [set0=2 set1=4, set0=4 set1=2] ;
set0=3 set1=7
Miranda
```

Each node now represents a two element SCOAP controllability measure. The 0-controllability is given first, followed by the 1-controllability. These results are shown in Figure 3.

Consider the output of the OR gate. To set the output to 0 the top input has to be set to zero (requires 1 assignment) and the bottom input has to be set to 0 (requires 2 assignments). Adding on a depth penalty of 1 for the gate itself, this gives a **set0** (o) measure of $1+2+1 = 4$. The output of this OR gate can be set to 1 by setting either of the inputs to 1. The SCOAP rules choose the input which has the lower SCOAP 1-controllability i.e. min $[1, 2] = 1$ and then 1 is added as a depth penalty. This gives **set1** (o) = min $[1, 2] + 1 = 2$.

6.3 Implementing SCOAP Observability Measure

Figure 4 shows the example circuit decorated with controllability values with observability values on the nodes.

The fork combining form has been redefined to choose the set with the smaller observability values. The line n has two possible paths to the output: one of cost

8 (through the *OR* gate) and the other of cost 7 (through the *AND* gate). The backward interpretation takes as a parameter a selection function to choose a unique value for each node. Here, the selection function is *min*, the function returning the smallest value, so **obsv** (n) = min [8, 7] = 7.

This interpretation may be implemented as one non-standard interpretation by carrying around environment information and backtracking. However, this method is clumsy and very inefficient. It is nicer to break it down into two steps, corresponding to the two different directions of information flow. This then makes the problem solvable in a functional framework.

The interpretation system computes the observability measure in the following manner. The result of the controllability interpretation is crossed with the circuit description, resulting in a circuit annotated with controllability values (like Figure 3). These values are then 'shifted' to the left to associate with the correct nodes. Now this structure is in the right form for a backward interpretation and contains enough information in each node to compute the observability values.

This scheme was also implemented in Ada. The Ada program ran faster, but was much longer and more difficult to write. The Miranda interpretation is smaller and easier to understand. It highlights the different information flows present in the method and breaks the algorithm into two separate parts which can be understood independently.

7 Other Interpretations

Many other interpretations have been implemented including pretty-printers for Ruby expressions. Pictures of simple compositions have been generated by producing LaTeX picture format output. The most sophisticated interpretation implemented is an automatic test pattern generator. This is based on the D-Algorithm [6].

Many circuit analyses have a similar shape to the circuits they analyse. However, the nature of the information flow in the analysis may be different from the information flow in the standard interpretation. Interpretations for modelling unidirectional forward and backward information flow have been presented. Some analyses involve data flow that oscillates forwards and backwards. A new core interpreter based on the existing forward and backward interpreters is being built to characterise such analyses.

8 Conclusions

Non-standard interpretation has been used to help analyse circuits. The deductive fault simulation method and the SCOAP testability scheme have been successfully implemented by non-standard interpretations. Deductive fault simulation is an interpretation which is more complex than the standard interpretation whereas SCOAP is simpler but has more complicated data flow. It is possible to implement relational interpretations in a relational framework, but we have chosen to break the interpretation into two stages and solve each in a functional framework.

An interpretation system has been implemented which facilitates the construction of non standard and abstract interpretations. Only a relatively small effort is required to build an interpretation since the system provides the interpretation of the combining forms and the wiring primitives.

Non-standard interpretation had proved to be a good way of structuring these analyses and allows quick prototype implementations. Expressing an analysis as a non-standard interpretation can often make it easier to understand so it provides a valuable notation. This method also gives us greater confidence in the prototype implementation of an analysis since the circuit structure does not have to be respecified.

9 Acknowledgements

Much work has been done in the past to try and exploit circuit description to get extra information. Sheeran has used *alternative interpretations* [7] in Ruby to check that only 'sensible' circuits are composed. O'Donnell has used a similar technique to draw pictures of more elaborate circuits [8].

I am very grateful to Mary Sheeran and John Hughes for their help in producing this paper.

References

[1] Sheeran M. *Ruby - a language of relations and higher-order functions.* Proc 3rd Banff workshop on hardware verification, Springer 1990.

[2] Kahn G. *The Semantics of a Simple Language for Parallel Programming.* Information Processing 74, North Holland, 1974.

[3] Peyton-Jones SL. *The Implementation of Functional Programming Languages.* Prentice-Hall, 1987.

[4] Armstrong DB. *A Deductive Method for Simulating Faults in Large Circuits.* IEEE Trans. Computers, **C-21**(5), 1972.

[5] Goldstein LH. *Controllability/Observability Analysis of Digital Circuits.* IEEE Transactions on Circuits and Systems, Vol. CAS-**26**, No. 9, Sept. 1979.

[6] Roth JP. *Diagnosis of Automata Failures: A calculus and a Method.* IBM Journal of Research and Development, Vol. **10**, No. 4, p278-91, July 1966.

[7] Sheeran M. *Retiming and Slowdown in Ruby.* The Fusion of Hardware Design and Verification, July 1988.

[8] O'Donnell JT. *Hardware Description with Recursion Equations.* Indiana University Computer Science Department Technical Report No. 212, 1986.

A The Forward Interpretation

The complete code for the forward interpretation is presented below.

```
The forward interpretation source.
Satnam Singh, 22.2.90.

> %include "../global/global"

> %free {t :: type ;
>        not_fn :: num->t->t ;
>        and_fn :: num->t->t->t ;
>        or_fn :: num->t->t->t ;}

The forward interpretation is paramerterised on the type
of the signals and the behaviour of the primitive elements.

> forward :: environment -> ast -> num -> data t ->
>            combinator (data t)

The forward interpreter takes as input:
(a) A environment containing parsed subset Ruby descriptions
(b) A parsed Ruby description
(c) The number to start node labelling with.
(d) An input data value to execute circuit (b)
The result is a structure of the same shape as the circuit,
containing the values of the nodes after interpretation rather than
the element constructors.

THE PRIMITIVE GATES

> forward env (BASIC NOT) n (ATOMIC x)
>  = BASIC (ATOMIC (not_fn n x))
> forward env (BASIC NOT) n other
>  = error ("NOT given shape " ++ (showsh (shapeof other))
>    ++ " at node " ++ (shownum n))

> forward env (BASIC AND) n (TUPLE [ATOMIC x, ATOMIC y])
>  = BASIC (ATOMIC (and_fn n x y))
> forward env (BASIC AND) n other
>  = error ("AND given shape " ++ (showsh (shapeof other))
>    ++ " at node " ++ (shownum n))

> forward env (BASIC OR) n (TUPLE [ATOMIC x, ATOMIC y])
>  = BASIC (ATOMIC (or_fn n x y))
> forward env (BASIC OR) n other
>  = error ("OR given shape " ++ (showsh (shapeof other))
```

```
>    ++ " at node " ++ (shownum n))
```

THE WIRING FUNCTIONS

```
> forward env (BASIC ID) n x
>  = BASIC x

> forward env (BASIC FORK) n x
>  = BASIC (TUPLE [x, x])
```

MODULE FUNCTIONS

```
> forward env (BASIC (BLOCK name)) n v
>  = forward env (lookup env name) n v

> forward env (BASIC (LET locals expr)) n v
>  = forward (locals++env) expr n v
```

COMPOSITION FUNCTIONS

```
> forward env (SER xs) n v
>  = SER (ser forward env xs n v)

> forward env (PAR xs) n (TUPLE ys)
>  = PAR (par forward env xs n ys)

> forward env (BASIC (WIRE pat body)) n v
>  = BASIC (plug (bindings pat v) body)
```

Simulating Multiprocessor Architectures for Compiled Graph-Reduction

J M Deschner

Computing Science Department
University of Glasgow
G12 8QQ

e-mail: deschner @ uk.ac.glasgow.cs

Abstract

Software simulations of hardware architectures are useful tools for evaluating a systems performance prior to its construction. This is especially true of multi-processor architectures where the design complexity is increased by orders of magnitude.

It is also necessary to be able to simulate accurately the behaviour of a parallel machine after it has been built. Statistics may then continue to be gathered without adversely affecting the behaviour of the hardware.

This paper describes in detail a system for simulating the parallel execution of functional programs based on compiled graph-reduction.

1 Introduction

Much research effort is being spent investigating parallel implementations of functional programming languages. In general, a software simulation is constructed to mimic as faithfully as possible the behaviour of the proposed architecture. These simulators are generally tied to the hardware under investigation in such a way that they cannot be used to model other systems without difficulty, such as the Rediflow system of [1,2], the simulation of the LAGER abstract machine in [3], or the novel technique described in [4] where a Miranda[1] literate script is used both as a formal specification of the HDG-Machine as well as a fully operational simulator of it.

Such simulators are used to provide such information as which compile-time analyses are most successful at discovering the available parallelism in a program, (e.g. the analysis described in [5]); which heuristics make accurate decisions as to the choice of task partitioning to perform; which scheduling strategies best distribute the available tasks over the given processor topology; and statistics on the program itself such as how long it would take to execute; what the size (or granularity) of the generated tasks was; its memory usage; etc. The GRIP multi-processor [6], currently under development at the University of Glasgow, is one such system which requires answers to questions of this form.

As well as being useful in providing pre-construction information for machine designers, simulators are also required to obtain detailed statistics on the performance of such machines after they have been built. Just recently it has become clear that it is impossible to gather accurate information on the performance of the hardware without necessarily affecting that performance [7]. This effect can be likened somewhat to that found when sampling the current through a circuit : the measured current is less than the actual current due to losses in the measuring device. As a result, only very superficial information could be obtained from the machine itself, such as overall execution time and number of active processors for a given program.

Traditional approaches to simulation involve interpreting the source code of some program, using data structures to mimic the processes (and processors) of the architecture being modelled. While this approach is straightforward and easy to implement, it suffers from the drawbacks of high memory usage and low execution speed, both factors mitigating strongly against simulating the execution of large programs (> 1,000,000 reductions, for instance).

A highly flexible simulation system is described, based on the Spineless Tagless G-machine [9], an abstract machine itself based on the G-machine [10] and the Spineless G-machine [11], and operationally very like TIM [12]. It is flexible in its ability to model

[1] Miranda [8] is a trademark of Research Software Ltd.

a wide variety of architectures, and allows a very general investigation of parallel implementations of compiled functional languages which does not follow the simplistic approach described above. By choosing a simpler representation of the program than its source code, it is hoped that it will allow the parallel simulation of larger programs than was previously possible. Although initially the system is only capable of simulating conservative parallelism, with major adjustment it could also be used to analyse speculative evaluation strategies. The initial idea and subsequent design of the system was very much influenced by [13], and a similar approach to simulating parallel logic programming described in [14].

2 Simulating Parallel Execution

The most common, and most flexible, approach to simulating a given architecture is to interpret the code which is going to be executed on it, building a "model" of the parallel execution in data. In effect, a cyclic queue of simulated processes is maintained. During one simulated "clock-tick" of the parallel machine, we travel around the queue once, allowing each process-node visited an arbitrary amount of time in which to do some work (see Fig. 1).

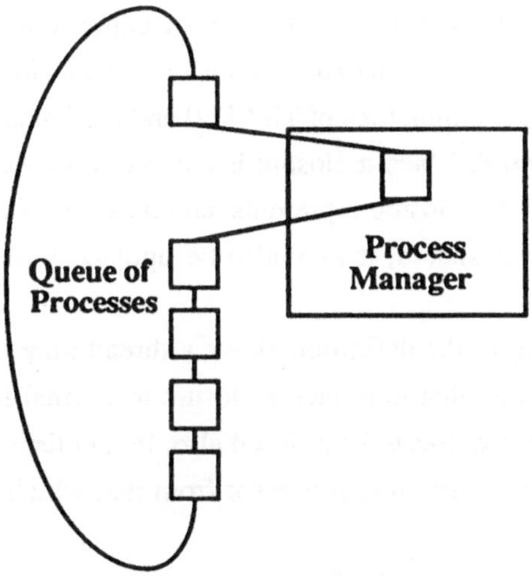

Fig. 1 A parallel simulator

This form of simulation system can be used to simulate any architecture and any scheduling/evaluation policy. Much of the simulators time, however, is spent simulating the execution of source code instructions which have nothing to do with parallelism. It is obviously necessary to have information about the work involved in executing such instructions in order to calculate an overall execution time for the program, but by choosing a different representation of the program which elides all these "non-interesting" details, we hope to both increase the speed of the resulting simulator and decrease the amount of run-time storage used. This would then allow us to simulate the execution of much larger programs.

Our choice of representation is dependent on our willingness to place a restriction on the generation of parallel tasks to only those that are known to do useful work. This is known as *conservative parallelism* and is the most common strategy employed. The alternative - *speculative parallelism* - is used if we wish to generate parallel tasks which we hope do useful work, but otherwise have little or no information about. To reduce the size of structures constructed during the simulation we will try and glean from a program just the information necessary in order to simulate its parallel execution.

2.1 What's the Minimum We Need To Know?

In a sequential environment, we envisage a single, sequential "thread" of computation. In a parallel world we envisage a *graph* of such threads, each thread forming a node of the graph and the sharing of nodes indicating explicitly where sharing of expressions takes place. What, though, is a thread?

For the purposes of this paper, we shall use the definition that a thread is a sequence of instructions which, when executed, causes an expression to be evaluated to its normal-form. When the value of an expression is required a *closure* is built to represent the expression and, in the terminology of TIM [12] and the Spineless Tagless G-machine [9], the closure is *entered*. When a closure is entered, code (a thread) is executed to evaluate the expression the closure represents, and its value is returned to the entering closure. If the closure is shared, it may also be updated with its value to avoid re-computation.

Note that according to the definition above a thread may cause sub-threads to be executed in the same way that to reduce a closure to normal-form may require other closures whose value it requires to be reduced also. Parallelism arises when we allow a thread to be executed on a different processor from that which is executing the parent thread.

We need at least three pieces of information, then:

- when a new thread is begun (i.e. when a closure is entered)
- when a thread has completed execution (i.e. when a closure is returned from)
- which thread caused the new thread to begin execution.

(We actually need more information than this - see §3.1).

The important point to note is that we can obtain all the above information without resorting to simulating the parallel execution of the program by the method described in §2.0. We can, in fact, get this information from a sequential run of the program!

While the compiled functional program is executing sequentially it is entering and returning from closures in exactly the same way as it would if it were running in parallel, the only difference being that when a new closure is entered, its code is executed on the same processor as the closure which entered it. We require a system which, whenever a closure is entered and returned from, we are given information about the fact. From this information, we can then construct a *precedence graph* of the threads of the program. This graph encodes a partial order of the execution of the threads, allowing us to simulate a different order of evaluation than that actually used when the program was executed initially. It is this freedom to re-order the execution of threads which allows us to simulate different process scheduling strategies.

3 The Simulation System

We begin with a program in some high-level functional language, such as LML [15] or Haskell [16]. This program is then compiled to a sequence of abstract machine code instructions, called Tcode, for the Spineless Tagless G-machine [9] to execute. In the normal course of events, each Tcode instruction is then simply "macro-expanded" into a sequence of native machine code instructions for a particular machine architecture. When executed, the code will cause the result of the program to be calculated and output.

Our simulator requires a *trace* of the execution of the program. This trace is obtained by placing extra code in the program. When executed, these additional instructions will output the trace.

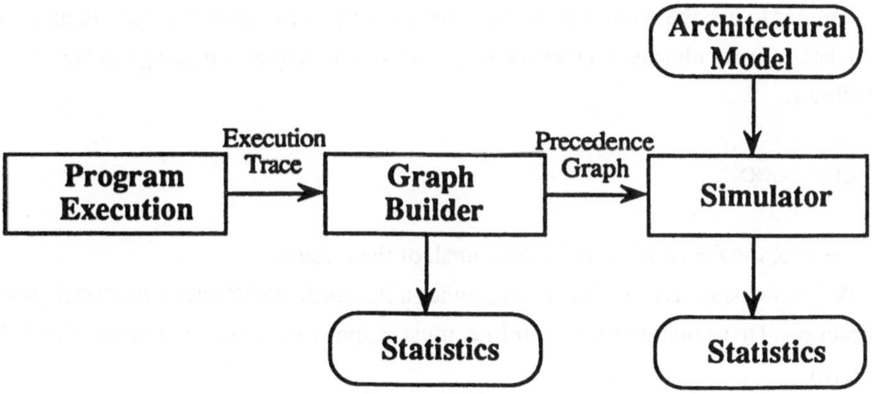

Fig. 2 The overall design of the simulation system

From such a trace, a graph may be constructed, encoding only information about those parts of the program which were executed in order to evaluate it. Information about all other parts of the program (e.g. those branches of an if-expression **not** evaluated) will have been lost (it is for this reason that only conservative parallelism may be modelled by the system as it currently stands).

The information in this graph can then be interpreted by an event driven simulator, which will allow the modelling of the parallel execution of the program using given partitioning and scheduling strategies (see Fig. 2).

3.1 Tracing

The abstract machine is modified to produce code which, when executed, will not only evaluate the program, but as it is doing so, output information to a trace file of its actions. This information details such things as when a closure is entered, when it is updated, etc. The trace information will be stored for later use by a *precedence graph builder.*

The modifications required to the abstract machine are to certain Tcode instructions and to the run-time system. The machine code sequences which implements each Tcode instruction will be expanded with code to output trace information.

3.1.1 Modifying the Machine

We wish to know when a closure is entered, when it has become evaluated to normal form and if it has been updated with its normal form. To do so, we require some method of uniquely identifying closures. We could simply assign an identifier to each closure but it is simpler to use the unique identifiers already assigned to each closure - their address in the heap. Every closure is given a code prefix which outputs a message to the trace file as follows:

```
ENT XXXX
```

(where `XXXX` is the address, in hexadecimal, of the closure).

When a closure returns it executes either a `RETURN_CONSTR` or `RETURN_BASIC` instruction. These instructions, therefore, must output a message to the trace file. It is of the form

```
RET XXXX
```

(where `XXXX` is the address, in hexadecimal, of the closure being returned). We can now look at the trace file and see when a particular closure is entered, and by matching RET's with ENT's, see when that closure is exited.

The closure being evaluated to normal-form may be shared, in which case it is imperative that it is overwritten by the closure returned as the result of the evaluation (or, more precisely, by an indirection to that closure). In order to identify which threads in the program were updated, a message is output to the trace file of the form

```
UPD XXXX
```

(where XXXX is the address of the result closure) to indicate that the immediately preceding thread is updated after evaluation.

We also wish to know where a particular closure resides. This allows us to model the communications delay sustained when the value of a non-local closure is required. This amounts to knowing when, in the sequential execution of the program, a closure is built. When this occurs (by executing a MAKE_CLOSURE instruction), a message of the form

```
CRE XXXX
```

(where XXXX is the address of the closure being built) is output to the trace file.

We also need to be informed when a SPARK instruction is executed. It is by executing these instructions that parallel tasks will be generated. The message output is of the form

```
SPK XXXX
```

(where XXXX is the address of the closure being sparked). Since the sparked closure will be evaluated later (due to the conservative parallelism restriction), we can then calculate how much effort would have been saved if we had given the closure to another processor at the time of the SPARK instruction to be evaluated in parallel, rather than evaluating it *in-line*.

As well as knowing when certain instructions were executed, we also need information on how much work is involved in executing all Tcode instructions. This information is obtained by giving every Tcode instruction (including those that already output trace information) knowledge of their own complexity. We assign each a small integer which represents some measure of how long they take to execute. Whenever an instruction is executed it outputs this integer value to the trace file in the form

```
WRK XXXX
```

(where XXXX is the time, in some arbitrary units, the instruction takes to execute). By using this WRK information we circumvent the necessity of interpreting every source code instruction, as do the simulators of §2.0.

3.1.2 Garbage Collection

Using the address of a closure to uniquely identify it is clearly going to require special handling whenever a garbage collection takes place, since the address of a closure could alter. The garbage collector used in the Spineless Tagless G-machine is a specialised form of a two-space copying collector. We, therefore, require from the garbage collector a pair of addresses, associating the old address of each evacuated closure with its new one. The output for the trace file is of the form

```
GAC XXXX YYYY
```

(where XXXX is the original address of the evacuated closure, and YYYY is the new address of the evacuated closure).

A trace file, then, will appear something like the example of Fig. 3.

```
CRE 2e59c WRK 23 CRE 2e590 WRK 14 CRE 2e584 WRK 15
CRE 221d8 WRK 18 WRK 42 SPK 221d8 WRK 11 CRE 221d0
...
WRK 22 ENT 21b60 WRK 9 RET 21b60 UPD 21b48 RET 21b60
GAC 222a8 332a6 GAC 223f6 332b0 GAC 23452 332b8
GAC 20adc 3c4f8 GAC 21b48 3c504 GAC 21b58 3c50c
...
GAC 21620 3c514 GAC 21b70 3c51c GAC 21620 3c514
WRK 23 RET 2f498 UPD 2f488 RET 2f498
...
RET 20f64 ENT 2f1a4 WRK 4 RET 20af4
```

Fig. 3 A portion of an example trace file

3.2 The Precedence Graph

The trace file produced by executing the program will be given as input to the *precedence graph builder*. Ultimately the precedence graph will be stored in a file so as to allow its re-use on different simulated architectures, but it will initially be constructed as an in-memory structure.

The graph can be thought of as a representation of just those parts of the program which were executed. It is acyclic, since all iteration and recursion has been unfolded from the original program. Each node of the graph, representing a sequential thread of the program, contains a list of pairs, the first element of each pair being a numeric quantity signifying the amount of time taken to carry out all "non-interesting" computation, such as arithmetic. The second element of the pair signifies some operation on another thread, such as creation, entering, updating, returning from or sparked. The second element, then, consists of a tagged pointer to another node (thread) in the graph. A small portion of a graph is shown in Fig. 4 (with different arcs signifying different tags).

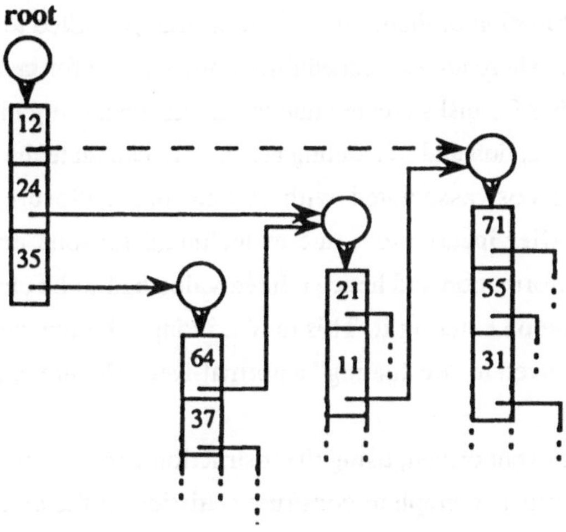

Fig. 4 Portion of an example precedence graph

This form of graph is necessary to allow all sharing of threads to be made explicit. All threads must be constructed separately and pointed to from all other threads which reference it. If a sharing analysis was carried out on the information in the trace file, the graph could be flattened somewhat by placing un-shared threads in-line where they are referenced. This may become necessary to reduce the amount of memory used to store the graph.

3.3 The Simulator

The precedence graph is used as one input to the simulator. The second input is a description of the architecture we wish to simulate. The description details

- the number of processors in the machine (1 .. ∞)
- the task-pool size (0 .. ∞)
- the task partitioning predicate to use
- the process scheduling policies to use
- the cost associated with distributing a task
- the cost associated with scheduling a task
- the cost associated with resuming a previously blocked task
- the cost associated with re-entering a closure.

The task partitioning predicate decides, when a "spark"-tagged thread is encountered in the graph, whether or not it should be placed in the task-pool. The process scheduling policies decide in what order tasks should be pulled out of the task-pool (e.g. FIFO, LIFO, or some combination of them. In addition a strategy called *lazy task creation* [17] will be investigated). There are two scheduling policies, one for tasks created as a result of a spark, and another for tasks created due to threads becoming un-blocked. The costs associated with task creation and scheduling are used to calculate the overhead introduced by parallelism. The cost associated with re-entering a closure may no longer be necessary. In an earlier incarnation, due to technical reasons normal-form closures produced no trace information and hence a fixed value had to be chosen to represent the amount of work done on entering it. This may no longer be the case, however, and the amount of work involved in "evaluating" a normal-form closure is available in the trace file.

The simulator is event driven, using the instruction complexity information given in the nodes of the precedence graph to construct statistics on the amount of work done to execute the program, and the resources consumed, on a parallel architecture.

Initially, the root of the precedence graph is given to a single processor. At any point during its execution, the simulator allows the most retarded active processor to do some work, i.e. that processor with the lowest clock value which has a thread to execute.

When the current processor encounters a numeric complexity value, it increments its clock by that amount.

When it encounters an "enter"-tagged pointer to another thread, it carries out a context switch and the thread to be entered becomes the current thread of that processor (assuming that another processor is not executing the thread, in which case the entering thread becomes blocked).

When a "spark"-tagged pointer is encountered, the thread pointed to may be placed in the task pool for another processor to execute, depending on the value of the partitioning predicate being employed.

In the current simulator, only shared memory machines may be simulated, with all tasks assumed to be globally visible to all processors. All "create"-tagged threads are ignored, therefore, since this information is only required to simulate locality.

4 Summary

This work is still at an early stage of development. The majority of the effort expended on the project has been in the graph building and simulation stages of the system, and consequently the output of trace information is not yet quite complete.

From correspondence with Ken Zink [18], the major limiting factor on their system was the size of the trace file produced. After some initial tests, it appears that it will also be the case with our system (since the tracing stage is still incomplete, information on trace file size is inexact). However, it is hoped that some data compression techniques can be used to reduce the size.

The project will continue firstly by completing the alterations to the Spineless Tagless G-machine [9] as described above to produce the trace information for a program. A more long term goal is to introduce locality to the modelled architectures, by using the closure creation information in the trace file to decide on which processor of the architecture a closure is resident. This will then allow communications latency to be modelled, and locality information to be taken into account when distributing work.

Once a fully-operational simulator is available it is hoped that statistics derived from its use will allow the author to make a general investigation of partitioning and scheduling strategies over a number of different parallel architectures, as well as being used to direct the work on the parallel compiler and run-time system of the GRIP project [6].

Acknowledgements

Firstly, I must thank the Computing Science Department as a whole and particularly the functional programming community within it for providing such a stimulating work environment. For providing the initial impetus for this research thanks must go to my supervisor, Professor Simon L. Peyton Jones. When inspiration or ideas are lacking he has an abundance. I thank Steve Tighe and Ken Zink who took the time to send additional information on their work, and to Phil Trinder for giving much useful advice on an earlier draft of this paper.

Always, and in particular for waiting so patiently, I thank my future wife Anjie.

References

[1] R M Keller, F C H Lin, "Simulated Performance of a Reduction-Based Multiprocessor", IEEE Computer, Vol. 17:7, 70-82, July, 1984.

[2] R M Keller, F C H Lin, P R Badovinatz, "The Rediflow Simulator", Dept. of Computer Science, University of Utah, 1982.

[3] I Watson, "Simulation of a Physical EDS Machine Architecture", Dept. of Computer Science, University of Manchester, Sept, 1989.

[4] D R Lester, G L Burn, "An Executable Specification of the HDG-Machine", GEC Hirst Research Centre, Nov, 1989.

[5] G L Burn, C L Hankin, S Abramsky, "Strictness Analysis for Higher-Order Functions", Science of Computer Programming, Vol 7, 249-278, Nov, 1986.

[6] S L Peyton Jones, C Clack, J Salkild, M Hardie, "GRIP - a high performance architecture for parallel graph reduction" in *Proc IFIP Conference on Functional Programming Languages and Computer Architecture*, Portland, G Khan, ed., Springer Verlag LNCS 274, 98-112, Sept, 1987.

[7] A D Malony, D A Reed, J W Arendt, R A Aydt, D Grabas, B K Totty, "An Integrated Performance Data Collection, Analysis and Visualisation System", Dept. of Computer Science, University of Illinois at Urbana-Champaign, Report no. UIUCDCS-R-89-1504, March, 1989

[8] D A Turner, "Miranda - a non-strict functional language with polymorphic types" in *ACM Conference on Functional Programming and Computer Architecture*, Nancy, Sept, 1985.

[9] S L Peyton Jones, J Salkild, "The Spineless Tagless G-machine" in *Proceedings of the Conference on Functional Programming Languages and Computer Architecture*, London, England, September 1989.

[10] T Johnsson, "Compiling lazy functional languages Part I", PhD thesis, PMG, Chalmers University, Goteborg, Sweden, 1987.

[11] G L Burn, S L Peyton Jones, J Robson, "The Spineless G-machine" in *Proc ACM Conference on Lisp and Functional Programming*, Snowbird, 244-258, July, 1988.

[12] J Fairbairn, S Wray, "TIM - a simple lazy abstract machine to execute supercombinators" in *Proc IFIP Conference on Functional Programming and Computer Architecture*, Portland, G Khan, ed., Springer Verlag LNCS 274, 34-45, Sept, 1987.

[13] S Tighe, K Zink, R Brice, "A Flexible Approach to the Study of Graph Reduction Architectures" in *Proc Conference on Systems Science*, Hawaii, June, 1986.

[14] J C de Kergommeaux, U C Baron, W Rapp, M Ratcliffe, "Performance analysis of a parallel Prolog: a correlated approach" in *Proc Parallel Architectures and Languages Europe (PARLE)*, E Odijk, M Rem, J C Syre, eds., LNCS 366, Springer Verlag, June, 1989.

[15] L Augustsson, "Compiling lazy functional languages Part II", PhD thesis, Dept. of Computer Science, Chalmers University, Sweden, 1987.

[16] P Hudak, P Wadler et al, "Report on the functional programming language Haskell", Dept. of Computer Science, Yale University, Dec, 1988.

[17] E Mohr, D A Kranz, R H Halstead, "Lazy task creation - a technique for increasing the granularity of parallel programs", Dept. of Computer Science, Yale University, Nov, 1989.

[18] K Zink, private communication, July, 1989.

Dependent Sums Express Separation of Binding Times

John Launchbury
University of Glasgow

Abstract

In partial evaluation, the separation between static and dynamic components of a data structure has traditionally been expressed in terms of products. However, this corresponds to a special case only, and there are many common examples where it is insufficiently descriptive. In this paper we show that domain projections define decompositions of domains into dependent sums. As domain projections may be used to pinpoint static values within data structures containing both static and dynamic parts, the two components of the dependent sum may be seen as descriptions of the static and dynamic parts respectively. This gives a more precise descriptive framework than before. In addition, previously *ad hoc* optimisations, such as type-tag removal and arity raising, arise as natural consequences of the theory.

1 Introduction

Decomposition is a standard tool in the mathematician's tool box. Integers may be factorised into a unique product of powers of primes, polynomials into products of irreducibles, and so on. Such decompositions reveal some fundamental structure of the object being decomposed, but there are other types of decomposition which are also useful. For example, an integer n may be expressed as a pair $(n\ div\ k,\ n\ mod\ k)$ for any integer k (here *div* is truncated division). This factorisation is driven by a choice of k and different choices will give different results. We may choose to decompose integers in this way to highlight some particular property of a number, its parity for instance.

The same sort of thing occurs in partial evaluation. At its simplest, partial evaluation may be thought of as *currying on programs*. From a program describing a function $f : A \times B \rightarrow Y$ and a description of a value $a \in A$, a partial evaluator produces a program describing the corresponding specialised function $f_a : B \rightarrow Y$. The new program should be an optimised version of the old, having taken the input value into account. It is a very powerful technique with applications ranging from the generation of compilers from interpreters, to the automatic optimisation of expert systems or theorem provers. The process is described in detail in [1, 2, 3] and in many of the papers in [4].

The situation above represents the simplest case and, in general, there is no reason to expect things to be so straightforward. For example, the program may have many arguments with data supplied for the first and third, say. Alternatively, there may be incomplete information given about a single argument—we might know that the value of an argument is a list of three elements, for example, but know nothing about the values of those elements. In the general case a partial evaluator takes a program describing a function $f : X \to Y$, where X and Y are arbitrary domains defined within the type system of the programming language, and a partial description of an input value $x \in X$ for f.

If it were always possible to decompose the domain X into two factors A and B such that $X \cong A \times B$ and such that the partial description about the input value x could always be transformed into a total description of the corresponding value $a \in A$, then we might hope it would always be possible to reduce the general case to the simplest case. Unfortunately, non-trivial solutions to equations of the form $X \cong A \times B$ are quite rare—many domain structures are just not expressible as products—so this hope is not realistic. However, by generalising the notion of domain product we can find non-trivial solutions to the corresponding decomposition problem in many more cases, which then allows us to provide a description of the general case of partial evaluation. The generalisation we use is dependent sum.

While we assume some knowledge about partial evaluation, very little detailed domain theory is required to follow most of the paper. We assume the reader is familiar with the basic concepts of least upper bound, monotonicity and continuity. We use Scott domains [5] so not only are the domains complete partial orders with bottom elements but they are also *consistently complete* and *ω-algebraic*. A domain is consistently complete if every set of elements that has an upper bound also has a least upper bound; and ω-algebraic if there is a countable set of *finite* or *basis* elements such that every element is the least upper bound of its finite approximations.

2 Static Values

The portion of the input data supplied for partial evaluation is called *static*, the remainder *dynamic*. As there is no *a priori* reason for whole parameters to be either completely static or completely dynamic, we need some general framework to describe which parts of a value are static and which are dynamic. Producing such a framework is the purpose of this paper. Of course, to be of use in practice, we also need some sort of *binding time analysis* to allow such information to be derived automatically. However, in this paper we omit any discussion of binding time analysis itself. A binding time analyser defined within the framework developed here may be found in [6].

To describe the static part of a value, we use a function from the argument domain to some domain of static values. If we make the static domain a sub-domain of the original we can simply "blank out" the dynamic part (i.e. the unknown part) of the argument and leave the static part unchanged. We use $\perp$ to represent the static part of dynamic data. Here $\perp$ has its fundamental meaning of "no information"—we get no static information from a dynamic value ($\perp$ is often associated with non-termination, but this is a secondary and derived interpretation. As a non-terminating computation gives no information about its result, $\perp$ is its natural value).

As an example, suppose that the original domain is $A \times B$ where B's value is static and A's dynamic. Then the function that selects the static part will be the map $(a, b) \mapsto (\bot, b)$. We can generalise this example to arbitrary domains by using *domain projections.*

Definition
A *projection* γ on a domain D is a continuous function $\gamma : D \to D$ such that (i) $\gamma \sqsubseteq ID$, and (ii) $\gamma \circ \gamma = \gamma$ (idempotence).

The first condition ensures that a projection adds no new information. This accords with the intuition that we can know no more about the static part of a value than we knew about the value originally. The second condition ensures that the function picks out the static part in one go. We will not need to repeatedly apply the function to check that the result we have really does represent the static part.

There are two important projections, ID and ABS which crop up frequently. ID is the identity function—used when the argument is completely static—and ABS is the constant function that always returns $\bot$—used when the argument is completely dynamic.

In general we cannot hope to find a projection that selects *all* the static part of an argument, but we should guarantee that what is selected is actually static. This means that we will often make do with a projection that is smaller than ideal (under the usual function ordering), for if a projection γ selects only static information from some argument then any projection smaller than γ does also. The description "static", therefore, means "definitely available during partial evaluation".

2.1 Finite Domains of Projections

The ultimate aim of the framework developed in this paper is to provide a grounding for machine-based analyses. Many such analyses rely on the existence of a finite domain of values in order to ensure termination. As not all projections are particularly suitable for our purposes (some are even uncomputable, for example) we will define a system of types (defining a class of domains) and derive a finite domain of projections over each type. Not only will the projections be computable, but they will also reflect the construction of the domain on which they act.

2.1.1 Types

To be fully formal we would need to provide a syntax for types and a semantic mapping of syntactic descriptions into corresponding domains. However, the extra notational overhead tends to obscure rather than clarify and so for the most part we ignore any distinction between the two and use the same notation for each.

We assume a language in which new types may be defined. There are the usual basic types such as *Integer* and *Boolean* etc. but in addition types may be defined through the use of (tagged) separated sum, product, and recursion. Thus, if $X_1, \ldots, X_n$ are types then each of $c_1\ X_1 + \cdots + c_n\ X_n$ and $X_1 \times \cdots \times X_n$ are types, and if $T(X)$ is a type for any type X then $\mu t.T(t)$ is also a type. The empty product is a type, written $\mathbf{1}$, and corresponds to the one point domain.

These type (domain) operations can be extended in the usual way to act on functions.

Definition
If $\{\gamma_i : X_i \to X_i\}_{\{1 \le i \le n\}}$ are functions, then define,

$$
\begin{aligned}
&(\gamma_1 \times \cdots \times \gamma_n) : (X_1, \ldots, X_n) \to (X_1, \ldots, X_n) \\
&(\gamma_1 \times \cdots \times \gamma_n)\ (x_1, \ldots, x_n) \ = \ (\gamma_1\ x_1, \ldots, \gamma_n\ x_n)
\end{aligned}
$$

$$
\begin{aligned}
&(c_1\ \gamma_1 + \cdots + c_n\ \gamma_n) : (c_1\ X_1 + \cdots + c_n\ X_n) \to (c_1\ X_1 + \cdots + c_n\ X_n) \\
&(c_1\ \gamma_1 + \cdots + c_n\ \gamma_n)\ \ \bot \ = \ \bot \\
&(c_1\ \gamma_1 + \cdots + c_n\ \gamma_n)\ (c_1\ x_1) \ = \ c_1\ (\gamma_1\ x_1) \\
&\qquad \vdots \\
&(c_1\ \gamma_1 + \cdots + c_n\ \gamma_n)\ (c_n\ x_n) \ = \ c_n\ (\gamma_n\ x_n)
\end{aligned}
$$

If $P(\gamma) : T(X) \to T(X)$ is a function for all functions $\gamma : X \to X$, then define

$$
\begin{aligned}
&\mu\gamma.P(\gamma) : \mu t.T(t) \to \mu t.T(t) \\
&\mu\gamma.P(\gamma) \ = \ \bigsqcup_{k=0}^{\infty} P^k(ABS)
\end{aligned}
$$

(i.e. the least fixed point of P).

2.1.2 Projections

For each type X we give an explicit construction of a finite domain of projections based on the form of the type definition defining X. The finite domains (called $FinProj_X$ for each particular X) are defined by the inference rules below. A projection $\gamma : X \to X$ is in $FinProj_X$ if γ **proj** X can be inferred using these rules.

ABS **proj** *Integer* [likewise for **1**, *Boolean* etc.]

ID **proj** *Integer* [likewise for **1**, *Boolean* etc.]

ABS **proj** $c_1\ T_1 + \cdots + c_n\ T_n$

$$\frac{P_1 \ \mathbf{proj}\ T_1 \quad \cdots \quad P_n \ \mathbf{proj}\ T_n}{c_1\ P_1 + \cdots + c_n\ P_n \ \ \mathbf{proj} \ \ c_1\ T_1 + \cdots + c_n\ T_n}$$

$$\frac{P_1 \ \mathbf{proj}\ T_1 \quad \cdots \quad P_n \ \mathbf{proj}\ T_n}{P_1 \times \cdots \times P_n \ \ \mathbf{proj} \ \ (T_1, \ldots, T_n)}$$

$$\frac{P(\gamma)\ \mathbf{proj}\ T(t) \quad [\gamma\ \mathbf{proj}\ t]}{\mu\gamma.P(\gamma)\ \mathbf{proj}\ \mu t.T(t)}$$

The final rule should be read, "if $P(\gamma)$ **proj** $T(t)$ can be inferred under the assumption that γ **proj** t then $\mu\gamma.P(\gamma)$ **proj** $\mu t.T(t)$ can be inferred."

Because type definitions are finite, it is easy to see that if any type X is defined using the base types and $+$, $\times$ and μ then $FinProj_X$ is a finite domain.

Which projections are included in $FinProj_X$? Certainly ABS always is (possibly occurring as $ABS \times ABS$ or $\mu\gamma.ABS$). ID also is always included, though this may not be immediately obvious, particularly in the recursive case. However, if $P(\gamma)$ **proj** $T(t)$ (under the assumption that γ **proj** t) and if $P(ID_t) = ID_{T(t)}$, then $\mu\gamma.P(\gamma) = ID_{\mu t.T(t)}$ as required. Over a product domain we have only those projections which act on the components separately. If X is a sum domain then $FinProj_X$ contains the ABS projection and, in addition, projections which discriminate between all the injective tags. The only projections we have over recursive domains are those which treat every level of recursion identically. Finally, we note that $ABS_1 = ID_1$ as there is only one projection on the one point domain.

2.1.3 Examples

To make the description clearer, we will consider three examples. Suppose that for some types X and Y, $FinProj_X = \{ABS, ID\} = FinProj_Y$. Then the elements of $FinProj_{(X,Y)}$ are given by

$$\begin{aligned} FinProj_{(X,Y)} &= \{ABS \times ABS,\ ID \times ABS,\ ABS \times ID,\ ID \times ID\} \\ &= \{ABS,\ LEFT,\ RIGHT,\ ID\} \end{aligned}$$

To take another example, suppose that the type *Num* is a tagged union of integers, reals, and complex numbers. That is,

$$Num = Int\ Integer + Re\ Real + Comp\ (Real \times Real)$$

The elements of $FinProj_{Num}$ are ABS, TAG (which retains the tag but discards everything else), ID, and eight projections lying between TAG and ID which variously discard values in one or more of the summed domains. This means that, not only can we model total presence or absence of information, but we can also model partial information—knowing only the tag but not the associated value, for example. If we have a function that operates on a tagged union our partial evaluator may, at least potentially, be able to evaluate away the tags to provide separate functions specialised to arguments of the different types. This is a key idea in the development of Section 4.

Finally, consider association lists as used to implement environments. Assuming we have two other types *Var* (variable names) and *Val* (values) we could define,

$$Assoc = End + More\ (Var \times Val \times Assoc)$$

The projections in $FinProj_{Assoc}$ include ABS and ID as usual. In addition we have $STRUCT$ (where only the recursive structure is known) and $STRUCT(LEFT)$ and $STRUCT(RIGHT)$ which discard the *Val* are *Var* parts respectively. These are ordered as follows.

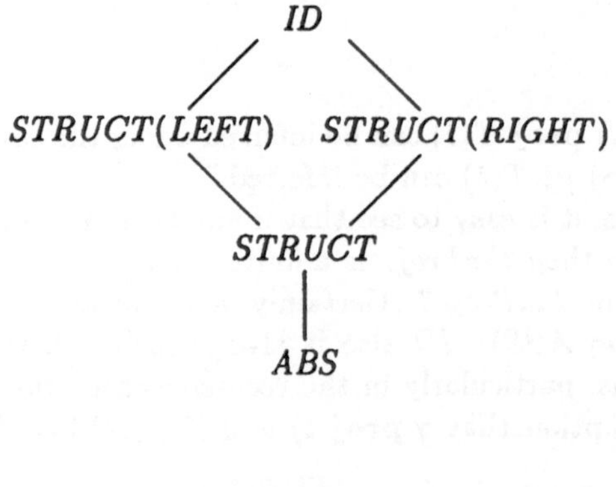

Using these projections, we can model the situation where we know only the names in an environment but not the values, for example. This situation is likely to occur during partial evaluation of an interpreter. It means that it should not be necessary to write interpreters with separate name and value lists in order to benefit from partial evaluation.

3 Run-Time Arguments

The static projection tells us which part of a function's argument will be present during partial evaluation. In any particular call of the function, this part of the argument is used in the production of a residual function. However, this still leaves the question as to which part of the argument should be given to the residual function at run-time? Obviously we could pass the whole argument if we wanted to, but we can do a lot better. After all, the partial evaluator will have taken the static part into account in producing the residual function. It ought to be unnecessary to supply the residual function with the same information all over again.

We need a way to select the run-time information. The original argument to a function must be factorised, or decomposed, into static and dynamic factors, and this factorisation should be as complete as possible. That is, the amount of static information which is also regarded as dynamic should be minimised. Then, when we pass the dynamic argument to the residual function, we will be passing as little information at run-time as possible.

3.1 Projection Complements

The simplest definition for a partial evaluator assumes that the program argument is defined on a product of the static and dynamic domains. In this section we justify the claim that this is not sufficiently descriptive to capture the general case, though it may be adequate for some purposes.

If $f : X \to Y$ is a function defined in the program, we would like to regard it as having the type $f : A \times B \to Y$, where A is static and B dynamic. Assuming we are suppled with a static projection γ for f we can produce A—it is just the range of the static projection, which we write as $\gamma(\!|X|\!)$ (this is a domain as all the elements of each $FinProj_X$ are finitary projections). Ideally, we would like to pick another projection, δ say, so that $B = \delta(\!|X|\!)$ and $X \cong A \times B$. Unfortunately, as we noted in the introduction, this is not possible in general. However, while we cannot achieve isomorphism we can ensure that, in some sense, X is a sub-domain of $A \times B$. A trivial solution to this is for δ to be the identity function and then B would equal X. Fortunately we can do better.

Suppose we are given a static projection and want the dynamic function to be a projection also. This dynamic projection must be a *complement* of the static.

Definition
If $\gamma : D \to D$ and $\delta : D \to D$ are projections, and if $\gamma \sqcup \delta = ID$, then δ is a *complement* of γ (and vice versa).

There may be many projections which are complements of a projection γ. We will choose one in particular and describe it as *the* complement of γ, written $\overline{\gamma}$. From the definition it is clear that for each value $x \in X$ the property that $\gamma\ x \sqcup \overline{\gamma}\ x = x$ holds. In other words, between a projection and its complement no information is lost. But for it to be a good choice, the complement should discard as much as possible consistent with this. That is, the complement should be as small as possible. In general there is no least complement, but as we are only interested in static projections drawn from an appropriate $FinProj_X$ we will take its complement from there also. If we do this then we can choose one which is minimal.

It is clear that X can be embedded in $\gamma(\!|X|\!) \times \delta(\!|X|\!)$ when γ and δ are complements because the canonical map $<\gamma, \delta>: X \rightarrow \gamma(\!|X|\!) \times \delta(\!|X|\!)$ is injective (that is, if $(\gamma\ x,\ \delta\ x) = (\gamma\ x',\ \delta\ x')$ for $x, x' \in X$ then $x = \gamma\ x \sqcup \delta\ x = \gamma\ x' \sqcup \delta\ x' = x'$). However, an example will show that the factorisation is not always exact. Consider the domain (*inl Boolean* + *inr Boolean*) with the projection *TAG* (which, as before, retains only the injection tags). The smallest possible complement of *TAG* is the projection which fixes the maximal elements but maps everything else to $\perp$ (its range is isomorphic to the coalesced sum of *Boolean* and *Boolean*). The range of *TAG* has 3 elements and the range of its complement has 5. The product of these domains has 15 elements, therefore, and so cannot possibly be isomorphic to the original domain which has 7 elements. Note that this problem is not a consequence of restricting ourselves to a particular finite domain of projections because the choice of the complement was unrestricted—it was the smallest possible. If we had restricted ourselves, as we would expect to in practice, then the least complement we could have chosen would have been *ID* itself, making the situation even worse.

4 Domain-Theoretic Dependent Sum

There are times when product can express an exact factorisation, but in general it is too restrictive. We need some more general operation from which product arises as a special case. That more general operation is *dependent sum*.

Dependent sum is usually thought of as a set construction and is often associated with constructive type (set) theory [7] where it occurs as a primitive. However, it made its debut as a domain construction in an exercise in Plotkin's lecture notes in 1978 [8]. Since then it has been used to provide models for the polymorphic λ-calculus [9]. Categorically speaking, dependent sum is a Grothendieck construction where the underlying domain is viewed as a category. This aspect is particularly relevant later on.

In order to develop a basic understanding we will give a set theoretic definition of dependent sum, and then show how to extend it to domains.

Definition

Let A be a set and $\{B_a\}$ a family of sets indexed by elements of A. Then the *dependent sum* $\sum_{a\in A} B_a$ is the set,

$$\sum_{a\in A} B_a = \{(a,b) \mid a \in A,\ b \in B_a\}$$

The dependent sum is a (possibly infinite) tagged union of the family of sets $\{B_a\}$. If the family is constant, i.e. if there exists some set B such that $B_a = B$ for every $a \in A$ then $\sum_{a\in A} B_a$ reduces to the set product $A \times B$.

Now suppose that A and the family $\{B_a\}_{a\in A}$ are domains and not just sets. Let us consider what it means to index a family of domains by a domain. It is clear what it means to index by a set, but a domain has more structure and this should be taken into account. We might quite reasonably require that as we move up a chain in the indexing domain, the corresponding domains in the family become larger. That is, if $a, a' \in A$ are indexing elements such that $a \sqsubseteq a'$ then there must be an embedding $\phi_{a,a'} : B_a \to B_{a'}$ which embeds B_a into $B_{a'}$. Of course, the embeddings should be such that if $a \sqsubseteq a' \sqsubseteq a''$ then $\phi_{a,a''} = \phi_{a',a''} \circ \phi_{a,a'}$. This much reflects the ordering relation on the domain. We must also express completeness. If we have a directed set $V \subseteq A$ then we require that $B_{\bigsqcup V} = \bigsqcup\{B_a \mid a \in V\}$ and that for any $a \sqsubseteq \bigsqcup V$ the embedding $\phi_{a,\bigsqcup V}$ is given by $\phi_{a,\bigsqcup V} = \bigsqcup\{\phi_{a,a'} \mid a' \in V\}$ (we use the least upper bound of domains following Scott's information systems; in some other framework it may be replaced by a union, for example).

This may be expressed very concisely categorically. If we view the indexing domain as a category, then the indexed family corresponds to a continuous functor from this category into the category of domains Dom^{ep} whose arrows are embedding/projection pairs (that is, pairs of functions $\phi : X \to Y$, $\psi : Y \to X$ such that $\psi \circ \phi = id_X$ and $\phi \circ \psi \sqsubseteq id_Y$).

Now that we know what a domain-indexed family of domains is, we can construct the dependent sum.

Definition (Domain Dependent Sum)
If $\{B_a\}_{a\in A}$ is a domain-indexed family of domains, then the *dependent sum* of the family is given by,

$$\sum_{a\in A} B_a = \{(a, b) \mid a \in A,\ b \in B_a\}$$

with the ordering

$$(a, b) \sqsubseteq_\Sigma (a', b') \Leftrightarrow (a \sqsubseteq_A a') \wedge (\phi_{a,a'}(a) \sqsubseteq_{B_{a'}} a')$$

Lemma 1
The dependent sum of a domain-indexed family of domains is a domain.

Sketch Proof
A complete proof that this construction results in a Scott domain appears in [9] but we will give an outline here. We need to show that the sum is an ω-algebraic, consistently complete, complete partial order. It is clear that it has a bottom element, given by $(\bot_A, \bot_{B_{\bot_A}})$, and the fact that the relation $\sqsubseteq$ over the elements of the sum is a partial order follows almost immediately from the fact that $\sqsubseteq_A$ and the $\sqsubseteq_{B_a}$ are all partial orders.

To construct the least upper bound of a directed set of elements drawn from the sum we initially consider the set of first components. These form a directed set in A which will have a least upper bound. If all the second components of the original directed set are injected into the domain indexed by this least upper bound, then again we obtain a directed set which will itself have a least upper bound. The pair, whose components are the two least upper bounds, is an element of the dependent sum and is the least upper bound of the original set. We can form the least upper bound of a consistent set in the same way.

To show algebraicity we have to characterise the finite elements. An element (a,b) of the sum is finite exactly when a is finite in A and b is finite in B_a. The set of finite approximations to an element form a directed set. Because A and the $\{B_a\}$ are algebraic, and because the indexing is continuous, the least upper bound of this directed set will be the original element. Finally, because A and the $\{B_a\}$ have countable bases, the set of finite elements is countable. □

As we might expect, domain product is a special case of domain dependent sum. To see this suppose that $B_a = B$ for every $a \in A$. The elements of the sum are then just the elements of the product. Furthermore, all the embeddings are constrained to be the identity, and so the order relation simplifies to the usual product ordering.

We have retained the set style notation for dependent sum even though it does not make the embeddings explicit. To be fully formal we should work with the functors given by the categorical view. Later on, when we do need the formality, we will do this. Elsewhere, however, we will use the set notation in the belief that familiar notation is helpful.

5 Projection Factorisation

Let us summarise what we have done. We started with a domain-indexed family of domains. From this, we produced a sum domain that respects the structure of the indexing domain. In this section we do things the other way around. We start off with a single domain and discover a domain-indexed family of domains sitting inside it. This allow us to express the original domain as a dependent sum.

We have already noted that domain-theoretic dependent sum is a special case of the (covariant) Grothendieck construction. This (very general) construction has a corresponding decomposition, namely the Grothendieck cofibration. Cofibrations have the property that they give rise to an indexed family whose Grothendieck construction reconstructs the original structure. It turns out that cofibration is precisely the concept we require in order to generalise our earlier notions of projection complements.

Consider a call of some function, $(f\ x)$ say, and suppose that γ is the static projection for f. During partial evaluation, we will be able to compute the static portion of x using γ. Call this value a. Hence $a = \gamma\ x$. At partial evaluation time, the value a represents the sum total of our knowledge about the value x. Prior to calculating the static value, all we would have known about x was its type, X say. Now, however, we can be more precise. Not only must x lie in X, but it must also lie in the inverse image of a under γ. That is, $x \in \gamma^{-1}\{a\}$. This might provide fairly tight constraints on the possible value of x. How tight the constraints are will depend on γ, of course. If γ is a large projection (indicating lots of static information) its inverse images (or *fibres*) will be relatively small but, conversely, if γ is small (not much static information) its fibres will be large.

A question naturally arises. Given that the fibres are subsets of the domain, what sort of structure do they have? The precise answers depends on the projections. The fibres of any projection form consistently complete cpos but they will not necessarily be algebraic. However, for the projections we use (members of an appropriate $\mathit{FinProj}_X$), not only are all the fibres Scott domains, but they also correspond to types which may be defined using the constructions of Section 2.

With these observations our overall strategy should have become clear. The range of the static projection forms a domain which indexes the family of its fibres, each of these being domains. It should, therefore, be possible to express the original domain as a dependent sum, where each of the summands is the inverse image of some static value. In any particular function application, we will know that the dynamic value must be constrained to the fibre corresponding to the static value, and so may express the type of the residual function accordingly.

Towards the end of the paper we will see some examples of this in practice, but in the meantime we show that the strategy may be realised.

5.1 Cofibration

When is a projection a cofibration? That is, when does it give rise to a family of domains whose dependent sum is isomorphic to the original domain? Rather than attempt to give a complete answer we will show that the projections we use do indeed have this property. Unsurprisingly, we induct over the projection constructions. This approach is sufficiently flexible so that if another domain construction were added to those of Section 2, then it alone would need to be checked.

For the present we will take on trust that all the fibres form domains. We will present a lemma shortly which gives a stronger result. Our immediate task is to demonstrate that appropriate embeddings exist. We do this in the following definition and lemma.

Definition
Let $\gamma : X \to X$ be a projection in *FinProj*$_X$ with $x, x' \in \gamma(\!|X|\!)$ such that $x \sqsubseteq x'$. Then $\widehat{\gamma}_{x,x'} : \gamma^{-1}\{x\} \to \gamma^{-1}\{x'\}$ is a mapping from $\gamma^{-1}\{x\}$ into $\gamma^{-1}\{x'\}$ where the $\widehat{\ }$ operation is defined inductively by

$$\widehat{(\gamma \times \delta)}_{(x,y),\,(x',y')} = \widehat{\gamma}_{x,x'} \times \widehat{\delta}_{y,y'}$$

$$\widehat{ABS}_{\bot,\bot} = id$$

$$\widehat{(inl\ \gamma + inr\ \delta)}_{\bot,\ inl\ x'} = \lambda x.x' \qquad \text{(likewise for } inr\text{)}$$

$$\widehat{(inl\ \gamma + inr\ \delta)}_{inl\ x,\ inl\ x'} = \widehat{\gamma}_{x,x'} + id \qquad \text{(likewise for } inr\text{)}$$

$$\widehat{\mu\gamma.P(\gamma)}_{x,x'} = \bigsqcup_n (\phi_n \circ \widehat{P^n(ABS)}_{\psi_n x,\ \psi_n x'} \circ \psi_n)$$

where $(\phi_n, \psi_n) : T^n(1) \to \mu t.T(t)$ is the usual embedding/projection pair.

Lemma 2
Let $\gamma : X \to X$ be a projection in *FinProj*$_X$ with $x, x' \in \gamma(\!|X|\!)$ such that $x \sqsubseteq x'$. Then $\widehat{\gamma}_{x,x'} : \gamma^{-1}\{x\} \to \gamma^{-1}\{x'\}$ is an order-preserving embedding (i.e. $a \sqsubseteq a' \Leftrightarrow \widehat{\gamma}_{x,x'}(a) \sqsubseteq a'$ for any $a \in \gamma^{-1}\{x\}$ and $a' \in \gamma^{-1}\{x'\}$).

Proof
The only case in which the result is not immediately obvious is the recursive case. To simplify notation we will write P^n for $P^n(ABS)$ and P^ω for $\mu\gamma.P(\gamma)$. We need to show three things. Firstly that $\widehat{P^\omega}_{x,x'}$ does indeed map elements of the x fibre to

elements of the x' fibre. Secondly that the map is an embedding, and finally that it preserves order.

Let a be an element in the x fibre (that is, $P^\omega\ a = x$). In order to show that $\widehat{P^\omega}_{x,x'}$ maps elements of the x fibre into the x' fibre, we must show that $P^\omega\ (\widehat{P^\omega}_{x,x'}\ a) = x'$.

$$
\begin{array}{lll}
& (P^\omega \circ \widehat{P^\omega}_{x,x'})\ (a) & \\
= & (P^\omega \circ (\bigsqcup_n\ \phi_n \circ \widehat{P^n}_{\psi_n x,\ \psi_n x'} \circ \psi_n))\ (a) & [\text{defn of } \widehat{P^\omega}] \\
= & (\bigsqcup_n\ P^\omega \circ \phi_n \circ \widehat{P^n}_{\psi_n x,\ \psi_n x'} \circ \psi_n)\ (a) & [\text{continuity}] \\
= & (\bigsqcup_n \bigsqcup_k\ \phi_k \circ P^k \circ \psi_k \circ \phi_n \circ \widehat{P^n}_{\psi_n x,\ \psi_n x'} \circ \psi_n)\ (a) & [\text{defn of } P^\omega] \\
= & (\bigsqcup_n\ \phi_n \circ P^n \circ \psi_n \circ \phi_n \circ \widehat{P^n}_{\psi_n x,\ \psi_n x'} \circ \psi_n)\ (a) & [\text{rearranging}] \\
= & (\bigsqcup_n\ \phi_n \circ P^n \circ \widehat{P^n}_{\psi_n x,\ \psi_n x'} \circ \psi_n)\ (a) & [\psi_n \circ \phi_n = id] \\
= & \bigsqcup_n\ \phi_n\ (P^n\ (\widehat{P^n}_{\psi_n x,\ \psi_n x'}\ (\psi_n\ a))) & \\
= & \bigsqcup_n\ \phi_n\ (\psi_n\ x') & [\text{finite induction}] \\
= & x' & [\text{algebraicity}]
\end{array}
$$

To see that $\widehat{P^\omega}_{x,x'}$ is an embedding we only need to note that (by finite induction) its approximations are all embeddings on larger and larger subdomains. In the limit we obtain an embedding on the whole domain. Finally, suppose that $a \sqsubseteq a'$ (where $a \in \gamma^{-1}\{x\}$ and $a' \in \gamma^{-1}\{x'\}$). As order between the finite approximations of a and a' (namely, $\psi_n\ a$ and $\psi_n\ a'$) is preserved by the approximations to $\widehat{P^\omega}_{x,x'}$ (an easy induction), then order is also preserved in the limit. □

We are now in a position to show that all the projections in $FinProj_X$ are cofibrations. Their fibres form an indexed family of domains such that, when we construct their dependent sum, we obtain a domain isomorphic to the original. This, our main result, is expressed in the following theorem.

Theorem 3 (Projection Factorisation)
If $\gamma : X \rightarrow X$ is an element of $FinProj_X$ then

$$X \cong \sum_{a \in \gamma(X)} \gamma^{-1}\{a\}$$

Proof
The elements of the sum are all of the form $(\gamma\ x,\ x)$ and so are in one-to-one correspondence with the elements of X. Furthermore, both X and the sum have the same ordering, for

$$
\begin{array}{lll}
& (\gamma\ x,\ x) \sqsubseteq_\Sigma (\gamma\ x',\ x') & \\
\Leftrightarrow & (\gamma\ x \sqsubseteq_X \gamma\ x') \wedge (\widehat{\gamma}_{\gamma x, \gamma x'}(x) \sqsubseteq_X x') & [\text{definition}] \\
\Leftrightarrow & (\gamma\ x \sqsubseteq_X \gamma\ x') \wedge (x \sqsubseteq_X x') & [\text{lemma 2}] \\
\Leftrightarrow & x \sqsubseteq_X x' & [\gamma \text{ monotonic}]
\end{array}
$$

which completes the proof. □

The projection factorisation theorem allows an arbitrary domain to be decomposed in many different ways depending on the choice of projection. In contrast with using projection complements, this factorisation is exact. However, there is still an issue open. We must show that all the fibres form domains. We actually want something stronger than this. As the fibres correspond to the domain of possible dynamic values we would like to produce a residual function whose argument type corresponds to the fibre. We need to know, therefore, whether the fibres are expressible in the type system. Fortunately, in most cases they are. We will consider a few examples before proving the result in general.

Consider the *Assoc* type again, together with the projection *STRUCT* that discards all the elements but retains the spine. The element *More* $(\perp, \perp, End)$ is in the range of *STRUCT* and its inverse image is isomorphic to the domain $Var \times Val$. Similarly, the element *More* $(\perp, \perp, More\ (\perp, \perp, End))$ is also in the range of *STRUCT*. Its inverse image is isomorphic to the domain $Var \times Val \times Var \times Val$. To take another example consider the *Num* type together with the projection *TAG* which discards everything except the injection tags. The element *Int* $\perp$ is in the range of *TAG* and its inverse image is isomorphic to *Integer*. These examples are typical and may be generalised to any finite element in the range of a projection, as the following theorem makes clear.

Theorem 4
Let X be a domain and $\gamma \in FinProj_X$ a projection. If $a \in \gamma(\!|X|\!)$ is a finite element then there exists a domain $B_a \cong \gamma^{-1}\{a\}$ such that B_a is expressible in the type system.

Sketch Proof
The proof is by induction over the static projection constructions. If the projection is *ABS* then the inverse image is just one of the domains we started with and so is expressible in the type system. In the sum and product cases the induction is straightforward. For the recursive case we appeal to the restriction that the static value is finite. In this case we only need to unfold the recursive type finitely often, and so will end up with a finite product of domains each expressible in the type system. □

The restriction in the theorem to finite elements ensures that we will never need to construct an infinite product. In principle, there is no reason why we should not, except that many languages exclude such constructions. Nonetheless, this is not a serious restriction. Attempting to specialise a function to an infinite value will cause the partial evaluator to loop. Conversely, if the partial evaluator halts, then no infinite values will have arisen.

5.2 Domain Dependent Products

In order to describe the action of the partial evaluator we need to define dependent products. Again these are more familiar in set theory than domain theory, but we may define them quite easily after having defined dependent sum.

Definition (Domain Dependent Product)
If $\{B_a\}_{a\in A}$ is a domain-indexed family of domains then the *dependent product* of the family is given by,

$$\prod_{a\in A} B_a = \{f \mid f_a \in B_a\}$$

where the elements f are continuous families indexed by A with the ordering

$$f \sqsubseteq_{\Pi} g \Leftrightarrow \forall a \in A.\ f_a \sqsubseteq_{B_a} g_a$$

The elements of the product are like functions except that their range is not very clearly defined. Supplying an indexing element $a \in A$ produces an element of the corresponding B_a. Each family is continuous, so if $a \sqsubseteq a'$ then $\phi_{a,a'}(f_a) \sqsubseteq_{B_a} f_{a'}$ and if $a = \bigsqcup\{a_i\}$ then $f_a = \bigsqcup\{\phi_{a_i,a}(f_{a_i})\}$.

A proof that dependent product is a Scott domain appears in [9]. An equivalent formulation defines the elements of the product to be the continuous sections of the first projection from the dependent sum. That is, the elements are functions $f : A \rightarrow \sum(A, B)$ such that $fst \circ f = id_A$. Such functions must have the form $f\ a = (a, b)$ where $b \in B_a$. This formulation makes it very clear that, if the family of domains is constant, then the dependent product $\prod_{a\in A} B$ is isomorphic to the function space $(A \rightarrow B)$.

There is an important isomorphism between function spaces from dependent sums and dependent products of function spaces.

Lemma 5
If $\{B_a\}_{a\in A}$ is a domain-indexed family of domains, and if C is some domain, then

$$(\sum_{a\in A} B_a) \rightarrow C \;\cong\; \prod_{a\in A}(B_a \rightarrow C)$$

Proof
This can be proved directly for the case of domains, but we can give an elegant category theoretic proof (communicated to me by Andrew Pitts). The details may be skipped without serious consequences.

The isomorphism is a consequence of the following adjoint situation. Let *Dom* be the usual category of domains and continuous functions, Dom^{ep} be the category of domains with embedding/projection pairs, and $[A \rightarrow Dom^{ep}]$ be the category of continuous functors from the domain A (viewed as a category) to Dom^{ep}. This latter category corresponds to domain-indexed families of domains. There is a functor $\Delta : Dom \rightarrow [A \rightarrow Dom^{ep}]$ (called the *diagonal functor*) which maps any domain D into the constant functor Δ_D (i.e the constant family $\{D\}_{a\in A}$). This functor has both a left and a right adjoint which are dependent sum and product, respectively (written $\sum \dashv \Delta \dashv \prod$). Let X be an arbitrary domain and $B : A \rightarrow Dom^{ep}$ be a functor corresponding to an indexed family of domains $\{B_a\}_{a\in A}$. Then all the following are natural isomorphisms:

$$\begin{array}{lll} Hom(X,\ (\sum B) \rightarrow C) & & \\ \quad \cong\ Hom(\sum B,\ X \rightarrow C) & & \text{[currying twice and product commutative]} \\ \quad \cong\ Hom(B,\ \Delta(X \rightarrow C)) & & [\Sigma \dashv \Delta] \\ \quad \cong\ Hom(B,\ \Delta X \rightarrow \Delta C) & & [\Delta \text{ preserves } \rightarrow] \\ \quad \cong\ Hom(\Delta X,\ B \rightarrow \Delta C) & & \text{[currying twice and product commutative]} \\ \quad \cong\ Hom(X,\ \prod(B \rightarrow \Delta C)) & & [\Delta \dashv \Pi] \end{array}$$

Thus, $Hom(\ \_\ ,\ (\sum B) \rightarrow C)$ is naturally isomorphic to $Hom(\ \_\ ,\ \prod(B \rightarrow \Delta C))$ and so, by the Yoneda lemma, $(\sum B) \rightarrow C \cong \prod(B \rightarrow \Delta C)$. Written in the notation of families this is just $(\sum_{a\in A} B_a) \rightarrow C \cong \prod_{a\in A}(B_a \rightarrow C)$. $\square$

Using this isomorphism, we are able to describe the action of a partial evaluator. Suppose we start with some function $f : X \to Y$ together with a partial description of a value $x \in X$. Let $\gamma : X \to X$ be the static projection, so that the partial description of the value $x \in X$ gives us complete information about the value $\gamma\ x \in \gamma(X)$. As the domain X is isomorphic to the domain $\sum_{a \in \gamma(X)}(\gamma^{-1}\{a\})$, we may view f as a function $f : (\sum_{a \in \gamma(X)}(\gamma^{-1}\{a\})) \to Y$. Now, we are in a position to appeal to the isomorphism above, and so also view f as an indexed family $f \in \prod_{a \in \gamma(X)}(\gamma^{-1}\{a\} \to Y)$. Supplying the index value $(\gamma\ x)$ gives us the corresponding residual function $f_{(\gamma\ x)} : \gamma^{-1}\{a\} \to Y$.

It is important to remember that a partial evaluator actually manipulates programs (i.e. representations of functions) rather than functions themselves. As such, each of the steps above require a fair amount of symbolic manipulation to achieve in practice. The description above expresses *extensionally* what happens to the functions, but says very little about the algorithms that achieve it through *intensional* manipulation.

If, in the isomorphism demonstrated above, we reduce the dependent sum and dependent product to their special cases of product and function space respectively, then the isomorphism reduces to currying. Thus, as a special case, currying remains a useful idiom for discussing partial evaluation. However, it fails to exhibit one important point: in general, the *type* of a residual function depends on the static *value* used to produce it. It is because of this fact that the use of dependent sum is unavoidable in general.

5.3 Examples

We return to the *Assoc* and *Num* types for our examples (Section 2). Suppose that, as we suggested earlier, we attempt to specialise an interpreter containing an environment in which the variable names are static but the values are dynamic. Commonly, there will be some sort of environment lookup function which will need to be specialised to the static portion of the environment. Assuming a standard definition for ***lookup***, what will its residual versions look like? The following is a typical example. Suppose the static part of the association list is

More ("X", $\perp$, *More* ("Y", $\perp$, *More* ("Z", $\perp$, ***End***)))

and that we apply ***lookup*** to it with index "Y". The residual function would be,

$$lookup_1\ (a, b, c) \ = \ b$$

The residual function now has three arguments whereas the original only had one. This is an example of *arity raising* as described by Sestoft [2] and Romanenko [10]. Sestoft reports that residual functions can have a significantly greater efficiency if arity raising is performed, but relied on hand placed annotations in the program to obtain it. In contrast, Romanenko performed a post processing analysis and achieved arity raising automatically. More recently, Mogensen [11] used the results of binding time analysis for the same purpose. However, each of these approaches were fairly *ad hoc*. With dependent sum factorisation, arity raising arises as a natural consequence of the theory.

Arity raising is not the only optimisation that dependent sum factorisation provides automatically. Another is tag removal. Consider the following coercion function which operates on elements of the *Num* type,

$$
\begin{aligned}
&\mathit{make\_complex} : \mathit{Num} \rightarrow (\mathit{Real} \times \mathit{Real})\\
&\mathit{make\_complex}\ x \;=\; \mathit{case}\ x\ \mathit{in}\\
&\qquad \mathit{Int}\ n \;\rightarrow\; (\mathit{make\_real}\ (\mathit{Int}\ n),\ 0.0);\\
&\qquad \mathit{Re}\ r \;\rightarrow\; (r,\ 0.0);\\
&\qquad \mathit{Comp}\ c \;\rightarrow\; c;
\end{aligned}
$$

Suppose that binding time analysis determines that the projection *TAG* specifies the static portion of the input to the function *make_complex*. Then the possible specialisations of *make_complex* are the functions,

$$
\begin{aligned}
&\mathit{make\_complex}_{(\mathit{Int}\ \bot)} : \mathit{Integer} \rightarrow (\mathit{Real} \times \mathit{Real})\\
&\mathit{make\_complex}_{(\mathit{Int}\ \bot)}\ n \;=\; (\mathit{make\_real}_{(\mathit{Int}\ \bot)}\ n,\ 0.0)
\end{aligned}
$$

$$
\begin{aligned}
&\mathit{make\_complex}_{(\mathit{Re}\ \bot)} : \mathit{Real} \rightarrow (\mathit{Real} \times \mathit{Real})\\
&\mathit{make\_complex}_{(\mathit{Re}\ \bot)}\ r \;=\; (r,\ 0.0)
\end{aligned}
$$

$$
\begin{aligned}
&\mathit{make\_complex}_{(\mathit{Comp}\ \bot)} : (\mathit{Real} \times \mathit{Real}) \rightarrow (\mathit{Real} \times \mathit{Real})\\
&\mathit{make\_complex}_{(\mathit{Comp}\ \bot)}\ c \;=\; c
\end{aligned}
$$

Not only has the run-time test been eliminated (and, presumably, another test in *make_real*) but so has the unnecessary packaging and unpackaging that occurred with complements. The arguments to the residual functions are optimal in that they contains no static information at all.

6 Acknowledgements

This work forms part of my Ph.D. research undertaken at Glasgow University funded by a research studentship from S.E.R.C. My thanks to all the members of the Computing Science department at Glasgow for providing an active and stimulating environment but particularly to John Hughes my supervisor—a never ending source of ideas—and also to Fairouz Kamerradine for our numerous discussions. Further afield, I would also like to thank the members of the MIX group at DIKU, but especially Neil Jones, Torben Mogensen and Peter Sestoft, for their helpful feedback and suggestions. Finally, I am very grateful to Dave Schmidt, Andy Pitts and Thierry Coquand for their guidance with the mathematics.

References

[1] N. Jones, P. Sestoft and H. Søndergaard. *An Experiment in Partial Evaluation: The Generation of a Compiler Generator.* In *Rewriting Techniques and Applications*, editor J.-P. Jouannaud, LNCS 202, pages 124-140, 1985.

[2] P. Sestoft. *The Structure of a Self-Applicable Partial Evaluator.* In *Programs as Data Objects*, editors H. Ganzinger and N. Jones, LNCS 217, pages 236-256, 1986.

[3] N. Jones, P. Sestoft and H. Søndergaard. *Mix: A Self-Applicable Partial Evaluator for Experiments in Compiler Generation.* Lisp and Symbolic Computation, 2, pages 9-50, 1989.

[4] D. Bjørner, A. Ershov and N. Jones (Editors). *Partial Evaluation and Mixed Computation.* Proceedings IFIP TC2 Workshop, Gammel Avernæs, Denmark, October 1987. North-Holland, 1988.

[5] D. Scott and C. Gunter. *Semantic Domains.* Draft, in *Handbook of Theoretical Computer Science*, North Holland, to appear.

[6] J. Launchbury. *Projection Factorisations in Partial Evaluation.* Ph.D. Thesis, Glasgow University, 1989.

[7] P. Martin-Löf. *Intuitionistic Type Theory.* Bibliopolis, 1980.

[8] G. Plotkin. *Complete Partial Orders, a Tool for Making Meanings.* Lecture notes for the Pisa Summerschool, 1978.

[9] T. Coquand, C. Gunter, and G. Winskel. *Domain Theoretic Models of Polymorphism.* Technical Report 116, University of Cambridge, 1987.

[10] S. Romanenko. *A Compiler Generator Produced by a Self-Applicable Specializer Can Have a Surprisingly Natural and Understandable Structure.* In [4], pages 445-463, 1988.

[11] T. Mogensen. *Binding Time Aspects of Partial Evaluation.* Ph.D. Thesis, DIKU, University of Copenhagen, 1989.

Type inference and type classes

Stephen Blott
Department of Computing Science
University of Glasgow

Type classes were developed in association with the lazy functional programming language Haskell [1] to handle overloading since no satisfactory off-the-shelf solution was available. The motivation and description of type classes is given in [2].

Type classes can be implemented by an extension to a traditional Hindley/Milner type-checker [3, 4, 5, 6] which follows the schema outlined below.

- Firstly, a set of overloadings of operators and identifiers can be defined in a the standard prelude or by the programmer.
- The program is then type-checked under an extension to the Hindley/Milner algorithm which resloves overloading when the context of an identifier's use allows. If a defintion is ambiguous (not resolved by context) then the new identifier is implicitly overloaded.
- Associated with each typing is a translation, the implementation of the program at the given type. Definitions of implicitly overloaded identifiers are replaced with equivalent parametrised definitions which can then be specialised to particular overloaded instances.

The Glasgow Haskell impementation is currently nearing completion and a report on the experience gained in the implementation of type classes may be found in [7].

This note presentes the type system, type inference algorithm, and principal type property and discusses implementation. It can viewed as an extension to that work which appears in the appendix of [2] and which will appear in a complete form in [8].

The presentation, in the main, is fairly terse; the motivation is left to [2]. Luis Damas' thesis [9] has been followed fairly closely, in particular, the proof of completeness.

1 The type system

This section outlines the type system; it is based on that which appears in the appendix of [2]. The main change is the separation of the translation from a typing. Further, examination of the principal type theorem has required several other more subtle changes.

Typings are of the form $A \vdash e : \sigma$, that is, under the *assumption set* A the expression e can be assigned type-scheme σ. We start with some definitions.

Identifiers	x	Types	τ
Expressions	e	Predicated types	ρ
Type Variables	α	Type-schemes	σ
Type Constructors	χ		

$$\begin{array}{lcl} e & ::= & x \mid e_0\ e_1 \mid \lambda x.e \\ & \mid & \textbf{let } x = e_0 \textbf{ in } e_1 \\ & \mid & \textbf{over } x : \sigma \textbf{ in } e \\ & \mid & \textbf{inst } x : \sigma = e_0 \textbf{ in } e_1 \end{array} \qquad \begin{array}{lcl} \tau & ::= & \alpha \mid \tau \rightarrow \tau' \\ & \mid & \chi(\tau_1, ..., \tau_n) \\ \rho & ::= & (x : \tau).\rho \mid \tau \\ \sigma & ::= & \forall \alpha.\sigma \mid \rho \end{array}$$

Figure 1: The grammar of expressions and types

1.1 Definitions

Types, predicated types, type-schemes and expressions are all defined as previously, see Figure 1. Predicates represent a form of bounded quantification, a requirement that an overloaded identifier have an instance at a given type; and **over** and **inst** expressions introcuce overloaded identifiers and instances thereof respectively.

An assumption set[1] is an assignment of type information to program identifiers. Lambda and let bound identifiers are associated with a type scheme (as in [5]) while overloaded identifiers require extra information regarding the instances which are in scope. There are three forms of assumption:

- $x : \sigma$, the typing of an identifier;
- $x :_o \sigma$, the signature of overloaded identifiers; and
- $x :_i \sigma$, instances of overloaded identifiers.

Subsequently we will restrict assumption sets by requiring them to be *valid.* The essential idea is that instances of overloaded identifiers must *make sense* within the given context, as must the predicates within the type-schemes.

We use A (also A' etc.) to denote assumption sets. We use P to denote segments of assumption sets containing only bindings of the form $x :_i \sigma$.

A substitution S is a mapping from type variables to types. Substitutions can also be applied to types, type-schemes and assumption sets under the obvious generalisations. Robinson's unification algorithm U is used [10] to find the most general substitution which unifies two types (if such a substitution exists). Id denotes the identity substitution.

[1] Assumption sets are misnamed, they are essentially bags. I wish to differentiate between two assumptions of a single instance. There is some question as to whether sets would be a better choice. This may be so; however, in order to maintain consistency, for this report they should be viewed as bags. Further, use of the ∪ operator on assumption sets should be viewed a bag union or concatenation, not set union.

TAUT $\sigma \geq_{A'} \sigma$

GEN $$\frac{\sigma \geq_A \sigma'}{\sigma \geq_A \forall\alpha.\sigma'} \quad \alpha \notin FV(\sigma)$$

SPEC $$\frac{\sigma \geq_A \forall\alpha.\sigma'}{\sigma \geq_A [\alpha \setminus \tau]\sigma'}$$

PRED $$\frac{\sigma \geq_{A;x:_i\tau} \rho}{\sigma \geq_A (x:\tau).\rho}$$

REL $$\frac{\sigma \geq_A (x:\tau).\rho}{\sigma \geq_A \rho} \quad x :_i \sigma' \in A, \quad \sigma' \geq_A \tau$$

Figure 2: Instance rules for type-schemes

We call one assumption set A' an instance of another A, as witnessed by S, if for some P

$$SA \cup P = A'.$$

That is, if by applying S to A and adding some set of predicate assumptions, one can construct A'.

We construct a relation $\sigma \geq_A \sigma'$ on type schemes to describe when, in a given context A, one type-scheme σ is *more general* than another σ'. In the absence of predicates, this definition subsumes that of [5, 9]; for predicates, it makes use of the instance information in scope to allow specialisation of typings to particular instances. The definition is given in Figure 2. The rules parallel the TAUT, GEN, SPEC, PRED and REL typing rules as Damas-Milner's instance rule does TAUT, GEN and SPEC.

1.2 Validity of type-schemes and assumption sets

As will be seen shortly, predicates move freely between the predicate part of a type-scheme and instance assumptions in an assumption set. Thus, to ensure that all environments are meaningful we require that predicates in type-scehmes be well-formed.

$\forall\alpha_1 \cdots \forall\alpha_n.(x_1:\tau_1)\cdots(x_m:\tau_m).\tau$ is *valid* in context A iff, for each τ_i (for i in 1 to m), there is a binding $x_i :_o \forall\beta_1 \cdots \forall\beta_p.(x'_1:\tau'_1)\cdots(x'_q:\tau'_q).\tau' \in A$ such that there is a substitution S of types for $\beta_1 \cdots \beta_p$ with $\tau_i = S\tau'$. That is, all the predicates in a type-scheme are well formed with respect to the environment; must have a corresponding overloading in a.

All assumption sets used within proofs must be valid. Valid assumption sets are defined inductively as follows.

- *Empty.* The empty set of assumptions, $\{\}$, is valid.
- *Normal identifier.* If A is a valid assumption set, σ is a valid type-scheme in context A, and x is not bound in A, then

$$A; x : \sigma$$

  is a valid assumption set.
- *Overloaded identifiers.* If A is a valid assumption set, and x is not bound in A, then

$$A;\ x :_o \sigma$$

  is valid.
- *Instances.* If A is a valid assumption set, σ is a valid type-scheme, and $x :_o \sigma \in A$, then

$$A;\ x :_i \sigma_1;\ ...;\ x :_i \sigma_n$$

  is valid iff, for i from 1 to n, σ_i is a valid type-scheme and $\sigma \geq_A \sigma_i$.

1.3 The typing rules

We are now in a position to present the typing rules. There are two groups of rules: the Damas/Milner rules (modulo the extension the the syntax of types and expressions), and the new rules.

There are five new rules: TAUT_i types overloaded identifiers with some instance in the environment; PRED and REL introduce and eliminate predicates (as GEN and SPEC do bound type variables); and OVER and INST type the new forms of expression.

Note that PRED and REL are the most significant typing rules; they characterise how we handle overloading. Notice also the relationship between the pair PRED and REL and the pair ABS and COMB, this is significant when we come to consider the translation.

2 Type inference algorithm

In this section we will describe a type inference algorithm O which infers typings for the type system outlined herein as W [5, 9] does for the Hindley-Milner type system.

Throughout this section we will assume that expressions are in the presence of a fixed set of overloadings. That is, no expressions contain **over** or **inst** sub-expression. We further assume that no overloaded identifiers have super-types.

β is used to denote a *fresh* type variable, that is, one which has not been used and will not be used elsewhere within the activation.

TAUT $A;\ x : \sigma \vdash x : \sigma$

SPEC $$\frac{A \vdash e : \forall \alpha.\, \sigma}{A \vdash e : [\alpha \setminus \tau]\sigma}$$

GEN $$\frac{A \vdash e : \sigma}{A \vdash e : \forall \alpha.\, \sigma} \qquad \alpha \notin FV(A)$$

COMB $$\frac{A \vdash e : (\tau' \rightarrow \tau) \quad A \vdash e' : \tau'}{A \vdash (e\ e') : \tau}$$

ABS $$\frac{A_x;\ x : \tau' \vdash e : \tau}{A \vdash (\lambda x.\, e) : (\tau' \rightarrow \tau)}$$

LET $$\frac{A \vdash e : \sigma \quad A_x;\ x : \sigma \vdash e' : \tau}{A \vdash (\mathbf{let}\ x = e\ \mathbf{in}\ e') : \tau}$$

Figure 3: The Damas/Milner typing rules

$$\textbf{TAUT}_i \quad A;\ x :_i \sigma \vdash x : \sigma$$

$$\textbf{PRED} \quad \frac{A;\ x :_i \tau \vdash e : \rho}{A \vdash e : (x : \tau).\rho}$$

$$\textbf{REL} \quad \frac{A \vdash e : (x : \tau).\rho \qquad A \vdash x : \tau}{A \vdash e : \rho}$$

$$\textbf{OVER} \quad \frac{A_x;\ x :_o \sigma \vdash e : \tau'}{A \vdash (\textbf{over}\ x : \sigma\ \textbf{in}\ e) : \tau'}$$

$$\textbf{INST} \quad \frac{A;\ x :_i \sigma' \vdash e' : \sigma' \qquad A;\ x :_i \sigma' \vdash e : \tau}{A \vdash (\textbf{inst}\ x : \sigma' = e'\ \textbf{in}\ e) : \tau}$$

Figure 4: The new typing rules

Still further notation is required. We extend the notion of *generalising a typing* of [5] to the bounded quantification described by predicates. Generalisation, as appears in the **let** clause below, is written $\overline{A}(P, \tau)$ and is defined as follows.

$$\overline{A}(\{x_1 ::_i \tau_1; \cdots; x_m ::_i \tau_m\}, \tau) = \forall\alpha_1 \cdots \forall\alpha_n.(x_1 : \tau_1) \cdots (x_m : \tau_m).\tau$$

where $\alpha_1, ..., \alpha_n$ are those type variables free in $\{\tau, \tau_1, ..., \tau_m\}$ but not in A.

O extends W by returning an extra result, a predicate assumption set. The new characterisation rule for O is

$$O(A, e) = (S, \tau, P) \text{ implies } SA \cup P \vdash e : \tau$$

P contains the instances of overloaded identifiers which were required to be assumed in order that the typing proceed. Therefore, the generalisation of the typing is also a typing, bounded by the instance assumptions P.

$$O(A, e) = (S, \tau, P) \text{ implies } SA \vdash e : \overline{SA}(P, \tau).$$

2.1 Algorithm O

O is then a simple extension to W. All type variables β are *fresh*, that is, they do not appear elsewhere in the activation. The algorithm is presented in Figure 5. The first line in the identifier cases are assertions with respect to binding in A, the first one deals with lambda and let bound identifiers while the second handles overloaded identifiers. If that or any of the unifications fail then the whole algorithm fails.

This is the most basic inference algorithm satisfying the requirements. It treats predicates in a passive way; they are synthesized from identifiers at the leaves and bound at **let** expressions. In particular, no attempt is made to establish whether a predicate is satisfied by an instance in the environment. As such, this algorithm is not intended to be an *implementation*, it is useful since it computes *principal typings*.

3 Results!

In this section we give the two main results: the syntactic soundness and completeness results for O which lead in turn to the existence of principal typings. We require two restrictions:

- firstly, that the expressions under consideration contain no **over** or **inst** sub-expressions, that all the overloading is in the environment; and
- secondly, that all $::_o$ bindings are of the form $\forall\alpha_1 \cdots \alpha_n.\tau$, that is, we are not considering any super-type relationships between overloaded operators.

The former assumption is fundamental, we can show that principal types do not exist if it is omitted. The latter, however, is a restriction on the scope of the work attempted so far. It is hoped that this will be dropped in the future.

This section, as with all the Sections hereafter, should be viewed as a summary of those which will appear in [8].

$$
\begin{array}{lcl}
O(A,x) & = & x : \forall\alpha_1 \cdots \forall\alpha_n.(x_1 : \tau_1)\cdots(x_m : \tau_m).\tau \in A \\
 & & S' = [\beta_1/\alpha_1; \cdots ; \beta_n/\alpha_n] \\
 & & (Id, S'\tau, \{x_1 :_i S'\tau_1; \cdots ; x_m :_i S'\tau_m\}) \\
 & & \\
O(A,x) & = & x :_o \forall\alpha_1 \cdots \forall\alpha_n.\tau \in A \\
 & & S' = [\beta_1/\alpha_1; \cdots ; \beta_n/\alpha_n] \\
 & & (Id, S'\tau, \{x :_i S'\tau\}) \\
 & & \\
O(A, \lambda x.e) & = & (S_1, \tau_1, P_1) = O(A_x; x : \beta,\ e) \\
 & & (S_1, S_1\beta \rightarrow \tau_1, P_1) \\
 & & \\
O(A, (e_1\ e_2)) & = & (S_1, \tau_1, P_1) = O(A, e_1) \\
 & & (S_2, \tau_2, P_2) = O(S_1 A, e_2) \\
 & & V = U(S_2\tau_1, \tau_2 \rightarrow \beta) \\
 & & (VS_2S_1, V\beta, VP_1 \cup VS_2P_1) \\
 & & \\
O(A, \mathbf{let}\ x = e_1\ \mathbf{in}\ e_2) & = & (S_1, \tau_1, P_1) = O(A, e_1) \\
 & & (S_2, \tau_2, P_2) = O(S_1 A_x; x : \overline{S_1 A}(P_1, \tau_1),\ e_2) \\
 & & (S_2S_1, \tau_2, P_2)
\end{array}
$$

Figure 5: Algorithm O

$$
\begin{array}{lcl}
R(A,P) & = & \text{let } P' = R'(A, P, \{\}) \text{ in} \\
 & & \text{if } P' = P \text{ then } P \text{ else } R(A, P') \\
 & & \\
R'(A, \{\}, P') & = & P' \\
R'(A, \{x : \tau\} \cup P, P') & = & \text{if } \exists x :_i \sigma \in A \text{ and } \exists \tau_i' \text{ such that} \\
 & & \quad \forall\alpha_1 ... \forall\alpha_n.(x_1 : \tau_1)...(x_m : \tau_m).\tau' = \sigma \\
 & & \quad S = [\tau_1'/\alpha_1, ..., \tau_n'/\alpha_n] \\
 & & \quad\ \text{such that } S\tau' = \tau \\
 & & \text{then} \\
 & & \quad Q = \{x_1 : S\tau_1, ..., x_n : S\tau_m\} \\
 & & \quad R'(A, P, Q \cup P') \\
 & & \text{else} \\
 & & \quad R'(A, P, \{x : \tau\} \cup P')
\end{array}
$$

Figure 6: Discharging of predicates

3.1 Syntactic soundness of O

O is *sound.* If O computes a typing then such a typing is provable within the type system. The theorem is as follows.

Theorem 1 *Soundness of* O*. If* $O(A,e) = (S,P,\tau)$ *then* $SA \cup P \vdash e : \tau$

Proof

The proof is by structural induction on e. It has been omitted for brevity from the current note.

3.2 Syntactic completeness of O

O is complete. If a typing exists, then O will compute a typing which *characterises* the given one. The theorem is as follows.

Theorem 2 *Completeness of* O*. Given* A *and* e*, and that* A' *is an instance of* A*, if* $A' \vdash e : \sigma'$ *then*

1. $O(A,e) = (S,P,\tau)$ *terminates ;*
2. A' *is an instance (minimal witness* R*) of* SA*; and*
3. *taking* $\sigma = \overline{SA}(P,\tau)$*,* $R\sigma \geq_{A'} \sigma'$*.*

Proof

The proof follows, in the main, that of the equivalent result in [9]. It is in two parts: we first show by an inductive argumment that the theorem holds if the last step of the derivation $A' \vdash e : \sigma'$ is a GEN, SPEC, PRED, or INST; we continue by structural induction on e assuming the last rule applied in each case was the appropriate structural rule TAUT, ABS, COMB or LET. Again, the proof has benn omitted on the grounds of brevity.

3.3 Principal typings: corollarys

We say that a type scheme σ is a *principal type-scheme of* e *under* A iff

1. $A \vdash e : \sigma$;
2. if $A \vdash e : \sigma'$ then $\sigma \geq_A \sigma'$.

Corollary 1

If $O(A,e)$ succeeds with (S,P,τ) then $\overline{SA}(P,\tau)$ is a principal type-scheme of e under PA.

Proof: exactly as in [9].

Corollary 2

If it is possible to derive a type-scheme for e under A then there is a principal type-scheme for e under A.

Proof: exactly as in [9].

4 Translation

In [2] the translation was associated directly with the typing, that is, typings are of the form $A \vdash e : \sigma \setminus \bar{e}$. In this section we discuss briefly how the translation, or semantics, of the new calculus is defined.

The translation of a term clearly depends on the typing; an overloaded identifier can be typed in as many ways as there are instance assumptions for it in the environment, each with a different meaning. Following [11] we assign a semantics to each typing derivation. That is, we map derivations in our system to derivations in the calculus of Damas/Milner. Here we give only the translation of assumption sets and type-schemes to give a feeling for the semantics.

We denote the translation (a projection) by *. Assumption sets and type-schemes are projected as follows. Bounded quantification in type-schemes is replaced with function types

$$(\forall\alpha_1 \cdots \forall\alpha_n.(x_1 : \tau_1) \cdots (x_m : \tau_m).\tau)^* = \forall\alpha_1 \cdots \forall\alpha_n.\tau_1 \to \tau_2 \to \cdots \to \tau_m \to \tau$$

and the projection is mapped across assumption sets.

$$\begin{array}{lcl} \{\}^* & = & \{\} \\ (A;\ x : \sigma)^* & = & A^*;\ x : \sigma^* \\ (A;\ x :_o \sigma)^* & = & A^* \\ (A;\ x :_i \sigma)^* & = & A^*;\ \overline{x :_i \sigma} : \sigma^* \end{array}$$

The notation $\overline{x :_i \sigma}$ denotes an implementation identifier associated with each instance assumption.

This translation will be treated more fully in [8] along with the *coherance* of the semantics (do derivations of the same typing have the same meaning).

5 Implementation

As mentioned previously, the algorithm herein treats predicates in a passive way, they are merely synthesized. This is not however the typing described in [2]; predicates which are satisfied by instances in the environment are eliminated. In this Section we give an algorithm which constructs such typings. A more detailed discussion of implementation issues appears in [7].

Figure 6 contains an algorithm R for discharing predicate assumptions, that is, releasing predicate assumptions which have been specialised such that there now exists an instance in A which satisfies them. In the case where an instance is predicated itself, these new predicates are introduced as new predicate assumptions. R is repeated until its application does not change the set of predicate assumptions.

R has been shown to be sound, in particular R corresponds to the following derived typing rule for some expression e and type τ.

$$\frac{A \cup P \vdash e : \tau}{A \cup P' \vdash e : \tau} \quad R(A, P) = P'$$

R can be incorporated in O at **let** expressions in order to eliminate predicates. However,

References

[1] P. Hudak, and P. Wadler (editors), Report on the functional programming language Haskell, Technical report YALEU/DCS/RR656, Yale University, Department of Computer Science, November 1988.

[2] Phil Wadler and Stephen Blott, How to make *ad-hoc* polymorphism less ad hoc, In *Proceedings of the 16'th Annual Symposium on Principles of Programming Languages*, Austin, Texas, January 1989.

[3] R. Hindley, The principal type scheme of an object in combinatory logic. In *Trans. Am. Math. Soc. 146*, pp. 29–60, December 1969.

[4] R. Milner, A theory of type polymorphism in programming. In *J. Comput. Syst. Sci. 17*, pp. 348–375, 1978.

[5] L. Damas and R. Milner, Principal type schemes for functional programs. In *Proceedings of the 9'th Annual Symposium on Principles of Programming Languages*, Albuquerque, N.M., January 1982.

[6] Luca Cardelli, Basic polymorphic typechecking, Computing Science tech. report 119, AT and T Bell laboratories, Murray Hill, NJ, 1984.

[7] Kevin Hammond, De-Mysticifying type classes, in *Proceedings of the 2nd Glasgow FP group workshop*, Fraserburgh, Scotland, 1989.

[8] S. Blott, Thesis, Computing Science Dept., University of Glasgow, (in preparation).

[9] L. Damas, Type assignment in programming languages, Thesis, University of Edinburgh, 1985.

[10] J. A. Robinson, A machine orientated logic based on the resolution principal. JACM 12, 1, pp. 23-41, 1965.

[11] V. Breazu, T. Coquand, C. A. Gunter, and S. Scedrov. *Inheritance and explicit coercion (preliminary report)*, V. Breazu, Department of Computer and Information Sciences, University of Pensylvania, Philidelphia, PA 19104, USA. October 1988.

Implementing Haskell Type Classes

K. Hammond and S. Blott,
Glasgow University*.

Abstract

This paper describes the implementation of the type class mechanism for the functional language Haskell. A simple introduction to type classes discusses the methods used to select operators and dictionaries in the Glasgow Haskell compiler. A solution to the problem of selecting super-class dictionaries, not considered by the original paper on type classes, is also presented. The modifications which must be made to a standard Hindley/Milner type-checker to allow the transformation of operators in the type-checking pass are described, and a revised definition of the type-checking algorithm *W* is provided. Finally, a set of performance figures compares the run-time efficiency of Haskell and LML code, indicating the overhead involved in the original naïve method of operator selection, and the improvement which may be obtained through simple optimisations.

1 Introduction

Haskell is a non-strict pure functional programming language [1,2], designed by a committee of functional programmers[1]. Haskell is named after the logician Haskell B. Curry whose seminal work in combinatory logic and lambda calculus forms the underpinning of much recent research in functional programming. Its raison d'être is to act as a common base for functional programming research, applications development and teaching.

As a framework for future research, Haskell incorporates many recent innovations in functional language design, in addition to features which are well understood. The

* Authors' address: Department of Computing, 17 Lilybank Gardens, Glasgow, UK.
Electronic mail: kh@cs.glasgow.ac.uk, blott@cs.glasgow.ac.uk.

1 The Haskell committee comprises: Arvind, Brian Boutel, Jon Fairbairn, Joe Fasel, Kevin Hammond, Paul Hudak, John Hughes, Thomas Johnsson, Simon Peyton Jones, Dick Kieburtz, Rishiyur Nikhil, Mike Reeve, Phil Wadler, David Wise and Jonathon Young.

language is non-strict, polymorphically typed, with higher-order functions and extensive pattern matching facilities; it posseses a module system, guarded equations, user-defined algebraic types, list comprehensions, lambda abstractions and a rich set of predefined data types, including complex numbers, arbitrary-precision integers, ratios, floating point numbers and arrays as well as the more usual fixed-precision integers, lists and characters. Programs are laid out in accordance with a simple layout rule which may be overridden at will. The language is more than just an amalgam of existing functional language designs, however. Features such as the type class system whose implementation is described in this paper give Haskell a distinctive flavour and considerable flexibility.

Throughout this paper Haskell version 1.0 is used [2]. This is the version described in the document previewed at FPCA '89 [1]. Haskell version 2.0 will be released one year after the definitive release of version 1.0 and will incorporate improvements suggested by the practical use of this and other implementations, such as that being undertaken at Yale University. Some more experimental features may also be added, based on experience gained from trailblazer implementations.

The implementation which is presented here is based on the Chalmers LML compiler, descriptions of which may be found in [3,4,5], itself written in LML. Several passes have been inserted into the basic Chalmers cycle (notably to deal with classes and irrefutable patterns), and others have been heavily modified (principally those connected with the type-checker). The structure of the new compiler is shown below. Passes which are new, or heavily modified are italicised. The names of the passes reflect the language features which they handle. *Rename* ensures the uniqueness of function names and also deals with imports of standard prelude functions. *Flatten* transforms a structured program graph into a list of declarations. *Convert* transforms the program graph into a simpler form for later passes to manipulate. *Unrec* removes unnecessary recursion (this is even more important in Haskell than LML since by default definitions use the equivalent of *letrec*). *Dopt* optimises type class dictionaries, as described below. The omitted passes handle lambda-lifting, strictness analysis and the other global optimisations performed by the LML compiler. These passes are unchanged in the Haskell compiler.

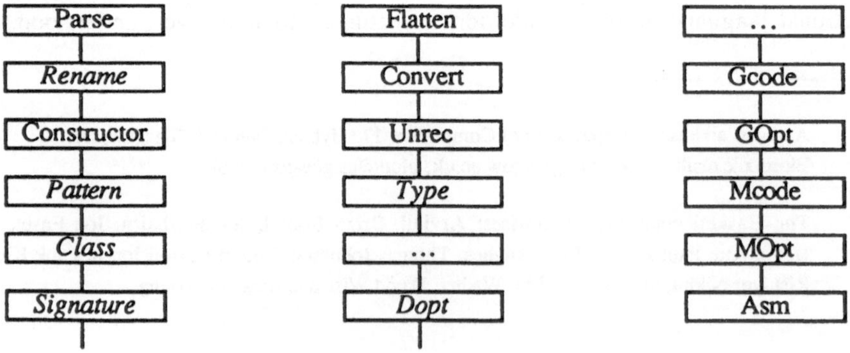

Figure 1: Haskell Compiler Passes

Because the compiler must retain considerably more information in order to compile Haskell programs, it is consequently slower and less memory efficient than the LML compiler. The restructuring which is intended with the next version of the Haskell compiler (written in Haskell) should rectify this to some extent.

2 Overview of Type Classes

Type classes provide a novel alternative to the traditional approaches to ad-hoc polymorphism [6]. They permit the definition of overloaded operators in a more rigorous and general manner than is possible with the type systems of other polymorphic languages such as Standard ML [7,8]. A formal treatment of type classes, with full motivation for their introduction, may be found in [6]. This section provides a brief overview only.

2.1 Alternative Approaches to ad-hoc Polymorphism

To understand the motivation for the introduction of type classes, consider the problem of typing arithmetic operators. In Standard ML, the arithmetic operators +, –, and * have type *Num → Num → Num*, where *Num* may be either *Int* or *Real* consistently. The appropriate type (*Int→Int→Int* or *Real→Real→Real*) is inferred depending on the type of the operands, an error resulting if insufficient type information is available. Thus,

```
fun succ n  =  n + 1
```

would have type *succ: Int→Int*, and

```
fun myadd a b  =  a + b
```

would be illegal. Note that under this scheme it is impossible to write the polymorphic successor function with type *Num → Num:* two functions with types *Int→Int* and *Real→Real* must be defined instead. Similar restrictions apply to the relational operators. The possibility of resolving ambiguity by allowing *succ* to define two or more functions does not seem generally acceptable since this may lead to exponental growth in the number of functions defined. Hope+ has adopted this approach, however [9]. An alternative approach of allowing run-time resolution of overloading through tagging constants and other expressions introduces space and time overheads which it seems desirable to avoid.

Equality represents a special case. It is presumably unacceptable to define equality over unrestricted function types, for instance (though certain languages allow this as function identity at the implementation level), so equality cannot be truly polymorphic (with type $\alpha \rightarrow \alpha \rightarrow Bool$); however the set of types which admit equality cannot be fixed, since it is usually desirable to permit equality tests over user-defined algebraic types, for example. In Standard ML, equality is defined for all "eqtypes" (which includes most algebraic data types). This imposes an additional burden on the type-checking algorithm, and is highly non-orthogonal.

Type classes solve the problem of ad-hoc polymorphism by allowing the definition of *classes* of overloaded operators with fixed generic types. *Instances* of these classes specify the functions which implement these overloaded operators for a given type. Where overloading cannot be resolved at compile-time (as in the definition of a polymorphic successor function), run-time parameter passing is used to ensure that the correct "method" is available to the operator.

2.2 Class Declarations

A class declaration introduces a new type class with its associated set of operators, and specifies the generic types of those operators. For example:

```
class Eq a where
        (==), (/=) :: a -> a -> Bool

class Eq a => Ord a where
        (<), (<=), (>), (>=) :: a -> a -> Bool
        max, min :: a -> a -> a
```

introduces the classes *Eq* and *Ord* with their associated operators ==, /=, <, <=, >, >=, *max* and *min* whose typings are *(==), (/=) :: Eq a => a → a → Bool, (<), (<=) , (>), (>=) :: Ord a => a →a →Bool* and *max, min :: Ord a => a →a →a*. Default methods may be attached to class operators if desired, their implementation is not considered here.

The *context* of an operator (before the =>) imposes restrictions on the applicability of the operator which must be satisfied wherever the operator is to be used. These restrictions are additional to the normal type constraints which apply to a program. Thus == may be used exactly where its operands are both of the same type α and it can be determined that α is an instance of the class *Eq*. For example:

```
checkeq a b c  =  if a == b then c else error "checkeq"
```

has typing *Eq a => a →a →b→b*, as is to be expected.

The declarations above also specify that *Eq* is a *super-class* of *Ord* (*Eq a => Ord a*): every type which is an instance of *Ord* must also be an instance of *Eq* if the program is to be correct. Obviously it is necessary to define such super-class relationships carefully (whilst it is reasonable to expect equality to be defined for all types which may be compared using < or <=, the reverse is not necessarily so). A type class may have several super-classes, and it need not possess any operators. An example from the Haskell standard prelude is the class *Data*, which unifies the classes *Enum*, *Text* and *Binary*:

```
class (Enum a, Text a, Binary a) => Data a
```

In any situation where it can be determined that a type is an instance of *Data*, that type must also be an instance of *Enum*, *Text* and *Binary*.

In Haskell, only one type variable may be bound by a class declaration (so *Eq a* is legal, but *Eq a b* is not): extensions to handle multiple type variables should be possible but are currently unexplored. As can be seen from the examples, the scope of the bound type variable extends to the **where** clause of the class declaration and to the super-class list in the obvious manner. It is an error to introduce a type variable in the super-class list which is not bound by the class declaration.

2.3 Instance Declarations

Instance declarations specify that a type is an instance of a class and introduce the concrete functions used to implement the class operators for that type. For example, *Char* could be declared to be an instance of class *Ord* by:

```
instance Ord Char where
        (<), (<=) :: Char -> Char -> Bool
        c < d   =  ord c <  ord d
        c <= d  =  ord c <= ord d
```

The type signatures could be derived if preferred. Default methods are used for the other operators of *Ord*. To preserve the super-class relation it is necessary to check (recursively) that *Char* is also an instance of each of the super-classes of *Ord* (that is that an instance declaration exists for *Eq Char* in this case). Since super-class information is a property of the class, it does not appear in the instance declaration. Only a single instance of a type may be specified for a given class, thus ambiguity resulting from the direct overlapping of instances is prohibited.

Types which are instances of a class may be simple or structured, but must be non-variable and no more than one level deep. Hence it is possible to define an instance of *Char* or *[a]*, but not *[Char]* for example. The motivation for this restriction is to avoid the ambiguity which would result where instances overlapped. For example:

```
instance Eq (a, [b]) where ...
```

would overlap with:

```
instance Eq (Int,[[a]]) where ...
```

Ambiguity would arise where both instances were simultaneously in scope: for example, given the definitions above, it would be impossible to determine which definition of == to use when comparing items of type *(Int, [[Char]])*. A syntactic restriction in Haskell avoids the need to check for such ambiguity. This is not a limitation on the basic method of [6], however.

Now whenever characters are compared using < or <=, the appropriate instance operator may be used. For example:

```
isasciictrl c  =  c < ' '
```

would use the definition of < for *Char* (denoted $<_{\text{Char}}$), whilst

```
isneg n  =  n < (0::Int)
```

would use $<_{\text{Int}}$ The signatures of these functions are simply *isasciictrl :: Char → Bool* and *isneg :: Int → Bool*. Note the explicit type signature attached to the constant 0. In Haskell, all numeric constants are overloaded. The function *fromInteger :: Num a => Integer → a* is implicitly applied to all *Integer* constants. Similarly the function *fromRational :: Floating a => Rational → a* is applied to all *Rational* constants. The default mechanism described later allows a default type to be assigned in all ambiguous cases, thus minimising the use of explicit type signatures for numeric constants.

Instances of Non-Flat Domains

Operations on structured types are more interesting, as shown by the instance declaration of *Eq List*, which defines structural equality over lists:

```
instance Eq a => Eq [a] where
        (==) :: [a] -> [a] -> Bool
        [] == []    =          True
        (a:as) == []   =       False
        [] == (b:bs)   =       False
        (a:as) == (b:bs)    =  a == b && as == bs
```

Note the overloaded use of == in the final equation. The elements forming the heads of the lists are tested for equality, then the tails of the lists are recursively tested for equality. The context of the instance limits the applicability of list equality to exactly those lists where equality is defined on the elements of the lists. Thus lists of arbitrary functions will not admit equality, but lists of lists of *Char* will.

The context of an instance must *imply* the super-classes of the instance as specified in the class header, so the context of the instance *Ord [a]* must imply *Eq [a]* etc. The signatures of operators in an instance declaration may not include a context; rather they inherit the context of the instance header. The scope of the type variables in the instance header thus extends to the signatures of the instance operators.

Now there is a problem. It is impossible to statically determine the instance of == to use for list elements, since this will vary with the type of the list. The solution adopted by [6], and used here, is to introduce dictionaries of operators. Each instance declaration creates a dictionary of the functions which implement the class operators for that instance. The appropriate function may be selected from the dictionary using the generic selector function for an operator. Each instance operator for a non-flat domain may require dictionaries to be passed to instantiate its type variables. For example,

```
null  =  (==) []
```

has the typing *Eq a => [a] →Bool*. Under the rules given in [6,10] it is translated as:

$$\texttt{null dict.Eq.a = (==)}_{\texttt{List}}\texttt{ dict.Eq.a []}$$

The last equation in the definition of *Eq List* has the translation:

$$\texttt{(==)}_{\texttt{List}}\texttt{ dict.Eq.a (a:as) (b:bs) =}$$
$$\texttt{(==)}_{\texttt{Eq}}\texttt{ dict.Eq.a a b \&\& (==)}_{\texttt{List}}\texttt{ dict.Eq.a as bs}$$

where $(==)_{Eq}$ represents the generic selector function for *(==)* from dictionaries of instances of *Eq* (in this case the identity function). The dictionary for *Eq List* would be simply:

$$\texttt{dict.Eq.List = ((==)}_{\texttt{List}}\texttt{, (/=)}_{\texttt{List}}\texttt{)}$$

Ambiguity

One significant problem with overloading is that of ambiguity. For example, the type of *a* in the following definition cannot be consistently defined given the typings for *put* and *get* in the standard prelude (*put :: Text a => a → String, get :: Text a => String → [(a, String)]*):

```
putget d s = put a "" where (a,s') = head (get s)
```

putget will have the derived typing *putget :: Text a => String*. Such typings are erroneous, and may be statically detected without difficulty. The definition may be disambiguated by using type signatures to fix the type of *a* to be a monomorphic type.

Ambiguity is defined to occur exactly when the typing of an expression *e* is *e :: C => T* and *C* contains at least one type variable *a* which occurs in *C*, but not *T* such that *a* is *not free* in the current type environment (it will not be free if, for example, it represents part of the type of a lambda variable).

Thus, the following is not ambiguous, even though the typing of *showaddn* is *showaddn :: Text a => String*, since *a* here would be bound to the type of the lambda variable *n* (note that *read :: Text a => a*):

```
add n s   =   s ++ " + " ++ show n ++ " is " ++ showaddn
                where showaddn = put (read s + n) ""
```

Where a numeric class (*Num, Real, Integral, Fractional, RealFrac, Floating, RealFloat*) is involved, *defaults* may be used to resolve the ambiguity (see section 3.5).

3 Implementing the Type Class Mechanism

This section describes the implementation of the type class mechanism introduced above. Some sample translations generated using these rules are listed in Appendix I.

3.1 Classes

Dictionary and Operator Templates.

Consider a class declaration:

```
class C => Z a where
        o₁  ::  τ₁
        :
        oₙ  ::  τₙ
```

where C = (S_1 a_1, ..., S_m a_m) (the S_i a_i are not necessarily distinct). The following selector function declarations may be produced:

```
op.Z.o₁   (i₁, ..., iₙ, s₁, ..., sₘ)   =   (i₁ :: Z a => τ₁)
:
op.Z.oₙ   (i₁, ..., iₙ, s₁, ..., sₘ)   =   (iₙ :: Z a => τₙ)
```

```
sup.Z.S1 (i1, ..., in, s1, ..., sm)  =  s1
:
sup.Z.Sm (i1, ..., in, s1, ..., sm)  =  sm
```

Each $op.Z.o_i$ selects the appropriate operator from an instance dictionary of the given form. The $sup.Z.S_i$ select super-class dictionaries from instance dictionaries, as described below. Where there is only a single operator or super-class, the selector function is simply the identity function, and might be compiled out, as suggested in [6]. A class with no operators and no superclasses could theoretically be defined in Haskell, but then of course no selector functions are needed. So for example:

```
class Eq a => Ord a where
      (<), (<=), (>), (>=) :: a -> a -> Bool
      min, max :: a -> a -> a
```

generates the following set of selector functions:

```
op.Ord.<, op.Ord.<=, op.Ord.>,
   op.Ord.>= :: Ord a => a -> a -> Bool
op.Ord.min, op.Ord.max :: Ord a => a -> a -> a

op.Ord.<   (lt,le,gt,ge,min,max,eqD)  =  lt
:
op.Ord.max (lt,le,gt,ge,min,max,eqD)  =  max

sup.Ord.Eq (lt,le,gt,ge,min,max,eqD)  =  eqD
```

Information Extracted from a Class Declaration

The information in the declarations is extracted and retained in the form of a list of *ClassInfo*, *classinfo* where:

```
classinfo :: [ClassInfo]
type ClassInfo = (Class, Context, [(Id,Type)])
```

This is used in the type-checking process to generate the transitive closure of the super-classes of a class, and to generate the appropriate dictionaries during the type-checking pass.

The function *clookup* is defined as follows:

```
clookup info class =
      let is = [i: i = (z,c,ops) ∈ info ∧ z = class] in
      if #is = 1 then is↓1 else ⊥
```

where ⊥ should be interpreted as an error, # is the length function and $is{\downarrow}i$ selects element i from is.

Non-Immediate Super-Class Selectors

The selectors defined above permit the selection of immediate super-class dictionaries, but they could not be used directly to select a dictionary for *Num a* from that given for *Integral a*, for instance. This can be achieved in two ways: by defining super-class selectors for all non-immediate super-classes of a class, or by constructing the selectors as necessary for individual functions. The former method has the advantage that selector functions need be defined once only: this is the approach taken.by the Haskell compiler.

```
∀c,c': issuper z c ∧ issuper* c c'
sup.z.c' = sup.c.c' ∘ sup.z.c
```

where *issuper** is the transitive closure of the super-class relation. Since the super-class relation need not be tree-structured, it is possible to generate several operators *sup.z.s* for some *z*, *s*, the conflict is resolved trivially by eliminating duplicate definitions from those created. In this case, the "shortest path" between two classes should be retained.

3.2 Instances

Instance declarations indicate that a class can be overloaded to a stated type, and define the versions of the class operators which must be used when those operators are known to overloaded to that type. Instance declarations of the form:

```
instance C' => Z T where
        o1  =  ε1
        :
        on  =  εn
```

where $C' = (S'_1\ a'_1, \ldots, S'_m\ a'_m)$, and $T = (t\ b_1 \ldots b_q)$, are transformed into:

```
iop.Z.t.o1 = ε1 :: C' -> τ'1
:
iop.Z.t.on = εn :: C' -> τ'n

dict.Z.t =
   (iop.Z.t.o1 :: , ..., iop.Z.t.on,
    dict.S1.t, ... , dict.Sm.t) ::
   C', C'' => (τ'1, ..., τ'n, σ1, ..., σm)
```

where $C'' = C\ [T/a]$, $\tau'_i = \tau_i\ [T/a]$, and the σ_j are the types of the relevant dictionaries. C and the S_i are obtained from the appropriate *ClassInfo* record. Note that the type signature obtained may include contexts which may not be written in Haskell (for example *Num Int*), this is quite harmless (and in fact necessary).

Additionally, all type signatures U_i in the instance declaration (or strictly, only those referring to instance operators) are replaced by $C' \Rightarrow U_i$. References to the o_i in the body of the ε_j are not transformed at this stage. For example:

```
instance Ord Char where
        a < b   =  ord a < ord b
        a <= b  =  ord a <= ord b
```

is transformed into:

```
iop.Ord.Char.<, iop.Ord.Char.<=,
    iop.Ord.Char.>, iop.Ord.Char.>= :: Char->Char->Bool
iop.Ord.Char.min, iop.Ord.Char.max :: Char->Char->Char

iop.Ord.Char.<  a b  =  (ord a < ord b)
iop.Ord.Char.<= a b  =  (ord a <= ord b)

dict.Ord.Char  =
      (iop.Ord.Char.<, iop.Ord.Char.<=, iop.Ord.Char.>,
       iop.Ord.Char.min, iop.Ord.Char.max, dict.Eq.Char)
```

Instances of operators may now be selected from the relevant dictionary using the *op.Z.o*$_i$ functions, and dictionaries of immediate super-classes may be selected using the *sup.Z.S* functions. So the < operator over *Char* may be obtained from:

```
op.Ord.<  dict.Ord.Char
```

or if sufficient type information is available, by:

```
iop.Ord.Char.<
```

The translation of an instance declaration where a context is involved is similar:

```
instance  Ord a => Ord [a]  where
      as < bs  =  ... {- 1 -}
```

is transformed into:

```
iop.Ord.List.<, iop.Ord.List.<=, iop.Ord.List.>,
    iop.Ord.List.>= :: Ord a =>[a]->[a]->Bool
iop.Ord.List.min, iop.Ord.List.max :: Ord a =>[a]->[a]->[a]

iop.Ord.List.<  as bs  = ... {- 1 -}
...

dict.Ord.List =
    (iop.Ord.List.<, iop.Ord.List.<=, iop.Ord.List.>,
     iop.Ord.List.>=, iop.Ord.List.min, iop.Ord.List.max,
     dict.Eq.List)
  :: Ord a => ([a]->[a]->Bool, [a]->[a]->Bool, [a]->[a]-
>Bool,
                  [a]->[a]->Bool, [a]->[a]->[a],  [a]->[a]->[a],
                  τEq List)
```

The typings assigned to the operators and dictionary ensure that these are translated with dictionaries inserted appropriately.

Information Extracted from an Instance Declaration

Additionally, the information contained in the instance declarations is transformed into a list of *InstanceInfo*, *instinfo* where:

```
instinfo :: [InstanceInfo]
type InstanceInfo = (Class, Context, Type)
```

The *Context* is used to generate dictionary parameters, and to extend the implication rule for instances.

Given this list and the list of *ClassInfo* described above, it is possible to check that the super-class relations hold for all declared instances. Specifically, the following predicates must hold:

```
∀i: i ∈ instinfo,
      let (z,c,(χ α1 .. αn)) = i in
      ∀s: issuper* z s, isinstance χ s
```

It is also necessary to check the validity of the contexts of all instances:

```
∀i: i ∈ instinfo,
      let (z,c',(χ α1 .. αn)) = i in
      let (z,c,ops) = clookup classinfo z in
      implies c'[(χ α1 .. αn)/α] c
```

where $\alpha = FV(c')$, the single free variable in *c'*. The function *ilookup* is defined analogously to *clookup:*

```
ilookup info class type =
      let   is = [i:  i = (z,c,t) ∈ info
                      ∧ z = class ∧ t = type] in
      if #is = 1 then is1 else ⊥
```

3.3 Derived Instances

Datatypes may be declared such that instances may be automatically derived for some or all of the Haskell classes *Text, Binary, Ix, Enum, Ord* and *Eq*. Instances created in this fashion are in general processed identically to explicitly declared instances: it may, however, be possible to exploit certain properties of these instances during optimisation.

3.4 Type Checking

Polymorphic types were known in combinatory logic as type schemas [11]. The first practical polymorphic type-checker was implemented by Milner, who also showed that the type system is semantically sound [12]. [13] is an approachable introduction to the theory and practice of polymorphic type checking, which can be recommended to those unfamiliar with this subject.

Definition of the Type-Checking Algorithm

The type-checker used in the Haskell compiler is a modified version of the standard algorithms described in the papers mentioned above. In particular, under the new type-checker, a translation is synthesised during type-checking.

The polymorphic type-checking algorithm $\mathcal{W}$ of e.g. [14] must therefore be modified to take account of type classes and the dictionary translations. For simplicity, only a few critical cases are considered here, but the principle is easily extended to other constructs such as case statements. This definition is based on the rules given in [6] and [10].

	TypeInfo =	Subst × Type × Dicts × Expr
δ ∈	Dicts	[Id×Assertion]
ε ∈	Expr	
ρ ∈	Env =	Id → Typing
υ ∈	Typing =	Context × Type
σ ∈	Subst =	Typing → Typing
κ ∈	Context =	[Assertion]
α ∈	Assertion =	ClassId × Type
η ∈	InstEnv =	[ClassId × Context × Type]
τ ∈	Type =	TyVar + TyCon × Type*
τ ∈	Type	
χ ∈	TyCon	
β ∈	TyVar	
ι ∈	Id	
ω ∈	Ids =	[Id]
ζ ∈	ClassId	

```
W : Env → Expr → InstEnv →  Ids → TypeInfo
W ρ (ε1 ε2) η ω =
      let (σ1, τ1, δ1, ε̄1) = W ρ ε1 η ω
      and (σ2, τ2, δ2, ε̄2) = W (σ1 ρ) ε2 η ω
      and σ = Unify (σ2 τ1) (τ2 -> β) where β is new in
      (σ.σ2.σ1, σβ, σ(o2δ1 ++ δ2), (ε̄1 ε̄2))

W ρ ι η ω =
      let υ = ρ ι and [α1, ... , αn] = FV(υ) -- ω
      and β1 ... βn be new in
      let υ' = υ [β1/α1 ... βn/αn] in
      let (σ,δ,ε) = D ι υ' (λυ.υ) in
      (σ, υ', δ, ε)

W ρ (\ ι -> ε) η ω =
      let β be new in
      let (σ, τ, δ, ε̄) = W (ρ[β/ι]) ε η (ω ++ [ι]) in
      (σ, (σβ → υ), δ, (\ ι -> ε̄))
```

```
W ρ (let ι = ε1 in ε2) η ω =
      let (σ1, τ1, δ1, ε̄1) = W ρ ε1 η ω in
      let δ1' = B δ1 and υ1 = (C δ1', τ1) in
      let (σ2, τ2, δ2, ε̄2) = W (ρ[υ1/ι]) ε2 η ω in
      let [α1, ..., αm] = C δ1' and n = #δ1 in
      let ∀i: 1 ≤ i ≤ m, εi' = G' αi η
      and ∀j: 1 ≤ j ≤ n, (ιj,εj'') = G (δ1↓j) η in
      (σ2, τ2, δ2,
       let ι = \ε1' -> ... \εm' -> let ι1 = ε1'' in ... let ιn = εn'' in ε̄1
       in ε̄2)
```

where it is assumed that substitutions may be composed, applied to lists etc. in the obvious fashion. The initial value of η is *instinfo*. FV(υ) gives a list of type variables which are free in υ.

The algorithms *D* and *G* handle dictionary generation and insertion.

```
D : Expr → Typing → Subst → Subst × Dicts × Expr
D ε ([],τ) σ = (σ, [],ε)
D ε (κ,τ) σ =
      let n = #κ
      and β1 ... βn be new type variables
      and ι1 ... ιn be new identifiers in
      let ε̄ = ( ... (ε ι1) ... ιn)
      and δ = [(ι1,κ↓1), ..., (ιn,κ↓n)] in
      (σ[β1/ι1, ..., βn/ιn], δ, ε̄)
```

```
G : Id × Assertion → InstEnv → Id × Expr
G (ι,α) η = (ι,G' α η)
```

```
G' : Assertion → InstEnv → Expr
G' (ζ β) η = "dict.ζ.β"
G' (ζ (χτ1 ... τn)) η =
      let (ζ,κ',(χβ1 ... βn)) = ilookup η ζ χ
      and [α1 ... αm] = κ'[τ1/β1, ..., τn/βn] in
      "dict.ζ.χ" (G' α1 η) ... (G' αm η)
```

The *dict.ζ.β* will need to be generated using super-class operators and dictionaries from the context κ if they do not occur in κ; the *dict.ζ.χ* may also require the use of super-class operators.

B eliminates type assertions which may be implied by other type assertions in a context.

```
B : [Id ×Assertion] → [Id ×Assertion]
B [(ι1,α1), ..., (ιn,αn)] =
      [(ιi,αi): ∀i: 0 < i ≤ n,
       ¬ (∃j: 0 < k < i ∧ αj = αi)  ∧  ¬ V αi  ∧
       ¬ (∃k: 0 < k ≤ n ∧ αk implies αi) ]
```

V determines whether its argument is an assertion concerning a type variable.

```
V : Assertion → Bool
V (ζ β) =                 true
V (ζ (χ τ1 ... τn)) =     false
```

C transforms a dictionary into a context.

```
C : [Id × Assertion] → Context
C [(ι1,α1), ..., (ιn,αn)] = [α1, ..., αn]
```

Validity of Contexts

A context is valid if each class assertion in the context is valid. An individual class assertion is valid if it can be determined that the type component of the assertion is a valid instance of the class component. It is unnecessary to check that the super-class relation holds at this point since this has already been verified.

```
validc c = ∀i: 1 ≤ i ≤ #c, valida ci

valida (class (χ τ1 .. τn)) =
      isinstance χ class ∧
      let (class,c,(χ β1 .. βn)) =
            ilookup instinfo class χ in
      validc c[τ1/β1, .., τn/βn]
```

Class assertions may be eliminated from a unified context if they contain no type variables or if they are *implied* by some other class assertion in the context. For example the typing of:

```
isodd n = (n + 1) `mod` 2 == 0
```

is *isodd :: Integral a => a → a → Bool* and not *isodd :: (Eq a, Num a, Integral a) => a → a → Bool*. The translation of *isodd* involves the use of super-class selectors (for simplicity the necessary *fromInteger* conversions are not shown):

```
isodd dict.Integral.n n =
      op.Eq.== dict.Eq.n
      (op.Integral.mod dict.Integral.n
            ((+) dict.Num.n n 1) 2) 0
   where
      dict.Eq.n =  sup.Integral.Eq  dict.Integral.n
      dict.Num.n = sup.Integral.Num dict.Integral.n
```

The Implies Relation

The notions of context and type assertion implication have hitherto been used without explanation. This section provides a formal definition of these relations. The implementation of this definition is straightforward.

Definition: Context Implication

```
A context C1 implies a context C2 if:
∀a ∈ C2, ∃b ∈ C1: b implies a
```

Definition: Type Assertion Implication

```
A type assertion S s implies a type assertion T t if:
s = t ∧ (S = T ∨ issuper* S T) ∨
t = χ τ1 .. τn ∧
      ∃z: isinstance χ z ∧
            let (z,(χ α1 .. αn),c') = ilookup instinfo z χ
            and c = c'[τ1/α1, .., τn/αn] in
            validc c ∧ S s implies c ∧ c implies T t
```

It follows that the following are valid:

```
Integral a          implies       Eq a
Eq a                implies       Eq [a]
Ord a               implies       Eq [a]
(Num a, Data a)     implies       Ord a
```

3.5 Default Types

Since ambiguity (in the sense of section 2.3) frequently arises when typing functions involving numeric literals, Haskell provides a mechanism which allows the programmer to indicate how the ambiguity should be resolved. A module may specify a (possibly empty) list of "default types" which may be used to resolve any ambiguity which arises during type-checking of that module. If no **default** declaration is given, **default** *(Int, Double)* is assumed. For example:

```
default Integer
```

declares that all numeric ambiguity should be resolved using type *Integer* where possible. Where several types are given in a default list the first type, if any, which is an instance of all classes C_i, such that $C_i\ a$ is a type assertion in the ambiguous context and a is an ambiguous type variable, is chosen as the default. Ambiguity is only resolved in this fashion if at least one of the C_i is a "numeric" class (one of *Num, Real, Integral, Fractional, RealFrac, Floating, RealFloat*). For example, given *putp::Text a => Int → a → String → String* and *read :: Text a => a*, defaults can be used to resolve the ambiguity of *addone*:

```
default (Integer, Float)
addone l = putp 0 ((read l)+1.0) ""
```

Here the typing of *addone* would be *addone :: Fractional a => [Char] → [Char]* without the default, which is clearly ambiguous (*a* is unbound). Using the default, the ambiguity is resolved such that the value returned by the *read* is a *Float* (since no instance of *Integer* exists for *Fractional*, this cannot be used to resolve the ambiguity), and the typing of *addone* is *addone :: [Char] → [Char]*.

The effect on the implementation is to require that the ambiguity check which is necessary when typing a function definition also takes into account any default declarations which are in scope. The translation may be modified as a result of substituting the default type for the ambiguous variable, since a known dictionary must now be used, rather than parameterising the function definition. For example, *addone* above would have the translation:

```
addone l = op.Put.putp dict.Text.Float (0::Int)
      (op.Num.+ dict.Num.Float
            (read dict.Text.Float l) (1.0::Float)) ""
```

where, for clarity, the two constants have been converted to their base forms.

3.6 Optimisations Employed

Four basic optimisations are employed at present (the first and last are suggested by [6]):

- introduction of instance operators;
- reduction of standard instance operators to primitive machine operations;
- reduction of *fromInteger* and *fromRational* when applied to a constant;
- elimination of generic operators for simple classes.

The first optimisation eliminates dictionaries, reducing the generic operator selector functions to instance operators in those cases where sufficient type information is available.

```
op.C.op  dict.C.T    =>   iop.C.T.op             if T ∉ Var
```

where *Var* is the set of type variables. For example:

```
op.Num.+  dict.Num.Int    =>    iop.Num.Int.+
```

This simplifies the reductions which must be performed at run-time.

The second set of optimisations further reduces instance operators for standard types and classes to their machine equivalents (*Int* and *Bool* have equivalent internal representations in the original G-Machine):

```
iop.Num.Int.+    a  b   =>   Padd  a  b
...
iop.Eq.Int.==    a  b   =>   Peq   a  b
...
iop.Eq.Bool.==   a  b   =>   Peq   a  b
...
```

For instance:

```
    iop.Num.Int.+  (iop.Num.Int.*  n  n)  5
 => Padd  (Pmul  n  n)  5
```

The third set of optimisations transforms *fromInteger* and *fromRational* applications into literal constants. The actual optimisations are:

```
iop.Num.Int.fromInteger  i                  =>   Itoi i
iop.Num.Integer.fromInteger  i              =>   i
iop.Fractional.fromRational.Float  r        =>   Rtof r
```

where *i* is an *Integer* constant, *r* is a *Rational* constant, *Itoi* converts an *Integer* to an *Int* and *Rtof* converts a *Rational* to a *Float*. The latter are compile-time conversions, of course. This optimisation proves to be surprisingly important: in the *Nfib* benchmark below, a factor of 4 was regained by employing this optimisation. The first three optimisations must be applied in order.

The final optimisation eliminates dictionaries for classes which have only one operator or super-class (but not both). This optimisation applies only if the first does not.

```
op.C.T.op  dict.C.T   =>   dict.C.T
if   T ∈ Var ∧ #ops(C) + #supers(C) = 1
```

This optimisation is of fairly limited utility (no standard classes have this property), but is simple to implement.

Further optimisations might attempt to reduce the run-time overheads of super-class selectors. John Hughes has, for instance, suggested packaging all super-class selectors in each instance dictionary. This and other optimisations might well repay investigation.

4 Performance Evaluation

The following table reports performance results obtained with the Haskell compiler. The first set of figures in each group refers to the original Chalmers LML compiler; the second refers to the unoptimised Haskell compiler; a final set refers to the Haskell compiler optimised as shown above. Comparison of the Haskell figures with the first set allows the isolation of the overhead introduced by the type class mechanism.

CPU is the total CPU time used by the test in seconds, excluding time spent in garbage collection, on an unloaded Sun-3/60 (averaged over 10 runs); *GC* indicates the number of garbage collections which occurred during the run; *Mem* is the memory usage in bytes; CPU_{Rel} is the speed of the implementation relative to Chalmers LML; and Mem_{Rel} is the memory usage relative to the LML base. All these figures are preliminary, referring only to the prototype compiler, and thus should not be taken as representative of the performance which might be achieved by a production compiler.

Test	CPU	CPU_{Rel}	GC	Mem	Mem_{Rel}
8 Queens	2.88	1.00	6	1.7M	1.00
	32.51	11.29	193	48.9M	28.76
	7.90	2.74	42	11.3M	6.65

Test	CPU	CPU_{Rel}	GC	Mem	Mem_{Rel}
Primes	4.89 47.54 10.08	1.00 9.72 2.06	19 204 47	5.3M 54.5M 13.0M	1.00 10.28 2.45
Nfib	21.65 221.65 21.30	1.00 10.24 0.98	161 1382 161	40.4M 349.0M 42.0M	1.00 8.64 1.03
KWIC	7.07 34.55 31.62	1.00 4.89 4.47	15 109 53	6.3M 47.8M 45.0M	1.00 7.59 7.14

The tests used were:

8 Queens	Solving the 8 Queens problem, uses a lot of arithmetic and lists;
Primes	the sum of the first 400 prime numbers, uses a lot of arithmetic and lists;
Nfib	Calculating nfib 28, uses a lot of arithmetic and function calls;
KWIC	Keywords in Context applied to a 40 line document, uses a lot of lists.

All the Haskell versions involve considerable use of overloading.

It is obvious from these results that the naïve translation using dictionaries is grossly inefficient (especially for examples involving arithmetic). The simple optimisations outlined above regain a proportion of the performance lost by the use of the type class system (in terms of both time and memory), especially where full specialisation of functions is required (as for Nfib). There is clearly scope for further optimisations in the Haskell compiler: in particular it will be necessary to compare the object code generated by the various versions of the compiler to determine what optimisations should be applied.

5 Summary and Conclusions

This paper has described in detail the implementation of type classes in the Glasgow University Haskell compiler. The implementation follows closely the description in [6], but uses lambda abstraction rather than tuples for passing dictionaries, and tuples rather than algebraic types for the dictionaries themselves. The modified definition of the type-checking algorithm derives from the inference rules provided in the former paper, but is presented here in the interests of clarity. The implementation of super-class selectors is a novel feature not described in [6].

The type class system itself is flexible, and quite intuitive. The preponderance of type classes in Haskell causes some confusion, however, and the super-class relationships are not always obvious (for example the relationship of *RealFloat* to *Num*). The definition of functions with a given typing can be hard, since the range of functions which may be used in the definition is diminished compared with a normal polymorphic type system. This mainly arises with instance definitions, but also applies to some standard functions.

Run-time performance is significantly impaired compared with LML-style overloading if a naïve translation is applied. Inspection of the code produced in each case suggests that much of the performance penalty may be overcome by application of the obvious optimisations, and indeed may even be superior for some overloaded operators (e.g. equality). Further work is needed to determine the optimisations which it is sensible to apply. The compiler itself is, inevitably, larger and slower as a consequence of the additional complexity of the Haskell language.

Acknowledgements

We would like to thank those who have read and commented on previous drafts of this paper, especially Phil Wadler, Sean Hayes and Amir Kishon. Amir Kishon provided particularly useful feedback by basing his implementation of type classes (incorporated in the Yale compiler) on an earlier version of this paper. This work was supported by a grant from Glasgow University.

References

1. Hudak P, Wadler PL et al. Report on the functional programming language Haskell, version 1.0 pre-release. Distributed at FPCA '89, London, September 1989.

2. Hudak P, Wadler PL et al. Report on the functional programming language Haskell, version 1.0. Glasgow University, April 1990.

3. Augustsson L. A compiler for Lazy ML. *Proc. ACM Symposium on Lisp and Functional Programming Languages*, Austin, Texas, 1984.

4. Augustsson L. *Compiling lazy functional languages, Part II*. PhD thesis, Chalmers University of Technology, Göteborg, 1987.

5. Johnsson T. *Compiling lazy functional languages, Part I*. PhD thesis, Chalmers University of Technology, Göteborg, 1987.

6. Wadler PL, Blott S. How to make ad-hoc polymorphism less ad hoc. *In: Proc. 16'th ACM Symposium on Principles of Programming Languages*, Austin, Texas, 1989, pp 60-76.

7. Harper R, MacQueen D, Milner R. Standard ML. *Report EFS-LFCS-86-2*, Dept. of Computer Science, Edinburgh University, 1986.

8. Harper R, Milner R, Tofte M. The definition of Standard ML, version 2. *Report EFS-LFCS-88-62*, Dept. of Computer Science, Edinburgh University, 1988.

9. Perry N. Hope+. *Internal Report IC/FPR/LANG/2.5.1/7*, Dept. of Computing, Imperial College, London, 1988.

10. Blott S. Type inference for type classes. *In this proceedings*, 1990.

11. Curry HB, Feys R. *Combinatory logic*. North-Holland, Amsterdam, 1958.

12. Milner R. A theory of type polymorphism in programming. *Journal of Computing Science,* 1978;17(3):348-375.

13. Cardelli L. Basic polymorphic typechecking. *Science of Computer Programming,* 1987;8:147-172.

14. Damas L, Milner R. Principal type schemes for functional programs. *In: Proc. 9th ACM Symposium on Principles of Programming Languages,* Albuquerque, New Mexico, 1982, pp 207-212.

Appendix I Sample Translations

These translations are taken directly from the compiler output, edited to remove clutter. 1L is the *Integer* value 1. Only the naïve translation is shown.

```
Glasgow University Haskell Compiler, version 0.2 (pre-release)
G-Code version Haskell Tue Jun 20 14:29:12 BST 1989

{-
    module Nfib(nfib) where
    nfib 0 = 1
    nfib 1 = 1
    nfib n = nfib (n-1) + nfib (n-2) + 1
-}

module Nfib(nfib) where
nfib = \ dict.Num.2319 -> \ dict.Num.2328 -> \ A1 ->
   case Peq A1  (op.Num.fromInteger dict.Num.2319 1L) of
      Pfalse ->
         case Peq A1 (op.Num.fromInteger dict.Num.2319 0L) of
            Pfalse ->
               op.Num.+ dict.Num.2328
                  (op.Num.+ dict.Num.2328
                     (nfib dict.Num.2319 dict.Num.2328
                        (op.Num.- dict.Num.2319 A1
                           (op.Num.fromInteger dict.Num.2319 1L)))
                     (nfib dict.Num.2319 dict.Num.2328
                        (op.Num.- dict.Num.2319 A1
                           (op.Num.fromInteger dict.Num.2319 2L))))
                  (op.Num.fromInteger dict.Num.2328 1L)
            Ptrue -> op.Num.fromInteger dict.Num.2328 1L
            default : DEFAULT_0
      Ptrue -> op.Num.fromInteger dict.Num.2328 1L
      default : DEFAULT_0
```

Translation 1: Generic nfib

```
Glasgow University Haskell Compiler, version 0.2 (pre-release)
G-Code version Haskell Wed Jul 19 18:12:23 BST 1989

{-
    module Ord_list(...) where

    instance Eq a => Eq [a] where
       [] == [] = True
       (x:xs) == (y:ys) = x == y && xs == ys
       [] == _  = False
       _  == [] = False

    instance Ord a => Ord [a] where
       [] < [] = False
       [] < (_:_) = True
       (_:_) < [] = False
       (x:xs) < (y:ys) = x < y || (x == y && xs < ys)

       [] <= [] = True
       [] <= (_:_) = True
       (_:_) <= [] = False
       (x:xs) <= (y:ys) = x < y || (x == y && xs <= ys)
    ...
-}


module Ord_List(...) where

iop.Eq.List.== = (\ dict.Eq.2280 -> \ A1 -> \ A2 ->
      case A1 of
         Pnil ->
             case A2 of
                Pnil -> Ptrue
                P: _ _ -> Pfalse
                default : DEFAULT_0
         P: I2230 I2231 ->
            case A2 of
               Pnil -> DEFAULT_1
               P: I2232 I2233 ->
                  ((&& (op.Eq.== dict.2304 I2230 I2232)
                       (op.Eq.== dict.2309 I2231 I2233))
               default :
                  case A2 of
                     Pnil -> Pfalse
                     P: _ _ -> Pfail "No match in ==\n"
                     default : DEFAULT_0
          default : DEFAULT_0) :: Eq a => [a] -> [a] -> Bool
      where
         dict.2304 = dict.Eq.2280
         dict.2309 = (dict.Eq.List dict.Eq.2280)

dict.Eq.List =
    (\ dict.Eq.2282 -> (iop.Eq.List.== dict.Eq.2282))
       :: Eq a => [a] -> [a] -> Bool
```

Translation 2a: Source and Instance of Eq [a]

```
iop.Ord.List.< = (\ dict.Ord.2286 -> \ A1 -> \ A2 ->
   case A1 of
      Pnil ->
         case A2 of
            Pnil -> Pfalse
            P: I2240 I2241 -> Ptrue
            default : DEFAULT_0
      P: I2234 I2235 ->
          case A2 of
              Pnil -> Pfalse
              P: I2238 I2239 ->
            ((|| (op.Ord.< dict.2324 I2234 I2238)
                  (&& (op.Eq.== dict.2329 I2234 I2238)
                      (op.Ord.< dict.2334 I2235 I2239)))
              default : DEFAULT_0
      default : DEFAULT_0) :: Ord a => [a] -> [a] -> Bool
    where {- rec -}
      dict.2324 = dict.Ord.2286
      dict.2329 = dict.Eq.2286
      dict.2334 = dict.Ord.List dict.Ord.2286
   where {- rec -}
      dict.Eq.2286 = sup.Ord.Eq dict.Ord.2286

iop.Ord.List.<= =
   (\ dict.Ord.2288 -> A1 -> \ A2 ->
      case A1 of
          Pnil ->
             case A2 of
                Pnil -> Ptrue
                P: I2248 I2249 -> Ptrue
                default : DEFAULT_0
           P: I2242 I2243 ->
          case A2 of
              Pnil -> Pfalse
              P: I2246 I2247 ->
                  ((|| (op.Ord.< dict.2349 I2242 I2246)
                        (&& (op.Eq.== dict.2354 I2242 I2246)
                            (op.Ord.<= dict.2359 I2243 I2247)))
              default : DEFAULT_0
          default : DEFAULT_0) :: Ord a => [a] -> [a] -> Bool
     where {- rec -}
        dict.2349 = dict.Ord.2288
        dict.2354 = dict.Eq.2288
        dict.2359 = dict.Ord.List dict.Ord.2288
   where {- rec -}
      dict.Eq.2288 = sup.Ord.Eq dict.Ord.2288

dict.Ord.List =
   (\ dict.Ord.2292 ->
       (iop.Ord.List.< dict.Ord.2292,
        iop.Ord.List.<= dict.Ord.2292,
        dict.Eq.List dict.Eq.2292))
      :: Ord a => ([a] -> [a] -> Bool, [a] -> [a] -> Bool,
                   Eq a => [a] -> [a] -> Bool)
    where {- rec -}
       dict.Eq.2292 = sup.Ord.Eq dict.Ord.2292
```

Translation 2b: Instance of Ord [a]

Implementing Functional Languages on the Transputer

Stuart Cox, Imperial College, London
Hugh Glaser, University of Southampton
Mike Reeve, ECRC, Munich

1 Introduction

The use of functional languages is now of increasing interest in program development and maintenance, however their efficient implementation on conventional processors is still a significant research issue[1, 2]. The aim of the work presented here is to develop a method for implementing lazy, curried functional languages for such architectures, giving performance comparable with imperative languages and supporting interlanguage working.

An important aspect of our approach is to compile in a way that can effectively use the information from the static analysis techniques that have been developed for functional languages, such as strictness analysis, to overcome the inherent inefficiences of functional languages, and in particular those due to lazy evaluation. If such analysis is successful, and we can hence put much of the lazy evaluation to one side, then if we consider the construction of a compiler for a pure functional language using traditional techniques, the referential transparency of the language means that many optimisations can be used irrespective of context. In particular, the compiler writer need have no concern about aliasing or side effects. Thus the optimisations that require considerable global knowledge in conventional languages can be more easily used for functional languages. Consequently we expect to import much of the experience that exists in the compiler writing discipline and which has perhaps not been largely applied to functional languages.

Interlanguage working allows the components of a large system to be written in the most appropriate language. It also allows the programmer to interface to the sort of libraries one would normally expect to be available, such as a database or windows standards. It is fair to say that hitherto, the functional language implementor has not laid great emphasis on the question of interlanguage working. Part of the reason for this is the difficulty of establishing the correct communication standards between conventional languages and pure functional languages required to implement lazy evaluation semantics. We believe that interlanguage working is possible in functional languages, and it is closely connected with the ability of the system to deal with complex questions of strictness analysis within the functional language component of a mixed language system. The question of the semantics of foreign language calls is still unresolved, but must be faced. From the language implementor's viewpoint, however, the requirement is to support interlanguage working; any restrictions on the use of such facilities must be left to the programming environment. The system described in this paper conforms to the interlanguage standards of the transputer and, for example, as a result it can use a functional language to map a C function over a list that has been constructed by the functional program.

2 Compilation to Tuki Code

The first stage in the system is to translate the functions of the source language into an intermediate code, known as Tuki code. The code is defined in terms of an abstract machine[3], but here we will simply illustrate the system by showing an example of the translation for a very simple function, the **nfib** function:

```
nfib(n) ⇐ if n<2
          then 1
          else nfib(n-1)+nfib(n-2)+1
```

Firstly we represent this function by the data flow graph of Figure 1. The meaning of the graph can be intuitively understood as allowing data to flow from top to bottom, with the values being transformed as they arrive at, and "fire", each node. This (data-driven) view is indeed the correct interpretation if the graph is to be executed to give call-by-value semantics. If call-by-need semantics are required, it should be viewed rather differently. Instead of each of the operations actually firing the primitive operator or user-defined function, they form a closure which is passed on as the result of the operator or function. Ultimately this closure may encounter a strict operation, such as the outer level printer, which will cause the suspension to be unwound. It is thus possible to view the Data Flow Graph as being neutral with respect to the evaluation mechanism. This neutrality is very useful when analysing the graph to determine which operations can be called by value.

In this graph, arcs have been labelled, and constants are indicated by a preceding "#". The label of each arc (and ultimately the value on that arc) does not change until an operation has been applied to it (eg *sub* or a recursive call on **nfib**). The only other comments that need to be made relate to the *iftrue* and *endif* constructs. *iftrue* directs its right input onto its left output if the left input is TRUE, the input is directed onto the right output if the value is FALSE. In this graph, the input is no longer needed if the truth value is TRUE and so is passed to a sink. For each *iftrue* construct there must be a corresponding *endif* construct. The *endif* construct acts as a merge, if the right input is a null value (as it will be if the iftrue construct selected the left output arc) then the left input is used, if not, then the right input is used. (The use of the *source* instruction in this function is a slight idiosyncrasy of the system, resulting from the constant appearing on its own, and not in an argument position to a simple operator or function; the right bias of the merge will cause the correct behaviour in this case.)

The generation of the Tuki code is performed by creating a textual representation of a total ordering of this graph. (The choice of total ordering from the partially ordered graph is beyond the scope of this paper.) The Tuki code that represents the graph in Figure 1 is shown in Figure 2.

A few comments should be made about the code. Firstly, the number after the name of the function specifies the number of formal parameters the function takes.

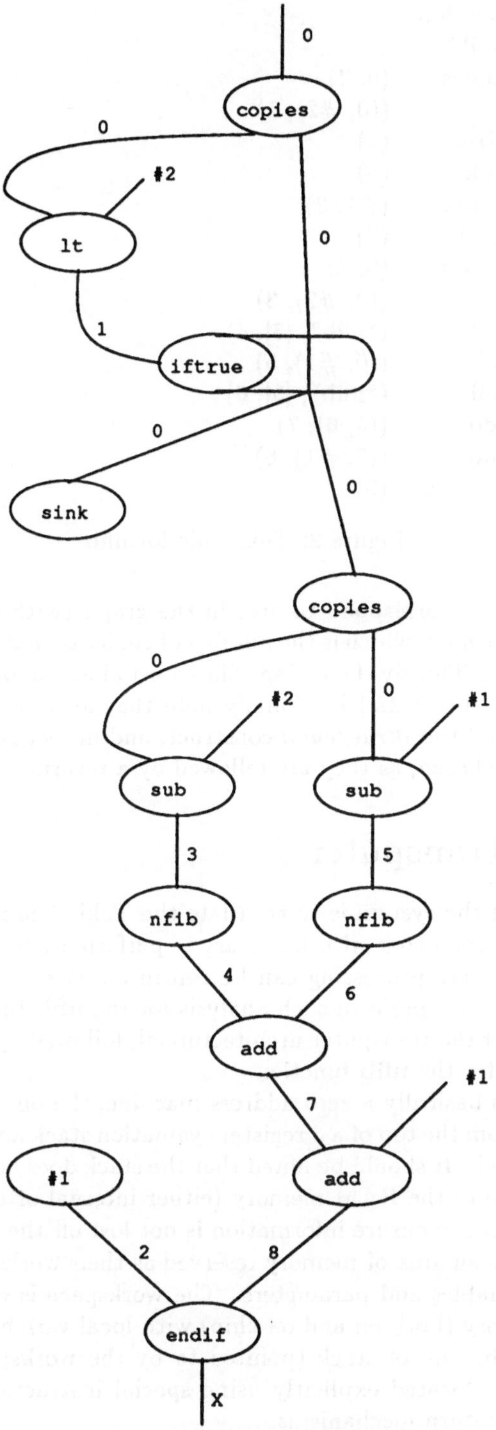

Figure 1: Data Flow Graph for nfib

```
function
"nfib"      1
copies      (0, 2)
lt          ((0, #2), 1)
iftrue      (1)
sink        (0)
source      (#1, 2)
retelse     (2)
copies      (0, 2)
sub         ((0, #2), 3)
call        ("nfib", [3], 4)
sub         ((0, #1), 5)
call        ("nfib", [5], 6)
add         ((4, 6), 7)
add         ((7, #1), 8)
retendif    (8)
```

Figure 2: Tuki code for nfib

Secondly, the numbers correspond to arcs in the graph (with the exception of the second argument to *copies*, which is the number of copies to make), and constants are represented by "#n". Thirdly the *call* specifies a list of actual parameters (indicated by the use of square brackets [ ]). Finally note that an *else* has been introduced to delimit the parts of the *iftrue/endif* construct, and in fact special versions of the *else* and *endif* were chosen, as they are followed by a return.

3 Tuki to Transputer

The second stage of the system is to translate the Tuki code into transputer code. In order to generate good code, it is necessary to perform static analysis to ascertain that the function we are processing can be run in an eager (data-driven) manner. Clearly the compiler can perform such analysis for the **nfib** function. We now give a brief description of the transputer architecture[4], followed by a description of the translation process for the **nfib** function.

The processor is basically a zero address machine, the operands to the instructions being taken from the top of a 3 register evaluation stack and the result returned to the top of the stack. It should be noted that the stack does not push down beyond the three registers into the RAM memory (either internal or external) and careful control has to be kept to ensure information is not lost off the end of the stack. All processes must have an area of memory reserved as their workspace - this holds the processes' local variables and parameters. The workspace is organised as a falling stack in main memory (both on and off-chip) with local variables addressed as positive offsets from the end of stack (pointed to by the workspace pointer). Space is allocated and deallocated explicitly using special instructions, and also by the procedure call and return mechanisms.

The area of code generation that makes a successful transputer implementation is the register/workspace allocation strategy and this is now described in some detail.

The compiler maintains a state which represents the location of all the active arcs at runtime. A Tuki statement is compiled in three phases. Phase one determines the current location of the arcs involved in the Tuki instruction by examining the current state of the machine. This may cause code to be generated that moves representations of arcs between the transputer's evaluation stack and the workspace associated with the process. Having ensured that the correct values are on the evaluation stack and that they are in the correct order, phase two can be started. This is the point at which the code required to perform the operation is generated. Most Tuki instructions will generate only one or two transputer instructions. The third, and final, phase updates the state of the machine (in the compiler) to take into account the effects of the Tuki instruction. Typically this will involve deleting the input arcs from the state and entering the output arc. The transputer always leaves the result of an operation on the evaluation stack and as one of the inputs to the next instruction can often be made to be the output of the previous instruction, this means that the representations of arcs are not moved unnecessarily.

In functional languages there are no loop structures, and repetitive processes are specified recursively. Consequently there are no loop structures in Tuki, and the compiler needs only one pass through the Tuki code. The only complex statement that must be handled is the Tuki *iftrue/else/endif* structure. The state of the machine just after the compilation of the *iftrue* statement is stacked (in case of nested if structures) and then restored when the corresponding else part is reached. This ensures that the two mutually exclusive branches of the if construct operate on the same initial state.

The basic job of the compiler is to allocate memory cells to the various arcs of the data flow graph. Each arc of the graph is used only once but can be replicated and so a count is associated with each cell at compile time. Once this count reaches zero, the cell can be used to represent another arc of the graph. Because of the pure, functional nature of the language, it is possible to take this very simple view of the data flow. The possible locations for these cells fall into three groups.. The first consists of only one cell and is the A-Register of the evaluation stack. Only one register is used here (rather than all three registers) as it is not possible to access registers on an individual basis. (Future versions of the compiler may make more sophisticated use of the B and C registers.) The two other locations for cells are both within the workspace of the function; these are the parameter area, allocated as part of the calling sequence, and any additional workspace claimed by the function (by adjusting the workspace pointer.)

The compiler maintains three lists, one for each of the cell areas outlined above. The length of the lists depends on the number of available cells in that area, in the case of the evaluation stack list it is always 1. The parameter area list is dependent on the number of parameters used by the function, but will never be less than 2, since the transputer calling mechanism always allocates space for three parameters (the third cell is used to hold the static link to support interlanguage working; see below.) The third list, representing additional workspace, is initially empty but might grow as the compiler proceeds through the graph. In general the compiler tries to use the cells in this order as this increases the probability that one of the operands is already in the evaluation stack and reduces the need for additional workspace.

The initial state of the compiler for the **nfib** function can be described as follows (where X indicates a cell that is available):-

The evaluation list is [X]
The parameter list is [0.1, X]
The workspace list is [ ]

The parameter has been placed on arc 0 and each arc has a reference count associated with it (separated from the arc by a "."), initially 1 for arc 0. Note the difference between the empty list [] indicating that no cells are available in this area and the X which indicates that there is a cell available which is not being used to represent an arc. This state is represented as a triple:

([X], [0.1, X], [])

The following annotated listing shows how the Tuki code is compiled to transputer code and how the state changes. When referring to parameters, the local offset is increased by 1 to allow for the static link in argument position 1, but which is not shown in the state triple. Thus *ldl 2* (load local at offset 2) refers to argument 1. The Tuki code is shown on the left in **bold**, the transputer code generated is in the centre, and the compiler state is shown to the right.

		([X], [0.1, X], [])
copies (0, 2)		([X], [0.2, X], [])

The **copies** does not generate any code, but changes the reference count for the arc.

lt ((0, #2), 1)

The **lt** (which translates into a *gt* in the instruction set, see [4]) requires a constant and the value on arc 0 to be on the evaluation stack and so generates the code to load the values and perform the operation, updating the state.

	ldc 2	
	ldl 2	
	gt	([1.1], [0.1, X], [])

iftrue (1)

The input arc is already available in the evaluation stack and so it is only necessary to perform the conditional jump. The state at this point is stacked, ready to be restored for the else part.

	cj EPnfib	([X], [0.1, X], []))

sink (0)

The **sink** will not generate any code but will reduce the reference count by 1; in this case the cell becomes free.

([X], [X, X], [])

source (#1, 2)

The evaluation stack is free and so code can be generated and the state updated.

	ldc 1	([2.1], [X, X], [])

retelse (2)

The value to return is on the evaluation stack and so a return instruction can be generated and the state restored to that which was saved earlier.

```
                ret
        epnfib:                                   ([X], [0.1, X], [])
```

copies (0, 2)

The **copies** does not generate any code, but changes the reference count for the arc.

```
                                                  ([X], [0.2, X], [])
```

sub ((0, #2), 3)

The **sub** loads the required constant and the value on arc 0 onto the evaluation stack and generates the operation, updating the state.

```
                ldl 2
                ldc 2
                sub                               ([3.1], [0.1, X], [])
```

call ("nfib", [3], 4)

The actual parameter of the call is already on the evaluation stack, however the call sequence requires the static link to be pushed onto the stack as well. The calling convention says that the static link is available as the first cell of the parameter area and so the following code must be generated.

```
                ldl 1
                call nfib                         ([4.1], [0.1, X], [])
```

sub ((0, #1), 5)

This **sub** does not use arc 4 which is currently represented by the evaluation stack and so it must be preserved. The compiler searches the lists to find the first X cell and generates code to save the evaluation stack there.

```
                stl 3                             ([X], [0.1, 4.1], [])
```

The code is now similar to the previous **sub**.

```
                ldl 2
                ldc 1
                sub                               ([5.1], [X, 4.1], [])
```

call ("nfib", [5], 6)

The call proceeds as before.

```
                ldl 1
                call nfib                         ([6.1], [X, 4.1], [])
```

add ((4, 6), 7)

The **add** requires the values on arcs 4 and 6 to be on the evaluation stack and so generates the code to retrieve arc 4, making use of the commutativity of addition (arc 6 is already on the evaluation stack.)

```
                ldl 3
```

The actual code to perform the addition is then generated and the state updated.

```
                add                               ([7.1], [X, X], [])
```

add ((7, #1), 8)

The **add** requires a constant and the value on arc 7 to be on the evaluation stack, this can be combined into one operation.

adc 1 ([8.1], [X, X], [])

retendif (8)

The value to return is on the evaluation stack and so a return instruction can be generated and the state adjusted.

ret ([X], [X, X], [])

4 Conclusions

The following performance measures have been obtained using our prototype system running on an INMOS B008 board with a B405 Transputer Module (T800 with 8M bytes of external memory).

The main benchmark used to evaluate the performance of the system is the familiar nfib function (see above), which counts the number of function calls it has made.

A value for n of 30 results in 2,692,537 function calls. If interlanguage working were not supported, then a speed of 689,652 function calls per second is achieved. With interlanguage working, the rate drops to 645,692 calls per second.

The second area in which some experiments have been performed is list processing. Using a lazy garbage collection system (written in C) a naive reverse of a 200 element list can be performed in 0.415 seconds. This represents a rate of 48,406 calls to append per second.

We have found the transputer to be a suitable target processor for our prototype system. Frequently we found that the code sequences we generated were the only possible ones (due to the RISC nature of the processor) but also that if we were to have a more complex repertoire of instructions we would still end up using those provided.

We have shown that functional languages can be implemented with performance as good as (and sometimes better than) conventional languages in the case of small eager functions. It remains to be seen if the compiler can generate code for very large, or lazy functions that matches that produced by compilers specifically orientated toward lazy evaluation (such as the G machine[1] and Tim[2]).

We have demonstrated that inter-language working can be supported with only negligible performance impact. As we were able to prototype the garbage collector in C, and also have access to all the C libraries, we found that the advantages of being able to perform interlanguage working were considerable.

The benefits of the Tuki route were based around the closeness of its notation to conventional technology which meant that many compiler optimisation techniques could be easily used. This, along with the fundamental simplicity of its constructs resulted in a small and efficient compiler of data flow graphs. Additionally the concentration on data flow meant that static analysis could detect a function that would run eagerly and generate an appropriate graph.

References

[1] T. Johnson, *Efficient compilation of lazy evaluation, In Proceedings of the SIGPLAN '84 Symposium on Compiler Construction*, pages 58-69, Montreal, 1984

[2] J. Fairbairn and S Wray, *Tim: A Simple, Lazy Abstract Machine to Execute Supercombinators*, Functional Programming Languages and Computer Architecture, 274, Springer-Verlag LNCS, 1987

[3] H. Glaser and S. Hayes, *Another Implementation Technique for Applicative Languages*, ESOP 86, Springer-Verlag LNCS 213, 1986.

[4] INMOS, *The Transputer Instruction Set, a Compiler Writers' Guide*, Prentice Hall, 1988

Hope^{+} on Flagship

Iain B. Robertson
ICL Mainframe Systems
Wenlock Way
West Gorton
Manchester
M12 5DR

Abstract

The Flagship project has aimed to develop a prototype parallel machine which would support a declarative programming style. The functional language Hope^{+} was chosen as the programming language. A compiler route from Hope^{+} has been developed through the intermediate language DACTL. This defines a graph reduction model of computation from which code can be produced to execute in parallel on the machine.

The results of Flagship using Hope^{+} are presented here. Aspects discussed are program design, implementation, performance and ease of modification of code. A range of applications are considered, from trivial benchmarks such as the Fibonacci Series to more complex applications such as the DebitCredit transaction processing benchmark.

1 Introduction

The ICL Fifth Generation Programme is motivated by the need to improve programmer productivity, software maintenance and software engineering methodology [1]. To address these problems, the programme includes development of declarative languages, compilers, tools, a parallel machine, a system environment and object managers to hold knowledge bases. The declarative approach relieves the programmer from the burden of expressing temporal sequence which ties conventional programs to the Von Neumann model of computation, improves software productivity and reduces errors. The inherent parallelism is exploited by the hardware to give potentially unlimited performance. The functional language Hope^{+} [2] has been used to develop a number of applications from which the results are presented here. This offers several extensions to the language first developed and implemented at Edinburgh [3] including:

- The basic type Num has been extended to include negative integers.
- A standard module to handle Vectors has been included.
- Hope modules are supported to allow separate compilation.
- Lazy evaluation is introduced for all data constructors. Function arguments are evaluated eagerly until a constructor exists at the outermost level.

- An 8-bit ISO character set has been adopted as the internal character set.
- Partial parameterisation of function calls is supported to facilitate work with higher-order functions.

The following extensions were not supported in the development route used during the experiments outlined in this paper.

- A basic type Real to support positive and negative real numbers.
- Recursive lets. Full local mutual recursion is not supported.
- Rule selection using pattern matching to permit overlapping patterns - resolution is based on order and not a tightest-fit strategy (although this is now available in the latest release of the development route).
- Error values - exceptions cause the program to abort rather than return an error value.

This paper gives a brief overview of Flagship - the hardware, computational model and development route in Chapter 2. The results obtained using functional programming are presented in Chapter 3 together with some performance comparisons and discussion. Chapter 4 summarises the benefits and weaknesses associated with our implementation of functional programming.

2 Flagship - an Overview

The Flagship machine consists of closely coupled processor-store pairs connected by a high bandwidth packet switched Delta network. The Flagship emulator is a 15 node machine with one service node. The design is scaleable up to 256 processing elements. Communication is based on message passing. The network can distribute packets to any node or, using an 'activity level' generated by each node, can perform load balancing by sending work to the least busy processor.

A packet based graph reduction model of computation [4] is implemented in assembler and 'C'. Executable packets are scheduled using a variable size queue and a stack. Garbage collection is done by weighted reference counting on every packet. References to remote packets result in either packet copying or, if it has only a single reference, a move. Applications which reference a remote 'stateholder' packet are exported to the remote node.

A development route is in place for implementing application software. Formal descriptions can be written in SPADE [5] and transformed to Hope$^+$. This allows program correctness to be determined. Hope$^+$ is compiled through the intermediate language DACTL [6] to the Flagship assembler language IIS (Idealised Instruction Set) [7]. IIS is compiled to 68020 machine code which can be run on the emulator.

3 Analysis of Results of Functional Programs

The following sections describe the benchmarks we have evaluated using Hope$^+$ and makes comparisons with other implementations. These comparisons are particularly between:

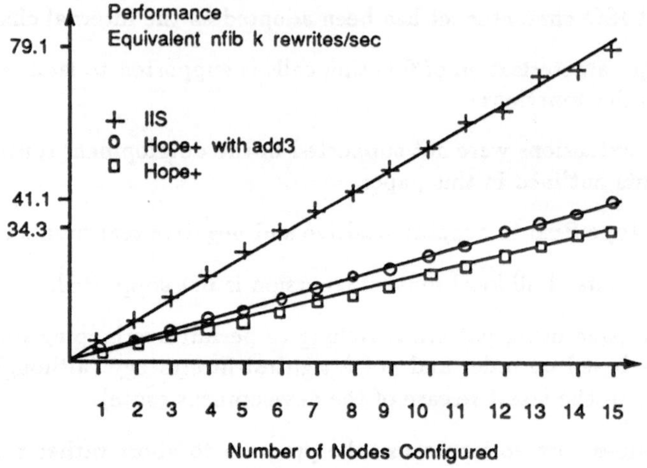

Figure 1: Nfib Performance

- Hope$^+$ compiled through our development route and run on a 15 node machine;
- hand-written code at the Flagship assembler level run on a 15 node machine;
- Hope$^+$ compiled by the FPM route and run on a SUN 3/50 or a SUN 3/260;

together with some performance figures from other machines.

3.1 Simple Benchmarks

3.1.1 Nfib

This is a modified version of the Fibonacci Series which adds one to the last two entries of the series. In Hope$^+$ it is written as:

```
module nfib ;

dec nfib : num -> num ;
--- nfib(0) <= 1 ;
--- nfib(1) <= 1 ;
--- nfib(n) <= 1 + nfib(n-1) + nfib(n-2) ;

nfib(28) ;

end;
```

Figure 1 shows the performance speed-up with nodes configured for a number of versions of the program. The performance is measured as 'equivalent nfib rewrites/sec' because each version performs a different number of rewrites to execute an 'nfib rewrite'. Plot 1 shows the results for nfib written as above in Hope$^+$. Written this way, the compiler produces separate rewrites for each addition, but plants in-line code for the subtractions. Plot 2 uses an extra function, defining a three-way-add as follows:

```
module nfib_a3 ;

dec add3 : num # num # num -> num ;
--- add3(x,y,z) <= x + y + z ;

dec nfib : num -> num ;
--- nfib(0) <= 1 ;
--- nfib(1) <= 1 ;
--- nfib(n) <= add3(1,nfib(n-1),nfib(n-2)) ;

nfib(28) ;

end;
```

This allows the compiler to plant the additions in-line in the add3 code. This reduces the number of rewrites generated by each recursion from four to three. Plot 3 shows results for the hand-written Flagship assembler (IIS) nfib which executes in the same number of rewrites as plot 2. The compiler overheads reduce performance by 50%. Various other hand-generated versions have produced performances of upto 4.65 M equivalent nfib rewrites/sec by using iteration within rewrites. This effectively makes rewrites large grain and therefore more efficient as the ratio of scheduling to useful work done is improved. As IIS is an idealised instruction set, it offers a large number of abstract registers (8 bytes each). The compilation from IIS to native assembler makes no register optimisations and therefore memory accesses are frequent. Optimisations of this sort would improve the performance of all the benchmarks described here.

3.1.2 Nqueens

This is a classic example of a program which illustrates 'back-tracking', ie. solutions to a problem are searched for along various possible paths and where these fail the program drops back to the last untested option and tries again. In practice, on the Flagship machine these options may be executed in parallel by using a suitable algorithm.

The objective of the exercise is to place N queens on an NxN chessboard such that no queens are attacking each other (ie. no two are placed on the same Rank, File or Diagonal).

The Hope$^+$ version is given in Appendix A. The program starts by placing a first queen on each File along Rank[1] thus giving an immediate 8-way parallelism in the search . It then attempts to place a second queen on Rank[2] in all possible non-attacking positions, each of these potential solutions is used in turn to generate further searches on Rank[3] etc, whilst accumulating a list of the successful File positions . If any potential solution fails to place a queen then that search is terminated at the Rank reached . If Rank[8] is reached then the list of the File indices of all 8 queens are used to encode a solution.

The minimum sized board is 4x4 which has a total of 2 valid solutions (including rotational and reflective symmetry) . The total numbers of solutions for larger sizes are shown below:-

```
  8 x 8  =  92  solutions
  9 x 9  = 352  solutions
10 x 10  = 724  solutions
```

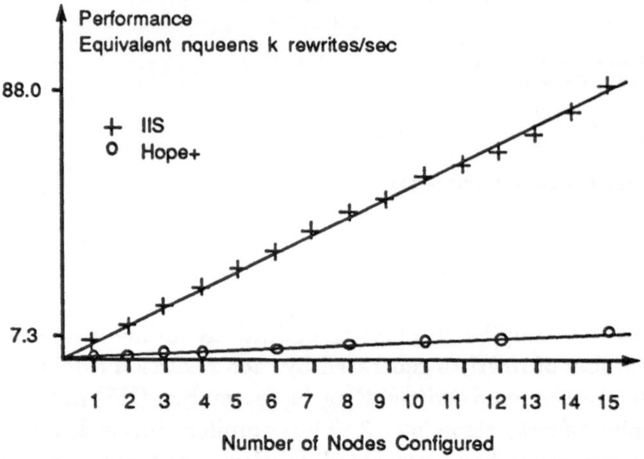

Figure 2: Nqueens Performance

MACHINE	LANGUAGE	RUN-TIME (SEC)
FLAGSHIP	IIS	1.0
FLAGSHIP	$Hope^+$	11.0
SUN 3/260	$Hope^+$(FPM)	1.1
SUN 3/50	$Hope^+$(FPM)	3.5

The two plots shown in Figure 2 show the results for Nqueens as a $Hope^+$ and an IIS version. The $Hope^+$ version can determine all 92 solutions of the 8x8 board using 422,956 rewrites. By writing in Flagship IIS the number of rewrites used can be reduced to only 80,659. The overheads using $Hope^+$ and the associated compiler route reduces performance to one-eleventh of hand-generated Flagship IIS. This large ratio is partly due to the optimisations possible at the IIS level:

- Vectors. By maintaining board positions as vectors of size N, we eliminate the inefficiency of list structures. Packed integer data guarantees locality of data whereas lists may be linked across several nodes. If processors require remote data, they will make copies. This process is especially inefficient for list structures as each element is wrapped in a packet with a 16byte header and holds 8 byte items - all items being tagged with type.
- Locality. It is possible in Flagship IIS to deliberately schedule work on the local node. Nqueens IIS has been written to give 90% locality.
- Iteration. By explicitly making parts of the computation local it is possible to use iteration in the *compatible* function - this relies on the vector format.

3.1.3 Tak

Tak is a recursive algorithm with cubic explosion. The $Hope^+$ program is given in Appendix A. Comparisons are given below for Tak(28,12,6).

MACHINE	LANGUAGE	RUN-TIME (SEC)
FLAGSHIP	IIS	18
FLAGSHIP	Hope$^+$	172
SUN 3/260	Hope$^+$(FPM)	6.9
SUN 3/50	Hope$^+$(FPM)	19.1

The Hope$^+$ version uses an extra rewrite for performing each subtraction. This is clearly inefficient as it causes extra scheduling for a simple operation. Our implementation of the computational model takes 50μs to schedule a rewrite packet for execution [8]. This is intolerable if the computation is as short as an arithmetic operation.

3.1.4 Triangle

This concurrent version of the Gabriel benchmark finds all the solutions to the "triangle game". The game consists of a triangular board with 15 holes. A peg is placed in every hole except the middle. The player makes a move by jumping over a peg into a vacant hole and removing the jumped peg. The object of the game is to remove all the pegs but one.

There are many possible sequences of moves, but only 1550 sequences result in a single remaining peg. The Gabriel version of the algorithm finds 775 solutions, the others being symmetrically identical (only one of the two possible initial moves is taken by the benchmark algorithm).

The table below shows Flagship's performance relative to some other machines.

MACHINE	LANGUAGE	RUN-TIME (SEC)
FLAGSHIP	IIS	80
FLAGSHIP	Hope$^+$	2400
SUN 3/260	Hope$^+$(FPM)	387
SUN 3/50	Hope$^+$(FPM)	1088
iPSC - 16 nodes	CCLISP	68

The Hope$^+$ version takes ten hours to complete on a single node. The figure given in the table extrapolates the estimated performance for a fifteen node machine. The poor performance is due to the inefficiency of maintaining legal move data as list structures. The IIS version achieves its performance by using vectors and iteration.

3.2 DebitCredit

This examplar is based on the Transaction Processing benchmark defined in [9]. Our objectives in implementing DebitCredit were:

- To evaluate the credibility of the Flagship technology as the basis of a relational database system.
- To obtain experience of the implementation of the central mechanisms of a relational database system on Flagship.
- To build the basis of a system which can be used as a testbed for the development of the database technology.

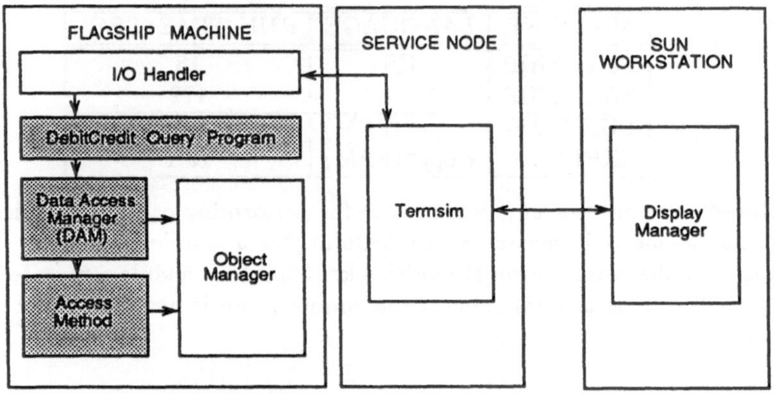

Figure 3: DebitCredit architecture

The demonstrator comprises three main components [10] as shown in Figure 3. The shaded areas show modules implemented in Hope$^+$.

1. The DataStore. This module consists of the following components:

   - an I/O handler, which communicates between the machine and a Terminal Simulator.
   - a query program which represents parameterised SQL in our form of relational algebra.
   - the Data Access Manager (DAM) provides the relational algebra runtime library and calls the Access Methods and Object Manager.
   - the Access Method is responsible for the primitive data structures representing the database and for operations on them.
   - the Object Manager which is responsible for the locking of data structures. A choice had to be made for the implementation of the Object Manager. Streams were considered too complicated and obscured the issues of shared store [11], continuations were felt to be a poor 'goto' style of programming and Hope$^+$C was not available at the time. The method adopted has been to use stateholders [4] to guard graphs of data. All computations accessing stateholders are executed on the processing element which holds that stateholder. The locking relies on this fact and that rewrites are guaranteed to be atomic.

2. Terminal Simulator. This module simulates a large population of terminals (teller machines), and a transaction processing monitor. It communicates with the Display Manager.

3. The Display Manager. This controls a DebitCredit session providing monitoring information and allowing input of parameters.

MACHINE	TPS
FLAGSHIP	140
SUN Hope$^+$(FPM)	5
IBM 4381-P22	22.1
DEC VAX 8830	27

The Flagship Transactions Per Second (TPS) are for running DebitCredit on a database of three relations - 200000 account records, 3000 teller records and 3000 bank records. The Flagship DebitCredit demonstrator is not a full impementation of the benchmark as defined in [9]. For example, no history records are maintained and the relation sizes are limited by the memory capacity of the nodes of the machine. Our implementation does not, however, take advantage of the 85% locality of the three relations - banks, tellers and accounts, as allowed by the definition of the benchmark. This states that 85% of transactions are made at the branch where the customer's account is held. By optimising the distribution of elements, it is possible to ensure that accounts associated with certain branches are held on the same node. In addition, all tellers can be arranged to be local to their branches. Hope$^+$ allowed us to implement a large part of the system in very little time compared with generating modules in Flagship assembler. The Access Methods were written in Hope$^+$ in one week, but took more than a month to write in IIS. It has been possible to experiment with variations of the Hope$^+$ DAM and Access Methods - attempts to alter IIS modules are time consuming and require considerable debugging. Most errors encountered in the project occurred in the IIS modules or as a result of inconsistent interfaces between Hope$^+$ and IIS modules. Of the errors which were traced to the DAM, many were the result of lazy evaluation not returning results when required by the Object Manager. The temporal constraints imposed by our locking mechanisms often required some special Hope$^+$ constructs to force their evaluation. Comparisons with dummy values were required in several functions to demand evaluation. The efficiency of the DAM module was increased by using M4 macros. This eliminated the need for a rewrite for each constant referenced. Further improvements in efficiency would be possible if our compilation route supported recursive let statements, and if a more complete Vectors module were available. Current experiments with the Hope$^+$modules are improving the performance considerably from early implementations which ran at around 30TPS.

4 Conclusions

Our experience with Hope$^+$ on the Flagship emulator has revealed many of the advantages of programming in a declarative style: formal specification, transformations, rapid development, fewer programming errors and easier modification of code. The ideal of linear performance speed-up through parallelism is shown to be possible on a real machine for programs like Nfib and Nqueens (Figures 1 and 2). Early indications for DebitCredit also show near linear performance speed-up.

While Flagship performance is excellent for hand-generated IIS versions (e.g. iterative nfib, triangle), the Hope$^+$ versions are relatively slow. The table below summarises the performance of Hope$^+$ benchmarks relative to IIS versions running on the Flagship machine and FPM running on a SUN 3/260.

BENCHMARK	REWRITES (FLAGSHIP) Hope$^+$:IIS	EXECUTION TIME (FLAGSHIP) Hope$^+$:IIS	Hope$^+$on FLAG:SUN(FPM)
Nfib	1:1	2:1	-
Nqueens	5:1	11:1	11:1
tak	7:4	10:1	5:2
triangle	-	30:1	7:1

There are several factors which lead to the loss of performance in Hope$^+$ programs:

- Rewrites are too finely grained. Our implementation of the computational model takes 50μs to schedule a rewrite packet for execution [8]. The Hope$^+$ rewrite execution rate is approximately 3 - 4 kRewrites/sec. This means that 20% of the execution is in scheduling costs. This ratio needs to be reduced to give more efficient performance.
- The fine grain rewrites often include StandardArithmetic functions which could be calculated in-line given more sophisticated compilers.
- List data constructs prove very inefficient. Copying in Flagship is packet based, therefore, remote access to list data structures is excessively burdensome (the model takes 190μs to perform one packet copy [8]).
- Packet overheads are too large and too much tagging is required. Every rewrite must perform considerable decoding and item analysis before executing the supercombinator code. Simple rewrites are therefore penalised as the execution mechanism must perform the same checks as for more complex rewrites. More sophisticated compilers would be able to plant rewrites which performed only as much checking as is necessary.

We now have features which eliminate some inefficiencies: annotations [12] can be used to specify computational order and locality; a vectors module can be used to implement data constructs more efficiently. As yet, few results have been obtained using these new features.

A Programs:

A.1 Nqueens

```
module nqueens;

! nqueens benchmark based upon Steve Noble's iis version
! Started 17th June 1988

! Changes Log
! 02-12-88 ADK Dactl version added module name & end statement


uses StandardXfer;

dec find : num X num X num X list(num) -> num;

dec first : num X num X num X list(num) -> num;

dec firstcond : num X num X num X list(num)  X truval -> num;
```

```
dec compatible : num X num X num X list(num) -> truval;

dec Abs : num -> num;

---find(rank,file,N,board)<=
        if file>N then 0 ! no more solutions on this rank
        else
          if rank>N then 1 ! a solution has been found
          else first(rank,file,N,board) + find(rank,file+1,N,board);

---first(rank,file,N,board)<=
         firstcond(rank,file,N,board,
                   compatible(rank,file,rank-1,board));

---firstcond(rank,file,N,board,false)<=0;
---firstcond(rank,file,N,board,true)<=
             find(rank+1,1,N,file::board);

---compatible(rank,file,row,nil)<=true;
---compatible(rank,file,row,h::t)<=
              if (h=file) or (Abs(h-file)=Abs(row-rank)) then false
              else compatible(rank,file,row-1,t);

---Abs(n)<= if n<0 then -n else n;

termout(numtostr(find(1,1,10,nil)));

end;
```

A.2 Tak

```
module tak ;

dec tak : num # num # num -> num ;

--- tak(x,y,z) <= if not (y<x) then z
                  else tak( tak(x-1,y,z),
                            tak(y-1,z,x),
                            tak(z-1,x,y) ) ;

tak(18,12,6) ;

end ;
```

A.3 Triangle

```
module triangle;


! Hope+ version of Gabriel Triangle Benchmark Program !

! Started by A D Kitto on January 26th 1988 !

! Changes Log                                  !
! Version five 29th February 1988              !
!  Used vector type for boardstate             !
!  Prints the number of soultions found        !
!  Use termout instead of pr for hc2.0         !
!  Metrics comments added                      !

uses StandardXfer, StandardVectors;

type boardlist     == list ( truval ) ;
type boardstate    == vector(truval);

dec boardbegin : boardstate ;
---boardbegin<=listtovector([true,true,true,true,false,true,true,
                             true,true,true,true,true,true,true,true]);

type move          == (num X num X num);
```

```
type sequence      == list ( move ) ;
type solution      == list ( move )  ;
type solutions     == list(solution);

dec leg1 : sequence ;
--- leg1 <= [( 1, 2, 4) , ( 2, 4, 7) , ( 4, 7,11) , ( 3, 5, 8) ,
            ( 5, 8,12) , ( 6, 9,13) , ( 1, 3, 6) , ( 3, 6,10) ,
            ( 6,10,15) , ( 2, 5, 9) , ( 5, 9,14) , ( 4, 8,13) ,
            (11,12,13) , (12,13,14) , (13,14,15) , ( 7, 8, 9) ,
            ( 8, 9,10) , ( 4, 5, 6) , ( 4, 2, 1) , ( 7, 4, 2) ] ;

dec leg2 : sequence ;
--- leg2 <= [ (11, 7, 4) , ( 8, 5, 3) , (12, 8, 5) , (13, 9, 6) ,
             ( 6, 3, 1) , (10, 6, 3) , (15,10, 6) , ( 9, 5, 2) ,
             (14, 9, 5) , (13, 8, 4) , (13,12,11) , (14,13,12) ,
             (15,14,13) , ( 9, 8, 7) , (10, 9, 8) , ( 6, 5, 4)];


dec legalmoves : sequence ;

---legalmoves<= leg1 <> leg2 ;

dec validmovep : move X boardstate -> truval ;
---validmovep((i,j,k),B)<= B@i and ( B@j and ( not ( B@k ) ) ) ;

dec makemove : move X boardstate -> boardstate ;
dec set : boardlist X num -> boardlist;
dec unset : boardlist X num -> boardlist;

---makemove((i,j,k),B)<= listtovector(set(unset(unset(vectortolist(B),i),j),k));

---set(nil,x)<= nil;
---set(h::t,x)<= if x=1 then true::t else h::set(t,x-1);
---unset(nil,x)<= nil;
---unset(h::t,x)<= if x=1 then false::t else h::unset(t,x-1);

dec try : num X boardstate X sequence X solution X sequence -> num;

!       depth X current position X possible move X partial solution so far !
!       -> number of solutions                                            !

---try(depth,B,nil,seq,restart)<=
          if depth=14 then 1 else 0 ; ! run out of moves !
---try(depth,B,h::t,seq,restart)<= if depth = 14 then 1   ! a solution found !
                                   else
                                     if validmovep(h,B) then
                                        try(depth+1,
                                            makemove(h,B),
                                            restart,
                                            h::seq,
                                            restart)
                                         +                 ! two search paths !
                                        try(depth,
                                            B,
                                            t,
                                            seq,
                                            restart)
                                     else try(depth,B,t,seq,restart);

let x==try(1,boardbegin,[(12,8,5)],nil,legalmoves) in termout(numtostr(x));
                                               ! find 775 solutions !

!  5,802,572 calls to try                  !
!  7,820,920 references to board           !
!    971,616 stores to board               !

end;
```

References

[1] Proctor BJ, Skelton CJ. What is Fifth Generation - the scope of the ICL programme. ICL Mainframe Systems Division. ICL Technical Journal, Volume 5, Issue 3, 1987

[2] Perry N. Hope+. Imperial College, London. IC/FPR/LANG/2.5.1/7 1988

[3] Burstall RM. et al. HOPE: An experimental applicative language. Edinburgh University Report. CSR-62-80, 1981

[4] Watson P. A super-combinator model of computation. Computer Science Deptartment. Manchester University, FS/MU/PW/021-87, 1987

[5] Boddy GS. SPADE - Specification processing and dependency extraction. ICL Mainframe Systems Division, FLAG/UD/3DR.003

[6] Glauert JRW, Kennaway JR, Sleep M.R. Dactl: a computational model and complier target language based on graph reduction. Declarative Systems Project, University of East Anglia. ICL Technical Journal, Volume 5, Issue 3, 1987

[7] Sargeant J. An idealised instruction set for a packet rewrite machine. Manchester University Computer Science Deptartment, 1988

[8] Robertson IB. Performance primitive test programs. ICL Mainframe Systems Division, FLAG/DD/4TP.003, 1989

[9] Sawyer T, Serlin O. DebitCredit benchmark - minimum requirements and compliance list. Codd & Date Consulting Group, San Jose

[10] Kellett SM. Definition of the DebitCredit benchmark for the initial EDS DBMS model. ICL Mainframe Systems Division, FLAG/WP/3BM.001, 1989

[11] Broughton P, Leunig SR, Prior S, Thompson CM. Designing system software for parallel declarative systems. ICL Mainframe Systems Division. ICL Technical Journal, Volume 5, Issue 3, 1987

[12] Glynn K, Kewley J, Watson P, While L. Annotations for Hope+. IC/FPR/PROG/1.1.1/5 Imperial College, London 1988

Expressing and Reasoning About Non-deterministic Functional Programs

John Hughes and John O'Donnell

1. Introduction

For some time functional language researchers have experimented with non-deterministic constructs for these otherwise deterministic languages. One strong motivation to do so is the desire to express necessarily non-deterministic programs, such as operating systems and interactive systems that service requests from several terminals in the order in which they are made. Another motivation is that some parallel algorithms are internally non-deterministic even though their result is not. Since functional languages are claimed to be well suited to parallel programming we certainly wish to be able to express such algorithms. Non-determinism can also be related to program refinement: a non-deterministic function may be considered to be a specification which is refined to a deterministic implementation. We will not address this third aspect here.

The catch is that adding non-determinism to a functional language interferes with reasoning. Many attempts have been made to sidestep this, but none is wholly satisfactory. In this paper we introduce a new way of expressing non-determinism functionally. Our approach is unsurprising — we simply add sets of possible values as a new datatype — yet it avoids many of the pitfalls of earlier attempts. We are able to prove theorems about non-deterministic programs using equational reasoning, just as we do in the deterministic case.

This paper is organised as follows. In the next section we review several previous approaches. In section 3 we introduce our own. After that we show how a number of well-known examples can be expressed using our operators. In section 5 we discuss our denotational semantics and its limitations, and prove some theorems about our example functions. Finally we develop some simple parallel tree algorithms that are internally non-deterministic, and prove their correctness.

2. Previous Approaches

Quite a variety of ways of adding non-determinism to functional languages have been explored. All introduce some obstacle to reasoning. In some cases the obstacle is blatant — referential transparency is lost. In other cases it is more subtle. In this section we briefly discuss four alternatives.

2.1 Add Non-deterministic Functions

Perhaps the most direct approach is simply to add functions whose result is not completely determined by their arguments. The simplest such function is McCarthy's amb [1].

amb x y = either x or y

Intuitively, amb evaluates its two arguments in parallel and returns the first to yield a value. This makes amb "bottom-avoiding":

$\text{amb}\ \bot\ x = x$
$\text{amb}\ x\ \bot = x$

It also allows us to write programs that respond to stimuli in their (temporal) order of arrival, which is useful.

Other researchers have chosen different functions as their non-deterministic primitives. Henderson chose merge, which interleaves two streams in the order in which their elements become available. He used it to express some simple operating systems [2]. His work was developed further by Jones [3] and Abramsky and Sykes [4]. Friedman and Wise instead defined frons, which adds an element to a list at a position determined by the time its value becomes available [5]. O'Donnell built a functional operating system based on frons [6].

The flaw in this general approach is well-known — it sacrifices referential transparency. That is, variables can no longer be replaced by their values, and equational reasoning becomes invalid. For example, given

double x = x + x

it is *not* true that

double (amb 1 2) = amb 1 2 + amb 1 2

because the left hand side can evaluate only to 2 or 4, while the right hand side can also give 3. Since equational reasoning is the fundamental tool for proving and transforming functional programs, it is difficult to see how to construct proofs without it.

Nevertheless, this approach has a big advantage — it makes non-determinism very easy to use. Indeed, non-deterministic functions are exactly as easy to use as deterministic ones! It is useful therefore to compare the convenience of other approaches with this one, since a method which makes non-deterministic programming much more difficult is unlikely to curry favour with pragmatists.

2.2 Add a Non-deterministic Environment

An alternative to providing non-deterministic functions is to run the program in an environment that performs non-deterministic operations for it. This idea was pioneered by Stoye: his functional operating system runs processes which are themselves deterministic stream functions, routing messages from one process to another and non-deterministically mergeing messages from different sources [7]. Referential transparency is retained because all the non-deterministic operations occur outside the programming language. Turner and Cupitt have followed this approach [8], and it has also been adopted by the Haskell design committee [9].

This approach is to some extent inconvenient, since any program which uses non-determinism internally must be split into several communicating processes, but the advantage is that referential transparency is not compromised. However, this does *not* mean that programs running under Stoye's system are easy to reason about — referential transparency is not the end of the story! Although we can prove theorems about individual processes in the usual way, there is no way to prove properties of the *whole system*. Indeed, Stoye gives no formal way of relating events in different processes. Worse, it is not even possible in principle to prove a subsystem correct in isolation, since any process may send a message to any other. Despite its referential transparency, Stoye's approach is unattractive to the program prover.

2.3 Add a Non-deterministic Language Level

A suggestion that has attracted much interest recently is to combine a functional language with an established process notation such as CCS or CSP. The functional language would be used to express individual deterministic processes, and the process notation would be used to express their combination and support non-determinism. A rigid separation between the two levels would enable existing proof techniques to be used within each level. An early example of such a two-level language is Holmstrom's PFL, which combined ML with CCS [10].

The main drawback of this approach is that it has not yet been shown to work. The central thesis — that separation of a program into two levels allows its proof of correctness to be factored similarly — remains unproven.

2.4 Add Oracles

An ingenious suggestion due to Burton is to parameterise non-deterministic choices by 'oracles' — essentially booleans that tell the operator which choice to make. The primitive non-deterministic operator is thus

```
choose :: oracle -> * -> * -> *
```

A program is provided with an infinite supply of oracles by the operating system, but cannot create new oracles internally. However, the operating system leaves oracle values undetermined until the first use in a choice. At that point the second and third arguments of choose are evaluated in parallel, and the first one to yield a value chosen. The choice is recorded in the oracle, so that subsequent uses of the same oracle can just make the same choice as the first use.

The choose function does not interfere with referential transparency. Consider

```
double x = x + x
```

It *is* true that

```
double (choose o 1 2) = choose o 1 2 + choose o 1 2
```

because the use of the same oracle in each choice on the right forces them to be made in the same way. On the other hand, provided oracles are used at most once, and the oracles supplied by the system start off unused, then an oracular program behaves as though all the choices were made by amb!

The oracular approach is not without its problems. First of all, choose is *not* bottom-avoiding unless the oracle it is supplied with is unused. Thus when correctness depends on bottom-avoidance, the best that can be proved is correct behaviour for suitable values of the oracle parameters. It may often be necessary to prove that oracles are used only once. It is hard to say how much of a burden this will turn out to be without more experience of proving oracular programs correct.

The oracular style is also rather less convenient than the amb-style. The programmer is responsible for passing oracular parameters to each non-deterministic function, and for organising suitable 'plumbing' to communicate these parameters from the outermost level of the program to the point where they are used. The plumbing is extra code that an amb-programmer would not need to write. A new class of errors — plumbing errors — is made possible, which lead to accidental re-use of oracle values. And the plumbing is ultimately unnecessary, because in a correct program the choices can be replaced by amb anyway!

3. Adding a Set Datatype

Our alternative proposal is very simple: we add an explicit set datatype to the programming language to represent the sets of possible values of a non-deterministic expression. Thus for every type t, there is a type {t} whose elements are sets of values of type t. 'Non-deterministic' functions are just those whose result is a set. The 'non-deterministic primitives' we provide are ordinary set operations such as union and cartesian product. Adding this new datatype clearly cannot threaten referential transparency, which would be compromised only if we provided a choice 'function'

```
choose :: {*} -> *
```

We will not do so.

Our intended representation of a set value is by a representative element chosen non-deterministically from it. Thus although t and {t} are quite different types, they have the same representation. This constrains the set operations we can provide; for example, we cannot provide intersection since it is impossible to choose an element of $S \cap T$ given only a representative of S and a representative of T. However, we can provide union: an element of $S \cup T$ can be chosen by making an arbitrary choice between the representatives of S and T. This is our non-deterministic choice operator. In fact we will use 'bottom-avoiding union', which makes the arbitrary choice by taking the first to yield a value. As a consequence we can assume that

$$\{\bot\} \cup S = S$$

which looks strange, but is indeed true in our denotational semantics.

Sets are built in the first place using the singleton former: {x} is a set containing only x. The implementation of singleton formation is a no-op — that is, the element chosen from {x} is x. Cartesian products of sets $S \times T$ can be formed — the implementation just builds a pair of the representatives of each component. And functions may be mapped over sets: we define

$$f * S = \{f\, x \mid x \in S\}$$

The implementation of mapping is function application: the function is applied to the representative of S.

Given mapping and product we can support a limited form of set comprehension:

$$\{f(x_1 \ldots x_n) \mid x_i \in S_i\}$$

can be expressed as

$$f * (S_1 \times \ldots \times S_n)$$

The comprehension notation is often convenient. Note that we *cannot* provide 'filtering' of a set — it's not possible to choose an element of $\{x \mid x \in S, x>0\}$ by choosing an arbitrary representative of S and then comparing it with zero.

We will need a generalised union operator

$$\bigcup :: \{\{*\}\} \text{ -> } \{*\}$$

whose implementation is again a no-op. $\bigcup$ is necessary when we compose non-deterministic functions. To see why, consider the functions

f, g :: int -> {int}

We might expect to be able to compose f and g, giving another function of the same type. In fact f has the wrong type to be *applied* to the result of g; it must be *mapped* over it instead:

h x = f * g n

But the type of h is now

h :: int -> {{int}}

We can use $\bigcup$ to eliminate the unwanted level of set bracketing:

$$h\, x = \bigcup (f * g\, n)$$

defines a function with the same type as f and g.

Just as we can write f * S to map a unary function over one set, it is sometimes convenient to map a curried function over *several* sets. We might try writing f * S * T for

$\{f\ s\ t \mid s \in S,\ t \in T\}$

but this is not correct. Assuming that * is left associative, f * S is a *set* of functions (a set of partial applications of f) and so cannot be mapped over another set. We need another operator to map a set of functions over a set of arguments:

$F ** S = \{f\ s \mid f \in F,\ s \in S\}$

Now we can map f over two sets by writing f * S ** T, and in fact we can map an n-ary function over n sets; for example

$f * S ** T ** U ** V = \{f\ s\ t\ u\ v \mid s \in S,\ t \in T,\ u \in U,\ v \in V\}$

(It would be more uniform, though less concise, to replace f * S in this expression by the equivalent {f} ** S). Like *, ** is implemented as function application.

We will sometimes use *sections* of operators to construct the functions we map over sets: for any operator ⊕, the sections (a⊕) and (⊕b) are the (unary) functions defined by

$(a\oplus)\ b = a \oplus b$
$(\oplus b)\ a = a \oplus b$

For example, (1/) is the reciprocal function and (/2) is the halving function. Using the operators *, **, and sections, functions on sets can often be made to look very similar to functions written using impure non-determinism.

Finally, an operator that is very helpful in controlling bottom-avoiding choices is *serialisation*:

$a \gg b \quad = \bot \quad \text{if } a = \bot$
$\qquad\quad = b \quad \text{otherwise}$

4. Examples of Non-deterministic Programming

In this section we give examples of non-deterministic programming in the set style. We begin by showing how the other proposed primitives, amb, merge and frons, can be expressed, and then we go on to use them in a few small operating system components similar to those developed by Henderson, Jones, and Abramsky and Sykes. We hope to demonstrate that our notation is not unreasonably heavy. In the following section we will discuss semantics and prove a few simple theorems about these functions.

First let us try to express McCarthy's amb. It's type, in the impure style, is

amb :: * -> * -> *

but since its result is non-deterministic we will give it the type

amb :: * -> * -> {*}

Now it is simply expressed as

$\text{amb}\ a\ b = \{a\} \cup \{b\}$

which makes an arbitrary choice between the values of a and b.

A less trivial example is merge. Since merge is non-deterministic its result will be a *set* of possible merged streams:

```
merge :: [*] -> [*] -> {[*]}
```

If we define a *biased* merge which favours its first argument for one step only, then we can define

```
merge xs ys = bias xs ys ∪ bias ys xs
```

Biased merge can be defined by

```
bias [] ys          = {ys}
bias (x:xs) ys      = (x:) * merge xs ys
```

Since bias is strict in its first argument, the bottom-avoiding choice in merge will not select an element from a stream whose value is not yet available:

```
merge xs ⊥          = bias xs ⊥ ∪ bias ⊥ xs
                    = bias xs ⊥ ∪ ⊥
                    = bias xs ⊥
```

and so the first element chosen will be from xs.

Although merge as we have defined it will not select an element from an undefined stream, it *may* select an undefined *element* from a stream. This is because

```
bias (⊥:xs) ys      = (⊥:) * merge xs ys
```

and the chosen result, ⊥:something, is not undefined and so is not avoided by the subsequent choice. We can ensure this doesn't happen by forcing the stream's elements to be computed before the cons-cells containing them. The function hs (for head-strict) does this.

```
hs []               = []
hs (x:xs)           = x » x:hs xs
```

A 'head-strict merge' can now be defined by

```
hsmerge xs ys       = merge (hs xs) (hs ys)
```

A restricted version of Friedman and Wise's frons operator, which is supposed to insert an element into a list in a position depending on the time its value becomes available, can be defined in terms of merge.

```
frons :: * -> [*] -> {[*]}
frons x xs = merge (x » [x]) (hs xs)
```

Now let us discuss some examples of functional 'systems programming'. The first example we consider is Jones' interrupt handler [3]. We take a functional interrupt to be a boolean expression which evaluates to True *when a real interrupt happens*. That is, both its value and its time of evaluation are significant. For example, if keyboard is a stream of characters typed by the user, then

```
member keyboard '^C'
```

is an interrupt — it evaluates to True when a control-C is typed, and to False on end-of-file, when it is clear no further interrupt can occur. Jones' interrupt handler may be used to terminate the execution of a program when an interrupt occurs. It is a function applied to the program's output stream which returns the prefix of the stream produced before the interrupt. We define it as follows:

```
interrupt int xs =
        (when int » {[]})
    ∪   case xs of
            []     -> {[]}
            x:xs' -> (x:) * interrupt int xs'

when True = True
when False = ⊥
```

The serialisation ensures that the first alternative cannot be chosen before the interrupt is ready.

For our next example we describe a process network of the kind Henderson built his operating systems from [2]. We will take as an example a simple network containing only two processes, an editor and a database. The processes communicate via streams: the editor communicates with the keyboard, the screen, and the database, while the database communicates only with the editor. Using Henderson's diagrammatic notation the network can be drawn as shown:

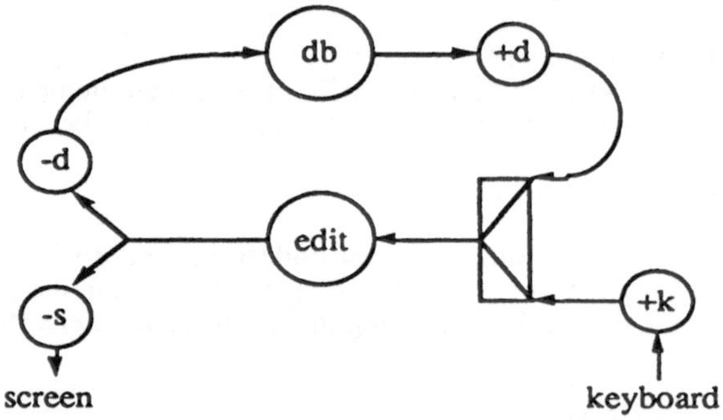

Here the square box with an arrowhead in it represents a merge, +k and +d represent tagging processes that enable edit to identify the source of messages in its merged input stream, and -d and -s represent untagging processes that filter edit's output to separate the messages intended from the screen from those intended for the database.

The tagging functions are deterministic and can be defined as follows:

```
data tagged * = Tag char *

tag :: char -> [*] -> [tagged *]
tag c []          = []
tag c (m:ms)      = Tag c m : tag c ms

untag :: char -> [tagged *] -> [*]
untag c []        = []
untag c (Tag c' m : ms)
                  = m : untag c ms                    if c = c'
                  = untag c ms                        if c ≠ c'
```

Now assuming the functions edit and db are deterministic and given, Henderson would describe the whole network by the equations

```
screen  = untag 's' edits
dbs     = db (untag 'd' edits)
edits   = edit (merge (tag 'k' keyboard) (tag 'd' dbs))
```

We need make relatively little alteration to express the same system using sets. The values of the streams screen, dbs, and edits are non-deterministic, and so each must be replaced by a set of streams. Then we need only change applications of functions to these streams to map functions over them instead:

screen = untag 's' * edits
dbs = db * (untag 'd' * edits)
edits = edit * $\bigcup$ (merge (tag 'k' keyboard) * (tag 'd' * dbs))

As a final example, we program an operating system kernel supporting process spawning and interprocess communication, taken from an example by Abramsky and Sykes. The running system looks like this:

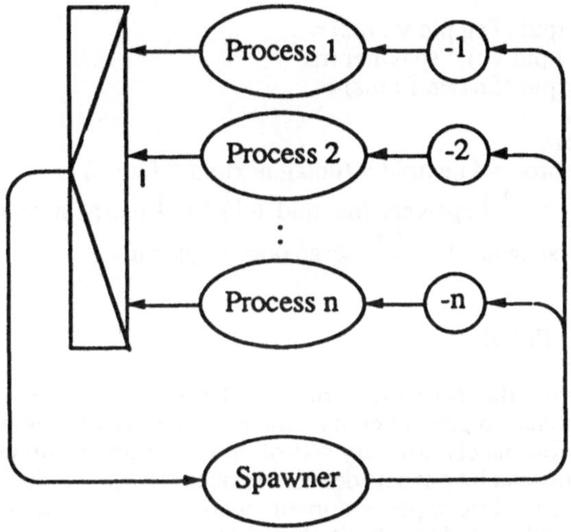

Processes may place two kinds of message in their output streams: data tagged with a process address which are simply forwarded by the spawner to be filtered out by the appropriate untag, and spawn messages which cause the spawner to create a new process. The latter contain a function to invoke as the process body, which is passed the new process' address and its input stream. Messages have the type

data message = Tag int value | Spawn (int -> [message] -> [message])

The spawner creates a process by becoming a mini process network containing the new process and a new invocation of itself:

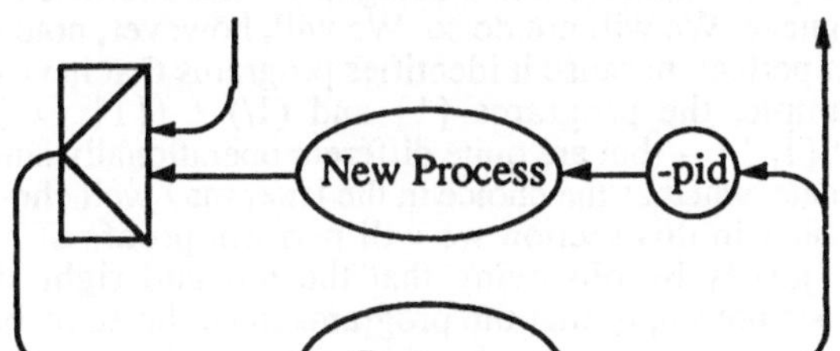

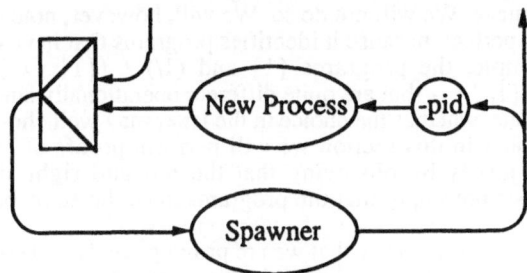

The effect is to add a new process to the process table.

The spawner can be expressed in the impure style as follows:

```
spawner nextpid (Tag pid v : ms) =
        Tag pid v : spawner ms
spawner nextpid (Spawn f : ms) =
        future
        where   newproc = f nextpid (untag nextpid future)
                future = spawner (nextpid + 1) (merge ms newproc)
```

Suppose there is a start-up process called boot; a complete system can then be expressed as

```
system = spawner 1 (merge boot system)
```

To re-express this in our framework we must replace the spawner by a function returning a *set* of streams. Once again, we only need to change selected function applications to maps.

```
spawner nextpid (Tag pid v : ms) =
        (Tag pid v :) * spawner ms
spawner nextpid (Spawn f : ms) =
        future
        where
        newproc = f nextpid * (untag nextpid * future)
        future = ⋃ spawner (nextpid + 1) * (⋃ merge ms * newproc)
system = ⋃ spawner 1 * (⋃ merge boot * system)
```

5. Semantics and Proofs

It is well-known that the semantics of non-deterministic functional languages is problematic. In particular, to give a denotational semantics of our language we must decide what sets denote. Unfortunately arbitrary sets of domain elements do not themselves form a domain — we must instead let out sets denote elements of a powerdomain.

We choose to use the Hoare powerdomain, whose elements are non-empty closed sets that are both *downward-closed* and *limit-closed.* (S is downward-closed if whenever $x \leq y$ and $y \in S$, then $x \in S$, and it is limit closed if whenever all the elements of a chain lie in S, so does the limit). Sets are ordered by inclusion, and the least set is $\{\bot\}$. Every set S in the Hoare powerdomain contains $\bot$ (by downward closure) and so

$$S \cup \{\bot\} = S$$

Thus $\cup$ is 'bottom-avoiding' in this powerdomain, and this is why we choose it — set operations in the Hoare powerdomain have properties consistent with our operational understanding. We will understand sets we write down to stand for the corresponding powerdomain element — that is, their downward- and limit-closure.

Having chosen a powerdomain it is a straightforward exercise to give a denotational semantics to our language. We will not do so. We will, however, note that this denotational semantics is far from perfect, because it identifies programs that have different operational behaviour. For example, the programs $\{1\}$ and $(1/) * (\{1\} \cup \{0\})$ have the same denotation — the set $\{1, \bot\}$ — but are quite different operationally since the former cannot actually fail to terminate, whereas the choice in the latter may well choose zero, leading to $\bot$ as the final result. Later in this section we will perform proofs of program equivalence using laws that we justify by observing that the left and right sides have the same denotation. If this does not imply that the programs have the same behaviour, what have we actually proved?

One way to answer this is to say that we are proving *partial correctness* only. Because powerdomain elements must be downward closed, the denotational semantics cannot distinguish non-deterministic programs that definitely terminate from those that may not. Thus if we prove

$$f\,x = \{y\}$$

we have shown only that running f will choose an element approximating y as its result, or to put it another way, that if f x terminates its result will be y.

There is another, potentially more satisfactory way to answer the question. That is to argue that the laws used in the proofs, although justified in this paper by referring to the Hoare powerdomain, could also be justified from the operational semantics. In other words, twe restrict ourselves to laws that *do* relate programs with identical behaviour, and so our theorems in fact show total correctness. To make this argument properly it is necessary to give a formal operational semantics, justify the laws used, and indeed explain what proofs by fixpoint induction now mean! We leave this for the future and satisfy ourselves with partial correctness proofs; however, we will point out cases where laws true in the Hoare powerdomain are clearly *untrue* of program behaviours.

The laws we use are as follows:

$$\bot_{\{t\}} = \{\bot_t\}$$

$$S \cup S = S \qquad \cup \text{ is idempotent}$$

$$S \cup T = T \cup S \qquad \cup \text{ is commutative}$$

$$S \cup (T \cup U) = (S \cup T) \cup U \qquad \cup \text{ is associative}$$

$$\{\bot\} \cup S = S \qquad \cup \text{ is bottom-avoiding}$$

In the Hoare powerdomain a stronger law is true:

$$x \leq y \Rightarrow \{x\} \cup \{y\} = \{y\}$$

but this does not hold operationally and we will not use it.
There are several laws about map:

$$f * \{x\} = \{f\,x\}$$

$$f * S = \{f\,\bot\} \qquad \text{if f is a constant function}$$

$$f * (g * S) = (f \cdot g) * S$$

The latter may be more readable expressed using comprehension notation:

$$f * \{e \mid \ldots\} = \{f\,e \mid \ldots\}$$

where the ellipses stand for the same thing on each side.

Serialisation may be moved in and out of set brackets:

$$x \gg \{y\} = \{x \gg y\}$$

$$x \gg (f * S) = ((x\gg) \cdot f) * S$$

The latter can be rewritten using comprehensions:

$$x \gg \{e \mid \ldots\} = \{x \gg e \mid \ldots\}$$

Generalised union can be related to map and singleton:

$$\bigcup \{S\} = S$$

$$\bigcup \{\{e\} \mid \ldots\} = \{e \mid \ldots\}$$

$$f * \bigcup S \quad = \quad \bigcup ((f*) * S)$$

Finally, it is true in the Hoare powerdomain that

$$f * (S \cup T) \quad = \quad f * S \cup f * T$$

but operationally this law is *not* true, because the bottom-avoiding choice avoids a different bottom in each case. For example,

{1/0} ∪ {1/1}

(which always chooses 1) is certainly not equivalent to

(1/) * ({0} ∪ {1})

which may choose 0 and then fail. However, the law *does* hold if f 'preserves bottoms', that is, if

f x = ⊥ if and only if x = ⊥.

Now let us prove some simple theorems about the functions in the previous section. We begin with merge: recall its definition

```
merge xs ys      = bias xs ys ∪ bias ys xs
bias [] ys       = {ys}
bias (x:xs) ys   = (x:) * merge xs ys
```

It is immediately clear that merge is commutative; we will prove that it is bottom-avoiding.

Theorem merge xs ⊥ = {xs ++ ⊥}
Proof
We prove the theorem for all *finite* xs by structural induction on xs. The theorem then follows for infinite xs by taking limits.

Case []

merge [] ⊥
= bias [] ⊥ ∪ bias ⊥ []
= {⊥} ∪ ⊥ unfolding bias, and because bias is strict in its first argument
= {⊥} ∪ {⊥}
= {⊥}
= {[] ++ ⊥}

Case ⊥ is similar.

Case x:xs

merge (x:xs) ⊥
= bias (x:xs) ⊥ ∪ bias ⊥ (x:xs)
= bias (x:xs) ⊥ ∪ {⊥} because bias is strict in its first argument
= bias (x:xs) ⊥ because ∪ is bottom-avoiding
= (x:) * merge xs ⊥
= (x:) * {xs ++ ⊥} induction hypothesis
= {x:xs ++ ⊥} map over a singleton

End of proof

A similar proof shows that merge xs [] = {xs}.

Next we'll prove two properties of the interrupt handler. Recall its definition:

```
interrupt int xs =
        (when int » {[]})
    ∪   case xs of
          []      -> {[]}
          x:xs' -> (x:) * interrupt int xs'
```

First we show that if no interrupt occurs, the handler simply copies its input to its output.

Theorem If int≠True then interrupt int xs = {xs}

Proof

We first simplify the body of the handler:

```
interrupt int xs
= (when int » {[]}) ∪ case xs of [] -> {[]}, x:xs -> (x:) * interrupt int xs'
= {⊥} ∪ case xs of ...
= case xs of [] -> {[]}, x:xs -> (x:) * interrupt int xs'
```

We complete the proof by structural induction on xs.

Case [] interrupt ⊥ [] = {[]}

Case ⊥ interrupt ⊥ ⊥ = {⊥}

Case x:xs

```
interrupt ⊥ (x:xs)
= (x:) * interrupt ⊥ xs
= (x:) * {xs}                                   (by induction hypothesis)
= {x:xs}
```

End of proof

On the other hand, if an interrupt does happen then the handler returns a prefix of its input. We need an auxiliary function to define a prefix:

```
take 0 xs            = []
take (n+1) []        = []
take (n+1) (x:xs) = x : take n xs
```

Theorem interrupt True xs = {take n xs | n ∈ {0,1...}}

Proof

We can simplify the body of the handler to

```
interrupt True xs =
        {[]}
    ∪   case xs of
          []      -> {[]}
          x:xs' -> (x:) * interrupt True xs'
```

Now we use structural induction on xs.

Case []

```
interrupt True []
= {[]} ∪ {[]}
= {[]}
= {take n [] | n ∈ {0,1...}}                    because take n [] is constant
```

Case ⊥

```
interrupt True ⊥
= {[]} ∪ {⊥}
= {take 0 ⊥} ∪ {take n ⊥ | n ∈ {1,2...}}    because take n ⊥ is constant for n>0
```

= {take n ⊥ | n ∈ {0,1...}}
(We'll discuss this last step after the end of the proof).

Case x:xs
interrupt True (x:xs)
= {[]} ∪ (x:) * interrupt True xs
= {[]} ∪ (x:) * {take n xs | n ∈ {0,1...}} by the induction hypothesis
= {[]} ∪ {x:take n xs | n ∈ {0,1...}}
= {take 0 (x:xs)} ∪ {take n (x:xs) | n ∈ {1,2...}}
= {take n xs | n ∈ {0,1...}}
End of proof

Let us return to the last step in the ⊥ case. Although it looks innocuous, we are in fact using the law

f * ({0} ∪ {1,2...}) = f * {0} ∪ f * {1,2...}

with f equal to λn.take n ⊥. Unless f is bottom-preserving this law may relate programs with different behaviours, and in this case f is *not* bottom preserving since it maps zero to []. Indeed, there is an operational difference between the programs on the left and right sides of the theorem: the program interrupt True ⊥ *cannot* ignore the interrupt and wait forever for the other input, while the program {take n xs | n ∈ {0,1...}} may well do so if a value of n other than zero is chosen. Our proof therefore shows partial correctness only.

Finally we prove another theorem about merge: that tagged streams can be recovered from their merge. For simplicity we assume the streams are infinite. We need the following lemma about tagging functions:

Lemma Let a and b be distinct defined tags, and let xs be an approximation to an infinite stream. Then
untag a (tag a xs) = xs
untag a (tag b xs) = ⊥
tag a xs = tag a xs ++ ⊥

Theorem Let a and b be distinct defined tags, and let xs and ys be infinite streams. Then
untag a * merge (tag a xs) (tag b ys) = {xs}

Proof
We first prove the theorem for finite approximations to infinite streams and then take limits. It does not suffice to use structural induction on either xs or ys separately, so we instead use induction on the total (finite) number of defined elements in xs and ys together. There are three cases to consider: xs=⊥, ys=⊥, and xs=x:xs', ys=y:ys'.

Case xs = ⊥
untag a * merge (tag a ⊥) (tag b ys)
= untag a * merge ⊥ (tag b ys)
= untag a * {tag b ys ++ ⊥}
= untag a * {tag b ys}
= {⊥}

Case ys = ⊥
untag a * merge (tag a xs) (tag b ⊥)
= untag a * merge (tag a xs) ⊥
= untag a * {tag a xs ++ ⊥}
= untag a * {tag a xs}
= {xs}

Case xs=x:xs', ys=y:ys'

untag a * merge (tag a (x:xs')) (tag b (y:ys'))
= untag a * (bias (tag a (x:xs')) (tag b (y:ys'))
∪ bias (tag b (y:ys')) (tag a (x:xs')))
= untag a * ((Tag a x:) * merge (tag a xs') (tag b (y:ys'))
∪ (Tag b y:) * merge (tag b ys') (tag a (x:xs')))

Now we want to distribute the untag a* over the union, but since untag a is not bottom-preserving this may change the operational behaviour. We return to this point at the end of the proof.

= untag a * (Tag a x:) * merge (tag a xs') (tag b (y:ys'))
∪ untag a * (Tag b y:) * merge (tag b ys') (tag a (x:xs'))

= (x:) * untag a * merge (tag a xs') (tag b (y:ys'))
∪ untag a * merge (tag b ys') (tag a (x:xs'))

= (x:) * {xs'} ∪ {x:xs'} using the induction hypothesis twice
= {x:xs'} ∪ {x:xs'}
= {x:xs'}
End of proof

This theorem appears to prove a very remarkable result — that merge is fair! It suggests that, even if ys is infinite, merge will not ignore xs infinitely often. This would be surprising if true, but in fact the proof shows only partial correctness, so the operational interpretation of the result is just that the value chosen from the set on the left hand side is an approximation to xs. The implementation of merge may well be unfair.

One reason why the proof shows only partial correctness is the step noted above; another is that the induction proves the result for finite approximations only, and fairness is a property of infinite values. The assumption that a program is fair for infinite inputs if it looks 'fair' for finite ones is wrong.

6. Parallel Algorithms

In this section we develop a few simple parallel tree searching algorithms. All operate on binary labelled trees:

data tree * = Leaf * | Node (tree *) (tree *)

Our algorithms search for a given leaf, the *quarry*; we begin with programs that simply determine whether or not the quarry occurs in the given tree, and go on to algorithms that find the minimum depth at which it does so.

A simple algorithm to test for the presence of the quarry is the following:

present q (Leaf v) = (q=v)
present q (Node l r) = present q l ∨ present q r

We assume that ∨ is defined by

True ∨ a = True
False ∨ a = a

so that it evaluates its arguments from left to right, and does not evaluate the second one at all if the first is True. With these assumptions, our tree searching algorithm works sequentially from left to right, and returns True as soon as the quarry is found. We will make an improved algorithm that searches the entire tree in parallel, returning True as soon as *any* parallel task finds the quarry.

One simple way to do this is to replace *sequential* or by *parallel* or, which satisfies

True |v| a	= True	(even if a=⊥)
a |v| True	= True	(even if a=⊥)
a |v| b	= a ∨ b	otherwise

Parallel or evaluates both arguments in parallel, returning True immediately either one evaluates to True, but otherwise behaving just like sequential or. Parallel or obviously cannot be defined in a sequential functional language, and indeed we cannot define it using sets — but we *can* define a close approximation:

por a b = {a ∨ b} ∪ {b ∨ a}

Theorem por a b = {a |v| b}

Proof

We check that por satisfies the three properties of |v|. First,

```
por True b   = {True ∨ b} ∪ {b ∨ True}
             = {True} ∪ {b ∨ True}
             = {True}                     since b ∨ True = ⊥ or True
```

By symmetry

```
por b True   = {True}
```

Finally, if neither a nor b is True, then a ∨ b = b ∨ a and so

```
por a b = {a ∨ b} ∪ {b ∨ a}
        = {a ∨ b}
```

End of proof

Now we define a version of present that returns a set of booleans, replacing ∨ by por.

```
present' q (Leaf v) = {q=v}
present' q (Node l r) = ⋃ por * present' q l ** present' q r
```

To prove the correctness of this function, we first observe that if a≠⊥ then por a b = {a∨b}, and that for finite trees t, present q t ≠ ⊥.

Theorem If t is a finite tree then
present' q t = {present q t}

Proof

By structural induction on t.

Case Leaf v:

```
present' q (Leaf v)
= {q=v}
= {present q (Leaf v)}
```

Case Node l r:

```
present' q (Node l r)
= ⋃ por * present' q l ** present' q r
= ⋃ por * {present q l} ** {present q r}        by the inductive hypothesis
= ⋃ {por (present q l) (present q r)}
= por (present q l) (present q r)
```

= {present q l ∨ present q r}   since present q l ≠ ⊥
= {present q (Node l r)}

End of proof

For our final example, we develop a parallel algorithm to find the minimum depth at which the quarry occurs. A simple sequential algorithm for this problem is

mindepth d q root = mind 1 q root

mind d q (Leaf v) = d   if q=v
= ∞   if q≠v
mind d q (Node l r) = mind (d+1) q l <u>min</u> mind (d+1) q r

We assume a binary operator <u>min</u>, and, for simplicity, that it has a unit ∞.

It would be straightforward to define a parallel <u>min</u> analogous to parallel or, and construct a parallel algorithm just like our previous example, but we can do better than this. We exploit that fact that, once the quarry has been found at a particular depth, there is no point in searching for occurrences at a greater depth. We aim therefore to make the parallel tasks communicate, so that as soon as any task finds the quarry at depth d, tasks searching at a greater depth give up. The proof of correctness of this algorithm is quite involved, so for brevity we will omit the proofs of the many straightforward lemmata needed.

First let us define a parallel searching algorithm which communicates the depths of occurrences of the quarry as it finds them. We express it as a function whose result is a set of lists of depths at which the quarry has been found:

srch d q (Leaf v) = {[d]}   if q=v
= {[]}   if q≠v
srch d q (Node l r) = ⋃ merge * srch (d+1) q l ** srch (d+1) q r

Let min be the function that finds the minimum of a list; then a straightforward induction on t proves

Lemma   min * srch d q t = {mind d q t}

and so srch can be used to solve our original problem.

Although srch is a parellel algorithm, it always searches the whole tree. We are interested in an algorithm that interrupts searches whose results are no longer relevant. For the time being, let us assume we have a function beaten, such that beaten d evaluates to True once it is known that searches at depth d can be abandoned. We can program an optimised algorithm as follows:

srch' d q t = interrupt (beaten d) (s d q t)

s d q (Leaf v) = {[d]}   if q=v
= {[]}   if q≠v
s d q (Node l r) = ⋃ merge * srch' (d+1) q l ** srch' (d+1) q r

We will need to make an assumption about the function beaten. Let M be mindepth q root; we will assume that d≤M implies beaten d≠True. This will guarantee that no search that might yet find the minimum depth occurrence can be erroneously interrupted.

We obviously cannot prove that srch' produces the same result as srch: it does not. Instead we will prove that srch' finds the same *minimal depth occurrences* as srch — that is,

filter (≤M) * srch' d q t = filter (≤M) * srch d q t

We need the following easy lemma:

Lemma filter p * merge xs ys = merge (filter p xs) (filter p ys)

Theorem filter (≤M) * srch' d q t = filter (≤M) * srch d q t
Proof
We first note that the result is obvious in the case d>M — since srch and srch' both return sets of lists of values greater than or equal to d, each side takes the value {[]}. But for d≤M, by assumption beaten d≠True, and so

interrupt (beaten d) xs = {xs}

which implies

⋃ interrupt (beaten d) * S = S

So in this case the interrupt in the body of srch' can be dropped, giving

srch' d q (Leaf v) = {[d]} if q=v
= {[]} if q≠v
srch' d q (Node l r) = ⋃ merge * srch' (d+1) q l ** srch' (d+1) q r

It is now clear that the theorem holds in the Leaf case, since srch and srch' are identical in this case. In the Node case we have

filter (≤M) * srch' d q (Node l r)
= filter (≤M) * (⋃ merge * srch' (d+1) q l ** srch' (d+1) q r)
= ⋃ merge * (filter (≤M) * srch' (d+1) q l) ** (filter (≤M) * srch' (d+1) q r)

Similarly

filter (≤M) * srch d q (Node l r)
= ⋃ merge * (filter (≤M) * srch (d+1) q l) ** (filter (≤M) * srch (d+1) q r)

We can therefore complete the proof by induction on M-d+1: the induction hypothesis can be applied here twice to allow us to conclude that the left- and right-hand sides of the theorem are equal.

End of proof

Now, the following lemma tells us that filtering out non-minimal elements from a list does not affect its minimum:

Lemma min xs = min (filter (≤min xs) xs)

We can now prove

Theorem min * srch' 1 q root = {M}
Proof
{M}
= {mind 1 q root}
= min * srch 1 q root
= min * (filter (≤M) * srch 1 q root) by the preceding lemma
= min * (filter (≤M) * srch' 1 q root)
= min * srch' 1 q root
End of proof

Our work is almost complete: we just need to find a suitable definition of beaten. Consider the following function:

```
btn d []        = False
btn d (x:xs)    = x<d ∨ btn d xs
```

It it easy to prove:

Lemma btn d * merge xs ys = por (btn d xs) (btn d ys)
btn d * interrupt True xs = {False} ∪ {btn d xs}

Now we can show

Theorem If $d \leq M$ then btn d * srch' 1 q root = {False}
Proof
We prove by induction on t that if $d \leq M \leq$ mind d' q t then

btn d * srch' d' q t = {False}

First note that

btn d * srch' d' q t
= btn d * ($\bigcup$ interrupt (beaten d') * s d' q t)

If beaten d' = True, this is

{False} ∪ btn d * s d' q t

and if beaten d' ≠ True, it is just

btn d * s d' q t

So it suffices to prove that this latter expression equals {False}.

Case Leaf q, q=v:
btn d * s d' q (Leaf v)
= btn d * {[d']}
= {d'<d}
= {False} since $d \leq M \leq$ mind d' q (Leaf v)=d'

Case Leaf q, q≠v:
btn d * s d' q (Leaf v)
= btn d * {[]}
= {False}

Case Node l r:
btn d * s d' q (Node l r)
= btn d * ($\bigcup$ merge * srch' (d+1) q l ** srch' (d+1) q r)
= $\bigcup$ por * (btn d * srch' (d+1) q l) ** (btn d * srch' (d+1) q r)
= $\bigcup$ por * {False} ** {False} by the induction hypothesis
= {False}

End of proof

So if xs∈ srch' 1 q root, then

```
beaten d = btn d xs
```

satisfies the assumptions about beaten that we made above.

Putting all this together, we can define our search algorithm by

```
mindepth' q root = min * occurrences
where   occurrences = ⋃ search * occurrences
        search occs = srch' 1 q root
        where  srch' d q t        = interrupt (beaten d) (s d q t)
               s d q (Leaf v)     = {[d]}                                    if q=v
                                  = {[]}                                     if q≠v
               s d q (Node l r)   = ⋃ merge * srch' (d+1) q l ** srch' (d+1) q r
               beaten d           = btn d occs
```

and now

```
mindepth' q root
= min * occurrences
= min * (⋃ search * occurrences)
= min * (⋃ {srch' 1 q root | occs∈ occurrences})
= ⋃ {min * srch' 1 q root | occs∈ occurrences})
= ⋃ {{mindepth q root}}          since beaten d satisfies the assumed conditions
= {mindepth q root}
```

which shows the correctness of the algorithm.

The algorithm described does not guarantee that the lists of occurrences found are decreasing, although this is likely to be the case. It is possible, say, that the quarry is found at depth 5, but that a process searching at depth 10 finds and reports an occurrence before it can be interrupted. Such 'out of order' occurrences must then be examined by each call of beaten, which is wasteful. We can improve the algorithm slightly by replacing the definition of occurrences by

```
occurrences = discard ∞ * (⋃ search * occurrences)

discard best []         = []
discard best (x:xs)     = x : discard x xs                 if x < best
                        = discard best xs                  if x ≥ best
```

which is justified because

```
min (discard ∞ xs) = min xs
btn d (discard ∞ xs) = btn d xs
```

We end by noting a subtlety in the algorithm and a limitation of our proof technique. In the algorithm we have developed, a search is interrupted only if its best possible result has already been *bettered*. It is tempting to modify this to interrupt searches whose best possible result has already been *matched* — changing the less than in btn to a less than or equal. If we do so, the algorithm remains correct, but cannot be proved correct by these methods!

The reason for this lies in the odd behaviour of non-deterministic recursive definitions. Consider a simple example:

```
nats = {0} ∪ {n+1 | n∈ nats}
```

Operationally, the choice in nats can only select zero. Any other choice would require the choice to have been made before it was made! But the denotation of nats in our semantics is the set of all natural numbers. Essentially, this is because the semantics of recursion is infinite unfolding, which turns the single choice in the equation above into infinitely many choices that can all be made differently.

Surprisingly, the modification we proposed depends for its correctness on the choice of a representative element of occurrences being made only once! To see why, suppose we were to unfold the recursion in its definition just once, giving

$$\text{occurrences} = \bigcup \text{search} * (\bigcup \text{search} * \text{occurrences})$$

which is semantically identical. Then it is possible that the inner call of search might choose a list of occurrences of the quarry including the minimum depth one, which could lead the outer call to interrupt *all* its searches and choose an *empty* list of occurrences as its result — since the minimum has 'already' been found. This clearly gives the wrong answer.

The modified algorithm is more efficient, and one may regard our inability to prove it correct as a serious flaw. On the other hand, unfolding recursions is a useful proof technique, and if we wish to have it available we cannot hope to verify the second algorithm. Moreover, the version we have proved correct does have some compensating advantages — it works even if the implementation makes *different* choices from the *same* set at different times. While this may seem unlikely, some distributed implementations do copy unevaluated expressions, and thereafter potentially evaluate them several times. Such implementations are likely to make different choices from the same set occasionally, unless special and expensive precautions are taken to prevent it.

7. Conclusions

We have presented a referentially transparent extension for functional languages that allows non-deterministic programs to be expressed. Non-deterministic programs can be written without any great contortions, and resemble annotated versions of programs written using impure non-deterministic functions.

We have addressed the issue of reasoning about non-deterministic functional programs, and shown how the familiar techniques of equational reasoning can be used to prove partial correctness in many cases. This represents an advance on previous work, which in many cases went no further than discussing whether or not the proposed languages were referentially transparent. However, we have no formal way of showing total correctness at present.

We have programmed, and proved theorems about, a number of familiar 'systems programming' examples, and developed and proved correct an optimised parallel tree-search algorithm.

Acknowledgements

We are grateful to the Glasgow Functional Programming Group for their stimulating company, and especially to Simon Jones who gave a talk that sparked off this work.

References

[1] John McCarthy, "A basis for a mathematical theory of computation," in *Computer Programming and Formal Systems*, P. Braffort and D. Hirschberg (eds.), North-Holland (1963) 33-70.

[2] Peter Henderson, "Purely functional operating systems," *Functional Programming and its Applications*, J. Darlington, P. Henderson and D. A. Turner (eds.), Cambridge University Press (1982) 177-192.

[3] Simon B. Jones, "A range of operating systems written in a purely functional style," Programming Research Group Technical Monograph PRG-42, Oxford University Computing Laboratory (1984).
[4] S. Abramsky and R. Sykes, "Secd-m: a virtual machine for applicative programming," *Functional Programming Languages and Computer Architecture* , LNCS 201, Springer-Verlag (1985) 81-98.
[5] Daniel Friedman and David Wise, "An indeterminate constructor for applicative programming," *Conference Record of the 7th Symposium on Principals of Programming Languages* (1980).
[6] John O'Donnell, "Implementation techniques for an applicative programming environment," *Proc. Workshop on Complex Functional Systems*, TR-HCI-15, European Computer-Industry Research Centre (1989).
[7] William Stoye, "A new scheme for writing functional operating systems," Technical Report 56, Cambridge University Computer Laboratory (1984).
[8] John Cupitt, "KAOS - An operating system written in a functional language," *Proc. Workshop on Complex Functional Systems*, TR-HCI-15, European Computer-Industry Research Centre (1989).
[9] Paul Hudak and Philip Wadler (eds.), "Report on the Haskell programming language" (draft), SIGPLAN Notices (to appear).
[10] Søren Holmstrøm, "PFL: A functional language for parallel programming and its implementation," Technical Report PMG-R7, Chalmers University (1983).

Evaluation Annotations for Hope$^+$

John M. Kewley* Kevin Glynn†

ICL Mainframe Systems
Wenlock Way
West Gorton
Manchester
M12 5DR

Abstract

To fully exploit the parallelism of the Flagship Machine it is desirable to be able to experiment with a variety of evaluation strategies. The ability to control the behaviour of individual functions via annotations is of enormous help in understanding the behaviour of a parallel system and permits the comparison of "lazy" and "eager" versions of languages as well as providing the oportunity to intermix the two evaluation orders.

The primary functional language used by the Flagship project is Hope$^+$[1]. Hope$^+$ has a mixed evaluation strategy, with strict function application combined with lazy data constructors. This can result in both unnecessary evaluation and loss of parallelism. Annotations enable user-control of the evaluation strategy so that such problems are avoided.

1 Introduction

Throughout this document the word "user" refers to both the programmer and any analysis tools present in the compilation route that might need to generate annotations.

Functions (and constructors) can be annotated when they are defined or when they are called. If a constructor or function is infix then the evaluation annotations are written as if it is prefix.

First we define three normal forms and associated evaluators which form the basis of the rest of this paper. We then go on to describe three different types of annotation that use these normal forms.

2 Normal Forms And Flagship Evaluators

In this section we define three normal forms, weak head-normal-form, spine-normal-form and irreducible-normal-form, and show how Hope$^+$ can support them.

*Email: `jk@uk.co.stc.stl.nw`

†Email: `keving@uk.co.stc.stl.nw`

2.1 Weak Head-Normal-Form (*WH*)

An expression of the form

$$C(e_1, e_2, \ldots, e_n)$$

is in weak head-normal-form if and only if C is a constructor. Any function (or partial application) is also considered to be in weak head-normal-form, a lambda being considered a constructor.

2.2 Spine-Normal-Form (*SN*)

In order to define spine-normal-form, we introduce some terminology from structured types.

There is a general form for structured type definitions, of which all definitions are an instance :

```
data T ==
        C1(T1,1 # T1,2 # ... T1,a1) ++
        C2(T2,1 # T2,2 # ... T2,a2) ++
          ⋮
        Cn(Tn,1 # Tn,2 # ... Tn,an);
```

where the $T_{i,j}$ are types and the C_i are constructors of arity a_i. Consider a constructor C_i. There will be a, possibly empty, subset of recursive arguments where $T_{i,j} = T$.

For example consider the definition of tree :

```
data tree(alpha) ==
        empty ++
        node(tree(alpha) # alpha # tree(alpha));
```

The first and third arguments of node are of type tree. Now we can define spine-normal-form. Consider an expression of type T

$$C_i(e_1, e_2, \ldots, e_n),$$

This expression is in spine-normal-form if and only if it is in weak head-normal-form and all expressions, e_j (where $T_{i,j} = T$, from the definition of T) are in spine-normal-form.

It is possible to automatically generate a function which will evaluate an expression to spine-normal-form, given its type definition. The function has an equation for each constructor and if that constructor has no recursive arguments then it returns the input expression otherwise it returns the expression but with itself called on all the recursive arguments. So a spine-normal-form evaluator for an expression of type tree would be :

```
dec SN_tree : tree(alpha) ⟶ tree(alpha);
```

— SN_tree(empty) <= empty;
— SN_tree(node(a,b,c)) <= node(SN_tree(a),b,SN_tree(c));

2.3 Irreducible-Normal-Form (*IN*)

Consider an expression

$$f(e_1, e_2, \ldots, e_n)$$

This is in irreducible-normal-form if and only if it is in weak head-normal-form and all the arguments e_1 to e_n are in irreducible-normal-form.

It will be possible to provide a built-in function which can take any expression and reduce it to irreducible-normal-form. It will first fire the expression to reduce it to weak head-normal-form. Then it will call itself on any unevaluated pointers in the arguments of the resultant constructor.

2.4 Other Forms

We now have a definition, an evaluator and a syntax (*WH*, *SN*, *IN*) for three normal forms. It is also useful to have a syntax to represent an unevaluated expression, where we don't know its form. We call this unevaluated, *UN*.

We need a syntax for defining a normal form of a tuple of expressions, product normal form, where each component expression is in a particular normal form. We use parentheses and separate the normal form descriptions by commas, i.e.,

$$(nf_1, nf_2, \ldots, nf_n)$$

This signifies that an expression is a tuple of n arguments, the ith expression is in normal form nf_i (for i = 1...n). An evaluator for this is straightforward : it returns a tuple of n arguments where the ith argument has had the evaluator for nf_i applied to it.

We also need to be able to refer to the default normal form that would be used if the annotation was not present. The default normal form is specified using the underscore character, _.

3 Strictness Annotations

We take the view that strictness annotations are making statements about properties of the program and the machine should be free to make use of them as is thought appropriate. This allows us to make use of strictness analysers written for other environments as long as their annotations produced can be mapped onto ours.

If an expression is fully-strict[1], it is not good enough to force the programmer or tool to say an expression is weak head-strict because the machine is usually more efficient at evaluation to weak head-normal-form. Instead the machine should treat the fully-strict annotation as allowing it to perform weak head-strict evaluation.

[1]Can be fully evaluated safely, i.e., is strict to irreducible-normal-form

To specify the strictness properties of a function or constructor we propose that the programmer uses a *ST nf* annotation, where *nf* is some normal form as described above. This means that it is safe to evaluate that argument to the given normal form.

For example consider the following operations on lists :

```
dec head : !# ST WH #!
        list alpha
  →     alpha;

dec length : !# ST SN #!
        list alpha
  →     num;

dec sum : !# ST IN #!
        list num
  →     num;
```

"head" is weak head-strict, "length" is spine-strict and "sum" is fully-strict in their arguments.

It should be noted that if the normal form *UN* is specified then that expression should not be evaluated until its value is demanded. This can be used to override the built-in evaluation orders of Hope$^+$.

So append can be written :

```
dec append : !# ST(WH,UN) #!
        (list alpha # list alpha)
  →     list alpha;
```

The strictness of a function/constructor application is determined by the function definition and any given strictness annotations on the application as described in Section 6.

4 Forcing Parallelism

Making use of strictness information to evaluate arguments to greater than weak head-normal-form would require using auxiliary functions (the evaluators given above) which will usually be less efficient. However in some circumstances it would be beneficial to evaluate the argument in parallel with evaluating the body of a function. e.g., consider the following function on a list :

```
dec f : !# ST SN #!
        list alpha
  →     beta;

--- f(nil) <= ...
```

```
— f(h::t) <=
      let x == loadsawork in
      g(h,x,f(t));
```

and the call :

```
f(complicated_expression)
```

In this example f performs a lot of work in between recursing down the list. The list to which it is being applied requires a lot of work to deliver each cons cell. In this situation it would be desirable to evaluate complicated_expression to spine strict form in parallel with f. In order to do this the user should annotate the argument with a keen annotation, *KN nf*, this tells the compiler to evaluate the argument to the normal form *nf* in parallel with evaluating the function, i.e.,

```
!# KN SN #! f(complicated_expression)
```

The compiler must transform the application into one which calls the appropriate evaluator, from Section 2, on the functions argument, e.g.,

```
dec SN_list : list alpha ⟶ list alpha;
— SN_list(nil) <= nil;
— SN_list(h::t) <= !# ST (_,SN) #! h::SN_list(t);
```

the application now becomes :

```
f(SN_list(complicated_expression))
```

to give the required result.

Of course we must ensure that the compiler doesn't optimise out these quasi-identity functions.

Care must be taken with such "speculative" computation; if the main computation finds it no longer needs this parallel work it must either halt it, which may not be straight-forward, or let it continue, wasting machine resources. This problem is compounded for a non-terminating piece of computation, such as *!# KN SN #!* applied to an infinite list.

5 Dependency Annotations

Dependency annotations on a function or constructor application indicate that the specified argument must be evaluated to some, given, normal form before the body of that function/constructor can be executed. Again the annotations can be placed on either the definition or the application of a function, and the effective annotation will be the highest of the two in the strictness ordering. The Dependency annotation, *DD st* states that its argument must be evaluated to form *st* before the body is evaluated.

Four possible reasons for using dependency annotations are

1. The function pattern matches on that argument.

2. The order of evaluation is being controlled for experimental reasons, such as timing.

3. It is necessary to control the machine's resources for some reason (e.g., minimal store is available).

4. The arguments have side-effects[2] have occurred before that function is executed. which must have completed before that function is executed.

The dependency annotation must always be respected by the compiler. Applications must be planted so that the body is only invoked when the arguments are in the required form. e.g.,

dec f : *!# DD (WH,_,IN) #!*

⋮

— g(x) <= f(e_1,e_2,e_3)

the application of f must be compiled to something like :

##f[^*E_1 E_2 ^*Fully_eval[E_3]]

where E_n is the DACTL[3] version of e_n, n = 1...3. Fully_eval will be a built-in function which will take E_3 and evaluate it to irreducible normal form before returning.

Incidently the data-dependency annotation to simulate Hope$^+$'s "eager" semantics is *!# DD WH #!* for each argument. Likewise that for "lazy" is *!# DD UN #!*.

6 How the compilers can use the Annotations

In this section we describe the actions the Flagship Hope$^+$ compiler could take in order to compile the evaluation annotations into DACTL markings and auxiliary functions. We first describe an ordering relation for the normal forms described in Section 2 such that any expression in a certain normal form must also be in any normal forms below that one in the ordering relation. We then give an algorithm for combining normal form annotations. The result is the least normal form which is greater than or equal to the input normal forms in the ordering relation. Finally we describe how the annotations interact to give the required DACTL program.

The ordering function for normal forms must be such that any expression in normal form *nf* must also be in the normal form of *nf'*, for all $nf' < nf$. To find the position of some normal form, *nf*, in the relation :

1. Convert it to canonical form : If *nf* is a product normal form and all its components are *UN* then replace it with *SN* (note it is also in *WH*). If *nf* is a product normal form and all its components are *IN* then replace it with *IN*.

[2] e.g., I/O in many otherwise pure functional languages.

[3] Declarative Alvey Compiler Target Language[2]

2. The ordering relation is : *UN* < *WH* < *SN* < *product normal form* < *IN*

We can now use this ordering relation to give an algorithm which will combine two normal forms, nf_1 and nf_2, to give a normal form which is the least normal form greater than or equal to nf_1 and nf_2 :

1. Convert nf_1 and nf_2 to canonical form.
2. If $nf_1 = nf_2$ then nf_1.

   Else, if either nf_1 or nf_2 are in {*UN*, *WH*, *SN*, *IN*} then the highest in the ordering relation.

   Else, nf_1 and nf_2 must both be product normal forms of arity n. The result is the canonical form of a product normal form of arity n where the ith component is the result of combining the ith components of nf_1 and nf_2, for i = 1...n.

Some examples of this combining function :
combine(*WH,SN*) = *SN*
combine(*(UN,UN,UN,UN),WH*) = combine(*SN,WH*) = *SN*
combine(*UN,UN*) = *UN*
combine(*(WH,UN),(UN,WH)*) = *(WH,WH)*

It will be necessary to have two forms of the evaluators described in Section 2. One, the dependent evaluator, doesn't return to its parent until the whole of the expression is in the required normal form. The other, the keen evaluator, causes all the evaluations to be done in parallel with the main thread of computation.

When the dependent evaluator produces a piece of active graph it plants it with a notification arc and adds one to the suspended count of the graph's parent. The keen evaluator just produces the active graph. So if tree is defined as :

```
data tree(alpha) ==
        empty ++
        node(tree(alpha) # alpha # node(alpha));
```

The dependent *SN* evaluator can be written as :

```
D_SNtree[ %empty ] => *%empty;
D_SNtree[ %node[ a b c ] ] =>
        ##%node[ ^*D_SNtree[ a ] b ^*D_SNtree[ c ] ];
```

The keen evaluator can be written as :

```
K_SNtree[ %empty ] => *%empty;
K_SNtree[ %node[ a b c ] ] =>
        *%node[ *K_SNtree[ a ] b *K_SNtree[ c ] ];
```

Two versions of the built-in *IN* evaluator will also have to be provided, one dependent and one keen.

We can now describe the DACTL code which will be planted by the Hope$^+$ compiler to take advantage of the annotations. When the compiler plants a function or constructor application it will have three sorts of annotations : *ST*, *KN*, *DD* (not forgetting any default annotations as a result of the language definition). Each of these classes will have two versions of the annotation, the one on the application and the one on the declaration of the function or constructor.

1. Using the algorithm above combine the normal forms for each class on the declaration and application. This gives *ST nfs*, *KN nfk* and *DD nfd*.

2. If *nfd* > *UN* then plant the application packet suspended on the result of the relevant dependent nfd evaluator. If *nfk* > *nfd* then the argument of this evaluator is an active keen *nfk* evaluator on the original argument otherwise it is the original argument.

   Else, if *nfk* > *UN* then plant an active keen evaluator on the argument and make the application packet active.

   Else, if *nfs* > *UN* then plant the argument active and make the application packet active. (Note : This assumes strictness information is only useful to cause us to leave function arguments unevaluated or allow us to plant keen to weak head-normal-form evaluations. If the compiler can make better use of this information then it may do so, as described in Section 2.

The following examples show the DACTL which should be produced with the given annotations and the application f(a) where f may be a function or a constructor. %f is the DACTL symbol which corresponds to f and A is the DACTL equivalent of a.

ST UN, *KN UN*, *DD UN* = *%f[A]
ST IN, *KN SN*, *DD UN* = *%f[#K_SNatype[^*A]]
ST IN, *KN WH*, *DD IN* = #%f[^#D_Fully_eval[^*A]]
ST SN, *KN IN*, *DD WH* = #%f[^*K_Fully_eval[*A]]

7 Summary

This paper has introduced three classes of evaluation annotations : strict, keen and dependent. Each annotation takes a normal form as argument. The normal forms supported are :

UN : unevaluated expression
WH : weak head-normal-form
SN : spine-normal-form
IN : irreducible-normal-form
($nf_1, nf_2, \ldots, nf_n$) : product normal form, the ith component expression is in normal form nf_i.
_ : represents the default normal form

These annotations may appear both on the function declarations and function/constructor applications. We have described how these annotations interact to produce DACTL with the required annotations and auxiliary evaluator functions.

The evaluation annotations proposed here differ from those in [3]. The strictness annotations are generalised, but the equivalent of the CONS_HEAD_STRICT strictness annotation[4] is not obtainable in our framework. This would require an argument to *SN* to say what normal form the non-reflexive arguments of the constructors are in. Specifying this information would cause severe difficulties with any types more complex than trees.

We have introduced a new annotation, keen, which will force the machine to evaluate arguments to desired normal forms in parallel with the main thread of computation.

To control the evaluation order we provide only one annotation, *DD*, which takes a normal form as argument and causes the argument to be evaluated to that normal form before the application is evaluated.

It is felt that the annotations and compiler actions specified here will be sufficient to write efficient parallel programs and experiment with Hope$^+$ on the Flagship Machine.

References

[1] Perry N. Hope$^+$. Imperial College, London. IC/FPR/LANG/2.5.1/7, 1988

[2] Glauert JRW, Kennaway JR, Sleep MR. Specification of Core DACTL1. Declarative Systems Project, University of East Anglia, 1987

[3] While L, Glynn K, Kewley J, Watson P, Hayes S. Annotations for Hope$^+$. Imperial College London. IC/FPR/PROG/1.1.1/5, 1988

[4]CONS_HEAD_STRICT can be used to state that whenever a cons cell is identified, its head should be fired.

Some Ideas On Parallel Functional Programming

Paul Roe

Department of Computing Science,
The University,
17, Lilybank Gardens,
Glasgow. G12 8QQ

email:proe@uk.ac.glasgow.cs

Abstract

This paper argues that parallel functional programs must be efficient in order to achieve speed-up on parallel machines. To this end parallelism expression and parallelism efficiency are discussed. Different classes of parallel algorithms and their expression are considered, along with two particular sources of inefficiency: task size and expression re-evaluation.

1 Introduction

To exploit parallel machines we must write parallel programs; in general we cannot re-use old programs since they are usually inherently sequential and contain no expression of any parallelism in them.

Writing programs is hard; writing parallel programs is even harder. This is because parallelism introduces an extra dimension into programs, which complicates thinking and reasoning about them. Parallelism must be considered throughout program construction. An alternative to this is to constrain languages to only allow expression of parallel algorithms; this has been advocated in [1].

There are two issues involved in the construction of any program:

- correctness - does the program compute the correct values?
- operation - how efficient is the computation?

Why use a parallel functional language then? An advantage of parallel functional programming (pfp) over parallel imperative programming is that for conservative parallelism correctness is independent of evaluation order. Hence for pfp correctness may be addressed independently of parallelism; this is not true for parallel imperative programming. (There are exceptions to this: for example synchronous programming for SIMD machines.)

In the context of pfp several interesting questions arise:

- how can parallelism be expressed?
- how can parallelism be made efficient?
  (speed-up on a parallel machines can only be achieved with efficient parallel programs)
- how do you 'get' a parallel program in the first place?

The following sections express some ideas concerning each of these three questions.

Overall it seems that a shift of emphasis away from conventional functional programming will be necessary in order to write parallel functional programs.

2 Parallelism expression

A program for a parallel machine must contain parallelism. In this section it is argued that the programmer must explicitly express the parallelism in a program and some examples of doing this are shown.

2.1 Is parallelism expression needed?

Do we need to *explicitly* express the parallelism in our programs? Why not have the compiler find the parallelism and annotate the program accordingly? For simple programs this seems plausible. Programs could be strictness analysed and then parallel annotations could be added. However strictness analysis is not enough, particularly to produce efficient parallel programs. Also this process is in some ways redundant. The programmer must know exactly where in their program the parallelism is, in order to be certain of its parallel operation. If they do not know exactly where the parallelism is, how can they be certain of their program's parallel operation?

2.2 What needs to be expressed?

Quinn [2] identifies three categories of parallel algorithms:

- Partitioned. A problem is divided into homogeneous subproblems which are solved in parallel. This is typified by divide and conquer algorithms.
- Pipelined. A problem is divided into different subproblems. These are connected such that the output of one subproblem feeds the input of another. The different phases of a complier are an example of a pipeline.
- Relaxation. Such algorithms are characterised by tasks working with the most recently available data; there is little synchronisation between tasks. These algorithms compute nondeterministically but their results maybe deterministic: for example parallel branch and bound algorithms.

We would like to express all of these in our parallel functional language. (Low level issues such as mapping tasks to processors are not discussed here.)

2.3 Parallelism expression in pfp

2.3.1 Primitive combinators

Many different parallelism annotations for functional languages have been proposed: for example [3], [4], and [5]. There are many advantages if annotations are combinators: ease of handling in a compiler, ability to form abstractions with them and partial evaluation possibilities.

To express algorithms in the first two categories two primitive combinators are sufficient: seq and par.

```
seq: * -> ** -> **

seq x y       = y,        x ~= Bottom
              = Bottom, otherwise

par: * -> ** -> **

par x y       = y
```

seq evaluates its first argument and then returns its second argument. par spawns its first argument as a task and returns its second argument.

In [6] it was recognised that two forms of parallelism annotation are required: one for functions and one for applications. These may both be expressed using par thus:

```
-- functions e.g. f x = exp

f x           = par x exp

-- applications e.g. app = f exp

app           = par e (f e)
                where e = exp
```

At first it seems curious that sequential combinators must be used in a parallel system. There are two reasons for needing seq:

Firstly for strict operators whose order of argument evaluation must be changed. For example (assuming left to right argument evaluation):

```
... par x (if cond then seq y (x+y) else seq z (x-z)) ...
```

The un-spawned variables in the arithmetic expressions must be evaluated or spawned before trying to evaluate the spawned variables. Otherwise evaluation might block on the spawned variables and parallelism will be lost. If the evaluation order of strict operators is specified then some, but not all, seq combinators may be removed.

Secondly, seq may be used for evaluating a data structure 'further' than WHNF. Typically this occurs in conjunction with pars so that tasks may evaluate data structures more than normally would occur. par could be used in place of seq here, but this is not always desirable for efficiency reasons.

Quinn's categories of parallel algorithms are now used to examine the expressiveness of these three combinators.

2.3.2 Partitioned algorithms

An example of a partitioned parallel algorithm is quicksort:

```
psort []        = []
psort (e:xs)    = (par qlo o par qhi) (qlo ++ [e] ++ qhi)
                  where
                  qlo = psort [x| x<-xs; x<e]
                  qhi = psort [x| x<-xs; x>=e]
```

(o is function composition.) This illustrates that partitioned algorithms can be easily expressed using the parallel combinators; albeit with a slight loss of clarity.

2.3.3 Pipelined algorithms

pfp can achieve pipelining with *any* data structure, unlike strict languages with streams.

A pipelining example is the list of all the prime numbers less than one thousand, using the sieve of Eratosthenes:

```
primes1           = (pseqspine o sieve1) [2..1000]

sieve1 []         = []
sieve1 (p:nos)    = par (seqspine filtnos) (p:sieve1 filtnos)
                        where
                        filtnos     = filter pred nos
                        pred n      = n mod p ~= 0

pseqspine l       = par (seqspine l) l

seqspine []       = []
seqspine (x:xs)   = seqspine xs
```

pseqspine has been found to be another useful combinator; it is used to force the spine of a list to WHNF. Above it is first used to eagerly force the evaluation of the whole list of primes (in the **primes** equation). This allows elements of **primes** to be consumed as they are generated. Secondly **seqspine** is used in **sieve** to evaluate the list of filtered numbers (**filtnos**). Each filtering removes multiples of the newly discovered prime from the remaining numbers. The meaning of this algorithm is reasonably clear but its operation is less clear.

Usually we want to restrain pipelined parallelism by buffering. This entails only 'evaluating ahead' a fixed portion of a list from the last element demanded. This is what John Hughes' buffered lists do [7]. A modified version of these is shown below:

```
pipe k l              = par (seqspine (take k l)) (next l (drop k l))

next xs []            = xs
next (x:xs) (y:ys)    = par y (x:next xs ys)
```

A more interesting primes problem is to produce the first one hundred primes numbers (with no knowledge of how big the one hundredth prime number is). There are no bounds on this search, hence a parallel solution to this problem must use some speculative evaluation - this has also been discovered in [4]. One possible way of implementing this is to use Hughes buffered lists to control speculative parallelism. Each filtering operation speculatively evaluates a few list elements in advance.

2.3.4 Relaxation algorithms

Relaxation algorithms are a problem for functional languages since they compute non-deterministically; however, their results may still be deterministic. They are also an important class of parallel algorithms. There have been several proposals for handling non-determinism and relaxation algorithms.

Burton has a particularly interesting idea for handling parallel branch and bound style algorithms [8]. This uses the notion of improving values; which are based on the observation that the global bound in branch and bound algorithms monotonically improves. A problem with his idea is that it requires speculative evaluation which is notoriously hard to manage [9]. Also there is a constraint on the search order to ensure determinism; this can lead to extra computation.

Two interesting papers in this proceedings discuss other techniques for dealing with relaxation algorithms. LeMetayer and Banatre have a non-deterministic re-writing model of computation, which allows them to derive and prove correct, relaxation algorithms [10]. Hughes and O'Donnell introduce a special form of sets into a functional language which allows relaxation algorithms to be expressed [11] .

A very limited form of non-deterministic computation is possible with bags (multisets) which maybe incorporated into a functional language [12].

2.4 Abstraction

Parallelism annotations complicate programs as can be seen in the earlier examples. Thus it is desirable to factor out parallelism from programs. It is also useful to express common patterns of parallel computation. This has been extensively advocated by Cole [1], where common patterns of computation are expressed as higher order combinators.

For example a combinator to evaluate the elements of a list in parallel:

```
parlist: (* -> **) -> [*] -> [*]

parlist f l          = par (p l) l
                       where
                       p []         = []
                       p (x:xs)     = par (f x) (p xs)
```

Thus `parall` which evaluates a list of objects to WHNF is `parlist id`. In many instances a Hughes style buffered version of `parlist` might be desirable.

There is scope for partial evaluation with parallelism abstractions: for example often the result of `parlist` is unused and hence p may be used instead.

`parlist` has been found useful in a real programs. For example to evaluate all of the second elements in a list of triples:

```
... parlist triple2 list_of_triples ...

triple2 (a,b,c) = b
```

parlist is only one example of a combinator for the parallel evaluation of a data structure. Such combinators may be written for any data structure; indeed they may even be derivable.

A combinator used extensively in the ZAPP project [13] is one for expressing divide and conquer algorithms. Reformulated this is:

```
dc div leaf solve x
        = solve x,                    leaf x
        = seq procs (combine procs),  otherwise
          where
          procs              = parmap id (dc div leaf solve) subprobs
          (combine, subprobs) = div x

parmap forcefun f l
        = par (parlist forcefun mapfl) mapfl
          where
          mapfl  = map f l
```

Notice how this uses another parallel combinator parmap. Thus psort maybe re-expressed:

```
psort          = dc qdiv (==[]) id
                 where
                 qdiv (e:xs)   = (comb, [lo,hi])
                                 where
                                 comb [l,h] = l ++ [e] ++ h
                                 lo         = [x| x<-xs; x<e]
                                 hi         = [x| x<-xs; x>=e]
```

It may be possible to encapsulate some non-deterministic computations, like parallel branch and bound algorithms, into combinators which take functional arguments. Such combinators may not be functional in their operation but under certain constraints they may yield determinate results. They could be reasoned about via laws and axioms describing them.

2.5 Evaluation Transformers

Burn's evaluation transformers [14] aid parallelism in two ways. Firstly, they allow list processing functions to be context sensitive; according to the context in which a function is used, different amounts of evaluation maybe done on its list arguments. Evaluation transformers are incorporated into the run-time system; this is especially useful since often the context in which a function occurs is unknown at compile time. If the context of a function is known at compile time a particular version of a function could be used. Secondly, evaluation transformers can prevent re-spawning of tasks; this is discussed further in the next section.

3 Removing parallelism

Once parallelism has been expressed in a program there is often too much of it! The number of tasks in a functional machine is usually controlled dynamically by its run-time system [15]. However, even under a conservative parallelism scheme some tasks are redundant:

- some may be too small
- some may be re-evaluating expressions

An efficient implementation of a parallel functional program must not create such redundant tasks.

3.1 Task size

Reviewing parallel quicksort it becomes obvious that some very small tasks will be created. In fact for a balanced tree of quicksort tasks, half of the tasks will evaluate `sort []`. This true for any divide and conquer algorithm with simple leaf tasks. The solution is to dynamically control the size of tasks.

3.1.1 Exact task size control

The task sizes in quicksort maybe controlled by sorting sequentially once the list to be sorted becomes sufficiently short. To do this generally for divide and conquer algorithms requires knowledge of the particular algorithm.

It is noticeable how the once classic parallel functional program now becomes less classic!

```
psort []        = []
psort (l=e:xs)  = sort l,                                  short l
                = (par qlo o par qhi) (qlo ++ [e] ++ qhi), otherwise
                  where
                  qlo = psort [x| x<-xs; x<e]
                  qhi = psort [x| x<-xs; x>=e]

-- sequential quicksort
sort []         = []
sort (x:xs)     = sort [e | e<-xs; e<x]
                  ++ [x] ++
                  sort [e | e<-xs; e>=x]

short l         = f l 1
                  where
                  f [] n     = true
                  f (x:xs) n = (n <= short_len) & f xs (n+1)
```

(It is important that & is left sequential.) The exact value of `short_len` would have to be determined by approximations and experimentation.

A subtle point arises: it is important for `short` to only examine a prefix of its argument, so that pipelining is maximised. Pipelining exists between successive recursive calls of quicksort; the recursive calls may commence before their list arguments are fully evaluated. If `short` was defined thus:

```
short l        = #l <= short_len
```

then the entire traversal of `l` would have to occur before either recursive call could commence. (This would not happen if numbers were lazy.) This shows how subtle parallelism can be and is part of the justification for the section on manipulation of parallel programs. The computation of `short` may be fused with the splitting of the list `l`, so that `l` is only traversed once; however care must be taken with the calculation of `short`.

If `psort` were to be a real program at least two other important optimisations would be made. The sequential sort `sort` should be an efficient sort for short lists: such as insertion sort. Rather than using lists, functional style difference lists could be used ensure the result lists are only traversed once when appended together. This may seem like a lot of work to go to for parallelising quicksort; but if we want it to be a 'real' parallel program for sorting thousands of elements, it must be efficient.

The divide and conquer combinator maybe extended to control task sizes thus:

```
par_dc p div leaf solve x
       = solve x,                     leaf x
       = seq_dc div leaf solve x,     p x             -- run sequential
       = seq procs (combine procs),   otherwise       -- run parallel
         where
         (combine, subprobs) = div x
         procs        = parmap id (par_dc p div leaf solve) subprobs

-- the sequential divide and conquer combinator
seq_dc div leaf solve x
       = solve x,                                         leaf x
       = combine ((map seq_dc div leaf solve) subprobs), otherwise
         where
         (combine, subprobs) = div x
```

Quicksort maybe formulated using `par_dc` similarly to previously, using `short` for the control predicate.

It should be clear that program control of task sizes is another reason why automatic parallelism expression seems unlikely. Deriving the code to determine when a task should be run sequentially is very hard. If the programmer is to produce this task size control code, then they need to all ready have the code for expressing the basic parallelism.

A possible way to automatically derive the task size control code is by using equation solving. Expressions must require at least a certain number of reductions to be candidate tasks. For example: quicksort maybe run backwards from its base equations until the appropriate number of reductions have been done; this could be done in a similar way to the absolute set abstraction extension to Hope [16]. The result of doing this would be a set of list permutations, each permutation requiring the specified number of reductions to reduce. The list lengths could then be calculated and hence a predicate formed for determining when to run sequentially. There are (at least !) a couple of problems with this. Firstly running arithmetic operations backwards is hard and running higher order functions backwards is impossible. Secondly to determine the predicate some notion of computational progress must be identified, to test on the set of results. In quicksort's case this is the decreasing length of the list; for divide and conquer factorial it is the convergence of the pair of numbers. In general this is not computable. This goes to show how difficult this would be to do automatically.

3.1.2 Delayed spawning

An alternative to explicitly programming task size control, is to use a heuristic. This heuristic is based on an idea by John Hughes and David Lester. The idea has an analogy with the Hewit and Liebermann style garbage collector. It is this: the longer a task has run the longer it is likely to run. Task size control corresponds to: if a task is likely to run a long time, it should spawn child tasks; if not, it should not spawn any tasks. I call this delayed spawning; rather than immediately spawning a task, the parent task delays its spawning - in case the parent task terminates. For example quicksort (again!):

```
dpsort l              = dps l []

dps [] l              = []

dps (e:xs) l          = seq sl (sl++[e]++sh),              #l<k
                        where
                        sl = dps [x| x<-xs; x<e] (l++[sh])
                        sh = dps [x| x<-xs; x>=e] []

                      = (par p o seq sl) (sl++[e]++sh),    #l=k
                        where
                        (p:ps) = l
                        sl     = dps [x| x<-xs; x<e] (ps++[sh])
                        sh     = dps [x| x<-xs; x>=e] []
```

The second argument to dpsort is a list of delayed spawns (a FIFO queue). The position of a delayed spawn in a task's queue is proportional to the amount of computation that the task has done since the delayed spawn. Thus once a delayed spawn reaches the head of the queue, the spawning task has done a sufficient amount of computation to warrant really spawning that task. On encountering a leaf, the delayed spawns in a tasks queue will not be spawned but will be evaluated sequentially (each delayed spawn may produce tasks though). Notice that once a task terminates the delayed spawns are visited sequentially in LIFO order. This is done purely for simplicity. It could be changed to FIFO, which would probably give better performance, by altering the base case equations.

The divide and conquer combinator maybe expressed to do delayed spawning thus:

```
dsdc      = dsdc' []

dsdc' l div leaf solve x
        = solve x, leaf x
        = seq this (combine (this:delayed)),                          #l<k
          where
          (combine, sp:sps) = div x
          delayed           = map (dsdc' [] div leaf solve) sps
          this              = dsdc' (l++[delayed]) div leaf solve sp

        = (par (parall p) o seq this) (combine (this:delayed)), #l=k
          where
          (p:ps)            = l
          (combine, sp:sps) = div x
          delayed           = map (dsdc' [] div leaf solve) sps
          this              = dsdc' (ps++[delayed]) div leaf solve sp

-- k probably needs to be a parameter to dsdc

parmap forcefun f l     = par (parlist forcefun mapfl) mapfl
                          where
                          mapfl  = map f l
```

It should be possible to mathematically analyse delayed spawning to determine its performance; alternatively it could be simulated.

3.2 Prevention of re-spawning

Lazy evaluation prevents re-evaluation of shared expressions. However, lazy evaluation does not, in general, prevent re-spawning (the spawning of all ready evaluated expressions). Although semantically harmless re-spawning will create redundant tasks, which are detrimental to a program's efficiency. Burn has proposed evaluation transformers as a solution to this problem. Unfortunately his transformers are not extensible. A solution is proposed: DIY evaluators.

3.2.1 Burn's evaluation transformers

Burn has proposed evaluation transformers to help alleviate the re-spawning problem with lists and to allow the context sensitive evaluation of lists and list processing functions. Here only the evaluator part of evaluation transformers is discussed.

Evaluators evaluate lists to varying degrees. They are ordered according to the amount of evaluation they do; which may be described using combinators thus:

```
E0 l       = Bottom                          -- no evaluation
E1 l       = l                               -- WHNF
E2 l       = pseqspine l                     -- structure only
E3 l       = parlist id l                    -- structure and elements

-- E0 < E1 < E2 < E3
```

To prevent re-evaluation list values are tagged with the strongest evaluator with which they have been evaluated. Any attempt to evaluate a list with an evaluator weaker than or equal to a previous evaluator does nothing. A stronger evaluator causes the list to be evaluated with that evaluator and its tag to be updated to reflect this.

Evaluators only capture four patterns of evaluation; there are an infinite number of patterns of evaluation possible. For example, a function may evaluate every other element of a list; this pattern of evaluation can only be approximated by `E2`. Head strictness is not captured by these evaluators either. Using combinators head strictness maybe expressed:

```
... f l ...            -- if f is head strict in l, this becomes:

... f (hd_strict l) ...

hd_strict []       = []
hd_strict (x:xs)   = par x (x:(hd_strict xs))
```

Unfortunately this creates a new list which is rather wasteful.

Head strictness is important for pipelining and other patterns of computation. For example with Burn's evaluators: if `l` has been evaluated with `E3` then `(l ++ m)` is evaluated with `E3`; `l` will again be evaluated with `E3`.

3.2.2 DIY evaluators

Burn's evaluators are restricted to lists because they are wired into the abstract machine. There are two reasons for this: efficiency and the low level nature of *recording* the amount by which a list has been evaluated. Essentially the latter point requires assignment. However, the parallel evaluation of any data structure may be done functionally, as has been shown. In other words the the only non-functional part of evaluators is the reading and updating of tags: indicating the strength of evaluator that has been applied to the value. If the reading and writing of tags was supported by the functional language the rest of the evaluators could be implemented in the functional language and all data structures and patterns of evaluation would be supported.

Supposing a side-effecting 'function' `assert_eval` is available. Burn's evaluators maybe implemented thus:

```
-- evaluation degree, 0 = unevaluated, 1 = WHNF, etc.

evaldeg    == Int

nullinfo   ::= Null

-- Evaluators, applied to lists
-- these correspond to Burn's evaluators

e0 l          = Bottom
e1 l          = l
```

```
e2 []          = []
e2 (l=x:xs)    = par (e2' l) l
e3 []          = []
e3 (l=x:xs)    = par (e3' l) l

e2' []         = []
e2' (l=x:xs)   = assert_eval (<=) e2' 2 xs
e3' []         = []
e3' (l=x:xs)   = par x (assert_eval (<=) e3' 3 xs)

-- assert_eval is a system supplied primitive
-- it asserts the evaluation (using eval) of
-- expression (exp) to degree (deg)

assert_eval:: (evaldeg -> evaldeg -> bool) ->
                      (* -> *) -> evaldeg -> * -> nullinfo

assert_eval less eval deg exp= seq (eval exp) Null, {exp.tag $less deg
                                                      exp.tag := deg}
                             = Null,                 otherwise
```

assert_eval asserts that an expression is evaluated to a given degree. It inspects an expression's tag and either evaluates the expression using the evaluation function and then returns **Null** or it immediately returns **Null**. Thus, modulo termination the result of **assert_eval** is always **Null**. Providing it is safe to evaluate the expression (**exp**) using the evaluation function (**eval**), **assert_eval** is safe. Note, the comparison and tag setting operations must be implemented as a single atomic operation on a parallel machine. Also, the **.tag** operation in **assert_eval** does not evaluate the expression it is applied to.

Whenever a closure is created its tag field is set to zero; evaluation of a closure, with a zero tag, to WHNF causes its tag to be set to one. These operation are done automatically by the system. Any further evaluation patterns must be implemented explicitly, using **assert_eval** (as has been done for Burn's evaluators). However, it is not the intention that the programmer should be directly programming all of these functions for an application. The functions could be provided as library routines or the functions could be derived by the compiler. Derivation could be fully automatic in conjunction with strictness analysis or the user could somehow specify the evaluators, and where they should be placed in the program. Once again a certain amount of partial evaluation is possible.

Most importantly there is a need to experiment with evaluators; this is part of the motivation for being able to express them in a functional language. It is even possible that if the danger of re-spawning only occurs in a simple way, then evaluators could be implemented with no additional language facilities. For example:

```
... (if .. then prod l else 0) + (if .. then sum l else 1)

prod  = fold 1 (*)
sum   = fold 0 (+)
```

Assuming left to right evaluation we could rewrite this as:

```
... res1 + res2
        where
        (res1, eval)     = if ..
                           then seq (parall l) (prod l, true)
                           else (0, false).

        res2             = if .. then (seq evaluate (sum l)) else 1
        evaluate         = if eval then Null else parall l
```

This is a rather contrived example; however if a program contains a few basic data structures from which parallelism was sought this approach might be feasible. The approach is to pass state between functions; this state describes the degree of evaluation of the major data structures in the program.

4 Parallel program manipulation

One of the reasons for wanting to use functional languages is that programs may be, mathematically, manipulated and derived. This usually entails applying meaning preserving transformations to a program to improve its operational behaviour.

The meaning of a parallel functional program is the same as the meaning of the sequential program formed by removing all of the parallel constructs from it. For example all expressions of the form `par e1 e2` mean the same as `e2`, providing: $(\texttt{e1} \neq \perp) \vee (\texttt{e1} = \perp \Rightarrow \texttt{e2} = \perp)$. However often extra computation to aid parallelism efficiency is also contained in a program. Therefore it is desirable to 'factor out' parallel code from a program: to ease understanding of the program's meaning. This could sometimes be done automatically by a dependency analysis. Alternatively an abstract version of the program containing no parallel constructs could be kept as part of the program's documentation.

The operational behaviour of a parallel functional program is very hard to understand, especially at the par combinator level. This is another good reason for using high level parallel combinators to express parallel computations. General theorems concerning the operational behaviour of such combinators can then be developed. These would then enable high level reasoning about parallel computations.

There follows a simple example of a parallel programs manipulation. It shows how some redundant parallelism may be removed from quicksort:

```
psort []       = []
psort (e:r)    = (par qlo o par qhi) (qlo ++ [e] ++ qhi)
                 where
                 qlo = psort [v| v <- r; v < e]
                 qhi = psort [v| v <- r; v >= e]
```

The laws below preserve operation and meaning. Idempotency reduces the number of tasks which are created.

```
par x o (par y o par z)    = (par x o par y) o par z    -- associative
par x o par y              = par y o par x              -- commutative
par x o par x              = par x                      -- idempotent
```

Also:

```
par l (l ++ m)          = l ++ m                        -- (*)
```

We may simplify the second psort equation thus:

```
  (par qlo o par qhi) (qlo ++ [e] ++ qhi)
= (par qhi o par qlo) (qlo ++ [e] ++ qhi)    -- by par commutativity
=  par qhi (par qlo (qlo ++ [e] ++ qhi))     -- composition def.
=  par qhi (qlo ++ [e] ++ qhi)               -- by (*) and ++ assoc.
```

psort maybe re-written:

```
psort []       = []
psort (e:r)    = par qhi (qlo ++ [e] ++ qhi)
                 where
                 qlo = psort [v| v <- r; v < e]
                 qhi = psort [v| v <- r; v >= e]
```

The above version of psort generates fewer tasks than the previous one, yet it has the same cost.

5 Conclusions

To achieve speed-up a parallel program must make efficient use of a parallel machine. It seems that to do this parallel programs must explicitly control some aspects of parallelism, notably task size and respawning prevention. However, producing efficient parallel programs is not easy and they certainly are not as clear as their sequential counterparts. Abstraction can hinder parallel efficiency, yet seems the only way of producing and manipulating parallel programs. The embarrassing lack of empirical studies with real sized programs and data prevents us from identifying the real efficiency issues in pfp.

Relaxation algorithms are problematical due to their non-deterministic nature. However several recent proposals have gone some way towards alleviating this problem.

Crucially, there is a great need for a framework within which to design parallel functional programs. We can only be certain of getting parallelism through parallel program design, *not accident!*

6 Acknowledgements

I would like to thank my supervisor, Professor Simon Peyton-Jones, for his help, encouragement and enthusiasm.

7 References

[1] Murray Cole, "Capturing the Structure of Efficient Parallel Computations as Higher Order Functions," Draft report, Dept. Computer Science, University of Glasgow, 1989.

[2] Michael J Quinn, in *Designing Efficient Algorithms for Parallel Computers*, McGraw-Hill International, 1987.

[3] F Warren Burton, "Annotations to Control Parallelism and Reduction Order in the Distributed Evaluation of Functional Languages," *ACM Trans. Programming Languages and Systems* 6 (April 1984), 159–174.

[4] Paul Hudak & Lauren Smith, "Para-Functional Programming: A Paradigm for Programming Multiprocessor Systems," Principles of Programming Languages, Florida, 1986.

[5] Paul Kelly, "Declarative Annotations for Distributed Functional Programming (Technical Summary)," Internal Report. Imperial College, London. SW7 2BZ, January 1988.

[6] Chris Hankin, Geoffrey Burn & Simon Peyton-Jones, "A Safe Approach To Parallel Combinator Reduction," *Theoretical Computer Science* 56 (1988), 17–36.

[7] John Hughes, "The Design and Implementation of Programming Languages," PhD thesis, PRG-40, Programming Research Group, Oxford University Computing Laboratory, 1983.

[8] F Warren Burton, "Indeterminate Behaviour with Determinate Semantics," CSS/LCCR TR 89-03, Centre for Systems Science, Simon Fraser University, BC, Canada, 1989.

[9] Paul Hudak, "Distributed Task and Memory Management," Proc. ACM Symposium on Principles of Distributed Programming 1983, August 1983.

[10] Jean-Pierre Banatre & Daniel LeMetayer, "Chemical Reaction as a Computational Model," in *Proceeding of Glasgow Workshop on Functional Programming, Fraserburgh, Scotland*, Springer Verlag, August 1989.

[11] John Hughes & John O'Donnel, "Expressing and Reasoning about Non-Deterministic Functional Programs," in *Proceeding of Glasgow Workshop on Functional Programming, Fraserburgh, Scotland*, Springer Verlag, August 1989.

[12] Paul Roe, "Bags: A functional data structure," Unpublished report, Dept. Computer Science, University College London, March 1989.

[13] D McBurney & M R Sleep, "Transputer-Based Experiments with the Zapp Architecture," Internal Report SYS-C86-10. UEA. Norwich, November 1986.

[14] Geoffrey Burn, "Evaluation Transformers - A Model for the Parallel Evaluation of Functional Languages (Extended Abstract)," in *Proc IFIP conference on Functional Programming Languages and Computer Architecture, Portland*, G Kahn, ed., Springer Verlag LNCS 274, Sept 1987, 446–470.

[15] Simon L Peyton-Jones & et al., "GRIP - a high performance architecture for parallel graph reduction," 3rd International Conference on Functional Languages Computer Architecture, 1987.

[16] J Darlington, A J Field & H Pull, "The Unification of Functional and Logic Languages," Imperial College Dept. of Computing Report, February 1985.

Parsing Using Combinators

Graham Hutton
Department of Computing Science
University of Glasgow
Scotland, UK

Abstract

In combinator parsing, the text of parsers resembles BNF notation. We present the basic method, and show how it may be extended to more practical parsers. We address the special problems of layout, and parsers with separate lexical and syntactic phases. In particular, an elegant new way of handling the offside rule is given. Many examples and comments are included.

1 Introduction

Broadly speaking, a parser may be defined as a program which analyses text to determine its logical structure. For example, the parsing phase in a compiler takes a program text as input, and produces a parse tree which expounds the structure of the program. Many programs can be improved by having their input parsed. The form of input which is acceptable is usually defined by a context-free grammar, using BNF notation. Parsers themselves may be built by hand, but are most often generated automatically using tools like Lex and Yacc from Unix [1].

Although there are many methods of parsing, one in particular has gained widespread acceptance for use in lazy functional languages. In *combinator parsing*, parsers are modelled directly as functions. Working in a higher-order language, it is quite natural to consider higher-order functions which combine or transform parsers. What may be surprising however, is that this approach leads to a parsing notation in which the text of parsers closely resembles BNF notation itself. In this manner, parsers are quick to build, and simple to understand and modify.

Combinator parsing is considerably more powerful than the commonly used methods, being able to handle ambiguous grammars, and providing full backtracking if it is needed. In fact, we can do more than just parsing. Arbitrary semantic actions may be added to parsers, allowing their results to be manipulated in any way we please. For example, we could imagine generating some form of abstract machine code as programs are parsed.

Although the underlying principles are widely known, dating back to [2], little has been written on combinator parsing itself. In this paper we present the basic method, and show how it may be extended to more practical parsers. The first section collects all the basic material, and includes many examples and comments. In the remainder of the paper, we address the special problems of layout, and parsers with separate lexical and syntactic phases. In particular, we present an elegant new way of handling the offside rule. After working through this paper, the reader should have sufficient knowledge to build a parser for a language like Miranda[1].

The techniques we present may be used in any lazy functional language with a higher-order/polymorphic style type system. However, all our programming examples are given in Miranda. The particular features and library functions of Miranda are explained as they are used. A library of parsing functions taken from this paper may be obtained by e-mail from the author, at ⟨graham@cs.glasgow.ac.uk⟩.

2 Parsing Using Combinators

A parser may be viewed as a function from a string of symbols to a result value. To be able to combine parsers in sequence, we also need to know how much of the input was used in producing the result. Thus, combinator parsers return a pair, comprising a result value and the unused suffix of the input string. Sometimes a parser may not be able to produce a result. For example, it may be looking for a letter, but find a digit. A parser produces a result only if there is successful recognition of the input string as a sentence of the grammar. In such cases the parser is said to have *succeeded*, otherwise it has *failed.*

To help us see how parsers fit together, it is useful to consider their types. From what has been seen already, the basic type is $[symbol] \rightarrow (value, [symbol])$. However, we must also take into account that a parser may fail. Rather than defining a new algebraic type for the success or failure of a parser, we choose to have parsers return a list of pairs as their result, with the empty list `[]` denoting failure, and a singleton list indicating success. Although this representation may seem a little strange at the moment, all will become clear later on.

Since we want to specify the type of any parser, regardless of the kind of symbols and values it works with, these types are included as extra parameters. In Miranda, such free type variables are indicated by stars.

```
parser * ** == [*] -> [(**,[*])]
```

For example, a parser for arithmetic expressions may have type (`parser char expr`), indicating that it takes a string of characters, and produces an expression tree. Notice that `parser` is not a new type as such, but an abbreviation (or synonym), whose sole purpose is to make types involving parsers easier to understand.

2.1 Primitive parsers

The primitive parsers are the building blocks of combinator parsing. The first of these corresponds to the ε symbol in BNF notation, denoting the empty string. The `succeed` parser always succeeds, without actually consuming any of the input string. Since the outcome does not depend upon the input, its result value must be completely pre-determined, so is included as an extra parameter to the parser.

```
succeed :: ** -> parser * **

succeed v inp = [(v,inp)]
```

[1]Miranda is a trademark of Research Software Limited.

This definition relies on partial application to work properly. The order of the arguments means that if succeed is only applied to its first argument, the result is a parser (i.e. a function) which always succeeds with this value. For example, (succeed 5) is a parser which always returns the value 5. Furthermore, even though succeed plainly has two arguments, its type would suggest that it has only one. There is no magic, the second argument has simply moved inside the type of the result, as would be clear upon expansion according to the parser synonym.

The second primitive parser is in some sense the opposite of the first, in that it always fails, regardless of the input.

```
fail :: parser * **

fail inp = []
```

The final primitive parser we define allows us to recognise individual symbols in the input string. Rather than enumerating the acceptable symbols, it is usually more convenient to provide the set implicitly, via a predicate which determines if an arbitrary symbol is a member. Not surprisingly, successful parses return the consumed symbol as their result value.

```
satisfy  :: (* -> bool) -> parser * *

satisfy p []     = fail []
satisfy p (x:xs) = succeed x xs  , p x
                 = fail xs       , otherwise
```

This parser may be regarded as *the* primitive or canonical parser, through which all others factor. In simpler words, all other parsers will ultimately be defined in terms of `satisfy`. Notice how `succeed` and `fail` are used in this example. Although they are not strictly necessary, their presence makes the parser easier to read. It is also important to note that `satisfy` trivially fails if there is no input.

Using `satisfy` we can define a parser for single symbols.

```
literal  :: * -> parser * *

literal x = satisfy (=x)
```

For example, applying the parser (`literal '3'`) to the input string "345" gives the result `[('3',"45")]`. In the definition of `literal`, `(=x)` is an example of an *operator section*, in this case denoting the function which compares its argument with `x`. Sectioning is a useful syntactic convention which enables us to partially apply infix operators. It is explained in more detail in the Miranda manual.

2.2 Combinators

Now that we have the basic building blocks, we consider how they should be put together to form useful parsers. In BNF notation, larger grammars are built piecewise from smaller ones using | to denote alternation, and juxtaposition to indicate sequencing. So that combinator parsers resemble BNF notation, we define two higher-order functions which correspond directly to these operators. Since higher-order functions like these combine parsers to form other parsers, they are often referred to as *combinators*[2] for short. We will use this term from now on.

The **alt** combinator corresponds to alternation in BNF. The parser (p1 $alt p2) recognises anything that either p1 or p2 would. Normally we would interpret *either* in a sequential (or exclusive) manner, returning the result of the first parser to succeed, and failure if neither does. This approach is taken in [3]. In combinator parsing however, we use inclusive *either*. That is, it is acceptable for both parsers to succeed, in which case we return both results. In other words, instead of restricting parsers to a single result, we allow an arbitrary number. This explains why we decided to have a parser return a list of results.

Under this interpretation, alt is implemented simply by appending (denoted by ++ in Miranda) the result of applying both parsers to the input string. In-keeping with the BNF notation, we use the Miranda $ notation and define this combinator as an infix operator. Just as for sectioning, the infix notation is merely a syntactic convenience. In particular, (x $f y) is equivalent to (f x y) in all contexts.

```
alt :: parser * ** -> parser * ** -> parser * **

(p1 $alt p2) inp = p1 inp ++ p2 inp
```

The reader may wish to verify that failure is the identity element for alternation. That is, (fail $alt p) = (p $alt fail) = p. In practical terms this means that alt has the expected behaviour if only one of the parsers succeeds.

There are two interesting implications in allowing parsers to produce more than one result. Perhaps the most obvious is that we can handle ambiguous grammars, with all possible parses being produced if so required. The feature has proved particularly useful in natural language processing [4]. More often that not however, we are only interested in the single longest parse of an input string (i.e. that which consumes the most symbols). For this reason, it is normal in combinator parsing to arrange for the parses to be returned in descending order of length. Although this may sound quite difficult, in practice it usually happens quite naturally without much special planning.

The second advantage is equally interesting. Under lazy evaluation, returning a list of results automatically gives us an equivalent to backtracking [2]. That is, even though a particular parse may fail, we do not necessarily need to start again. Some of the work in getting to failure may be re-used in trying the next parse. We need only go back to last alt where we haven't yet tried the second branch. In practical terms, this behaviour arises from the depth first traversal inherent in all top-down methods such as combinator parsing.

The then combinator corresponds to sequencing in BNF. The parser (p1 $then p2) recognises anything that both p1 and p2 would if placed in succession. Since the first parser may succeed with many results, each with an input stream suffix, the second parser must be applied to each of these in turn. In this manner, two results are produced for each successful parse, one from each of the parsers. They are combined (by pairing) to form a single result for each parse.

---

[2]Our informal use of this term is consistent with the standard λ-calculus meaning.

```
then :: parser * ** -> parser * *** -> parser * (**,***)

(p1 $then p2) inp = [((v1,v2),out2) | (v1,out1) <- p1 inp;
                                      (v2,out2) <- p2 out1]
```

This combinator is an excellent example of *list comprehension* notation, analogous to set comprehension in mathematics (e.g. $\{x^2 \mid x \in \mathrm{N} \wedge x < 10\}$ defines the first ten squares), except that lists replace sets, and elements are drawn in a determined order. Combinator parsing is not dependant upon list comprehension notation, but much of the elegance will be lost if it is not available.

Since alternation and sequencing are the primitive combining forms, it is important to consider how they interact with themselves, and each other. Firstly, it is easy to verify that alternation is associative. That is, (p $alt q) $alt r = p $alt (q $alt r). In practice this means we do not not need to worry about bracketing repeated alternation correctly. On the other hand, sequencing is not associative, due to the tupling of results from the component parsers. In Miranda, all infix operators defined using the $ notation are assumed to associate to the right. Thus, when we write (p $then q $then r) it is interpreted as p $then (q $then r).

When they appear together in the same expression, sequencing is normally assumed to have higher precedence than alternation. Unfortunately, in Miranda all user defined infix operators are deemed to have the same precedence. This means that extra bracketing will sometimes be needed to disambiguate expressions involving both alt and then. Even if such declarations are permitted in the language, it is usual to take a new line for each alternative in a lengthy expression.

2.3 Manipulating values

Part of the result from a combinator parser is a value. When two parsers are combined in sequence we get a pair of values. So that we are not limited to binary parse trees, we need some way of manipulating the default result values from parsers. This is the purpose of the using combinator. The parser (p $using f) has the same behaviour as p, except that the function f is applied to each of its result values.

```
using :: parser * ** -> (** -> ***) -> parser * ***

(p $using f) inp = [(f v,out) | (v,out) <- p inp]
```

Although this combinator has no counterpart in pure BNF notation, it does have much in common with the $\{\cdots\}$ operator in YACC notation [1]. In fact, the using combinator does not restrict use to building parse trees. Arbitrary semantic actions can be used, allowing values to be manipulated in any way we please. For example, in section 2.4 we show how to make an evaluator for arithmetic expressions from a parser for expressions, simply by changing the actions. In the remainder of this section we define some useful parsers and combinators.

In BNF notation, repetition occurs often enough to merit its own abbreviation. When zero or more repetitions of a phrase p are admissible, we simply write p^*. Formally, this notation is defined by the equation $p^* = p\,p^* \mid \varepsilon$. The many combinator corresponds directly to this operator, and is defined in much the same way.

```
many :: parser * ** -> parser * [**]

many p = ((p $then many p) $using cons) $alt (succeed [])
```

The action cons is the uncurried version of the list constructor (:), defined by **cons (x,xs)** = **x:xs**. Since combinator parsers return all possible parses according to a grammar, if failure occurs on the nth application of (many p), n results will be returned, one for each of the 0 to $n-1$ successful applications. Following convention, the results are returned in descending order of length. For example, applying the parser many (literal 'a') to the input "aaab" gives the output

```
[("aaa","b"),("aa","ab"),("a","aab"),("","aaab")]
```

Not surprisingly, the next parser corresponds to the other common iterative form, denoted by + in BNF notation. The parser (some p) has the same behaviour as (many p), except that it recognises one or more repetitions instead of zero or more. Note that (some p) may fail, whereas (many p) always succeeds.

```
some :: parser * ** -> parser * [**]

some p = (p $then many p) $using cons
```

Using this combinator we can build parsers for numbers and words. A number is simply a sequence of digits, and a word a sequence of letters.

```
number :: parser char [char]
word   :: parser char [char]

number = some (satisfy digit)
         where digit x = '0' <= x <= '9'

word = some (satisfy letter)
       where letter x = ('a' <= x <= 'z') \/ ('A' <= x <= 'Z')
```

The next combinator is a generalisation of the literal primitive in section 2.1, allowing us to recognise specific strings, instead of single symbols. The parser (string xs) recognises the complete sequence of symbols xs. In particular, the parser fails if only a prefix of the list is available.

```
string :: [*] -> parser * [*]

string []     = succeed []
string (x:xs) = (literal x $then string xs) $using cons
```

As well as being used the define other parsers, the using combinator is often used to prune unwanted components from a parse tree. Recall that two parsers composed in sequence produce a pair of results. Sometimes we are only interested in one of these components. For example, it is common to throw away reserved words such as "begin" and "where" during parsing. In such cases, two special versions of the sequential combinator are useful, which throw away either the left or right result values, as indicated by the position of the extra letter in their names.

```
xthen :: parser * ** -> parser * *** -> parser * ***
thenx :: parser * ** -> parser * *** -> parser * **

p1 $xthen p2 = (p1 $then p2) $using snd
p1 $thenx p2 = (p1 $then p2) $using fst
```

The actions **fst** and **snd** are the standard projection functions on pairs, defined by `fst (x,y) = x` and `snd (x,y) = y`. The two abbreviations **xthen** and **thenx** throw away selected components from a compound result. Sometimes we are not interested in the result values at all, only that the parser actually succeeds. For example, if we find a reserved word during lexical analysis, it may be convenient to return some short representation rather than the string itself. The **return** combinator is useful in such cases. The parser (`p $return v`) has the same behaviour as p, except that it returns the value v if successful.

```
return :: parser * ** -> *** -> parser * ***

p $return v = p $using (const v)
              where const x y = x
```

2.4 Example

To conclude our introduction to combinator parsing, we will work through the derivation of a simple parser. Our example is adapted from [5]. Suppose we have some programs which manipulate arithmetic expressions, defined in Miranda as follows:

```
expr ::= Num num | expr $Add expr | expr $Sub expr
                 | expr $Mul expr | expr $Div expr
```

While this representation is reasonable from a programming point of view, even small expressions are difficult to understand in this form. The obvious solution is to define a *pretty-printer* which converts expressions to a more readable form for display. For example, it is easy to define a function **showexpr** such that

```
showexpr ((Num 3) $Mul ((Num 6) $Add (Num 1))) = "3*(6+1)"
```

If expressions are to be viewed in short notation, it would seem equally reasonable that they should also be supplied in this form. While pretty-printing is notionally quite simple, the inverse operation of parsing is usually thought of as being much more involved. As we shall see however, a combinator parser for arithmetic expressions is no more complicated than a simple pretty-printer.

Before we start thinking about parsing, we must define a BNF grammar for expressions. To begin with, the algebraic type **expr** may itself be cast in BNF notation. All we need do is include parenthesised expressions as an extra case.

$$\begin{aligned} expn \;\; ::= \;\; & expn + expn \mid expn - expn \mid expn * expn \mid expn/expn \mid \\ & digit^{+} \mid (expn) \end{aligned}$$

Although this grammar could be used as the basis of the parser, in practice it is useful to impose a little more structure. To simplify expressions, multiplication and division are normally assumed to have higher precedence than addition and subtraction. For example, $3 + 5 * 2$ is interpreted as $3 + (5 * 2)$. In grammatical terms, this means introducing a new non-terminal for each level of precedence.

$$\begin{array}{lll} expn & ::= & term + term \mid term - term \mid term \\ term & ::= & factor * factor \mid factor / factor \mid factor \\ factor & ::= & digit^{+} \mid (expn) \end{array}$$

While addition and multiplication are clearly associative, division and subtraction are sometimes assumed to associate to the left. The natural way to express this convention in the grammar is with left recursive production rules (such as $expn ::= expn - term$). Unfortunately, in top-down methods such as combinator parsing, it is well known that left recursion leads to non-termination of the parser [1]. In section 4.1 we show how to transform a grammar to eliminate left recursion. For the present however, we will leave the grammar alone, and use parenthesis to disambiguate expressions involving repeated operations.

Now that we have a grammar for expressions, it is a simple step to build a combinator parser. The BNF description is simply re-written in combinator notation, and augmented with semantic actions to manipulate the result values. In fact, it is convenient to remove all non-numeric symbols within the parser itself, using the special sequential forms **xthen** and **thenx**.

```
expn   = ((term $then literal '+' $xthen term) $using plus)  $alt
         ((term $then literal '-' $xthen term) $using minus) $alt
         term

term   = ((factor $then literal '*' $xthen factor) $using times)  $alt
         ((factor $then literal '/' $xthen factor) $using divide) $alt
         factor

factor = (number $using value) $alt
         (literal '(' $xthen expn $thenx literal ')')
```

All that remains is to define the semantic actions which build the parse tree. Since the parser has already stripped the non-numeric components, the arithmetic actions simply take a pair as their argument. In the following, **numval** is the standard Miranda function which converts a numeric string to the corresponding number.

```
value  xs    = Num (numval xs)
plus   (x,y) = x $Add y
minus  (x,y) = x $Sub y
times  (x,y) = x $Mul y
divide (x,y) = x $Div y
```

This completes the parser. For example, **expn "2+(4-1)*3"** gives

```
[( Add (Num 2) (Mul (Sub (Num 4) (Num 1)) (Num 3)) , ""          ),
 ( Add (Num 2) (Sub (Num 4) (Num 1))               , "*3"        ),
 ( Num 2                                           , "+(4-1)*3" )]
```

More than one result is produced because the parser is not forced to consume all the input. As we would expect however, the longest parse is returned first. This behaviour results from the careful ordering of the alternatives in the parser.

Although a parse tree is the natural output from a parser, there is no such restriction in combinator parsing. For example, simply by replacing the standard semantic actions with the following set, we have an evaluator for arithmetic expressions:

```
value  xs    = numval xs
plus   (x,y) = x + y
minus  (x,y) = x - y
times  (x,y) = x * y
divide (x,y) = x div y
```

Under this interpretation,

```
expn "2+(4-1)*3" = [(11,""), (5,"*3"), (2,"+(4-1)*3")]
```

We could imagine many other useful interpretations. For example, in [5] actions are given which transform arithmetic expressions to postfix (reverse-polish) notation, for evaluation on a stack-based machine.

3 Layout Conventions

Unlike the arithmetic expression example of the previous section, most programming languages have a fairly large and involved syntax. To make life a little more pleasant for the programmer, there is usually a set of layout rules which specify how *white-space* (spaces, tabs and newlines) may be used to improve readability. In this section we consider two common layout conventions, and show how they may be interpreted in combinator parsing.

3.1 Free-format input

At the syntactic level, programs comprise a sequence of tokens. Many languages adopt *free-format input*, imposing few restrictions on the use of white-space. It is not permitted inside tokens, but may be freely inserted between them, although it is only strictly necessary when two tokens would otherwise form a single larger token. White-space is normally stripped out along with comments during a separate lexical phase, in which the program to be parsed it divided into its component tokens. This approach is developed in section 4.3.

For many simple parsers however, a separate lexer is not actually needed (as is the case for the arithmetic expression parser of the previous section), but we still might want to use white-space to make things easier to read. The `nibble` combinator provides a simple solution. The parser (`nibble p`) has the same behaviour as p, except that it eats up any white-space in the input string before or afterwards.

```
nibble :: parser char * -> parser char *

nibble p = white $xthen p $thenx white
           where white = many (any literal " \t\n")
```

The **any** combinator used in this definition can often be used to simplify parsers involving repeated use of `literal` or `string`. It is defined as follows.

```
any :: (* -> parser ** ***) -> [*] -> parser ** ***

any p = foldr (alt.p) fail
```

The library function `foldr` captures a common pattern of recursion over lists. It takes a list, a binary operator $\otimes$ and a value α, and replaces each constructor (`:`) in the list by $\otimes$, and the empty list `[]` at the end by α. Often α is chosen to be the right identity for $\otimes$. For example, `foldr (+) 0 [1,2,3]` = `1+(2+(3+0))` = 6. The infix dot (`.`) denotes function composition, defined by `(f.g) x = f (g x)`. It should be clear that **any** has the following behaviour:

```
any p [x1,x2,...,xn] = (p x1) $alt (p x2) $alt ... $alt (p xn)
```

If we now take a simple parser, and place a single `nibble` wherever we would like to allow white-space, we have an analogue to free-format input, without altering the structure of the parser at all. In practice, `nibble` is most often used with reserved words and symbols, so that following abbreviation is useful.

```
symbol :: [char] -> parser char [char]

symbol = nibble.string
```

For example, applying the parser (`symbol "hi"`) to the string `"   hi    there"`, gives `("hi","there")` as the first result. There are two points worth noting about free-format input. First of all, it is good practice to indent programs to reveal their structure. Although free-format input allows us to do this, it does not prevent us doing it wrongly. Secondly, extra symbols are usually needed in programs to guide the parser in determining their structure. The classic examples are "begin", "end" and semi-colon from Pascal. Experience has shown that such symbols can be a nuisance to the accomplished programmer, and a source of confusion to beginners.

3.2 The offside rule

Another approach to layout, as adopted by many functional languages, is to constrain the generality of free-format input *just* enough so that extra symbols to guide the parser are no longer needed. This is normally done by imposing a weak indentation strategy, and having the parser make intelligent use of layout to determine the structure of programs. For example, consider the following program:

```
a = b+c
    where
        b = 10
        c = 15-5
d = a*2
```

It is plainly obvious from the indention that a and d are intended to be top-level definitions, with b and c local to a. The constraint which guarantees that we can always determine the structure of programs in this manner is usually given by Landin's *offside rule* [6], defined as follows:

> If a syntactic class obeys the offside rule, every token of an object of the class must lie either directly below, or to the right of its first token. A token which breaks this rule is said to be *offside* with respect to the object, and terminates its parse.

In Miranda, the offside rule is applied to the body of definitions, so that extra symbols are not needed to separate definitions, or indicate block structuring. The offside does not force a specific way of indenting programs, so we are still free to use our own personal styles. It is worthwhile noting that there are other interpretations of the offside rule. For example, the languages Occam [7] and Haskell [8] both take a slightly different approach.

3.3 The offside combinator

Inkeeping with the spirit of combinator parsing, we would like to define a new combinator which encapsulates the offside rule, and hides all the messy details. Given a parser, the `offside` combinator should transform it to reflect the additional constraints imposed by the offside rule. That is, the parser (`offside p`) should only succeed if p consumes precisely those symbols which are onside with respect to the first symbol in the input string.

Although the `offside` combinator is easy to imagine in principle, it is perhaps not so obvious how it should be implemented. The problem is that parsers only see a suffix of the entire input string, having no knowledge of what has already been consumed by previous parsers. To implement the offside rule we need to know the context of the input, to decide which of the following symbols are onside. Our solution to this problem is the key to the `offside` combinator. Rather than actually passing an extra argument to parsers, we will simply assume that each symbol in the input string has been paired with its row/column position at some stage prior to parsing. To simplify to types of parsers involving the offside rule, we use the abbreviation (pos *) for a symbol of type * paired with its position:

```
pos * == (*,(num,num))
```

Since the input string is now assumed to contain the position of each symbol, the primitive parsing function `satisfy` must be changed slightly. As row/column numbers are present only to guide the parser, it is reasonable to have `satisfy` throw this information away from consumed symbols. In this manner, the annotations in the input string are of no concern when building parsers, being entirely hidden within the parsing notation itself. The other parsers defined in terms of `satisfy` need a minor change to their types, but otherwise remain the same.

```
satisfy :: (* -> bool) -> parser (pos *) *

satisfy p []      = fail []
```

```
satisfy p (x:xs) = succeed a xs , p a
                 = fail xs      , otherwise
                   where (a,(r,c)) = x
```

We are now able to define the offside combinator. The only complication is that white-space must be treated as a special case, since it is never offside. In fact, the white-space in the input is somewhat redundant, since having symbols paired with their position may be viewed as an extreme form of layout. It is therefore both convenient and reasonable to assume that white-space has been stripped from the input prior to parsing. Most parsers will have a separate lexical phase anyway, in which both comments and white-space are removed, so this is no great problem.

```
offside :: parser (pos *) ** -> parser (pos *) **

offside p inp = [(v,inpOFF) | (v,[]) <- p inpON]
                where
                   inpON  = takewhile (onside (hd inp)) inp
                   inpOFF = drop (#inpON) inp
                   onside (a,(r,c)) (b,(r',c')) = r'>=r & c'>=c
```

This combinator is quite unlike any of the others, so worth some explanation. The offside rule tells us that for `offside p` to succeed, it must consume precisely the onside symbols in the input string, so it is sufficient to only apply p to the longest onside prefix (`inpON`). The pattern `(v,[])` in the list comprehension filters out parses which do not consume all such symbols. For successful parses, we simply return the result value v, and remaining portion of the input string (`inpOFF`).

It is interesting to note that `offside` does not depend upon the structure of the symbols in the input, only that they are paired with their position. For example, it is irrelevant whether symbols are single characters or complete tokens.

For completeness, the four standard Miranda functions used in the definition of `offside` are as follows. The function (`takewhile p`) returns the longest prefix of a list, in which property p holds of each element. The function `hd` returns the first element of a list, defined by `hd (x:xs) = x`. The function (`drop n`) removes the first `n` elements from the front of a list. Finally, (`#`) denotes the length of a list.

4 Building Complete Parsers

Many simple grammars can be parsed in a single phase, but most programming languages need two distinct parsing phases - lexical and syntactic analysis. Since lexical analysis is nothing more than a simple form of parsing, it is not surprising that lexers themselves may be built as combinator parsers. In this section we work through an extended example, showing that by careful choice of notation, two-phase parsers are no more complicated to build than one-phase parsers.

4.1 Example language

We develop a parser for a small programming language, similar in form to Miranda. The following program shows all the syntactic features we are considering.

```
f x y = add a b
        where
           a = 25
           b = sub x y
answer = mult (f 3 7) 5"
```

If a program is well-formed, the parser should produce a parse tree, according to the following type. Even though local definitions are attached to definitions in our language, it is normal to have them at the expression level in the parse tree.

```
script ::= Script [def]
def    ::= Def var [var] expn
expn   ::= Var var | Num num | expn $Apply expn | expn $Where [def]

var == [char]
```

The context-free aspects of the syntax may be characterised by the following BNF grammar. Ambiguity is resolved by the offside rule, which is applied to the body of definitions, so that special symbols to separate definitions and delimit scope are not needed. The non-terminals *var* and *num* denote variables and numbers respectively, defined in the usual way.

$$\begin{array}{lll} prog & ::= & defn^* \\ defn & ::= & var^+ \text{ “=” } body \\ body & ::= & expr \text{ [“where” } defn^+\text{]} \\ expr & ::= & expr\ prim \mid prim \\ prim & ::= & var \mid num \mid \text{“(”} expr \text{“)”} \end{array}$$

As we would expect, the left associativity of function application is expressed with a left recursive production rule (i.e. $expr ::= expr\ prim \mid prim$). As already mentioned in section 2.4, left recursion and top-down parsing methods do not mix. If we are to build a combinator parser for this grammar, we must first eliminate the left recursion. Consider the canonical left recursive production rule:

$$\alpha \ ::= \ \alpha\beta \mid \gamma$$

What language is generated by α? By unwinding the recursion a few times, it is clear that a single γ, followed by any number of βs is acceptable. Thus, we would assert that $\alpha ::= \gamma\beta^*$ is equivalent to $\alpha ::= \alpha\beta \mid \gamma$. The proof is simple:

$$\begin{array}{llll} \gamma\beta^* & = & \gamma\,(\beta^*\beta \mid \varepsilon) & \text{[properties of } *\text{]} \\ & = & \gamma\beta^*\beta \mid \gamma\varepsilon & \text{[distributivity]} \\ & = & (\gamma\beta^*)\,\beta \mid \gamma & \text{[properties of sequencing]} \\ & = & \alpha\beta \mid \gamma & \text{[definition of } \alpha\text{]} \end{array}$$

In the context of our example language, this law means that we may safely replace the *expr* production rule with $expr ::= prim\ prim^*$, which simplifies to $expr ::= prim^+$. In other words, by applying a simple transformation to the grammar, we have eliminated left recursion in favour of iteration.

4.2 Layout analysis

Recall that the **offside** combinator assumes that white-space in the input is replaced by row/column annotations. To this end, each character is paired with its position during a simple layout phase prior to lexical analysis. Both white-space and comments will be stripped by the lexer itself, as is normal practice.

```
prelex = pl (0,0)
         where
            pl (r,c) []     = []
            pl (r,c) (x:xs) = (x,(r,c)) : pl (r,tab c) xs , x = '\t'
                            = (x,(r,c)) : pl  (r+1,0)  xs , x = '\n'
                            = (x,(r,c)) : pl  (r,c+1)  xs , otherwise
            tab c = ((c div 8)+1)*8
```

4.3 Lexical analysis

The primary function of lexical analysis is to divide the input string into its component tokens. Each token is made up of two separate parts – a *tag* and an *attribute value*. Two strings only have the same tag if they may be treated as equal during syntax analysis. When more than one string matches a token, sufficient information to tell them apart is returned as the attribute value of the token. In practice, it is convenient to return the string itself. Thus,

```
token == (tag,[char])
```

If a token is uniquely determined by its tag, the empty-string should be used as its attribute value. For example, we could imagine `(Ident,"add")` and `(Lpar,"")` as tokens corresponding to the strings `"add"` and `"("`. While it is fine to refer to identifiers and numbers by their tag during syntax analysis, having to invent and use tags for reserved words and symbols is somewhat tedious. For this reason, rather than having separate tags for each reserved word and symbol, we will bundle them all together under the single tag `Symbol`, with the string itself as the attribute value:

```
tag ::= Ident | Number | Symbol | Junk
```

For example, the tokens `(Number,"123")` and `(Symbol,"where")` correspond to the strings `"123"` and `"where"`. The special tag `Junk` is used for things like white-space and comments, which should be stripped before syntax analysis.

Like all other parsers, lexers will ultimately be defined in terms of the primitive parsing function `satisfy`. Earlier we decided that this was a good place to throw away the position of all consumed symbols. Now we actually need some of this information, since tokens must be paired with their position. Rather than changing `satisfy` again, and having row/column numbers visible everywhere, we define a new combinator which encapsulates the process of pairing a token with its position. Since it will be applied once to each parser corresponding to a complete token, it is a convenient place in which to tag each token as well.

The `tok` combinator takes a parser and a tag, and modifies the parser so that strings are built into tokens, and paired with the position of their first character. In other words, the `tok` combinator changes a parser with result type `[char]` into a parser with result type `(pos token)`.

```
tok :: parser (pos char) [char] -> tag -> parser (pos char) (pos token)

(p $tok t) inp = [(((t,xs),(r,c)),out) | (xs,out) <- p inp]
                 where (x,(r,c)) = hd inp
```

For example, (`string "where" $tok Symbol`) is a parser which produces the result `((Symbol,"where"),(r,c))` if successful, where `(r,c)` is the position of the `"w"` character in the input string. Notice that `tok` may fail with parsers which admit the empty string, in trying to select the position of the first character when none of the input string is left. It is reasonable to ignore this problem however, since tokens are always at least one character in length, to guarantee termination of the lexer.

We now turn our attention to lexical analysis itself. Thinking for a moment about what the lexer actually does, it should be clear that the general structure will be as follows, where each `p`*i* is a parser, and `t`*i* a tag:

```
many ((p1 $tok t1) $alt (p2 $tok t2) $alt ... $alt (pn $tok tn))
```

This structure will remain the same for all lexers. All that will change is the parsers and tags. It is therefore convenient to wrap the general structure up inside a definition which takes care of all the messy details. Given a list of parsers and tags `[(p1,t2),(p2,t2),...]`, the `lex` combinator builds a lexical analyser.

```
lex :: [(parser (pos char) [char],tag)] -> parser (pos char) [pos token]

lex = many.(foldr op fail)
      where (p,t) $op xs = (p $tok t) $alt xs
```

The standard functions `(.)` and `foldr` were explained in section 3.1. Using the `tok` abbreviation, we may define the lexer for our language as follows:

```
lexer :: parser (pos char) [pos token]

lexer = lex [( some (any literal " \t\n") , Junk   ),
             ( string "where"             , Symbol ),
             ( word                       , Ident  ),
             ( number                     , Number ),
             ( any string ["(",")","="]   , Symbol )]
```

One of the secondary functions of the lexer is to resolve lexical conflicts. There are basically two kinds. First of all, classes may overlap. For example, reserved words are usually also acceptable as identifiers. Secondly, some strings may be interpreted as different numbers of tokens. For example, `">="` could be seen either as a single token representing the operator (≥), or as two entirely separate tokens.

In our lexer, there is only one such conflict – the reserved word `"where"`. We arrange for the correct interpretation by ordering the tokens according to their relative priorities (e.g. reserved words appear before identifiers). Apart from the necessary ordering, in a large lexer it is a good idea to order tokens by probability of occurrence. This simple step can considerably improve performance.

4.4 Scanning

Since there is no natural identity element for the list constructor (:) used by `many` to build up the list of tokens, white-space and comments are not removed by the lexer itself, but tagged as junk to be removed afterwards. The `strip` function takes the output from the lexer, and removes all tokens with `Junk` as their tag:

```
strip :: [pos token] -> [pos token]

strip = filter ((~=Junk).fst.fst)
```

The standard function (`filter p`) retains only those elements of a list which satisfy the predicate `p`, defined by `filter p xs = [x | x <- xs ; p x]`. For example, `filter (>5) [1,6,2,7]` has value `[6,7]`.

4.5 Syntax analysis

Lexical analysis has made the initial jump from characters to tokens. Syntax analysis completes the parsing process, by combining tokens to form a parse tree. For things like identifiers and numbers, their precise value is not important during syntax analysis, only that they are in fact identifiers and numbers. Thus, we can imagine an analogue to the `literal` primitive, which matches any token of a given class, regardless of its attribute value. In fact, once we have parsed a token, its tag becomes somewhat redundant, in much the same way as its position becomes redundant after being consumed by the `satisfy` primitive. To this end, the parser (`kind t`) only recognises tokens of class `t`, returning their attribute value (i.e. spelling) if successful.

```
kind :: tag -> parser (pos token) [char]

kind t = (satisfy ((=t).fst)) $using snd
```

For example, (`kind Ident`) matches any identifier, returning its spelling if successful. Because reserved words and symbols are bundled under the single tag `Symbol`, the `kind` function is not much use in these cases. We need a special function which matches on the spelling of symbols. Thus, the parser (`lit xs`) only admits the token `(Symbol,xs)`. Again the tag is redundant after parsing.

```
lit :: [char] -> parser (pos token) [char]

lit xs = literal (Symbol,xs) $using snd
```

For example, (`lit "("`) only matches a left parenthesis. We may now build the syntax analyser itself. Recall the BNF description of our example language.

prog	::=	*defn**
defn	::=	*var*$^+$ "=" *body*
body	::=	*expr* ["`where`" *defn*$^+$]
expr	::=	*prim*$^+$
prim	::=	*var* | *num* | "("*expr*")"

As for the expression parser in section 2.4, we simply cast this description in combinator notation, and include semantic actions to build the parse tree. However we must take into account the offside rule, which is used to disambiguate the grammar. All we need do is apply the `offside` combinator to the body of definitions.

```
prog = many defn $using Script
defn = (some (kind Ident) $then lit "=" $xthen offside body) $using defnFN
body = (expr $then ((lit "where" $xthen some defn) $opt [])) $using bodyFN
expr = some prim $using (foldl1 Apply)
prim = (kind Ident  $using Var)   $alt
       (kind Number $using numFN) $alt
       (lit "(" $xthen expr $thenx lit ")")
```

The `opt` abbreviation used in this parser corresponds to the [· · ·] notation in BNF, denoting an optional phrase. It is defined by `p $opt v = p $alt (succeed v)`. To complete the parser, we must define the remaining semantic actions. But first, the somewhat strange action (`foldl1 Apply`) merits some explanation.

Recall that the original grammar in section 4.1 used left recursion to express the left associativity of application. By transforming the grammar slightly, the recursion was replaced by iteration. In combinator parsing, iteration corresponds to `many` and `some`. These operators produce a list as their result. What we really want in this case is a left recursive application spine. That is, if the result were the list `[x1,x2,x3,x4]`, it should be transformed to (((`x1 @ x2`) `@ x3`) `@ x4`), where `@` denotes the application constructor `Apply`. To do this, we use a directed reduction as for the `any` combinator in section 3.1, except that this time the operator should be bracketed to the left instead of the right. That is, `foldl` should be used instead of `foldr`. In fact we use `foldl1`, which is precisely the same, except that it only works with non-empty lists, and hence we don't need to supply a base case.

Of the three remaining semantic actions, the first two are quite straightforward, simply converting the default result values to the internal form. The final action takes into account that local declarations are found at the expression level in the parse tree, while they are attached to definitions in the grammar.

```
defnFN (f:xs,e) = Def f xs e
numFN  xs       = Num (numval xs)

bodyFN (e,[])   = e
bodyFN (e,d:ds) = e $Where (d:ds)
```

4.6 The complete parser

The complete parser is obtained by composing the four phases. For simplicity, we ignore the possibility of errors, assuming that both lexical and syntactic analysis are always successful. Since only the first result value from each parser is required, the function (`fst.hd`) is used to select this component.

```
parse :: [char] -> prg

parse = fst.hd.prog.strip.fst.hd.lexer.prelex
```

There are two points to be noted from this example. Firstly, through careful choice of notation, two-phase parsers are no more complicated to build than one-phase parsers. Secondly, the `offside` combinator succinctly implements the assumption that the offside rule is used to disambiguate the grammar.

5 Summary

We started with a tutorial on the basic aspects of combinator parsing, going on to develop the notation further, so that parsers for real programming languages could be built, with separate lexical and syntactic phases. Special mention was given to layout conventions, and in particular the offside rule. We demonstrated that a parser for a Miranda style language could be built quickly and simply.

Many interesting and important aspects of combinator parsing have been omitted. In particular, it is well known that combinator parsers may have unexpected space and time behaviour, and are often not as lazy as we would expect. Simple solutions to these problems are discussed in both [2] and [5].

Acknowledgements

Thanks are due to John Launchbury, David Murphy, Duncan Sinclair and Mary Sheeran for their comments on various drafts of this paper. John in particular has contributed a great deal. His comments, and interest in combinator parsing, radically changed both the form and content of the paper.

References

[1] Alfred Aho, Ravi Sethi and Jeffrey Ullman. *Compilers - Principles, Techniques and Tools.* Addison-Wesley, 1986.

[2] Philip Wadler. *How to Replace Failure by a List of Successes.* FPCA 85, LNCS 201, 1985.

[3] John Fairbairn. *Making Form Follow Function.* Glasgow University, 1986.

[4] Richard Frost and John Launchbury. *Constructing Natural Language Interpreters in Lazy Functional Languages.* Glasgow University, 1988.

[5] John Launchbury. *Parsing in a Functional Language using Higher Order Combinators.* Glasgow University, 1988. (Unpublished)

[6] Peter Landin. *The Next 700 Programming Languages.* CACM Vol. 9, March 1966.

[7] Geraint Jones. *Programming in occam.* Prentice-Hall International, 1987.

[8] Paul Hudak and Philip Wadler (editors). *Report on the Programming Language Haskell.* Glasgow University and Yale University. 1989. (Draft)

Gerald: An Exceptional Lazy Functional Programming Language

A.C. Reeves, D.A. Harrison, A.F. Sinclair, P. Williamson
Department of Computing Science,
University of Stirling,
Stirling FK9 4LA

Abstract

The availability of an exception handling mechanism can, with judicious use, greatly aid the clarity of code, allowing the programmer to separate the code to handle unusual situations from the code for the normal case. We describe an exception handling mechanism for a lazy functional language. The system proposed allows expressions which might raise an exception to be evaluated lazily, preserves referential transparency and has no dependence on reduction sequence. Exceptions are parameterised and are statically bound to recovery code. There are two strategies for recovery: `resume` which replaces the expression signaling an exception with the recovery code; and `terminate` which replaces the expression signaling the exception at the nearest *firewall* with the recovery code. *Firewalls* are used to bound `terminate` handlers, this allows the preservation of lazy evaluation where exceptions may be raised. A system of priorities is introduced on exceptions, which allow the programmer to indicate which exception is more serious, should a conflict occur. We discuss the approach proposed with reference to present systems.

1 Introduction

Frequently a program to solve an apparently trivial problem can become extremely complex when the programmer wishes to write *robust* software to deal with unusual or exceptional situations. These exceptional situations may be system generated like division by zero, or programmer defined if the programmer wishes to treat a particular case in an unusual way. We contend that the availability of an exception handling construct can greatly reduce the complexity of code. The code is simplified because the programmer is able to separate the text which recovers from an unusual situation from the code to deal with the normal situation.

Cristian [1, 2], Goodenough [3], and Yemini and Berry [4, 5] have done fundamental work on exception handling. The replacement model of Yemini and Berry has a number of very desirable features: it allows exceptions to be parameterised, and allows a number of different handling options. The handling options include terminating, resuming, or retrying the interrupted operation using input produced by evaluating some recovery expression.

Bretz and Ebert [6] took the Yemini and Berry model into the realm of functional programming by introducing ALEX, an ISWIM-like [7] language which supports the features listed above. To illustrate the ALEX exception handling mechanism consider the following function.

```
f x = if x < 0 then (signal bad x) + 5 else x
```

This function signals the exception `bad` with parameter `x`, if it is applied to a negative value. The function can be applied in the following ways.

1. `handle bad by \x.0 terminate in f (-1)`
   When `f` signals the exception the recovery code `(\x.0) -1` evaluates to `0`. This value replaces the call of `f`, therefore the value of the expression is `0`.

2. `handle bad by \x.-x resume in f (-1)`
   The recovery code `(\x.-x) -1` is evaluated to `1`. The function application resumes where it was interrupted, replacing the signal by the value of the recovery code. Thus the value of the expression is `6`.

3. `handle bad by \x.-x retry in f (-1)`
   Again the recovery code evaluates to `1`. The function `f` is then re-invoked using the value of its recovery code as its argument so the result of this expression is the value of `f 1` (i.e. `1`).

Two of the major problems involved in the introduction of an exception handling construct into a lazy functional programming language are:

1. The `terminate` and `retry` handling options given by Bretz and Ebert can change the strictness properties of a function. For example consider `inclist`, a function to add one to every element in a list of positive integers.

   ```
   inclist l = if l = [] then []
               else if hd l >= 0 then hd l + 1 : inclist (tl l)
               else (signal Bad_num (hd l)) + 1 : inclist (tl l)
   ```

   Without signals this function would obviously be defined on infinite lists, only the head of a list need be forced to increment the next element. The value of the expression

   $$\texttt{inclist (1 : 2 : }\perp\texttt{)}$$

   should be

   $$2 : 3 : \perp$$

   Now consider the following call of `inclist` using ALEX semantics:

```
handle Bad_num by \x.[] terminate in inclist (1 : 2 : ⊥)
```

Any expression, which is not a handler, containing the `Bad_num` signal as a sub-expression becomes the signal `Bad_num` when it is evaluated. We refer to this as ***up-propagation.*** The result of the expression above is `[]`, as defined by the recovery code, if `Bad_num` is signaled at any point in the evaluation of `inclist`. Since it is possible that $\perp$ in the argument approximates a list which contains a negative number, the result of the whole computation must remain $\perp$ until `inclist` has terminated or signaled `Bad_num`. This call of `inclist` is therefore ***hyper***-strict since the presence of $\perp$ in any part of its argument produces $\perp$ as a result. Use of a retry handler also converts `inclist` into a ***hyper***-strict function. This is because of the up-propagation of signals to handlers.

2. A functional programming notation typically contains no information about the order in which sub-expressions are to be evaluated. This can cause problems where an expression contains more than one sub-expression which can signal an exception. Consider the expression:

```
(signal bad x) + (signal worse y)
```

Unless we know the order in which `+` evaluates its arguments it is not possible to tell whether the expression will signal `bad` or `worse`. Since the handlers for `bad` and `worse` may define different recovery code it is not possible to determine the value of the expression unless we know which sub-expression is evaluated first.

Most modern functional programming languages do not have powerful exception handling facilities. One notable exception to this is Standard ML [8] which does support a strong exception handling construct. Standard ML solves the problems outlined above by having a call by value (strict), sequential semantics.

In this paper we introduce the concept of ***down-propagation*** of handlers which allows non-strict functions to signal exceptions. The notion of a ***firewall*** is introduced to control the action of a handler on `terminate`, when handlers are down propagated. We will avoid the need to specify the sequence of evaluation by introducing a system of ***priorities*** on exceptions; when more than one component of an expression signals an exception, the exception with the highest priority will be signaled.

2 Informal Description

2.1 Down-Propagation and Firewalls

Above we describe how up-propagation of signals transforms an otherwise non-strict function into a ***hyper***-strict function. It is worth examining this statement in more detail. When a signal is raised within an expression there may be many operators (or function applications) between the signal and its associated handler. For example, in the expression below where `lazy` is defined to be any non-strict binary operator:

```
handle bad by \x.0 terminate in (2 + (signal bad 3)) lazy 4
```

there are two operators, namely `+` and `lazy` between the signal `bad` and its handler. Somehow the signal and its handler must be united so that the handler can be applied to the signal. When this is done by up-propagation the signal is propagated upwards through the `+` and `lazy` operators. Although `lazy` is defined to be non-strict in both arguments, the up-propagation of signals through it transforms it into a strict operator. We must evaluate an expression to determine whether or not it produces a signal. If we have up-propagation of signals through non-strict operators, like `lazy`, we must evaluate their arguments, making them strict. Clearly we cannot allow up-propagation of signals through non-strict operators.

As an alternative to up-propagation of signals we can use down-propagation of handlers to unite signals and their handlers. Using down-propagation, every sub-expression inherits a local version of every handler which is in scope for the expression. Every signal is now handled as locally as possible. Using this scheme the expression given above is equivalent to:

```
(2 + handle bad by \x.0 terminate in (signal bad 3)) lazy 4
```

Unfortunately both `terminate` and `resume` have the same semantics as function application when pure down-propagation is used. It is also less than clear what (if anything) `retry` means with pure down-propagation. Some sort of compromise between up and down-propagation is obviously required. The desired semantics can be obtained by removing the `retry` handling option and introducing the concept of a *firewall.*

Signals raised within a firewall are propagated to that firewall, but will not propagate through the firewall. This gives *up-propagation* of signals to firewalls. Handlers declared outside a firewall are inherited by that firewall. This gives *down-propagation* of handlers to firewalls. All operators construct firewalls around any argument in which they are non-strict. Firewalls are also constructed around handler blocks, function arguments, and the bodies of functions. The mechanism described here obviously allows a handler to be defined for any arbitrary expression, not just a function application.

The exception handling mechanism is statically bound and therefore an exception may only be handled within a defining handler block. A handler is a *first class* value which may be either passed as an argument to, or returned as the result of, a function. Considering a handler as a first class value allows the programmer to define functions which handle the same exception in different ways depending on how they are called. To create a handler we suffix a λ-expression with the keyword `terminate` or with `resume`, e.g.: `\x.4 terminate` or `\y.-y resume`.

The expression shown above would be firewalled as follows (where `|[` *expression* `]|` denotes an implicitly firewalled expression).

```
|[ handle bad by \x.0 terminate
   in
         |[ (2 + (signal bad 3)) ]| lazy |[ 4 ]|
]|
```

Using down-propagation and firewalling the effect of `terminate` is to replace the whole of an expression within a firewall by the result of the handler. The result of the above expression is therefore `0 lazy 4`. As before `resume` is handled as locally as possible, by replacing the signal with the result of the handler. Using `resume` instead of `terminate` in the expression above would produce the result `(2 + 0) lazy 4`.

The combination of down-propagation and firewalls provides an extremely powerful and flexible construct for exception handling. The strictness of a function which signals exceptions is controlled in exactly the same way as the strictness of a function which does not, by the strictness of the operators contained in its body.

For example consider fully lazy `inclist`.

```
inclist l handler =
   handle Bad_num by handler
   in
       if l = [] then []
       else if hd l >= 0 then hd l + 1 : inclist (tl l) handler
       else (signal Bad_num (hd l)) + 1 : inclist (tl l) handler
```

As : is non-strict in both arguments they are firewalled. Any call of this function with a `terminate` handler will replace the signal `Bad_num`, at the nearest firewall, with the value given by application of the handler to the signal parameter. In this example, the firewall nearest to an occurrence of the `Bad_num` signal is around the list element containing the signal. Use of a `terminate` handler will replace a complete element of the list *without* adding 1 to the result.

For example:	`inclist (1 : 2 : -1 : ⊥) (\x.0 terminate)`
will evaluate to	`(1+1) : (2+1) : 0 : ⊥`

Using a `resume` handler, the signal will be replaced as locally as possible, a list element containing a signal will be replaced with the value defined by the handler plus 1.

So	`inclist (1 : 2 : -1 : ⊥) (\x.0 resume)`
evaluates to	`(1+1) : (2+1) : (0+1) : ⊥`

Compare this behaviour with the behaviour of `incstream`. In the sequel we shall use ! to denote head-strict list construction. Head-strict lists are typically used to construct I/O streams.

```
incstream s handler =
   handle Bad_num by handler
   in
      if s = [] then []
      else if hd s >= 0 then hd s + 1 ! incstream (tl s) handler
      else (signal Bad_num (hd s)) + 1 ! incstream (tl s) handler
```

Since this function uses the ! operator, which constructs a firewall around its second argument but not its first, we can construct calls of incstream which are head-strict shown below.

1. Terminate the resulting expression by replacing the whole unevaluated tail of the stream by the result returned by the handler.

   ```
   incstream (1 !  2 !  -1 !  ⊥) (\x.[] terminate)
   ```

   which evaluates to `2 !  3 !  []`

2. Resume using a modified value in place of the signal.

   ```
   incstream (1 !  2 !  -1 !  ⊥) (\x.-x resume)
   ```

   which returns `2 !  3 !  2 !  ⊥`

2.2 Exceptions with Priorities

The second problem outlined above concerned the need to know the sequence in which an operator evaluates its arguments. To recap: the expression shown below is ambiguous when called with a terminate handler which can replace the +, unless the order in which + evaluates its arguments is known.

```
(signal bad 3) + (signal worse 4)
```

If the + operator evaluates its left argument first this function will invoke the handler for bad. A + operator which evaluates its right argument first will invoke the handler for worse. This situation occurs because + must evaluate more than one argument *before* it can return a result. One of the strengths of functional programming is the fact that the sequence of evaluation of sub-expressions is irrelevant to its result. It is a retrograde step to lose this property.

We should note that the above expression is not ambiguous if either bad or worse is handled using a handler which resumes the computation. A **resume** handler will handle the signal by replacing it as locally as possible. When a **resume** handler is used there can be no interaction between signals because at least one signal is replaced before any interaction can occur. It is only if the terminate option is used to handle both signals that the expression is ambiguous.

A possible solution to the problem is to prioritise the + operator so that a signal from the left hand argument takes priority over a signal from the right hand argument. Hammond uses this approach for PSML [9] a lazy, parallel purely functional language derived from Standard ML. One minor drawback of this approach is that no operator which is prioritised in this manner can be commutative. So we cannot guarantee

```
x + y = y + x
```

when both x and y can signal an exception.

To remove the need for sequential semantics, without giving up the commutative property of + and other operators, we introduce a system of priorities on signals. Let us assume that two signal bindings are given.

```
handle bad   by \x.4 * x terminate
handle worse by \x.-x terminate
```

We will also assume that the signals have been assigned a priority so that the signal worse has a higher priority than the signal bad. This priority is to be used to resolve any ambiguity in an expression which signals more than one exception. The expression

```
(signal bad 3) + (signal worse 4)
```

would therefore be handled by the handler for worse and so would have the value -4. By assuming the existence of a method for assigning a priority to a signal we can eliminate the need to know the order in which + and other strict operators evaluate their arguments. We can now decide which handler will be invoked by examining the relative priorities of the signals.

The method chosen to assign priorities to signals is based on the normal scoping rules for nested non-recursive let abstractions. Where handler blocks are nested, the signals bound in the inner block have higher priority than those defined in the outer block. When a handler block binds more than one signal; the signal most recently bound, i.e. the one nearest the end of the list, has highest priority. For example the signals bad and worse could be bound to handlers with the appropriate priorities, in either way shown below.

```
handle bad by \x.4 * x terminate
in
          handle worse by \x.-x terminate
          in
                    (signal bad 3) + (signal worse 4)
```

This binds the signal worse with a higher priority than the signal bad because it is the more local of the two. Alternatively both signals could be bound at the same level.

```
handle bad   by \x.4 * x terminate
         worse by \x.-x terminate
in
         (signal bad 3) + (signal worse 4)
```

In this situation the signal bound closest to the end of the list of definitions (i.e. textually closest to the expression) has highest priority, so again the handler for `worse` is invoked. Priorities are assigned depending on the position of the signal binding so it is impossible for two signals to be bound with the same priority. It should be noted that although the signal priority mechanism is based on *non*-recursive `let` abstraction the handlers are actually bound using similar semantics to recursive `let` or `letrec` abstraction. A handler may signal an exception which is handled by another handler bound in the same handler block. A handler may even signal the exception which it handles itself.

There is one problem which remains to be solved. It is possible for both arguments of a strict operator to signal the same exception with *different* parameters. The priority mechanism cannot resolve this conflict since both signals should be handled by the *same* handler. The signal cannot simply be given to the handler because we have to decide which signal parameter is to be used. It is not possible to solve the problem by arbitrarily deciding to signal the exception with one or other parameter without either introducing non-determinism, sequentialising the semantics of the `+` operator, or making `+` non-commutative. The situation is dealt with by introducing a new version of the signal which has a `void` parameter. Obviously, the programmer must now be able to specify a handler which can accept, either the ordinary parameter of the signal, or a `void` parameter. This is done by allowing the programmer to add a second handler definition to any handler which uses the `terminate` handling option.

```
handle bad by \x.4 * x terminate 42 multiple
in
          (signal bad 3) + (signal bad 4)
```

Since the handler to be used for multiple signals is handling signals which have a `void` parameter the recovery code must be a constant expression. Using this scheme the expression given above would evaluate to 42.

One final point to note is that the priority and firewall mechanism is consistent with the notion of strictness. Before we invoke a handler we must evaluate every argument in which an operator is strict so that we can be sure that we invoke the correct handler. If an operator is not strict in a particular argument there is no need to evaluate it since it is surrounded by a firewall and cannot contribute a signal to the current evaluation.

2.3 System Exceptions

The exception handling mechanism provides a set of system exceptions to allow recovery from common error situations, such as division by zero. The system exceptions are defined by adding a notional outer handler block to all programs. This handler block defines handlers for the system exceptions such as division by zero, `DBZ`. The predefined system exception handlers simply return the value `failure`. Operations which can raise system exceptions are notionally transformed to signal the system exceptions as appropriate. For example the division operator is defined as:

```
div x y = if y =/= 0 then x / y else signal DBZ void
```

All system exceptions are raised with a void parameter. When the programmer defines a new handler to handle a system exception, the operators which raise this exception are implicitly re-defined within the handler block so that they use the new version of the signal, rather than the one which is defined in the outer notional handler block. The effect of this is to transform the program as shown below.

```
handle DBZ by \x.0 terminate in 1 div 0 + 1
```

is transformed into

```
handle DBZ by \x.0 terminate
in      1 div 0 + 1
        where div x y = if y =/= 0 then x / y
                        else signal DBZ void
```

It should be stressed that the re-definition of operators can be done automatically by a compiler and is only necessary because the exception mechanism we propose has static binding. Without automatic re-definition of operators which raise system exceptions the programmer would be unable to write code to trap system exceptions. The notional outermost handler for a system exception would be invoked whenever that exception was signaled. We do not give a list of system exceptions as this may be language dependent.

3 Discussion

3.1 Summary

This paper has examined the relationship between functional programming and exception handling. The examination focussed on two points.

1. Any exception handling mechanism based on pure *up-propagation* of signals to handlers must force any function which signals an exception to be strict when that signal is handled by terminating the evaluation. Standard ML has a strict semantics and ALEX, which has a lazy semantics, must be strict when an expression can signal an exception.

   To allow non-strict functions to signal exceptions, the notions of *firewalling* and *down-propagation* were introduced. The idea can be summed up by saying that signals propagate upwards only as far as a firewall. Using down-propagation, firewalls are erected around any sub-expression which need not be evaluated for the enclosing expression to be defined. A firewall inherits a local version of every signal which is in scope. This gives the programmer control not only of the strictness of any expression he or she defines but also control over the precise behaviour of the `terminate` handling option.

2. The need for sequential semantics in a language with an exception handling construct was also examined. We found that sequential semantics are only required to *disambiguate* an expression in which more than one argument of a strict, commutative operator signals an exception. To remove the need for sequential semantics, without removing the commutative property of normally commutative operators, we introduced a system of priorities for exception handlers. The use of a priority mechanism removes the need for an explicitly sequential semantics at no real cost. The only requirement for implementation of the priority system is that an operator should evaluate every argument in which it is strict *before* it returns a result.

3.2 Applications

In the introduction it was stated that one of the main uses of an exception handling construct is to allow the programmer to separate error recovery code from normal code. This can improve the readability of a large program. There are however application areas where the availability of an exception handling construct may be more than a textual convenience.

1. Real-Time applications and fault tolerance.
   In a real-time environment the ability to deal with exceptional conditions which arise may be crucial for system reliability and safety. Work is and has been done on the application of functional programming in a real-time environment [10, 11, 12, 13].

2. Operating System Design and Implementation.
   The use of functional languages for the programming of operating systems has been researched intermittently in the last eight years. Early work was done independently by Karlsson [14], Henderson and Jones [15, 16] and Abramsky [17]. More recently Stoye [18] implemented a multiprocessing operating system with purely functional processes. Currently Perry [19] is working on functional operating systems using Hope$^+$C, and one of the authors, Sinclair [20], is working on functional operating systems, concentrating on I/O. This area is a major application for exception handling: an operating system must be extremely robust, since it must be able to recover from errors caused by user processes.

3.3 Future Work

The work described in this paper is by no means complete. In this section we outline two of the major areas which we believe require further work.

1. Compatibility with strong polymorphic type checking.
   This paper has said nothing about type checking in the discussion of exception handling. Bretz and Ebert constructed a set of type inference rules for ALEX. There may be some problems providing a similar set of rules for the exception handling construct discussed here. Because of down-propagation and firewalls

the type checker must be able to decide which firewalls a particular signal can be raised at, so that it can check that a terminate handler produces the correct result. Construction of such a type checker is a non-trivial task.

2. Introduction into an accepted functional programming language.
   It was *not* the purpose of this paper to add to the functional programming Tower Of Babel by introducing yet another functional programming language. The exception handling mechanism discussed here is designed as far as possible to be compatible with existing functional programming notations. A denotational semantics for Gerald, a primitive lazy functional language containing the exception handling construct discussed here is given in the appendix. It would appear to us to be a worthwhile exercise to spend some time adding the exception handling construct to an existing modern functional programming language such as Miranda [1] [21] or Lazy ML [22]. This would involve considerable extension of the semantics to include the high level features of modern lazy functional programming languages, such as pattern matching.

Finally, it should be stated that the exception handling mechanism discussed here is extremely powerful and allows a large range of conditions to be dealt with. Like any other powerful construct it is of course open to abuse. It is possible to write bad programs in any language, there is no reason for a language containing an exception handling construct to be an exception.

4 Acknowledgements

We would like to thank Phil Collier, Kevin Hammond, and Simon Jones for their helpful suggestions and criticisms of this work. Andrew Reeves and Andrew Sinclair are supported by SERC studentships. Dave Harrison and Paul Williamson are supported by the ESPRIT project PANGLOSS. Sections of the text of this paper are reproduced from the proceedings of TENCON '89 with the permission of the I.E.E.E. .

A The Denotational Semantics of Gerald

A.1 Syntactic Domains

E	∈ Expression	BO	∈ Binary_Operator
I	∈ Identifier	UO	∈ Unary_Operator
HD	∈ Handler_Definition	B	∈ Boolean
H	∈ Handler	N	∈ Integer
D	∈ Definition	Y	∈ String

[1] Miranda is a Trademark of Research Software.

A.2 Abstract Syntax

E ::= N | B | Y | I | (E) | E BO E | UO E | E ! E | E : E | *hd* E | *tl* E | *nil* | *eos* | *let* D *in* E | *if* E *then* E *else* E | *lambda* I . E | E E | *signal* I E | H | *handle* HD *in* E | (E , E , ... , E)

N	::=	0 | 1 | etc	UO	::=	− | *not* | ...
B	::=	*true* | *false*	D	::=	I = E D |
Y	::=	"any finite string"	HD	::=	I *by* E HD |
BO	::=	+ | − | * | / | \\ | *and* | *or* | ...	H	::=	E *terminate* [E *multiple*] | E *resume*

A.3 Semantic Domains

v,e	∈ VAL	= ATOM ⊕ STREAM ⊕ LIST ⊕ TUPLE ⊕ FUNC ⊕ SIGNAL ⊕ HANDLER ⊕ UNDEF
	ATOM	= NUM ⊕ BOOL ⊕ STRING
st, v !: *lift* (st)	∈ STREAM	= (VAL ⊗ $\text{STREAM}_\perp$) ⊕ SNIL
l, *lift* (v :: l)	∈ LIST	= $(\text{VAL} \times \text{LIST})_\perp$ ⊕ LNIL
tp, *lift* (v) :! tp	∈ TUPLE	= ($\text{VAL}_\perp$ ⊗ TUPLE) ⊕ TNIL
	SNIL	= NIL
	LNIL	= NIL
	TNIL	= NIL
	NIL	= $\{ \text{Nil} \}_\perp$
	VOID	= $\{ \text{Void} \}_\perp$
f	∈ FUNC	: VAL → VAL
s, ⟨I,v⟩	∈ SIGNAL	= Identifier ⊗ ($\text{VAL}_\perp$ ⊕ VOID)
	HANDLER	= TERM ⊕ RES
InRES f	∈ RES	= FUNC
InTERM f v	∈ TERM	= FUNC × VAL
ρ	∈ ENV	= Identifier → VAL
	UNDEF	= $\{ \text{Undef} \}_\perp$

Note: We are also giving ourselves predicates to determine whether objects are in a particular domain; i.e. IsVAL, IsATOM, ... IsUNDEF. The projection functions for the VAL domain are OutATOM, OutSTREAM, ... OutUNDEF and injections are InATOM, InSTREAM, ... InUNDEF. Similar naming conventions are used for other domains. In addition we shall use:
InLEFTLIST : $(\text{VAL} \times \text{VAL})_\perp \rightarrow$ LIST

InLEFTSTREAM : $(\mathsf{VAL} \otimes \mathsf{STREAM}_\perp) \to \mathsf{STREAM}$
InLEFTTUPLE : $(\mathsf{VAL}_\perp \otimes \mathsf{TUPLE}) \to \mathsf{TUPLE}$.

A.4 Semantic Functions

Since HANDLER and SIGNAL are sub-domains of VAL they can be placed in ENV. This does mean that a normal binding and a handler binding cannot exist for the same identifier at the same point.

ϕ : ENV
$[\_ \mapsto \_]$: Identifier $\to$ VAL $\to$ ENV
$\_ \,\&\, \_$: ENV $\to$ ENV $\to$ ENV

$\phi\,[\![\mathrm{I}]\!] = \mathsf{InUNDEF\ Undef}$

$$\begin{aligned} [\mathrm{I} \mapsto \mathsf{v}]\,[\![\mathrm{I}']\!] &= \mathsf{v} && \text{if } \mathrm{I} = \mathrm{I}' \\ &= \mathsf{InUNDEF\ Undef} && \text{otherwise} \end{aligned}$$

$$\begin{aligned} (\rho \,\&\, \rho')\,[\![\mathrm{I}]\!] &= \rho[\![\mathrm{I}]\!] && \text{if IsUNDEF } (\rho'[\![\mathrm{I}]\!]) \\ &= \rho'[\![\mathrm{I}]\!] && \text{otherwise} \end{aligned}$$

ref : Identifier $\to$ ENV $\to$ VAL

$$\begin{aligned} \mathsf{ref}\,[\![\mathrm{I}]\!]\,\rho &= \perp && \text{if IsUNDEF } (\rho[\![\mathrm{I}]\!]) \\ &= \rho[\![\mathrm{I}]\!] && \text{otherwise} \end{aligned}$$

The next function is just for use with signals. It decides which of two signals is bound the closest in an environment and returns it. Also, if given the same exception name twice it discards the arguments and returns a signal with the exception name and a Void argument.

closest : SIGNAL $\to$ SIGNAL $\to$ ENV $\to$ VAL

$$\begin{aligned} \mathsf{closest\ s1\ s2}\ \rho &= \perp && \text{if close s1 s2 } \rho = \perp \text{ or IsUNDEF (close s1 s2 } \rho) \\ &= \mathsf{close\ s1\ s2}\ \rho && \text{otherwise} \end{aligned}$$

close : SIGNAL $\to$ SIGNAL $\to$ ENV $\to$ VAL

$\mathsf{close\ s} \perp \rho = \perp$

$\mathsf{close} \perp \mathsf{s}\ \rho = \perp$

$\mathsf{close}\ \langle \mathrm{I1,v1} \rangle\ \langle \mathrm{I2,v2} \rangle\ \phi = \mathsf{InUNDEF\ Undef}$

$$\begin{aligned}
\text{close } \langle I1,v1\rangle\ \langle I2,v2\rangle\ [I \mapsto h] &= \text{InSIGNAL } (\langle I,v1\rangle) && \text{if } I = I1 \text{ and } I \neq I2\\
&= \text{InSIGNAL } (\langle I,v2\rangle) && \text{if } I \neq I1 \text{ and } I = I2\\
&= \text{InSIGNAL } (\langle I,\text{Void}\rangle) && \text{if } I = I1 \text{ and } I = I2\\
&= \text{InUNDEF Undef} && \text{otherwise}
\end{aligned}$$

$$\begin{aligned}
&\text{close } \langle I1,v1\rangle\ \langle I2,v2\rangle\ (\rho 1\ \&\ \rho 2)\\
&\quad = \bot && \text{if close } \langle I1,v1\rangle\ \langle I2,v2\rangle\ \rho 2 = \bot\\
&\quad = \text{closest } \langle I1,v1\rangle\ \langle I2,v2\rangle\ \rho 1 && \text{if IsUNDEF (close } \langle I1,v1\rangle\ \langle I2,v2\rangle\ \rho 2)\\
&\quad = \text{closest } \langle I1,v1\rangle\ \langle I2,v2\rangle\ \rho 2 && \text{otherwise}
\end{aligned}$$

handle tries to apply a *resume* handler to a signaled exception, but leaves the signal unhandled if the signal is to be handled by a *terminate* handler. Note that *lift* in a pattern to match denotes drop in the function body, i.e. f (*lift* v) = v $\equiv$ f (v) = *drop* v.

handle : VAL $\to$ ENV $\to$ VAL

handle $\bot$ $\rho = \bot$

$$\begin{aligned}
\text{handle e } \rho &= \text{hand (OutSIGNAL e) } \rho && \text{if IsSIGNAL e}\\
&= \text{e} && \text{otherwise}
\end{aligned}$$

hand : SIGNAL $\to$ ENV $\to$ VAL

hand $\bot$ $\rho = \bot$

$$\begin{aligned}
\text{hand } \langle I, \textit{lift}\ v\rangle\ \rho &= \text{handle ((OutRES f) v) } \rho && \text{if IsRES f}\\
&= \text{InSIGNAL } (\langle I, \textit{lift}\ (v)\rangle) && \text{otherwise}\\
&\text{where}\\
&\quad f = \text{OutHANDLER (ref I } \rho)
\end{aligned}$$

hand $\langle$I, Void$\rangle$ ρ = InSIGNAL ($\langle$I, Void$\rangle$)

This gives the semantics of firewalls and is therefore responsible for the application of *terminate* handlers to signals. Note that the environment of a firewall is fixed when the firewall is constructed.

firewall : ENV $\to$ VAL $\to$ VAL

$$\begin{aligned}
\text{firewall } \rho \text{ e} &= \text{wall } \rho \text{ (OutSIGNAL e)} && \text{if IsSIGNAL e}\\
&= \text{e} && \text{otherwise}
\end{aligned}$$

wall : ENV $\to$ SIGNAL $\to$ VAL

wall ρ $\bot = \bot$

$$\text{wall } \rho \ \langle I,v\rangle = \bot \qquad \text{if ref I } \rho = \bot$$
$$= \text{apply } \rho \text{ v (OutSIGNAL (ref I } \rho)) \qquad \text{otherwise}$$

apply : ENV → (VAL$_\bot$⊕ Void) → HANDLER → VAL

apply ρ e ⊥ = ⊥

apply ρ ⊥ h = ⊥

apply ρ (*lift* e) (InRES f) = firewall ρ (f e)

apply ρ Void (InRES f) = ⊥

apply ρ (*lift* e) (InTERM f v) = firewall ρ (f e)

apply ρ Void (InTERM f v) = ⊥   if v = ⊥ or IsUNDEF v
= firewall ρ v   otherwise

apply is included to make the definition of firewall more readable. Note that in the last case, where we have a multiple signal (the argument is Void) and there is no *multiple* case (the constant value is Undef) the result is ⊥.

Note: a tuple is simply a tail-strict list.

sel : TUPLE → NUM → VAL

sel ⊥ n = ⊥

sel tp ⊥ = ⊥

sel (InTNIL Nil) n = ⊥

sel (InLEFTTUPLE (*lift* (v) :! tp)) n = v   if n = 0
= sel tp (n-1)   otherwise

Note that tuples are numbered from left to right starting at 0. Also, the Nil case could be handled with a system exception if desired.

head : (LIST ⊕ STREAM) → VAL

head ⊥ = ⊥

head (InLEFTLIST (*lift* (v :: l))) = v

head (InLEFTSTREAM (v !: (*lift* st))) = v

tail : (LIST ⊕ STREAM) → VAL

tail ⊥ = ⊥

tail (InLEFTLIST (*lift* (v :: l))) = InLIST l

tail (InLEFTSTREAM (v !: (*lift* st))) = InSTREAM st

A.5 Semantic Equations

$\mathcal{E}$: Expression → ENV → VAL
$\mathcal{D}$: Definition → ENV → ENV
$\mathcal{H}$: Handler_Definition → ENV → ENV
$\mathcal{N}$: Integer → VAL
$\mathcal{B}$: Boolean → VAL
$\mathcal{S}$: String → VAL

$\mathcal{E}[\![\mathrm{N}]\!]\rho = \mathcal{N}[\![\mathrm{N}]\!]$

$\mathcal{E}[\![\mathrm{B}]\!]\rho = \mathcal{B}[\![\mathrm{B}]\!]$

$\mathcal{E}[\![\mathrm{Y}]\!]\rho = \mathcal{S}[\![\mathrm{Y}]\!]$

$\mathcal{E}[\![\mathrm{I}]\!]\rho = \textsf{handle (ref } \mathrm{I}\ \rho)\ \rho$

$\mathcal{E}[\![(\mathrm{E})]\!]\rho = \mathcal{E}[\![\mathrm{E}]\!]\rho$

$\mathcal{E}[\![\mathit{signal}\ \mathrm{I\ E}]\!]\rho = \textsf{handle (InSIGNAL } \langle \mathrm{I}, \mathit{lift}\ (\textsf{firewall } \rho\ (\mathcal{E}[\![\mathrm{E}]\!]\rho))\rangle)\ \rho$

Note the possibility for E to produce a Signal thus allowing a Signal to be the value argument to a Handler.

In the next equation ⊙ is any strict binary operator except tuple projection and α is the semantic operator corresponding to it.

$\mathcal{E}[\![\mathrm{E1} \odot \mathrm{E2}]\!]\rho$ = ⊥ if e1 = ⊥ or e2 = ⊥
= handle (e1 α e2) ρ if not (IsSIGNAL e1) and not (IsSIGNAL e2)
= e1 if IsSIGNAL e1 and not (IsSIGNAL e2)
= e2 if not (IsSIGNAL e1) and IsSIGNAL e2
= priority_signal otherwise
where
e1 = handle ($\mathcal{E}[\![\mathrm{E1}]\!]\rho$) ρ
e2 = handle ($\mathcal{E}[\![\mathrm{E2}]\!]\rho$) ρ
priority_signal = closest (OutSIGNAL e1) (OutSIGNAL e2) ρ

In the next equation % is any strict unary operator and % is the semantic operator corresponding to it.

$$\mathcal{E}[\![\ \%\ \mathrm{E}\ ]\!]\rho = \bot \quad \text{if e} = \bot$$
$$= \text{e} \quad \text{if IsSIGNAL e}$$
$$= \text{handle } (\%\ \text{e})\ \rho \quad \text{otherwise}$$
$$\text{where}$$
$$\text{e} = \text{handle } (\mathcal{E}[\![\ \mathrm{E}\ ]\!]\rho)\ \rho$$

$$\mathcal{E}[\![\ \textit{if}\ \mathrm{E1}\ \textit{then}\ \mathrm{E2}\ \textit{else}\ \mathrm{E3}\ ]\!]\rho$$
$$= \bot \quad \text{if e1} = \bot \text{ or (not (IsBOOL e1) and not (IsSIGNAL e1))}$$
$$= \text{e1} \quad \text{if IsSIGNAL e1}$$
$$= \text{e2} \quad \text{if OutBOOL (OutATOM e1)} = \text{true}$$
$$= \text{e3} \quad \text{otherwise}$$
$$\text{where}$$
$$\text{e1} = \text{handle } (\mathcal{E}[\![\ \mathrm{E1}\ ]\!]\rho)\ \rho$$
$$\text{e2} = \text{handle } (\mathcal{E}[\![\ \mathrm{E2}\ ]\!]\rho)\ \rho$$
$$\text{e3} = \text{handle } (\mathcal{E}[\![\ \mathrm{E3}\ ]\!]\rho)\ \rho$$

$$\mathcal{E}[\![\ \textit{let}\ \mathrm{D}\ \textit{in}\ \mathrm{E}\ ]\!]\rho = \mathcal{E}[\![\ \mathrm{E}\ ]\!]\ (\text{fix } (\lambda\rho'.\ \rho\ \&\ \mathcal{D}[\![\ \mathrm{D}\ ]\!]\rho'\ ))$$

$$\mathcal{E}[\![\ \mathrm{E}\ \textit{terminate}]\!]\rho = \text{InHANDLER (InTERM } (\mathcal{E}[\![\ \mathrm{E}\ ]\!]\rho) \text{ (InUNDEF Undef))}$$

$$\mathcal{E}[\![\ \mathrm{E1}\ \textit{terminate}\ \mathrm{E2}\ \textit{multiple}\ ]\!]\rho = \text{InHANDLER (InTERM } (\mathcal{E}[\![\ \mathrm{E1}\ ]\!]\rho)\ (\mathcal{E}[\![\ \mathrm{E2}\ ]\!]\rho))$$

$$\mathcal{E}[\![\ \mathrm{E}\ \textit{resume}]\!]\rho = \text{InHANDLER (InRES (OutFUNC } (\mathcal{E}[\![\ \mathrm{E}\ ]\!]\rho)))$$

$$\mathcal{E}[\![\ \textit{handle}\ \mathrm{HD}\ \textit{in}\ \mathrm{E}\ ]\!]\rho = \text{firewall } \rho'\ (\mathcal{E}[\![\ \mathrm{E}\ ]\!]\rho')$$
$$\text{where}$$
$$\rho' = \text{fix } (\lambda\rho''.\ \rho\ \&\ \mathcal{H}[\![\ \mathrm{HD}\ ]\!]\rho'')$$

$$\mathcal{E}[\![\ \textit{lambda}\ \mathrm{I}\ .\ \mathrm{E}\ ]\!]\rho = \text{InFUNC } (\lambda\ \text{e}\ .\ \text{firewall } \rho'(\mathcal{E}[\![\ \mathrm{E}\ ]\!]\rho'))$$
$$\text{where}$$
$$\rho' = (\rho\ \&\ [\mathrm{I}\mapsto\text{e}])$$

$$\mathcal{E}[\![\ \mathrm{E1}\ \mathrm{E2}\ ]\!]\rho = \bot \quad \text{if e1} = \bot$$
$$= \text{e1} \quad \text{if IsSIGNAL e1}$$
$$= \text{(OutFUNC e1) e2} \quad \text{otherwise}$$
$$\text{where}$$
$$\text{e1} = \text{handle } (\mathcal{E}[\![\ \mathrm{E1}\ ]\!]\rho)\ \rho$$
$$\text{e2} = \text{firewall } \rho\ (\mathcal{E}[\![\ \mathrm{E2}\ ]\!]\rho)$$

$$\mathcal{E}[\![\ \textit{nil}\ ]\!]\rho = \text{InLIST (InLNIL Nil)}$$

$$\mathcal{E}[\![\ \textit{eos}\ ]\!]\rho = \text{InSTREAM (InSNIL Nil)}$$

$\mathcal{E}[\![\mathrm{E1} : \mathrm{E2}]\!]\rho$
= InLIST (InLEFTLIST (*lift* (firewall ρ e1 :: OutLIST (firewall ρ e2))))
where
e1 = $\mathcal{E}[\![\mathrm{E1}]\!]\rho$
e2 = $\mathcal{E}[\![\mathrm{E2}]\!]\rho$

$\mathcal{E}[\![\mathrm{E1} \; ! \; \mathrm{E2}]\!]\rho$
= $\perp$ if e1 = $\perp$
= e1 if IsSIGNAL e1
= st otherwise
where
e1 = handle ($\mathcal{E}[\![\mathrm{E1}]\!]\rho$) ρ
e2 = $\mathcal{E}[\![\mathrm{E2}]\!]\rho$
st = InSTREAM (InLEFTSTREAM (e1 !: OutSTREAM (*lift* (firewall ρ e2))))

$\mathcal{E}[\![\mathit{hd}\ \mathrm{E}]\!]\rho$ = $\perp$ if e = $\perp$
= e if IsSIGNAL e
= head (OutLIST e) if IsLIST e
= head (OutSTREAM e) if IsSTREAM e
= $\perp$ otherwise
where
e = handle ($\mathcal{E}[\![\mathrm{E}]\!]\rho$) ρ

$\mathcal{E}[\![\mathit{tl}\ \mathrm{E}]\!]\rho$ = $\perp$ if e = $\perp$
= e if IsSIGNAL e
= tail (OutLIST e) if IsLIST e
= tail (OutSTREAM e) if IsSTREAM e
= $\perp$ otherwise
where
e = handle ($\mathcal{E}[\![\mathrm{E}]\!]\rho$) ρ

$\mathcal{E}[\![(\mathrm{E1}\ ,\ \mathrm{E2}\ ,\ \ldots\ ,\ \mathrm{Em})]\!]\rho$
= InTUPLE (InLEFTTUPLE (*lift* (firewall ρ ($\mathcal{E}[\![\mathrm{E1}]\!]\rho$)) :!
(InLEFTTUPLE (*lift* (firewall ρ ($\mathcal{E}[\![\mathrm{E2}]\!]\rho$)) :! ...
(InLEFTTUPLE (*lift* (firewall ρ ($\mathcal{E}[\![\mathrm{Em}]\!]\rho$)) :!
lift (InTNIL Nil))) ...))))

Here we use # to represent tuple projection.

$\mathcal{E}[\![$ E1 # E2 $]\!]\rho$

$= \bot$	if e1 $= \bot$ or e2 $= \bot$
$=$ handle v ρ	if not (IsSIGNAL e1) and not (IsSIGNAL e2)
$=$ e1	if IsSIGNAL e1 and not (IsSIGNAL e2)
$=$ e2	if not (IsSIGNAL e1) and IsSIGNAL e2
$=$ priority_signal	otherwise

where

v	$=$ sel (OutTUPLE e1) (OutNUM (OutATOM e2))
e1	$=$ handle ($\mathcal{E}[\![$ E1 $]\!]\rho$) ρ
e2	$=$ handle ($\mathcal{E}[\![$ E2 $]\!]\rho$) ρ
priority_signal	$=$ closest (OutSIGNAL e1) (OutSIGNAL e2) ρ

$\mathcal{D}[\![\ ]\!]\rho = \phi$

$\mathcal{D}[\![$ I = E D $]\!]\rho = [$ I $\mapsto \mathcal{E}[\![$ E $]\!]\rho$] & $\mathcal{D}[\![$ D $]\!]\rho$

$\mathcal{H}[\![\ ]\!]\rho = \phi$

$\mathcal{H}[\![$ I *by* H HD $]\!]\rho = [$I $\mapsto \mathcal{E}[\![$ H $]\!]\rho]$ & $\mathcal{H}[\![$ HD $]\!]\rho$

References

[1] Cristian F.; *Robust data types*, Acta Informatica 17, 1982, pp365–397.

[2] Cristian F.; *Dependable programs: Concepts and terminology*, IBM Research laboratory San Jose, C.A., 1986 (Technical Report).

[3] Goodenough J.B.; *Exception handling: Issues and a proposed notation*, Comm ACM, Vol 18, No 12, 1975, pp513–519.

[4] Yemini S., Berry D.M.; *A modular verifiable exception handling mechanism*, ACM TOPLAS, Vol 7, No 2, 1985, pp214–243.

[5] Yemini S., Berry D.M.; *An axiomatic treatment of exception handling in an expression-oriented language*, ACM TOPLAS, Vol 9, No 3, 1987, pp390–407.

[6] Bretz M., Ebert J.; *An exception handling construct for functional languages*, Proceedings ESOP88, 2nd European Symposium on Programming, Nancy, France, March 1988, LNCS 300, Springer-Verlag.

[7] Landin P.J.; *The next 700 programming languages*, Comm ACM, Vol 6, No 3, 1966, pp157–166.

[8] Harper R., MacQueen D., Milner R.; *Standard ML*, LFCS-86-2. Laboratory for Foundations of Computer Science, University of Edinburgh, March 1986.

[9] Hammond K.; *Error Handling in the Parallel Implementation of a Lazy Functional Language*, Internal Report SYS–C89–01, School of Information Systems, University of East Anglia, 1988.

[10] Broy M.; *Applicative Real-Time Programming*, Proceedings IFIP 1983. North-Holland Information Processing 83.

[11] Caspi P., Pilaud D., Halbwachs N., Plaice J.A.; *LUSTRE : A Declarative Language for Programming Synchronous Systems*, Conference Record of the 14th Annual ACM Symposium on Principles of Programming Languages, January 1987.

[12] Harrison D.; *RUTH : A Functional Language for Real-Time Programming*, Proceedings Parallel Architectures and Languages Europe, Eindhoven, June 1987, LNCS 259, Springer-Verlag.

[13] Harrison D.; *Functional Real-Time Programming : The Language Ruth And Its Semantics*, Ph.D. Thesis, University of Stirling, Stirling, Scotland, Submitted September 1988.

[14] Karlsson K.; *Nebula – A functional operating system*, Laboratory for Programming Methodology, Department of Computer Science, Chalmers University, 1981.

[15] Henderson P.; *Purely functional operating systems*, In *Functional programming and its applications*, Eds Darlington, Henderson and Turner, CUP, 1982.

[16] Jones S.B.; *A range of operating systems written in a purely functional style*, Programming Research Group Technical Monograph PRG-42, Oxford University, September 1984.

[17] Abramsky S.; *Dynamically reconfigurable process networks: an applicative approach*, Internal report, Computer Systems Laboratory, Queen Mary College, 1982.

[18] Stoye W.; *The implementation of functional languages using custom hardware*, Ph.D. Thesis, Technical Report 81, University of Cambridge, December 1985.

[19] Perry N.; *Hope$^+$C, A continuation extension for Hope$^+$*, IC FPR LANG 2.5.1 21, Department of Computing, Imperial College, November 1987.

[20] Jones S.B., Sinclair A.F.; *Functional programming and operating systems*, The Computer Journal, Vol 32, No 2, 1989, pp162–174.

[21] Turner D.A.; *An introduction to Miranda*, In *The Implementation of Functional Programming Languages* by S. L. Peyton Jones. Prentice Hall International Series in Computer Science. Ed C. A. R. Hoare. London 1987.

[22] Johnsson T.; *Compiling lazy functional languages*, Ph.D. Thesis, Chalmers University of Technology, Goteborg, Sweden, 1987.

Geometrization for Interactive Software Development

Kieran Clenaghan
Department of Computing Science
University of Glasgow, Scotland

1. Introduction

This paper introduces an approach to making computable algebraic specifications *interactive*. We present the structure of a specification-independent sequential machine, and examine what is needed to equip a specification so that it can be used interactively on this machine. This machine serves as our operating system and user-interface management system for specification use. An objective is to keep this machine as simple as possible, so that the burden of providing sophistication rests with the specification being used and the way it is equipped for use. We are particularly interested in how modularity in specifications can induce a modular approach to specifying interaction.

Our machine structure regards the user-interface as a *geometric* object, and requires a specification to be equipped with a *geometrization system* for interactive use. A geometrization system comprises a collection of *geometors* which map symbolic objects of a specification onto the geometry of the user-interface. A specification equipped in this way is called an *interactive specification*. The machine we describe is therefore generic, being parameterised with respect to an arbitrary interactive specification.

In this paper we present the *architecture* of our machine and some basic properties of geometrization systems. Our account is introductory and motivational. The implementation of the machine, and the notational presentation of geometrization systems form the basis of further work. In this light, the paper merely scratches the surface of a substantial research programme, but we will be happy if we convince the reader that this programme is interesting and worthwhile.

The paper is organised as follows. Section 2 presents an example specification which is used throughout the paper. Sections 3, 4, and 5 introduce machines Mach1, Mach2, and Mach3 respectively. These are successively more detailed with respect to interaction. Mach3 depends on geometrization, and section 5 discusses the basic structure of geometrization systems and their use, and how they might be developed. Finally, section 6 puts the work properly in context, and discusses the significance of the new directions offered by it.

2. An Example Specification, NAT

We restrict our attention to specifications whose intended computable models are realised by canonical term rewriting systems[1]. This class of specifications will be denoted CSPEC. The restriction is chosen to make the notion of execution simple, and to avoid immediate concern for non-termination. Specifications in CSPEC should also

[1]A canonical term rewriting system is a rewriting system in which each term has a unique normal form that is computed in a finite number of rewriting steps.

be broadly familiar to a wide audience (especially those acquainted with a functional programming language), and we can identify them with *programs*. The algebraic approach is chosen because it enjoys a rich theoretical background. It also places emphasis on modularity [1], [2], and opens avenues to more expressive specification frameworks [3], both of which are seen as important to the future development of our work.

For the introductory purposes of this paper we choose to develop our ideas relative to a specific simple example. It is a fragment of a specification of the natural numbers, and we call it NAT. This specification has the benefit of familiarity, and needs no motivation or explanation. Therefore, we omit the specification of its rewrite rules, and we provide only its signature as follows:

NAT =	**sorts**	Nat		
	opns	zero:		$\rightarrow$ Nat
		s:	Nat	$\rightarrow$ Nat
		_+_:	Nat, Nat	$\rightarrow$ Nat
		_*_:	Nat, Nat	$\rightarrow$ Nat

It should be clear that NAT can be equipped with rewrite rules to satisfy membership of CSPEC. The signature of NAT, denoted Sig[NAT], defines a set of well-formed terms and a term algebra in the usual way (see [4]). We denote this term algebra and its carrier by T_{NAT}. It is assumed that the rewrite rules of NAT define a morphism, E_{NAT}: $T_{NAT} \rightarrow C_{NAT}$. This morphism is the *evaluation* homomorphism for NAT. Its target is the *canonical term algebra,* C_{NAT}, which is a sub-algebra of T_{NAT} containing only the normal-form terms (see [5]).

If SP is an arbitrary specification, then Sig[SP], E_{SP}, T_{SP}, and C_{SP} apply as in the examples above. Terms of an arbitrary sort *s* are referred to as *s-sorted* terms. Since T_{SP} is determined by just the signature of SP, say Σ=Sig[SP], we allow the notation T_Σ for the term algebra determined by Σ.

3. A Simple Machine: Mach1

Probably the simplest machine for NAT is a realisation of E_{NAT} extended to a monoid[2] homomorphism: E_{NAT}^*: $T_{NAT}^* \rightarrow C_{NAT}^*$. E_{NAT}^* serves as an abstract model of a pocket calculator without a storage facility. It is simple to add a storage facility to this model. This is done by modeling the store as a total function σ:X$\rightarrow$Can, where X is a finite set of variable symbols. X is drawn from a global set, V, of variable symbols disjoint from the constant symbols of Sig[NAT] (i.e. V does not contain 'zero' in this case).

The signature Sig[NAT] can be extended to include the symbols of X. Let us denote this extension by Sig[NAT(X)], and the resulting term algebra by $T_{NAT(X)}$. A new evaluation homomorphism for NAT *over* store σ is obtained, which we denote $E_{NAT(\sigma)}$: $T_{NAT(X)} \rightarrow C_{NAT}$. See [4] or [5] for details of these standard constructions.

[2]Following standard convention we use the superscript * for constructing monoids in the usual way. The symb λ denotes the unit element of a monoid, and $\cdot$ denotes concatenation.

Thus, we can present a model of a finite machine that facilitates the use of NAT over store σ. For simplicity, we shall provide only two machine operations: (i) an ***evaluation*** operation which "displays" the value of a given term, and (ii) an ***assignment*** operation for updating the store (but performs no "display"). These are defined at a ***meta-level*** because of their use of variables. However, we may characterise them as building new terms using terms in $T_{NAT(X)}$ as follows:

_ eval:	$T_{NAT(X)}$	$\rightarrow$ Command
_ _ assign:	$T_{NAT(X)}$, V	$\rightarrow$ Command

The underscores indicate argument positions, so these operators are both postfix. Let the set of Command-sorted terms be denoted Calc. We now define a machine, Mach1[NAT], as the 6-tuple (Calc, Display, State, init, show, dyn), where

Calc is the set of *inputs*.

Display $=_{def}$ $Can_{\perp}$, is the set of possible *outputs*. $Can_{\perp} = Can \cup \{\perp\}$.

State$=_{def}$ Store$\times$Display, is the set of *states*, where Store=(V$\rightarrow$Can).

init $=_{def}$ $(\emptyset,\perp)$, is the *initial* state.

show: State $\rightarrow$ Display is the (trivial) *output function:* Show $(\sigma,d) = d$.

dyn: Calc$\times$State $\rightarrow$ State is the *dynamics,* defined below.

$$\text{dyn}((t\ \text{eval}),(\sigma,d)) = (\sigma, E_{NAT(\sigma)}(t))$$

$$\text{dyn}((t\ y\ \text{assign}),(\sigma,d)) = (\sigma[y\leftarrow E_{NAT(\sigma)}(t)],d)$$

The function _[_$\leftarrow$_]: (V$\rightarrow$Can)$\times$V$\times$Can $\rightarrow$ (V$\rightarrow$Can) updates a function in the obvious way.

We could re-define this machine for some arbitrary SP$\in$CSPEC and denote it by Mach1[SP]. The underlying machine structure is therefore generic, and we denote it by Mach1.

3.1 Notes from Classical Automata Theory

This definition of Mach1[NAT] is extremely simple. However, it establishes a link between program use and automata-theoretic formulations of machines. We wish to build upon this link by investigating how to scale up the above mathematical model to cope with both larger programs and increased sophistication of program use.

The automata-theoretic link has the advantage of providing a number of notions that have been studied in a general framework, and which are of practical concern. We discuss two of these. First let us recall some standard definitions. The definitions are relative to Mach1[NAT], but they generalise easily to Mach1.

Let c$\in$ Calc, cs$\in$ Calc*, and s$\in$ State.

The *reachability map,* reach: Calc* $\rightarrow$State, maps each sequence of input to the state reached from the initial state by this input. It is defined here via another function, reachfrom, which is useful in the next definition.

reach cs = reachfrom init cs

reachfrom s λ = s

reachfrom s (cs· c) = dyn (c, reachfrom s cs)

The *observability map,* obs: State $\rightarrow$ (Calc*$\rightarrow$Display), maps each state to a *response map* for this state, that takes sequences of inputs to displays. If two states have the same response map then they cannot be distinguished via the display, i.e. thay are observably the same, otherwise they are observably distinct. It is defined:

obs s = show $\circ$ (reachfrom s)

Immediately, we can express the following:

Definition 3.1 (Machine Properties)

(a) Mach1[NAT] is *reachable* if reach is surjective.
(b) Mach1[NAT] is *observable* if obs is injective.

Reachability of Mach1[NAT] requires (i) that any X-indexed set of normal-forms, i.e. any element of Store, can be constructed using assign, where X is a finite subset of V, and (ii) that any normal-form, i.e. any element of Display, can be constructed using eval. It also requires that all pairs of these elements are reachable. Thus, the reachability requirement can be decomposed into Store-reachability, Display-reachability, and the independence of these. From a practical point of view, this is clearly a basic requirement for using NAT.

Observability of Mach1[NAT] requires that for each s$\in$ State=Store$\times$Display, there is a unique response map. Again, we would like to decompose this requirement into Store-observability, Display-observability, and the independence of these. In practice this would require that the user can independently distinguish each distinct store and each distinct display using the output function.

So far, we have just borrowed a framework for asking some important formal questions. We now want to develop this framework in order to refine the questions and to make answering them feasible. In particular, we are interested in some details about *how* states can be reached and observed. For example, we would like to stipulate that any term in $T_{NAT(X)}$ can be the argument to eval, which is not captured by the properties as given above. The question of reachability arises again in sections 4.1 and 5.4, and the question of observability arises again in section 5.3.

3.2 An Important Factorisation

An important decision in our approach is that for any specification, SP, we regard E_{SP} as a "black-box". Its extension, $E_{SP(\sigma)}$, to work over a store, σ, is such that E_{SP} remains invariant under changes to σ; alternatively, one can obtain E_{SP} from $E_{SP(\sigma)}$ by simply forgetting about σ. These notions have a formal rendering using free and forgetful functors, but we shall not pursue the technicalities here. However, it is worth noting that we could compose E_{SP} in this "free" way with a more sophisticated notion of a store, for example one with a database structure.

This factors the reachability and observability requirements into (i) those which apply to E_{SP} and (ii) those which apply to the store (or more precisely the state). Case (i) is not considered here; there is a substantial literature on the subject, see for example [6]. Case (ii) is our main concern (for which there is scant literature).

3.3 Review of the Simple Model

There are a number of shortcomings of the above (naive) model of Mach1[NAT] for providing use of NAT. The main ones are:

(a) It is assumed that the user can supply any element of Calc as input. This ignores a very significant and potentially complex component of a practical machine: that which enables the construction and editing of terms.

(b) The output set is based on Term. This neglects the mapping of terms onto some model of the user-interface hardware. We need to recover the distinction between the abstract syntax for defining the semantics of a program and the concrete syntax for using a program, and observing its results.

(c) The dynamics does not capture the interactive nature of program use. We need a concept of an *interaction* that is "excited" by an input and that "responds" with an output, and includes a state-transition. A simple example is the effect of typing a character: the character is echoed and causes some state-transition, for example it is inserted into a string component of the state.

(d) Assumptions about the user of the machine are left implicit. An explicit model of certain aspects of the user is needed to complete the interactive scenario.

Section 4 addresses shortcoming 3.3(a); section 5 addresses shortcomings 3.3(b) and (c); shortcoming 3.3(d) is beyond the scope of the paper.

4. Term Editing

In Mach1[NAT], the definition of dyn specifies the interpretation of the language Calc. As pointed out in 3.3(a), it leaves the problem of constructing a sentence of Calc. This may be generalised to the problem of constructing terms generated by an arbitrary algebraic signature Σ. We address this general case, referring to the term algebra of Σ and its carrier by T_Σ. The particular case Calc will serve as our example.

Consider an arbitrary term in Calc, e.g. "(x+y) eval". There are two stages in effecting a state-transition based on such a term[3]. The first stage is the *presentation* of the term; and the second stage is the *evaluation* of the term. Two common practices in presenting terms are the following:

(i) Present a string of characters representing a term, and parse this string to produce the (abstract) term. Typically a string-oriented (i.e. text) editor is

[3] Alternative models which are not considered here are possible. For example, many pocket calculators avoid any construction of a term, and only construct (in bottom-up style) a value for a term.

involved.

(ii) Present the term piece-meal using a term editor. Such an editor is called a *structure* editor (cf. [7]).

These practices are mutually complementary rather than mutually exclusive. We consider the former approach to be subsumed in the latter, since ultimately, the presentation of a string requires term editing, albeit for simple terms. Notice that, given a suitable parsing function, Parse:String $\rightarrow T_{NAT(X)}$, then $(E_{NAT(\sigma)} \circ \mathrm{Parse})^*$: String$^* \rightarrow C_{NAT}{}^*$ is only a slight variation on the $E_{NAT(\sigma)}{}^*$ of section 3, with the input terms specialised to String-sorted terms. This allows us to assume that parsing can be "built into" $E_{NAT(\sigma)}$. For especially relevant literature on parsing see [8]. Here, our attention is on term editing.

4.1 A Term-Editing Machine: Mach2

Term editing has received considerable practical and theoretical research attention in the special case of "structure-oriented program editing" (see the references in [7]). However its utility in other cases is open to further study. For example, interesting cases of term editing arise in electronic spreadsheets, computer-aided circuit design, and in more general CAD systems. These cases are beyond the scope of the present work, but they provide some impetus for a more general approach than that in [7]. What follows in this section is a good deal less sophisticated than [7], but its role is only to lay bare a formal basis for the ideas of section 5, where we begin to depart from the approach of [7].

Two key aspects of term editing that need to be reconciled are (a) practical user-oriented requirements; and (b) formal description of a machine for realising term editing. Unfortunately, it is not yet possible to achieve this reconciliation, since the formal aspect is not well enough developed. Therefore, a simplistic set of user-oriented requirements is taken that provides a non-trivial but tractable formal description problem. These requirements centre on the ability to construct a term via a succession of so-called *partial* terms. To explain this more precisely we need to recall some standard formal definitions.

Let $\Sigma=\langle S,\Omega\rangle$ be an algebraic signature, where S is a set of sorts, and Ω is an $S^*\times S$-indexed set of operator symbols. The S-indexed set of terms over Σ, T_Σ, is defined inductively as follows:

(i) $\Omega_{\lambda,s} \subseteq (T_\Sigma)_s$

(ii) $f(t_1 \ldots t_n) \in (T_\Sigma)_s$, for $f \in \Omega_{w,s}$, $w=s_1 \ldots s_n$, and $t_i \in (T_\Sigma)_{s_i}$, for $1 \leq i \leq n$.

We define the set of partial terms over S as a super-set of T_Σ by adding new constants $\perp_s \in \Omega_{\lambda,s}$ for $s \in S$. The simple idea is that $\perp_s$ serves as a place-holder for a term of sort s. Terms with no place-holders are called *complete* terms. Using partial terms we illustrate the piece-meal construction of the term "x+y" as follows:

$\perp_{Nat}$	*Select the sort* Nat.
$(\perp_{Nat} + \perp_{Nat})$	*Replace the place-holder by the operator +.*
$(x + \perp_{Nat})$	*Replace the first place-holder by* x.
$(x + y)$	*Replace the second place-holder by* y.

In this construction, we assume that both x and y are assigned to Nat terms in the store. Note that each of the above operations is described by (i) a partial term; (ii) a place-holder selection; and (iii) an operator or variable. An obvious development for term editing is to extend place-holder selection to arbitrary sub-term selection[4]. This leads to the definition of an *indexed* term.

An *indexed* term is a pair, (t,i), where t is a (partial) term, and i is an index into t. For $t \in T_\Sigma$, we define the set of indices of t, denoted Ind(t), as a subset of strings of naturals as follows:

$$\mathrm{Ind}(f_{\lambda,s}) = \{\lambda\}$$
$$\mathrm{Ind}(f_{w,s}(t_1 \ldots t_n)) = \{\lambda\} \cup \{k \cdot i \mid 1 \le k \le n,\ i \in \mathrm{Ind}(t_k)\}$$

Given a term t, and any index in Ind(t) one can generate any other index of t using a sequence of the operators up, down, left, and right which are defined below. These operators are called *index movement* operators.

(a) up λ $= \lambda$
up $(i \cdot k)$ $= i$

(b) down i $= (i \cdot 1)$, if $(i \cdot 1) \in \mathrm{Ind}(t)$
$= i$, otherwise

(c) left λ $= \lambda$
left $(i \cdot k)$ $= i \cdot (k-1)$, if $k \neq 1$
$= i \cdot k$, otherwise

(d) right λ $= \lambda$
right $(i \cdot k)$ $= i \cdot (k+1)$, if $i \cdot (k+1) \in \mathrm{Ind}(t)$
$= i \cdot k$, otherwise

Now we define (informally) a machine, Mach2, whose state is an indexed term plus a store. The indexed term is the term being edited, called the *editing term*. The basic structure of interaction that we want to develop is independent of the store model, so we shall assume that the store is fixed from now on, and relegate discussion of store updates to appendix 2. The input set of Mach2 comprises the following.

- The sorts S.
- The operators Ω.
- Variables defined in the store.
- The index movement operators, up, down ,left, right.
- An evaluation operator, eval.

The interpretation by Mach2 (as state-transitions) of the sorts and operators is defined in appendix 1, but can be inferred from the example above. In term construction, variables are interpreted as nullary operators. The interpretation of the index movement operators follows their definitions. Finally, eval is defined only for complete terms, and evaluates the sub-term at the index of the editing term.

[4]The addition of useful editing operations such as cut and paste is easy; we omit them for brevity only.

As promised in section 3.1, we raise the question of reachability again. For Mach2, reachability means the reachability of all possible indexed terms, and all possible stores. It should be no surprise that all partial terms can be reached and, by inclusion, all complete terms can be reached. A sketch of the proof of term reachability is given in appendix 1. Reachability of all possible stores requires the assignment operator, and is discussed in appendix 2.

We let Mach2[NAT] denote Mach2 specialised for the specification NAT.

4.2 Concrete Inputs to Mach2

Mach2 does not satisfactorily resolve 3.3(a) since we still need to define how the user can select appropriate inputs. The definition is based on practical screen-oriented systems. In such systems, it is typical for output to "prompt" the user for input, and for selectable input to be related to some portion of the output.

For uniformity we shall assume that each element of the set of outputs comprises an entire user-interface which determines the set of possible inputs. For simplicity we shall assume that outputs and inputs are deterministically interleaved. Figure 4.1 is a picture image of the user interface to a machine supporting the use of NAT (no attempt has been made to take the "human factors" of this interface into consideration!).

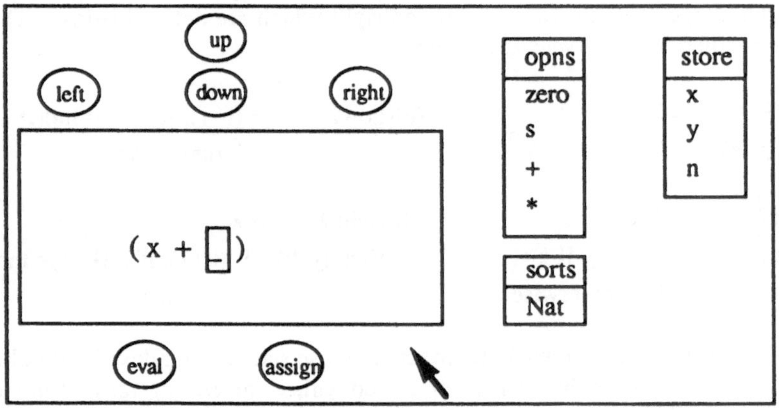

Figure 4.1

From experience of a (simulation of a) pocket calculator, one can easily infer the functionality of the interface in fig 4.1. The available inputs are displayed as names. It is assumed that each input can be selected by a *pointing* device (depicted as a dark arrow). The term being edited is the *editing term;* its *image* is shown within the largest inner rectangle, and the index into the editing term, called the *editing index,* is represented by highlighting the indexed sub-term. In spite of its apparent simplicity this user-interface is sufficiently rich to provide a good focus for developing some general aspects of interaction.

We begin by noting that the entire user interface itself may be considered to be an image, ui_image, of some term, ui_source, generated by a suitably complex signature. By using the pointing device to pick an index (or point) in ui_image one selects as input a sub-term of ui_source. This involves associating each index in ui_image with a unique index in ui_source.

It follows that each selectable sub-term must have a state-transition interpretation associated with it. For example, selection of a sub-term of the editing term will reset the editing index. The state-transitions associated with the other entities shown were discussed at the end of the previous section, 4.1.

5. Realising a User-Interface by Geometrization: Mach3

We need a map that takes terms to their user-interface images. We call terms that are given images *source terms*. The map that takes source terms to their images is called a *geometor*. The acts of specifying and applying this map are, context-sensitively, both called *geometrization*. In this section we want to investigate the structure of a machine, Mach3, that is based on geometrization, and thus more detailed with respect to interaction than Mach2. To obtain Mach2[NAT] we did not need to add structure to NAT. By contrast, to obtain Mach3[NAT] we need two extra mappings based on NAT. One is a geometor that will produce user-interface images of terms in T_{NAT}. The other is a geometor for Sig[NAT], the store σ, $E_{NAT(\sigma)}$, and the editing operators. Only the former mapping is discussed, but we consider an arbitrary signature, so we implicitly cover many of the issues in the definition of the latter mapping as well.

A geometor serves two basic functions: *(A)* it projects computational objects, i.e. terms, onto the user interface for sensory perception by a user; and *(B)* it provides a mapping from the user interface to components of terms. From a minimalist formal perspective, function *A* is governed by observability conditions, and function *B* is governed by reachability conditions. However, from a pragmatic point of view, both are influenced by effectiveness and aesthetics. We shall take a minimalist, but general, formal perspective which we hope leaves room for pragmatic adjustments on an individual specification basis.

5.1 Definition of a Geometor and its Use

We define geometors as arrows in a category[5] so that we insist upon associative composition and an identity. There are two categories of geometors: **Geom**, containing simply *geometors*, and **IA-Geom**, containing *index-association geometors*. The former category can be obtained from the latter by a simple forgetful functor U:**IA-Geom**$\rightarrow$**Geom**. The term *geometor* will mean *index-association geometor*, unless otherwise clear from context.

The category **Geom** is a sub-category of the category of sets and functions. An arrow in **Geom**, $UG:T_\Sigma\rightarrow T_{\Sigma'}$, is a function between terms over signatures Σ and Σ', respectively. For t a term, UG(t) is the *image* of t *through* UG.

An arrow in **IA-Geom**, $G:F_\Sigma\rightarrow F_{\Sigma'}$, is a geometor as in **Geom**, extended such that for a term t, G(t) is a pair, (g,r), where g is the image of t, and $r:Ind(g)\rightarrow Ind(t)$ is a partial *index-association* function from g to t. Identity arrows are $id_\Sigma:T_\Sigma\rightarrow T_\Sigma: t \mapsto (t,id_{Ind(t)})$. The composition of geometors $G:T_\Sigma\rightarrow T_{\Sigma'}$ and $G':T_{\Sigma'}\rightarrow T_{\Sigma''}$ is defined by $(G'\cdot G)(t)= (g',r\circ r')$, where $(g',r')=G'(g)$, $(g,r)=G(t)$. The forgetful functor U just

[5]Elementary categorical language is used here more in anticipation of its worth in future developments than for any contribution to descriptive clarity in this paper.

forgets the index association functions.

By these definitions, geometors could be trivial; sections 5.3 and 5.4 suggest ways of stipulating that they are non-trivial.

The following informal specification of a cycle of Mach3 illustrates the application of a geometor, G, which produces the user interface from the machine's state.

- Let (User-Interface, r) = G(State)
- Show the User-Interface
- Accept a User-Interface coordinate c, and a value x
- Get the State index i = r(c)
- Get the semantics dyn associated with index i of State.
- Generate the new state dyn(x,State)

The value x may denote "selection", or some more informative value. For example, the value could be "single mouse-click" or "double mouse-click", or it could be a colour, or a measure of force.

A more succinct specification of the basic control structure of Mach3 is given below. G is the geometor for the entire state, and U:**IA-Geom**→**Geom** is as defined previously. Each input is a pair, (c,x), a coordinate (or index) and a value. The function iter has type iter:State × Input* → Display*, where State, Input, and Display are left unspecified. The function sem which gives the semantics associated with an index of the state is also left unspecified.

$$
\begin{aligned}
\text{iter}\ (s,\lambda) &= (U(G))\ (s) \\
\text{iter}\ (s,(c,x)\cdot \text{inputs}) &= \text{ui}\cdot\ (\text{iter}(\text{dyn}(x,s),\ \text{inputs}) \\
&\quad \text{where} \\
&\quad (\text{ui},\ r) = G(s) \\
&\quad \text{dyn} = \text{sem}(s,\ r(c))
\end{aligned}
$$

5.2 Example Geometors

A simple example of a geometor is a mapping taking Nat-terms to terms representing lists of characters. This can be presented as a straightforward unparsing function. We shall just sketch its presentation here. The presentation of geometors is a subject for further work.

The following is the signature for list terms.

```
LIST =   CHAR +
         sorts    List
         opns     nil : → List
                  _:_ : Char, List → List
```

The translation, denoted G, from Nat-terms to List-terms can be presented using rules such as the following:

Let $e, e_1, e_2 \in T_{NAT(X)}$

$$
\begin{aligned}
G(e_1 * e_2) &= G(e_1) \mathbin{++} \text{"*"} \mathbin{++} G(e_2) \\
G(e\ \text{eval}) &= G(e) \mathbin{++} \text{"eval"}
\end{aligned}
$$

The ++ operator is list concatenation; it is not included in the LIST signature since it is used only in the computation of lists, and appears only in the language expressing the translation. The quoted strings are convenient representations for lists of characters.

Now consider the index association functions. Only example functions are given; we do not yet have a scheme for specifying their generation. However, the examples illustrate what is involved. Below, the indices of terms are explicitly placed as superscripted prefixes, e.g. $^{\lambda}({}^{1}e1 * {}^{2}e2)$. The following is an example geometrization:

$$^{\lambda}({}^{1}zero \ * \ {}^{2}zero) \quad => \quad {}^{\lambda}({}^{1}\text{'0'} \ : \ {}^{2}({}^{2\cdot 1}\text{'*'} \ : \ {}^{2\cdot 2}({}^{2\cdot 2\cdot 1}\text{'0'} \ : \ {}^{2\cdot 2\cdot 2}nil)))$$

To accompany this translation we want an association of indices, r, defined:

$$r = \{1 \mapsto 1,\ 2\cdot 1 \mapsto \lambda,\ 2\cdot 2\cdot 1 \mapsto 2\}.$$

Now we define a geometor that takes List-terms to so-called *lines*. A line is a term $L_n(c_1, ..., c_n)$, where each c_i, $1 \le i \le n$, is a character. Ignoring the name, L_n, of the constructor, this is isomorphic to a function, $L_n : \{1..n\} \to Char$. For convenience, we use the function representation for lines in defining the geometor G'. It is given by G'(t) = H(t,1), where H is defined as follows:

$$H(nil,i) \quad = \varnothing$$
$$H(x{:}xs,i) \quad = \{(i,x)\} \cup H(xs,i+1)$$

To accompany this translation we want an association of indices, r', defined:

$$r' = \{1 \mapsto 1,\ 2 \mapsto 2\cdot 1,\ 3 \mapsto 2\cdot 2\cdot 1\}$$

Thus, $r \circ r'$ is defined to be:

$$r \circ r' = \{1 \mapsto 1,\ 2 \mapsto \lambda,\ 3 \mapsto 2\}$$

The motivation behind this example is that there is a user-interface device which enables the user to select any of the indices 1, 2 or 3. A selection of an index i would generate the input (i,select), which could be interpreted as a command to set the index of the editing term to $(r \circ r')(i)$. The geometor H could be more elaborate by providing images for _:_ and nil. In that case r would be strictly partial on the range of r'.

5.3 Geometrization Systems

We must now ask what properties of geometors are important. We begin with the question of observable distinction. Should a geometor preserve inequality? Well, consider the geometrization of a character, x, and the geometrization of a string containing just x in a specification where these are distinct values. It is commonly desirable to project these as identical images. Therefore, a geometor need not preserve inequality. This is an example of "ellipsis": the deliberate hiding of detail. The hiding of rulers in a text editor display is another well-known case. Other examples, which are not necessarily deliberate, arise when the image space is not rich enough in some sense. The projection of information onto a lower-dimensional space, and the loss of accuracy through "poor resolution" are such examples.

However, we do want an extended notion of geometrization that at least approximately preserves inequality. The proposed notion is that of a *geometrization system*. A geometrization system is a collection of geometors and geometor *transformers*. For example, in the case of strings cited above, we may have two geometors which differ on whether or not they distinguish an element and the unit string containing it. A geometor transformer for this case could be just a command to alternate between the available geometors. Having a collection of geometors is therefore similar to having multiple unparsing schemes as in [7].

More generally, the idea is that to each term, t, is associated an *observation* function: obs(t): $\Gamma^* \rightarrow$Image, where Γ is the set of geometor transformers, and Image is the set of images. Inequality is observable if obs is injective (cf. observability in 3.1). If obs is not injective then we would like it to preserve some "distance" of inequality. For example, the inequality of two real numbers may be preserved up to n decimal places.

All geometors in a geometrization system must have the same source and target types (i.e. geometor transformers preserve the source and target of the geometors) in order that geometrization systems can be composed via geometor composition. A specification equipped with a geometrization system is called an *interactive* specification.

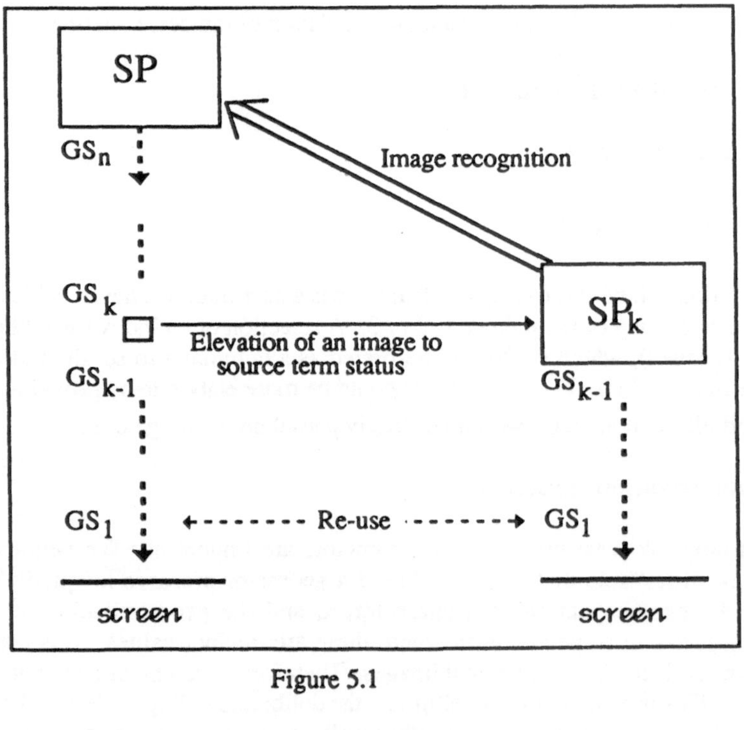

Figure 5.1

5.4 Reachability and Inverse Geometrization

The definition of a geometor allows the empty index-association function. However, reachability of any term (or state) requires that *some* input can be selected via an index-association function. This determines a minimal requirement. Criteria for strengthening the definition are specification-specific. For example, in order to exploit the (near) constant-time access of an image coordinate on a screen, one might like to maximise the range of an index-association function. This kind of criteria may be crucial to the effectiveness of certain interactive specifications.

In section 4 we dismissed parsing as part of "black-box" evaluation. It is worth reviewing the role of parsing in the light of geometrization. Figure 5.1 gives a rather general picture of the relationships between two interactive specifications SP and SP_k. It illustrates the use of SP via a composition of geometrization systems, $GS_1 \circ \ldots \circ GS_n$, where it is assumed that image terms of GS_k are source terms of some specification, SP_k, and it depicts the re-use of $GS_1 \circ \ldots \circ GS_{k-1}$ for SP_k.

Parsing may be viewed, with reference to this picture, as a special form of image recognition. If we assume that objects in SP_k are strings, and that $GS_k \circ \ldots \circ GS_n$ is just an unparsing function, then we may have a partial inverse function: a parser. In practice SP_k could provide text editing facilities; thus there is a natural notion of elevating a term (e.g. a string) that is an image of another term (a term of SP) to become a source term in its own right (i.e. a term of SP_k).

The elevation of an image with respect to one specification to the status of a source term with respect to some other specification may be desired for other reasons. For example, a screen image may be elevated in this way so that it could be "touched up".

5.5 Faithfulness of Geometric Representations

An intriguing aspect of geometrization is the opportunity to formalise some notion of representation *faithfulness* in the geometry of images. A simple example is the image of a *list* of values: one expects that the geometric layout of the values in the image will "respect" the access ordering of the values in the list. By contrast, a *set* of values might be laid out arbitrarily in an image. In both cases, however, we might insist that the size of the image is proportional to the size of the list or set.

The notion of representation faithfulness is fundamental to questions concerning the accuracy of information communication via a geometric medium. We have already discussed the faithful representation of inequality. The list example above has illustrated a need for specification-dependent faithfulness constraints. There are many other examples, such as constraints on tree layout (cf. [9]), and especially the geometrization of terms which originate as abstractions of intrinsically geometric objects (cf. [10]).

The constraints concerning faithfulness can be coded rigidly into presentations of geometors, where for any term one obtains exactly one image. However this injectivity property should be relaxed. A well-known motivation comes from the desire to be able to layout a program text according to taste by adjusting the use of whitespace (i.e. a geometric characteristic). Thus, the abstract syntax tree of a program can be associated with a (theoretically unbounded) number of program texts (i.e. geometrical images).

This leads to a formulation of "degrees of freedom" in images. We wish to specify geometors such that each source term is associated with a congruence class of images. This is easily seen in the list example, where we may like to convey the access order of the list but allow this to be represented in a number of ways. For example, all elements could be laid out horizontally with uniform, but unspecified, spacing. We could relax this further; for example the spacing need not be uniform, and the direction need not be specified.

Other examples of degrees of freedom include the ability to scale or rotate an image, and the more *ad hoc* ability to change font. Having degrees of freedom associated with images allows *constrained* direct manipulation of images, that is, where an image can be altered to another congruent form. This is a relatively novel aspect that deserves research, and is particularly interesting in the context of the composition and re-use of geometrization systems (as illustrated in fig. 5.1). The presentation of degrees of freedom in geometors is a subject for further work.

6. Discussion

This paper has attempted to set out some problems in the design of a generic interactive machine. The contribution of the paper lies in the proposed machine architecture. This architecture lends itself well to the precise formulation of machine properties which are of practical interest. This is, of course, just a beginning. Four strands of further development are now underway: completion of the mathematical description of the machine; modular presentations of geometrization systems including degrees of freedom; analysis of interaction styles supported by the machine; and a prototype implementation.

A number of further issues remain to be investigated. Two of these are identified as particularly interesting. One is the store organisation of the machine, where, following the work reported in [11], we can explore the association between stored values and the specifications which define them. Another is the self-application of the geometrization paradigm to the specification of a system supporting the development of interactive specifications. These are related, since in the latter, specifications become objects which reside in the store of some *meta*-specification.

In the remainder of this section we make a few remarks about the background to this work, and conclude with two aspects which are presently in the foreground of our continuing work.

6.1 Background

This work started by considering how to formally specify an interactive system. The Cornell Synthesiser Generator (CSG) [7] provided encouragement to separate computational and interactive aspects. The CSG work, however, does not focus on geometrization. Motivation to focus on geometrization has come from a number of sources, but mainly the declarative construction of graphical images and the re-usability of such constructions. Literature on this is scarce, see for example [12], [13], and [14], and the references therein. It was also noted that the lack of development in this area coincided with a major problem of user-interface management systems, the problem of handling application-defined data types uniformly; see [15], [16].

This problem arises when the language for expressing interaction is divorced from the language for writing applications, such that the building blocks used in the application language do not correspond naturally to building blocks in the language of interaction. For example, types might be defined hierarchically in an application language without a corresponding hierarchical mechanism in the interaction language for visualising and interacting with the types. We tackle this problem by considering how to specify interaction as a function of the generative definition of an application language (this is analogous to the definition of language semantics as a function of the generative abstract syntax of a language).

A variety of approaches to the formal specification of interaction appear in the literature, see for example [16], [17], [18], [19], [20], [21], and [22]. For lack of space we do not discuss the individual contributions, but note that a common conclusion of all these works is that this area is under-developed. Geometrization as proposed here is a new contribution to this area.

Our choice of the algebraic framework was motivated in section 2, and is further motivated in the next section. A number of systems have been designed to support the development of algebraic specification, for example [23], [24], [25], [26], [27], and [28]. Unfortunately, none of these has developed graphical interaction related to geometrization. Most attention has been on logic issues and computation by rewriting.

6.2 Modular Specification Development and Geometor Re-use

The re-use of software components is a major research area. Contributions come from theory and techniques which enable generic specification. Examples are modular and parameterised specification languages, higher-order and polymorphic function definitions, inheritance systems, user-interface management systems, graphics toolkits, and persistent storage management systems. Geometrization systems provide a new example.

A major goal is to integrate geometrization into a theoretical framework for modular software development, for example that of [29,30] or [31]. The basic idea is to align the specification of geometrization systems with the specification of modules. Some of the issues are listed below, where "geometrization" is used to mean "specification of geometrization systems".

- modular geometrization and composition rules
- commutativity of geometrization with module composition
- preservation of geometrization through module refinement

To approach these issues it would be necessary to define a category of *specifications of geometrization systems,* and relate this to a category of program specifications. In particular, specification morphisms should induce appropriate morphisms on geometrization systems.

Certain specification-building operations have been shown to depend on only some very basic properties of the underlying logical system [3]. Possession of these properties characterises a logical system as an *institution*. In [32], it is proposed that the "game" of formulating a (more concrete) specification framework is "to identify a minimal set of extra assumptions necessary for a particular purpose". In this spirit, it would be interesting to identify how to minimally extend the notion of an institution to entail geometrization systems. Success at this would, in principle, provide a basis for developing the interactive use of specifications written in any of a number of logics.

6.3 Flexible Interaction

We have proposed a separation between "black-box" evaluation and interaction. This agrees to some extent with the discipline of separability in user-interface management systems, but it may be considered rather severe. However, our notion of term evaluation does not attempt to encompass all of an application's specification. Instead, we see the specification of an application as involving both term evaluation parts and interaction parts. There is no prejudice: some applications may be interaction-biased, and some may be evaluation-biased.

Our separation allows the evaluation engine to be free of any requirements to support interactive programming. This frees the implementor of the evaluator to employ optimisation techniques, such as lazy or parallel evaluation, without interfering with the coding of interaction. The other side of the coin is that we must provide sufficient flexibility for specifying interaction. To address this we need to study the flexibility in the underlying machine architecture, and user-supplied contributions to the function *sem* of section 5.1. This study is the subject of a forthcoming report.

Acknowledgements

Thanks go to David Watt for detailed comments on a draft of this paper.

Appendix 1: Term Reachability in Mach2

A sketch of the proof of term reachability for Mach2 as defined in section 4.1 is given here. We also define more precisely the interpretation of sorts and operators as inputs to Mach2. The proof is specification-independent, and we assume an arbitrary specification with signature $\Sigma=(S,\Omega)$. The following assumption and lemma are used.

Assumption
We assume that the user is able to select all inputs as specified in section 4.1

Lemma
Given a state (t,i), the state can be transformed into (t,j) for any $j\in Ind(t)$. Proof of this using the operators up, down, left and right is straightforward.

Theorem
The state (t,i) for any $t\in T_\Sigma$, and $i\in Ind(t)$ can be reached from any other state.
Notation: t[i] denotes the sub-term of t at index i; $t[i\leftarrow t']$ denotes the replacement of t[i] by t' in t (cf. [33]).
Proof. The lemma deals with the i component; the following proof deals with the t component. First, an input $s\in S$ is interpreted as setting the editing term to $(\bot_s,\lambda)$. Note that $\bot_s[\lambda]=\bot_s$. We show by induction on the structure of terms that for a state (t,i) with $t[i]=\bot_s$, any element $t_s\in(T_\Sigma)_s$ can be constructed at t[i].

Base case. $t_s = f_{\lambda,s}$. Choose $f_{\lambda,s}$ as input, which is interpreted as sending (t,i) to $(t[i\leftarrow f_{\lambda,s}],i)$.

Induction Step. $t_s = f_{w,s}(t_1, ..., t_n)$, where $w=s_1 ... s_n$.
Inductive Hypothesis. For arbitrary state (t,i) with $t[i]=\bot_s$, any element $t_s\in(T_\Sigma)_s$ can be constructed at t[i].

Choose $f_{w,s}$ as input, which sends (t,i) to $(t[i \leftarrow f_{w,s}(\bot_{s_1}, ..., \bot_{s_n})],i)$. Then, for $1 \le x \le n$, we can use the lemma to obtain the state (t,ix), and since $t[ix]=\bot_{s_x}$ we can use the inductive hypothesis to construct t_x at t[ix].

(End of proof)

There is an alternative machine structure in [34], where it is proved that all terms can be constructed using a stack and post-fix presentation of terms. However, it is motivated by the proof of a compiler, and does not offer the editing flexibility that we desire here.

Appendix 2: Store Updates

There are many ways in which one could facilitate store updates. The canonical requirement is that the user can apply the assignment operator (cf. section 3) to arbitrary valid arguments. We have discussed the construction of any term, which accounts for the first argument to the assignment operator. The second argument to assign is an element of V, the global set of variables. We can see how the user might select, by pointing, any element of $X \subset V$, i.e. those variables already defined by the store, but we need a further facility to enable the selection of variables in $V \backslash X$. This can be done by providing a pervasive specification of strings of characters, with sort String and sort Char, that is included in all interactive specifications. We can then provide a "parse" operator from sort String into V. Let us call this operator parse_id, so that, for example, parse_id "x" denotes the variable $x \in V$.

We now present one possible facility for effecting store updates. We stick to a simple method, placing focus on store reachability, rather than addressing user-oriented design issues. However, we believe that our method provides a good basis for an effective user-oriented design.

The method is explained for Mach2[SP]. A *naming* operation, $name_s$: V, s $\rightarrow$ s, is added for each sort s in Sig[SP], and we define $E_{SP}(name_s(v,t)) = t$. Thus, using this operation, the user can innocuously name arbitrary sub-terms of the editing term. The benefit is that we can define the assignment operator at named subterms: at $name_s(v,t)$, it takes t as its first argument and v as its second argument. The v of this subterm could be constructed by parse_id, or it might be selected from the display of variables already in the store (or, more precisely, in X).

This method provides an easy way of asserting reachability of all stores, since it (almost) reduces to the reachability of all terms as before, extended to include Char-sorted and String-sorted terms and the additional family of naming operators. One key operation is omitted. It is a *deletion* operation that removes variables from the domain of the store. To complete our claim of reachability we can interpret the assign operator at $name_s(v,\bot_s)$ to mean the deletion of v from the domain of the store. The design of a more practically convenient deletion mechanism is rather straightforward and does not provide further insight into store reachability as pursued here.

7. References

(Note: LNCS n = Lecture Notes in Computer Science, Volume n)

[1] Joseph A. Goguen. *Parameterised Programming*. IEEE Trans. Soft. Eng., Vol. Se-10, No. 5, 1984.

[2] H. Weber and H. Ehrig. *Specification of Modular Systems*. IEEE Trans. on Software Eng., SE-12, 7, 1986.

[3] J.A. Goguen and R.M. Burstall. *Introducing Institutions*. LNCS 164, pp.221-256, 1984.

[4] H. Ehrig and B. Mahr. *Fundamentals of Algebraic Specification 1*. Springer Verlag, 1985.

[5] J. Meseguer and J.A. Goguen. *Initiality, Induction and Computability*. In *Algebraic Methods in Semantics*, eds. M. Nivat, & J.C. Reynolds, Cambridge Univ. Press, 1985.

[6] D. Sannella and A. Tarlecki. *On Observational Equivalence and Algebraic Specification.*. JCSS, vol. 34, pp 150-178, 1987.

[7] Thomas W. Reps and Tim Teitelbaum. *The Synthesizer Generator: A System for Constructing Language-Based Editors*. Springer-Verlag 1989.

[8] F. Voisin. *CIGALE: A Tool for Interactive Grammar Construction and Expression Parsing*. Sci. Comp. Prog., Vol. 7, pp 61-86, 1986.

[9] Kenneth J. Supowit and Edward M.Reingold. *The Complexity of Drawing Trees Nicely*. Acta Informatica, Vol.18, pp 377-392, 1983.

[10] W. Leler. *Constraint Programming Languages: Their Specification and Generation*. Addison-Wesley, 1988.

[11] M.P. Atkinson, O.P. Buneman, and R.Morrison. *Data Types and Persistence*. Springer Verlag, 1988.

[12] K. Arya. *A Functional Approach to Animation*. Computer Graphics Forum, Vol. 5, No. 4, 1986.

[13] R. Helm and K. Marriott. *Declarative Graphics*. LNCS 225, pp 513-527, 1986.

[14] P. Lucas and S. Zilles. *Graphics in an Applicative Context.*. IBM Research Report, San Jose, 1987.

[15] G.E. Pfaff (Ed). *User Interface Management Systems*. Springer Verlag, 1985.

[16] Special issue of ACM TOGS on User Interface Management Systems. Vol. 5, 3, 1986.

[17] B. Sufrin. *Formal Specification of a Display-Oriented Editor*. Sci. Comp. Prog. 1, 3, 1982.

[18] H. Ehrig, W. Fey, and H. Hansen. *Towards Abstract User Interfaces For Formal System Specifications*. In H-J. Kreowksi (Ed.) Recent Trends in Data Type Specifications, Springer-Verlag, IFB 116, 1985.

[19] H. Alexander. *ECS- A Technique for the Formal Specification and Rapid Prototyping of Human-Computer Interaction*. In *People and Computers: Designing for Usability,* Eds. M.D. Harrison and A.F. Monk, Cambridge Univ. Press, 1986.

[20] S.O. Anderson. *Proving Properties of Interactive Systems*. In *People and Computers: Designing for Usability,* Eds. M.D. Harrison and A.F. Monk, Cambridge Univ. Press, 1986.

[21] L. Marshall. *A Formal Description Method for User Interfaces*. Ph.D. Thesis (1986) and Tech. Rep. UMCS-87-1-2, University of Manchester.

[22] A.J. Dix, M.D. Harrison, C. Runciman, and H.W. Thimbleby. *Interaction models and the principled design of interactive systems*. European Software Engineering Conference, Strasbourg, 1987.

[23] M. Bidoit & C. Choppy. *ASSPEGIQUE; An Integrated Environment for Algebraic Specifications*. LNCS 185, pp 246-260, 1985.

[24] M. Broy, A. Geser and H. Hussman. *Towards Advanced Programming Environments Based on Algebraic Concepts*. LNCS 244, 1986.

[25] J. Dick. *ERIL- Equational Reasoning, an Interactive Laboratory*. Res. Report, Rutherford Labs, Didcot, Eng., 1986.

[26] H. Hansen. *The ACT-System. Experiences and Future Enhancements - (Draft).* Report, Technische Universitat Berlin, 1987.

[27] R. Kneuper. *Symbolic Execution of Specifications: User Interface and Scenarios*. Tech. Report, UMCS-87-12-6, University of Manchester, 1987.

[28] J.A. Goguen and T. Winkler. *OBJ3 User's Manual*. SRI, 1988.

[29] D. Sannella and A. Tarlecki. *Specifications in an Arbitrary Institution*. Information and Computation, 76, pp 165-210, 1988.

[30] D. Sannella and A. Tarlecki. *Towards Formal Development of Programs from Algebraic Specifications: implementations revisted.* Acta Informatica, 25, pp 233-281, 1988

[31] H. Ehrig, W. Fey, H. Hansen, M. Lowe, and F. Parisi-Presicce. *Algebraic Theory of Modular Program Development*. Report 87-06, Technische Universitat Berlin, 1987.

[32] D. Sannella and A. Tarlecki. *Extended ML: an institution - independent framework for formal program development*. Res. Report ECS-LFCS-86-16, University of Edinburgh, 1986.

[33] G.Huet. *Confluent Reductions: Abstract Properties and Applications to Term Rewriting Systems*. JACM 27, 4, pp 797-821, 1980.

[34] R. Burstall and P. Landin. *Programs and their proofs: an algebraic approach*. Machine Intelligence 4, 1970.

Author Index